W·E·S·T·E·R·N
W·I·N·D

Western wind, when will thou blow,
The small rain down can rain?
Christ! if my love were in my arms,
And I in my bed again!

W·E·S·T·E·R·N
W·I·N·D
AN INTRODUCTION TO POETRY
•second edition•

John Frederick Nims
University of Illinois at Chicago

McGRAW-HILL PUBLISHING COMPANY
New York   St. Louis   San Francisco   Auckland   Bogotá   Caracas
Hamburg   Lisbon   London   Madrid   Mexico   Milan   Montreal
New Delhi   Oklahoma City   Paris   San Juan   São Paulo
Singapore   Sydney   Tokyo   Toronto

Second Edition
9
Western Wind Copyright © 1983, 1974 by McGraw-Hill, Inc.

Library of Congress Cataloging in Publication Data
Nims, John Frederick, 1913–
Western wind.

Includes index.
1. Poetics. 2. Poetry—Collections. I. Title.
PN1042.N6   1983   809.1   82–16504
ISBN 0-07-554405-9

Book design: Dana Kasarsky Design
Cover: Sculpture by Antoine Pevsner, *Developable Column,* 1942. Brass and
oxidized bronze, 20¾" high, base 19⅜" diameter. Collection, Museum of
Modern Art, New York. Purchase.

Preface

This second edition of *Western Wind* has been modified along lines suggested by students and teachers who have used the first edition since its appearance eight years ago. Two major changes have been made: some material has been omitted, some reorganized, so that the original twenty-three chapters are now compacted into fourteen; and an anthology of about two hundred poems, over one-fourth of them new to this edition, now supplements the one hundred and eighty poems included in the chapters. Among those added are—in accordance with the wishes of a number of instructors—many of the familiar masterpieces of the language. Other new poems represent some of the best of our younger poets.

The original structure of *Western Wind*, which is based on human nature and the ways of the world we live in, has been retained. The book begins, as our lives do, with sense impressions and the emotions they arouse. It then proceeds to the words with which the poet, like the rest of us, has to express such images and emotions. It goes on to consider the qualities of these words as poets use them: their sounds as well as their meanings, the rhythms they assume, the forms, traditional or free, in which they find expression.

Individual instructors, who will have their own preferences about the way to approach poetry, are not bound to this sequence. The order of the book, like most things human, is flexible; teachers may move about in it as they choose, lingering over one section, dealing more briefly with another. Some instructors have preferred to begin with the sections on rhythm. The flexibility of this design allows for the

PREFACE

differences one finds in the aptitudes and interests of individual classes and individual students. Some will be happier doing more or less than the typical class or typical individual.

The exercises are suggestive, designed not so much to test a knowledge of facts as to lure the student into thinking creatively. As many or as few may be used as will suit the levels and interests of classes using the book. Questions more elementary and more general than those given will suggest themselves to instructors, who will have their own favorite ways of formulating basic exercises in, for example, paraphrasing, scanning, analyzing, or comparing poems. The writing exercises should be useful to many classes.

Year after year, wherever writers gather, no piece of advice is heard more often than "Show; don't tell!" Good writers *show* us a world. In critical writing and teaching, too, this advice applies. It is more important, for instance, to show students examples of metaphor than to discuss its nature, more important to let them taste ten tangy metaphors than to spoon-feed them the cold gruel of definition. *Western Wind* is richer in examples, many of them contemporary, than other introductions to poetry known to the author. This feature has been retained, with more than two hundred and fifty brief examples either added to or substituted for earlier ones.

I am grateful to the editors who worked with me on this project: to David Dushkin, who first encouraged it, to James Smith, who took over for him, and to Helen Litton, whose editorial care did much for the first edition. For encouraging the present edition I have to thank David Follmer, Richard Garretson, and Steven Pensinger; for editorial assistance with it I am indebted to John Sturman and Liz Israel. I also wish to thank the many instructors and students who have written me with suggestions over the years, and most of all the many younger poets who have made use of *Western Wind* in workshops and classes they have given.

J. F. N.

Contents

BEFORE WE BEGIN   **xxv**

· I ·
THE SENSES
1

1 WHERE EXPERIENCE STARTS: THE IMAGE   **3**

THE ROLE OF THE SENSES	3
Anonymous, *Western Wind*	6
Archibald MacLeish, *Eleven*	7
Sappho, *There's a Man*	8
T. S. Eliot, *Preludes*	9
Anonymous, *Brief Autumnal*	10
THE SPECIFIC IMAGE	12
Ezra Pound, *In a Station of the Metro*	12
Alba ("As cool as the pale wet leaves . . .")	12
Anthony Hecht, *The End of the Weekend*	12
Anonymous, *Sir Patrick Spens*	14
EXERCISES AND DIVERSIONS	16
Brewster Ghiselin, *Rattler, Alert*	16
Sappho, *Leaving Crete, Come Visit Again*	18

CONTENTS

2 WHAT'S IT LIKE? SIMILE, METAPHOR, AND OTHER FIGURES 19

SIMILE AND METAPHOR	19
Robinson Jeffers, *The Purse-Seine*	20
John Ciardi, *Most Like an Arch This Marriage*	23
Emily Dickinson, *My Life Had Stood—A Loaded Gun*	26
William Butler Yeats, *No Second Troy*	28
Robert Frost, *A Patch of Old Snow*	30
Walter de la Mare, *Afraid*	30
Helen Chasin, *City Pigeons*	31
ANALOGY	32
Walter de la Mare, *All But Blind*	33
SYNESTHESIA	36
ALLUSION	39
Alexander Pope, *Intended for Sir Isaac Newton*	39
PERSONIFICATION, MYTHOLOGY	39
Karl Shapiro, *A Cut Flower*	41
William Butler Yeats, *Leda and the Swan*	42
Walter Savage Landor, *Dirce*	42
EXERCISES AND DIVERSIONS	43

3 THE BROKEN COIN: THE USE OF SYMBOL 47

SYNECDOCHE, METONYMY	47
THE SYMBOL	50
Howard Nemerov, *Money*	52
Plato, *The Apple*	54
George Herbert, *Hope*	55
William Blake, *The Sick Rose*	56
Robert Frost, *Acquainted with the Night*	56
Saint John of the Cross, *The Dark Night*	57
THING-POEMS	58
Rainer Maria Rilke, *The Merry-Go-Round*	58
William Carlos Williams, *Nantucket*	59
Karl Shapiro, *Girls Working in Banks*	60
ALLEGORY	61
Sir Thomas Wyatt, *My Galley Chargèd with Forgetfulness*	62
Kingsley Amis, *A Note on Wyatt*	62

CONTENTS

EXERCISES AND DIVERSIONS   64
John Crowe Ransom, *Good Ships*   66
Carl Sandburg, *A Fence*   67

4 BINOCULAR VISION: ANTIPOETRY, PARADOX, IRONY, THE WITHHELD IMAGE   69

ANTIPOETRY   69
William Shakespeare, *Winter*   70
Francis P. Osgood, *Winter Fairyland in Vermont*   71
Elizabeth Bishop, *Filling Station*   71
Walt Whitman, *Beauty*   73
William Shakespeare, *Sonnet 130*   74
Robert Graves, *The Face in the Mirror*   74

PARADOX   76
Alexander Pope, from *An Essay on Man*   77

IRONY   80

UNDERSTATEMENT—THE WITHHELD IMAGE   81
Simonides, *On the Spartan Dead at Thermopylae*   83
X. J. Kennedy, *Loose Woman*   84

OVERSTATEMENT   86
Robert Graves, *Spoils*   87

EXERCISES AND DIVERSIONS   88
Rod Taylor, *Dakota: October, 1822, Hunkpapa Warrior*   88
Wallace Stevens, *The Emperor of Ice-Cream*   90

· II ·
THE EMOTIONS
93

5 THE COLOR OF THOUGHT: THE EMOTIONS IN POETRY   95

THE ROLE OF EMOTION   95
William Butler Yeats, *The Spur*   100
Walter Savage Landor, *Alas! 'Tis Very Sad to Hear*   101
Ammianus, *Epitaph of Nearchos*   101
W. H. Auden, *The Shield of Achilles*   102

SENSE AND SENTIMENTALITY   103
Anonymous, *The Unquiet Grave*   104
Anonymous, *Papa's Letter*   107
John Crowe Ransom, *Bells for John Whiteside's Daughter*   109
Algernon Charles Swinburne, *Étude Réaliste (I)*   110

James Wright, *A Song for the Middle of the Night*   *110*
Will Allen Dromgoole, *Old Ladies*   *111*
John Crowe Ransom, *Blue Girls*   *112*
May Swenson, *Cat & the Weather*   *114*
William Stafford, *Traveling Through the Dark*   *115*
Mary Thacher Higginson, *Ghost-Flowers*   *116*
Theodore Roethke, *The Geranium*   *117*
Laurence Hope, *Youth*   *118*

EXERCISES AND DIVERSIONS   118
Kenneth Fearing, *Yes, The Agency Can Handle That*   *121*

· III ·

THE WORDS
123

6   MACHINE FOR MAGIC:
THE FRESH USUAL WORDS   125

LIVING WORDS   125
Kenneth Patchen, *Moon, Sun, Sleep, Birds, Live*   *128*
Robert Frost, *Dust of Snow*   *132*
         Neither out Far Nor in Deep   *134*
Emily Dickinson, *A Narrow Fellow in the Grass*   *135*

LESS IS MORE   136
Alfred, Lord Tennyson, *Break, Break, Break*   *137*
A. E. Housman, *Along the Field as We Came By*   *138*
William Butler Yeats, *An Irish Airman Foresees His Death*   *139*
Ezra Pound, *The Bath Tub*   *141*
Hilaire Belloc, *On His Books*   *144*
Robert Frost, *The Wrights' Biplane*   *145*
W. H. Auden, *The Wanderer*   *145*

EXERCISES AND DIVERSIONS   149
Randall Jarrell, *The Knight, Death, and the Devil*   *152*
Mahlon Leonard Fisher, *In Cool, Green Haunts*   *155*

· IV ·

THE SOUNDS
157

7   GOLD IN THE ORE: THE SOUNDS OF ENGLISH   159

VOWELS   161
Dylan Thomas, *Do Not Go Gentle into That Good Night*   *163*

CONTENTS

Robert Frost, *Once by the Pacific*   164
E. E. Cummings, *Chansons Innocentes, I*   169

CONSONANTS   171

EXERCISES AND DIVERSIONS   180
John Milton, *On the Late Massacre in Piedmont*   183
Anonymous, *Love and Death*   183

8 WORKING WITH GOLD:
THE DEVICES OF SOUND   184

LANGUAGE AS MIMICRY   184
John Updike, *Player Piano*   187

A REASON FOR RHYME?   190
Ezra Pound, *Alba* ("When the nightingale . . .")   192
Robert Browning, *Meeting at Night*   194
W. H. Auden, *Musée des Beaux Arts*   198

OFF-RHYME   199
Wilfred Owen, *Anthem for Doomed Youth*   200
          Arms and the Boy   200

THE MUSIC OF POETRY   201
William Butler Yeats, *The Lake Isle of Innisfree*   205

EXERCISES AND DIVERSIONS   208
T. S. Eliot, *New Hampshire*   210
William Butler Yeats, *Under Ben Bulben, VI*   210
Edwin Arlington Robinson, *The Dark Hills*   212

· V ·
THE RHYTHMS
215

9 THE DANCER AND THE DANCE:
THE PLAY OF RHYTHMS   217

RHYTHM   217

REPETITION AS RHYTHM   219
Robert Graves, *Counting the Beats*   220
Walt Whitman, *Leaves of Grass, 21*   221
Ted Joans, *The .38*   222

THE RHYTHM OF ACCENT   224

CONTENTS

A NOTE ON SCANSION 226
Christian Morgenstern, *Fish's Nightsong* 228

IAMBIC PENTAMETER 229

VARIATIONS ON IAMBIC 231
William Shakespeare, *Sonnet 66* 232

METER AND RHYTHM 238
William Butler Yeats, *The Second Coming* 240

LINE LENGTH 242
Matthew Arnold, *Dover Beach* 243
A. E. Housman, *I to My Perils* 244
Theodore Roethke, *My Papa's Waltz* 244

EXERCISES AND DIVERSIONS 246
William Browne, *On the Countess Dowager of Pembroke* 250

10   DIFFERENT DRUMMERS: RHYTHMS OLD AND NEW   252

OTHER SYLLABLE-STRESS RHYTHMS 252
George Gordon, Lord Byron, *The Destruction of Sennacherib* 255
William Blake, *Ah Sun-Flower* 256

STRONG-STRESS RHYTHMS 258
Anonymous, *I Have Labored Sore* 260
Richard Wilbur, *Junk* 260
Anonymous, from *Ubi Sunt Qui Ante Nos Fuerunt?* 262
E. E. Cummings, *if everything happens that can't be done* 263
Dudley Randall, *Blackberry Sweet* 265

SPRUNG RHYTHM 266

A WORD ABOUT QUANTITY 266
William Meredith, *Effort at Speech* 267

SYLLABIC METER 268
James Tate, *Miss Cho Composes in the Cafeteria* 268
Sylvia Plath, *Mushrooms* 269
Dave Etter, *Romp* 271

FREE VERSE, FREE RHYTHMS 272
Ezra Pound, *The Return* 273
Stephen Crane, *A Man Said to the Universe* 274
"Think as I Think" 274

THE VARIABLE FOOT 277
William Carlos Williams, *The Descent* 277

CONTENTS

CONCRETE POETRY 279
Emmett Williams, *Like Attracts Like* 279
Reinhard Döhl, *Pattern Poem with an Elusive Intruder* 280
Hansjörg Mayer, *Oil* 281

THE PROSE POEM 281

EXERCISES AND DIVERSIONS 282
William Carlos Williams, *Iris* 284

· VI ·
THE MIND
287

11   THE SHAPE OF THOUGHT: WE GO A-SENTENCING   289

THE SENTENCE 289
Eugenio Montale, *The Eel* 291
Gwendolyn Brooks, *We Real Cool* 291

USE OF CONNECTIVES 292
Robert Frost, *"Out, Out—"* 292
Jacques Prévert, *The Message* 294

PARALLELISM 294
Walt Whitman, *I Hear America Singing* 294

SENTENCE STRUCTURE 296
E. E. Cummings, *Me up at does* 297
Peter Viereck, *To Helen of Troy (N.Y.)* 299
Robert Frost, *Beyond Words* 299
Kenneth Patchen, *O All Down Within the Pretty Meadow* 300
John Clare, *Remember Dear Mary* 300

LEVELS OF LANGUAGE 301
Robert Graves, *The Persian Version* 302
Edward Field, *Curse of the Cat Woman* 302
Miller Williams, *Sale* 303

NEW WORDS, NEW LANGUAGE 304
E. E. Cummings, *wherelings whenlings* 306

EXERCISES AND DIVERSIONS 308

12   GOLDEN NUMBERS: ON NATURE AND FORM   312

William Butler Yeats, *The Statues* 319
John Donne, *The Anniversary* 323
William Butler Yeats, *The Lover Mourns for the Loss of Love* 325

CONTENTS

FIXED STANZA FORMS   325
John Ciardi, *Exit Line*   327
Howard Nemerov, *"Good-bye," Said the River,*
   "I'm Going Downstream"   327
Sir Henry Wotton, *Upon the Death of Sir Albert Morton's Wife*   327
John Williams, *On Reading Aloud My Early Poems*   327
Robert Herrick, *Upon Julia's Clothes*   328
William Wordsworth, *A Slumber Did My Spirit Seal*   329
Edgar Allan Poe, *To Helen*   330

FIXED FORMS FOR POEMS   333
George Meredith, *Lucifer in Starlight*   334
John Berryman, *Sigh as it Ends*   335
William Shakespeare, *Sonnet 29*   335
Howard Nemerov, *A Primer of the Daily Round*   336
Edmund Spenser, *Sonnet LXXV*   336
Gwendolyn Brooks, *The Rites for Cousin Vit*   337
Gerard Manley Hopkins, *Pied Beauty*   337
Elizabeth Bishop, *Sestina*   338
François Villon, *Ballade to His Mistress*   339
Frances Cornford, *To a Fat Lady Seen from the Train*   340
Lady Izumi Shikibu, *Lying Here Alone*   341
Adelaide Crapsey, *Cinquain: A Warning*   342
Bashō, *On a Withered Branch*   342
        Lightning in the Clouds!   342
Richard Wilbur, *Sleepless at Crown Point*   342
Anonymous, *Sir Isaac Newton*   343
E. William Seaman, *Higgledy-piggledy*   343
Paul Pascal, *Tact*   343
Anonymous, *There Was a Young Lady of Tottenham*   344

EXERCISES AND DIVERSIONS   345
A. E. Housman, *With Rue My Heart is Laden*   345
Thomas Hardy, *I Look into My Glass*   347

13   A HEAD ON ITS SHOULDERS:
     COMMON SENSE, UNCOMMON SENSE   349

COMMON SENSE   349
D. H. Lawrence, *To Women, as Far as I'm Concerned*   349
R. D. Laing, *Jill*   350
John Berryman, *He Resigns*   352
William Wordsworth, *The Solitary Reaper*   353
Will Allen Dromgoole, *Building the Bridge*   355

UNCOMMON SENSE   358
Jean Arp, *What the Violins Sing in Their Baconfat Bed*   359

CONTENTS

Andrew Glaze, *Zeppelin*   363
Thomas Lux, *My Grandmother's Funeral*   364
Lisel Mueller, *Palindrome*   365
Stevie Smith, *Our Bog is Dood*   366
Federico García Lorca, *Sleepwalkers' Ballad*   369

EXERCISES AND DIVERSIONS   371
Anonymous, *I Never Plucked—a Bumblebee*   372

14   ADAM'S CURSE: INSPIRATION AND EFFORT   **375**

Robert W. Service, *Inspiration*   375
Dylan Thomas, *In My Craft or Sullen Art*   376
D. H. Lawrence, *The Piano*   385
              Piano   386

EXERCISES AND DIVERSIONS   390
A. E. Housman, *I Hoed and Trenched and Weeded*   390
William Butler Yeats, *The Lamentation of the Old Pensioner*   392

ANTHOLOGY
395

ANONYMOUS
Adam Lay Ibounden   397
A Lyke-Wake Dirge   397
Lully, Lulley, Lully, Lulley   398
Edward, Edward   399
Lord Randal   400
The Demon Lover   401

SIR THOMAS WYATT
They Flee from Me   403

SIR EDWARD DYER
The Lowest Trees Have Tops   403

CHRISTOPHER MARLOWE
The Passionate Shepherd to His Love   404

SIR WALTER RALEIGH
The Nymph's Reply to the Shepherd   404

SIR PHILIP SIDNEY
With How Sad Steps, O Moon   405

WILLIAM SHAKESPEARE
Sonnet 18   406

CONTENTS

Sonnet 33   406
Sonnet 73   406
Sonnet 116   407
Sonnet 129   407

THOMAS CAMPION
My Sweetest Lesbia, Let Us Live and Love   408
It Fell on a Summer's Day   408
Thrice Toss These Oaken Ashes in the Air   409

THOMAS NASHE
Adieu, Farewell Earth's Bliss   409

CHIDIOCK TICHBORNE
Elegy   410

JOHN DONNE
The Sun Rising   411
A Valediction: Of Weeping   412
A Valediction: Forbidding Mourning   413
Death Be Not Proud   414

BEN JONSON
On My First Son   414
Still to Be Neat, Still to Be Dressed   415

ANONYMOUS
Loving Mad Tom   415

ROBERT HERRICK
Delight in Disorder   417

GEORGE HERBERT
Easter-Wings   418
Redemption   418
The Collar   419
Love   420

EDMUND WALLER
Go, Lovely Rose   420

JOHN MILTON
Lycidas   421
On His Blindness   427
On His Dead Wife   427

ANNE BRADSTREET
To My Dear and Loving Husband   427

CONTENTS

RICHARD LOVELACE
To Lucasta, Going to the Wars — 428

ANDREW MARVELL
A Dialogue Between the Soul and Body — 428
To His Coy Mistress — 429

HENRY VAUGHAN
Peace — 431

JOHN DRYDEN
Song from *The Secular Masque* — 431

KATHERINE PHILIPS
An Answer to Another Persuading a Lady to Marriage — 431

APHRA BEHN
Song: Love Armed — 432

JOHN WILMOT, EARL OF ROCHESTER
The Disabled Debauchee — 432

JONATHAN SWIFT
A Description of the Morning — 434

THOMAS GRAY
Elegy Written in a Country Churchyard — 434

CHRISTOPHER SMART
from *Jubilate Agno* — 438

WILLIAM BLAKE
The Tyger — 440
London — 441
A Poison Tree — 441
Epilogue to *The Gates of Paradise* — 442

WILLIAM WORDSWORTH
She Dwelt Among the Untrodden Ways — 442
The World Is Too Much With Us — 442
Composed upon Westminster Bridge — 443

SAMUEL TAYLOR COLERIDGE
Kubla Khan — 443

WALTER SAVAGE LANDOR
Rose Aylmer — 445
On Seeing a Hair of Lucretia Borgia — 445
Past Ruined Ilion Helen Lives — 445

THOMAS LOVE PEACOCK
The War-Song of Dinas Vawr — 445

CONTENTS

GEORGE GORDON, LORD BYRON
So We'll Go No More A-Roving   447

PERCY BYSSHE SHELLEY
Ozymandias   447
Ode to the West Wind   448

JOHN CLARE
Badger   450
Autumn   451

JOHN KEATS
La Belle Dame Sans Merci   451
Ode to a Nightingale   453
To Autumn   455
The Eve of St. Agnes   456

EDWARD FITZGERALD
from *The Rubáiyát of Omar Khayyám*   466

ALFRED, LORD TENNYSON
Ulysses   468
Tears, Idle Tears   470

ROBERT BROWNING
My Last Duchess   470

EDWARD LEAR
How Pleasant to Know Mr. Lear!   472

EMILY BRONTË
Remembrance   473

ARTHUR HUGH CLOUGH
The Latest Decalogue   474

WALT WHITMAN
from *Leaves of Grass* (1855)   474
Out of the Cradle Endlessly Rocking   475
When I Heard the Learn'd Astronomer   480
Reconciliation   480

DANTE GABRIEL ROSSETTI
The Woodspurge   481

CHRISTINA ROSSETTI
Up-Hill   481

EMILY DICKINSON
Went Up a Year This Evening   482

CONTENTS

How Many Times These Low Feet Staggered 482
I Heard a Fly Buzz—When I Died 483
I Started Early—Took My Dog 483
Because I Could Not Stop for Death 484
The Wind Begun to Knead the Grass 484
Tell All the Truth But Tell It Slant 485

WILLIAM MORRIS
The Haystack in the Floods 485

ALGERNON CHARLES SWINBURNE
Chorus from *Atalanta in Calydon* 489

THOMAS HARDY
The Ruined Maid 491
Drummer Hodge 492
The Self-Unseeing 492
The Man He Killed 493
The Oxen 494
In Time of "The Breaking of Nations" 494

GERARD MANLEY HOPKINS
God's Grandeur 495
The Windhover 495
Felix Randal 496
Spring and Fall 496

A. E. HOUSMAN
To an Athlete Dying Young 497
Loveliest of Trees, the Cherry Now 498

WILLIAM BUTLER YEATS
The Cold Heaven 498
Sailing to Byzantium 498
Among School Children 499
A Last Confession 502

EDWIN ARLINGTON ROBINSON
The Mill 502
Mr. Flood's Party 503

WALTER DE LA MARE
The Listeners 504

ROBERT FROST
Mending Wall 505
Provide, Provide 506
The Most of It 507
The Subverted Flower 507

CONTENTS

WALLACE STEVENS
Sunday Morning   509
The Snow Man   512
A Postcard from the Volcano   513
The Sense of the Sleight-of-Hand Man   513

WILLIAM CARLOS WILLIAMS
To Waken an Old Lady   514
The Red Wheelbarrow   514
The Dance   515

EZRA POUND
The River-Merchant's Wife: A Letter   515

EDWIN MUIR
The Horses   516

MARIANNE MOORE
A Grave   517
The Steeple-Jack   518
A Carriage from Sweden   520

T. S. ELIOT
The Love Song of J. Alfred Prufrock   522
Sweeney Among the Nightingales   526

CONRAD AIKEN
The Things   527

ARCHIBALD MACLEISH
Ars Poetica   529
You, Andrew Marvell   530

E. E. CUMMINGS
anyone lived in a pretty how town   531

JEAN TOOMER
Reapers   532

HART CRANE
Praise for an Urn   532
Proem: To Brooklyn Bridge   533

ALLEN TATE
The Mediterranean   534

ROBERT FRANCIS
Pitcher   535
Swimmer   536

CONTENTS

LANGSTON HUGHES
Dream Variations   536
The Negro Speaks of Rivers   537

KENNETH FEARING
Love, 20¢ the First Quarter Mile   537

OGDEN NASH
Very Like a Whale   538

STEVIE SMITH
Not Waving but Drowning   539

ROBERT PENN WARREN
Myth on Mediterranean Beach: Aphrodite as Logos   539

W. H. AUDEN
Lullaby   542
In Memory of W. B. Yeats   543

THEODORE ROETHKE
Elegy for Jane   545
The Waking   546

BERNARD SPENCER
Castanets   546

ROBERT FITZGERALD
Cobb Would Have Caught It   547

ELIZABETH BISHOP
The Fish   547

MURIEL RUKEYSER
Effort at Speech Between Two People   549

ROBERT HAYDEN
Those Winter Sundays   550
O Daedalus, Fly Away Home   550

KARL SHAPIRO
The Leg   551
The Two-Year-Old Has Had a Motherless Week   552

RANDALL JARRELL
Next Day   553

JOHN BERRYMAN
Dream Songs, 4, 22   554

DYLAN THOMAS
Fern Hill   555

CONTENTS

JOHN CIARDI
Snowy Heron 557
Faces 557

ROBERT LOWELL
Skunk Hour 558
For the Union Dead 560

GWENDOLYN BROOKS
The Bean Eaters 562

MAY SWENSON
Painting the Gate 562

HOWARD NEMEROV
Learning by Doing 563
Because You Asked About the Line Between Prose and Poetry 564

RICHARD WILBUR
A Grasshopper 564
Playboy 565

PHILIP LARKIN
Lines on a Young Lady's Photograph Album 566
At Grass 567
The Explosion 568

JAMES DICKEY
Cherrylog Road 568

MAXINE KUMIN
The Retrieval System 571

A. R. AMMONS
The Constant 572
Cut the Grass 573

JAMES MERRILL
The Broken Home 574

DAVID WAGONER
Staying Alive 577

JOHN ASHBERY
The Instruction Manual 578

JAMES WRIGHT
Speak 581

CONTENTS

PETER DAVISON
My Lady the Lake   582

ANNE SEXTON
Pain for a Daughter   583

PHILIP LEVINE
Keep Talking   584

GARY SNYDER
Mother Earth: Her Whales   585

TED HUGHES
Pike   588

DEREK WALCOTT
Sabbaths, W.I.   589

SYLVIA PLATH
Tulips   590

MARK STRAND
The Tunnel   592
Where Are the Waters of Childhood?   593

CHARLES SIMIC
Baby Pictures of Famous Dictators   594

SEAMUS HEANEY
Death of a Naturalist   594

MARGARET ATWOOD
Siren Song   595

LOUISE GLÜCK
The School Children   596

ALICE WALKER
Even as I Hold You   597
"Good Night, Willie Lee, I'll See You in the Morning"   597

ROBERT MORGAN
Finding an Old Newspaper in the Woods   598
Bees Awater   598

CONTENTS

ELIZABETH LIBBEY
The Gesture   598

KATHA POLLITT
Turning Thirty   599

GARY SOTO
Summer   600

INDEX OF POETS AND POEMS   603

INDEX OF FIRST LINES   617

INDEX OF PRINCIPAL TERMS AND TOPICS   625

PERMISSIONS ACKNOWLEDGMENTS   627

Before We Begin

Sometimes we feel like jumping a fence for the fun of jumping, or we burst into song for the fun of singing, or we string words together just for the fun of saying them. What we do "for fun" we do for the pleasure of doing it, without having any other purpose in mind. Fun is an expression of the exuberance we feel at being alive, an overflow of the spirit of play that characterizes so much human activity, though it may be less evident in adults than in children, less common in our time than in earlier and simpler ages. When we *imagine* anything, we are playing with images, combining them as they have never been combined before, perhaps not even in nature itself. Out of such playing with images came primitive ritual and the mythologies of early religion. Out of our playing with rocks and herbs and the mystery of fire came early science. Out of our playing with hollow reeds or tightened sinews or the beat of bone on deerskin came early music; musicians still "play" on their pianos or guitars. And out of our playing with words, with their sounds and shapes and rhythms and the images they conjured, came early poetry, so wonderful that in all parts of the world it seemed a kind of magic.

To some of us today, poetry may seem an artificial refinement of natural speech. But in the literature of every country poetry comes before prose does. It is closer than prose to the origins of language. We can even say it is more natural: more primitive, more basic, a more total expression of the muscular, sensuous, emotional, rhythmical nature of the human animal. The ancient Greeks, childlike for all their sophistication, considered the poet an "athlete of the word." In the universities of a truly humane society, they might have felt, poetry would belong at least as much to departments of physical education as to departments of literary criticism.

But what *is* poetry? That is the question this book is setting out to answer. Whatever it is, it is so closely related to the other activities of our life that we will find ourselves dealing with many curious questions about man and his world. Some of them are:

If a baby were born with no senses, would it know it exists?
How can we see sounds and hear colors?
Why do cats dislike getting their feet wet?
Why did the thought of a line of poetry make A. E. Housman stop shaving?
When do singers get a sore throat listening to other singers?
Why does the pitch get higher if we play a 33⅓ rpm record at 78 rpm?
Why do charms against the devil fail to work in translation?
Why do French dogs say "ouâ-ouâ" instead of "bow-wow"?
What kind of rhyme is like a blue note in music?
What American president wrote a treatise on the nature of rhythm in poetry?
Why do metronomes have a poor sense of rhythm?
Why did Picasso say, "Man invented the alarm clock"?

Poetry—like so much we are closest to and know best—is not easy to define. We can begin by saying what it is not. Poetry is not the same as *verse*. Verse is any singsong with rhythm and rhyme, as in

> Thirty days hath September,
> April, June, and November. . . .

The word "verse" refers only to the shape an expression takes, not to its content or quality.

Poetry *may* be in verse, and often does use some kind of verse-like structure. Many poets, for example, have been attracted by the shape of the sonnet, which arranges rhythms and rhymes in a definite formation. But the sonnet in itself is only a verse-form; a sonnet may be poetry or it may not. Poetry is not poetry *because* it is in verse; to the shape of verse it has to add qualities of imagination and emotion and of language itself. Such qualities, not easy to describe briefly, are what this book is about.

Much about verse (as opposed to poetry) is arbitrary, just as the rules of a game are arbitrary. The limerick, for instance, has five lines of regulation length, as in Arthur Buller's Einsteinian example:

BEFORE WE BEGIN

> There was a young lady named Bright,
> Whose speed was far faster than light;
>   She set out one day
>   In a relative way,
> And returned home the previous night.   5

The longer lines, 1, 2, and 5, are bound together by one rhyme; the shorter ones, 3 and 4, by another. There is nothing in nature that says a limerick should have this form, just as there is nothing in nature that says we should have four balls and three strikes in baseball, or four downs to make ten yards in football.

But though verse is arbitrary, poetry is not. Everything in poetry is an expression of what is natural: It is the way it is because we are the way we are.

The whole approach of this book will be based upon this certainty: The nature of poetry follows from our own human nature. The main divisions are organized as we ourselves are. Human experience begins when the senses give us

(1)

IMAGES of ourself or of the world outside. These images arouse

(2)

EMOTIONS, which (with their images) we express in

(3)

WORDS, which are physically produced and have

(4)

SOUND, which comes to our ear riding the air on waves of

(5)

RHYTHM. The whole process, from the beginning, is fostered and overseen by an organizing

(6)

MIND, acting with the common sense of our everyday life, even when dealing with the uncommon sense of dreams or visions.

In a good poem the elements work together as a unit, just as our own combination of body and mind works together. But if we were studying body-and-mind as medical students do, we would soon realize that it is impossible to consider all parts of it at once. The way to deal with a complicated subject is to look at it part by part. In medical school we would expect separate lectures on the heart, the stomach, the lungs, and so forth, even though we realize no organ can function apart from the others. And so with poetry: We have to talk separately about the elements that make it up—such as imagery, diction, rhythm—even though we know they cannot exist in isolation.

Although poetry is not bound by such arbitrary rules as games are, it does fall under the influence of certain natural laws, like those we call the rules of health, or like those that govern mountain climbing. Mountain climbers are not subject to anything as formal as the three-strike rule in baseball, but they cannot forget that they have only so many arms and legs, that some kinds of rock crumble and some do not, and that the law of gravitation can exact more severe penalties than any man-made rule book. Poetry may not have rules and regulations, but, as we shall see, it has to make sense in terms of our own human nature.

In such a study as this, specific examples are more persuasive than definitions. It is helpful to give the definition of a metaphor; it is even more helpful to give enough examples so that—as in life itself—we can come to our own conclusions about what it is.

We can also learn about things by observing what they are not. Just as rudeness can teach us to value courtesy, so a bad line or bad stanza can teach us to appreciate a good one. Some of our bad examples are so clumsy we may find ourselves laughing at them. Nothing wrong with that: A sense of humor is a sense of proportion. It is also a sense of delight—delight in noting that life has its incongruities and absurdities and that we can live in spite of them. Only a fool, said the French poet Paul Valéry, thinks a man cannot joke and be serious.

Our attitude to poetry—as to any subject—should be a questioning one. We might think of nearly every sentence in this book as ending with a ghostly question mark. Is this statement—we should ask ourselves—really true? We can decide only by considering the evidence we have: the poems we have read, the poems we are reading, and what we know of our own nature.

Although we will have to make some general statements about poetry, we can find exceptions to nearly all of them. A recent cartoon showed a professor of mathematics who had written $2 + 2 = 4$ on the blackboard. He was beginning his lecture with a "However. . . ." Readers may come across sentences in this book that they would like to see followed by a "However. . . ." They are certainly free to supply their own. This is a book to live with and be alive with; being alive is often a process of disagreement.

As individual human beings we differ greatly. In a time of increasing standardization, when more and more things and more and more people are being referred to by number instead of by name, it is important to cherish these differences. It seems to be a part of the general sameness of our culture that we are expected to give indiscriminate approval to accepted values. If we say we like poetry, it is assumed we like all poetry. But why should we? It is only human to have what Robert Frost called "passionate preferences." Not all readers are going to like all the poems in this book; nor should they expect to. Nor are these chapters like a tape to be fed into a computer, every millimeter of which is to be processed in exactly the same way. Human attention, like everything human, has its rhythms: Now we concentrate, now we relax, pretty much as our interests dictate. Individual teachers and individual classes, as well as individual students, will have their preferences. There is no reason they should read every poem or every chapter with equal interest. Some groups may prefer to skim or skip certain sections so that they can concentrate on others that are more to their liking. Some may prefer to read, here and there, only the poems, which are always more important than what is being said about them. We should not be misled into thinking that the poems are here only to illustrate something about poetry. Any poem might be cited to illustrate many points besides the one being made in the text that accompanies it. Over and above their relevance to any context, however, is the importance the poems have in themselves.

If we confined ourselves to poetry that belonged to the always changing world of "now," this could be a much shorter book than it is. Some years ago we would not have needed many introductory remarks to understand the lyrics of the Beatles. We would hardly have needed a book at all; we could have learned what we needed to know by going around with a transistor plugged into one ear. But the trouble with the "now" poetry of a season or two is that it fades with the season— whereas poetry, in a phrase of Ezra Pound, ought to be "news that stays news." What Emily Dickinson had to say a hundred years ago is as fresh today as when she said it. So is much of what Shakespeare said nearly four hundred years ago. Many of the lines of Sappho, from about 2600 years ago, are as vivid as news flashes.

If most of the world's great poetry is a product of the past—which is the sum of all our nows—it is only for statistical reasons: More great poets lived in those many centuries than are alive today. In discussing such a body of poetry, we can save time by resorting to what look like technical terms. These may put off some readers, who forget that they themselves make extensive use of such terms in speaking of their own interests. Referring to a midline pause in a poem as a "caesura" is no more pedantic than referring to split T's or tight ends or topspin or a chipshot or fuel-injection. Such technical terms are nothing but convenient shortcuts.

There are people who think that knowledge destroys their spontaneous reaction to anything beautiful. They are seldom right; generally, the more we know, the more we see to appreciate. There are people who think that to analyze a poem or, as they like to say, to "tear it apart," is to destroy it. But one no more destroys a poem by means of analysis than one destroys birds or flowers or anything else by means of a diagram.

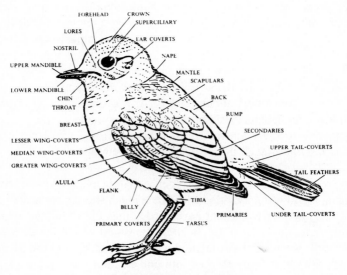

The Main Parts of a Bird

There is no reason to worry about this bird. It has not been injured or "taken apart." If one is interested in birds, one likes to be able to tell one from another—a catbird from a mockingbird, a great rackettail drongo from a blue-faced booby. The diagram shows where points of difference lie. And so with poems. Diagrams and analyses no more substitute for them than our drawing substitutes for a bird. But they may help to make a point or two.

With poetry we have to return to the reading habits of a more primitive age than our own. Poetry has no use for the kind of speed-reading techniques we are encouraged to practice with informational materials. In speed-reading, we are told not to fixate on any one word,

BEFORE WE BEGIN

not to backtrack over what we have already read, and not to sub-vocalize, by half pronouncing the words or by moving our lips. But in reading poetry we have to dwell on the words to savor their implications and relationships; we have to glance back and reread whenever we have a mind to; and we have to feel the words alive in our mouths, even if we move our lips to do so. We may have to read a poem several times to feel we know it—and then (as with a favorite record) return to it as many times as we want for further pleasure. In a world increasingly sophisticated, poetry is one of the few ways in which we can still afford to be primitive.

O · N · E

THE SENSES

I

Where Experience Starts
THE IMAGE

THE ROLE OF THE SENSES

Our first contact with reality begins with what we call an **image**—a piece of news from the world outside or from our own bodies which is brought into the light of consciousness through one of the senses. It may come through the eye as color, through the ear as sound, through the tongue as taste, or through one of the other senses as another kind of physical information. When we remember with any vividness, we remember in images. It is difficult to reason without using them; our dreams are wholly made up of them.

We can think of images as differing from ideas or thoughts in that images are always made up of sense data: They deal in such impressions as color or sound or taste or smell or temperature or the feeling of physical contact. Ideas and thoughts may involve images, but they do not necessarily do so. We can think "Charity is a virtue" or "Exercise is good for the health" without having impressions of color, sound, smell, or other sense data.

Poets (like children, like primitive tribesmen, like all of us when we dream) naturally think in images. "I no sooner have an idea," said Goethe, "than it turns into an image." But it *was* an image even before it was an idea, because that is how the mind—or the inseparable mind-body combination—naturally works. Juliet, thinking of the family feud that threatens her love for Romeo, wonders, "What's in a name?" Immediately images of color and fragrance well up: "That which we call a rose/By any other name would smell as sweet." Juliet knew the smell and feel and color of a flower long before she speculated about problems of nomenclature. About three-fourths of our brain area is given over to processing data produced by sight and hearing and smell. Poets use imagery because it makes up so much of the human experience. We can hardly imagine anything we value or despise that does not come home to us in terms of physical sensation. The poet Conrad Aiken, looking back on his life, found it made up of "The Things" (see Anthology, p. 527).

If a child could be born with no senses whatsoever—with no feeling even of warmth—it would have no way of knowing it existed. If we know that we are, and if we know that what we call the outside world seems to exist, from the page at our fingertip to the farthest reach of the newest telescope, we know it only through the senses. Even imagination is dependent upon them for the elements it rearranges in fantasy.

How the senses work is largely mysterious. The eye gives us information about light rays, but nobody understands how the cells of the retina react photochemically to the rays, or how these chemical reactions turn into electrical impulses along the optic nerve, or how these impulses are perceived by sight-centers in the brain not as flickers of electricity but as "sundance gold" or "Capri blue" or "apple green." All we know is that some kind of stimulus to the cells in the eye (or in the ear or fingertip or any other part of the body) triggers a reaction, creating a current that travels along the nerve circuits. Like a telephoned series of *click click click*, which is essentially the same for all the senses, the current is somehow turned by the brain into perceptions of tulips or tennis courts or another's hand warm in our own as moonlight plays on the lake and night wind stirs in the pine trees. The images of poetry are based on the fantastic realities of body and mind.

An image is anything presented to the consciousness as a bodily sensation. We call such images **concrete** (from the Latin word for *solid*), as opposed to ideas that may be **abstract** (Latin, *withdrawn*)—stripped, that is, of physical detail. Such words as "violet," "bread," "sunlight," "surf," and "blond" are concrete; such words as "entity," "nutrition," "meteorology," "recurrence," and "blondeness" are abstract.

Poetry is immediately concerned with the concrete, the specific, the particular, with the *bread* and *sunlight* of our life; it has only occasional use for its *nutrition* and *meteorology*. The great English poet William Blake reacted as any poet would when he once read a sentence in praise of abstraction and generality: against it in the margin he wrote, in indignant capitals, "To Generalize is to be an

WHERE EXPERIENCE STARTS

Idiot. To Particularize is the Alone Distinction of Merit. . . ." A few pages later he added another marginal comment: "Singular & Particular detail"—or what we are calling sense imagery—"is the Foundation of the Sublime." The twentieth-century Spanish poet Federico García Lorca put the matter even more directly when he said, "The poet is a professor of the five bodily senses." A nineteenth-century canon of Saint Paul's Cathedral in London might have been speaking of a bad poet when he spoke of someone as having "Not body enough to cover his mind decently with; his intellect is improperly exposed."

The senses are given us; all creation demands that we use them. When the God of Genesis chose to reveal Himself to humanity, He made a physical world of things in which to do so. When He made the human soul, He formed a physical body in which it could reside. Whatever we know of the divine has expressed itself in matter. As Ralph Waldo Emerson said, "There seems to be a necessity in spirit to manifest itself in material forms; and day and night, river and storm, beast and bird, acid and alkali, preexist in necessary Ideas in the mind of God, and are what they are by virtue of . . . the world of spirit." It is necessary to stress the dignity of physical imagery because there are those who think poets demean themselves in descending to the world of matter instead of dealing directly with the world of spirit. They forget that the poet's word, like the Word of the Evangelist, is not even apparent to us until it is "made flesh."

"We think in generalities," said the mathematician and philosopher Alfred North Whitehead, "but we live in detail." It is these details, these things of this world, that poets choose from to create their own world of poetry. Ezra Pound, one of the great innovators of modern literature, insisted that "The artist seeks out the luminous detail and presents it. He does not comment." There is no piece of advice young writers hear more frequently than "Show, don't tell." *Show* us the world as you see it, they are advised; do not—unless you are an editorial writer—give us your comments on it. So Pound, when he wishes to convince us of the beauty of a Chinese girl named Rafu, does not simply *tell* us she is beautiful; he *shows* us the effect her beauty has on men who see her:

> And when men going by look on Rafu
> They set down their burdens,
> They stand and twirl their moustaches.

So Herman Melville, when he wishes to conclude a poem by reminding us that danger and possibly evil are ever present in life, does not simply *tell* us so; he closes with an image that shows us the danger and possible evil in action:

> —The shark
> Glides white through the phosphorus sea.

So Chaucer, long before, did not simply *tell* us that a certain individual was a treacherous hypocrite; he showed us

> The smiler with the knife under the cloak.

This is the way of poets; they no sooner have an idea than it turns into an image. It is the way of any speaker or writer concerned with effective communication.

"Western Wind" is a little poem that was found, with its music, in an early sixteenth-century manuscript.

> Westron wynde when wyll thow blow
> the smalle rayne downe can rayne
> Chryst yf my love wer in my armys
> and I yn my bed agayne

> *Anonymous (c. 1500)*

Or, more comfortably in modern spelling:

> Western wind, when will thou blow,
> The small rain down can rain?
> Christ! if my love were in my arms,
> And I in my bed again!

The poet misses someone he loves and wishes spring would come so he could see her. The prose meaning of the poem—its ideas—might look like this:

> Characteristic of the coming of spring in Europe is the fact that prevailing winds are from the west; with them comes a marked increase of rainfall, though the spring rains tend to be gentle. I look forward with impatience to its coming, because at that time circumstances will be such that I will be reunited with the person I love and be given an opportunity to express that love in the normal human way.

For the anonymous poet the experience is all *one*, and all sensuous, as in reality. Spring means the wind and the rain on his cheek, so real that he addresses the wind as if it were alive—as it might seem alive to

WHERE EXPERIENCE STARTS

a child or to a simple tribesman untouched by the complexities of modern society. He imagines the reunion, too, in its physical reality. The poem does not come just from a mind; it comes from a mind in, and very aware of, a body. Aware of two bodies. Aware of the world. It sounds—though from long ago—like a real voice speaking. If we do not believe the voice in a poem, nothing else matters: The poet has left a credibility gap we will never bridge. Whatever else a poem may be, unless it seems a real voice in a real body in a real world, it is not likely to affect us deeply.

Our preference for sense detail has been embedded in the human psyche for well over a million years. It surfaces most vividly in the free-floating world of dreams and hallucinations, in the poetry of people farthest from the schooling of civilization, and in the thoughts of children before they too, at about the age of thirteen, give up their poetically concrete way of experiencing for the abstractions of adulthood. The child of MacLeish's poem is still living in the richly sensuous "antithink" world of the body.

• ELEVEN •

And summer mornings the mute child, rebellious,
Stupid, hating the words, the meanings, hating
The Think now, Think, the Oh but Think! would leave
On tiptoe the three chairs on the verandah
And crossing tree by tree the empty lawn   5
Push back the shed door and upon the sill
Stand pressing out the sunlight from his eyes
And enter and with outstretched fingers feel
The grindstone and behind it the bare wall
And turn and in the corner on the cool   10
Hard earth sit listening. And one by one,
Out of the dazzled shadow in the room,
The shapes would gather, the brown plowshare, spades,
Mattocks, the polished helves of picks, a scythe
Hung from the rafters, shovels, slender tines   15
Glinting across the curve of sickles—shapes
Older than men were, the wise tools, the iron
Friendly with earth. And sit there, quiet, breathing
The harsh dry smell of withered bulbs, the faint
Odor of dung, the silence. And outside   20
Beyond the half-shut door the blind leaves
And the corn moving. And at noon would come,
Up from the garden, his hard crooked hands
Gentle with earth, his knees still earth-stained, smelling
Of sun, of summer, the old gardener, like   25

THE SENSES

A priest, like an interpreter, and bend
Over his baskets.
                    And they would not speak:
They would say nothing. And the child would sit there
Happy as though he had no name, as though   *30*
He had been no one: like a leaf, a stem,
Like a root growing—

Archibald MacLeish (1892–1982)

Hardly a line without a physical image.

Poems rarely limit themselves to one or two senses; most range as our minds do, using whatever sense gives the most relevant information. Nor are the senses limited to five: We can feel what our muscles are doing, can keep our balance, can sense a hot stove in a dark room, can feel pain and other bodily intimations. The mechanisms that give us our "body image" or self-awareness are called proprioceptive; in health they operate so smoothly we are not aware they exist.

One of the most celebrated of proprioceptive poems is by Sappho, who wrote some very modern poems in the sixth century B.C. In it, she tells how it feels to see someone sitting casually next to the person she is in love with. She lets us share the whole force of her passion by detailing, almost without comment, her physical symptoms. The poem begins:

There's a man I really believe's in heaven
—over there, *that* man. To be sitting near you,
knee to knee so close to you, hear your voice, your
          cozy low laughter,
close to *you*—enough in the very thought to   *5*
put my heart at once in a palpitation.
I, come face to face with you on a sudden,
          stand in a stupor:
tongue a lump, unable to lift; elusive
little flames play over the skin and smolder   *10*
under. Eyes go blind in a flash; and ears hear
          only their own din.
Head to toe I'm cold with a sudden moisture;
knees are faint; my cheeks, in an instant, drain to
pale as grass. I think to myself, the end? I'm   *15*
          really going under? . . .

Sappho (fl. c. 600 B.C.)

In an early poem T. S. Eliot wants to tell us that life in a big crowded modern city can be lonely, depressing, sordid, hurried, anonymous, that it can leave human beings nervous, dissatisfied, frustrated.

These are abstract ideas, which Eliot never states directly in his poem. As poet, his problem is to find the images that will embody these ideas; in the poem that results, there is hardly a line not made up of sense imagery.

• PRELUDES •

I

The winter evening settles down
With smell of steaks in passageways.
Six o'clock.
The burnt-out ends of smoky days.
And now a gusty shower wraps   5
The grimy scraps
Of withered leaves about your feet
And newspapers from vacant lots;
The showers beat
On broken blinds and chimney-pots,   10
And at the corner of the street
A lonely cab-horse steams and stamps.
And then the lighting of the lamps.

II

The morning comes to consciousness
Of faint stale smells of beer   15
From the sawdust-trampled street
With all its muddy feet that press
To early coffee-stands.
With the other masquerades
That time resumes,   20
One thinks of all the hands
That are raising dingy shades
In a thousand furnished rooms.

III

You tossed a blanket from the bed,
You lay upon your back, and waited;   25
You dozed, and watched the night revealing
The thousand sordid images
Of which your soul was constituted;
They flickered against the ceiling.
And when all the world came back   30
And the light crept up between the shutters
And you heard the sparrows in the gutters,
You had such a vision of the street
As the street hardly understands;
Sitting along the bed's edge, where   35

You curled the papers from your hair,
Or clasped the yellow soles of feet
In the palms of both soiled hands.

IV

His soul stretched tight across the skies
That fade behind a city block,   40
Or trampled by insistent feet
At four and five and six o'clock;
And short square fingers stuffing pipes,
And evening newspapers, and eyes
Assured of certain certainties,   45
The conscience of a blackened street
Impatient to assume the world.

    I am moved by fancies that are curled
Around these images, and cling:
The notion of some infinitely gentle   50
Infinitely suffering thing.

    Wipe your hand across your mouth, and laugh;
The worlds revolve like ancient women
Gathering fuel in vacant lots.

T. S. Eliot (1888–1965)

    Operating with imagery is more than a preference of the mind; it is an actual necessity. When people are sense-deprived, left alone in darkness and silence, they begin to hallucinate. We find something like this hallucination in the poetry of John Keats, who said, "O for a life of Sensations rather than of Thoughts!" His "Ode to a Nightingale" (see Anthology, p. 453), which begins with proprioceptive sensations, whirls away on images of sight, sound, touch, taste, and smell, escaping into pure imagination in spite of the interference of "the dull brain." The fifth stanza is an example of compensatory dreaming: Unable to see what flowers—imaginary flowers—are around him, Keats proceeds to identify them by their imaginary smells.

    Poets in all ages have turned ideas into images, as the ancient Greek poet did when he lamented that a lady who had rejected him in youth and middle age was still rejecting him.

• BRIEF AUTUMNAL •

Green grape, and you refused me.
Ripe grape, and you sent me packing.
Must you deny me a bite of your raisin?

Anonymous (date uncertain)
(Translated by Dudley Fitts, 1903–1968)

•abstract/concrete•

"I no sooner have an idea," said Goethe, "than it turns into an image." That, typically, is the way the poetic mind works. Here are examples, all from Shakespeare, of how abstract ideas are turned into concrete images—images, for the most part, of *things*, simple and familiar.

ABSTRACT IDEAS

CONCRETE IMAGES

We mean you no harm.
> To you our swords have leaden points, Mark Antony . . .

Just because you're so proper, does that mean other people cannot enjoy themselves?
> Dost thou think, because thou art virtuous,
> There shall be no more cakes and ale?

Though he is prosperous and secure, you can annoy him in little ways.
> And though he in a fertile climate dwell,
> Plague him with flies.

Make the best of it.
> Men do their broken weapons rather use
> Than their bare hands.

We cannot trust anyone.
> Where we are,
> There's daggers in men's smiles . . .

Ungrateful children are a source of suffering to their parents.
> How sharper than a serpent's tooth it is
> To have a thankless child.

I have much to worry about.
> O, full of scorpions is my mind, dear wife!

People who fail lose many friends.
> Men shut their doors against a setting sun.

I often change my mind.
> I am a feather for each wind that blows.

You are cowardly, stupid, and unreliable.
> He that trusts to you,
> Where he should find you lions, finds you hares;
> Where foxes, geese; you are no surer, no,
> Than is the coal of fire upon the ice
> Or hailstone in the sun.

THE SPECIFIC IMAGE

Our senses note only particulars. We never see color, we see particular colors; we never just touch, we touch something. For a long time philosophers have been saying that being exists only in individual things. "The individual," says Carl Jung, "is the only reality." E. E. Cummings puts it more catchily: "There's nothing as something as one." *Humanity* does not exist as a thing we can see; but *this* person does, *that* person does. This human preference for the particular is shown in many primitive languages, which may have no word for "tree" but which may have many such words as "oak," "pine," "maple," and "elm." Poets, like primitives and children, prefer the specific image. Pound, who urged writers to go in fear of abstractions, and who believed "It is better to present one image in a lifetime than to produce voluminous works," has given us some memorable images.

· IN A STATION OF THE METRO ·

The apparition of these faces in the crowd;
Petals on a wet, black bough.

Ezra Pound (1885–1972)

· ALBA ·

As cool as the pale wet leaves of lily-of-the-valley
She lay beside me in the dawn.

Ezra Pound (1885–1972)

Frequently a poem (like life itself) offers only sense details; it professes neither a meaning nor a moral, though it may embody both. The interpretation (as in life itself) will be up to us.

· THE END OF THE WEEKEND ·

A dying firelight slides along the quirt
Of the cast-iron cowboy where he leans
Against my father's books. The lariat
Whirls into darkness. My girl, in skin-tight jeans,
Fingers a page of Captain Marryat,
Inviting insolent shadows to her shirt.

5

WHERE EXPERIENCE STARTS

We rise together to the second floor.
Outside, across the lake, an endless wind
Whips at the headstones of the dead and wails
In the trees for all who have and have not sinned.   *10*
She rubs against me and I feel her nails.
Although we are alone, I lock the door.

The eventual shapes of all our formless prayers,
This dark, this cabin of loose imaginings,
Wind, lake, lip, everything awaits   *15*
The slow unloosening of her underthings.
And then the noise. Something is dropped. It grates
Against the attic beams.
                              I climb the stairs,

Armed with a belt.   *20*
                        A long magnesium strip
Of moonlight from the dormer cuts a path
Among the shattered skeletons of mice.
A great black presence beats its wings in wrath.
Above the boneyard burn its golden eyes.   *25*
Some small grey fur is pulsing in its grip.

Anthony Hecht (b. 1923)

The author presents his evidence—shows what happens—without comment. We decide on the meaning, each of us, as if each had been present in that lakeside cottage.

Film makers often use imagery in a similar way.

There is a famous sequence at the end of Lewis Milestone's *All Quiet on the Western Front* in which the hero, Paul, a German soldier, is shot by a French sniper. The sniper is shown carefully aiming his rifle but all we see of Paul is his hand stretching out to try and touch a butterfly that has come to rest. We recognize it as Paul's hand because we already know he is a butterfly collector, and, because of the sniper, watch it stretching farther in anxious suspense. Then there is a shot, the hand jerks, slowly drops, and lies still. Paul's death is as vivid as if we had seen a full picture of him dying. . . .*

The rifle, the hand, the butterfly—these are the kind of images the poet also uses. A good way to check on the *visual* imagery in a poem is to ask: What kind of camerawork would it take to present this image? Could it be filmed at all?

---

* R. Stephenson and Jean R. Debrix, *The Cinema as Art* (Baltimore: Penguin, 1965), p. 207.

For examples of a technique like that of cinema we can go to some of the oldest poems in English, the folk ballads, which move, through graphic scenes generally without transition, from emotional high point to emotional high point.

• SIR PATRICK SPENS •

The king sits in Dumferling toune,
    Drinking the blude-reid wine:
"O whar will I get guid sailor,
    To sail this schip of mine?"

Up and spak an eldern knicht,   5
    Sat at the kings richt kne:
"Sir Patrick Spens is the best sailor,
    That sails upon the se."

The king has written a braid letter,
    And signd it wi' his hand;   10
And sent it to Sir Patrick Spens,
    Was walking on the sand.

The first line that Sir Patrick red,
    A loud lauch lauched he:
The next line that Sir Patrick red,   15
    The teir blinded his ee.

"O wha is this has don this deid,
    This ill deid don to me;
To send me out this time o' the yeir,
    To sail upon the se?   20

"Mak haste, mak haste, my mirry men all,
    Our guid schip sails the morne."
"O say na sae, my master deir,
    For I feir a deadlie storme.

"Late, late yestreen I saw the new moone   25
    Wi' the auld moone in hir arme;
And I feir, I feir, my deir master,
    That we will cum to harme."

9/**braid:** *broad, long*   23/**na sae:** *not so*
14/**lauch:** *laugh*   25/**yestreen:** *yesterday evening*
16/**ee:** *eye*   26/**auld:** *old*
17/**wha:** *who*

WHERE EXPERIENCE STARTS

O our Scots nobles wer richt laith
   To weet their cork-heild shoone;   *30*
Bot lang owre a' the play wer playd,
   Thair hats they swam aboone.

O lang, lang, may thair ladies sit
   Wi' thair fans into their hand,
Or eir they se Sir Patrick Spens   *35*
   Cum sailing to the land.

O lang, lang, may the ladies stand,
   Wi' thair gold kems in their hair,
Waiting for thair ain deir lords,
   For they'll se thame na mair.   *40*

Haf owre, haf owre to Aberdour,
   It's fiftie fadom deip,
And thair lies guid Sir Patrick Spens,
   Wi' the Scots lords at his feit.

Anonymous (date uncertain)

One can imagine the action here filmed as a short art movie, following the order of the stanzas. The scenario for the first three might run as follows:

1. Shot of king, surrounded by councillors. King's fingers move nervously on stem of wine goblet. He glances at window; storm outside. Tossing branches, fast-moving clouds. King asks his question.
2. Camera goes from face to face of councillors. They look toward window. Gradually all look toward old knight. He answers. Reluctantly?
3. Shot of king's hand, signing letter with great flourish. Shot of Sir Patrick Spens, walking by surf. Stormy background. Small medieval ships drawn up on shore. His men nearby. He is handed the letter.

---

[29]/**richt laith:** *right loth*
[30]/**weet . . . shoone:** *wet . . . shoes*
[31]/**Bot lang owre a':** *but long before all*
[32]/**swam aboon:** *floated above*

[35]/**Or eir:** *before ever*
[38]/**kems:** *combs*
[40]/**na mair:** *no more*
[41]/**Haf owre:** *half way over*

exercises & diversions

A. Effective writing avoids the abstract and general; it prefers the concrete and particular. This is as true of advertising and other forms of popular communication as it is of poetry. Writers for the media, we notice, make rich use of most of the poetic devices discussed in this book. The cartoon below is not about one team versus another, but about the abstract versus the concrete. Think of examples of the kind of concrete detail whose absence in the words of the first speaker provokes the critical outburst of the second.

(By permission of John Hart and Field Enterprises, Inc.)

B. Since snakes do not have the same sensory equipment as we have, special problems come up for the poet who tries to get into the consciousness of a snake. How successfully is it done here?

RATTLER, ALERT

Slowly he sways that head that cannot hear,
Two-jeweled cone of horn the yellow of rust,
Pooled on the current of his listening fear.
His length is on the tympanum of earth,
And by his tendril tongue's tasting the air   5
He sips, perhaps, a secret of his race
Or feels for the known vibrations, heat, or trace
Of smoother satin than the hillwind's thrust
Through grass: the aspirate of my half-held breath,
The crushing of my weight upon the dust,   10
My foamless heart, the bloodleap at my wrist.

Brewster Ghiselin (b. 1903)

Rattlesnakes, which are deaf, are very sensitive to vibrations of the earth, their "tympanum" or eardrum. Their flickering tongues are "chemoreceptive," providing them with a chemical analysis of the environment. They also have infrared temperature-differential

exercises & diversions

receptors to help locate warm-blooded prey. These are the scientific facts. How does the poet present them?

After several lines of "he . . . his" (referring to the snake), we suddenly get the "my" of the observer in the last three lines. What proprioceptive clues are there to the observer's emotional state?

Most of the lines end with a *th* sound or an *s* sound or an *st* sound. Could this use of sound be meaningful? Could the *t*'s of line 5? The *h*'s of line 9?

In the last line, why is "foamless" used of the heart? Why is "bloodleap" a better word here than "pulse"?

C. There is no point in trying to "speed-read" a poem. Most have to be read slowly, with attention to the weight and suggestions of the words. Read and reread "The End of the Weekend" until you feel you understand the situation. Ask yourself such questions as these:

1. Does it matter that the firelight is "dying"?
2. Why is the girl "inviting" shadows? Why are they "insolent"?
3. Why are the imaginings "loose"?
4. Is there any special reason, in the poem, for the girl to be fingering a book by Captain Marryat, a naval officer who wrote adventurous sea stories?
5. If they are alone, why does the man lock the door?
6. What does the image of the "great black presence" have to do with the love affair? What effect, if any, did it probably have on the lovers?

D. O that 'twere possible
After long grief and pain
To find the arms of my true love
Round me once again!

Tennyson, in this excerpt from "Maud," is saying about the same thing as the author of "Western Wind." Most readers would probably feel that he is saying it less memorably. Would you agree? Find as many *specific* reasons as you can for the superiority of whichever version you prefer.

E. 1. Instead of the abstraction "nutriment" one might use such an image as "juicy cheeseburger on dark rye with dill pickle." What concrete images can you think of that might be used to stand for the following abstractions: exercise, amusement, wretchedness, locality, velocity, attraction, dryness, spiciness, agitation, deception, insufficiency, authority, success?
2. A traffic signal might be used as an image to stand for such abstractions as safety or control. While walking, driving, or idling, make a list of ten objects that come to your attention. What abstrac-

tions (qualities, conditions, processes) could each stand for if mentioned in a poem?

F. In this fragment, Sappho invites the goddess Aphrodite to come visit her in a temple garden. In her description, how many of our senses does the poet involve?

Leaving Crete, come visit again our temple,
please, for me. So holy a place, a pleasant
stand of apple trees, and the altar wreathed in
    cedary incense.
Once within, you've water that chuckles cool through   *5*
mazy apple paths, with a dusk of roses
overgrown. There's sleep in the air: the wind and
    leaves are like magic.
Once within, you've pasture for horses grazing;
Maytime flowers are rich in the grass, the friendly   *10*
heavens breathe . . .

G. 1. Complete the scenario of "Sir Patrick Spens," using, where effective, concrete details not mentioned in the text but suggested by it. What other poems in this chapter would lend themselves to cinematic treatment?
2. A poem that directly expresses the emotion of its real or imagined speaker is called a **lyric.** It tends to be brief and in some way song-like—originally, a lyric was a poem sung to the music of a lyre. (We still speak of the "lyrics" of popular songs.) "Western Wind" is a perfect example of the lyric cry: the direct outpouring of the love and longing felt by the speaker. When lyric feeling chooses to express itself more self-consciously, at more length, in a more elaborate form, it is often called an **ode,** as in Keats' "Ode to a Nightingale" (see Anthology, p. 453).

If Keats *had* expressed the feelings of his ode in a four-line lyric, what might he have said? If the author of "Western Wind" *had* written a six-stanza ode to his absent love, what might have been the substance of each of the six stanzas?

2

What's It Like?
SIMILE, METAPHOR,
AND OTHER FIGURES

SIMILE AND METAPHOR

The poet's preference for thinking in images, as we have seen, is not merely a literary mannerism; it is based on the way our body and mind put us in touch with the universe.

In the next two chapters we are going to consider how all of us—including the poets—compare and relate the images that come into our minds. To begin with, we organize them according to resemblances. A thought pattern we use many times a day takes such forms as, "What is she really like?" "What's it like, being in college?" "What's it *like*?" Our effort to understand anything starts by relating it to something better known that it resembles. The earliest mention of coal in Chinese literature refers to it as "ice-charcoal"; all that the poet could do with the unfamiliar substance was to relate it to others that he knew. Over twenty centuries later, two of our astronauts, working in moon dust they had never seen before, could use nothing but *like*'s to describe it:

"When you put your scoop in, it smoothes it out—just like plaster."

"I was going to say—like cement."

When *Viking I* landed on Mars a few years later, scientists were puzzled by the physical make-up of its surface; comparing samples with lunar dust, sand, and other substances, they decided it was most like wet clay. When *Voyager I* reached Saturn in 1980, the same kind of problem arose with phenomena never encountered before. "When you find stuff you don't understand," one scientist said, "you ask yourself, does it look like anything you've ever seen before?"

The mind itself operates by finding likenesses. When a new piece of information is fed into the brain, it is whirled around the circuits until it finds its place with similar things. Otherwise we would not only learn nothing; we would not even long survive in a world full of hazards we have to identify.

Poets are only acting the way other people do in wondering what things are like. "To what shall I compare thee, dear bridegroom?" asks Sappho. "Shall I compare thee," Shakespeare wonders, "to a summer's day?" The Song of Songs from the Bible delights in telling what things are like: "As the lily among thorns, so is my love among the daughters. As the apple tree among the trees of the wood, so is my beloved among the sons." The best-known of the Psalms begins, "The Lord is my shepherd."

This need to compare is psychological and emotional. To describe the nature of moon dust, the astronauts had to relate it to something familiar. But poets are not merely trying to convey information; they feel pleasure and give us pleasure in discovering resemblances that no one had noticed before. *It's true*, we feel, when coming on a good comparison, *It's true, but I never realized it!* Such comparisons, the poet James Dickey reminds us, are adventurous.

A California poet, Robinson Jeffers, feeling how "beautiful . . . and a little terrible" it was to watch schools of sardines being netted at night, was reminded that civilizations too are doomed and that a fate like that of the sardines may await our world as well. Although we may not agree with his gloomy prognosis, there is something exciting and even beautiful in the way he relates his two sets of images. The discovery of any surprising likeness is one more clue to the suspicion that there seems to be an order, however deep and mysterious, in the universe.

• THE PURSE-SEINE •

Our sardine fishermen work at night in the dark of the moon; daylight
    or moonlight
They could not tell where to spread the net, unable to see the
    phosphorescence of the shoals of fish.
They work northward from Monterey, coasting Santa Cruz; off
    New Year's Point or off Pigeon Point
The look-out man will see some lakes of milk-color light on the sea's
    night-purple; he points, and the helmsman
Turns the dark prow, the motor-boat circles the gleaming shoal and
    drifts out her seine-net. They close the circle   5
And purse the bottom of the net, then with great labor haul it in.

WHAT'S IT LIKE?

        I cannot tell you
How beautiful the scene is, and a little terrible, then, when the
    crowded fish
Know they are caught, and wildly beat from one wall to the other of
    their closing destiny the phosphorescent
Water to a pool of flame, each beautiful slender body sheeted with
    flame, like a live rocket
A comet's tail wake of clear yellow flame; while outside the narrowing *10*
Floats and cordage of the net great sea-lions come up to watch,
    sighing in the dark; the vast walls of night
Stand erect to the stars.

        Lately I was looking from a night mountain-top
On a wide city, the colored splendor, galaxies of light: how could I
    help but recall the seine-net
Gathering the luminous fish? I cannot tell you how beautiful the city
    appeared, and a little terrible.
I thought, We have geared the machines and locked all together into
    interdependence; we have built the great cities; now   *15*
There is no escape. We have gathered vast populations incapable of
    free survival, insulated
From the strong earth, each person in himself helpless, on all
    dependent. The circle is closed, and the net
Is being hauled in. They hardly feel the cords drawing, yet they shine
    already. The inevitable mass-disasters
Will not come in our time nor in our children's, but we and our
    children
Must watch the net draw narrower, government take all powers—
    or revolution, and the new government   *20*
Take more than all, add to kept bodies kept souls—or anarchy, the
    mass-disasters.

        These things are Progress;
Do you marvel our verse is troubled or frowning, while it keeps its
    reason? Or it lets go, lets the mood flow
In the manner of the recent young men into mere hysteria, splintered
    gleams, cracked laughter. But they are quite wrong.
There is no reason for amazement: surely one always knew that
    cultures decay, and life's end is death.

                                Robinson Jeffers (1887–1962)

The discovery of likeness is often expressed by the figures of speech
called **simile** and **metaphor**.

"Simile" is the Latin word for *like*; we use simile when we say one
thing is *like* another. "Metaphor" is from the Greek word for *transfer*;

in using it we transfer to one thing the name of something else we associate with it, as when we say that the heart of a cruel man is a stone or that a grumpy man is a bear. The obvious difference between simile and metaphor is that the first, by means of a word such as "like," "as," "as if," "than," compares two terms or images ("I feel like a wreck"); the second omits the linking word and seems to identify the two more wholeheartedly ("I'm a wreck!"). Metaphor, since unqualified, is stronger than simile; since more concentrated, it hits with greater impact. The two terms cover different intensities of the same process, as the surrealist leader André Breton recognized when he said, "The most exalting word is the word LIKE, whether it is pronounced or implied." We can see how language itself developed out of metaphor by noting the fossil metaphors it still contains: the *leg* of a table, the *mouth* of a river, the *teeth* of the wind.

There may be readers who think that "figures of speech" are artificial or fancy ways of saying what a plain-speaking man could say simply. But the important figures of speech are not mere tricks of rhetoric; they are modes in which our minds really operate.

Our minds work naturally in metaphor; without it they would fail to function productively. When we say our minds "work" and "function productively," we are relying on a metaphor: The mind is [like] a machine. Our everyday conversation is built ("built" is metaphorical) on a foundation of many such metaphors. The nature of, for example, time is hard to grasp in any physical way. Money is more material: We can jingle it in our pocket or put it folded into our wallet. So it is convenient to think *time is money*; that way we physicalize it, put it in terms we can handle. We say we *save* time, *waste* time, *spend* time, have *extra* time *to give* someone, *invest* time in projects, *run out of* time, *budget* our time, live on *borrowed* time. All of these, and many such expressions, are based on the metaphor *time is money*. Many things in our experience make sense to us only with the help of a metaphor. This has always been true in religion, in which we think of God as a father, as a shepherd, as a lord of hosts, and so on. It is equally true in science, and never more so than today, when we are trying to understand the invisible particles in the atom. Niels Bohr, the Nobel Prize winning physicist, said: "When it comes to atoms, language can only be used as in poetry. The poet, too, is not nearly so concerned with describing facts as with creating images." J. Bronowski has explained further: "All our ways of picturing the invisible are metaphors, likenesses that we snatch from the larger world of eye and ear and touch." A recent book on metaphor concludes with: "Metaphor is as much a part of our functioning as our sense of touch, and as precious."* We should not forget that language itself is nothing but "figure of speech": We use a word when we mean a thing or an action.

When we say "A is [like] B," we are trying to show, in a fresh and vivid way, something about the nature of A. A good figure jolts us out of accustomed ruts of thinking and surprises us into a pleasant shock of recognition. But since it is the A that is being clarified for us ("Moon dust is like plaster"), the B should be better known, more familiar, in some respect more vivid than the A. The greatest writers prefer very common, "unpoetic" objects for their B's, as Dante does when he compares a winged monster, resting his forepaws on the brink of a cliff, to *a scow* on a riverbank, or when he says that people passing in the moonlight squint, in order to recognize each other, like *an old tailor threading his needle,* or that the mind rests in the truth it has been seeking like *an animal in its den*; or as Villon does when he says that the teeth of a starving man stand out from his shrunken gums like those of *a rake,* or that the body of a hanged man on which the birds feed is more pecked at than *a thimble.*

The B is also likely to be the more concrete of the two terms, as in John Donne's

> Let falsehood like a *discord* anger you. . . .

or in his

> If they are good it would be seen;
> Good is as visible as *green.* . . .

Sometimes a simile or metaphor will determine the structure of an entire poem, as we saw in "The Purse-Seine" and as we see in the following poem.

· MOST LIKE AN ARCH THIS MARRIAGE ·

> Most like an arch—an entrance which upholds
> and shores the stone-crush up the air like lace.
> Mass made idea, and idea held in place.
> A lock in time. Inside half-heaven unfolds.
>
> Most like an arch—two weaknesses that lean   5
> into a strength. Two fallings become firm.
> Two joined abeyances become a term
> naming the fact that teaches fact to mean.

---

* George Lakoff and Mark Johnson, *Metaphors We Live By* (Chicago: University of Chicago Press, 1980), p. 239. The *time is money* metaphor is discussed there.

· *simile* ·

For now I trust to have, doubtless,
More joy than there be stitches in my shirt . . .

Charles d'Orléans

[God] hangs in shades the orange bright,
Like golden lamps in a green night.

Andrew Marvell

Deep in the sun-searched growths the dragon-fly
Hangs like a blue thread loosened from the sky. . . .

Dante Gabriel Rossetti

[Camel] With 'is silly neck a-bobbin' like a
          basket full o' snakes . . .

Rudyard Kipling

Her eyes were like a stormy sea,
     Forlorn, and vast, and grey;
Wherein a little beaten ship
     Flew through the spray.

Walter de la Mare

Not quite that? Not much less. World as it is,
what's strong and separate falters. All I do   10
at piling stone on stone apart from you
is roofless around nothing. Till we kiss

I am no more than upright and unset.
It is by falling in and in we make
the all-bearing point, for one another's sake,   15
in faultless failing, raised by our own weight.

John Ciardi (b. 1916)

· *simile* ·

I farm a pasture where the boulders lie
As touching as a basket full of eggs . . .

Robert Frost

The attic wasps went missing by like bullets . . .

Robert Frost

She rides her hips as
it were a horse

William Carlos Williams

[The blue bird] runs in the snow like a bit of blue metal . . .
You acid-blue metallic bird . . .
You copper-sulphate blue bird!

D. H. Lawrence

Wi' minds like the look on a hen's face . . .

Hugh MacDiarmid

We walk a great deal when the weather allows,
The women in shoes that look like baked potatoes. . . .

Hollis Summers

It was cold . . .
A ragman passed with his horses, their breaths
Blooming like white peonies. . . .

Donald Hall

The first stanza—to oversimplify its implications—shows the marriage like an arch in that it is an entrance to a holy place (the arch and the "like lace" suggest a Gothic cathedral), which somehow makes burdens seem light. The second stanza shows the marriage like an arch in that it is composed of two individuals weak in themselves but strong when joined. Each half arch needs the other for support; alone, it would collapse. "Two fallings become firm," because it is actually gravitation, pulling the stones of the arch earthward, that wedges them firmly in place. The third and fourth stanzas mean that alone, as half arch, the speaker would come to nothing; without the support of the other half arch, all he did would be "roofless." The poem ends with the paradox (see Chapter 3) that it is the very tendency of the marriage partners to fall, their very "failing," that lifts on high the cathedral-like structure of their marriage.

As that poem was based on a simile, the next one is based on a metaphor.

· MY LIFE HAD STOOD—A LOADED GUN ·

My Life had stood—a Loaded Gun—
In Corners—till a Day
The Owner passed—identified—
And carried Me away—

And now We roam the Sovereign Woods—   5
And now We hunt the Doe—
And every time I speak for Him
The Mountains straight reply—

And do I smile, such cordial light
Upon the Valley glow—   10
It is as a Vesuvian face
Had let its pleasure through—

And when at Night—Our good Day done—
I guard My Master's Head—
'Tis better than the Eider-Duck's   15
Deep Pillow—to have shared—

To foe of His—I'm deadly foe—
None stir the second time—
On whom I lay a Yellow Eye—
Or an emphatic Thumb—   20

Though I than He—may longer live
He longer must—than I—
For I have but the power to kill,
Without—the power to die—

Emily Dickinson (1830–1886)

The speaker says her life is a loaded gun—a surprising metaphor for this poem of faithful love. Once that statement has been made, in line 1, the poet is committed to that image: Everything else in the poem should make sense in terms of both life and gun, as, in the

WHAT'S IT LIKE?

preceding poem, everything made sense in terms of both marriage and arch. Here, the life of the speaker belongs to its "owner," the one she is in love with. She enjoys the companionship of that owner among the echoing mountains of their life; the flash of the gun is like an affectionate smile. She is also his lifelong protector. In the last stanza, though the words are very simple, their connections may be more difficult: The lines seem to mean that the person loved *must* (has just *got* to!) live longer than the lover, because without him she would have no function in life, nothing to live for.

In both of these poems, the figures of speech are explicit. Merely to imply a metaphor can also be effective: to say A is like B without ever naming B, but giving clues to B's identity.

> . . . I looked, and Stella spied,
> Who, hard by, made a window send forth light. . . .
>
> *Sir Philip Sidney*

Stella's beauty is like a candle, a lamp, or some other source of light.

Since "motley" is the many-colored costume of a fool, a poet implies he lives among fools when he writes

> Being certain that they and I
> But lived where motley is worn . . .
>
> *William Butler Yeats*

Metaphors are implied but not identified in the following lines:

> When we first met and loved, I did not build
> Upon the event with marble . . .
>
> *Elizabeth Barrett Browning*

> The freighted clouds at anchor lie . . .
>
> *Henry Wadsworth Longfellow*

> Out in the porch's sagging floor,
> Leaves got up in a coil and hissed,
> Blindly struck at my knee and missed. . . .
>
> *Robert Frost*

THE SENSES

In "Went Up a Year This Evening" (see Anthology, p. 482), Emily Dickinson writes an entire poem that describes a death in imagery of a balloon ascension—without ever mentioning the balloon.

In "No Second Troy," Yeats has written about a woman whose beauty and intensity are likely to bring trouble to the world; he implies she is like Helen of Troy, whose glamour led to the destruction of a kingdom.

• NO SECOND TROY •

Why should I blame her that she filled my days
With misery, or that she would of late
Have taught to ignorant men most violent ways,
Or hurled the little streets upon the great,
Had they but courage equal to desire?   5
What could have made her peaceful with a mind
That nobleness made simple as a fire,
With beauty like a tightened bow, a kind
That is not natural in an age like this,
Being high and solitary and most stern?   10
Why, what could she have done, being what she is?
Was there another Troy for her to burn?

William Butler Yeats (1865–1939)

In addition to the implied image, the poem has two others of an especially powerful sort. Besides being like A, the B is charged with other suggestions that throw light on A. The woman has a mind "that nobleness made simple as a fire." Fire is simple, yes; but, like all basic images, it is ambivalent. It is beautiful, vivid, life-giving; it is also ominous and destructive, as the woman is. Her nobility may be simple, but—watch out! Her beauty is "like a tightened bow," its lines gracefully and dynamically curved. But a tightened bow is also threatening, like a pointed revolver. The apparently simple images carry what we could call a *supercharge*.

Or the opposite may happen. The A-is-B equivalence may be sound in one respect, but the B may carry other suggestions that weaken the metaphor. Honey and vinegar, for example, are about the same color. We might say that rich blonde hair or sun-tanned skin was honey-colored, but we could not safely say it was vinegar-colored. The suggestion of sourness in the vinegar image disqualifies it as a metaphor for anything lovely, no matter how right its color might be. We find the same fault in the following lines:

WHAT'S IT LIKE?

> Once more at dawn I drive
> The weary cattle of my soul to the mud hole of your eyes.

However desirable a mud hole may be for cattle, it is hardly a flattering image for a lovely eye.

Another common weakness is what is called a *mixed metaphor*—that is, a metaphor made up of components that do not go together. "Skating on thin ice" and "being in hot water" are sensible enough metaphors (though trite) for hazardous actions and embarrassing predicaments. But if a person says, "People who skate on thin ice are likely to find themselves in hot water," he or she is mixing a metaphor and, unless humor is intended, is writing awkwardly. Mixed metaphors are like double exposures in photography. Some may be deliberate, some may accidentally result in a good picture. Most are plain failures, with results comic, ugly, or merely blurred. We get something like the comedy of mixed metaphor in the "Irish bulls" Carl Sandburg quotes in *The People, Yes*:

> I can never get these boots on till I have worn
>   them for a while . . .
> If all the world were blind what a melancholy sight
>   it would be . . .
> They would cut us into mince-meat and throw our
>   bleeding heads on the table to stare us in the face . . .
> On the dim and faroff shore of the future we can see
>   the footprint of an unseen hand . . .

John Ciardi, in describing the fields just after a spring thaw, begins, "The paper fields. . . ." "Paper," then, is his metaphor. He continues the line, ". . . lay crumpled by the road." If the fields are paper, they have to do something paperlike; they have to be "crumpled." A less skillful writer might have said, "The paper fields lie shattered by the road," forgetting that paper cannot shatter. Pablo Neruda, as translated by W. S. Merwin, writes:

> The clouds travel like white handkerchiefs of goodbye. . . .

and then continues the image with:

> The wind, travelling, waving them in its hands. . . .

Suppose he had written:

> The clouds travel like white handkerchiefs of goodbye;
> The wind is balancing them like a juggler. . . .

The image would have been ridiculous: handkerchiefs are hard to balance.

Sometimes, as we saw in "Most Like an Arch This Marriage" and "My Life Had Stood—A Loaded Gun," an image is sustained throughout a poem. A small poem by Robert Frost is a good example:

· A PATCH OF OLD SNOW ·

There's a patch of old snow in a corner
    That I should have guessed
Was a blow-away paper the rain
    Had brought to rest.

It is speckled with grime as if   5
    Small print overspread it,
The news of a day I've forgotten—
    If I ever read it.

Robert Frost (1874–1963)

The metaphor ("patch of old snow" equals "a blow-away paper") is sustained by three words in the second stanza: "print," "news," and "read." A careless writer might easily have forgotten his newspaper imagery and written something like

It is speckled with grime as if
    It were polka-dot cotton,
Like some mystical code in a dream,
    Or a tune I've forgotten.

But newspapers are not made out of cotton, nor are polka dots much like a "code," nor is a "tune" related to newspapers or polka dots or a code.

Consistency of imagery holds together a little poem for a little girl.

· AFRAID ·

Here lies, but seven years old, our little maid,
Once of the darkness Oh, so sore afraid!
Light of the World—remember that small fear,
And when nor moon nor stars do shine, draw near!

Walter de la Mare (1873–1956)

WHAT'S IT LIKE?

Here it is imagery of light and darkness that unifies the poem. It would be easy to destroy it by abandoning the "Light-of-the-World" metaphor:

> Here lies, but seven years old, our little maid,
> Once of the darkness Oh, so sore afraid!
> Great Lord of Hosts, remember that small fear,
> And when she lies beneath the earth, draw near!

For longer poems that sustain a single metaphor, see George Herbert's "Redemption" (Anthology, p. 418) and William Carlos Williams' "To Waken an Old Lady" (Anthology, p. 514). Both are based on a metaphor; the following poem, on a simile. Again the basic figure ("Old people are like birds") makes sense on both levels (that of people and that of birds) throughout the poem.

• CITY PIGEONS •

> Old people are like birds:
> the same words flock to the mind's eye
> in speaking of them.
> They perch in public places,
> scratch for the world's crumbs, seek   5
> its shiny trifles—
> easily ruffled
> are quick to realight, alert
> and nodding,
> cheeky occupants of plazas,   10
> monuments' companions, supplicants
> in lime-specked groves
> to dirty mysteries.

Helen Chasin (b. 1938)

On the other hand, images may be sustained at too great a cost, as they are in this anonymous little verse:

> God took our flower—our little Nell.
> He thought He too would like a smell.

· *metaphor* ·

Now is the winter of our discontent
Made glorious summer by this sun of York:
And all the clouds that loured upon our house
In the deep bosom of the ocean buried . . .

William Shakespeare

Hark! she bids all her friends adieu;
Some angel calls her to the spheres;
Our eyes the radiant saint pursue
Through liquid telescopes of tears . . .

Isaac Watts

The haughty thistle o'er all danger towers,
In every place the very wasp of flowers.

John Clare

A bird . . .
And he unrolled his feathers
And rowed him softer home—

Than oars divide the ocean
Too silver for a seam.

Emily Dickinson

Thought is a garment and the soul's a bride
That cannot in that trash and tinsel hide . . .

William Butler Yeats

ANALOGY

Any resemblance, in form or function, between unlike objects can be
called **analogy**, which is a kind of reasoning based on metaphor. Since
A is like B in some respects, it is possible to suppose that other re-
semblances follow. The poet's mind—like the subconscious mind of
the dreamer and the prelogical mind of the child—is more moved by
similarities and parallels than by stricter forms of logic; analogy seems
to be the poet's favorite form of reasoning. When Sidney writes

> Thus noble gold down to the bottom goes,
> When worthless cork aloft doth floating lie. . . .

· *metaphor* ·

Out of the chimney of the court-house
A greyhound of smoke leapt and chased
The northwest wind. . . .

Edgar Lee Masters

The old star-eaten blanket of the sky . . .

T. E. Hulme

. . . an eagle
Was perched on the jag of a burnt pine,
Insolent and gorged, cloaked in the folded storms
    of his shoulders . . .

Robinson Jeffers

. . . snakes' hypodermic teeth . . .

Marianne Moore

. . . the lion's ferocious chrysanthemum head. . . .

Marianne Moore

She held out
Her deck of smiles, I cut, and she dealt. . . .

Randall Jarrell

. . . If you can beg the
money for it, dial God, and if a
creed answers, hang up.

John Ciardi

he means that since certain values in life are good as gold and others cheap and lightweight as cork, perhaps these values behave like gold and cork in the current of life: The best may sink from sight, the worst stay conspicuously on top.

Sometimes we find an entire poem structured on analogy.

· ALL BUT BLIND ·

All but blind
    In his chambered hole
Gropes for worms
    The four-clawed Mole.

·*analogy*·

And why take ye thought for raiment? Consider the lilies of the field, how they grow; they toil not, neither do they spin: and yet I say unto you, That even Solomon in all his glory was not arrayed like one of these.

Matt. 6:28

Old wood inflamed, doth yield the bravest fire,
When younger doth in smoke his virtue spend. . . .

Sir Philip Sidney

No more be grieved at that which thou hast done:
Roses have thorns, and silver fountains mud;
Clouds and eclipses stain both moon and sun,
And loathsome canker lives in sweetest bud.

William Shakespeare

Thin airy things extend themselves in space,
   Things solid take up little place. . . .

Abraham Cowley

Errors like straws upon the surface flow;
He who would search for pearls must dive below. . . .

John Dryden

But 'tis too much on so despised a theme:
No man would dabble in a dirty stream. . . .

The Earl of Rochester

All but blind
   In the evening sky   5
The hooded Bat
   Twirls softly by.

All but blind
   In the burning day   10
The Barn-Owl blunders
   On her way.

·*analogy*·

Nothing in progression can rest on its original plan. We may as well think of rocking a grown man in the cradle of an infant.

Edmund Burke

True ease in writing comes from art, not chance,
As those move easiest who have learned to dance.

Alexander Pope

No mud can soil us but the mud we throw . . .

James Russell Lowell

Try as he will, no man breaks wholly loose
    From his first love, no matter who she be.
Oh, was there ever sailor free to choose,
    That didn't settle somewhere near the sea?

Rudyard Kipling

                    But enough,
For when we have blamed the wind we can blame love . . .

William Butler Yeats

If we must speak, then let us humbly speak;
humbly becomes the great, and great we are;
ice is the silent language of the peak;
and fire the silent language of the star . . .

Conrad Aiken

And blind as are
    These three to me,
So, blind to Some-One   15
    I must be.

Walter de la Mare (1873–1956)

See also Sir Edward Dyer's "The Lowest Trees Have Tops" (Anthology, p. 403).

· *synesthesia* ·

Eyes are vocal, tears have tongues,
And there are words not made with lungs . . .

Richard Crashaw

The voice of the seneschal flared like a torch . . .

James Russell Lowell

To the bugle, every color is red.

Emily Dickinson

Dark hills at evening in the west,
Where sunset hovers like a sound
Of golden horns that sang to rest
Old bones of warriors underground . . .

Edwin Arlington Robinson

And Cortez rode up, reining tautly in—
Firmly as coffee grips the taste—and away!—

Hart Crane

When we were children words were colored
(Harlot and murder were dark purple). . . .

Louis MacNeice

Baskets of ripe fruit in air
The bird's song seem. . . .

Edith Sitwell

Analogies, like the other figures of speech we are considering, also thrive outside the literary world. When a football coach near the end of a winning season was asked if he would change his strategy for the last game, "No," he analogized, "I'm going to dance with the girl that brought me."

SYNESTHESIA

One kind of analogy that works with intersense relationships is called **synesthesia**, from Greek words that mean *blended feeling*. It is the perception or interpretation of the data of one sense in terms of an-

•*synesthesia*•

Cathedral evening, tinkle of candles
On the frosted air. . . .

Kenneth Patchen

. . . the sun blared like a brass. . . .

Gray Burr

[Of daffodils]
Yellow telephones
in a row in the garden
are ringing
shrill with light. . . .

May Swenson

It's funny early spring weather, mild and washy
the color of a head cold.

James Schuyler

A woman so skinny I could smell her bones
hugged me because I'd turned away from sin. . . .

Miller Williams

The apple nestles in the air
Humming its color. . . .

Jeanne Murray Walker

other. The process itself has been seen as regressive. Early in human history, it seems we did not distinguish between the senses as sharply as we do now. Sense data tended to overlap, as they still do in young children. But not only in children: Sir Isaac Newton associated colors with musical notes—red with C, orange with D, and so on. There are reports of musicians who see vivid colors when they compose or conduct. Sense centers in the brain, when stimulated, can apparently arouse associated centers. There is a basis then in the nature of our minds for synesthesia, which we frequently use in speech without being aware we are doing so. Words like "sweet," "sour," and "bitter" are taste words, but we speak of a sweet smile, a sour note, a bitter sight. Although "stink" is a smell word, we apply it to anything that affects us unpleasantly. "Loud" is a sound word, yet we speak of a loud necktie. We feel blue; we listen to cold words; we see dull colors; we drink dry martinis (which taste smooth). Wine experts would be lost without synesthesia: a glance at one of the standard guides reveals that the following words are used to describe various vintages: hard, soft, light, heavy, smooth, rough, dry, spotty, fat, round, green, flinty, strong, sturdy, velvety, satiny, firm, sunny, harsh. Speech itself, which turns all of our experiences into sound, has been considered a kind of synesthesia.

Synesthesia was a mode of imagery favored by the French Symbolist poets of the nineteenth century (see Chapter 3, p. 61). Charles Baudelaire imagined

> There are perfumes cool as the flesh of children,
> Sweet as oboes, green as the meadows . . .

and Arthur Rimbaud wrote a sonnet to the color of vowels, which begins

> A black, E white, I red, U green, O blue . . .

He was thinking about the French vowels; we might feel differently about their "color" in English.

ALLUSION

Another recognition of similarity is **allusion**, which follows an "it-reminds-me-of" pattern. An allusion is an incomplete reference to something that those who share our knowledge or background will understand. In conversation we often use such allusions as "There he goes acting like Bill!" or "I hope this evening won't be like the last one." To an outsider, the meaning of such an allusion would be obscure. Poets, naturally at home with poetry, sometimes quote from or allude to other writers (as Pablo Picasso liked to "quote" from other painters by including details from their work in his own paintings). When Frost, writing about the accidental death of a farm boy, calls his poem " 'Out, Out—,' " he assumes we will remember Macbeth's famous remarks on life and death,

> Out, out, brief candle!
> Life's but a walking shadow. . . .

and that his poem will pick up an added pathos from the memory. When Alexander Pope writes his "Intended for Sir Isaac Newton," he trusts we will all hear the allusion to the first chapter of Genesis.

• INTENDED FOR SIR ISAAC NEWTON •

> Nature and Nature's laws lay hid in Night:
> God said, *Let Newton be!* and all was Light.

Alexander Pope (1688–1744)

Such modern poets as Ezra Pound and T. S. Eliot have been particularly fond of referring by partial quotation to the work of other poets. For examples, see Eliot's "The Love Song of J. Alfred Prufrock" (Anthology, p. 522).

PERSONIFICATION, MYTHOLOGY

Since we have more in common with people than with other objects of our experience, it is not surprising that many of our comparisons relate things to people. We personify, or see as people, not only inanimate things but also abstractions, movements, or events. In the childhood of the individual, in the childhood of the race, in the mind of the dreamer, we find extensive use of such **personification.** The child may pet or punish his toy wagon for being good or bad. Early human societies show a tendency toward animism or psychism, toward attributing life to lifeless things. Even in our civilized society adults reduced to primitive rage break their golf club or kick their flat tire. We speak of "friendly" colors or "timid" arguments or "yawning" chasms or chemical "reactions." We project our moods onto landscapes or onto the weather. Robert Burns, when unhappy, wondered how nature could go on being its happy self.

> Ye banks and braes o' bonnie Doon,
>   How can ye bloom so fresh and fair?
> How can ye chant, ye little birds,
>   And I so weary, full o' care. . . .

Eliot called April the "cruellest" month. Projecting the qualities of living things onto the nonliving is what John Ruskin called the "pathetic fallacy." When used mechanically or sentimentally, it can be ridiculous

·personification·

Grim-visaged War hath smoothed his wrinkled front,
And now, instead of mounting barbèd steeds
To fright the souls of fearful adversaries,
He capers nimbly in a lady's chamber
To the lascivious pleasing of a lute . . .

William Shakespeare

When well-appareled April on the heel
Of limping Winter treads . . .

William Shakespeare

The grey-eyed morn smiles on the frowning night.
And fleckèd darkness like a drunkard reels
From forth day's path . . .

William Shakespeare

. . . Danger knows full well
That Caesar is more dangerous than he.

William Shakespeare

I had for my winter evening walk—
No one at all with whom to talk,
But I had the cottages in a row
Up to their shining eyes in snow.

Robert Frost

When I am dead and over me bright April
    Shakes out her rain-drenched hair . . .

Sara Teasdale

Come, my songs, let us express our baser passions,
Let us express our envy of the man with a steady job
        and no worry about the future.
You are very idle, my songs.
I fear you will come to a bad end.
You stand about on the streets,
You loiter at the corners and bus-stops,
You do next to nothing at all . . .
Insolent little beasts, shameless, devoid of clothing! . . .

Ezra Pound

or maudlin. Used sensitively, it can be vigorous: Seeing a tree in a wind-
storm, one might imagine tree and storm as wrestling antagonists.
Today we have our own personifications: "Football is king . . .";
"Medical science tells us . . ."; "The economy demands . . ."; "In-
flation is threatening . . .". We speak of Jack Frost, Old Man River
("He must know something"), Mr. Clean, Lady Luck. More than one
modern poet has transferred his soul into a plant.

· A CUT FLOWER ·

I stand on slenderness all fresh and fair,
I feel root-firmness in the earth far down,
I catch in the wind and loose my scent for bees
That sack my throat for kisses and suck love.
What is the wind that brings thy body over?   5
Wind, I am beautiful and sick. I long
For rain that strikes and bites like cold and hurts.
Be angry, rain, for dew is kind to me
When I am cool from sleep and take my bath.

Who softens the sweet earth about my feet,   10
Touches my face so often and brings water?
Where does she go, taller than any sunflower
Over the grass like birds? Has she a root?
These are great animals that kneel to us,
Sent by the sun perhaps to help us grow.   15
I have seen death. The colors went away,
The petals grasped at nothing and curled tight.
Then the whole head fell off and left the sky.

She tended me and held me by my stalk.
Yesterday I was well, and then the gleam,   20
The thing sharper than frost cut me in half.
I fainted and was lifted high. I feel
Waist-deep in rain. My face is dry and drawn.
My beauty leaks into the glass like rain.
When first I opened to the sun I thought   25
My colors would be parched. Where are my bees?
Must I die now? Is this a part of life?

Karl Shapiro (b. 1913)

In "To Autumn" (see Anthology, p. 455), John Keats personifies the
spirit of that season.

We still like to make up stories, just as our earliest ancestors did,
which use personification to explain the great forces of our existence.
Such stories, which might explain how the world began or where the

sun goes when it sets, we call myths. **Mythology** is a natural product of the symbolizing mind; poets, when not making up myths of their own, are still commenting on the ancient ones. Yeats tells us how, at a time when he thought the world was in need of guidance from above, his imagination "began to play with Leda and the Swan for metaphor." But, as he was writing, "bird and lady took such possession of the scene that all politics went out of it." He concentrated on the imagined experience itself, which, for poetry, may be more important than any "ideas" expressed. What would it really be like, he wondered, for a girl to be loved by Zeus in the form of a swan?

• LEDA AND THE SWAN •

A sudden blow: the great wings beating still
Above the staggering girl, her thighs caressed
By the dark webs, her nape caught in his bill,
He holds her helpless breast upon his breast.

How can those terrified vague fingers push   5
The feathered glory from her loosening thighs?
And how can body, laid in that white rush,
But feel the strange heart beating where it lies?

A shudder in the loins engenders there
The broken wall, the burning roof and tower   10
And Agamemnon dead.
                              Being so caught up,
So mastered by the brute blood of the air,
Did she put on his knowledge with his power
Before the indifferent beak could let her drop?   15

William Butler Yeats (1865–1939)

A poet may merely refer to an ancient myth, as Walter Savage Landor does when he puts to new use the story about Charon, the aged ferryman who in classical mythology took the souls of the dead across the River Styx in the underworld.

• DIRCE •

Stand close around, ye Stygian set,
    With Dirce in one boat conveyed!
Or Charon, seeing, may forget
    That he is old and she a shade.

Walter Savage Landor (1775–1864)

Landor's quietly written poem is about a girl so beautiful that even when dead and a mere "shade" she might have brought out the potential ravisher in Charon, old as he is.

exercises & diversions

A. Ponder the similes and metaphors in the following lines. Which do you think succeed? Which fail?

1. Fair under these [her lips] doth stately grow
   The handle of this pleasant work,
   The neck. . . .

   Sir Philip Sidney

2. Money is like muck, not good except it be spread.

   Sir Francis Bacon

3. Love melts the rigor which the rocks have bred;
   A flint will break upon a feather-bed. . . .

   John Cleveland

4. Slow time, with woollen feet make thy soft pace,
   And leave no tracks in the snow of her pure face. . . .

   Richard Lovelace

5. Fain would I kiss my Julia's dainty leg,
   Which is as white and hairless as an egg.

   Robert Herrick

6. Sweet marmalade of kisses newly gathered. . . .

   Margaret Cavendish

7. Sweet maidens with tanned faces,
   And bosoms fit to broil. . . .

   John Clare

8. The rushes whistle, sedges rustle,
   The grass is buzzing round like bees. . . .

   John Clare

9. Silently one by one, in the infinite meadows of heaven,
   Blossom the lovely stars, the forget-me-nots of the angels. . . .

   Henry Wadsworth Longfellow

10. The lamps, just lit, began to outloom,
    Like dandelion-globes in the gloom. . . .

    Thomas Hardy

11. And then Llewellyn leapt and fled
    Like one with hornets in his hair. . . .

    Edwin Arlington Robinson

12. the goldfinches
    leap up about my
    feet like angry
    dandelions

    Yvor Winters

13.   . . . a sow
    Displaying a valentine rump. . . .

    Adrien Stoutenburg

B. 1. How are metaphors used in the following lines of William Stafford?
   ("Cat's-paws" are movements of the wind as shown on the surface of water.)

   I watched his face swept by cat's-paws
   when we found the camp tumbledown,
   and back of cabins drunken Chryslers,
   Hudsons even—old elephants—fallen
   on alder swords through their ribs. . . .

   2. How well do you think the imagery (lake, skates, saint, thin ice) works in the following love poem, published early in this century?

   Her bosom's like a frozen lake
       On whose cold brink I stand;
   Oh, buckle on my spirit's skates,
       And take me by the hand!

   And lead thou, loving saint, the way
       To where the ice is thin
   That it may break beneath my feet
       And let a lover in.

C. Identify and evaluate the examples of analogy, synesthesia, and personification in the following lines.

   1. Gnats are unnoted wheresoe'er they fly,
      But eagles gazed upon with every eye . . .

      William Shakespeare

2. And the hapless soldier's sigh
Runs in blood down palace walls . . .

William Blake

3. Let no Sunrise' yellow noise
Interrupt this Ground . . .

Emily Dickinson

4. The sun had laid his chin on the grey wood,
Weary, with all his poppies gathered round him. . . .

William Butler Yeats

5. We would kiss each other, laughing . . . under the deep foliage.
All that could be heard would be the heat of the sun.

Francis Jammes

6. And music flowing through me seemed to open
Mine eyes upon new colors . . .

Ezra Pound

7. And Tian said, with his hand on the strings of his lute,
The low sounds continuing
after his hand left the strings,
And the sound went up like smoke, under the leaves . . .

Ezra Pound

8. You cannot light a match on a crumbling wall.

Hugh MacDiarmid

9. How trumpet and drum paraded before
The marching young men, how they led
Us, green and dumb, where the war
Opened his mouth to be fed . . .

Howard Nemerov

10. it was almost dark when the wind
breathless from playing
with water
came over and stopped
resting in the bare trees and dry grass . . .

A. R. Ammons

11. . . . Near the gate
A lone iris was panting, purple-tongued . . .

James Merrill

12. The old snow gets up and moves taking its
Birds with it . . .

W. S. Merwin

13. A bulldozer grinding and slobbering
Sideslipping and belching on top of
The skinned-up bodies of still-live bushes . . .

Gary Snyder

D. 1. In attacking the notion, held by some linguists, that there is no such thing as "good English," and that the only standard is what people say, Theodore M. Bernstein, in *The Careful Writer*, uses three analogies: There are more bad fiddlers than good, yet no one hesitates to say there is such a thing as good violin playing; there are more golfers who shoot in the nineties than in the seventies, yet we know there is a right way to play golf; there are more awkward do-it-yourself carpenters than competent professionals, yet we know there are right and wrong ways of doing carpentry work. "In language alone," he concludes, "are the bunglers blessed." Do his analogies constitute good metaphoric reasoning?

(By permission of John Hart and Field Enterprises, Inc.)

2. In the cartoon above, the use of metaphor has led to a failure of communication. Has the poet chosen his metaphors badly? Or has the bird misinterpreted them? Through malice? Through stupidity? (The lazy mind hates metaphor, says Diana in George Meredith's *Diana of the Crossways.*)

E. 1. Make up five deliberately mixed metaphors.
2. Marianne Moore found a simple, true, and original comparison in her line ". . . the elephants with their *fog-colored* skin. . . ." Can you think of a comparison, at once simple, true, and original, to fill in the blank ". . . the lions with their _____-colored skin (or fur) . . ."? Replace "lions" with "zebras," "giraffes," "polar bears," "toads," and then fill in the blanks.
3. Sylvia Plath found a simple, true, and original simile for ripening pears in the orchard when she wrote "The pears fatten like little buddhas." With what verb and what simile would you fill in the blanks in "The bananas _____ like _____"? What if the fruit were peaches, grapes, coconuts, strawberries?

3

The Broken Coin
THE USE OF SYMBOL

Chapter 2 focused on simile and metaphor: on how we can illustrate the nature or quality of something by comparing it to something else with which we are more familiar, or which possesses that quality more vividly. This chapter will focus on another of the ways we handle imagery: on our habit of mentioning an object so that it refers not only to itself but to other realities associated with it.

Our central concern here is with symbolism, but two figures of speech afford a handy introduction to it. Their names are exotic (like so many in medicine, law, and other fields) because given them by the scholars in Greece who noticed long ago that they are shortcuts we employ regularly in our thinking and in our speech.

SYNECDOCHE, METONYMY

Synecdoche (the Greek means something like *taking as a whole*) is commonly defined as "a part for the whole." A way of perceiving and thinking as well as of speaking, in its commonest form it singles out some part of a thing as important enough to stand for the whole thing, as when we say "A *sail!*" meaning a whole ship, or "All *hands* on deck," or "Let's count *noses*," or "We need new *blood* in this department." (Or we may use a broader term for a narrower one, as when we see a police officer coming and say "Here comes the law!") Without

•*synecdoche, metonymy*•

Scepter and crown
Must tumble down,
And in the dust be equal made
With the poor crooked scythe and spade.

James Shirley

O 'tis not Spanish, but 'tis heaven she speaks!

Richard Crashaw

Thy beauty shall no more be found,
Nor, in thy marble vault, shall sound
My echoing song; then worms shall try
That long preserved virginity,
And your quaint honor turn to dust,
And into ashes all my lust . . .

Andrew Marvell

He stood among a crowd at Dromahair;
His heart hung all upon a silken dress . . .

William Butler Yeats

The boy's first outcry was a rueful laugh,
As he swung toward them holding up the [mangled] hand
Half in appeal, but half as if to keep
The life from spilling . . .

Robert Frost

I should have been a pair of ragged claws
Scuttling across the floors of silent seas.

T. S. Eliot

synecdoche, the mind itself would have trouble operating. As Robert
Frost writes:

. . . The present
Is too much for the senses,
Too crowding, too confusing—
Too present to imagine.

· *synecdoche, metonymy* ·

[Of students on a school bus]
When a cough came from the compound interest problem,
And a sneeze from the third chapter of the Civicsbook. . . .

John Ciardi

Once at the Plaza. . . .
I heard three hundred-thousand-dollar bills
Talking at breakfast. One was male and two were female. . . .

Randall Jarrell

They took my lover's tallness off to war . . .

Gwendolyn Brooks

Here and there the snowball fights began
As boys shaped white invective to be hurled. . . .

Gray Burr

Great pain was in the world before we came.
The shriek had learned to answer to the claw
Before we came; the gasp, the sigh, the groan,
Did not need our invention. . . .

Howard Nemerov

And riding the trolley homeward this afternoon
With the errands in my lap. . . .

Eleanor Ross Taylor

We listen while a dustpan eats
the scattered pieces of a quarrel. . . .

Vern Rutsala

men with wall street in their brief cases. . . .

Victor Hernández Cruz

From the great welter of sensations fed into our brain every second
(100 million, according to scientists), our attention focuses on some as
standing for larger configurations—that is, we see "a part for the
whole." A cave man coming suddenly upon his enemy, perhaps a more
primitive type with snarling teeth bared, might later report to his cave
wife, "Guess what I saw today! The Fang!" Like so many "rhetorical

devices," synecdoche was nearer and dearer to primitive people than to us—for them, the part *was* the whole. This is a common assumption of magic all over the world. Get any part of a person—a lock of his hair, a fingernail, or even learn his real name (Rumpelstiltskin!)— and that person is subject to your magic power.

We often talk in synecdoche: "She was all eyes" or "Look at Nosey!" or "Here comes Big Mouth" or "She's really a brain" or "How's Twinkletoes?" When we ask in prayer for "our daily bread" we have more in mind than an all-starch diet. "That's life" is a synecdoche; we see one incident or situation as standing for the nature of existence.

Metonymy is so close it overlaps. If our cave man had run into a hostile but more advanced type of enemy, he might have been especially impressed by something the stranger was carrying: a sharp rock fastened with deer hide thongs to a stout stick. If he had had a second escape, he might have reported later, "I saw The Axe today!" A metonymy—the cave man is referring to one thing by using the name of something associated with it. Children use metonymy when they call a dog a "bow-wow," from the associated sound. We use it when we say things like "Are there going to be any big names at the party?" or "His backhand [that is, the ball hit by his backhand] just nicked the line," or "I've been reading Shakespeare," or "I ate the whole plate" (even though the plate is still on the table), or "I drank two bottles." The last is that old favorite—container for thing contained. (James Thurber once thought up its opposite: "Get away from me or I'll hit you with the milk!") Metonymy is used by Shakespeare when he means to tell us that kings, scholars, and physicians must all die in time:

> The scepter, learning, physic must
> All follow this, and come to dust.

THE SYMBOL

In Chapter 2 we saw that a typical metaphor has an A-is-B pattern, as in "life is a dream." (Even though we express this as "the dream of life" or "this dream-life we live," we are still relying on our basic equation.) In such a pattern, the focus is on the A; we are being told more about the nature of life than about the nature of dreams.

We also saw that in metaphor the B is likely to be better known, more concrete, more of a sense image than the A: The nature of a dream is more readily grasped than the nature of life.

The **symbol,** an image that stands for more than it denotes literally, is like metaphor in that it transfers meaning from one thing to another. But with symbol the current of interest is reversed: Our concern is directed from the first term to the second. The A is better known, more concrete, more of a sense image than what should be the B—which is often an abstraction the user does not even identify. If the poet mentions a rose, but is really thinking of the nature of beauty, then he is using *rose* as a symbol of beauty. If he mentions that he is halfway along a road, but is really thinking that he is in his middle thirties, then he is using *road* as a symbol of his life span. If he uses his *rose* and *road* symbols well, he need not refer to beauty or life at all; we will know that he has something more in mind than a real rose or a real road. If we think of the metaphoric process as "A-is-B," we might think of the symbolic one as "A-is-X," with the X usually unidentified.

Symbolic images often are physical objects: a hill, a well, a river. They symbolize such abstractions as spiritual ascent, vitality, time. A lion is a symbol for fierceness or courage; a fox, for cunning; a rock, for firmness; a torch, for learning. Light is a symbol for knowledge; darkness for ignorance. "Who looks upon a river in a meditative hour," wondered Emerson, "and is not reminded of the flux of all things?" A river, that is, is a symbol for time or change. "Every natural fact," Emerson believed, "is a symbol of some spiritual fact." We often find symbolic meaning in the details of life, as Portia does in *The Merchant of Venice* when she exclaims:

> How far that little candle throws his beams!
> So shines a good deed in a naughty world.

A candle, then, becomes a symbol for the power of virtue. Shelley, perpetually on the lookout for objects he could use as symbols, once admitted to a friend, "You know I always seek in what I see the manifestation of something beyond the present and tangible object. . . ." This is why, in "To a Skylark," he is able to address the skylark with "Bird thou never wert."

In Federico García Lorca's "Sleepwalkers' Ballad" (p. 369), a young man, dying of gunshot wounds, comes to see for the last time the woman he loves. To her father he says:

> "Friend, what I want is to trade
> this horse of mine for your house,
> this saddle of mine for your mirror,
> this knife of mine for your blanket."

THE SENSES

None of this is meant literally; the young man would not have inserted in a Córdoba newspaper a want ad reading: "Will trade horse, saddle, knife for house, mirror, blanket." The objects mentioned are symbols of two ways of life; the dying man means, "I wish I could settle down and marry your daughter."

The use of such symbols, like that of other poetic "devices," is based on the way the mind really works. Our senses are affected by something. They send their electrical message to the brain, which interprets it as an image, a symbol of the original object that moved them. We express the image by using a word that is a symbol of that symbol. When we say anything we have already built symbol on symbol.

A baby begins to think symbolically early in its development, associating the opening of a door with food-mother-warmth. Later, the adult dreams in symbols. For people in the uncivilized state, almost everything is symbolic, stands for something else. The most meaningful symbols are such natural ones as fire, water, air, and earth. Although these symbols are few in number, they have been significant to us for the hundreds of thousands of years of human existence. "No genius," says Carl Jung, "has ever sat down with a pen or a brush in his hand and said, 'Now I am going to invent a symbol.'"

Not a natural symbol, that is. There seem to be symbols we do make up. Most words are invented symbols; so are flags, coats of arms, traffic signs, valentine hearts, mathematical symbols, and the like. Scholars of language would rather refer to these inventions as *signs*, reserving the word "symbol" for what has a natural basis in reality and itself embodies the quality it stands for. A rose, for example, may be a symbol for beauty; it really exists and really is beautiful. When a snowy owl, generally an arctic bird, appeared in Chicago during a recent winter, newspaper accounts described it as "a symbol of desolation"; amid the skyscrapers or along the frozen lakefront, it seemed to embody that very quality.

Howard Nemerov gives us an introductory lecture, with illustrations, on the symbolism of a coin.

· MONEY ·

an introductory lecture

This morning we shall spend a few minutes
Upon the study of symbolism, which is basic
To the nature of money. I show you this nickel.
Icons and cryptograms are written all over
The nickel: one side shows a hunchbacked bison

5

THE BROKEN COIN

Bending his head and curling his tail to accommodate
The circular nature of money. Over him arches
UNITED STATES OF AMERICA, and, squinched in
Between that and his rump, E PLURIBUS UNUM,
A Roman reminiscence that appears to mean   10
An indeterminately large number of things
All of which are the same. Under the bison
A straight line giving him a ground to stand on
Reads FIVE CENTS. And on the other side of our nickel
There is the profile of a man with long hair   15
And a couple of feathers in the hair; we know
Somehow that he is an American Indian, and
He wears the number nineteen-thirty-six.
Right in front of his eyes the word LIBERTY, bent
To conform with the curve of the rim, appears
To be falling out of the sky Y first; the Indian   20
Keeps his eyes downcast and does not notice this;
To notice it, indeed, would be shortsighted of him.
So much for the iconography of one of our nickels,
Which is now becoming a rarity and something of   25
A collectors' item: for as a matter of fact
There is almost nothing you can buy with a nickel,
The representative American Indian was destroyed
A hundred years or so ago, and his descendants'
Relations with liberty are maintained with reservations,   30
Or primitive concentration camps; while the bison,
Except for a few examples kept in cages,
Is now extinct. Something like that, I think,
Is what Keats must have meant in his celebrated
Ode on a Grecian Urn.   35

          Notice, in conclusion,
A number of circumstances sometimes overlooked
Even by experts: (*a*) Indian and bison,
Confined to obverse and reverse of the coin,
Can never see each other; (*b*) they are looking   40
In opposite directions, the bison past
The Indian's feathers, the Indian past
The bison's tail; (*c*) they are upside down
To one another; (*d*) the bison has a human face
Somewhat resembling that of Jupiter Ammon.   45
I hope that our studies today will have shown you
Something of the import of symbolism
With respect to the understanding of what is symbolized.

Howard Nemerov (b. 1920)

(Photo by   20
Edwin J. Gross)

It helps to remember that the Greek word *symbolon* means some-
thing *put together*—originally a coin (or potsherd) broken into two
pieces, one of which was given to each of the parties in a legal agree-

ment as identification. This half coin became a *symbol*: It hinted that something more was needed to complete its meaning.

A poem ascribed to Plato uses the apple symbolically. To toss an apple in someone's direction meant to make a "pass" at this person; it was a way of saying, "I want your love." But the apple in Plato's poem means even more: It stands for the brevity of natural life and beauty. The poem is saying, as so many have said, "Now is the time for love; man does not have forever."

· THE APPLE ·

I've tossed an apple at you; if you can love me,
take it. Give me your girlhood in exchange.
If you think what I hope you won't, though,
take it, look at it:
consider how briefly its beauty is going to last.   5

Plato (late fifth and early fourth centuries B.C.*)*

The apple is a natural symbol—no mere sign—for what is beautiful and enjoyable, a natural symbol also for beauty and enjoyment that cannot last. In our A-is-X pattern, A is for apple, a real apple that really rolled along the marble of a portico in Greece. But its appleness is not the main point; if the Greek girl had simply picked it up, taken a big bite and munched away, with a mere "Thank you" for the tosser, she would have misunderstood the meaning of the apple. The main point is the X and its cluster of associations: love, beauty, mortality.

One of our problems is to know a symbol when we see one. Sigmund Freud, twitted because his cigars suggested Freudian symbols, replied tartly that sometimes a cigar was just a cigar. Sometimes the images in a poem are just themselves. An apple is an apple; a rose is a rose. They are impoverished, not enriched, by being seen as symbols. When the poet says "bed" in "Western Wind," we can be pretty sure he means an actual bed. One could read the poem symbolically and decide the lines mean: "When will the breath of the Spirit descend on me with life-giving grace, so that I may rest in the security of true belief with what I love the most—my virtue?" Common sense tells us such a reading is improbable. Finding symbols where there are no symbols can lead to serious distortions of the poems we read, and to distortions of the reality they would show us.

In our daily conversations common sense tells us when symbols are really symbols. When we hear remarks like "I never promised you a rose garden," we know that the promise of a real rose garden is unlikely in the world we live in, so we take it as standing for something else. And so in poems: When physical objects, though they seem to make sense in the context of the poem, make incomplete sense in the world as we know it, we may find we are dealing with symbols. This seems to be happening with the rather odd exchange of property in the poem that follows.

• HOPE •

I gave to Hope a watch of mine: but he
    An anchor gave to me.
Then an old prayer-book I did present:
    And he an optic sent.
With that I gave a vial full of tears: 5
    But he a few green ears.
Ah loiterer! I'll no more, no more I'll bring:
    I did expect a ring.

George Herbert (1593–1633)

Even if we assumed that "Hope" was not a personification of the virtue of that name, but an actual person named, say, Wilbur P. Hope, junk-shop owner, it is difficult to imagine such an exchange taking place. The third transaction is particularly bizarre—but so is this whole way of doing business. None of this, we soon suspect, is meant literally. The watch suggests, "It's time!" The anchor, a traditional symbol of faith, suggests, "Hold on a while." The old prayer book, "But I've been devout for a long time!" The "optic" or telescope, "Look beyond." The vial, "I've suffered and longed!" The green ears, "Some day the time will be ripe." The ring, "But I want fulfillment, complete joy— like that of a marriage."

For a poem in which the symbolism is less direct than in the ones we have seen, we can look at "Lully, Lulley, Lully, Lulley" (see Anthology, p. 398). Much of the appeal of these lines, which are at least as old as "Western Wind," lies in their mystery. We feel that something significant is going on, but are not quite sure what. The symbolic situation could stand for many things in the drama of life and death.

Symbolic poems are not less satisfactory when we cannot provide the symbols with an exact meaning. In fact, it often seems the most compelling symbols direct us to an area of speculation rather than to any single reality.

· THE SICK ROSE ·

O Rose, thou art sick!
The invisible worm
That flies in the night,
In the howling storm,

Has found out thy bed   5
Of crimson joy:
And his dark secret love
Does thy life destroy.

William Blake (1757–1827)

The rose, traditionally a symbol of love and beauty, is here something
that has life and is in a bed of vivid joy. The worm is a source of cor-
ruption, is secret, works in the dark, is associated with a violent dis-
order in nature. Many kinds of beauty and love are threatened by many
kinds of destructive secret forces. The poem is more powerful in not
compelling us to fix on any one of the possibilities; we are free to
range among them, feeling the force of now one, now another. A
symbol that has to explain itself, that feels apologetic about its presence,
is not a healthy symbol.

Robert Frost can be a tricky writer, faking out a hasty reader in
poem after poem. Frost himself said he never wrote a nature poem.
Instead, he got a great deal of fun—to use a favorite word of his—out
of saying one thing and meaning another.

· ACQUAINTED WITH THE NIGHT ·

I have been one acquainted with the night.
I have walked out in rain—and back in rain.
I have outwalked the furthest city light.

I have looked down the saddest city lane.
I have passed by the watchman on his beat   5
And dropped my eyes, unwilling to explain.

I have stood still and stopped the sound of feet
When far away an interrupted cry
Came over houses from another street,

But not to call me back or say good-by;   10
And further still at an unearthly height,
One luminary clock against the sky

Proclaimed the time was neither wrong nor right.
I have been one acquainted with the night.

Robert Frost (1874–1963)

THE BROKEN COIN

Frost knew about walks in the city at night. Everything about his poem
is authentic—and yet suggestions, like widening ripples, fade off into
remoteness and mystery. The poem would be poorer if it simply said:
"I have known the dark side of life, the loneliness and misery and
violence and oppression, the inability of all of our standards to give
any ultimately satisfying answer."

Poets who work in symbols are likely to give more care to the
vividness of their images than to the abstractions the images stand for.
Images can sometimes be so real that we are not at first aware they
are symbols, though something a little strange about them may lead
us to feel, perhaps only half consciously, that more is going on than
we are aware of. If we came to the poem below with no knowledge
about the author, we might take it for a literal love poem: A young
woman steals away from her house secretly at night, makes her way
through the darkness of a sleeping town, meets her lover in a cedar
grove by a castle wall, and is made so ecstatically happy that she
almost loses consciousness.

• THE DARK NIGHT •

Once in the dark of night
when love burned bright with yearning, I arose
(O windfall of delight!)
and how I left none knows—
dead to the world my house, in deep repose;   *5*

in the dark, where all goes right,
thanks to a secret ladder, other clothes
(O windfall of delight!)
in the dark, enwrapped in those—
dead to the world my house, in deep repose.   *10*

There in the lucky dark,
none to observe me; darkness far and wide;
no sign for me to mark,
no other light, no guide
except for my heart—the fire, the fire inside!   *15*

That led me on
true as the very noon is—truer too!—
to where there waited one
I knew—how well I knew!—
in a place where no one was in view.   *20*

O dark of night, my guide!
night dearer than anything all your dawns discover!
O night drawing side to side
the loved and lover—
she that the lover loves, lost in the lover!   *25*

Upon my flowering breast,
kept for his pleasure garden, his alone,
the lover was sunk in rest;
I cherished him—my own!—
there in air from plumes of the cedar blown.   *30*

In air from the castle wall,
as my hand in his hair moved lovingly at play,
he let cool fingers fall
and the fire there where they lay!
all senses in oblivion drift away.   *35*

I stayed, not minding me;
my forehead on the lover I reclined.
Earth ending, I went free,
left all my care behind
among the lilies falling and out of mind.   *40*

Saint John of the Cross (1549–1591)

But the poet, one of the greatest of Spanish mystics, is writing about
the love between God and the human soul. Günter Grass, the con-
temporary German novelist, has said, "I don't know about God. I
couldn't write about God in detail. The only things I know are what I
see, hear, feel and smell." If a person can know anything about God,
Saint John probably knew it—but he also knew that one writes a poem
in images of what he sees, hears, feels, smells—images that, as symbols,
carry far more than their physical references.

THING-POEMS

Sometimes a poem that seems to be a description of an object will offer
a basis for a symbolic reading. Such poems—as written by Rainer
Maria Rilke, for example—have been called *Dinggedichte*, or "thing-
poems."

• THE MERRY-GO-ROUND •
Jardin du Luxembourg

Under the roof and the roof's shadow turns
this train of painted horses for a while
in this bright land that lingers
before it perishes. In what brave style
they prance—though some pull wagons.   *5*

THE BROKEN COIN

And there burns
a wicked lion red with anger . . .

and now and then a big white elephant.

Even a stag runs here, as in the wood,
save that he bears a saddle where, upright,   *10*
a little girl in blue sits, buckled tight.

And on the lion whitely rides a young
boy who clings with little sweaty hands,
the while the lion shows his teeth and tongue.

And now and then a big white elephant.   *15*

And on the horses swiftly going by
are shining girls who have outgrown this play;
in the middle of the flight they let their eyes
glance here and there and near and far away—

and now and then a big white elephant.   *20*

And all this hurries toward the end, so fast,
whirling futilely, evermore the same.
A flash of red, of green, of gray, goes past,
and then a little scarce-begun profile.
And oftentimes a blissful dazzling smile   *25*
vanishes in this blind and breathless game.

Rainer Maria Rilke (1875–1926)
(Translated by C. F. MacIntyre, 1900–1967)

While vividly realistic, the details hint at something beyond themselves
—at life itself or some aspect of it.

"No ideas," William Carlos Williams liked to say, "but in things."
His "Nantucket" is a thing-poem, though at first it may seem as objec-
tive as a well-made Kodachrome.

· NANTUCKET ·

Flowers through the window
lavender and yellow

changed by white curtains—
Smell of cleanliness—

THE SENSES

Sunshine of late afternoon—   5
On the glass tray

a glass pitcher, the tumbler
turned down, by which

a key is lying—And the
immaculate white bed   10

William Carlos Williams (1883–1963)

    Karl Shapiro's poem, while professing merely to describe, is also
telling us something about the nature of banks and the kind of civiliza-
tion in which they are important.

• GIRLS WORKING IN BANKS •

Girls working in banks wear bouffant hair and shed
In their passage over the rather magnificent floors
Tiny shreds of perforated paper, like body flakes.
They walk through rows of youngish vice-presidents
With faraway looks, who dandle pencils and tend to ignore   5
The little tigerish lights flashing on their telephones.
When the girls return to their stations behind a friendly grid
They give out money neatly or graciously take it,
For not far from them the great interior glow of a vault
Built out of beaten dimes, stands open, shines,   10
Beaming security without ostentation.
If you glance inside it there's nothing to be seen
But burnished drawers and polished steel elbows
Of the great machine of the door. It's a speckless world
With nobody inside it, like the best room in the gallery   15
Awaiting the picture which is still in a crate.
The girls change places frequently, moving their own addresses
From Open to Closed, Next Counter, or they walk away
With surprising freedom behind a wall or rise up on escalators
Past aging and well-groomed guards whose pistols seem   20
Almost apologetic as they watch people
Bending over Formica stand-up desks writing
With ballpoint pens attached to rosary chains,
After which the people select a queue in which they stand
Pious, abashed at the papery transactions,   25
And eventually walk with the subtlest sense of relief
Out of revolving doors into the glorious anonymous streets.

Karl Shapiro (b. 1913)

THE BROKEN COIN

Marianne Moore has written a number of poems that go deeper than the descriptions they seem to be. In "A Carriage from Sweden" (see Anthology, p. 520), she admires a country cart because, in a world of increasingly shoddy productions, it is lovingly and honestly made: symbolic of a culture and a way of life she values.

Any poet who uses symbols may be called a symbolist. The label "Symbolist" is given specifically to a school of French poets of the nineteenth century and those poets of other languages, including English, influenced by them. Such poets as Baudelaire, Rimbaud, and Mallarmé shunned direct statement in favor of the magic and musicality of language and the suggestibility of symbols, in their case symbols sometimes highly personal and obscure to others. Baudelaire saw the whole world as a "forest of symbols."

ALLEGORY

The line between metaphor and symbol is not as distinct as that separating mathematical concepts; one cannot always say with assurance where one ends and the other begins. Nor is it clear exactly where symbol gives way to **allegory,** which can be defined as a narrative in which characters and events stand for ideas and actions on another level. Such fables as those of Aesop are a simple form of allegory; they seem to be telling us about animals but are really telling us about human behavior. Such parables as those in the Bible are often allegories; they seem to be telling us about the shepherd and his sheep or the bridegroom and his bride when they are really telling us about God and human beings. Most allegory has a narrative framework, either a short incident or a long story.

A mountain may be a symbol of salvation, a traveler may be a symbol of a human being in his life. But if the traveler takes as much as one step toward the mountain, it seems that traveler and mountain become allegorical figures, because a story has now begun. Even a landscape can be called allegorical if a continuity is found in the symbolism used to describe it—if everything mentioned, that is, stands for something else.

In other ages, when people thought that everything happening in our world corresponded to something in a spiritual world, it was easy to see things allegorically. Today we rarely have this kind of double vision. The modern objection to allegory is to its artificiality. It is easy enough to see that natural objects like rivers and mountains can serve as symbols for a cluster of associations, but when we force such objects, and human characters as well, into a continuous narrative in which they "really mean" something else, it seems we are regimenting them into an unnatural order in which things can no longer be themselves. What is felt to be the main difference between symbolism and allegory is that the symbolic detail is a real thing which suggests other things— as we know a real thing can do. But the allegorical detail exists primarily to stand for something else; the emphasis is more on the abstraction it stands for than on the image itself.

Allegories tend to be long; in a book like this we can consider only such miniature allegories as the sonnet below, which Sir Thomas Wyatt translated from Petrarch. The ship itself is not very real; it exists only to stand for love and its troubles. The cargo is forgetfulness (for which there is not much market in the real world); the oars are desperate thoughts; the wind is the lover's gust of sighs; the rain, the lover's tears. Any one of these similes or metaphors might work in itself; the attempt to coordinate so many may seem oppressively contrived.

· MY GALLEY CHARGÈD WITH FORGETFULNESS ·

My galley chargèd with forgetfulness
Through sharp seas in winter nights doth pass
'Tween rock and rock, and eke mine enemy, Alas!
That is my lord, steereth with cruelness;
And every oar a thought in readiness   5
As though that death were light in such a case;
An endless wind doth tear the sail apace
Of forcèd sighs and trusty fearfulness.
A rain of tears, a cloud of dark disdain
Hath done the wearèd cords great hinderance,   10
Wreathed with error and eke with ignorance.
The stars be hid that led me to this pain;
Drownèd is reason that should me comfort,
And I remain despairing of the port.

Sir Thomas Wyatt (1503–1542)

Kingsley Amis is alluding to Wyatt's poem, not without seriousness, when he describes a modern girl.

· A NOTE ON WYATT ·

See her come bearing down, a tidy craft!
Gaily her topsails bulge, her sidelights burn!
There's jigging in her rigging fore and aft,
And beauty's self, not name, limned on her stern.

¹/**chargèd:** *loaded, cargoed*   ³/**eke:** *also, moreover*

THE BROKEN COIN

See at her head the Jolly Roger flutters!   5
"God, is she fully manned? If she's one short . . ."
Cadet, bargee, longshoreman, shellback mutters;
Drowned is reason that should me comfort.

But habit, like a cork, rides the dark flood,
And, like a cork, keeps her in walls of glass;   *10*
Faint legacies of brine tingle my blood,
The tide-wind's fading echoes, as I pass.

Now, jolly ship, sign on a jolly crew:
God bless you, dear, and all who sail in you.

Kingsley Amis (b. 1922)

Details are handled allegorically. What saves the poem is the feeling that Amis is having affectionate fun with a rather burdensome convention.

Wyatt leaves no doubt that his ship poem is allegorical. We would be mistaken, however, if we read his "They Flee from Me" (see Anthology, p. 403) as if it were (although in puritanical times it has been so read, in the belief that it was improper for a real woman to show up barefoot and in a loose gown in the poet's bedroom). In that poem, Wyatt is complaining, as men will, about the fickleness of women—real women, not allegorical statues. A few decades after Wyatt, Sir Philip Sidney warned his readers that when he named a woman he meant a *woman*:

> You that with allegory's curious frame
>   Of other's children changelings use to make,
>   With me those pains, for God's sake, do not take . . .
> When I say "Stella," I do mean the same. . . .

His word "curious" ("elaborate" or "worked over") sums up the objection to allegory, which William Blake characterized as an "inferior kind of poetry."

For the use of allegory in art, see Albrecht Dürer's engraving "The Knight, Death, and the Devil" (p. 153), which shows the Christian knight—or simply the good man—ignoring such spooks and phantoms as death and the devil as he journeys through life toward the castle of salvation.

exercises & diversions

A. In the lines that follow, identify and evaluate the synecdoches and metonymies.

1. O you hard hearts, you cruel men of Rome!

William Shakespeare

2. Old families last not three oaks.

Sir Thomas Browne

3. Hark! she is called, the parting hour is come.
   Take thy farewell, poor world! heaven must go home. . . .

Richard Crashaw

4. The tortoise and the elephant unite,
   Transformed to combs, the speckled and the white. . . .

Alexander Pope

5. To see a world in a grain of sand
   And a heaven in a wild flower,
   Hold infinity in the palm of your hand
   And eternity in an hour.

William Blake

6. Today I heard a sweet voice carolling
   In the woodlot paths, with laugh and careless cry
   Leading her happy mates: apart I stept,
   And while the laugh and song went lightly by,
       In the wild bushes I sat down and wept.

Frederick Goddard Tuckerman

7. A fool there was and he made his prayer
   (Even as you and I)
   To a rag and a bone and a hank of hair
   (We called her the woman who did not care)
   But the fool he called her his lady fair—
   (Even as you and I!)

Rudyard Kipling

8. Your enemy, an old foul mouth, had set
   The pack upon him. . . .

William Butler Yeats

exercises & diversions

9.　　　　. . . She was starting down,
Looking back over her shoulder at some fear. . . .

Robert Frost

10. Under her eyelids the footlights were swarming,
Out in the dark was a murmur of faces. . . .

Conrad Aiken

11. The brown enormous odor [of pigs] he lived by
was too close, with its breathing and thick hair. . . .

Elizabeth Bishop

12. At the newsstand in the lobby, a cigar
Was talking: "Since I've been in this town
I've seen one likely woman. . . ."

Louis Simpson

B. In the cartoon on page 66, the literary person is happy to detect metaphors in natural objects. A road or way can stand for the possible ("No way!" we say, for the impossible), a rock for stability, a running brook for change, rising ground for aspiration. His metaphors could equally well serve as symbols. A flower would have served as a "Metaphor for Love" if Robert Burns had omitted the "like" in his love poem, "O my love's [like] a red, red rose." There A equals B, and the B tells us something about the nature of the A. But the same rose serves as a symbol in William Blake's "O rose, thou art sick . . ."; there the rose stands for an unnamed something (A equals X), which we take to be Love, Beauty, or some other quality.

1. If there were room to label these other objects in the cartoon, what qualities, processes, or the like, might each stand for: the leaves, the trunk and branches, the horizon, the sky, the book, the wrist watch, the glasses, the clothing, the beard, the nose, the signs themselves?
2. In Dürer's engraving "The Knight, Death, and the Devil" (p. 152) what qualities, processes, or the like, might the following objects serve as symbols for: the hourglass, the dog, the horse, the castle, the towers, the skull, the reins, the thorn trees, the armor, the sword, the lizard? Do you see other objects of possible metaphoric or symbolic use?

C. 1. In "Good Ships" (pp. 66–67) two attractive young people meet at a party, but nothing comes of the encounter. The poet seems to feel that it is sad that convention smothers the possibilities of romance.

(Drawing by Koren; © 1979, The New Yorker Magazine, Inc.)

GOOD SHIPS

Fleet ships encountering on the high seas
Who speak, and then unto the vast diverge,
Two hailed each other, poised on the loud surge
Of one of Mrs. Grundy's Tuesday teas,
Nor trimmed one sail to baffle the driving breeze.   5

[4]/**Mrs. Grundy:** *a symbol for conventional behavior.*

A macaroon absorbed all her emotion;
His hue was ruddy but an effect of ocean;
They exchanged the nautical technicalities.

It was only a nothing or so until they parted.
Away they went, most certainly bound for port,   10
So seaworthy one felt they could not sink;
Still there was a tremor shook them, I should think,
Beautiful timbers fit for storm and sport
And unto miserly merchant hulks converted.

John Crowe Ransom (1888–1974)

a. Is the ship imagery allegorical? Metaphoric? Symbolic?
b. Can all three overlap?
c. Does the "macaroon" stand for anything?
d. Instead of "ruddy" in line 7, the poet originally wrote "ashy."
Which word fits in better with the sea imagery and the situation?

2. A FENCE

Now the stone house on the lake front is finished and the work-
    men are beginning the fence.
The palings are made of iron bars with steel points that can stab
    the life out of any man who falls on them.
As a fence, it is a masterpiece, and will shut off the rabble and   5
    all vagabonds and hungry men and all wandering children
    looking for a place to play.
Passing through the bars and over the steel points will go nothing
    except Death and the Rain and Tomorrow.

Carl Sandburg (1878–1967)

Is it true that this fence, which begins as a real one, becomes more
symbolic in every line? Do you think the personifications of the last
line (indicated by the capital letters) make the symbolism too in-
sistent?

D. 1. "Lully, Lulley, Lully, Lulley" (p. 398) has been given an historical
interpretation. One scholar believes that the weeping lady is Catherine
of Aragon, lamenting the loss of her husband Henry VIII to Anne
Boleyn, whose heraldic emblem was a white falcon. Do the details
of the poem seem to support such a reading? Does it make the sym-
bolism richer or poorer?
2. Would you agree with the following explication of William Carlos
Williams' "Nantucket"? Or do you think the critic, Guy T. Wise, is
"reading things into" the poem?

exercises & diversions

Dr. Williams has written a sharp attack on the New England ethos and its prevailing Puritanism in this deceptively simple little poem. There is nothing vital, nothing natural in the world he shows us— except the flowers, and notice that they are *outside* the room, their actual color "changed" by the veil of curtains they are seen through. There is a "smell of cleanliness"—but we all know what cleanliness is next to, and Dr. Williams knows we know. The sunshine is "late afternoon" sunshine—tired and weak, as sunshine goes. The tray and the pitcher are both glass—a colorless and monotonous little still-life: glass has no character of its own, but simply reflects or shows that of other things. The tumbler, now. Is it fanciful to propose that although Dr. Williams means a drinking-glass, he would like us to think also, by contrast, of the colorful tumblers, or acrobats, of the circus world, so unlike the staid New Englanders? The tumbler, anyway, is turned down. The expression implies a refusal; the very image in itself is negative. One cannot fill a downturned tumbler—folly to try. Next to the tumbler is a key, obvious symbol of exclusion. There is unmistakable irony in the heavy "And" of the last sentence. The bed is not only dead white, it is "immaculate," which suggests a hypocritical spirituality hardly appropriate to a hotel-room bed.

E. Write a poem, in any form, that describes a simple object or situation so that it picks up symbolic overtones as the poem progresses.

4

Binocular Vision
ANTIPOETRY, PARADOX, IRONY,
THE WITHHELD IMAGE

Up to now we have been concerned with sense perception, the source of human awareness; with how our mind deals with the images the senses provide, with how it relates and compares them, condensing some into symbols, narrowing its focus onto parts of others. In this chapter we will consider how our mind—and the poet's—handles the conflicting evidence that its images sometimes present, and also how the poet sometimes prefers to withhold an image rather than present it at all.

ANTIPOETRY

Dante mentions that Providence has written the word for "man" (*omo*) in the bone structure of the human face. This fancy may no longer strike us with wonder, but perhaps Nature is trying to tell us something by the way she positions our eyes: Everything we see, we see from two points of view. The world we perceive is made up of data both good and bad, with a wide range of the pleasant and unpleasant between the two extremes. If we look back over poems we have read, we find a number of sense details that are not conventionally appealing.

T. S. Eliot mentions "faint stale smells of beer" and

THE SENSES

> . . . the yellow soles of feet
> In the palms of both soiled hands.

One false view of poets is that their mission is to give us "beauty" by seeing only the good, the noble, the inspiring in reality. What they show us is likely to be a more meaningful world than the unselective senses give, but not a "nicer" world, not a censored distortion of reality. They avoid images that are conventionally pretty and, for that reason, overused in middling poems of the past. Often their best work is made up of materials previously overlooked and therefore as fresh and unspoiled as experience itself is. The more consciously "poetic" (in the conventional sense) the materials out of which a poem is made, the poorer the poem is likely to be. Shakespeare goes out of his way to be unpretty in what may be the best winter poem in English.

• WINTER •

When icicles hang by the wall,
And Dick the shepherd blows his nail,
And Tom bears logs into the hall,
And milk comes frozen home in pail;
When blood is nipped and ways be foul,   *5*
Then nightly sings the staring owl,
To-whit to-who, a merry note,
While greasy Joan doth keel the pot.

When all aloud the wind doth blow,
And coughing drowns the parson's saw,   *10*
And birds sit brooding in the snow,
And Marion's nose looks red and raw;
When roasted crabs hiss in the bowl,
Then nightly sings the staring owl,
To-whit to-who, a merry note,   *15*
While greasy Joan doth keel the pot.

William Shakespeare (1564–1616)

Not a Christmas-card touch: no decorations, candles, carols. Yet out of this unpromising material Shakespeare has made a poem that gives a feeling of the energy and exhilaration of winter, of the challenge and vitality and sheer fun of it, such as no pretty poem could ever do.

8/**keel:** *cool by stirring*   13/**crabs:** *crabapples*
10/**saw:** *platitude*

BINOCULAR VISION

· WINTER FAIRYLAND IN VERMONT ·
(after Shakespeare)

When icicles by silver eaves
Proclaim old Winter's jolly reign,
When woodfires gleam like golden sheaves,
And Frost is blazoning the pane,
When lanes are fairylands in white,   5
And downy owls bejewel the night,
Joan baking, in a flowery blouse,
Sends rich aroma through the house.

When breezes carol merrily,
And herald angels tread the snows,   10
Wee chickadees are fluffs o' glee
And Marion's cheek a blushing rose.
When bowls of popcorn twinkle bright
And downy owls bejewel the night,
Joan baking, in a flowery blouse,   15
Sends rich aroma through the house.

Francis P. Osgood (b. 1910)

No gloomy birds or chapped noses here; everything is directed toward greeting-card charm. But if the roughness has gone out of the poem, so has the life, the convincing vitality.

The poet who sees only those details that flatter our fondest hopes has one eye closed to reality. But no more so than the poet who sees only what is ugly or shocking:

When icicles like frozen spit
Are drooling from the roof's mustache,
When roads are white as chicken sheds,
And pimpled skin's a scabby rash. . . .

Seeing everything as foul and joyless has become a more fashionable extreme—more warranted, some believe, by the world we live in. Yet dark glasses falsify as surely as rose-colored ones.

Elizabeth Bishop goes beyond the plain to the gorgeously dirty.

· FILLING STATION ·

Oh, but it is dirty!
—this little filling station,
oil-soaked, oil-permeated
to a disturbing, over-all
black translucency.   5
Be careful with that match!

THE SENSES

Father wears a dirty,
oil-soaked monkey suit
that cuts him under the arms,
and several quick and saucy   *10*
and greasy sons assist him
(it's a family filling station),
all quite thoroughly dirty.

Do they live in the station?
It has a cement porch   *15*
behind the pumps, and on it
a set of crushed and grease-
impregnated wickerwork;
on the wicker sofa
a dirty dog, quite comfy.   *20*

Some comic books provide
the only note of color—
of certain color. They lie
upon a big dim doily
draping a taboret   *25*
(part of the set), beside
a big hirsute begonia.

Why the extraneous plant?
Why the taboret?
Why, oh why, the doily?   *30*
(Embroidered in daisy stitch
with marguerites, I think,
and heavy with gray crochet.)

Somebody embroidered the doily.
Somebody waters the plant,   *35*
or oils it, maybe. Somebody
arranges the rows of cans
so that they softly say:
ESSO—SO—SO—SO
to high-strung automobiles.   *40*
Somebody loves us all.

Elizabeth Bishop (1911–1979)

Emerson in "The American Scholar" pointed out that with the rise of democracy there came a change in literature: Instead of the sublime and beautiful, "the near, the low, the common, was explored and

---

25/**taboret:** *stool or small table*
39/ESSO: S.O. (Standard Oil), a brand name now replaced by Exxon in the United States.

poeticized." He rejoiced in the fact, finding in these new themes the presence of the spiritual. Emerson would have been pleased by Whitman's registering his preference for the worn, the ragged, the ordinary, instead of the conventionally beautiful, by jotting down a "series of comparisons" he may have intended to use in a poem.

• BEAUTY •

series of comparisons

not the beautiful youth with features of bloom & brightness
but the bronzed old farmer & father
not the soldiers trim in handsome uniforms marching off to sprightly
    music with measured step
but the remnant returning thinned out,
not the beautiful flag with stainless white, spangled with silver & gold   *5*
But the old rag just adhering to the staff, in tatters—the remnant of
    many battle-fields
not the beautiful girl or the elegant lady with   ?   complexion,
But the mechanic's wife at work or the mother of many children,
    middle-aged or old
Not the vaunted scenery of the tourist, picturesque,
But the plain landscape, the bleak sea shore, or the barren plain,
    with the common sky & sun,—or at night the moon & stars.   *10*

Walt Whitman (1819–1892)

But Whitman, like the other poets we have been reading, did not swing to the easy extreme of the repulsive. In our own century Wallace Stevens commended William Carlos Williams on his "passion for the anti-poetic," by which he meant "the real" as opposed to the sentimental.

The contemporary Chilean poet Nicanor Parra uses the term "antipoems" for poetry in which "there is humor, irony, sarcasm . . . the author is making fun of himself and so of humanity." His antipoetry is not opposed to poetry as antimatter is to matter; instead of swinging to an extreme of ugliness, it swings away from a rapt and humorless fixation on accepted beauty back toward the human center from which we see the world.

Such "antipoems" are not new or modern. Poets have always been aware that some of our most exciting experiences, if seen honestly, present us with contradictory data and arouse mixed feelings—a good example is Kenneth Fearing's poem "Love, 20¢ the First Quarter Mile" (see Anthology, p. 537).

For one of the most famous "antipoems," we can go to Shakespeare:

THE SENSES

· SONNET 130 ·

My mistress' eyes are nothing like the sun;
Coral is far more red than her lips' red;
If snow be white, why then her breasts are dun;
If hairs be wires, black wires grow on her head.
I have seen roses damasked, red and white,   5
But no such roses see I in her cheeks;
And in some perfumes is there more delight
Than in the breath that from my mistress reeks.
I love to hear her speak, yet well I know
That music hath a far more pleasing sound.   10
I grant I never saw a goddess go;
My mistress when she walks treads on the ground:
  And yet, by heaven! I think my love as rare
  As any she, belied with false compare.

William Shakespeare (1564–1616)

5/**damasked:** *of mingled colors*   8/**reeks:** *is exhaled* (not the modern meaning)

Refusing to be taken in by the clichés of second-rate poetry, Shakespeare looks objectively at the woman he is in love with and tells us only the exciting truth about her.

Robert Graves (whose picture we see opposite) can look objectively even at his own face in the mirror, but his realistic scrutiny does not interfere with romantic enthusiasm.

· THE FACE IN THE MIRROR ·

Grey haunted eyes, absent-mindedly glaring
From wide, uneven orbits; one brow drooping
Somewhat over the eye
Because of a missile fragment still inhering,
Skin deep, as a foolish record of old-world fighting.   5

Crookedly broken nose—low tackling caused it;
Cheeks, furrowed; coarse grey hair, flying frenetic;
Forehead, wrinkled and high;
Jowls, prominent; ears, large; jaw, pugilistic;
Teeth, few; lips, full and ruddy; mouth, ascetic.   10

I pause with razor poised, scowling derision
At the mirrored man whose beard needs my attention,
And once more ask him why
He still stands ready, with a boy's presumption,
To court the queen in her high silk pavilion.   15

Robert Graves (b. 1895)

Robert Graves *(Wide World Photos)*

"Antipoems" are not automatically better than other poems. They do come to us with a guarantee of authenticity, but the authentic need not be, in itself, interesting or moving. Boring people are no less boring because they really exist. Wordsworth in "Composed upon Westminster Bridge" and Jonathan Swift in "A Description of the Morning" (see Anthology, pp. 443 and 434) have both written morning poems. Wordsworth is solemn, even reverent. Swift, more in the manner of the antipoet, mentions, not without humor, things that are scandalous or ugly. He gives us a different poem but not necessarily a better one.

PARADOX

Our minds operate on balanced opposites (we even say a malfunctioning mind is "unbalanced"). If our instincts of love and death, of love and aggression are in conflict, that inner tension corresponds with what we find outside. "The sad truth is that man's real life consists of a complex of inexorable opposites—," said Carl Jung, "day and night, birth and death, happiness and misery, good and evil . . . if it were not so, existence would come to an end." We could easily add to Jung's list: woman and man, ebb and flow, heat and cold, inhaling and exhaling—and so on for as long as we wish. Physics would give us examples: Sir Isaac Newton saw the universe itself as made up of equal and opposite pairs, every action having a reaction. So would physiology: We can stand erect only because for every muscle (called an "agonist") pulling us in one direction, there is a paired muscle (called an "antagonist") pulling us the opposite way. Creation and destruction seem to work curiously together.

The way in which the fundamental dualities of life coexist is represented by the Oriental symbol for the Yin and Yang. Originally meaning only the shady side and sunny side of a hill—darkness and light—the words came to stand for the cosmic polarities that make up our existence. The symbol is not merely a neatly halved circle of two colors. The dualities interact and interpenetrate, so that the semicircle of one curves into the semicircle of the other. In the midst of each colored area is a small circle of its opposite: In everything beautiful,

BINOCULAR VISION

there is something ugly; in everything true, something false; in everything male, something female. Poetry has said this in many ways. Shelley wrote:

> Our sincerest laughter
> With some pain is fraught;
> Our sweetest songs are those that tell of saddest thought.

Paradox—a statement that seems to imply a contradiction—was a fact of life long before it was a literary figure. In its Greek form, the word meant *contrary to expectation*. We say a person is a paradox when we cannot reconcile his or her apparently contradictory tendencies. We say, "It wasn't like him to do that" or "I wasn't myself last night." No one can miss the fact that human nature is deeply contradictory. Alexander Pope, who had in mind Blaise Pascal's remarks on the "greatness and misery" of man, developed the theme in this excerpt:

• From AN ESSAY ON MAN •

> Placed on this isthmus of a middle state,
> A being darkly wise, and rudely great:
> With too much knowledge for the Sceptic side,
> With too much weakness for the Stoic's pride,
> He hangs between; in doubt to act, or rest,　　　　5
> In doubt to deem himself a God, or Beast;
> In doubt his Mind or Body to prefer,
> Born but to die, and reasoning but to err;
> Alike in ignorance, his reason such,
> Whether he thinks too little, or too much:　　　　10
> Chaos of Thought and Passion, all confused;
> Still by himself abused, or disabused;
> Created half to rise, and half to fall;
> Great lord of all things, yet a prey to all;
> Sole judge of Truth, in endless Error hurled:　　　15
> The glory, jest, and riddle of the world!

Alexander Pope (1688–1744)

It is easy to see how Pope's very style is affected by the play of contraries, with line sometimes balanced against line (lines 3 to 4), half line against half line (lines 8 and 13).

In a poem based entirely on the paradoxes that arose from the very events of his life, Chidiock Tichborne, executed at eighteen, during the reign of Queen Elizabeth I, meditates on his early death in his "Elegy" (see Anthology, p. 410).

•*oxymoron*•

Yes, brother, you may live.
There is a devilish mercy in the judge,
If you'll implore it, that will free your life
But fetter you till death . . .

William Shakespeare

A dungeon horrible, on all sides round
As one great furnace flamed; yet from those flames
No light, but rather darkness visible. . . .

John Milton

[Fish] Legless, unloving, infamously chaste . . .

Leigh Hunt

. . . seas less hideously serene . . .

Edgar Allan Poe

. . . the sweet hell within . . .

Walt Whitman

Dancing to a frenzied drum,
Out of the murderous innocence of the sea.

William Butler Yeats

. . . a soft tumult
of thy hair. . . .

James Joyce

. . . the ladies in their imperious humility . . .

Marianne Moore

Paradox has been found even in Wordsworth's apparently naïve "Composed upon Westminster Bridge" (see Anthology, p. 443)— paradoxical in that the poet attributes to the man-made city such beauty as a romantic poet expects to find only in the things of nature.

Awareness of paradox is often expressed by means of **oxymoron**, which might be translated from the Greek as *cleverly stupid* or para-

•*oxymoron*•

The rough but tender voice, the wide-mouthed grin,
The unsteady-steady hand that poured the gin . . .

Conrad Aiken

He was the splendidest fool I ever knew. . . .

Conrad Aiken

My father moved through dooms of love
through sames of am through haves of give,
singing each morning out of each night
my father moved through depths of height

E. E. Cummings

I eye the statue with an awed contempt. . . .

Robert Lowell

. . . darkly auspicious as
The ace of spades.

Richard Wilbur

The lines blaze with a constant light, displayed
As in the maple's cold and fiery shade. . . .

Howard Nemerov

Robert Frost
who said either we write
out of a strong weakness (poets
love oxymoronic forms). . . .

Richard Howard

phrased as *absurd on purpose*. It links, in one syntactical unit, words that seem to cancel each other out: "honest thief," "saintly devil," "beautifully ugly," "terrible beauty," "boring excitement," "dull fun," "militant pacifist," "lucky disaster," "frigid kiss," "living death," "hurry slowly." "Superette" (for a little supermarket) is a kind of one-word oxymoron; so is the much older "bittersweet."

IRONY

Irony directs our attention, in any of several ways, to a relation of opposites. The most familiar form of irony is the statement that means its contrary, as when, in the middle of an icy downpour, we comment, "Lovely weather!" Or "More good news!" on looking at the evening headlines. Sometimes the person to whom irony is directed does not know that the words have a double meaning, or even the speaker may not be aware that they have. When Othello is confronted by an armed posse, he greets them with quiet irony:

> Keep up your bright swords, for the dew will rust them.

He is ironic in professing concern for the prettiness of their weapons; ironic too in implying that their swords are more likely to be stained by dew than by blood.

There is another kind of irony in Romeo's saying,

> If I may trust the flattering truth of sleep,
> My dreams presage some joyful news at hand. . . .

because we know that at any moment he is going to receive the report that Juliet is dead.

Macbeth, after committing murder, looks at his bloody hand and thinks:

> Will all great Neptune's ocean wash this blood
> Clean from my hand? No, this my hand will rather
> The multitudinous seas incarnadine,
> Making the green, one red.

He knows the truth of his situation. Lady Macbeth does not: It is ironic when she enters almost immediately with the remark:

> A little water clears us of this deed. . . .

We say that situations in life are ironic when there is some striking illustration of the way in which qualities, events, and the like contain something of their opposite—when a result, for example, is the contrary of what was intended. If one has just been given a driver's license, has just been congratulated by the instructor, and, when driving off, goes into reverse by mistake and backs up over someone, it is especially satisfactory—as irony!—if the person run over is the instructor. Such irony seems to imply pattern or design of some mischievous sort, as if a supreme jokester were planning the scenario of our lives. A writer who has made a study of the worst disasters of the twentieth century warns us to avoid any ship, plane, or building that is publicized as being especially safe.

Thomas Hardy was a poet fascinated by irony. In poem after poem he seems on the lookout for the little circle of the Yin in the asymmetrical half circle of the Yang. One of the best known of his ironic poems, "The Ruined Maid" (see Anthology, p. 491), is about the hypocritical discrepancy, in Victorian England, between the way virtue was extolled and its opposite rewarded. Amelia, a girl from the country, has been "ruined" (seduced) with the result that she now lives in luxury.

In "The Latest Decalogue" (see Anthology, p. 474), Arthur Hugh Clough gives an ironic reading of the ten commandments as they might be observed by a cynical materialist.

The ironic view of life has been a favorite with many twentieth-century poets, perhaps because the events of our time have brought home to us the conviction that there is no simple way of looking at things.

In speech, we can make any statement ironic by the tone in which we utter it, the facial expression we assume, the gestures we dramatize it with. The poets' problem is to make irony clear without any of the aids we have in speech. They have only words on the page to work with. They need our intelligent collaboration; we have to be more wide awake than usual when reading poets given to irony. In the following lines, Ramon Guthrie is writing about a political figure posing for press photographers. Most of us will feel that the apparent innocence of the last two lines is really tongue-in-cheek, really ironic, and that the statement is all the more cutting for seeming naïve.

> He poses for press photographers
> with bowed head, thumb holding his right eyelid shut,
> auricular performing the same service for the left,
> his three other fingers poised against his forehead.
> It takes a very pious man to pray that fervently
> with flash-light bulbs exploding all around him. . . .

UNDERSTATEMENT—THE WITHHELD IMAGE

Up to now we have seen what kind of images poets give us as they select details from the whole range of our experience and not only from what is considered beautiful or pleasant. We turn now to the images they do not give us.

If each of the millions of images pouring in from the senses had an equal claim on our attention, the mind, unable to handle that dazzling overload, would go into shock. Fortunately, we have mechanisms to keep from consciousness all but the most significant details.

Poets too, though they may think in images, work selectively; they give us only so much of what could be a confusing abundance—often give us synecdoches, for example, instead of totalities. They know too how silence sometimes speaks louder than words, and how an image can be most vividly present to us when it is not mentioned at all.

It was Voltaire who said that the way to bore people is to tell them everything. What *not* to say or *not* to do is the secret of many arts. Dizzy Gillespie, the jazz trumpeter, said, "It took me all my life to learn the biggest music lesson of them all—what NOT to play." Robert Frost would agree that the same holds for poetry: "The unsaid part is the best part."

We like to complete meanings for ourselves. A poem that starts us out on a process of discovery involves us more pleasurably than one in which the poet tells us all. For most people, the drawing on this page is more interesting in its incomplete form than if the missing lines were filled in and the label "Washerwoman with Bucket" affixed beneath. Children who have exciting news to tell are acting like poets when they dash up to us with a "Guess what?"

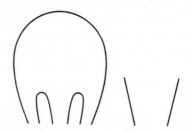

In 480 B.C., a few hundred Greek soldiers found themselves in the narrow pass at Thermopylae, between the mountains and the sea, facing an overwhelmingly larger Persian army. As the foreign troops came on, advance units were surprised to see the Spartans stretched out casually along the shore combing their long hair. A. E. Housman, in "The Oracles," describes the scene:

> *The King with half the East at heel is marched from lands of morning;*
> *Their fighters drink the rivers up, their shafts benight the air.*
> *And he that stands will die for nought, and home there's no returning.*
> The Spartans on the sea-wet rock sat down and combed their hair.

BINOCULAR VISION

The first three lines are somewhat pompous and overwritten. They suggest the awe one is supposed to feel before the army of a king so great that he is referred to simply as "*the* King." The last line is different in tone; Housman uses only a detail or two to stir our feelings.

The poet Simonides, writing soon after the battle, was even more terse:

• ON THE SPARTAN DEAD AT THERMOPYLAE •

> Go tell at Sparta, traveler passing by,
> That here obedient to her laws we lie.

Simonides (556?–468 B.C.*)*

This poet was enough of a "professor of the five senses" to recognize one of the times he need not invoke them. Only too many of those he was talking to would have their own memories of a son or a father dead, their own knowledge of what a spear or sword can do to the human flesh one loves. Such images may be more effective when not mentioned at all. Every good writer, poet or not, knows this: Never tell a reader what will leap to his mind without your telling.

What we might call the **withheld image** can be as powerful as the presented one. It is difficult to imagine that "Western Wind" would have been better if it had been explicit, as current fiction often is, about the bedtime activities of the lovers.

The most famous example of the withheld image is in the love scene in which Paolo and Francesca, the adulterous lovers, pause to tell Dante about the day that spelled their ruin:

> One day, for pleasure, we were reading about Lancelot, how love compelled him; we were all alone, unsuspected, unsuspecting. Our eyes met often over the reading, and often our faces went suddenly pale—and then in a single moment we were overcome. When we read how the smiling lips that Lancelot longed for were kissed by so great a lover, this one here, who will never leave me, kissed me all trembling on the mouth—

And then the withheld image. Instead of giving us the love scene, Dante merely adds:

> That was the end of our reading for the day.

The movie camera might show their fingers relaxing on the book, then the book itself slipping to the floor.

The question of what to withhold may come up most urgently with themes of sex and violence, always among the great concerns of literature.

Such ballads as "Lord Randal" (see Anthology, p. 400) provide us with examples. In it the main images are all withheld. Lord Randal has been meeting his "true-love," and yet there is no love scene. He has just been poisoned, and yet there is no poisoning scene. He is now dying, and yet there is no death scene.

No one would hold that crucial images should always be withheld, love scenes and deathbed scenes never presented. "Lord Randal" shows that powerful effects can be achieved by holding something back—not only certain images but certain facts, the meaning of which we piece together only gradually. Lord Randal might have entered, crying, "Mother, I'm poisoned!" but then his later revelations would have been less gripping than they now are. The poet might have shown the young man swelling and dying; it is probably better he did not. Both sex and violence are such highly charged subjects that any lack of sureness in describing them may set off the safety valve of laughter.

Other poets, in dealing with such horrors, have preferred a different strategy. In Edwin Arlington Robinson's "The Mill" (see Anthology, p. 502), we are given only such clues as will enable us, detective-fashion, to discover the central event. When we realize, without being told directly, that the lines are about a double suicide, the shock will be greater—as if we had stumbled on the bodies in real life.

A contemporary poet, X. J. Kennedy, has presented an unsolved killing so that many details such as the motive and the killer's identity are withheld from us, just as they often are in crimes that make the headlines and puzzle the authorities.

• LOOSE WOMAN •

Someone who well knew how she'd toss her chin
    Passing the firehouse oglers, at their taunt,
    Let it be flung up higher than she'd want,
Just held fast by a little hinge of skin.
Two boys come from the river kicked a thatch   5
    Of underbrush and stopped. One wrecked a pair
    Of sneakers blundering into her hair
And that day made a different sort of catch.

Her next-best talent, setting tongues to buzz,
    Lasts longer than her best. It still occurs   10
    To wonder had she been our fault or hers
And had she loved him. Who the bastard was,

Though long they asked and notebooked round about
And turned up not a few who would have known
That white inch where her neck met shoulderbone,   *15*
Was one thing more we never did find out.

X. J. Kennedy (b. 1929)

The withheld image is part of a good writer's overall strategy. Unskillful writers inflate their style so as to give their material more substance than it has, just as the puffer, or swellfish, gulps in water when panicked so as to appear larger and more formidable than it is. An old anecdote has a preacher writing in the margin of a sermon these directions to himself: "Argument weak here. Shout and pound pulpit." Weak writers rely on language that shouts and pounds. They like "unleashed titanic angers, throbbing and surging; awesome, specter-haunted anguish stalking the blood-soaked realm!"

More mature writers prefer to understate, to say less than they might rather than more, so that the meaning can explode *within the reader*, not just within the words on the page.

In "Michael," Wordsworth ends an account of the heartbreak of an old man by telling how he used to go out to the stone sheepfold he had been working on:

> . . . many and many a day he thither went
> And never lifted up a single stone.

Wordsworth does not have to tell why the man did not lift a stone; the meaning is more powerful if it bursts on us. A lesser poet might have said something like

> . . . many and many a day he thither went
> To pour forth tears of anguish and despair.

Frost concludes his story of the accidental death of a farm boy (p. 292) by having the doctor listening to his heartbeat:

> Little—less—nothing! and that ended it.
> No more to build on there. And they, since they
> Were not the one dead, turned to their affairs.

When we realize what hopes the parents must have had for the boy's future, the "No more to build on there" is deeply moving. We might have remained unaffected if we had been told how the parents' horror-stricken eyes were fathomless pools of grief and anguish as they saw their brightest hopes trodden underfoot by callous Fate. The last line and a half is so understated it sounds cold, and yet Frost himself found the poem too moving to read in public. If the parents "turned to their affairs"—which would include not only milking the cows but getting in touch with the undertaker—we know with how heavy a heart they did so.

A form of understatement we all use is called **litotes.** It asserts a truth by denying its opposite. We say, "Not bad!" of a good cup of coffee, or "She's no Miss America!" of a plain woman. E. E. Cummings concludes a lyric with a litotes based on grammar:

> we are for each other: then
> laugh, leaning back in my arms
> for life's not a paragraph
>
> and death i think is no parenthesis

He gives what may be the supreme litotes of all time in his poem on the death of a politician he did not like. If he had not died, says Cummings,

> somebody might hardly never not have been unsorry, perhaps

OVERSTATEMENT

There is a place too for the kind of overstatement called **hyperbole** (in Greek, *throwing beyond the mark*). We frequently say things like "the best evening I ever had" or "the nicest dress I ever saw" or "I never heard such a lie!" Without hyperbole, some teen-agers—to use a hyperbole—could hardly get through a sentence. Slang relies on it: "He's the most!" "That music is too much!" A magazine writer calls it the chronic P.R. malady—we all know that in advertising everything is the best of its kind.

The characters in Shakespeare frequently make remarks that we recognize as hyperbole. When Miranda, in *The Tempest*, wants to tell her father that what he has just said is very interesting, she remarks:

> Your tale, sir, would cure deafness.

The lovesick Duke in *Twelfth Night* ascribes similar curative powers to what he admires:

BINOCULAR VISION

> Oh, when mine eyes did see Olivia first,
> Methought she purged the air of pestilence!

Hyperbole is not so much a way of writing as a way of seeing—the wildest hyperbole may be expressed in simple words. Perhaps it is an especially American way of seeing; the tall tales of frontier days are based on it. In *The People, Yes*, Sandburg gives a series of American hyperboles:

> They have yarns
> Of a skyscraper so tall they had to put hinges
> On the two top stories so to let the moon go by,
> Of one corn crop in Missouri when the roots
> Went so deep and drew off so much water
> The Mississippi riverbed that year was dry,
> Of pancakes so thin they had only one side,
> Of "a fog so thick we shingled the barn and six feet out on the fog,"
> Of Pecos Pete straddling a cyclone in Texas and riding it to the west
>   coast where "it rained out under him,"
> Of the man who drove a swarm of bees across the Rocky Mountains
>   and the Desert "and didn't lose a bee. . . ."

Hyperboles are not lies; only the very naïve would take them literally. Graves, in making the concluding statement of "Spoils," is not necessarily ignorant of the properties of matter or of the techniques of safe-cracking.

• SPOILS •

When all is over and you march for home,
The spoils of war are easily disposed of:
Standards, weapons of combat, helmets, drums
May decorate a staircase or a study,
While lesser gleanings of the battlefield—   5
Coins, watches, wedding-rings, gold teeth and such—
Are sold anonymously for solid cash.

The spoils of love present a different case,
When all is over and you march for home:
That lock of hair, these letters and the portrait   10
May not be publicly displayed; nor sold;
Nor burned; nor returned (the heart being obstinate)—
Yet never dare entrust them to a safe
For fear they burn a hole through two-foot steel.

Robert Graves (b. 1895)

His conclusion, mistaken as it might seem to a metallurgist, makes perfect sense in terms of the nature of emotion, whose effect cannot be insulated by any physical substance: Love letters can continue to sear us, and the writer, wherever we keep them.

exercises & diversions

A. The great example of irony in literature is the story of Oedipus as told by Sophocles in his play *Oedipus Rex*. The very steps Oedipus takes to avoid killing his father bring about the crime. Sophocles has Oedipus say many things that we know have a different meaning from what the hero intends. He pronounces, for example, a solemn curse on the killer and says he will investigate the case as thoroughly as if the murdered man had been his father.

Does the following poem have the same kind of "dramatic irony"? The Hunkpapa were a tribe of the Dakota (or Sioux), the most impressive and prosperous of the American Indians. The year 1822 would have been a happy one for them; much of the rest of the century was not.

DAKOTA: OCTOBER, 1822
HUNKPAPA WARRIOR

New air has come around us.
It is cold enough to make us know we are different
from the things we touch. Before dark, we ride
along the high places or go deep in the long
grass at the edge of our people
and watch for enemies.
We are the strongest tribe of the Sioux. Buffalo
are plentiful, our women beautiful. Life
is good.
What bad thing can be done against us?

Rod Taylor (b. 1947)

1. Is the time of year symbolic or otherwise significant in the poem?

2. Is the time of day?

B. What elements of "antipoetry" are there in T. S. Eliot's "Preludes" (pp. 9–10)?

exercises & diversions

C. How effective as paradox do you consider each of these examples?

1. Hope is a good breakfast, but it is a bad supper.

Sir Francis Bacon

2. Greatly his foes he dreads, but more his friends;
He hurts me most who lavishly commends.

Charles Churchill

3. Beware the fury of a patient man.

John Dryden

4. He who praises everybody praises nobody.

Samuel Johnson

5. You purchase pain with all that joy can give,
And die of nothing but a rage to live.

Alexander Pope

6. Man learns from history that man learns nothing from history.

Hegel

7. You ought certainly to forgive them as a christian, but never to admit them in your sight, or allow their names to be mentioned in your hearing.

Jane Austen

8. While Adam slept, Eve from his side arose:
Strange his first sleep should be his last repose.

Anonymous

9. The greatest of faults, I should say, is to be conscious of none.

Thomas Carlyle

10. The last thing that a poet learns is how to throw away,
And how to make you thrill and creep with what he doesn't say.

J. R. Lowell

11. No people do so much harm as those who go about doing good.

Bishop Mandell Creighton

exercises & diversions

12. It has long been an axiom of mine that little things are infinitely the most important.

Sir Arthur Conan Doyle

13. Tennyson was not tennysonian.

Henry James

14. Packed in my skin from head to toe
Is one I know and do not know.

Edwin Muir

15. The cure for loneliness is solitude.

Marianne Moore

16. If time matters, and of course it does, take a plane;
If time is even more important, go by ship.

Hollis Summers

D. How much poets should withhold is their own decision. They may want to tantalize us into "exploratory behavior." Difficulty is part of the fun in guessing games and detective stories; we are willing to spend time examining anything that gets our interest. (Some obscure poems never do—they are merely boring.) The poem that follows has been called "a famous puzzle-piece."

THE EMPEROR OF ICE-CREAM

Call the roller of big cigars,
The muscular one, and bid him whip
In kitchen cups concupiscent curds.
Let the wenches dawdle in such dress
As they are used to wear, and let the boys   5
Bring flowers in last month's newspapers.
Let be be finale of seem.
The only emperor is the emperor of ice-cream.

Take from the dresser of deal,
Lacking the three glass knobs, that sheet   10
On which she embroidered fantails once
And spread it so as to cover her face.
If her horny feet protrude, they come
To show how cold she is, and dumb.
Let the lamp affix its beam.   15
The only emperor is the emperor of ice-cream.

Wallace Stevens (1879–1955)

exercises & diversions

The setting is a house in which preparations are being made for the final ceremonies for the dead.

1. (lines 1–2) Is there an element of irony, of play-of-opposites, in that the man making ice cream is the type he is?

2. (line 3) Why the highfalutin diction (not used elsewhere in the poem) and the gooey lushness of sound?

3. (lines 4–6) Why are the "wenches" described as "dawdling" in their everyday dresses? Why is it mentioned that the florists use last month's newspaper?

4. (line 7) Recall what a "finale" is. Some might paraphrase the line as meaning: Whatever seems to be true of life and death, whatever one likes to think about them, what we see in this house is the reality; ice cream and the horny feet of the dead are facts of our existence. Would you prefer to paraphrase it differently? How?

5. (line 8) Is the ice cream, which is real enough, also a symbol? If so, of what? Of the sweetness of life? Of the coldness of death? Of both combined?

6. (line 8) Is the emperor the "muscular one"? Or is the emperor the ruling principle that the ice cream represents? Or both?

7. (lines 9–16) Why does the diction change in the second stanza?

8. (line 10) Why does the poet bother to mention that the dresser has three missing knobs? Are they symbolic? (Trust your common sense.)

9. (lines 10–12) Is it ironic that the sheet she embroidered now covers the woman's face? "Fantails" can refer to either goldfish or pigeons. Stevens tells us he meant pigeons. Would the goldfish image have been as good? Are the pigeons (or goldfish) symbolic?

10. (line 13) Is it impolite or "not nice" of Stevens to mention that the dead woman has "horny feet"? With what tone does he seem to say this? Of fastidiousness? Of contempt? Or—?

11. (line 15) Is the lamp—what lamp?—to be affixed so that it focuses on the feet? Or on what?

12. After asking ourselves such questions, should we still feel that the poem is a puzzle, with too much withheld to make an interpretation possible?

13. At one time Stevens picked "The Emperor of Ice-Cream" as his favorite poem, giving what might seem paradoxical reasons. He said that it wore "a deliberately commonplace costume" and yet had "something of the essential gaudiness of poetry." Point out how—and why—the commonplace and the gaudy coexist in the poem.

E. 1. One can imagine an unliterary person giving a realistic account of a visit to the house of Stevens' poem, an account that would tally in all respects with the details which Stevens mentions. "I stopped in at poor Mrs. Foote's last night. What a scene! Smoke all over! There was this big guy in the kitchen, wearing a bowling shirt that said *ROMA ICE CREAM PARLOR.* . . ."

Write such an account in your own way, through the eyes of an imaginary visitor.

2. Write a short poem or a paragraph in which the chief effect you intend (beauty, sordidness, strength, weakness, for example) is combined with elements of its opposite.

T · W · O

THE EMOTIONS

5

The Color of Thought
THE EMOTIONS IN POETRY

THE ROLE OF EMOTION

Up to now (to repeat an outline given earlier) we have been concerned with the source of human awareness, sense perception: with how our mind deals with the images the senses provide; with how it relates and compares them, condensing some into symbols, narrowing its focus onto parts of others; with how it handles conflicting evidence; and with how it presents, or chooses not to present, all this in poetry.

This chapter will be about emotion, the reaction of the mind-body combination to the objects or situations that sense images make it aware of. Emotion, like imagery, is conditioned by our physiological history; we can no more feel a disembodied emotion than perceive a disembodied image.

Why do cats dislike getting their feet wet? Charles Darwin, fascinated by the behavior of animals, thought he knew. About 3000 B.C. the Egyptians domesticated the native wildcat to serve as a guard animal. As cats slowly spread over the world they retained the racial preferences of the almost waterless land of their ancestors.

Darwin also tried to account for human facial expressions as inherited from our ancestors. When we express scorn or rage by sneering, we curl back our lip to bare the once large canine teeth, although it has been a long time since we, in our endless armaments race, have considered our dental weaponry of much account.

Psychologists believe that the mind also inherits predispositions. Certain images affect us more powerfully than any experience of our

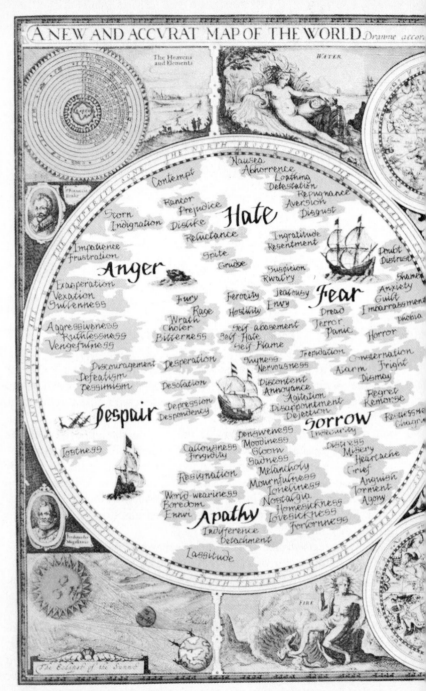

Map of the Emotions

THE EMOTIONS

own would seem to account for. Psychologists like Carl Jung, poets like William Butler Yeats believe that such images have an inherited potential: We are moved by them because of their significance for us throughout our history. These reactions have been encoded in the nervous system itself, in the biochemistries of memory. **Archetypal image** is the term Jung has used for those patternings whose unconscious charge can stir and disturb us. Birth, love, guilt, death, rebirth are examples of such archetypal themes. So are sibling rivalry, the need for or envy of a father figure or earth mother, the quest for some kind of Grail, ideas of heaven or hell. We can think of images that affect us as if from long ago: the sun, darkness, the sea, mountains, trees, caves, shelter, storms, war—all the basic realities that helped determine our happiness or misery, our survival or extinction, throughout our history.

Certain passages of poetry touch us as if there were indeed such memories.

> The Son of Morn in weary Night's decline,
> The lost Traveller's Dream under the Hill.

It is not necessary to know what Blake meant to find his lines strangely haunting. Almost every word is rich with emotions that go back as far as human memory.

Emotional experience: This, more than anything else, is what poetry gives us. And this is what we value as much as anything in life and what we are willing to go to almost any extreme for. Our lives—if fully human—are afloat on seas of emotion; we live more richly there than we live in any geographical world.

We do not have to believe in the ideas of a poem to share its experience: A pacifist can enjoy Homer; an atheist, Dante. But we do have to believe in its emotions. If the poem seems to fake anything there, it is not likely to involve us.

The poet, unlike the philosopher, is not primarily a thinker. "The poet who 'thinks,' " T. S. Eliot reminds us, "is merely the poet who can express the emotional equivalent of thought." Robert Frost said that a poem "is never a thought to begin with. . . . A poem begins with a lump in the throat . . . a home-sickness or a love-sickness. . . . A complete poem is one where an emotion has found its thought and the thought has found the words. . . ."

Though emotion may be hard to define, we know very well what it feels like. We know that strong emotion has a marked and instant physical effect on us. It influences our heartbeat, our breathing, the distribution of our blood flow (we flush or grow pale), our visceral activities, our glandular secretions, the temperature and electrical con-

THE COLOR OF THOUGHT

ductivity of our skin. Emotion affects all of our internal rhythms—and the rhythm of our poetry. Its physiological aspects could hardly be better illustrated than in the poem of Sappho we have read (p. 8); in it she describes herself as being almost paralyzed with fear and love.

If this seems to be a poetic flight of fancy we might recall that emotion releases adrenalin into the bloodstream, and that an excess of adrenalin, instead of assisting muscular activity, interferes with the reconversion of lactic acid to the needed glycogen, so that, under great emotional stress, we become muscularly handicapped. Sappho is right in feeling she may faint. A greatly increased heartbeat (*tachycardia*) will result in reduced circulation, since the heart then operates less efficiently as a pump; and as the brain gets less blood one becomes dizzy and may lose consciousness. Sappho did not know all this, but she did know what she was feeling, what her body image had become, and she did know that poets report in images.

It is no wonder that poetry, which is physical and emotional, affects sensitive readers in a physical way. William James, the psychologist, was susceptible: "In listening to poetry . . . we are often surprised at the cutaneous shiver which like a sudden wave flows over us, and at the heart-swelling and the lachrymal effusion that unexpectedly catch us at intervals. . . ." Emily Dickinson judged poetry by its physical effect:

> If I read a book [and] it makes my whole body so cold no fire ever can warm me I know *that* is poetry. If I feel physically as if the top of my head were taken off, I know *that* is poetry. These are the only way I know it. . . .

So did A. E. Housman: "Experience has taught me, when I am shaving of a morning, to keep watch over my thoughts, because, if a line of poetry strays into my memory, my skin bristles so that the razor ceases to act. . . ."

We can visualize the emotions as a color wheel (p. 100) like the ones we see in art-supply shops, a wheel in which selected colors are arranged, like spokes, according to their prismatic or "spectral" order. We make more colors by adding white to get "tints," black to get "shades." If we start blending the colors themselves there is no end to the number we can make, just as there is no end to the number or complexity of our emotions.

Colors opposite each other on *their* wheel are complementary: Mixed together, they cancel each other out, giving us black or a neutral shade of gray. But when emotions are mixed, as they usually are, each can remain distinct. When we feel a passionate love and hate for the same person, the blend is anything but gray.

THE EMOTIONS

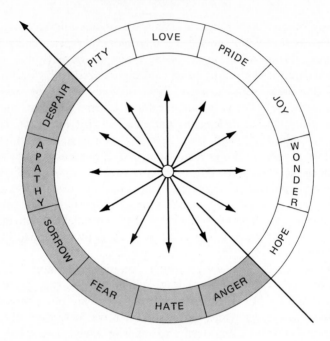

It would be possible to classify poems as belonging to this or that segment of the wheel. One could make collections of love poems, poems of joy, poems of wonder, and the rest. The more poems we read, the more we find they are not confined to the happier emotions, the brighter half of the wheel. Life never promised us a rose garden. Poets deal with all the possibilities of existence, with all that has happened to men and women before and after the fall in Eden. Dante, one of the greatest of poets, wrote an "Inferno" as well as a "Paradiso."

In "The Woodspurge" (see Anthology, p. 481), Dante Gabriel Rossetti has written a poem of "perfect grief." In "Tears, Idle Tears" (see Anthology, p. 470), Tennyson has written about "some divine despair." Yeats in his old age admits to unbecoming passions.

• THE SPUR •

You think it horrible that lust and rage
Should dance attention upon my old age;
They were not such a plague when I was young;
What else have I to spur me into song?

William Butler Yeats (1865–1939)

THE COLOR OF THOUGHT

Walter Savage Landor lives up to his middle name in the lines he wrote on an old and dying poet:

• ALAS! 'TIS VERY SAD TO HEAR •

Alas! 'tis very sad to hear,
You and your Muse's end draws near:
I only wish, if this be true,
To lie a little way from you.
The grave is cold enough for me   5
Without you and your poetry.

Walter Savage Landor (1775–1864)

Hate poetry, more or less witty, goes back at least to the ancient Greeks.

• EPITAPH OF NEARCHOS •

Rest lightly O Earth upon this wretched Nearchos
That the dogs may have no trouble in dragging him out.

Ammianus (second century A.D.*)*
(Translated by Dudley Fitts, 1903–1968)

One of the most outspoken poems of disgust, revulsion, and probably self-recrimination is Shakespeare's "Sonnet 129" (see Anthology, p. 407).

Though we could classify poems according to their predominant emotion, there is no particular gain in doing so. In most poems we get not one emotion in a solo, but rather duets or quartets or even symphonies of many emotions. W. H. Auden's poem "The Shield of Achilles" is about a contemporary world in which human beings have "lost their pride," or can be made to lose it. This depersonalized totalitarian world, hideous with the crime that accompanies poverty and urban demoralization, is contrasted with the world of dance, music, and "ritual pieties" that Homer has shown us. In the *Iliad*, Book xviii, the sea goddess Thetis, because of love for her son Achilles, asks the crippled blacksmith Hephaestus to make a new set of armor for him. As we read the poem, we are whirled completely around the wheel of emotion: Not a one is left untouched. Thetis looks in hope at the human possibilities and is brought to dismay—close to despair—by the contemporary reality.

THE EMOTIONS

• THE SHIELD OF ACHILLES •

     She looked over his shoulder
       For vines and olive trees,
     Marble well-governed cities
       And ships upon untamed seas,
     But there on the shining metal   *5*
       His hands had put instead
     An artificial wilderness
       And a sky like lead.

A plain without a feature, bare and brown,
     No blade of grass, no sign of neighbourhood,   *10*
Nothing to eat and nowhere to sit down,
     Yet, congregated on its blankness, stood
An unintelligible multitude,
A million eyes, a million boots in line,
Without expression, waiting for a sign.   *15*

Out of the air a voice without a face
     Proved by statistics that some cause was just
In tones as dry and level as the place:
     No one was cheered and nothing was discussed;
     Column by column in a cloud of dust   *20*
They marched away enduring a belief
Whose logic brought them, somewhere else, to grief.

     She looked over his shoulder
       For ritual pieties,
     White flower-garlanded heifers,   *25*
       Libation and sacrifice,
     But there on the shining metal
       Where the altar should have been,
     She saw by his flickering forge-light
       Quite another scene.   *30*

Barbed wire enclosed an arbitrary spot
     Where bored officials lounged (one cracked a joke)
And sentries sweated for the day was hot:
     A crowd of ordinary decent folk
     Watched from without and neither moved nor spoke   *35*
As three pale figures were led forth and bound
To three posts driven upright in the ground.

The mass and majesty of this world, all
     That carries weight and always weighs the same
Lay in the hands of others; they were small   *40*
     And could not hope for help and no help came:
     What their foes liked to do was done, their shame
Was all the worst could wish; they lost their pride
And died as men before their bodies died.

> She looked over his shoulder   45
>   For athletes at their games,
> Men and women in a dance
>   Moving their sweet limbs
> Quick, quick, to music,
>   But there on the shining shield   50
> His hands had set no dancing-floor
>   But a weed-choked field.
>
> A ragged urchin, aimless and alone,
>   Loitered about that vacancy; a bird
> Flew up to safety from his well-aimed stone: 55
>   That girls are raped, that two boys knife a third,
>   Were axioms to him, who'd never heard
> Of any world where promises were kept,
> Or one could weep because another wept.
>
>   The thin-lipped armourer,   60
>   Hephaestos, hobbled away,
>   Thetis of the shining breasts
>   Cried out in dismay
>   At what the god had wrought
>   To please her son, the strong   65
>   Iron-hearted man-slaying Achilles
>   Who would not live long.

W. H. Auden (1907–1973)

SENSE AND SENTIMENTALITY

Our remarks on emotion bring us back to where we began our discussion of poetry: back to the role of the senses and to the fact that the poet is, as Federico García Lorca said, a "professor of the five bodily senses." It is through the image that poetry can best convey emotion—either through the image of the object that arouses it, or through the image of its physical effect. Frost describes his walk at night (p. 56) and Marianne Moore her Swedish carriage (p. 520) so that, without being told what to feel, we share the writer's emotions.

Poems may not be subject to the same emotional disorders that bring certain of their readers to the psychoanalyst's couch, but they suffer from their own kinds of unbalance. These fall into the general classes of the "too little" and the "too much." Some poems fail to involve us because they seem to feel no passion and arouse none in us: frigid poems. Perhaps they substitute intellect or wit for passion; they may be nothing more than exercises in ingenuity. James Russell Lowell felt this in the work of Edgar Allan Poe,

> Who has written some things quite the best of their kind,
> But the heart somehow seems all squeezed out by the mind.

To an insensitive and unsympathetic reader, however, all poems are frigid. Because poets strong enough to be self-controlled may only imply their feelings instead of letting them gush forth, they may appear to be unfeeling to the insensitive reader. Often, instead of directly revealing emotion, poets will show us something that is a clue to it. Exactly as in real life: We can often tell from people's appearance and behavior what their emotional state is, though they say nothing about it. The less they say, the more moved we may be. Such reticence is characteristic of much of the world's great poetry. As the eleventh-century Chinese poet Wei T'ai puts it:

> Poetry presents the thing in order to convey the feeling. It should be precise about the thing and reticent about the feeling, for as soon as the mind [of the reader] responds and connects with the thing, the feeling shows in the words: this is how poetry enters deeply into us. If the poet presents directly feelings which overwhelm him, and keeps nothing back to linger as an aftertaste, he stirs us superficially; he cannot start the hands and feet involuntarily waving and tapping in time . . . set heaven and earth in motion and call up the spirits!*

A more common emotional malady is that of "too muchness" or **sentimentality**—emotion in excess of its object, emotion gone out of control and taking over, as cancer cells take over in the body. Sentiment itself—opinion colored by feeling—may be a very good thing: Lincoln's Gettysburg Address expresses noble sentiments. Sentimentality is the disease to which sentiment is subject.

That our grief for even the most worthy of objects can be excessive is the warning given in a folk ballad that probably goes back many centuries.

• THE UNQUIET GRAVE •

> "The wind doth blow today, my love,
>   And a few small drops of rain;
> I never had but one truelove,
>   In cold grave she was lain.

---

* Translated by A. C. Graham in *Poems of the Late T'ang* (London: Penguin, 1965).

"I'll do as much for my truelove   *5*
   As any young man may;
I'll sit and mourn all at her grave
   For a twelvemonth, and a day."

The twelvemonth and a day being up,
   The dead began to speak,   *10*
"Oh who sits weeping on my grave,
   And will not let me sleep?"

" 'Tis I, my love, sits on your grave
   And will not let you sleep,
For I crave one kiss of your clay-cold lips   *15*
   And that is all I seek."

"You crave one kiss of my clay-cold lips,
   But my breath smells earthy strong;
If you have one kiss of my clay-cold lips
   Your time will not be long: *20*

" 'Tis down in yonder garden green,
   Love, where we used to walk,
The finest flower that ere was seen
   Is withered to a stalk.

"The stalk is withered dry, my love,   *25*
   So will our hearts decay;
So make yourself content, my love,
   Till God calls you away."

Anonymous (date uncertain)

Excessive grief, which can turn into sentimental brooding, is a vexa-
tion to the dead—and so also to the living.

Apathy and despair can be sentimental. If we enjoy wallowing in
our own miseries, they become forms of self-pity. Love can be senti-
mental when the lover is "in love with love"—when he cares more
about tending his own emotional hothouse than about the well-being
of the person he loves. Or it can be sentimental when the object of his
feelings—an animal, perhaps—deserves less than the fullness of human
love.

Emotion is healthy when it is of the kind and in the amount that its
object deserves: when what we love is really lovable, when what we
fear is really fearful. It might seem better to love anything, to feel joy
in anything, than to love nothing and feel no joy. But is it? In a play
of Christopher Marlowe, there is a character who sends a pot of poi-

soned rice pudding to a community of nuns. When they all fall sick and die, he exclaims happily, "How sweet the bells ring, now the nuns are dead!" And he goes cheerfully on to his next project, that of poisoning all the monks in a neighboring monastery. The joy and love he feels in his activity will probably seem ill-conceived to most of us.

Excessive pity, even for a worthy cause, can quite incapacitate one for a normal life: The morning papers could keep someone who is pity-prone in futile tears the whole day long. Aristotle thought an overabundance of emotion so harmful to the psyche that he defended Greek tragedy as a necessary release from pity and fear. Healthy emotion is directed to something outside ourselves; sentimentality indulges our own feelings. Sentimentalists, concerned more with cherishing their own feelings than with the object of those feelings, are saying, in effect, "Look how tender I am! How sensitive to beauty! How capable of deep emotions! How rich in sympathy!" Since they may feel that their unusual sensitivity is unappreciated, they may easily fall into self-pity.

To experience any emotion is exciting—we never feel so alive as when we are emotionally aroused. So we are tempted to fake our emotions, to build them up deliberately into more than they are. To sustain such fake passion, we have to create or falsify its object. Sentimentalists hallucinate, turn the world into a warm nest in which they can coddle their own snug feelings. They see only so much of reality as confirms them in their enjoyment of the more tender and tearful emotions. They like things that are cute and quaint and tiny; they can, indeed, miniaturize even the strongest and noblest objects until they become of a size to merit pity and tears.

Writers of sentimental poetry like to play on our stock responses—those built-in automatic reactions we have to many things we think dear and familiar: childhood; barefoot boys; home, sweet home; the old porch swing; the old oaken bucket; old rocking chairs; dust-covered toys; the fidelity of dogs. It was no doubt the sentimentalists' doting views on dogs and toddlers that led W. C. Fields, a lifelong crusader against sentimentality in art and life, to behave so as to win the admiring tribute from Leo Rosten: "Any man who hates dogs and babies can't be all bad."

The innocent happiness of childhood is particularly dear to sentimentalists. They choose not to know (at least in their rosy moods) about unhappy childhoods—like that of Yeats, who said, "Indeed I remember little of childhood but its pain." Judging by psychiatric reports and newspaper stories, the lives of many children are unhappy: Only a mindlessly sentimental view of childhood would deny that. Nor are the parents invariably blissful: Any parent knows that children,

THE COLOR OF THOUGHT

lovable as they are, can be exasperating, simply because they are little individuals who want what they want. A parent of young children, coming home tired after a hard day at the office, is not likely to find the little ones in the pose described by William Cullen Bryant:

> And some to happy homes repair,
> Where children, pressing cheek to cheek,
> With mute caresses shall declare
> The tenderness they cannot speak.

Even Wordsworth, great poet as he was, slipped into sentimental child-worship when he hailed his "six years' darling of a pigmy size" as "best philosopher . . . Mighty prophet! Seer blest!"—titles that his philosophic friend Coleridge dryly dismissed with the remark that "Children at this age give us no such information of themselves."

"Papa's Letter" is the kind of sentimental falsification that shows up in anthologies of "best-loved poems." It plays shamelessly on a number of stock responses.

• PAPA'S LETTER •

I was sitting in my study,
    Writing letters when I heard
"Please, dear mama, Mary told me
    Mama mustn't be disturbed.

"But I's tired of the kitty;   5
    Want some ozzer fing to do.
Writing letters, is 'ou, mama?
    Tan't I wite a letter too?"

"Not now, darling, mama's busy;
    Run and play with kitty, now."   10
"No, no, mama, me wite letter;
    Tan, if 'ou will show me how."

THE EMOTIONS

I would paint my darling's portrait
    As his sweet eyes searched my face.
Hair of gold and eyes of azure,   *15*
    Form of childish, witching grace.

But the eager face was clouded,
    As I slowly shook my head,
Till I said: "I'll make a letter
    Of you, darling boy, instead."   *20*

So I parted back the tresses
    From his forehead high and white,
And a stamp in sport I pasted
    'Mid its waves of golden light.

Then I said, "Now, little letter,   *25*
    Go away and bear good news."
And I smiled as down the staircase
    Clattered loud the little shoes.
        . . .

Down the street the baby hastened
    Till he reached the office door.   *30*
"I'se a letter, Mr. Postman;
    Is there room for any more?

'Cause dis' letter's doin' to papa,
    Papa lives with God, 'ou know,
Mama sent me for a letter,   *35*
    Do 'ou fink 'at I tan go?"

But the clerk in wonder answered,
    "Not today, my little man."
"Den I'll find annozzer office,
    'Cause I must go if I tan."   *40*
        . . .

Suddenly the crowd was parted,
    People fled to left, to right,
As a pair of maddened horses
    At the moment dashed in sight.

No one saw the baby figure—   *45*
    No one saw the golden hair,
Till a voice of frightened sweetness
    Rang out on the autumn air.

'Twas too late—a moment only
    Stood the beauteous vision there,   *50*
Then the little face lay lifeless
    Covered o'er with golden hair.

THE COLOR OF THOUGHT

Rev'rently they raised my darling,
    Brushed away the curls of gold,
Saw the stamp upon the forehead   *55*
    Growing now so icy cold.

Not a mark the face disfigured,
    Showing where the hoof had trod;
But the little life was ended—
    "Papa's letter" was with God.   *60*

Anonymous (nineteenth century)

There are kind and sensitive people who would read this poem with guffaws of derision—not out of sadism, but simply because they find it unbelievable. They feel they are being had, that this tear-jerker is exploiting some of our deepest emotions in a contrived and cynical way, is using us as calculatingly as advertisers try to do. (Who ever saw in a beer ad anyone surly, pugnacious, or unshaven, although such beer drinkers exist?)

For an extreme contrast, suppose we look at one of the best poems about the death of a child.

• BELLS FOR JOHN WHITESIDE'S DAUGHTER •

There was such speed in her little body,
And such lightness in her footfall,
It is no wonder her brown study
Astonishes us all.

Her wars were bruited in our high window.   *5*
We looked among orchard trees and beyond
Where she took arms against her shadow,
Or harried unto the pond

The lazy geese, like a snow cloud
Dripping their snow on the green grass,   *10*
Tricking and stopping, sleepy and proud,
Who cried in goose, Alas,

For the tireless heart within the little
Lady with rod that made them rise
From their noon apple-dreams and scuttle   *15*
Goose-fashion under the skies!

---

³/**brown study:** *deep absorption, day-dreaming*   ⁵/**bruited:** *sounded*

But now go the bells, and we are ready,
In one house we are sternly stopped
To say we are vexed at her brown study,
Lying so primly propped.   20

John Crowe Ransom (1888–1974)

This is a real little girl. No doubt lovable—but still, in her vitality, a
vexation to those around. No escape from that little voice! She dies,
but there is nothing melodramatic about her death—no touching death-
bed scenes. Nor is her "angelic beauty" described as she lies there
"primly propped." There are no professions of anguish or despair or
of heavenly hope from the relatives. We know, without being told,
that here is a sorrow too deep for words, and that what we are con-
fronted with is one of the mysteries of our existence.

Here, for comparison, are two other baby poems, one sentimental
and one not.

• ÉTUDE RÉALISTE (I) •

A baby's feet, like sea-shells pink,
    Might tempt, should heaven see meet,
An angel's lips to kiss, we think,
    A baby's feet.

Like rose-hued sea-flowers toward the heat   5
    They stretch and spread and wink
Their ten soft buds that part and meet.

No flower-bells that expand and shrink
    Gleam half so heavenly sweet
As shine on life's untrodden brink   10
    A baby's feet.

Algernon Charles Swinburne (1837–1909)

(The poet-priest Gerard Manley Hopkins, though devoted to a holy
life, said of Swinburne's "*rot* about babies" that it made him side with
King Herod, notorious for his Massacre of the Innocents.)

• A SONG FOR THE MIDDLE OF THE NIGHT •

By way of explaining to my son the following curse by Eustace Deschamps:
"Happy is he who has no children; for babies bring nothing but crying and stench."

Now first of all he means the night
    You beat the crib and cried
And brought me spinning out of bed
    To powder your backside.

THE COLOR OF THOUGHT

I rolled your buttocks over   5
   And I could not complain:
Legs up, la la, legs down, la, la,
   Back to sleep again.

Now second of all he means the day
   You dabbled out of doors   10
And dragged a dead cat Billy-be-damned
   Across the kitchen floors.
I rolled your buttocks over
   And made you sing for pain:
Legs up, la la, legs down, la, la,   15
   Back to sleep again.

But third of all my father once
   Laid me across his knee
And solved the trouble when he beat
   The yowling out of me.   20
He rocked me on his shoulder
   When razor straps were vain:
Legs up, la la, legs down, la la,
   Back to sleep again.

So roll upon your belly, boy,   25
   And bother being cursed.
You turn the household upside down,
   But you are not the first.
Deschamps the poet blubbered too,
   For all his fool disdain: 30
Legs up, la la, legs down, la la,
   Back to sleep again.

James Wright (1927–1980)

One sentimental poet had such devotion to the saintly mother at whose knee she learned to prattle that she professes to see her virtues in all old ladies.

• OLD LADIES •

In every old lady I chance to meet
   Whoever, wherever she be,
From her snow-crowned head to her patient feet
   My own brave mother I see.

In every old lady whose patient eyes   5
   Are deeps of a fathomless sea,
So patient and tender and kind and wise
   My mother looks out at me.

THE EMOTIONS

In every old lady in silent prayer
    To God on her bended knee,   *10*
I vision my own mother kneeling there
    Praying a prayer for me.

In every old lady I bend above,
    Asleep in death's mystery,
I whisper, "Please carry my lone heart's love   *15*
    To my angel mother for me."

In every old lady I meet each day,
    The humble, or lofty and fine,
I see an angel stand, guarding the way,
    Somebody's mother and mine.   *20*

              Will Allen Dromgoole (1860–1934)*

It may be sweet of the poet to feel that way. But she must also be somewhat nearsighted or undiscriminating. We all know marvelous old ladies—brave, witty, beautiful. But are we really honoring their exceptional qualities by asserting that *all* old ladies are equally wonderful? Lady Macbeth, had she lived, might not have turned out so well. Nor did the mother in the old ballad "Edward, Edward," who, after apparently goading her son into murder, was told by him that she deserved "the curse of hell." But we need not turn to literature—we can easily find old ladies—at the races, on barstools—we might hesitate to compare our mothers to. John Crowe Ransom—again—gives us a frankly unsentimental view.

· BLUE GIRLS ·

Twirling your blue skirts, travelling the sward
Under the towers of your seminary,
Go listen to your teachers old and contrary
Without believing a word.

Tie the white fillets then about your hair   *5*
And think no more of what will come to pass
Than bluebirds that go walking on the grass
And chattering on the air.

---

* When the first edition of this book appeared, the poet Allen Tate wrote the author: ". . . where did you find Will Allen Dromgoole? As a very small boy, I knew her. She had a weekly page of verse and prose in the Nashville *Banner* some 60 years ago—or even 70. She wrote several children's books, among them *Hero Chums*, which my mother read to me before I was six. 'Miss Will Allen' was the first woman to have a commission in the Navy. . . ."

THE COLOR OF THOUGHT

Practise your beauty, blue girls, before it fail;
And I will cry with my loud lips and publish   *10*
Beauty which all our power shall never establish,
It is so frail.

For I could tell you a story which is true;
I know a lady with a terrible tongue,
Blear eyes fallen from blue,   *15*
All her perfections tarnished—yet it is not long
Since she was lovelier than any of you.

John Crowe Ransom (1888–1974)

What comes through in this poem of mixed emotions, this "story which is true," is more than dislike of the "terrible tongue" and the faded eyes. The poet remembers, with something like admiration and love, a lady once lovelier than any of the beautiful and careless young girls before him.

Sentimentalists tend to overvalue the companionship of an animal, since its response to them is less critical than that of a human being and, therefore, more flattering. All the better if the animal has a sad fate, which, by encouraging their own pity and self-pity, permits them to drop a gentle tear. We think of the "trembling maid, of her own gentle voice afraid" in Thomas Moore's "Lalla Rookh":

Oh! ever thus from childhood's hour,
I've seen my fondest hopes decay;
I never loved a tree or flower,
But 'twas the first to fade away.
I never nursed a dear gazelle,   *5*
To glad me with its soft black eye,
But when it came to know me well,
And love me, it was sure to die!

Such sentimentality arouses not only disbelief but derision in sensible readers. Few lines in English have been more honored with parody, which taunts our self-pitying little gazelle-nurser with such lines as those of James Payn:

I've never had a piece of toast
Particularly long and wide,
But fell upon the sanded floor,
And always on the buttered side.

Even cat lovers may feel that Rod McKuen goes overboard in his love for his cat Sloopy. For years, the poet tells us, it had been Rod and

Sloopy "against the world." Then one day Rod did not come home. A day later he came running through the snow, "screaming *Sloopy Sloopy*," only to find her gone!

> I was a madman
> to have stayed away
>   one minute more
> than the appointed hour.

Sloopy, he reflects, is now a bitter cat, and

> I'm bitter too
> and not a free man any more. . . .

>   Looking back
> perhaps she's been
> the only human thing   *5*
> that ever gave back love to me.

McKuen, sentimentally, treats Sloopy as if she were human. May Swenson, on the other hand, tries to imagine how a cat might really experience the world.

• CAT & THE WEATHER •

> Cat takes a look at the weather:
> snow;
> puts a paw on the sill;
> his perch is piled, is a pillow.
>
> Shape of his pad appears: *5*
> will it dig? No,
> not like sand,
> like his fur almost.
>
> But licked, not liked:
> too cold.   *10*
> Insects are flying, fainting down.
> He'll try
>
> to bat one against the pane.
> They have no body and no buzz,
> and now his feet are wet;   *15*
> it's a puzzle.
>
> Shakes each leg,
> then shakes his skin
> to get the white flies off;
> looks for his tail,   *20*

tells it to come on in
by the radiator.
World's turned queer
somehow: all white,

no smell. Well, here   25
inside it's still familiar.
He'll go to sleep until
it puts itself right.

May Swenson (b. 1919)

Emotions are to be evaluated with reference to their object. It is
precisely such an evaluation that William Stafford is concerned to make
in his poem about an unborn fawn: Should one risk human lives in a
probably vain effort to save the fawn?

• TRAVELING THROUGH THE DARK •

Traveling through the dark I found a deer
dead on the edge of the Wilson River road.
It is usually best to roll them into the canyon:
that road is narrow; to swerve might make more dead.

By glow of the tail-light I stumbled back of the car   5
and stood by the heap, a doe, a recent killing;
she had stiffened already, almost cold.
I dragged her off; she was large in the belly.

My fingers touching her side brought me the reason—
her side was warm; her fawn lay there waiting,   10
alive, still, never to be born.
Beside that mountain road I hesitated.

The car aimed ahead its lowered parking lights;
under the hood purred the steady engine.
I stood in the glare of the warm exhaust turning red;   15
around our group I could hear the wilderness listen.

I thought hard for us all—my only swerving—,
then pushed her over the edge into the river.

William Stafford (b. 1914)

Flowers, like other pretty things in nature, lend themselves to senti-
mental treatment. A page from *How to Know the Wild Flowers* (1900)
shows three ways of describing the corpse plant. Mary Thacher Higgin-

son's sonnet, which she called "Ghost-Flowers," associates the flower with qualities she thinks poetic—religion and virginity, for example. The writer of the prose paragraph, who is more realistic, points out that the flower has a tendency "to decompose and turn black when handled."

· **INDIAN-PIPE. CORPSE-PLANT. GHOST-FLOWER.** ·
Monotropa uniflora. Heath Family.

A low fleshy herb from three to eight inches high; without green foliage; of a wax-like appearance; with colorless bracts in the place of leaves. *Flower.*—White or pinkish; single; terminal; nodding. *Calyx* —Of two to four bract-like scales. *Corolla.*—Of four or five wedge-shaped petals. *Stamens.*—Eight or ten; with yellow anthers. *Pistil.*— One, with a disk-like, four or five-rayed stigma.

> In shining groups, each stem a pearly ray,
>   Weird flecks of light within the shadowed wood,
>   They dwell aloof, a spotless sisterhood.
>   No Angelus, except the wild bird's lay,
> Awakes these forest nuns; yet, night and day,   5
>   Their heads are bent, as if in prayerful mood.
>   A touch will mar their snow, and tempests rude
>   Defile; but in the mist fresh blossoms stray
> From spirit-gardens, just beyond our ken.
>   Each year we seek their virgin haunts, to look   10
>   Upon new loveliness, and watch again
> Their shy devotions near the singing brook;
>   Then, mingling in the dizzy stir of men,
>   Forget the vows made in that cloistered nook.*

The effect of a cluster of these nodding, wax-like flowers in the deep woods of summer is singularly fairy-like. They spring from a ball of matted rootlets, and are parasitic, drawing their nourishment from decaying vegetable matter. In fruit the plant erects itself and loses its striking resemblance to a pipe. Its clammy touch, and its disposition to decompose and turn black when handled, has earned it the name of corpse-plant. It was used by the Indians as an eye-lotion, and is still believed by some to possess healing properties.

* *Mary Thacher Higginson (nineteenth century)*

One protection against sentimentality is a sense of humor—which means a sense of proportion. Although Theodore Roethke's attitude toward his geranium is less pious than Higginson's toward the corpse plant, he seems to have more concern and affection for his plant than she has for hers.

• THE GERANIUM •

When I put her out, once, by the garbage pail,
She looked so limp and bedraggled,
So foolish and trusting, like a sick poodle,
Or a wizened aster in late September,
I brought her back in again   5
For a new routine—
Vitamins, water, and whatever
Sustenance seemed sensible
At the time: she'd lived
So long on gin, bobbie pins, half-smoked cigars, dead beer,   10
Her shriveled petals falling
On the faded carpet, the stale
Steak grease stuck to her fuzzy leaves.
(Dried-out, she creaked like a tulip.)

The things she endured!—   15
The dumb dames shrieking half the night
Or the two of us, alone, both seedy,
Me breathing booze at her,
She leaning out of her pot toward the window.

Near the end, she seemed almost to hear me—   20
And that was scary—
So when that snuffling cretin of a maid
Threw her, pot and all, into the trash-can,
I said nothing.

But I sacked the presumptuous hag the next week,   25
I was that lonely.

Theodore Roethke (1908–1963)

Sentimental poetry demands that we feel without thinking. If a man is handsome and attractive, aglow with youth, does it matter if he commits a few crimes here and there—or even as many as one can commit in a "thousand nights"? Not to Laurence Hope, who has not only a confused sense of justice but a naïve idea of how juries behave.

THE EMOTIONS

· YOUTH ·

I am not sure if I knew the truth
    What his case or crime might be,
I only know that he pleaded Youth,
    A beautiful, golden plea!

Youth, with its sunlit, passionate eyes,   5
    Its roseate velvet skin—
A plea to cancel a thousand lies,
    Or a thousand nights of sin.

The men who judged him were old and grey,
    Their eyes and their senses dim,   10
He brought the light of a warm Spring day
    To the Court-house bare and grim.

Could he plead guilty in a lovelier way?
His judges acquitted him.

Laurence Hope (1865–1904)

exercises & diversions

A. In "The Shield of Achilles" (p. 102), Auden shows the horror of a contemporary world by contrasting it with an ancient world of naturalness, order, "ritual pieties," and the dance. Many of his details are taken from the eighteenth book of the *Iliad*, but there the artwork on the shield is not as sweetly innocent as that which Thetis hopes for in Auden's poem. The world of Homer is less idealized: Hephaestus depicts a murder trial and a city at war, in which appear the figures of Discord, Tumult, and Fate, whose cloak is soaked red with human blood. In the peaceful countryside there is a gory scene of a lion gorging on a dead bull.

  1. Do you think Auden handles his contrast well by showing the ancient world as entirely idyllic and the contemporary one as entirely hideous?

  2. Is it ironic that Achilles, the representative of the ancient world, is himself "iron-hearted," "man-slaying," and doomed to an early death?

  3. In scenes of the modern world, what effective use is made of the withheld image? What is *not* shown?

exercises & diversions

4. What effective synecdoches or metonymies occur? Why is "boots" (line 14) a better word than "shoes"?

5. Auden's idea might be expressed (oversimply) as: the conditions of contemporary life do not permit man to develop his full human potential as well as older civilizations did. Show the steps by which the poet turns this idea into images.

6. Why would the contemporary civilization Auden shows be hostile to poetry? What details indicate that all emotion has been stifled?

7. Some readers will feel a Biblical allusion in the number of the victims of modern tyranny (line 36). Others may feel that when Auden says that his "multitude" is "waiting for a sign" (line 15), he is referring to the twelfth chapter of Saint Matthew, in which some of the scribes and Pharisees tell Christ they would like to see "a sign" (a miracle). Would the allusion—if it is there—seem ironic?

8. In Homer, there is no "sacrifice," no "flower-garlanded heifers," no "altar" (fourth stanza). All are found in John Keats' "Ode on a Grecian Urn":

> Who are these coming to the sacrifice?
> To what green altar, O mysterious priest,
> Lead'st thou that heifer lowing at the skies,
> And all her silken flanks with garlands dressed?

Would you guess that Auden is making a deliberate allusion to the Keats poem? Or is this an involuntary echo? A mere coincidence?

9. The urchin (line 53) is described as "aimless," but his stone is "well-aimed." In a freshman writing class would this be called "clumsy repetition," or is it intentional?

10. Other words seem to be used with special effect, so that we almost do a double take with them. With derivation (see dictionary) and connotations in mind, weigh the use of "artificial" (line 7), "feature" (line 9), "neighbourhood" (line 10), "congregated" (line 12), "unintelligible" (line 13), "cheered" (line 19), "enduring" (line 21), "arbitrary" (line 31), "vacancy" (line 54), "axioms" (line 57).

11. What is the effect of the unusually high percentage of monosyllabic words in the sixth stanza?

exercises & diversions

12. Why is Hephaestus described as "thin-lipped" (line 60)? The usual epithet for Thetis is ἀργυρόπεζα ("silver-footed"). Why, in line 62, did not Auden write "Thetis of the silver feet"?

13. When stanzas are used in a poem, they are generally the same throughout. We can see at a glance that two kinds of stanzas are used here. Why is the shift appropriate in this poem?

14. What is the inner logic of the stanzas? Do the second and third stanzas, for example, relate to the first? The fifth and sixth to the fourth?

15. Is it true that all the emotions named on the "emotion wheel" (p. 100) are felt as present in this poem?

16. The addition of one more stanza would make the structure symmetrical. Where should it be? Can you see any reason for its absence? (Heroic project for literary aspirants: Try writing the "missing" stanza so it fits in with the others in all respects.)

B. The philosopher Jean-Paul Sartre sees emotion as the process by which we escape, when frustrated by reality, into a make-believe world. For example, a man who gets the worst of it in an argument escapes from the world of logic (where he cannot win) to the world of fury (where he can win). His face reddens, his muscles swell, he jumps to his feet with a threatening "Oh yeah? Maybe you'd like a punch in the nose!" Or a rejected man sulks in a corner, his eyes dull so he cannot see the real world, his muscles lax so he cannot cope with it. He escapes into a despair that says the world is not worthwhile anyway. For Sartre, emotion is symbolic activity, magical behavior—a way of transforming what we cannot deal with.

1. Can you find poems in this chapter in which someone uses emotion as an escape from a reality he cannot face?

2. Can you recall poems in earlier chapters in which emotion was used in this way?

3. As opposed to Sartre, the physician-writer Gustav Eckstein holds, in *The Body Has a Head*, that "without emotion there is nothing that could be called mind. Clarification of thought depends on it." What poems have we read in which emotion seems to stimulate thought rather than distort it?

4. Do you feel that although Sartre's theory may not fit all emotions, it does fit sentimental ones, which are a kind of magical behavior aimed at transforming reality? Cite examples.

C. Sentimentality, which gives free access to unearned emotions, is at home in the popular arts—the movies, TV, best-selling fiction, advertising—which show us not the world as it is but the world as magically transformed to what we would like it to be.

YES, THE AGENCY CAN HANDLE THAT

You recommend that the motive, in Chapter 8, should be changed from ambition to a desire, on the heroine's part, for doing good; yes, that can be done.

Installment 9 could be more optimistic, as you point out, and it will not be hard to add a heartbreak to the class reunion in Chapter 10.

Script 11 may have, as you say, too much political intrigue of the sordid type; perhaps a diamond-in-the-rough approach would take care of this. And 12 has a reference to war that, as you suggest, had better be removed; yes.

This brings us to the holidays, that coincide with our prison sequence. With the convicts' Christmas supper, if you approve, we can go to town.

5 Yes, this should not be difficult. It can be done. Why not?

And script 600 brings us to the millennium, with all the fiends of hell singing Bach chorales.

And in 601 we explore the Valleys of the Moon (why not?), finding in each of them fresh Fountains of Youth.

And there is no mortal ill that cannot be cured by a little money, or lots of love, or by a friendly smile; no.

And few human hopes go unrealized; no.

10 And the rain does not ever, anywhere, fall upon corroded monuments and the graves of the forgotten dead.

Kenneth Fearing (1902–1961)

1. The "agency" is preparing a series of programs for mass presentation. Is it true that the revisions they are willing to make are all in the direction of sentimental treatment of the material?

2. Do you think the poem has the same speaker—an agency executive—throughout? Or does the poet himself begin to cut in with his own voice? If so, where?

3. What is the basis of the irony we get toward the close? Why does the irony become stronger as it becomes more concrete?

exercises & diversions

4. Is the poem essentially an attack on sentimental taste? On what grounds does the poet seem to think of sentimentality as a kind of falsehood?

5. "Yes, this should not be difficult" (line 14). Is it true that the sentimental treatment of a theme is easier than the emotionally honest treatment?

6. Write a poem or a paragraph about "the convicts' Christmas supper," the kind of writing that would "go to town" as an agency-pleaser.

D. 1. Poems not written as allegories can sometimes be read allegorically. Could Archibald MacLeish's "Eleven" (p. 7) be read as a poem about the poetic process, in that the child, hating the "Think now, Think . . . ," leaves the world of thought to get back to the world of sensation, imagination, and feeling?

2. Tennyson's "Tears, Idle Tears" (see Anthology, p. 470) takes on a peculiar coloring in its context. It occurs as a song in "The Princess" (1847), named after the progressive Princess Ida, who anticipated many of the ideas of the women's liberation movement. Wanting women to give up all "the tricks which make us toys of men," she founds an all-women's college. Any men found on the campus are to be executed. The unsentimental princess treats the song with some contempt, since it seems to be reactionary in praising the good old days, or, as she says, it "moans about the retrospect." It seems to her to be proestablishment because it fails to point out the injustices of the past.

Does the poem seem to have political or social overtones?

E. 1. All of us have personal images (of things, of people, of places, of seasons) that affect us deeply, perhaps because they condense memories and associations from childhood. Think of examples in your own mind. If you were writing poetry, how could you make use of these images so that others could be made to feel their power? Write a poem or prose paragraph around one or more of these personal images.

2. What objects do you think you yourself tend to be sentimental about? Let yourself write a frankly sentimental poem or prose paragraph about such an object.

Now rewrite it so that, while still heartfelt, it has no traces of sentimentality.

T·H·R·E·E

THE WORDS

6

Machine for Magic
THE FRESH USUAL WORDS

LIVING WORDS

Up to now we have been considering how the senses give us images that are a picture of our world, and how these images affect us with desire or aversion or any of the other emotions.

When we have given examples, however, we have had to anticipate still another element of poetry: the *words* through which the image and emotion are expressed.

In the mind of poets and their readers, image, emotion, and word all interact. And they interact with other elements we have not yet come to, such as sound and rhythm and the shape of sentences. Neither the poem nor the poet's mind is compartmentalized as neatly as a table of contents would seem to indicate. In trying to arrive at an understanding of any complicated object, the best we can do is take it part by part. In medical school, for example, students listen to lectures on various organs as if these were independent, though they are well aware that the organs cannot live separately. Nor are the students likely to object to their professors because they divide and classify.

The fact that we are moving on now to the role of words in poetry does not mean that we can put imagery and emotion behind us, as if we had "finished" them. What we have said about the two ought to be kept in mind and retested as we contemplate what is almost the only way we have of sharing them: the spoken word.

The painter Edgar Degas, not content with doing his graceful paintings of dancing girls, also wanted to write poems. Finding the literary work difficult, he complained to his friend, the celebrated poet Mallarmé, that he could not seem to write well, although he was "full of ideas." Mallarmé's famous answer was: "My dear Degas, poems are not made out of ideas; they're made out of *words.*" The best ideas, even though they turn into images, are of no avail *as poems* unless the words are right—just as a statue of even the noblest subject is a failure if the wood cracks or the marble shatters. Poems are made out of *words.*

And poets are necessarily in love with words. As the poet W. H. Auden has put it:

> . . . a poet is, before anything else, a person who is passionately in love with language . . . [this] is certainly the sign by which one recognizes whether a young man is potentially a poet or not. "Why do you want to write poetry?" If the young man answers: "I have important things to say," then he is not a poet. If he answers, "I like hanging around words listening to what they say," then maybe he is going to be a poet.*

Many poets have found their dictionary fascinating reading. "For several years," confessed Emily Dickinson, "my Lexicon—was my only companion." In his *Cantos* Ezra Pound quotes his friend Ford Madox Ford with approval:

> . . . get a dictionary
> and learn the meaning of words.

Many poets have told us that their poems started not with an idea but with a phrase or two that pleased them—phrases for which they then had to find the appropriate idea. This procedure, which will seem in reverse to most of us, is so common that the French poet Paul Valéry admitted that poets have more trouble finding ideas to fit their words than words to fit their ideas.

Poetry consists not so much in saying memorable things as in saying things memorably. The interplay of image and emotion is not yet poetry; without the word it would remain forever silent, unshared, locked in the core of the individual. The poets' job is to make out of words a machine that will transmit what is in their minds to the minds of others—a machine so finely built that those others will admire it at least as much for its own beauty as for the message it transmits.

---

* W. H. Auden, "Squares and Oblongs," in *Poets at Work*, ed. C. D. Abbott (New York: Harcourt, Brace & Co., 1948), p. 171.

MACHINE FOR MAGIC

To some, "machine" may seem too unpoetic a metaphor. And yet it was the poet William Carlos Williams who called a poem "a small (or large) machine made out of words." He was echoing what Valéry had already said more than once: "A poem is really a kind of machine for producing the poetic state of mind by means of words."

When poets are constructing one of their magic-machines, they are not so much *saying* something as *making* something out of words, just as a sculptor is making something out of stone, a painter something out of shapes and colors, a composer something out of sounds.

Much of our nonpoetic speech aims at communicating information. We say, "Jacksonville is five miles away," or "The room will cost thirty dollars a night." It does not matter what words we use provided the message is clear; we may forget the exact words once they have served their purpose. But poets care *how* they say what they say. "All the fun's in how you say a thing . . . ," said Robert Frost. Poets care about the sound and length of words, their suggestions, their rhythm when put together. They want to say something not only right for the occasion, but something that will keep forever. They are getting back, in short, to language as a kind of magic.

The words on pages 128–129 show us two kinds of diction. On the left-hand page we have words that are very much alive and have been so for centuries; these are the kind of words the best poets will prefer to use. On the right-hand page we have words and combinations of words that may once have been part of the living language but have long since lost their vitality; these are the kind of words the best poets will avoid.

"Moon, Sun, Sleep, Birds, Live" of Kenneth Patchen is like a working model of a poem, cut away to give us a vivid glimpse of the moving parts.

It might be hard to state the "meaning" of this page of poetry, in which the words of the title, dramatized by typography, stand out in a field of seven little poems. Around this composition is a frame of about a hundred words, some related by association of ideas. The page, capable of being read in many ways, seems to be notes for a meditation on existence and language, on words as expressing the basic realities of our lives. It is also a lesson in the language of poetry. The vocabulary it uses is taken from the best words available to the poet—nearly all are what Joseph Conrad called the "fresh usual words" and André Breton "les mots sans rides," the unwrinkled words. These have endured, as alive today as in Shakespeare's time. They are still the words we use for many of our deepest experiences. A large number come to us as sense impressions: "rain," "wind," "light," "cold," and others.

THE WORDS

· MOON, SUN, SLEEP, BIRDS, LIVE ·

rain wind light cold cold dark late stem gate bar flame knife garden blue

noise morning son loud art alive net tiger storm lily job tear maker shove

mirror **work**

coast **star**

deer **good**

Moon
SUN

frog **soul**

tunnel I am the music you make **book**

grave   the blue wings of the ocean **lift**

noose   the crying of the black swan **world**

supper **body**

SLEEP

beauty I am the friend **stone**

fear of your childhood **town**

heights **weave**

Birds

garden It is in my heart to wish you **center**

taste no sorrow **break**

climb no pain **afraid**

will no betrayal **skill**

for I am the will of your last being

look   the shudder of the breaking open **thing**

wing   of terrible gates **laugh**

valley O thou art good **grow**

rule I am the cave and the light and wise **three**

name the watch God keeps and kindling **keep**

knock when His children go mad a new fire **force**

LIVE

angel I am the death you seek **other**

shadow the life you are afraid **charm**

terror to know **soar**

quest *behold this eye of blood!* **fence**

power rise tree knowledge innocence fall hand thorn get father chain spool

law peace turtle grass snow prayer life black deep first tie hit see eye

Kenneth Patchen (1911–1972)

MACHINE FOR MAGIC

opalescent   proffered   beauteous   waning   haunting   witchery
ethereal   lightsome   behest   wrought   sought   supernal
sunder   sever   besmirch   benison   ope   sup   smite
darkling   thrice   rhapsodic   wend   illume   boon   waft
tranced   pageantry   array   mart   lave   rive   clime
crystal   pattern   filigree   silhouette   arabesque   furled   mute
enmeshed   cacophony   sere   symmetry   linger   frail   etched
mystic   morsel   abode   aureole   endowed   saraband
alchemy   sibylline   trancèd   labyrinthine   fray   plangent
design   rhythm (of life, etc.)   chaste (moonlight, etc.)
symphony (of life, of the city, etc.)   tracery (of branches, etc.)
happy haunts   endearing grace   eyes' tender light   fierce beauty
sadly yearn   one brief space   teeming life   life's evening
sunset glow   silvery laugh   unison divine   first faint blush of dawn
swaying in the breeze   wee fleeting touch   radiant smile
willing hands   heavy laden   wondrous tales   beauty's elixir
light and gay   friends of yesteryear   long-cherished dreams
piny grove   'neath the starlit canopy   the kiss of the breeze
kindly deeds   broken dreams   peacefully sleeping
mute orchestras of spring   murmured hymn   cannot fathom
thousands cheered   memories of lost days   snow-capped peaks
cadenced words of pure delight   dew-kissed flowers   allotted span
golden deeds   star-jeweled sky   earth's pageantries   rippling stream
bitter tears   mystic mingling   numbered days   softly pervades
seething humanity   rhapsodic balm   would that I could
falls in benediction   the young wind   harborward   sighing winds
timeless flight   the thrill of nature's lyre   ancient days
loved familiar things   the verdant earth in glad array
dream-fraught musings   amorous troubadours   haunting mood
the days of wine and roses   brooding quietude   solemn majesty
muted rage   soul aglow   naked trees   mountains towering high
quick suspicion   feathered songsters choiring in the blue
untethered sails   night's soft fragrance   the tender morn
caressing ripples   nocturnal paeans of glee   the star-sweet night
bleak winter tolls its knell   nameless grace   last aching memory
the musings fancy sired   the petalled flowers   sequestered ways
the rose dewy-eyed   woe-enfolded cypresses   dread surmise
rock-bound coast   heaven's vaulted reach   chill-winged rain

Most are "thing words" ("lily," "tiger," "star") rather than terms for abstractions; what we said about *concrete* and *abstract* in Chapter 1 holds too for the poet's vocabulary. Some directly express emotions; many more name objects that have long been charged with emotion: "flame," "knife," "garden," "morning," among them. All are rich in **connotation,** the suggestions that words accumulate in addition to their **denotation,** or dictionary meaning. (See the first Exercise, p. 149, for examples of these terms.)

The vitality of Patchen's vocabulary is clear if we contrast his page with a page of words that are dead or close to dying, words we would not be likely to use if we had anything urgent or passionate to say. One cannot insist that poets will never use any of these; sometimes they have their reasons for trying to revive a dead word, or even for laying it forth in state. Some words too have precise technical applications that retain their vigor, such as "opalescent" when used of gemstones, or "witchery" when used of superstitions in colonial New England. They shrivel and die when put to such use as "The heavenly rainbow wafts her opalescent witchery o'er the verdant earth." (Compare the simplicity of Wordsworth's "The rainbow comes and goes, / And lovely is the rose. . . .") A poem with a high percentage of such verbiage has little chance of coming to life. The deadest words are the merely "poetic" ones, words once alive but long since embalmed. Some readers, seeing them only in poetry of the past and thinking of them as uncontaminated by daily handling, may believe them especially worthy of the poet's attention. But devotion to such words or phrases is a kind of necrophilia.

A number of our examples of dead diction ("bitter tears," "thousands cheered") have become **clichés.** A "cliché" was originally a printing term for a single piece of type with words so often used together that it was handy to have them in one piece. Clichés have caught on because when first used they were apt and striking: "sadder but wiser," "tired but happy," "strong as an ox," "cool as a cucumber," "blissful ignorance," "get down to brass tacks," "far be it from me to . . . ," "this historic occasion," "add insult to injury," "last but not least," "at this point in time." The first man to compare the cheeks of a girl to a rose, said Salvador Dali, was obviously a poet; the first to repeat it was possibly an idiot.

Most revolutions in poetry aim at getting back to a more natural language. "The *norm* for a poet's language," said T. S. Eliot, "is the way his contemporaries talk." Pound has insisted on this norm again and again. "Good god! isn't there one of them that can write natural speech without copying clichés . . . ?" Poetry, he liked to repeat, ought to be at least as well written as prose. It ought to use no expression that one would not use under the stress of emotion in real life.

The greatness of Frost lies partly in that he was one of the few who brought poetry back to natural speech. One early poem, however, has about every fault that "poetic diction" can have, and is sentimental as well. Yet it has a couple of lines—one line in particular—that the young Frost recognized as prophetically good. The first third of the poem, "My Butterfly," reads:

> Thine emulous fond flowers are dead, too,
> And the daft sun-assaulter, he
> That frighted thee so oft, is fled or dead:
> Save only me
> (Nor is it sad to thee!)—   5
> Save only me
> There is none left to mourn thee in the fields.
>
> The gray grass is scarce dappled with the snow;
> Its two banks have not shut upon the river;
> But it is long ago—   10
> It seems forever—
> Since first I saw thee glance,
> With all thy dazzling other ones,
> In airy dalliance,
> Precipitate in love,   15
> Tossed, tangled, whirled and whirled above,
> Like a limp rose-wreath in a fairy dance. . . .

Amid much faded literary diction, the good line stands out in all its plainness:

> Its two banks have not shut upon the river.

The metaphor—ice like closing doors—is only implied. The plainest words are used—"shut," for example, instead of the more genteel "closed." A young person who liked his poetry "poetic" about 1890 might have written:

> King Winter hath not clanged
> His crystal portals o'er the finny chamber.

And typical readers might have thought, "How poetic!" perhaps remembering how James Russell Lowell had taken about thirty lines to tell how, when the chill wind blew,

THE WORDS

The little brook heard it and built a roof
'Neath which he could house him, winter-proof;
All night by the white stars' frosty gleams
He groined his arches and matched his beams;
Slender and clear were his crystal spars   *5*
As the lashes of light that trim the stars . . .
No mortal builders' most rare device
Could match this winter palace of ice . . .
Mimicked in fairy masonry
By the elfin builders . . .   *10*

But Frost, with rare independence, knew better than the other young poets and typical readers of his time. Once, when he went outside after a difficult or boring day, he felt a little tingle of pleasure at the way a crow powdered him with falling snow as it stirred. He wrote:

• DUST OF SNOW •

The way a crow
Shook down on me
The dust of snow
From a hemlock tree

Has given my heart   *5*
A change of mood
And saved some part
Of a day I had rued.

Robert Frost (1874–1963)

This is no more than a small poem about a small experience, like those so dear to writers of *haiku* (see p. 342). Although every word is fitted into a rhythm and about one out of four has a rhyming sound, all fall easily into their natural place. The feeling, communicated more through the little dance of rhythm and rhyme than through what is said, would have gone flat if Frost had merely annotated the experience:

The way that a crow
shook down right on me
some snow, rather like dust,
from a high hemlock bough
has given my heart   *5*
a different feeling about things,
and partly saved
a day I felt had been wasted.

For some, this constitutes "writing a poem"—just putting it down any old way. Frost made his statement memorable by giving it verve and lilt. A less direct poet might have felt such plain language was inadequate for such an experience; he might have inflated it with preachments and poetic diction:

• PULVEROUS SILVER ESSENCE! •

How dear the ways of Nature! Lo, yon crow
Precipitated earthward, even on me,
A pulverous silver essence, dust of snow,
White benefactions of a hemlock tree;

Bequeathing (legacy unto my heart!)   5
Transfigurations of an erstwhile mood,
Redeeming a jeweled modicum, wee part
Of one diurnal unit I had rued.

Many readers would consider our dressed-up version more "poetic" than Frost's unassuming sentence. Other readers, more cerebral, might prefer it this way:

• WITTGENSTEIN AND THE CROW •

Event
as instanced in
"the progress of phenomena":
Item: the avian
disbursal of elate frigidities   5
from a species Old Pop Longfellow saluted
as second in his paradigm of murmurers.
Which same
affords me *möglichkeit*
of shifting psyche-gears: 10
thereby reclaiming data stamped KAPUT.

It seems unlikely that either version would fix itself in the memory quite as successfully as Frost's original.

Some of the best poems are made up of very simple words:

all, along, any, ashore, back, bar, cannot, comes, day, deep, ever, far, glass, ground, gull, hull, keep, land, like, long, look, more, one, pass, people, raising, reflects, sand, sea, ship, standing, takes, truth, turn, vary, water, watch, way, wetter, when, wherever.

Not a rare word here, not a "poetic" one. And yet out of these words, plus a couple of *the*'s and *a*'s, Frost made a poem (about "the response of mankind to the empty immensity of the universe") that the critic Lionel Trilling said he often thinks "the most perfect poem of our time."

• NEITHER OUT FAR NOR IN DEEP •

The people along the sand
All turn and look one way.
They turn their back on the land.
They look at the sea all day.

As long as it takes to pass   5
A ship keeps raising its hull;
The wetter ground like glass
Reflects a standing gull.

The land may vary more;
But wherever the truth may be—   10
The water comes ashore,
And the people look at the sea.

They cannot look out far.
They cannot look in deep.
But when was that ever a bar   15
To any watch they keep?

Robert Frost (1874–1963)

Emily Dickinson is another poet who can get eye-opening effects, make us do the double take that fixes our attention, by using ordinary words in a way that is rich and strange. What could we make of a list of words like this?—

acre, alone, attended, barefoot, boggy, bone, boy, breathing, closes, comb, cool, cordiality, corn, divides, feel, feet, fellow, floor, further, gone, grass, know, likes, may, met, more, narrow, nature, never, noon, notice, occasionally, once, opens, passed, people, rides, secure, seen, several, shaft, spotted, stooping, sudden, sun, then, thought, tighter, too, transport, unbraiding, when, whiplash, with, without, wrinkled, zero.

Emily Dickinson managed. Out of these plain words she made one of the best poems ever written about one of God's creatures.

· A NARROW FELLOW IN THE GRASS ·

A narrow Fellow in the Grass
Occasionally rides—
You may have met Him—did you not
His notice sudden is—

The Grass divides as with a Comb—   5
A spotted shaft is seen—
And then it closes at your feet
And opens further on—

He likes a Boggy Acre
A Floor too cool for Corn—   10
Yet when a Boy, and Barefoot—
I more than once at Noon
Have passed, I thought, a Whip lash
Unbraiding in the Sun
When stooping to secure it   15
It wrinkled, and was gone—

Several of Nature's People
I know, and they know me—
I feel for them a transport
Of cordiality—   20

But never met this Fellow
Attended, or alone
Without a tighter breathing
And Zero at the Bone—

Emily Dickinson (1830–1886)

A more conventional poet might have shuddered, at the close, with

I gasp, and icy chills go
Up and down my spine!

But look at the originality of Emily Dickinson's last two lines!

Many of the words in the two lists above have one syllable. English, unlike Spanish or Italian, uses monosyllables for many of the basic realities: day, night, birth, death, boy, girl, love, hate, youth, age, and many others. Concentrations of monosyllables can have powerful effects, as in the last lines of Shakespeare's "Sonnet 18":

So long as men can breathe or eyes can see,
So long lives this, and this gives life to thee.

THE WORDS

They can be forceful too when played off against the longer Latinate words that English is rich in, as in the following lines from *Macbeth*:

> Will all great Neptune's ocean wash this blood
> Clean from my hand? No, this my hand will rather
> The multitudinous seas incarnadine,
> Making the green, one red.

There are exceptions—here as elsewhere—to almost everything we are saying. The bigger, rarer word may be the effective one:

> Sometimes these *cogitations* still amaze
> The troubled midnight and the noon's repose.

> T. S. Eliot (1888–1965)

Eliot uses "cogitations" with a kind of self-mockery: his speaker is not only a thinker, he is that more deliberate thing, a cogitator, and therefore all the more amazed to confront emotional realities. Keith Waldrop startles us with polysyllables:

> Some brat has chalked the word "screw"
> at the edge of my drive, and doodled
> around it *unequivocal hieroglyphics*.

"Unequivocal hieroglyphics" is ironic because of the very discrepancy between the level of the language and the crude reality it refers to.

LESS IS MORE

One quality of memorable speech is concentration: much in little. Of a mother punishing her child with such ineffectual fury that the child himself feels sorry for her weakness, John Ciardi writes:

> She beat so hard it hurt me not to hurt.

To describe how daughters drift away from their mothers:

> And still they grew away because they grew.

MACHINE FOR MAGIC

To describe the long period over which a widow received insurance payments:

Two mailmen died before his mail stopped coming.

The beauty of conciseness is like that of the globe or sphere (in many cultures a symbol of spiritual perfection)—both cover the greatest volume with the minimum surface area.

· BREAK, BREAK, BREAK ·

Break, break, break,
   On thy cold gray stones, O Sea!
And I would that my tongue could utter
   The thoughts that arise in me.

O well for the fisherman's boy,   *5*
   That he shouts with his sister at play!
O well for the sailor lad,
   That he sings in his boat on the bay!

And the stately ships go on
   To their haven under the hill;   *10*
But O for the touch of a vanish'd hand,
   And the sound of a voice that is still!

Break, break, break,
   At the foot of thy crags, O Sea!
But the tender grace of a day that is dead   *15*
   Will never come back to me.

Alfred, Lord Tennyson (1809–1892)

We appreciate the leanness of this lament for bygone days if we contrast it with another that has a high fat content. "Retrospection," an anonymous poem of the late nineteenth century, begins:

When we see our dreamships slipping
   From the verge of youth's green slope—
Loosening from the transient moorings
   At the golden shore of hope—
Vanishing, like airy bubbles,   *5*
   On the rough, tried sea of care,
Then the soul grows sick with longing
   That is almost wild despair.

Far behind lies sunny childhood—
  Fields of flowers our feet have trod   *10*
When our vision-bounded Eden
  Held no mystery but God;
When in dreams we spoke with angels,
  When awake, with brooks and birds,
Reading in the breeze and sunshine   *15*
  Love's unspoken, tender words. . . .

And so on, through five more stanzas of the same.

Poetry, as we quoted before, ought to be at least as well written
as prose. Some of the material in the rest of this chapter may seem to
refer not just to poetry but to prose as well—indeed to good writing
in general. And it does: Though good writing will not guarantee a
good poem, bad writing will guarantee a bad one.

Some parts of speech are more necessary than others. Nouns and
verbs are the most important, the most existential—nouns referring
to the forms that being can take, verbs to their activity. Adjectives
and adverbs are hangers-on, with little independent existence of their
own. Used weakly, they are decorative rather than structural, and hence
attractive to the apprentice writer, who needs surface decoration to
cover up the architectural flaws. Humpty Dumpty, in telling Alice about
words, says, "They've a temper some of them; particularly verbs,
they're the proudest—adjectives you can do anything with, but not
verbs. . . ." In his writings on style, Pound constantly warns against
adjectives. Perhaps nothing so weakens a poem as to have the nouns
"chaperoned" (as Pound said) by adjectives, or the verbs by adverbs.
Adjective fanciers are surprised at how many poems are almost with-
out their favorite part of speech. In the poems that follow, we might
notice how few adjectives there are, of what kind they are, and for
what occasions they seem to be saved.

· ALONG THE FIELD AS WE CAME BY ·

  Along the field as we came by
A year ago, my love and I,
The aspen over stile and stone
Was talking to itself alone.
'Oh who are these that kiss and pass?   *5*
A country lover and his lass;
Two lovers looking to be wed;
And time shall put them both to bed,
But she shall lie with earth above,
And he beside another love.'   *10*

---

³/**stile:** *steps over a wall or fence*

MACHINE FOR MAGIC

> And sure enough beneath the tree
> There walks another love with me,
> And overhead the aspen heaves
> Its rainy-sounding silver leaves;
> And I spell nothing in their stir,   *15*
> But now perhaps they speak to her,
> And plain for her to understand
> They talk about a time at hand
> When I shall sleep with clover clad,
> And she beside another lad.   *20*
>
> A. E. Housman (1859–1936)

One can imagine these lines bedizened—but hardly improved!—with modifiers:

> Along the fragrant summer fields as gaily we came by,
> One oh-so-happy year ago, my beauteous love and I,
> The trembling aspen over stile and over rugged stone
> Was softly talking, softly, to its brooding self alone:
> "Oh who are these impassioned ones that warmly kiss and pass?   *5*
> A sturdy country lover and his rosy-beaming lass.
> Two young and happy lovers looking sweetly to be wed;
> And brutal ruthless time shall put them dismally to bed.
> The much-lamented girl shall lie with dank old earth above;
> And he lie pleasantly beside another buxom love.   *10*

The airman in a poem of Yeats uses hardly an adjective in explaining why he took part in World War I. (As an Irishman, he could not hate the Germans or love the English; his impulse to enlist came from an existential love of adventure.)

· AN IRISH AIRMAN FORESEES HIS DEATH ·

> I know that I shall meet my fate
> Somewhere among the clouds above;
> Those that I fight I do not hate,
> Those that I guard I do not love;
> My country is Kiltartan Cross,   *5*
> My countrymen Kiltartan's poor,
> No likely end could bring them loss
> Or leave them happier than before.
> Nor law, nor duty bade me fight,
> Nor public men, nor cheering crowds,   *10*
> A lonely impulse of delight
> Drove to this tumult in the clouds;

THE WORDS

I balanced all, brought all to mind,
The years to come seemed waste of breath,
A waste of breath the years behind   *15*
In balance with this life, this death.

William Butler Yeats (1865–1939)

Gerard Manley Hopkins uses hardly any adjectives in "Spring and Fall" (see Anthology, p. 496), which is about the sorrow of a child as she watches the leaves drop. (She is really grieving, the poet tells her, over the fact of mortality—as Homer did when he said that the generations of men were like the generations of leaves.)

What we have been saying about modifiers is a caution, not a rule. Adjectives and adverbs tend to run to fat, to be sagging appendages on the bone and muscle of poetry. But just as we need some fat for the health and contour of the body, so we need some adjectives in poetry: for precision, for luxuriance, sometimes even for a needed sense of muchness.

The most useless adjectives duplicate the meaning of their noun, or express a quality implied by it. We have no need of them in such expressions as:

celestial stars, fragrant flowers, vernal spring, deep abyss, empty chasm, cold winter sun, flaming pyre, fair beauty, soft whispers, sweet perfume, loud strife, bleak waste, stimulating wine, dark forebodings, nobly enshrined.

If the nouns did not have their usual qualities—if the stars were *infernal*, or the spring *wintry*, or the strife *quiet*—the fact might be interesting enough to deserve an adjective.

Adjectives do little except dilute the poetry in such phrases from Bryant as:

hovering vulture, busy artisan, weary traveller, beaten drums, mighty ocean, golden grain, balmy evening, pathless desert, snow-capped peaks, stubborn flint, yielding wax, sultry July, chill north wind.

Doubled adjectives can add fat to a poem, especially when the meanings overlap, as in "flushed and angry cheek," "gay and gaudy hue," "bleak and barren mountains," "this region, desolate and drear," "icy Alpine height." Sometimes there are reasons for accumulating adjectives, as when Shakespeare wants to give a sense of the muchness of something in

MACHINE FOR MAGIC

> How weary, stale, flat and unprofitable
> Seem to me all the uses of the world!

or in

> . . . I grant him bloody,
> Luxurious, avaricious, false, deceitful,
> Sudden, malicious, smacking of every sin
> That has a name . . .

As many as three adjectives together tend to drag, but John Milton uses that very drag expressively in describing how his coy Eve yields to Adam with "sweet, reluctant, amorous delay. . . ."

Adjective-prone writers tend to favor such hyphenated expressions as "the day-tired town" or "her life-glad form" or "age-forgotten songs." Some hyphenated expressions are natural: "the spring-fed lake," "the air-conditioned theater," "salt-caked tugs." But new ones made up only for poetic effect call attention to themselves as unnatural intruders. They can also be imprecise. Does "She entered the wood, deer-cautious" mean she was cautious as a deer, or cautious because there were deer around? With such expressions as the following, we suspect the writer has made a self-conscious effort to lift natural English to a more "poetic" level: "brook-gladdened meadows," "hate-lashed storms," "terror-tinged yearning," "chimneys sulphur-flamed," "fruit-ripe with child," "thirst-inviting brook," "pine-bemurmured ridge." Pound, however, makes good use of elaborate hyphenization for mockery in the following little poem.

• THE BATH TUB •

> As a bathtub lined with white porcelain,
> When the hot water gives out or goes tepid,
> So is the slow cooling of our chivalrous passion,
> O my much praised but-not-altogether-satisfactory lady.

Ezra Pound (1885–1972)

A writer careful about adjectives and adverbs, keeping them in reserve for special effects, can make them vigorous and vivid.

> Like the fish of the bright and twittering fin. . . .

Herman Melville

THE WORDS

A raven low in the air, with stagnant eyes. . . .

Walter de la Mare

The horses jerked at the bridle-hands,
Nosing out a way for the stammering hooves
Along the rocks of a ribbed creek-bed. . . .

Robinson Jeffers

You lay still, brilliant with illness, behind glass. . . .

Thomas Kinsella

The old farmer, his scarlet face
Apologetic with whiskey. . . .

James Wright

Sometimes surprising effects can result from transferring a modifier from the noun it really belongs with to an associated noun. We often use such transfers in ordinary speech—as when we say we had a "noisy evening," even though it was the *we*, not the evening, that was noisy. We speak of "giddy heights," of a "shivery horror movie," of "dishonest money." Sir Philip Sidney said he did not "aspire to Caesar's bleeding fame." Other examples:

. . . clarions
That in the battle blowen bloody sounds. . . .

Geoffrey Chaucer

O, most wicked speed, to post
With such dexterity to incestuous sheets!

William Shakespeare

His brow is wet with honest sweat. . . .

Henry Wadsworth Longfellow

Contemporary poets are still transferring adjectives:

And all throughout a Breughel matinee
Those buxom waltzes ran. . . .

James Merrill

MACHINE FOR MAGIC

Humpty Dumpty may have found verbs the hardest words of all, but writers have coped with them. (John Berryman says of Ernest Hemingway, who prided himself on coping, "He verbed for forty years. . . .") Here are some interesting verbs performing:

> The day had been one cloud, but now a bird
> Shot into song. . . .
>
> *Frederick Goddard Tuckerman*

> . . . over a field
> Snapping with grasshoppers. . . .
>
> *Frederick Goddard Tuckerman*

> The lazy cows wrench many a scented flower. . . .
>
> *Robert Bridges*

> Knee-deep in straw the cattle twitched
> Sweet hay from crib and rack. . . .
>
> *Robert Bridges*

> . . . They heard the wind,
> Flustering below. . . .
>
> *Robinson Jeffers*

> Scolding your pipe against a tree. . . .
>
> *Marcia Masters*

> The Hammond organ lubricates the air. . . .
>
> *Miller Williams*

> Rudolph Reed was oaken.
> His wife was oaken too.
> And his two good girls and his good little man
> Oakened as they grew. . . .
>
> *Gwendolyn Brooks*

Such vivid verbs are often compressed metaphors: The Reeds are strong as oak; they *are* oak; as they grow stronger, they oaken.

Poets, like other writers, achieve concentration by packing double meanings into single words. This kind of double talk—these puns—are by no means confined to poetry. We often see slogans like:

DRIVE AS IF YOUR LIFE DEPENDED ON IT.

ARE YOU DYING FOR A CIGARETTE?

Today we think of puns as the kind of humor more likely to evoke groans than laughter. But puns were taken more seriously in earlier times. When John Donne put his future in jeopardy by marrying Sir George More's underage daughter without the father's consent, some-one—probably not Donne himself—composed a one-liner:

> John Donne,   Anne Donne,   Un-done.

Donne himself was not joking when he wrote, during an illness that might have been fatal, his poem "A Hymn to God the Father," with its punning:

> When Thou hast done, Thou hast not Donne,
> For I have more.

(Some critics even think that "more" is a pun on his wife's name.)

Some puns play on different meanings of the same word, as in George Starbuck's lines:

> The world has a glass center.
> I saw the sign for it.
> TOLEDO, GLASS CENTER OF THE WORLD.

Others play on different words that sound alike.

· ON HIS BOOKS ·

> When I am dead, I hope it may be said,
> "His sins were scarlet, but his books were red."

> *Hilaire Belloc (1870–1953)*

We should always be alert to the possibility of such double meanings, which may be anything but funny. When Herman Melville (better known as the author of *Moby-Dick* than as a poet) described how the carefree young Union soldiers went off to their first battle as to a picnic, he wrote:

> No berrying party, pleasure-wooed,
> No picnic party in the May,
> Ever went less loth than they
> Into that leafy neighborhood. . . .

We cannot fail to hear the grisly pun on *berrying party* and *burying party*.

MACHINE FOR MAGIC

When Frost writes about "a zealot full of fluid inspiration" we know that the inspiration is not only free-flowing and fluent, but also encouraged by alcohol. And when he came to compose his little poem in praise of Orville and Wilbur Wright, whose pioneer experiments with kites and gliders led to the first true airplane flight, he pivoted his poem on a Wright-write-right pun.

• THE WRIGHTS' BIPLANE •

This biplane is the shape of human flight.
Its name might better be First Motor Kite.
Its makers' name—Time cannot get that wrong,
For it was writ in heaven doubly Wright.

Robert Frost (1874–1963)

Besides storing their words with multiple meanings, writers can give them more charge by making full use of their connotations (see page 130). Words can, like people, be interesting because of their background, because of where they have been and the company they have kept in the past.

When the Normans came over from France in 1066, the language of the natives was Old English (or Anglo-Saxon), which gave us many of the words for down-to-earth realities. French became the language of the court; words of French ancestry are redolent of courtliness, chivalry, romance. For centuries Latin was the language of the church and of scholarship; words patently from the Latin can still suggest erudition or pedantry. In ordinary speech we do not separate these three components, but a high concentration of any one can make itself felt as unusual. In "The Wanderer," W. H. Auden makes use of Old English derivatives, some few of them odd enough to call for the dictionary. Such words, as opposed to the more cultivated French and Latin ones, evoke a rugged and heroic life in a primitive northern setting. Auden's poem is about the archetypal figure of the seeker, the adventurer, the pioneer who leaves his home, his establishment, to fare forth into new territory.

• THE WANDERER •

Doom is dark and deeper than any sea-dingle.
Upon what man it fall
In spring, day-wishing flowers appearing,
Avalanche sliding, white snow from rock-face,
That he should leave his house,   5

1/**dingle:** *deep cleft or hollow*

No cloud-soft hand can hold him, restraint by women;
But ever that man goes
Through place-keepers, through forest trees,
A stranger to strangers over undried sea,
Houses for fishes, suffocating water,   *10*
Or lonely on fell as chat,
By pot-holed becks
A bird stone-haunting, an unquiet bird.
There head falls forward, fatigued at evening,
And dreams of home,   *15*
Waving from window, spread of welcome,
Kissing of wife under single sheet;
But waking sees
Bird-flocks nameless to him, through doorway voices
Of new men making another love.   *20*

Save him from hostile capture,
From sudden tiger's leap at corner;
Protect his house,
His anxious house where days are counted
From thunderbolt protect,   *25*
From gradual ruin spreading like a stain;
Converting number from vague to certain,
Bring joy, bring day of his returning,
Lucky with day approaching, with leaning dawn.

W. H. Auden (1907–1973)

The first eighteen words are from Old English; not until we come to "flowers" do we have a word that derives, through Old French, from the Latin. We can see how different the poem would sound if we Latinized it:

Fate is more obscure and profound than any ocean-valley . . .

The vocabulary keeps us in an Old-English world until we reach

Save him from hostile capture,

which is pure Latin-French. So is

Converting number from vague to certain,

and words like "sudden," "protect," "anxious," "gradual." As the wanderer returns home, he returns to a more genteel vocabulary.

---

[11]/**fell:** *hill, ridge*   [12]/**becks:** *brooks*
  chat: *a kind of bird*

MACHINE FOR MAGIC

Hopkins, though a professor of Latin and Greek, favored native English words. In "The Windhover" (see Anthology, p. 495) there are almost no words whose Latin ancestry would be obvious. The vocabulary is basically Old English, but what is unusual is the large number of words, all crucial to the meaning, that suggest a French world of chivalry, adventure, and even romance: "minion," "dauphin," "falcon," "achieve," "mastery," "beauty," "valour," "buckle," "billion," "dangerous," "chevalier," "sillion," "vermilion." That the language has so French a cast is appropriate: The poet, seeing a kind of knightly adventurousness in the daring falcon, thinks of Christ, his chevalier or supreme knight-figure.

The eighteenth century was particularly fond of a sonorous Latinate vocabulary, as in these lines from Samuel Johnson's "The Vanity of Human Wishes":

> Let *Observation* with *extensive* view,
> Survey mankind from China to Peru. . . .
>
> *Delusive Fortune* hears the *incessant* call,
> They mount, they shine, *evaporate,* and fall. . . .
>
> The form *distorted justifies* the fall,
> And *detestation* rids the *indignant* wall. . . .

Even when such words are the natural ones for their meaning, an accumulation can sound learned or pompous.

man

tree

sun

Pound believed the ideograms that stand for words in Chinese to be pictograms, which look so much like the objects they denote that a sensitive observer "could read a certain amount of Chinese writing without ANY STUDY." Among the examples he gives are the three above, which, simple as they are, seem rather shaky support for his views. When we are told that the first means *man* or *person*, we can see that, yes, it is two-legged. But we might just as well have guessed that it meant *tent* or *mountain peak* or *arrowhead* or anything sharp. Only a minority of Chinese characters are actually pictograms; and a very few even of these bear a recognizable resemblance to the object.

But sometimes words come to us with a halo of ghostly images: apparitions from the underworld of etymology. "Deliberate" comes from the Latin *librare* (*to weigh*), which is itself from *libra* (a pound—whence our abbreviation *lb.*—and the *scales* on which *pounds* were weighed). When we remember that the word has to do with weights and balances, then it becomes a pictogram: we see the weighted mechanisms shifting as the bridge begins to rise in Richard Wilbur's line:

> Deliberately the drawbridge starts to rise. . . .

We become more sensitive to ordinary words by realizing how haunted they are. Merely turning the pages of a dictionary will stir up quite a few ghosts. "Alarm" is more exciting when we realize it is a cry, "To arms!" (*All' arme!* in Italian). An ordinary "derrick" becomes a grislier part of the industrial landscape if we remember that it was named after a certain Derrick, a famous London hangman. "Nonchalant" means *not heating up*. To be nonchalant is to "cool it." "Curfew" has a setting when we know it comes from two Old French words we would now spell *couvre-feu*: *cover the fire*—put it out for the night. A curfew for teen-agers picks up interesting symbolic overtones if we think of it as meaning "time to put the fires out." "Dexterity" refers to the right hand, most people's best hand; "sinister" refers to the left, or unlucky, side: To speak of a magician, or a ball handler, as having "sinister dexterity" gives us a curious punning oxymoron. Sensitive to the personality and history of words, writers make full use of them as resources. Frost has noticed that when a person says he is in favor of a *revolution* in any respect he means he wants to keep things exactly as they are: a *revolution* means that something wheel-like goes all the way around and ends up where it was. Revolutionaries should be in favor of half revolutions:

> Yes, revolutions are the only salves.
> But they're one thing that should be done by halves.

Many words become like pictograms in the light of their history. This is one more way in which the poet can concentrate meanings.

exercises & diversions

A. 1. When Federico García Lorca's speaker (p. 51) says he would like to trade his horse, saddle, and knife for a house, mirror, and blanket, he is not thinking of the **denotation** or dictionary meaning of the words ("**horse:** a large, solid-hoofed, herbivorous quadruped, *Equus caballus* . . .") but of the **connotation** or cluster of associations each has. The horse connotes an outdoor life of wandering, adventure, and peril; the saddle connotes homelessness, discomfort, and hardship; the knife, passion and violence. The objects for which he would like to trade connote safety, comfort, and settled domesticity. The words in Patchen's poem (p. 128) are rich in connotation. "Rain," in the upper-left-hand corner, suggests coolness, fertility, flowers, freshness, renewal, purity, snugness by the fire; but it also connotes chilliness, discomfort, loneliness, gloom, deprivation (as in "to save for a rainy day"). What association clusters go along with each of these words: gate, fence, flame, snow, garden, coast, lily, thorn, mirror, shadow, star, stone?

2. Do any other words in Patchen's poem strike you as being especially strong in connotation?

3. Does it seem to you that such words—or what they stand for—could be symbols of what they connote? Is "rain," for example, a fertility symbol?

B. Evaluate the worth of each adjective in the following examples:

1. This done, he took the bride about the neck
And kissed her lips with such a clamorous smack
That at the parting all the church did echo. . . .

William Shakespeare

2. Whate'er false shows of short and slippery good
Mix the mad sons of men in mutual blood. . . .

Richard Crashaw

3. Poor world, said I, what wilt thou do
    To entertain this starry Stranger?
Is this the best thou couldst bestow,
    A cold and not too cleanly manger?
Contend, ye powers of heaven and earth,
    To fit a bed for this huge birth.

Richard Crashaw

4. And far in the hazy distance
   Of that lovely night of June,
The blaze of the flaming furnace
   Gleamed redder than the moon. . . .

Henry Wadsworth Longfellow

5. From the pavements and the roofs
In shimmering volumes wound
The wrinkled heat. . . .

John Davidson

6.   . . . Never had I more
Excited, passionate, fantastical
Imagination. . . .

William Butler Yeats

7. For everything that's lovely is
But a brief, dreamy, kind delight. . . .

William Butler Yeats

8. The sky was like a waterdrop
   In shadow of a thorn,
Clear, tranquil, beautiful,
   Dark, forlorn. . . .

Walter de la Mare

9. The autumn night receives us, hoarse with rain. . . .

Louise Bogan

10. The responsible sound of the lawnmower. . . .

William Stafford

11.   . . . barefoot gulls
designing the sand. . . .

William Stafford

12. [Of a beggar]
How much money would erase him in a dream,
his lids inflamed, his bare feet biblical
with sores? . . . The bay across the street
is affluent with sun. . . .

Richard Hugo

C. In the light of matters discussed in this chapter, comment on the following quotations:

1. O shut the door! and when thou hast done so,
Come weep with me—past hope, past cure, past help!

William Shakespeare

2. Alas, sir, are you here? Things that love night
Love not such nights as these. . . .

William Shakespeare

3. And worse I may be yet. The worst is not
As long as we can say, "This is the worst."

William Shakespeare

4. And the ox, with sleek hide, and with low-swimming head;
And the sheep, little-kneed, with a quick-dipping nod;
And a girl, with her head carried on in a proud
Gait of walking, as smooth as an air-swimming cloud.

William Barnes

5. The loud vociferations of the street
Become an indistinguishable roar. . . .

Henry Wadsworth Longfellow

6. [Of a deer]
We do not discern those eyes
Watching in the snow . . .
We do not discern those eyes
Wondering, aglow,
Fourfooted, tiptoe. . . .

Thomas Hardy

exercises & diversions

7. *"Chelidon urbica urbica"*
I cried on the little bird,
Meticulously enunciating each syllable of each word. . . .

Walter de la Mare

8. Nay, let us have the marble peace of Rome. . . .

Vachel Lindsay

9. From what I've seen tacked up, you can't draw water.
Your plan is "going into art"? Oh, daughter,
What would you learn? How man bends at the knee?
Better bone up on such anatomy
At first hand. . . .

X. J. Kennedy

10. Mellifluous as bees, these brittle men
droning of Honeyed Homer give me hives. . . .

George Starbuck

D. In Jarrell's "The Knight, Death, and the Devil," which is based on Albrecht Dürer's engraving, there are many hyphenated modifiers. Do they seem to work here? Is there anything, for example, in the texture of the engraving itself to which they correspond?

THE KNIGHT, DEATH, AND THE DEVIL

Cowhorn-crowned, shockheaded, cornshuck-bearded,
Death is a scarecrow—his death's-head a teetotum
That tilts up toward man confidentially
But trimmed with adders; ringlet-maned, rope-bridled,
The mare he rides crops herbs beside a skull.   *5*
He holds up, warning, the crossed cones of time:
Here, narrowing into now, the Past and Future
Are quicksand.   A hoofed pikeman trots behind.
His pike's claw-hammer mocks—in duplicate, inverted—   *10*
The pocked, ribbed, soaring crescent of his horn.
A scapegoat aged into a steer; boar-snouted;
His great limp ears stuck sidelong out in air;
A dewlap bunched at his breast; a ram's-horn wound
Beneath each ear; a spur licked up and out   *15*
From the hide of his forehead; bat-winged, but in bone;

Albrecht Dürer, *The Knight, Death, and the Devil* (Detail)
(Courtesy, The Art Institute of Chicago, Clarence Buckingham Collection)

His eye a ring inside a ring inside a ring
That leers up, joyless, vile, in meek obscenity—
This is the devil. Flesh to flesh, he bleats
The herd back to the pit of being.   20
In fluted mail; upon his lance the bush
Of that old fox; a sheep-dog bounding at his stirrup,
In its eyes the cast of faithfulness (our help,
Our foolish help); his dun war-horse pacing
Beneath in strength, in ceremonious magnificence;   25
His castle—some man's castle—set on every crag:
So, companioned so, the knight moves through this world.
The fiend moos in amity, Death mouths, reminding:
He listens in assurance, has no glance
To spare for them, but looks past steadily   30
At—at—
        a man's look completes itself.

The death of his own flesh, set up outside him;
The flesh of his own soul, set up outside him—
Death and the devil, what are these to him?   35
His being accuses him—and yet his face is firm
In resolution, in absolute persistence;
The folds of smiling do for steadiness;
The face is its own fate—*a man does what he must*—
And the body underneath it says: *I am.*   40

Randall Jarrell (1914–1965)

E. What kind of pictures haunt these words from their etymological
past? (Consult a good dictionary.)

fool, generous, companion, lunacy, planet, maudlin, tawdry, sabotage,
pandemonium, tangerine, bungalow, chivalrous, cavalier, bedlam,
gargoyle, focus, exaggerate, disaster, dilapidated, carnival, carnation,
carnage, carnal, horde

F. 1. Contrast the use of adjectives in Karl Shapiro's "A Cut Flower"
(p. 41) with that in his "Girls Working in Banks" (p. 60). Why
the difference?

2. Examine the use of adjectives preceding their nouns in "The
Woodspurge" (p. 481), "Love, 20¢ the First Quarter Mile" (p. 537),
and "Spoils" (p. 87). Why is the use of adjectives so very different
in "Leda and the Swan" (p. 42)? Could any of the adjectives there
be omitted without loss?

exercises & diversions

G. 1. Recall that Eliot said that "the *norm* for a poet's language is the way his contemporaries talk," and that Pound was in favor of "natural speech." What would they probably think of the diction in this poem?

IN COOL, GREEN HAUNTS

A sweet, deep sense of mystery filled the wood.
  A star, like that which woke o'er Bethlehem,
  Shone on the still pool's brow for diadem—
  The first to fall of summer's multitude!
In cool, green haunts, where, haply, Robin Hood   5
  Ranged royally, of old, with all his train,
  A hushed expectance, such as augurs rain,
  Enthralled me and possessed me where I stood.

Then came the wind, with low word as he went;
  The quick wren, swift repeating what he said;   10
  A chattering chipmunk lured me on and led
Where scented brakes 'neath some wee burden bent:—
  One look—'twas this those wild things yearned to say:
  "A little brown-eyed fawn was born today!"

Mahlon Leonard Fisher (twentieth century)

2. Some would consider this sonnet sentimental. Does the kind of diction used contribute to the possibly sentimental effect?

3. This kind of language is sometimes called "sonnet diction." How would you characterize it?

4. Could this poem be saved if rewritten in the natural speech of your contemporaries? Try to write such a version.

H. Write a descriptive poem (of, say, a dozen lines, in any rhythm) about a familiar object, or anything of interest to you. Do not use any adjectives until the last line, and then try to use, effectively, a series of three.

F · O · U · R

THE SOUNDS

7

Gold in the Ore
THE SOUNDS OF ENGLISH

This chapter may look as if it were about some such abstraction as acoustical theory. It is actually about the way we use our bodies—instruments of flesh and bone—to produce the sounds we call voice: the sounds of poetry and all human speech. We can realize how sensitive the mouth is and what care the brain takes of it if we contemplate a "homunculus" (see p. 160)—a representation of the way human beings would look if the proportions of our body corresponded to the brain area devoted to each part. More brain-space is needed for the mouth than for all the rest of the body except the hands.

We can think of words as having not only a mind (their meanings) but also a body—the structure of sound in which their meaning lives. Most poets, who are not Platonic in their love for language, care as much for the body of their words as for the mind. They like to feel words in the mouth, as Andrew Glaze does with "freedom":

> FREEDOM!—roll it about on the tongue.
> It is certainly a spiritual sound.
> One vowel is like a running white horse.
> The other is like a drum blow. . . .

Wallace Stevens is speaking for many good poets when he says "words, above everything else, are, in poetry, sounds." The sound of poetry, what Robert Frost called "the gold in the ore," is what we turn to now.

A poem comes to us first as speech, on sound waves that register as barometric changes against the drums and gauges of the ear, an apparatus so sensitive it takes notice if the pressure against it varies by

THE SOUNDS

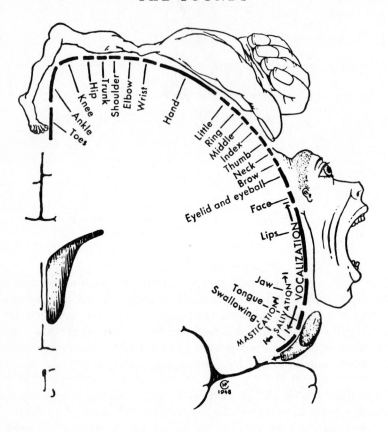

one part in ten billion. "A breath of the mouth becomes a picture of the world," said Johann Gottfried von Herder, ". . . everything that man has ever thought and willed . . . depends on a moving breath of air."

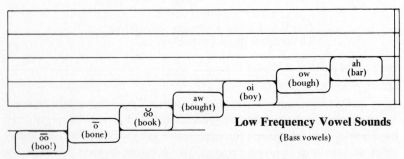

Low Frequency Vowel Sounds

(Bass vowels)

Frequency Scale of English Vowel Sounds

We hear poems even when we seem to be taking them silently from the page. Tiny wires attached to the speech areas of the throat have picked up electrical currents—evidence that the muscles were being stimulated during silent reading. The body participates sympathetically with what it experiences. Colors affect us physically: Experiments have shown that fixing the eyes on pure red for a time can raise our blood pressure and accelerate our heartbeat, whereas fixing our eyes on pure blue can have a tranquilizing effect. Images of sound must affect us no less profoundly, since as very young children we were more at home in the world of sound (which we had known even before birth) than in the world of sight. The rest of this chapter will be about the physical nature of speech. This is not theoretical material to be merely read; these are physical facts to be acted out physically—to be felt and tried in the mouth as we read.

VOWELS

Our speech sounds are conventionally divided into vowels and consonants. With vowels the airflow from the lungs is not impeded. If we pronounce a e i o u, we can feel that we are nowhere obstructing the breath but only, by raising our tongue, rounding our lips, and the like, reshaping the instrument it flows through. How we manage so complicated a process would astound us if we thought about it.

Our feats of hearing are equally incredible. We follow as many as twenty distinct sounds a second; we notice sounds that fade into nothingness in a few thousandths of a second; and we do so while turning this complicated acoustic input into electrochemical nerve impulses that the brain can process. The most complicated sound patterns a

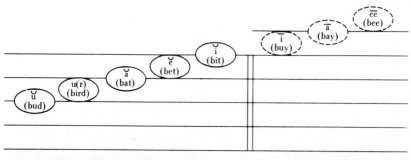

Middle Frequency Vowel Sounds

(Tenor Vowels)

High Frequency Vowel Sounds

(Alto Vowels)

poet ever uses are as nothing compared to the patterns we handle habitually.

Vowels are in a way like musical notes, so that we can set up a vowel scale (rather like a musical scale) based on the frequencies that the sounds have in themselves. Sound, as we know, travels in waves. Since it travels at constant speed, the shorter the waves, the more per second—the higher, that is, the frequency of the sound. Shortwave sounds are high-frequency sounds, shrill sounds, like the *ee* of "whee!" The longer the waves, the fewer per second, and the slower and deeper the sound seems to be. (We know that if a 78 rpm record is slowed down to the 33⅓ speed, the sound will get slower and deeper.) The *oo* of "moon" is a low-frequency sound.

A difficulty we run into in making up a vowel scale is that vowels are not notes but chords made up of tones and overtones from the resonating system of throat, mouth, and head. Some of our fifteen sounds, the diphthongs, are two chords sounded in sequence. The *i* sound of "good-by" is a run-together *áh-ee*. Several other sounds are also vowels in motion—"glides" from one sound into another. Our scale, though it would not provide a basis for laboratory experiment, is on the whole accurate for American speech, and it serves well enough for the reading of poetry.

The upness and downness of vowel sounds affect us physically in different ways. The *ee* sound, at the top of the scale, comes in a pattern of waves that could be diagramed like this:

ee

in contrast to the *oo* sound at the bottom:

oo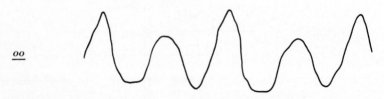

The high-frequency *ee* is busier, gives the ear more to process. Its greater activity suggests greater vitality, speed, excitement than the slower moving, more sluggish waves of the *oo*.

Few categories in our experience are richer in emotional suggestion

GOLD IN THE ORE

than upness and downness. We associate being "up" or "high" with an increase of vitality, being "down" or "low" with a lessening of it. Our heart "sinks" when we feel grief, the physical effect of which Charles Darwin describes as follows: "The muscles [become] flaccid; the eyelids droop; the head hangs on the contracted chest; the lips, cheeks, and lower jaw all sink downward from their own weight."* The last phrase explains why downness is bad: When we give up or lose strength, gravitation takes over. All growth, aspiration, striving is an upward thing, almost against the nature of matter itself.

High-frequency vowels go well with expressions of excitement, exhilaration, vivacity. James Joyce, one of the most sound-conscious of writers, provides a good example of their use in an exultant passage from *A Portrait of the Artist as a Young Man*:

> He was alone. He was unheeded, happy and near to the wild heart of life. He was alone and young and wilful and wildhearted, alone amid a waste of wild air and brackish waters and the seaharvest of shells and tangle and veiled grey sunlight and gayclad lightclad figures, of children and girls and voices childish and girlish in the air. . . .

Probably no poet has ever so deliberately written in the high-frequency range as Dylan Thomas did when he urged his dying father to keep up his courage to the end.

· DO NOT GO GENTLE INTO THAT GOOD NIGHT ·

Do not go gentle into that good night,
Old age should burn and rave at close of day;
Rage, rage against the dying of the light.

Though wise men at their end know dark is right,
Because their words had forked no lightning they   *5*
Do not go gentle into that good night.

Good men, the last wave by, crying how bright
Their frail deeds might have danced in a green bay,
Rage, rage against the dying of the light.

Wild men who caught and sang the sun in flight,   *10*
And learn, too late, they grieved it on its way,
Do not go gentle into that good night.

---

* Charles Darwin, *The Expression of the Emotions in Man and Animals* (The University of Chicago Press, 1965), p. 167.

THE SOUNDS

Grave men, near death, who see with blinding sight
Blind eyes could blaze like meteors and be gay,
Rage, rage against the dying of the light.   *15*

And you, my father, there on the sad height,
Curse, bless, me now with your fierce tears, I pray.
Do not go gentle into that good night.
Rage, rage against the dying of the light.

Dylan Thomas (1914–1953)

The rhyming sounds, throughout, are ī ("night") and ā ("day"). With
these are many high, bright ē's ("deed"). The effect is not only in the
high-frequency vowels themselves, but in the fact that they occur about
twice as often here as they do in the normal run of English speech.
The unlooked-for percentage must come as a shock of excitement, an
aural pick-me-up, to the sensitive, if largely subconscious, mechanisms
of the brain.

A more somber poem gives a very different concentration of sound:

• ONCE BY THE PACIFIC •

The shattered water made a misty din.
Great waves looked over others coming in,
And thought of doing something to the shore
That water never did to land before.
The clouds were low and hairy in the skies,   5
Like locks blown forward in the gleam of eyes.
You could not tell, and yet it looked as if
The shore was lucky in being backed by cliff,
The cliff in being backed by continent;
It looked as if a night of dark intent   10
Was coming, and not only a night, an age.
Someone had better be prepared for rage.
There would be more than ocean-water broken
Before God's last *Put out the Light* was spoken.

Robert Frost (1874–1963)

A scary poem. Something in the universe, it implies, is threatening our
existence; things are going to get worse before they get better. The
vowel sounds gravitate toward the lower, darker notes: There are more
than twice as many *aw*'s, *oo*'s, and *o*'s as we are used to hearing in
spoken English.

The larger an object is and the more volume it has, the more slowly it is likely to vibrate. The long strings in a piano give us the deep tones; a double bass can go lower than a violin. Avalanches and stormy seas have deeper reverberations than hailstones on the roof—not merely louder. The larger object produces a low-frequency sound.

Since low notes are related to largeness, they also evoke what is powerful or awesome or ominous or gloomy. We think of them as *dark* notes, perhaps because our experience of caverns and other reverberating hollows is associated with the dark. (The voice of the great singer Caruso was said to "darken" as over the years it changed from tenor to baritone.)

Vowels have their characteristic resonance from the shape and size of the cavities in which they resound—that is, from the way in which we make use of the resonating chambers of mouth and head. The larger the hollow in which a vowel sound vibrates, the deeper the sound and the more clearly our nerves and muscles tell us that *we ourselves* are embodying largeness, hollowness, darkness. If we could see—which heaven forbid!—a cross section of the head of a person pronouncing "*ee*," it would look rather like the left hand figure below. The front part of the tongue has been raised to permit only a narrow stream of air to pass through. Such a high front vowel, tensely produced, can suggest not only speed, brightness, and vitality but also littleness, as in "needle" or "teeny-weeny." It *is* a littleness, and we are doing a kind of charade of littleness by squeezing our mouth to the narrowest opening that permits any sound at all.

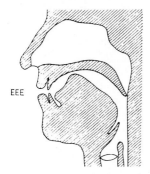
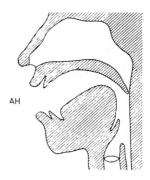

People producing an *ah* sound (right hand figure, above) have to make their mouth a noticeably larger resonating chamber: have to make a sensitive part of their body, very close to the brain, a more sonorous cavern for the deeper, more solemn, more awesome sound. Not only do the sounds we produce have certain qualities, but our bodies, in producing them, are trying to be *like* those very qualities.

Sounds also affect us through the memories they arouse of what we have heard in life. The 10 billion neurons of the brain have almost infinite interconnections. Hearing certain sounds cannot fail to remind us of surf or thunder or the hiss of a snake or the whine of the winter wind through telephone wires on the prairie. Or of feet echoing in an empty street at night, the scream of brakes, the siren of a fire truck. Sounds like these can be deeply emotional, bringing, as we have learned, their messages of life and death.

For many reasons, then, the sounds of human speech are charged with emotional potential. Poets have always felt this. When Shelley begins his "Ode to a Skylark" with a line that features the four highest-frequency vowels, he sets the poem in the key of these vowels:

> Hail to thee, blithe spirit!

When Frost uses almost all of the bass vowels in the first two lines of "An Old Man's Winter Night," his introductory chords prepare us to expect the worst:

> All out-of-doors looked darkly in at him
> Through the thin frost, almost in separate stars. . . .

Once we have uttered a sound, we take pleasure in repeating it. We find repetition in magic spells, in solemn oaths, in orations, in ads, as well as in the speech noises a baby makes for its own pleasure. When a sound is clearly struck in a poem, it tends to attract similar sounds. At the beginning of Gary Snyder's "Oil," many of the sounds that we hear can be heard again within the next few syllables:

> soft rainsqualls on the swells
> south of the Bonins, late at night. Light
> from the empty mess-hall
> throws back bulky shadows
> of winch and fairlead   5
> over the slanting fantail where I stand. . . .

Repetition of a vowel sound ("soft"/"squalls"; "rain"/"late") is known as **assonance**.

Each of the fifteen vowel sounds of our scale has its own character or tone color. Skillful writers and sensitive readers are aware of the differences, just as one is aware of the differences between the tones of a flute, a violin, and a bassoon. But since poets for the most part work with the language as it is, and since words that combine a desired sound and an appropriate meaning are not always available, the use of expressive sound in poetry is not to be expected as a regular thing. The most we can say is that poets are sensitive to the sounds they are making and use them expressively when they see the opportunity. The benefit that most of us, as readers, derive from meditating at least briefly on the quality of individual sounds is that we come to participate more completely, more physically, in the experience of the poem. The remarks that follow—we repeat—should be tested in the mouth.

Writers or readers who wanted to master the keyboard of sound could concentrate on each of the fifteen vowel sounds in turn, noticing what happens in their mouth when they pronounce it, listening to its quality and deciding on its emotional possibilities, thinking of words in which it seems especially expressive, and watching for it to turn up in the poetry they are reading. They would not be surprised to discover that, just as such symbols as "earth" and "sea" have room at the same time for opposite connotations, so one sound can be appropriate for opposite emotions—the shrill *i* of "strike" can serve for either exultation or despair. Sounding this diphthong, they would feel how it originates as an *ah* in the lax back region of the throat but climbs instantly into the vibrant *ee* region. They could feel it move in their mouth. They might guess that since more energy goes into its production than into that of a pure vowel, it has more energy to convey. They might well decide that it is the most dynamic of the high-frequency vowels, that it strikes the ear more forcibly than the others, has more audibility. They might come upon Sylvia Plath using it almost brutally for its cutting power in

> Christ! they are panes of ice,
> A vice of knives . . .

or upon James Tate dramatizing its shrillness in

> . . . sirens malign
> the sky . . .

or upon Coleridge using its brightness and sparkle in

> Or if the secret ministry of frost
> Shall hang them up in silent icicles,
> Quietly shining to the quiet moon.

We could work through all the vowel sounds in this way—though we do not have the time or space to do so here. Suppose we pick out only a few for examination.

THE SOUNDS

Even the dullest vowel sound has its individuality. The little *i* (of "bit") has been a favorite with writers trying to depict things that are brisk, quick, little, slim, glittery. Plato thought it especially apt for showing movement. Many would feel that "skinny-dipping" sounds more like what it means than "nude bathing" does. The effect is in the thin, glittery vowels. "Shivery hickory" sounds right for a baseball bat. Robert Fitzgerald uses it in his well-known baseball poem (p. 547), which has other quick-moving *i*-sequences as well:

> . . . the baseman
> Gathers a grounder in fat green grass,
> Picks it stinging and clipped as wit
> Into the leather: a swinging step
> Wings it deadeye down to first. . . .

It is easy to find other examples of expressive *i*'s:

> Slim pickerel glint
> in the water. . . .

Donald Hall

> near the winter river with silt like silver. . . .

William Stafford

> [a bird] flits nimble-winged in thickets. . . .

Sylvia Plath

The short *ŭ* sound, *u* or *uh*, has a definite but disreputable personality. It has been called the "shudder vowel"—the *uh* or *ugh* we make when feeling horror or disgust. Pronouncing it is like clearing the throat or ejecting something from the mouth. The slang word "upchuck" (for *vomit*) has the appropriate sound. (Slang is frequently more sound conscious than standard English.) An investigation of hundreds of monosyllables has shown that the *ŭ* of "mud" has generally undesirable connotations. One scholar has listed many *uh* words that express dislike, disgust, or scorn: "blunder," "bungle," "clumsy," "humdrum," "slum," "slush," "muck," "muddle," "slut." We could all think of others: "dump," "crummy," "sludge," "chump," "bunk," "punk," "runt," "pus," "muss," "fuzz," "puffy," "repugnant."

When we sort of push a grunt up, with tongue, cheek, and lips left slack, what comes out is an "*Uh*." We use it as the hesitation sound, when we don't, uh, quite know what to say. The archaic word "ugsome" meant *repulsive*.

GOLD IN THE ORE

Man saying "Ugh!"
(From Charles Darwin, *The Expression of the Emotions in Man and Animals*, No. 2, Plate V. University of Chicago Press, 1965, © 1872)

Any observation we make about sound and sense will have MANY exceptions. These in no way disprove the expressiveness of sound; they merely show that in some words that particular element is inert or subordinate to other considerations. We can all think of pleasant *uh* words: "young love," "summer," "cuddle," "comfort," "slumber," "lullaby," "yummy."

E. E. Cummings has combined the pleasant-unpleasant associations of *ŭ* and its slushy sound in his poem about the "mud-luscious," "puddle-wonderful" world of children.

• **CHANSONS INNOCENTES, I** •

in Just-
spring   when the world is mud-
luscious the little
lame balloonman

whistles   far   and wee   5

and eddieandbill come
running from marbles and
piracies and it's
spring

when the world is puddle-wonderful⠀⠀⠀⠀⠀⠀⠀⠀⠀⠀⠀⠀*10*

the queer
old balloonman whistles
far⠀⠀⠀and⠀⠀⠀wee
and bettyandisbel come dancing

from hop-scotch and jump-rope and⠀⠀⠀⠀⠀⠀*15*
it's
spring
and
⠀⠀⠀⠀the

⠀⠀⠀⠀⠀⠀goat-footed⠀⠀⠀⠀⠀⠀⠀⠀⠀⠀⠀⠀⠀⠀⠀⠀*20*

balloonMan⠀⠀⠀whistles
far
and
wee

⠀⠀⠀⠀⠀⠀⠀⠀⠀⠀⠀⠀⠀⠀⠀⠀*E. E. Cummings (1894–1962)*

The seven low-frequency vowel sounds, resonated from the back of the mouth, owe their deeper tone to the larger volume of air set in motion. They are more mouth-filling because they have more mouth to fill. To many, *aw* will seem the most powerful of the vowel sounds, a hollow reverberation from far back in the throat, rougher, grander, larger than the even lower-frequency *oh* and *oo* sounds. Some find the word "God" more impressive when they drop the vowel a couple of notes and pronounce it "Gawd." John Milton's "Lycidas" (p. 421) opens impressively with a string of three stressed *aw*'s:

⠀⠀⠀Yet once more, O ye laurels, and once more. . . .

There are a half-dozen in the opening lines of *Paradise Lost*:

⠀⠀⠀. . . that forbidden tree, whose mortal taste
⠀⠀⠀Brought death into the world, and all our woe,
⠀⠀⠀With loss of Eden, till one greater man
⠀⠀⠀Restore us. . . .

One of Yeats' most sonorous lines is built on *aw*:

GOLD IN THE ORE

That dolphin-torn, that gong-tormented sea.

The vowel sound of lowest frequency is the *oo* of "moon." Because the lips are more rounded than for *oh* and the tongue a bit higher, *oo* picks up a flutelike quality from the narrower aperture. It sounds smoother, less hollow than the other deep tones. Helped by *b* and *m* it can indeed go "boo!" or "boom!" But since one of its formants, or constituent sounds, is the same as for the much higher *ee*, and since *oo* is articulated high in the mouth, it can also have an eerie crooning quality. Better than any description is the range of emotions for which Plath uses it in the love-hate poem, all cooing and hooting, she wrote to the Teutonic "daddy" she felt had abandoned her by dying in her childhood. Of its eighty lines, over half end in *oo*, with such stanzas as:

> I have always been scared of *you,*
> With your Luftwaffe, your gobbledygoo.
> And your neat moustache
> And your Aryan eye, bright blue.
> Panzer-man, panzer-man, O You—. . . .   5
> Bit my pretty red heart in two.
> I was ten when they buried you.
> At twenty I tried to die
> And get back, back, back to you.
> I thought even the bones would do. . . .   10

CONSONANTS

Vowels are produced by an unimpeded flow of breath. Consonants are produced by interference that sets up an audible turbulence or cuts off the airflow completely. It might seem that the fewer consonants we use, the more musical our speech would be. But consonant power is one of the glories of English. Hawaiian, by contrast, has a high percentage of vowels and cannot pronounce two consonants together— "Merry Christmas" comes out "Mele Kalikimaka." Hawaiian may seem "prettier" than English, but its effect has been called childlike and effeminate. It is the consonants that give shape and energy to our speech. Richard Wilbur has this in mind in his poem on Saint Teresa of Ávila, who had to

> lock the O of ecstasy within
> The tempered consonants of discipline.

THE SOUNDS

Like vowels, consonants have their distinctive characters, which are felt more emphatically in repetition. Such repetition at the beginning of words or syllables is called **alliteration.**

The most vowel-like of the consonants are *w* and *y*. *W* is double *U*—an *oo* sound. When we read "Western Wind," we begin "*oo-estern oo-ind, hoo-en oo-ill* . . . ," with the *oo*'s gliding so rapidly into the following vowel that we are hardly aware of their *oo*ness at all. Vowel-like *w*'s alliterate smoothly.

> O sylvan Wye! thou wanderer through the woods. . . .
>
> *William Wordsworth*

> So let the day be wilder, windier, wetter. . . .
>
> *Frederick Goddard Tuckerman*

> It is a red bird that seeks out his choir
> Among the choirs of wind and wet and wing. . . .
>
> *Wallace Stevens*

It may be that the two *w*'s account for the popularity of the western wind among poets. The east wind seems to have had no such luck:

> When the wind is in the east,
> 'Tis good for neither man nor beast. . . .

Nor good for alliteration.

In the opinion of many, the common American *r* is more vowel than consonant. Except for custom, "bird" could just as well be spelled "brd." But since *r* has a dark throaty quality—especially when combined with a guttural like *g*—we use it to represent the growl or *grrrr* of an animal or angry man. Ben Jonson was not the first to call it the dog's letter. François Villon put his French *r* (then rolled) to amusing use when he wrote a ballade (p. 339) to a lady he was angry at; for twenty-eight lines his rhymes, all ending in *r*, snarl and snap at her.

The *r* and *l* are both called *liquids*. They seem to flow on or around the tongue instead of being clicked or popped or hissed forth. Probably *l* would win a popularity contest for the prettiest vowel sound. Lord Byron makes fun of the overuse of soft *l*'s:

> When amatory poets sing their loves
> In liquid lines mellifluously bland. . . .

GOLD IN THE ORE

He would probably not have objected to the less conspicuous *l*'s with which Yeats' old woman wonders:

> What lively lad most pleasured me
> Of all that with me lay?

Jonson said *l* was called a liquid because "it melteth in the sounding." More down-to-earth theorists have noticed that the sound seems to be formed low in the mouth, near the surface of the tongue and the inner surface of the lower teeth, which are more bathed in saliva than other parts of the mouth. Saliva-bathed or not, *l* does go well with liquidity:

> And on a sudden, lo! the level lake
> And the long glories of the winter moon.
>
> *Alfred, Lord Tennyson*

> I hear lake water lapping with low sounds
> by the shore. . . .
>
> *William Butler Yeats*

The *m, n,* and *ng* sounds are known as *nasals*. The airflow is diverted into the nasal passages to vibrate there. We can feel the change in our mouth by sounding the three in sequence: "bam," "ban," "bang."

We use an *m* sound—sometimes conventionalized as "yum!"—for warm appreciation. Probably no other consonant is so expressive by itself. In reply to "Do you like my dress?" a perfectly intelligible answer would be "Mmmmmmmm!" The sound is prolonged, not broken off; is internal (behind closed lips) and hence warm and cherished; is associated with the affectionate and sensitive lips, which bring the human child the first pleasure it knows—food and the warm presence of its mother. It has been noticed that *m* occurs in the word for "mother" in many languages, presumably because this is the sound happy babies make. Because it is about the only sound we can make with closed lips, we hum it when engaged in such pleasurable activities as eating something or kissing someone.

The sound of *n* is somewhat higher in tone, more a whine than a hum. It is smaller and sharper than an *m*; it seems to pick up a bony hardness from being sounded near the roof of the mouth. We might think of mosquitoes as going "*Nnnnnn,*" but not "*Mmmmmm.*" The suggestion has been made that its through-the-nose quality accounts for its presence in words of negation in many languages: "no," "non," and "nicht," among others.

The *ng* sound has a metallic resonance that qualifies it for many sound words: "bang," "boing," "bong," "clang," "ding-dong," "gong," "jangle," "ping," "ring."

The seven sounds we have so far discussed have been called semi-vowels; they would probably be thought of as the most musical of the consonants.

The sounds known as *fricatives* are produced by audible friction over something that interferes with the airflow from the lungs. They include: *h; f, c; th* ("thing"), *dh* ("that"); *s, z; sh, zh* ("pleasure"). The *h* is only a roughness in the breath, the rasp of air through the vocal cords as they get in place for the vowel that follows.

In *f* and *v*, turbulence is heard as the air passes between the lower lip and the upper teeth. Both sounds can be pleasantly soft, though they are not necessarily so.

> Duncan is in his grave;
> After life's fitful fever he sleeps well. . . .
>
> *William Shakespeare*

> Her tapering hand and rounded wrist
> Had facile power to form a fist. . . .
>
> *John Greenleaf Whittier*

> Snow falling and night falling fast, oh, fast
> In a field I looked into going past. . . .
>
> *Robert Frost*

When the breath hisses between tongue and teeth, the result is an *s* sound. Jonson spoke of it with mixed feelings: "a most easy and gentle letter, and softly hisseth against the teeth . . . it is called the serpent's letter." Ancient critics looked down on it as "more suited to a brute beast than to a rational being." Tennyson tried to get rid of *s*'s; he called it "kicking the geese out of the boat." Robert Graves says his deathbed advice will be: "The art of poetry consists in knowing exactly how to manipulate the letter S." Graves finds Shelley particularly crude in his handling of *s* sounds, as in these lines from "Ode to the West Wind":

GOLD IN THE ORE

Thou on whose stream, mid the steep sky's commotion,
Loose clouds like earth's decaying leaves are shed. . . .

> . . . when to outstrip thy skiey speed
> Scarce seemed a vision. . . .

In processing sound-tracks for recordings, technicians make use of a device called a *de-esser* to get rid of the hiss. Writers, however, sometimes make their lines hiss on purpose. One famous example is the conspiratorial whisper of Macbeth:

> . . . if the assassination
> Could trammel up the consequence and catch,
> With his surcease, success. . . .

Many of the sounds we have been considering can change their character in the company of other sounds. The *sn* and *st* might be taken as typical.

Woman saying "Sn—!"
(From Charles Darwin, *The Expression of the Emotions in Man and Animals,* No. 1, Plate IV. University of Chicago Press, 1965, © 1872)

Of the words that start with *sn*, only a few are pleasant: "snow," "snuggle," "snug," and some others. Most are unpleasant: "snag," "snare," "snake," "sneak," "snide," "snitch," "snob," "snoop," "snub." One large group of *sn* words has to do with the nose: "sneeze," "sniff," "snuffle," "snivel," "snoot," "snore," "snort," "snout," "snuff," "sneer." Darwin thought that "sneer" and "snarl" were related, and that both were produced by muscular contractions like those of a snarling dog, with lip drawn back to expose the threatening canine tooth.

Many words beginning with *st* mean things that "stand steady" or are "stable" or "stabilized"; or that support something, like "staff," "stake," "stem," "stilt," "stirrup," "strut," "stud"; or that are somehow strong, like "stern," "stiff," "strict," "stubborn," "sturdy," "stag," "steed"; or that show energetic action, like "stalk," "stamp," "storm," "stun."

> How bowed the woods beneath their sturdy stroke!
>
> *Thomas Gray*

> And she who seemed eaten by cankering care
> In statuesque sturdiness stalks. . . .
>
> *Thomas Hardy*

Robert Graves, often a skeptic in these matters, commends the muscular *str* words as being like what they mean: "strain," "strength," "strangle," "struggle," "strike," "strive," and many others.

Sh, sounded farther back in the mouth, is less sharp but has more body than *s*. We use it, as a kind of "white noise," to overpower other sounds when we say, "Shhhh!" or "Hush!"—whereas "Sssss!" is to get attention or express disapproval.

The final group of consonants—*p, b; t, d; k, g*—called *stops* (or *plosives* or *explosives*), are more drastic. They cut off the air for a moment, let pressure build up behind the barrier of lips or tongue, then release it with a tiny explosion. With *p* and *b*, the most forceful of the consonant sounds, it is the lips that block and explode the air. Repetitions of *p* call instant attention to themselves by sounding like the "Peter Piper picked . . ." tongue twister. The *b* can be almost as obstreperous. When Shakespeare wants to make fun of excessive alliteration (consonant repetition), *b* is the letter he chooses for his ridicule:

> Whereat, with blade, with bloody blameful blade,
> He bravely broached his boiling bloody breast. . . .

Plath uses *p* and *b* for the texture of rocky soil:

> What flinty pebbles the ploughblade upturns. . . .

Other contemporaries have used these stops for abrupt physical motion:

> The lobbed ball plops, then dribbles in the cup. . . .
>
> *Robert Lowell*

GOLD IN THE ORE

Plop, plop. The lobster toppled in the pot. . . .

John Berryman

Robert Browning put the exuberance of *b* to good use in describing the buxom abundance of a woman's body:

Was a lady such a lady, cheeks so round and lips so red,—
On her neck the small face buoyant, like a bell-flower on its bed,
O'er the breast's superb abundance where a man might base his head?

A *p* (and a *b* almost as well) can express rejection by holding back the air and then violently expelling it, as in "Pooh!" or "Bunk!" Comic strips use the spit sound "*Ptui!*" for disgust. (The classical Greek word for "spit" was almost the same—*ptuo.*) Such words originate, it seems, in the natural mouth movements of the act of spitting. When we pronounce *p* or *sp*, the muscles of the mouth mimic disgust—which means that, if disgust happens to be what we feel, we can throw ourselves more completely, with more body English, into what we are saying.

When we pronounce *t* or *d*, the air is stopped by the tongue tip, which is clicked against the ridge behind the teeth. The effect is neater, trimmer than with the more explosive *p* and *b*; clocks and watches show a sense of fitness in saying "ticktock" instead of "bing bang."

When we pronounce *k* or *g* (a hard *g*, as in "guttural," not as in "gesture"), the airflow is stopped farther back toward the throat by the bunched-up back of the tongue. Particularly when reinforced with *r* or the deeper vowels, these give us the most throaty sound available— as in "choke," "crow," "gag," "gargle."

Crows crowd croaking overhead. . . .

John Clare

Not only sands and gravels
Were once more on their travels,
But gulping muddy gallons
Great boulders off their balance
Bumped heads together dully   5
And started down the gully. . . .

Robert Frost

Alliteration is as old as language. Babies alliterate before they can speak a sentence: "da-da," "bye-bye." We all know what alliteration can do for a slogan or catch phrase. Political sloganeers revel in it.

THE SOUNDS

Alliterative phrases have entwined themselves into the language we use every day. One could find hundreds of examples like "house and home," "rack and ruin," "spick and span," "rough and ready," "a dime a dozen," "in the fourth and final quarter." Driving into Tennessee from the north, one passes a restaurant–gas station called "Tank 'n' Tummy," among fireworks dealers known as "Goofy Goober," "Lonely Luke," "Crazy Chris," and—with assonance—"Loco Joe." Somebody believes in sound values!

Alliteration can, like any useful thing, be vulgarized by overuse. Politicians and writers are probably the most flagrant offenders. But poets have also been at fault. Edmund Spenser, coming on the line

> For lofty love doth loathe a lowly eye . . .

objected to this "playing with the letter." Good alliteration, however, is much more than a literary gewgaw. It can create a bond of identity between words, hinting that if they have a sound in common, perhaps they have something more.

> Love me little, love me long,
> Is the burden of my song.
>
> *Anonymous*

> Lay hands upon these traitors and their trash. . . .
>
> *William Shakespeare*

> So all their praises are but prophecies
> Of this our time, all you prefiguring. . . .
>
> *William Shakespeare*

It can also represent, by its muchness of sound, any kind of muchness.

> Great England's glory and the world's wide wonder. . . .
>
> *Edmund Spenser*

> Before polygamy was made a sin;
> When man, on many, multiplied his kind,
> Ere one to one was cursedly confined. . . .
>
> *John Dryden*

> Fish, flesh and fowl, commend all summer long
> Whatever is begotten, born, and dies. . . .
>
> *William Butler Yeats*

GOLD IN THE ORE

Flammantia moenia mundi, Lucretius wrote,
Alliterating like a Saxon—all those M's mean majesty. . . .

Robinson Jeffers

Or weary repetition:

The plowman homeward plods his weary way. . . .

Thomas Gray

It may link words together by sound only to contrast their meaning:

The mighty mingling with the mean,
The lofty with the low.

John Greenleaf Whittier

The graceful with the gross combined,
The stately with the stinking. . . .

Arthur Hugh Clough

It may be a mark of abundant energy:

To leap large lengths of miles when thou art gone. . . .

William Shakespeare

Clinging alliteration can stand for clinging things:

Nor cast one longing lingering look behind . . .

Thomas Gray

And though it loved in misery
Close and cling so tight,
There's not a bird of day that dare
Extinguish that delight.

William Butler Yeats

. . . the stale
steak grease stuck to her fuzzy leaves. . . .

Theodore Roethke

In writing about the bewildering death of a little girl (p. 109), John Crowe Ransom uses stiff alliteration for two kinds of immobility:

> In one house we are sternly stopped
> To say we are vexed at her brown study,
> Lying so primly propped.

Assonance (p. 166) can serve the same purposes as alliteration, though often more subtly.

exercises & diversions

A. About such matters as we have been discussing in this chapter, the Roman critic Quintilian once wrote: "Studies of this kind harm only those who stick in them, not those who pass through them." Explore the implications of this remark, particularly in regard to our treatment of sound.

B. 1. *Whisper* the words "June," "Joan," "John," "Jan," "Jen," "Gin," "Jane," "Jean," in that order. Can you feel how the vowel sounds move progressively up the scale? Now *whisper* them in reverse order. Can you feel them move down the scale?

2. What do you notice about the use of sound in Pound's "Alba" (p. 12)?

3. Shakespeare's "Sonnet 129" (p. 407) was referred to earlier as a poem of disgust or revulsion. The poem is full of expressively ugly sounds. Point them out.

C. In each of the following lines of poetry, some sound effect is conspicuous. Decide, with each, if it is too conspicuous. Or are the sounds appropriate and expressive?

1. Thou wretched, rash, intruding fool, farewell!

William Shakespeare

2. I'll lug the guts into the neighbor room. . . .

William Shakespeare

3. But let determined things to destiny
Hold unbewailed their way. . . .

William Shakespeare

4. Oh for that night! When I in Him
Might live invisible and dim.

Henry Vaughan

5. I saw, alas! some dread event impend. . . .

Alexander Pope

6. "Lock the door, Lariston, lion of Liddisdale;
Lock the door, Lariston, Lowther comes on. . . ."

James Hogg

7. The fair breeze blew, the white foam flew,
The furrow followed free;
We were the first that ever burst
Into that silent sea.

Samuel Taylor Coleridge

8. From the sails the dew did drip. . . .

Samuel Taylor Coleridge

9. Over the water the old ghost strode. . . .

Thomas Lovell Beddoes

10. Because God's gifts put man's best dreams to shame.

Elizabeth Barrett Browning

11. Up many and many a marvellous shrine
Whose wreathèd friezes intertwine
The viol, the violet, and the vine. . . .

Edgar Allan Poe

12. Sometimes a troop of damsels glad,
An abbot on an ambling pad. . . .

Alfred, Lord Tennyson

13. Like some black mountain glooming huge aloof. . . .

James Russell Lowell

14. A vacant sameness grays the sky. . . .

Thomas Hardy

15. The mother looked him up and down,
And laughed—a scant laugh with a rattle.

Edwin Arlington Robinson

16. Some morning from the boulder-broken beach. . . .

Robert Frost

17. But the strangest thing: in the thick old thatch. . . .

Robert Frost

18. One hears the rustled stirring of a bell:
A small bell faintly clinked,
Sleepy and indistinct:
Or a deep bell which the winds forlornly toll. . . .

Conrad Aiken

19. Tossed
by the muscular sea,
we are lost,
and glad to be lost
in troughs of rough
love.

May Swenson

20.   . . . salt flats,
Gas tanks, factory stacks, that landscape. . . .

Sylvia Plath

D. 1. In 1655 Milton wrote one of his greatest sonnets to protest an atrocity of the time, the slaughter in the mountains of more than one thousand members of the Vaudois by the Duke of Savoy. How is sound used expressively? (Notice that sounds at the end of lines are especially prominent—even more so when they happen to rhyme.)

ON THE LATE MASSACRE IN PIEDMONT

Avenge, O Lord, thy slaughtered saints, whose bones
   Lie scattered on the Alpine mountains cold,
   Even them who kept thy truth so pure of old
   When all our fathers worshiped stocks and stones
Forget not: in thy book record their groans   5
   Who were thy sheep and in their ancient fold
   Slain by the bloody Piedmontese that rolled
   Mother with infant down the rocks. Their moans
The vales redoubled to the hills, and they
   To Heaven. Their martyred blood and ashes sow   10
   O'er all th' Italian fields where still doth sway
The triple tyrant: that from these may grow
   A hundredfold, who having learnt thy way
   Early may fly the Babylonian woe.

John Milton (1608–1674)

E. **1.** Think of ten common alliterating phrases like "might and main," "friend or foe," and the like.

2. We discussed words beginning with *sn* and *st*. Do you find any pattern in words beginning with *bl* and *br*? (Recall words you know, like "blare" and "brisk," or skim a dictionary.) The following little poem seems to mean that without the dark side of life we would not properly value the bright side. Is the sound appropriate?

LOVE AND DEATH

And yet a kiss (like blubber) 'd blur and slip,
Without the assuring skull beneath the lip.

F. Write a short poem or paragraph on an "up" theme, using many high-frequency vowels. Do the same with a "down" theme, using many low-frequency vowels.

    (You might also enjoy reversing the process to see what happens: write on an "up" theme using "down" vowels, and vice versa.)

8

Working with Gold
THE DEVICES OF SOUND

LANGUAGE AS MIMICRY

Poetry used to be magic. Far away and long ago, among people simpler than most of us, poetic formulas, perhaps in rhyme or some other form of sound-play, were thought to bring rain or put a curse on an enemy or charm someone into loving. In all such spells, as we recall from fairy tales, the sound was as important as the sense. Origen, the third-century theologian from Egypt who wrote in Greek, mentions certain charms found useful in ridding one's house of devils; he cautions, however, that they will not work in translation. Not because devils are poor linguists, but because the power of the formula lay in the sound itself. The aspects of language we will be concerned with in this chapter may seem more a matter of magic than of science.

Some 15,000 years ago, when the glaciers of the last Ice Age drove our ancestors into cave openings near the Mediterranean, reindeer, natives of the Arctic tundra, roamed freely over what are now the resort areas of the Riviera. Earth dwellers had been human for hundreds of thousands of years before the Ice Age, but they come before us with particular vividness when we see the cave drawings made in those centuries. These exist for us in a soundless world. "Many of the painted caves are really very terrifying places; the silence is intense, broken only occasionally by a distant boom when a drop of water falls from the roof into some silent pool below."* But the artist

---

* M. Burkitt, *The Old Stone Age* (New York: New York University Press, 1956), p. 216.

WORKING WITH GOLD

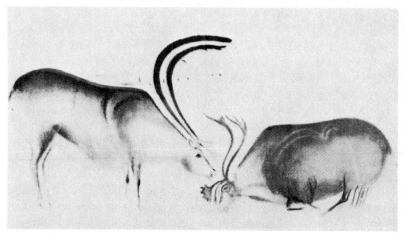

Reindeer from the Caverns of Font-de-Gaume, France
(*American Museum of Natural History*)

did not live in a world of silence. Ice and gravel crackled underfoot, thunder roared and re-echoed, animals made the same cries and growls that animals make today.

The people who did these sensitive drawings must have used their built-in sound systems to imitate animals or the sounds of nature. Crouched by the fire near the cave mouth and listening to thunder reverberating among the rocks, they must have amused or frightened themselves by making thunder sounds deep in the throat—probably bursting into wild, delighted laughter at their success or lack of it. Likely enough the earliest words for thunder would be thunder sounds —as "thunder" itself seems to be.

When our cave dwellers let rumbling sounds roll around in their throat, they were beginning to use what we call **onomatopoeia.** The Greek word means *name making,* as if something in nature made its own name by sounds associated with it—as a dog does for a child when it seems to say "bow-wow." These verbal mimicries are as deeply rooted in human nature as the desire to draw is; some people even think they account for the origin of language. We know that children find them expressive: Not only the "choo-choo" and "ticktock" they learn from others, but also the words they originate themselves, like the "ffttt" one little boy made up as a name for soda water or the "pooh" one little girl called a match, from the sound made in blowing it out. Onomatopoetic words occur in primitive languages all over the world. Comic strips rely heavily on them. One had this sound track for a fight sequence: "KAK . . . BTAK . . . FTAK . . . BUTOOP . . . YAGGHHHH . . . KAPOWK . . . FOOM . . . SZAK . . . BOK . . . THWIK . . . THAK . . . BRUP . . . KLIP!" "Thump," "thud," and other such words may have originated as *btak* or *foom* sounds long ago. Dictionaries show many words described as "of imitative origin"— "giggle," "gargle," "whiz," "bang," "pop," "sizzle," among them. A dictionary of American slang gives a long list of more recent inventions, such as "beep," "bebop," "boing," "burp," "clunk," "ding-a-ling," "plunk," "putt-putt," "smooch," "yackety-yak."

If our cave dwellers of 15,000 years ago did rumble their thunder sounds, they were doing no more than others had done long before them and would be doing long afterward. John Keats made thunder sounds in his way:

> A shout from the whole multitude arose,
> That lingered in the air like dying rolls
> Of abrupt thunder, when Ionian shoals
> Of dolphins bob their noses through the brine. . . .

Six deep *oh* sounds, the dull *u*'s of "abrupt thunder," and perhaps the *ah*'s of "dolphins bob."

Another cave painting shows men or long-haired girls climbing a high tree to rob a swarm of wild bees of its honey. The bees are swirling around the extended arms of one of the figures. The bee-robbers would surely have talked of their experience, and talking of it would surely have made sounds like *mmmmmmmmmmm* or *uuuuzzzz* or *buzzzz* to describe the angry bees. If so, they would have been doing what Tennyson did thousands of years later in his lines

> The moan of doves in immemorial elms,
> And murmuring of innumerable bees. . . .

Some are skeptical of onomatopoeia because, although dogs, cats, falling objects, thunder, and the like make the same sounds all over the world, speakers of different languages have different words to represent the sounds. We may think we hear "bow-wow" when a dog barks. But a Spaniard hears "¡guau! ¡guau!"; a Frenchman, "ouâ-ouâ"; a German, "wauwau"; a Swede, "vov-vov." Hawaiian dogs bark in vowels: "aoaoao." Russian dogs go "ГАВ, ГАВ." Ancient Greek dogs said, "βαύ, βαύ." If human beings cannot even agree on how a dog barks, some may feel, what good is onomatopoeia?

WORKING WITH GOLD

But these dog sounds do have something in common. One can hardly imagine a language in which barking would be represented by "tweetwee" or "sisszizz." The barks are unlike because different languages have different ways of putting sounds together. A French dog would not say "bow-wow" because French uses a *w* only in foreign words. Why should French dogs bark like foreigners in their own country?

Such sound words are produced by the limited resources of our vocal equipment, which pretends, not very successfully, to be something else. And which has to produce a word that can be written down. But how can we *spell* the way a dog barks? Or spell the sound of the rain or the rush of wind in the trees or any of the nonhuman sounds? Our onomatopoetic words are like imitations done in another medium —as when Sergei Prokofiev, in *Peter and the Wolf*, uses different musical instruments to represent human and animal noises. The sound of a clarinet is not really like that of a cat, nor an oboe like that of a duck, nor three French horns like that of a wolf. "Sizzle" is a good onomatopoetic word, yet we could stand in the kitchen and say "sizzle" until we were blue in the face and no one would really think bacon was cooking.

Since onomatopoeia, like other sound effects we have considered, communicates little by itself, it can only reinforce or dramatize a meaning we already know is there. Its utility, therefore, is very limited. We seldom find a poem constructed wholly for sound effects, like the one below.

· PLAYER PIANO ·

My stick fingers click with a snicker
And, chuckling, they knuckle the keys;
Light-footed, my steel feelers flicker
And pluck from these keys melodies.

My paper can caper; abandon   5
Is broadcast by dint of my din,
And no man or band has a hand in
The tones I turn on from within.

At times I'm a jumble of rumbles,
At others I'm light like the moon,   10
But never my numb plunker fumbles,
Misstrums me, or tries a new tune.

John Updike (b. 1932)

THE SOUNDS

In onomatopoeia, the sound of a word is supposed to imitate a sound associated with its meaning. Suppose we are dealing not with sound at all, but with some other category of experience. Are words then in any way like what they mean? Children think they are. A five-year-old, in Colorado for the first time, was heard to exclaim, "Those are mountains, daddy? There ought to be a bigger word for *those!*" So do poets. Alexander Pope was thinking like the child when he wrote:

> I'd call them mountains, but can't call them so,
> For fear to wrong them with a name too low. . . .

In an ideal language, some believe, sound and sense would be in perfect accord. Humpty Dumpty was thinking along these lines when he asked Alice what her name meant.

> "*Must* a name mean something?" Alice asked doubtfully.
> "Of course it must," Humpty Dumpty said with a short laugh, "my name means the shape I am—and a good handsome shape it is, too. With a name like yours, you might be any shape, almost."

Humpty Dumpty's idea of the meaningfulness of names is at least as old as the second chapter of Genesis: ". . . the Lord God formed every beast of the field, and every fowl of the air; and brought them unto Adam to see what he would call them: and whatsoever Adam called every living creature, that was the name thereof." Biblical scholars point out that for the Hebrews names were thought of as symbols, magic keys to the nature, character, or role of the bearer. John Hollander's poem "Adam's Task" is about Adam giving appropriate names to the strange beasts:

> Thou, paw-paw-paw; thou, glurd; thou, spotted
> Glurd; thou, whitestap, lurching through
> The high-grown brush; thou, pliant-footed,
> Implex; thou, awagabu. . . .

We would have to see these fabulous animals to judge the appropriateness of the names. A "glurd" might glow, like Blake's tiger (though in a sort of a blur), as it glides. An "awagabu" sounds waggy and sinuous—perhaps a bit like the "ongologo," a word some primitive tribes use for the centipede. An "ongologo" would have to have a lot of something.

Plato, in his *Cratylus*, may be the first philosopher to have discussed an ideal language based on sound. In the dialogue, Socrates

WORKING WITH GOLD

(who is sometimes joking) entertains the notion that words should not be merely arbitrary or conventional, but natural as well—something in their being should correspond to the nature of what they denote. The letter *r* belongs in words of motion because (in the trilled *r*) there is more activity in the mouth than for any other sound. *L* is for looseness or fluidity, since the tongue seems to slip in pronouncing it. But the heavier *g* in front of *l* will slow it down and make it sticky—as in our word "glue." If we could use such likenesses, says Socrates, "this would be the most perfect state of language."

Such a language might be ideal, and it would certainly be fun to use. But Plato knew that a language like that had never existed and probably never would, since there are only certain categories of objects, qualities, or experiences that can be matched up with certain sounds. Some sounds may be *harder, faster, larger, stickier* than other sounds, but how can they be more *possible*, more *true*, or more *virtuous*?

In everyday life, the sound of a word is not of much immediate importance. No one would refuse to cry "Fire!" or "Help!" out of a feeling that the word had an inappropriate combination of vowels and consonants.

But a good writer, the critic Herbert Read believes, will pick and choose among the existing words for those that "by some subtle combination of vowel and consonant suggest by a seeming appropriateness the quality or kind of object named." Beyond simple onomatopoeia, he finds two subtly appropriate classes of words: those in which movement of lips, tongue, and cheek, together with suggestive sound, simulate the action described—as in "blare," "flare," "brittle," "whistle," "creep," "scrabble," "puddle," "shiver," "fiddle," "sling," "globe"— and those in which sounds are not imitative, but suggestive musical equivalents—as in "swoon," "mood," "sheen," "horror," "smudge," "jelly."

We can figure out the "magic" of most of these. "Blare" and "flare" have a big, loose lip movement. "Brittle" breaks in two in the middle. "Sling" hisses—*sssss*—and then lets go suddenly—*llll-ING!* "Mood" is a deep-inside sound. "Horror" catches in the throat. Even some very ordinary words strike us as having a physical rightness about them. The word "match" moved a classical scholar to exclaim, "How admirably it catches the scrape of sulphurated stick on emery!" The Danish philologist Otto Jespersen likes the word "roll," as in *rolling along*. It is a word we can keep rolling around in our mouth; *r*, *o*, and *l* can all be sounded as long as we want or we have breath for. Whereas the Russian word for "roll" (*katat'* or *katit'*) sounds like something bumping along on square wheels. "Level" is a word like its meaning, sounding the same forward or backward and ending as levelly as it began. "Uneven," however, has that little bump of an accent sticking up in the middle. One well-known maker of jams and jellies has shown that it knows people are sensitive to sound suggestion by turning its own rather ugly name to account. "With a name like Smucker's," say the labels, "it has to be good."

What we are dealing with is a form of synesthesia (p. 36) that tries to provide an equivalent in sound for appearance, smell, taste, touch, and movement. Such "sound-images" occur in primitive languages all over the world. Most of us know that there are analogies between the senses, and that the imagination likes to play with them. Very hot curry, for example, has a taste that suggests a bright color—yellow or red—rather than a pastel gray or lavender. Anyone sensuously alive feels these correspondences. Saint Augustine, among other things a professor of rhetoric, was well aware of synesthesia as a source of vocal appropriateness. After speaking of sound-words used to denote actual sounds, he says, "But since there are things which have no sound, for these the analogy of touch comes into play: if they touch the sense smoothly or roughly, smoothness or roughness of touch is heard in the letters. . . ."

The reason why poets like to unite sound and sense should be clear from all we have been saying about poetry, which speaks not merely for the brain but for the whole human being, body and mind. When sound goes along with sense, the meaning of a poem becomes *physicalized*. It resists the authoritarianism of the intellect, which claims the right to force a meaning on any combination of sounds, regardless of their nature. Appropriate sound invites the body to participate in the being of a poem, just as the poet's body participated in its creation.

A REASON FOR RHYME?

When we say "neither rhyme nor reason," we imply that rhyme lies outside the domain of reason. In a way it does, though we can see some of the reasons for its appeal. If in the pages that follow we seem to be devoting inordinate attention to it, we are doing so because it can stand for those other "magical" devices of sound that poets use to keep their language from being too purely rational.

Poetry, of course, does not *have* to rhyme. Many of the poems we have read are without rhyme and live quite happily that way. All we

WORKING WITH GOLD

are doing in this section is investigating what rhyme has to contribute when it is present. With it we are back once more in the world of magic and unreason.

When George Gordon, Lord Byron writes

> There's not a sea the passenger e'er pukes in
> Turns up more dangerous breakers than the Euxine

his lines are vitalized by the rhyme. The effect is gone if we read:

> There's not a sea the passenger e'er pukes in
> Turns up more dangerous breakers than the Black Sea.

The ingenuity and impudence of linking by sound the folksy "pukes in" with the classical name for the Black Sea are what give these lines their electric tingle. Good rhyme likes to spark a current of thought or emotion between two poles.

Expressions like "fair and square," "rough and tough," "moaning and groaning," and such reduplicating ones as "shilly-shally," "hocus-pocus," "walkie-talkie," and "fender-bender," show how rhyme has worked itself into the fabric of the language. As fast as slang changes, it still retains its fondness for rhyme. One decade says, "See you later, alligator"; another says "super-duper" or "slick chick." Furry Lewis, the blues composer, says:

> The time when you get a blues . . . you have to go all over it again until you rhyme it. It got to be rhymed up if you call yourself being with the blues. If it ain't rhymed up it don't sound good to me or no-body else.

Probably the commonest objection to rhyme is that it prevents poets from saying what they want to say—which (defenders of rhyme would retort) is like hurdlers complaining that the hurdles get in their way. In any field, power shows itself in the ease with which obstacles are overcome.

Another objection is that rhyme is associated with so much bad poetry that it is no longer fit to associate with good poetry. Bad rhyming can be boring, can give us "the sure returns of still expected rhyme"—like the "June"/"moon" and the "breeze"/"trees" that Pope objected to:

> Where'er you find the cooling western breeze,
> In the next line it whispers through the trees. . . .

THE SOUNDS

There are other expected rhymes: "breath" can only bring up "death"; "mountains" are fond of "fountains"; "anguish" means that someone is bound to "languish"; and "kiss" leads to "bliss" so inevitably that Lord Byron could make fun of the pair:

> "Kiss" rhymes to "bliss" in fact as well as verse—
> I wish it never led to something worse. . . .

Rhyme is made up of a sameness plus a difference, as in *poet/ know it/show it.* The sameness, the fixed element, is an accented vowel sound (1). Sounds coming *after* the accented vowel sound must be the same (2). The difference, the variable, is what comes *before* the accented vowel sound (3).

1.	p	o	et	2.	po	et	3.	p	o et
	kn	ow	it		know	it		kn	ow it
	sh	ow	it		show	it		sh	ow it

Rhyme, by no means peculiar to English, seems to be an almost universal phenomenon. It is found in the poetry of many primitive peoples. Chances are it goes back, long before written records, to the very beginnings of verse. We do not have to be experts in African languages to recognize it in a song of the Gabon Pygmies:

> Msore i nia n'fare,
> Msore i nia n'sare.

Nor do we have to know Swahili to recognize the rhyme in four consecutive lines ending with *jehazi, ngazi, wazi, mjakazi.* Rhyme occurs in Chinese verse from the earliest times; one authority deplores that most translations give us no inkling of this. Long before the time of the medieval monks in England, rhyme flourished in Ireland and Wales. Irish missionaries may have brought it to the continent. Or perhaps it came from Arabia, whose culture may have given the Provençal poets of the twelfth century their interest in elaborate rhyming, of which Ezra Pound gives some idea in his adaptation of a little Provençal poem:

· ALBA ·

> When the nightingale to his mate
> Sings day-long and night late
> My love and I keep state
> In bower,
> In flower,

WORKING WITH GOLD

> 'Till the watchman on the tower
> Cry:
> > "Up! Thou rascal, Rise,
> > I see the white
> > > Light
> > > And the night
> > > > Flies."

                                          10

Ezra Pound (1885–1972)

Rhyme was so important in old Persian poetry that the quatrains of Omar Khayyám (p. 466) were arranged according to rhyming sounds. It is so built into the syntax of Greek and Latin (in which the endings of nouns, adjectives, and verbs make up a constant chiming) that there was no need to seek additional rhyme for the end of lines. This is true also of Japanese, in which all words end with a vowel or an *n*, so that it is almost impossible to find a haiku without rhyming words.

Many reasons have been given for the appeal of rhyme. One of the oldest is that we like to see any stunt skillfully performed: We like to watch acrobats and tightrope walkers and jugglers. Good rhyming is a feat of skill with words.

Another reason is based on a psychological tendency that we feel even more clearly in music. It has been called "the law of return," which holds that it is better to return to any starting point than not to return—a law that operates in both primitive melodies of two or three notes and in complex orchestral music. Prominent sounds arouse in us the expectation of hearing them again. Ogden Nash plays on this sense of expectation in a special way; we know that when one of his rhymes is about to come up it may be an outrageous one, and we wait for it with the kind of pleasure-pain with which we see an upheld tray of glassware tipping and about to crash to the floor. (See "Very Like a Whale," Anthology, p. 538.)

History, we say, repeats itself, and it does so with effects like those of rhyme. Characters today may remind us of Napoleon or Julius Caesar, as if individuals were rhyming with each other. Periods in history are like other periods. Pound uses such correspondences in his *Cantos*, and even uses the word "rhyme" to refer to them.

Then, too, our experience of physical reality accustoms us to corresponding pairs—left and right, up and down, far and near, and many others. Something like mirror-image rhyme has been found in Robert Browning's "Meeting at Night." In each six-line stanza the **rhyme scheme** (as we call the pattern of rhymes) begins with an *a b c* and then reverses itself with a *c b a*, forming the pattern *a b c c b a*—

perhaps (as a scientist has suggested) to represent the ebb and flow of sea waves. (Rhyme schemes are indicated by letters, with one letter standing for each rhyming sound. In *a b c c b a*, the first and sixth lines rhyme, the second and fifth, and the third and fourth.)

• MEETING AT NIGHT •

I

The gray sea and the long black land;
And the yellow half-moon large and low;
And the startled little waves that leap
In fiery ringlets from their sleep,
As I gain the cove with pushing prow,   5
And quench its speed i' the slushy sand.

II

Then a mile of warm sea-scented beach;
Three fields to cross till a farm appears;
A tap at the pane, the quick sharp scratch
And blue spurt of a lighted match,   10
And a voice less loud, thro' its joys and fears,
Than the two hearts beating each to each!

Robert Browning (1812–1889)

The supreme experience of bilateral symmetry is the human body, with its almost perfect correspondence of right and left. When we walk, our two sides swing forward not only in rhythm but in something very like rhyme—ankle rhymes with ankle, knee with knee, hip with hip, wrist with wrist, shoulder with shoulder. The best defense of the naturalness of rhyme is the sight of any healthy man or woman walking down the street—*a b a b*—rhyme in motion.

Another theory of the nature of rhyme is even more physical. According to Goethe, words rhyming are words making love, words snuggling, in as close a union as possible, almost fusing but—*vive la différence*—still a little different, just as the two sexes are different.

One sound, it seems, fits snugly with another.
And when a word is nestled in our ear,
Another comes beside it with caresses. . . .

English poets, long before Goethe's time, have spoken of "the kiss of rhyme."

A Defense of Rhyme
(© *Steven Caras/New York City Ballet, from Robbins'* Dances at a Gathering)

Some people imagine that rhyme interferes with the rational proc-
esses of thought by obliging us to say other things than we originally
had in mind. But are rational processes so important? In many of us,
even in poets, they can be dull and predictable. An interruption, a
few detours and unexpected turns, might make a trip with them less

THE SOUNDS

B. C.   **By Johnny Hart**

Does the bird understand or misunderstand the nature of rhyme?
(By permission of John Hart and Field Enterprises, Inc.)

routine. The necessity of finding a rhyme may jolt the mind out of its ruts, force it to turn wildly across the fields in some more exhilarating direction. Force it out of the world of reason into the world of mystery, magic, and imagination, in which relationships between sounds may be as exciting as a Great Idea. It is surprising that the intellectual Hegel defended rhyme by saying that without such devices words become "mentalized"—we forget they have a body and use them only as tools to communicate.

When two words rhyme, their meanings also interact: Each can take on something of the meaning of the other. This is what the young poet Jim Hall had in mind when he wrote

> Any kid knows that rhyming flowers
> with towers
> makes a rose all of a sudden a mile high. . . .

Rhyme can also intensify a word by amplifying its sound. When John Clare, in "The Parish," wanted to show us a pretentious ignoramus, he might have written:

> Young Farmer Bigg, of this same flimsy sort,
> Wise among fools, and with the wise an ass. . . .

"Ass," the key word, is not especially resonant here. But Clare wrote:

> Young Farmer Bigg, of this same flimsy class,
> Wise among fools, and with the wise an ass. . . .

WORKING WITH GOLD

And then we really hear the word.

Yet another reason for rhyme is in its structural possibilities. It can even serve as a scaffolding for poetry not yet built. Some of Shelley's manuscripts show that he left certain lines blank except for the rhyme, which furnished not only necessary sounds but key ideas. We can see how rhyme works as a kind of structural blueprint, below, in a complicated stanza like that of John Donne's "The Canonization," in which the speaker is telling others to do whatever they want as long as they do not interfere with his love.

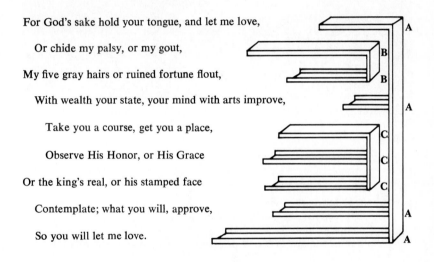

For God's sake hold your tongue, and let me love,   A

Or chide my palsy, or my gout,   B

My five gray hairs or ruined fortune flout,   B

With wealth your state, your mind with arts improve,   A

Take you a course, get you a place,   C

Observe His Honor, or His Grace   C

Or the king's real, or his stamped face   C

Contemplate; what you will, approve,   A

So you will let me love.   A

We can also set up a rhyme scheme to see how successfully we can resist it—by treating it as an opponent rather than as a teammate. This wrestling match with rhyme, which is now on top, now underneath, is seen in Browning's poem "My Last Duchess" (see Anthology, p. 470). The poem is in rhyming couplets, yet many of the rhymes are hurried over as if not there because the movement of the sentence will not allow us to pause for them.

In "Musée des Beaux Arts," W. H. Auden makes rhyme almost inconspicuous by having, in lines of uneven length, rhyming words the sense will not let us linger on. Some of these rhymes are far apart.

Pieter Brueghel the Elder, *Landscape with the Fall of Icarus*
(Musées Royaux des Beaux-Arts, Brussels; Photo: Marburg—Art Reference Bureau)

· MUSÉE DES BEAUX ARTS ·

About suffering they were never wrong,
The Old Masters: how well they understood
Its human position; how it takes place
While someone else is eating or opening a window or just walking
    dully along;   5
How, when the aged are reverently, passionately waiting
For the miraculous birth, there always must be
Children who did not specially want it to happen, skating
On a pond at the edge of the wood:
They never forgot   10
That even the dreadful martyrdom must run its course
Anyhow in a corner, some untidy spot
Where the dogs go on with their doggy life and the torturer's horse
Scratches its innocent behind on a tree.

In Brueghel's *Icarus,* for instance: how everything turns away   15
Quite leisurely from the disaster; the ploughman may
Have heard the splash, the forsaken cry,
But for him it was not an important failure; the sun shone
As it had to on the white legs disappearing into the green
Water; and the expensive delicate ship that must have seen   20
Something amazing, a boy falling out of the sky,
Had somewhere to get to and sailed calmly on.

                             W. H. Auden (1907–1973)

But perhaps the last reason for the use of rhyme is the best of all: People find it fun. Poetry has been seen as the supreme example of the play spirit in human beings. "The hitting of the mark by rhyme" is part of the game—as in the many target games we like to play. Children love all such word play; the use of rhyme has been seen as a subconscious recollection of the fun of childhood. "I rhyme for fun," declared Robert Burns. Gary Snyder says, "If you start teaching poetry on the grade school level, use rhyme, they love it. . . . Children love word play, music of language. . . ." There have always been re-formers, of course, who disapprove of fun, especially when they think they have something serious to say.

The rhyme we have been talking about and giving examples of is called **end rhyme.** Rhymes within the line, **internal rhymes,** are also common.

Once upon a midnight dreary, while I pondered, weak and weary. . . .

Marianne Moore uses internal rhyme as a structural principle in her "A Carriage from Sweden" (p. 520). We notice easily enough the end rhymes in lines 2 and 3 of each stanza. But one could probably read the poem for years and not notice that in the first line of every stanza the third syllable rhymes with the last one—"there"/"air," "may"/ "away," "resined"/"wind," and so on—or that in the last line of every stanza the first syllable rhymes with the eighth (in one stanza, the ninth)—"*some*thing"/"*home*," "*in*tegrity"/"*vein*," "*A*dolphus"/"*de-cay*," for example.

OFF-RHYME

What we call rhyme in Marianne Moore does not always fit the defini-tion given some pages back. "*Some*thing" and "*home*," "*in*tegrity" and "*vein*" do not have the same vowel sound; "some" calls for "hum," not "home"; "in" calls for "vin," not "vein." This kind of "imperfect rhyme"—also called "**off-rhyme**," "slant rhyme," "oblique rhyme," "near rhyme," "half rhyme"—has been deliberately employed by some earlier poets and many modern ones.

Emily Dickinson uses it so often that it becomes characteristic. Her earliest work shows she could rhyme perfectly when she wanted to, but for some reason she became fond of the little dissonance of off-rhyme. Instead of rhymes like "June"/"moon" she prefers "June"/

THE SOUNDS

"men," "June"/"mean," or "June"/"moan." She often has rhymes like "port"/"chart," "affair"/"more," or "wheel"/"mill." She seems to feel that a vowel can rhyme with any other vowel: "know"/"withdrew," "dough"/"sky," "sky"/"tree."

No poet has called attention to the expressive value of off-rhyme more movingly than Wilfred Owen in his poems of World War I. Owen wrote in both full rhyme, as in the first poem below, and off-rhyme, as in the second. The use of off-rhyme in itself does not guarantee a better or more original or even more "modern" poem, but it does offer a different kind of music.

• ANTHEM FOR DOOMED YOUTH •

What passing-bells for these who die as cattle?
    Only the monstrous anger of the guns.
    Only the stuttering rifles' rapid rattle
Can patter out their hasty orisons.
No mockeries now for them; no prayers nor bells,   *5*
    Nor any voice of mourning save the choirs,—
The shrill, demented choirs of wailing shells;
    And bugles calling for them from sad shires.

What candles may be held to speed them all?
    Not in the hands of boys, but in their eyes   *10*
Shall shine the holy glimmers of good-byes.
    The pallor of girls' brows shall be their pall;
Their flowers the tenderness of patient minds,
And each slow dusk a drawing-down of blinds.

Wilfred Owen (1893–1918)

• ARMS AND THE BOY •

Let the boy try along this bayonet-blade
How cold steel is, and keen with hunger of blood;
Blue with all malice, like a madman's flash;
And thinly drawn with famishing for flesh.

Lend him to stroke these blind, blunt bullet-leads   *5*
Which long to nuzzle in the hearts of lads,
Or give him cartridges of fine zinc teeth,
Sharp with the sharpness of grief and death.

For his teeth seem for laughing round an apple.
There lurk no claws behind his fingers supple;   *10*
And God will grow no talons at his heels,
Nor antlers through the thickness of his curls.

Wilfred Owen (1893–1918)

The rhymes in "Arms and the Boy" are all off-rhyme. But there is something special about the first three pairs: The vowel sounds change while the consonants before and after remain the same, so that we have a framing of "bl-d," "fl-sh," and "l-ds" with different vowel sounds in the middle. This pattern is known as **consonance.** Most of the rhyming pairs drop to a deeper vowel sound in the second word— an effect like that of a flatted "blue note" in music. Off-rhymes are like discords; they suggest that something is irregular and disturbed, has somehow failed or fallen short. They have been popular with many poets of our century, who feel that a discordant medium is appropriate for a discordant age.

When James Wright composed "Speak," his "rhyme be damned" poem "of flat defeat in a flat voice," off-rhyme gave him the blue notes he needed (see Anthology, p. 581).

THE MUSIC OF POETRY

What we call the "music" of poetry is only by analogy like the music we hear from the singing voice or from musical instruments. A number of poets have been unwilling to have their poems turned into songs; as one French poet said when a composer requested such permission, "I thought I had already set it to music." Vachel Lindsay went so far as to say "Sheet music, piano music, orchestras and the like should not be in the same room with verses, as a general rule." What the poets mean, of course, is that poetry makes its own kind of music, which is not that of singers or instrumentalists.

When we say that language is euphonious or has euphony we mean that it is pleasant to the ear. But we probably also mean that we pronounce it so easily that there is a pleasure in the physical movements, as there is in any muscular activity we perform with ease. (A French poet-critic has written a book of more than five hundred pages on the "muscular pleasure" of poetry.) Eurhythmics is the art of moving our body in harmony with music or the spoken word; euphony might be thought of as oral eurhythmics. Its opposite is cacophony, the harsh or inharmonious use of language—harsh to listen to because harsh to pronounce. We cannot, as we say, get our tongue around it.

But as Gilbert White says in *The Natural History and Antiquities of Selborne*:

> Sounds do not always give us pleasure according to their sweetness and melody; nor do harsh sounds always displease. We are more apt

to be captivated or disgusted with the associations which they promote than with the notes themselves. Thus the shrilling of the field-cricket, though sharp and stridulous, yet marvellously delights some hearers, filling their minds with a train of summer ideas of everything that is rural, verdurous, and joyous.

Harsh lines in poetry may also please us because their very harshness may help dramatize the meaning.

Poets deliberately write rough lines to give a sense of physical effort, as Pope did:

> When Ajax strives some rock's vast weight to throw,
> The line too labors, and the words move slow. . . .

Our tongue muscles have as much trouble with the *xstr*, *s/s*, *ksv*, and *t/t* of the first line as Ajax had with his rock.

In "The Haystack in the Floods," (see Anthology, p. 485) William Morris has lines that invite the participation of our facial muscles:

> . . . A wicked smile
> Wrinkled her face, her lips grew thin,
> A long way out she thrust her chin:
> "You know that I should strangle you
> While you were sleeping, or bite through 5
> Your throat, by God's help. . . ."

Such effects are more muscular than musical.

Even though we have found that it is possible to arrange vowels in a kind of scale, the relationships between them are not like those between musical notes. We can sing *do mi so do* and feel a pleasurable harmony in the intervals. There is no such pleasure in saying *o͞o ah ă ee*. The tones do get higher but the intervals are not related, although we sometimes get a general sense of vowels ascending, as in Shakespeare's lines

> Like to the lark at break of day arising
> From sullen earth, sings hymns at heaven's gate. . . .

or in this line by Robert Graves

> O love, be fed with apples while you may. . . .

Or we may feel the vowels dropping, as in Walt Whitman's evocation

> When lilacs last in the dooryard bloom'd. . . .

or Emily Dickinson's description

> The thunder gossiped low. . . .

WORKING WITH GOLD

The simplest way to make a sound ring out is to repeat it immediately, as Shakespeare does in phrases like "brave day" or "time's scythe." Or to repeat it after an unstressed syllable, as he does in "ragged hand" or "mortal war." Dickinson liked this simple figure—"stumbling buzz," "satin cash." So did Sylvia Plath—"gristly-bristled," "cuddly mother." Such linked repetitions of sound turn up everywhere in poetry:

> This fabulous shadow only the sea keeps.
>
> *Hart Crane*

> and bats with baby faces in the violet light. . . .
>
> *T. S. Eliot*

Often we find two sounds interlocked, as in Shakespeare's phrase "that in black ink."

> Under the glassy, cool, translucent wave. . . .
>
> *John Milton*

> . . . brown hair over the mouth blown. . . .
>
> *T. S. Eliot*

Or we find one pair of sounds bracketing another, as in Shakespeare's "outlive this powerful."

> And chaste Diana haunts the forest shade. . . .
>
> *Alexander Pope*

> In which sad light a carvèd dolphin swam. . . .
>
> *T. S. Eliot*

These three simple arrangements—linked, interlocked, bracketed—can be used to build up more involved combinations. Consonants can be patterned in the same way. Such figures are generally not systematic. What poets do is repeat sounds when they feel that the repetition would be pleasant or meaningful. If their repetitions happen to fall into a pattern, well and good.

Most poets, we find, care very much about such sound effects and work hard at them. A friend of Keats tells us that one of the poet's "favorite topics . . . was the principle of melody in verse . . . particularly in the management of open and close vowels ["height"/"hit,"

"load"/"lid," and the like]." Keats' theory, "worked out by himself
. . . was, that the vowels should be so managed as not to clash one
with another so as to mar the melody,—and yet that they should be
interchanged, like differing notes of music to prevent monotony."

Keats also believed that certain sounds are more or less appropriate
for certain feelings, and can be all the more expressive if skillfully
repeated. The first stanza of the "Ode to a Nightingale" (see Anthol-
ogy, p. 453) is a good example:

In the first line, dark, dull vowel sounds ("heart," "drowsy,"
"numbness") are contrasted with the shriller ones ("aches," "pains").
All the sounds of line 1 are repeated in the stanza, but none so much
as the dull *u* of "numbness," which recurs in "drunk," "some," "dull,"
"one," "sunk." The next sequence to notice is the short *e* followed by
a nasal—"sense," "hemlock," "emptied," "envy." The repetition of
this unexciting little vowel is monotonous, like the numbness that
Keats, for all his "aches" and "pains," says he is feeling. These *en*'s
and *em*'s are vitalized by the brighter vowel in the "beechen green" of
line 9. Rather gloomy vowels set the tone for the first few lines of the
stanza, but the song of the nightingale (which Keats thinks of as a
Dryad, or tree goddess) brings in a run of excited vowels such as we
have not heard before: "light-wingèd Dryad of the trees." The four
prominent syllables even make up a little tune or figure at the top of
the vowel scale. The keen *ee* sound becomes even clearer in "beechen
green." The last line is tonally interesting: The prominent syllables
slide down the scale to the throaty *oh*, only to rise to the very top in a
final *ee* that echoes the other happy *ee* sounds.

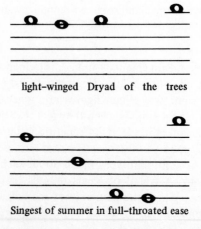

light–winged Dryad of the trees

Singest of summer in full–throated ease

WORKING WITH GOLD

An early poem of Yeats—which owed something to his reading of Thoreau's *Walden*—"set the professors agog," said Yeats, "by the arrangements of the vowel sounds."

· THE LAKE ISLE OF INNISFREE ·

I will arise and go now, and go to Innisfree,
And a small cabin build there, of clay and wattles made:
Nine bean-rows will I have there, a hive for the honeybee,
And live alone in the bee-loud glade.

And I shall have some peace there, for peace comes dropping slow, *5*
Dropping from the veils of the morning to where the cricket sings;
There midnight's all a glimmer, and noon a purple glow,
And evening full of the linnet's wings.

I will arise and go now, for always night and day
I hear lake water lapping with low sounds by the shore; *10*
While I stand on the roadway, or on the pavements grey,
I hear it in the deep heart's core.

William Butler Yeats (1865–1939)

All we find is what has been standard practice among sound-conscious poets—a pleasant variety of vowels that lets us range freely over the scale (as in the *ī*, *i*, *oh*, *ow*, and *ee* of the first line); certain clearly felt repetitions amid the variety (as in "clay"/"made," "nine"/"hive"); uses of vowel and consonant sounds that are right for their meaning (as the three little *i*'s of "cricket sings" and "linnet's wings"); and perhaps an occasional progression up or down the scale, as in the descending *ee ŭ ah oh* of "peace comes dropping slow" and the similar *ee ah aw* of "deep heart's core." In recordings made later, Yeats himself dwelt on the vowel sounds almost the way a singer would; he explained the strangeness of his reading by saying that he cared very much about the sound of his lines.

There are many pretty effects in this short poem. One we might overlook is in

I hear lake water lapping with low sounds by the shore . . .

Thirteen vowel sounds, eleven of them different. The sound of the water is always changing and yet is always the same too, as the continued *l*'s are hinting.

2/**wattles:** *interwoven sticks or branches*

THE SOUNDS

peace comes dropping slow

the deep   heart's core

Sometimes the music of a single good line can carry through a poem. One of Lord Byron's most famous lyrics opens with a series of six almost identical *oh* sounds, whose rich melancholy is re-echoed at the end. The sound is so compelling that we probably overlook the weakness of the second stanza, with its clumsy diction and imagery, and let sound carry the poem into its immortality. (See "So We'll Go No More A-Roving," Anthology, p. 447.)

Robert Penn Warren has spoken about the enjoyment we feel in participating physically in the experience of a poem: ". . . a pleasure, just the way the muscles get into play. In your whole vocal apparatus. . . . It's just a wonderful workout, a sense of kinetic involvement in the lines. This release, this muscular play . . . just the physical pleasure of a well-turned line is something. . . ."

The poem that aroused Warren's gymnastic sensibilities is Milton's "Lycidas" (see Anthology, p. 421). Edward King, a Cambridge acquaintance of Milton's, was drowned while on his way to visit his family in Ireland. King had written some poetry himself; he was planning to become a clergyman. Milton thought about himself: He too was a young student with plans and ambitions. Were they indeed worth the effort and sacrifice if life could be ended by a sudden mindless accident? He thought about the church of his time, which seemed in need of such young men as the one it had just lost. Milton dreamed of heaping his friend's body with all the flowers of the countryside, which themselves would grieve for the dead young man—but he was too tough and level-headed to go along with such poetic fancies, which he knew were a "false surmise" (line 153). The body itself had not been recovered. It was tossing somewhere in the hundreds of miles of wild ocean between the Hebrides and the far-off coast of Spain.

Milton has put some readers off by writing his poem in the form of a pastoral elegy: He imagines that he and his friends are song-loving shepherds in an idyllic culture. The use of such imagery was an old form of make-believe—it had its conventional rules just as games have theirs. What, after all, is more artificial in the world of nature than a tennis court or a golf course? And yet they offer us better scope for certain activities than natural terrain would. And so, for some, do such conventions as those of the pastoral. Milton chose to play the game that way, with an ancient form of "let's pretend" that no doubt represents our desire for a simple life in significant rapport with the environment. He knew poets had been playing that game for at least two thousand years. He takes the name "Lycidas" from earlier works of that type; he refers to places in Sicily and Italy because they are associated with Theocritus and Vergil, who wrote the best pastoral poetry of antiquity. But he also deliberately breaks with their kind of poetry by making his indignant attack on the corruption of the church, by referring to his own literary status and ambitions, and by admitting not only Apollo and Jove into his poetic world but also—and far more significantly—the founder of Christianity, who triumphantly walked the waves that had engulfed a young Christian. (An **elegy** is a lament for the dead, or a meditation on the thoughts that death arouses.)

The power of Milton's music makes itself felt in the first line with the three resonant *or* sounds, echoing within a few lines in "forced" and "before," and recurring in key passages later, most impressively in the six lines beginning with line 58: "Orpheus," "bore," "roar," "gory," "shore." Together, *aw* and *r* make up what must be the strongest combination of vowel and consonant in English. The virile *r*, which we are told Milton pronounced "very hard," seems to be a favorite sound of his—there are eighteen in the first five lines of "Lycidas." This is typical of the music of the poem, which is strong and resonant more often than conventionally melodious. Robert Lowell calls the brusque third line "a very great line in its context . . . largely through sound." The sound itself is "harsh and crude," a roughness in the mouth that is pleasantly chunky to munch on. Many of the most memorable lines are equally rough-textured—really a "workout."

exercises & diversions

A. 1. Say the following words over slowly to yourself, feeling them in the mouth. In which ones does the sound seem to go well with the sense? Can you always say why?

Slump, murmur, spoon, fork, encumber, cucumber, curt, fife, bassoon, abrupt, cluster, sullen, moody, lackadaisical, brisk, brusque, languid, robust, keen, dull, smooth, rough, woofer, tweeter, hiccup, glee, glum, glimmer, glow, flip, flop, fluff, drip, droop, creak, croak, glut, gulp, gobble, cantankerous, gleam, gloom, flabbergast, lollipop, gorge, oily, shudder, pomp, tinsel.

2. Could the meaning of any be reversed (where possible) without loss of expressiveness? Could "slump," for example, just as well mean to *straighten up,* "murmur" mean *to howl*?

3. List a dozen or so other words that seem to you to be like their meaning.

4. List a dozen or so that seem to be conspicuously unlike their meaning.

B. Think about the relationship between sound and sense in the following lines of poetry. What do you conclude about each?

> **1.** Life is as tedious as a twice-told tale
> Vexing the dull ear of a drowsy man. . . .
>
> *William Shakespeare*

> **2.** They err that would bring style so basely under:
> The lofty language of the law was thunder.
>
> *Thomas Randolph*

> **3.** The luscious clusters of the vine
> Upon my mouth do crush their wine. . . .
>
> *Andrew Marvell*

> **4.** Dear, damned, distracting town, farewell!
>
> *Alexander Pope*

> **5.** But when loud surges lash the sounding shore,
> The hoarse, rough verse should like the torrent roar. . . .
>
> *Alexander Pope*

6. Oh what a tangled web we weave,
   When first we practice to deceive!

Sir Walter Scott

7.   . . . Yet to the tender tooth
   The tongue still turneth. . . .

Frederick Goddard Tuckerman

8. [of a scarecrow]
   And stand, above the stubble, stiff
      As mail at morning-prime. . . .

Walter de la Mare

9.   . . . Lee Cauldwell
   Rode by the stable wondering why his lips
   Twitched with such bitter anger. . . .

Robinson Jeffers

10.   . . . old Jinny lying beside her
   Wakened at the word thunder and suddenly chuckling
   Began to mimic a storm, "whoo-whoo" for the wind
   And "boom-boom-boom" for thunder. . . .

Robinson Jeffers

11. And the gray air haunted with hawks. . . .

Robinson Jeffers

12. The mouth too loose with constant lippish thinking
   Of fevered kisses, and the little eyes
   Malicious and provocative that smear you
   With drivel of desire. . . .

Conrad Aiken

13. More beautiful and soft than any moth
   With burring furred antennae feeling its huge path
   Through dusk, the air liner with shut-off engines
   Glides over suburbs. . . .

Stephen Spender

14. Bolstered by bifocal
 Tinted glass
 And a transistor-batteried plastic
 Flesh-colored hearing aid. . . .

Hollis Summers

15. The trees
 say *Wesson. Mazola*
 replies a frog.

James Schuyler

C. How is rhyme used in these two poems?

NEW HAMPSHIRE

Children's voices in the orchard
Between the blossom- and the fruit-time:
Golden head, crimson head,
Between the green tip and the root.
Black wing, brown wing, hover over;   5
Twenty years and the spring is over;
To-day grieves, to-morrow grieves,
Cover me over, light-in-leaves;
Golden head, black wing,
Cling, swing,   10
Spring, sing,
Swing up into the apple tree.

T. S. Eliot (1888–1965)

UNDER BEN BULBEN, VI

Under bare Ben Bulben's head
In Drumcliff churchyard Yeats is laid.
An ancestor was rector there
Long years ago, a church stands near,
By the road an ancient cross.   5
No marble, no conventional phrase;
On limestone quarried near the spot
By his command these words are cut:

 *Cast a cold eye
 On life, on death.
 Horseman, pass by!*   10

William Butler Yeats (1865–1939)

exercises & diversions

D. Examine the use of rhyme in the following poems, noticing especially the rhyme scheme, the use of perfect rhyme and off-rhyme, the expressiveness of the rhyme.

1. "The End of the Weekend," p. 13.

2. "In My Craft or Sullen Art," p. 376.

3. "The Woodspurge," p. 481.

4. "Bells for John Whiteside's Daughter," p. 109.

5. "Traveling Through the Dark," p. 115.

6. "A Narrow Fellow in the Grass," p. 135.

E. What sound patterns—linked, interlocked, bracketed—do you find in the following lines?

1. Leave me, O love, which reachest but to dust,
And thou, my mind, aspire to higher things. . . .

Sir Philip Sidney

2. To see his active child do deeds of youth. . . .

William Shakespeare

3. The teeming autumn, big with rich increase. . . .

William Shakespeare

4. And time that gave doth now his gift confound. . . .

William Shakespeare

5. Now leaves the trees, and flowers adorn the ground. . . .

Alexander Pope

6. Rough satyrs dance, and Pan applauds the song:
The nymphs forsaking every cave and spring,
Their early fruit, and milk-white turtles bring. . . .

Alexander Pope

7. I cannot see what flowers are at my feet. . . .

John Keats

8. A scattered chapter, livid hieroglyph. . . .

Hart Crane

9. I walk through the long schoolroom questioning;
A kind old nun in a white hood replies. . . .

William Butler Yeats

10. . . . cardboard boxes, cigarette ends. . . .

T. S. Eliot

F. 1. How does Milton arrange his rhymes in "Lycidas"? What little figures, such as *a b a b* or *a b b a*, do you find? Are any lines left unrhymed? If so, does there seem to be a reason? Does Milton use offrhyme?

2. Pick out some lines that seem especially smooth. Some that seem especially rough.

G. 1. In the rest of the "Ode to a Nightingale" (see Anthology, p. 453), does Keats use sound as richly as in the first stanza? Pick out another stanza for close analysis.

2. How does Robinson use sound expressively in "The Dark Hills"?

THE DARK HILLS

Dark hills at evening in the west,
Where sunset hovers like a sound
Of golden horns that sang to rest
Old bones of warriors under ground,
Far now from all the bannered ways
Where flash the legions of the sun,
You fade—as if the last of days
Were fading, and all wars were done.

Edwin Arlington Robinson

H. Compose a poem in which the lines end with the words below in the order given. Find possible connections between the words, so that

exercises & diversions

your poem gives a logical account of something. Since we have not yet discussed rhythm, use any rhythm you want to, free or not. But if you do happen to use a line that has five beats (strong accents) as in

> What's in a name? That which we call a rose
> By any other name would smell as sweet. . . .

you will have written a Shakespearean sonnet.

_____ quiet

_____ kiss

_____ riot

_____ abyss

_____ trees

_____ June

_____ peas

_____ prune

_____ crystal

_____ bar

_____ pistol

_____ guitar

_____ brooded

_____ concluded

Such an exercise, called *bouts-rimés* (rhymed endings) has been a favorite game of poets.

F · I · V · E

THE RHYTHMS

9

The Dancer and the Dance
THE PLAY OF RHYTHMS

RHYTHM

Our very existence, like that of the universe we live in, is a system of rhythms. Biologists know of more than a dozen human rhythmical cycles, from that of the heart pulsing 100,000 times a day to that of the alpha waves of the brain pulsing almost ten times as fast. Even before we were born, consciousness may have come to us as an awareness of rhythm—the hammocklike swinging as our mother walked, the intimate beating of her heart and our own matching hers in double time. This first sound we hear is the basis of our sense of rhythm. As a writer in *Scientific American* puts it: "From the most primitive tribal drumbeats to the symphonies of Mozart and Beethoven there is a startling similarity to the rhythm of the human heart." Long ago people guessed that the heartbeat might be the source of our speech rhythms as well. The Greek physician Galen quotes an earlier medical writer as saying that the heart's weak-strong diastole and systole, whose sound is described as *lub-DUBB* or *ka-BOOM*, is like the weak-strong iambic foot (as in the word "alive"). By "foot" we mean one of the units whose repetition will give us a rhythm; the word goes back to primitive times when the swing of a rhythm might be accentuated by a stamping foot. This particular unit, a weaker syllable followed by a stronger one (*ka-BOOM*), has been called "iambic" since the Greeks identified and named it more than 2,000 years ago.

A basic rhythm in many languages, it may indeed be echoing the most basic of physical rhythms. The emotional importance we attach to the heart is shown by our taking it as the symbol of love, although it is not the heart but the hypothalamus at the base of the brain that is the physical source of our emotions. A shepherdess in Elizabethan poetry can rejoice that

> My true love hath my heart, and I have his,
> By just exchange, one for the other given. . . .

There is less demand among lovers for the hypothalamus. Researches have shown that the heartbeat rhythm, even produced mechanically, has a soothing effect on babies; not only Madonnas in art but live mothers in the supermart prefer to hold their babies so that the child's head is to the left, close to the beating heart of the mother.

> Hunched in the dark beneath his mother's heart,
> The fetus sleeps and listens; dropped into light,
> He seeks to lean his ear against the breast
> Where the known rhythm holds its secret place. . . .

> *John Updike*

Some have even held that, since the beat of the accents in most poetry is a little faster than the heartbeat, the rhythm acts as a tonic. In *The Emperor Jones*, Eugene O'Neill assumes such a relationship between external rhythms and the pulse rate:

> *From the distant hills comes the faint, steady thump of a tom-tom, low and vibrating. It starts at a rate exactly corresponding to normal pulse beat—72 to the minute—and continues at a gradually accelerating rate from this point uninterruptedly to the very end of the play.*

We know that excitement, anticipation, emotion can speed up the heart or cause it to spark contractions so close together we get the sensation of a skipped beat. Grief and depression can slow it down. One of Shakespeare's young women says of a false lover, "he grieves my very heart-strings . . . it makes me have a slow heart." We will see that all these effects have their correlation with the rhythms of poetry.

Walking, too, with our legs and arms swinging in pendulum time, has developed our feeling for rhythms. Goethe composed many of his poems while walking. So did the young Robert Frost, swinging as his pendulum the schoolbooks he carried at the end of a strap. The kind of work that men and women did for countless centuries—sowing, mowing, woodchopping, spinning, rocking the cradle—encouraged rhythmical expressions. Robert Graves believes that our most vigorous rhythms originated in the ringing of hammers on the anvil and the pulling of oars through the sea.

We feel rhythms also in the world outside, with its alternations of day and night, its revolving seasons, its pulsing of waves on the shore, and its swaying of trees in the wind. There are times when rhythm has a stronger hold on us than our most sacred concerns. Through rhythm, an authority on the dance has said, we reunite ourselves with the ecstasy and terror of a moving universe. No wonder people have been fascinated by the nature of rhythm. Thomas Jefferson, while serving as minister to France, even took time out from his diplomatic duties to write about it in his "Thoughts on English Prosody."

Though rhythm is not easy to define, we could agree that it is a pattern of recurrence: Something happens with such regularity that we can resonate with it, anticipate its return, and move our body in time with it.

The Elizabethan George Puttenham said that the effect of rhythm was "to inveigle and appassionate the mind"—to involve and excite us. A rhythm that we hear can set up sympathetic reactions—we tap a foot, drum with our fingers, nod in time to it. Rhythm can also affect the way we feel: Psychiatric research has discovered that rhythmical body movements can lead to altered states of consciousness. Rhythm is contagious. It is also hypnotic. We find it difficult, by the ocean, to count to a hundred waves without feeling our mind drift away into a kind of trance. In taking possession of us, it leaves less of our attention for other concerns. Its trancelike effect explains its connection with magic; the language used in primitive ceremonies all over the world is rhythmical. Its affinity with ecstasy (*being outside oneself*) is well known.

Rhythmical speech has also been thought of as distancing or framing (as in a picture or on a stage) the material it deals with. Its sustained cadence—not exactly what we are used to in actual speech—tells us we are in another world, a make-believe world like that of the theater, in which experience is presented to us without the obligations it involves in real life.

REPETITION AS RHYTHM

One of the simplest forms of rhythm, and one of the most emphatic and passionate, is repetition. Among the most emotional paragraphs in William Faulkner's *Absalom, Absalom!* is the last one, in which Quentin is asked why he hates the South.

"I dont hate it," Quentin said quickly, at once, immediately; "I dont hate it," he said. *I dont hate it,* he thought, panting in the cold air, the iron New England dark; *I dont I dont; I dont hate it! I dont hate it!*

Whenever poetry begins, it seems to begin with repetition—which is a form of *dwelling on* something. The African Bushmen have a song in celebration of the new moon, which is thought to bring rain:

> New moon, come out, give water for us,
> New moon, thunder down water for us.
> New moon, shake down water for us.

Such repetitions are fundamental to poetry, as in a wedding song of the Gabon Pygmies:

> Counting, counting your steps,
> Today you go away.
> With a large heart, with a weary heart,
> Go away, go away below!
> Counting, counting your steps,   5
> With a large heart, with a weary heart,
> Today you go away. . . .

They are no less stirring in the poetry of our own civilization:

· COUNTING THE BEATS ·

> You, love, and I,
> (He whispers) you and I,
> And if no more than only you and I
> What care you or I?
>
> Counting the beats,   5
> Counting the slow heart beats,
> The bleeding to death of time in slow heart beats,
> Wakeful they lie.
>
> Cloudless day,
> Night, and a cloudless day,   10
> Yet the huge storm will burst upon their heads one day
> From a bitter sky.
>
> Where shall we be,
> (She whispers) where shall we be,
> When death strikes home, O where then shall we be   15
> Who were you and I?

THE DANCER AND THE DANCE

Not there but here,
(He whispers) only here,
As we are, here, together, now and here,
Always you and I.   *20*

Counting the beats,
Counting the slow heart beats,
The bleeding to death of time in slow heart beats,
Wakeful they lie.

Robert Graves (b. 1895)

Probably no poet has made more systematic use of repetition as a rhythmical principle than Walt Whitman.

• LEAVES OF GRASS •
[21]

I am the poet of the body,
And I am the poet of the soul.

The pleasures of heaven are with me, and the pains of hell are
    with me,
The first I graft and increase upon myself . . . . the latter I
    translate into a new tongue.

I am the poet of the woman the same as the man,   *5*
And I say it is as great to be a woman as to be a man,
And I say there is nothing greater than the mother of men.

I chant a new chant of dilation or pride,
We have had ducking and deprecating about enough,
I show that size is only development.   *10*

Have you outstript the rest? Are you the President?
It is a trifle . . . . they will more than arrive there every one, and
    still pass on.

I am he that walks with the tender and growing night;
I call to the earth and sea half-held by the night.

Press close barebosomed night! Press close magnetic nourishing night! *15*
Night of south winds! Night of the large few stars!
Still nodding night! Mad naked summer night!

THE RHYTHMS

Smile O voluptuous coolbreathed earth!
Earth of the slumbering and liquid trees!
Earth of departed sunset! Earth of the mountains misty-topt!   20
Earth of the vitreous pour of the full moon just tinged with blue!
Earth of shine and dark mottling the tide of the river!
Earth of the limpid gray of clouds brighter and clearer for my sake!
Far-swooping elbowed earth! Rich apple-blossomed earth!
Smile, for your lover comes!   25

Prodigal! you have given me love! . . . . therefore I to you give love!
O unspeakable passionate love!

Thruster holding me tight and that I hold tight!
We hurt each other as the bridegroom and the bride hurt each other.

Walt Whitman (1819–1892)

A more recent poem shows how effective repetition can be. If we rewrite these lines without the repeated words at beginning and end, there is no longer the tension and suspense that carries us forward.

• THE .38 •

I hear the man downstairs slapping the hell out of his stupid wife again
I hear him push and shove her around the overcrowded room
I hear his wife scream and beg for mercy
I hear him tell her there is no mercy
I hear the blows as they land on her beautiful body   5
I hear glasses and pots and pans falling
I hear her fleeing from the room
I hear them running up the stairs
I hear her outside my door
I hear him coming toward her outside my door   10
I hear her banging on my door
I hear him bang her head on my door
I hear him trying to drag her away from my door
I hear her hands desperate on my doorknob
I hear the blows of her head against my door   15
I hear him drag her down the stairs
I hear her head bounce from step to step
I hear them again in their room
I hear a loud smack across her face (I guess)
I hear her groan—then   20
I hear the eerie silence
I hear him open the top drawer of his bureau (the .38 lives there)
I hear the fast beat of my heart
I hear the drops of perspiration fall from my brow
I hear him yell I warned you   25

THE DANCER AND THE DANCE

I hear him say damn you I warned you and now it's too late
I hear the loud report of the thirty eight caliber revolver then
I hear it again and again the Smith and Wesson
I hear the bang bang bang of four death dealing bullets
I hear my heart beat faster and louder—then again   30
I hear the eerie silence
I hear him walk out of their overcrowded room
I hear him walk up the steps
I hear him come toward my door
I hear his hand on the doorknob   35
I hear the doorknob click
I hear the door slowly open
I hear him step into my room
I hear the click of the thirty eight before the firing pin hits the bullet
I hear the loud blast of the powder exploding in the chamber of the .38 40
I hear the heavy lead nose of the bullet swiftly cutting its way through
   the barrel of the .38
I hear it emerge into space from the .38
I hear the bullet of death flying toward my head the .38
I hear it coming faster than sound the .38   45
I hear it coming closer to my sweaty forehead the .38
I hear its weird whistle the .38
I hear it give off a steamlike noise when it cuts through my sweat
   the .38
I hear it singe my skin as it enters my head the .38 and   50
I hear death saying, *Hello, I'm here!*

Ted Joans (b. 1928)

Such repetitions consist of patterns of word arrangement. Other elements of design can be repeated, so that we have a rhythm like that of a painting. If we "read" Kandinsky's *Lines of Marks* (p. 224), we find the artist repeating and varying a few simple motifs: the bar, the circle, the triangle, the crescent.

Dylan Thomas' "Fern Hill" (see Anthology, p. 555) has not only an elaborate rhythmical structure for the ear but also a painterly use of thematic materials. The colors green and gold (for grass and sunlight) are used throughout. Five of the six stanzas make mention of singing or music. There are many echoes in syntax or diction: "green and carefree," "green and golden," "green and dying"; "happy as the grass was green," "happy as the heart was long."

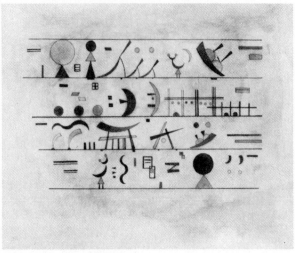

Wassily Kandinsky, *Lines of Marks*
(Oeffentliche Kunstsammlung Basel)

THE RHYTHM OF ACCENT

The repetition of words, images, or motifs gives us a kind of rhythm. But what we mean when speaking of the rhythm of poetry is more often a pattern of sound in the syllables themselves.

If we were writing in a language like ancient Greek, in which the length of syllables was prominent, we could make a pattern by alternating long and short ones, as if they were quarter notes and eighth notes. If we were writing in a tonal language like Chinese, we could make a pattern by alternating pitch. But in English, in which accent is more prominent than length or pitch, we generally make a pattern out of accented and unaccented syllables. There are several ways in which we can do this. The one we will consider first is the commonest in our poetry. Called **syllable-stress,** it takes into account both the number of syllables in the pattern and the arrangement of their accents.

Most of us have a practical grasp of what a syllable is, perhaps based on the way dictionaries divide up words: mo-lec-u-lar; syn-co-pat-ed; un-pre-ten-tious. We recognize syllables as the little lumps of sound words can be crumbled into—the vowel nucleus with whatever consonants may attach themselves to either side. There are occasional options. Words like "fire" or "hour" are pronounced sometimes as one syllable, sometimes as two (fi-er, hou-er). Other words have a certain play or give: cu-ri-ous or cur-yus; sen-su-al or sench-wul; fa-vor-ite or fav-rite; mur-der-ous or murd-rous.

Certain syllables are made more prominent than others by being *accented*—we also say *stressed* or *emphasized*. We put noticeably more energy into pronouncing them than we do into syllables that have no accent. Nearly all of us (unless tone-deaf) recognize accents when we hear them: What we *imPORT*, we call "IMports"; what we *reJECT*, we call "REjects." Speech has a tendency to alternate accented and unaccented syllables, much as we tend to impose a rhythm on any series of sounds. The language likes to rhythmicize itself. We shift the accent in "reSTORE" to get a better rhythm in "RESToreAtion." Longer words, as Jefferson noticed, move in rhythm: tubérculósis, enthúsiástically, indústriálizátion.

There are, of course, many degrees of the kind of emphasis we call accent. We need subtle differences to distinguish, in speaking, between "What's in the road ahead?" and "What's in the road—a head?" Or, to take two of the most hackneyed examples, between "the green-house," the green house," and "the Greene house"; and between "light-housekeeper," "lighthouse keeper," and "light [maybe blond] housekeeper." Linguists admit four degrees of stress, though no doubt, for anyone sensitive enough to catch them, there are many in between. But whether there are four or forty, all we need for the rhythms of poetry are *two*. Does a syllable have *more* or *less* stress, mass, energy than the syllables around it? How much more does not matter. More or less alone can make waves of sound. Like alternations of tension and relief, like the *lub-DUBB* of the heartbeat, like inhaling and exhaling, like Yin and Yang and the antithetical play of existence, rhythm is an interaction between *two* principles, *two* kinds of accent, not among three or more.

The writer who is using accents for his rhythm makes sure that they come in waves, as so much energy does in the physical world. What we feel in accentual rhythm is a regular surge of *more* and *less* in the natural flow of the language.

When we go surfing on a rhythm, we take the crests and hollows without particularly analyzing their dynamics. We ride the lines like this:

| | CUR | | TOLLS | | KNELL | | PART | | DAY, |
| The | | few | | the | | of | | ing | |

very much as we would have pronounced the words anyway, even if we had not been riding the rhythm (which ought to be in the *natural* pronunciation of the words, and not in any artificial singsong we impose on them). We may be content to take these waves of rhythm as they come, as one can be happy merely watching the surf along the shore. But if we really care about waves we have to immobilize the flux (as with a camera) to see the wave as a surge of rotating particles that themselves move forward hardly at all.

If we could similarly immobilize the waves of the commonest English rhythm (called "iambic"), we would find every unit of trough and crest to be made up of a dip and swell in the accents—of an unstressed syllable and a stressed one, as in "reJOICE," "to LOVE," "at HOME." The unit whose repetition makes up any rhythm is called a **foot,** a term that, as we said, takes us back to the supposed association of poetry with the dance, when each rhythmic unit was marked by a beat of the dancer's foot.

A NOTE ON SCANSION

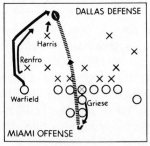

(*The New York Times*)

If we are to isolate any unit of rhythm-particles for our inspection, we need a set of symbols—some would say *signs*—to stop the action and show what is happening. The process of applying these symbols is what we call **scansion.** Many find it a dreary affair. It seems pedantic and destructive to represent a living line of verse by anything so lifeless as ∪—|∪—|∪—|∪—|∪—|. This is certainly not the same thing as a line of poetry. Agreed. But we take for granted the utility of such simplified schemes in many activities. Compared with the color and drama of a football game, the diagram of a play is also dry and

pedantic. Yet it is difficult to imagine a professional quarterback look-
ing at the diagram and snarling, "Who needs that kind of stuff? I just
want to get out there and throw!" Our line of scansion is misleadingly
stiff: It suggests that all accented syllables are exactly the same and all
unaccented ones exactly the same, rigid as the stone ups and downs
along a battlement. In fact they may be quite uneven, like a series of
waves on the lake or the undulations of a hilly horizon or any profile
in nature.

Musical notes are sometimes used with poetry to show how the
particles of rhythm are related. The first two lines of George Meredith's
"Love in the Valley" might be analyzed as:

Under yonder beech-tree single on the green-sward

Couched with her arms behind her golden head,

But speech has nothing like so metronomic a regularity. Music is in the
world of chronometric time; the metronome, even though the per-
former may tease and worry it now and then, sets the standard. But
the rhythm of poetry exists also in the free-flowing world of psycho-
logical time, the kind of time in which, as Romeo says, "Sad hours
seem long," or in which happiness, to paraphrase Goethe, can make
the day race by on flashing feathers. Time, in the rhythms of poetry, is
subjective—as elastic as Dali's famous watch, drooped like a pancake
over its tree branch. One could pause for a couple of seconds after a
word in poetry ("beech-tree," for example, in the first line of Meredith's
poem) and not affect the basic rhythm. Musical scansion is not of much
use to us.

A more modern type of scansion, that of structural linguistics, at-
tempts to show four degrees of stress, four degrees of pitch, and four
kinds of connective pauses between words. But a system that turns a
simple line of Yeats into

₂   _{2 3}   _{1 2}   ₃

ˏSpeéch + àftĕr + lóng˙sîlĕnce; ît + îs + right . . .

is more complex than we need. Readers do not listen that way; poets do not write that way. When Theodore Roethke quotes from a nursery rhyme:

Hinx, minx, the old witch winks,

he says he feels it as "five stresses [accents] out of a possible six." He does not say he feels it as "three primaries, a secondary, and a tertiary."

• FISH'S NIGHTSONG •

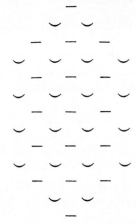

Christian Morgenstern (1871–1914)

All that matters is more or less; an easy way to indicate the two is the traditional one—a firm straight line for the accented syllable (—) and a sagging little curve for the slack one (◡), as in the famous "concrete" poem by Christian Morgenstern, in which the symbols stand for silent music as well as for waves and fishes. (Some scanners prefer to tilt the straight line skyward (′) to indicate accent.) Sometimes the pattern of accents is unmistakable,

The cŭr|fĕw tōlls| thĕ knēll| ŏf pārt|ĭng dāy. . . .

Nothing to hesitate over here. Where we find ourselves hesitating, the thing to do is to mark the accents we are sure of. There is no doubt about words like "dĕlīght," "rĕmēmbĕr," "āppĕtīte," or (usually) about phrases like "thĕ cāt," "tŏ thĕ stōre," "yŏu wānt tŏ." We generally get enough pieces of the pattern from the known words to complete the rest of it for ourselves by filling it in with matching parts—testing them by means of natural pronunciation to see if they really fit. Once we get into the swing of a rhythm we are pretty sure how it is going to continue. But scansion is not an exact science like mathematics. Stressed and unstressed syllables are not always as instantly identifiable as even and odd numbers are. Occasionally we come across a line that no two of us will scan in exactly the same way; we might even scan the same line a little differently on different days or in different moods. But even when we differ about details, we are generally in agreement about the basic rhythm.

IAMBIC PENTAMETER

The rhythmical line we will be using for the examples that follow in this section is the commonest line in the poetry of our language, the **iambic pentameter.** *Iambic* because for over twenty centuries that has been the name of the trough-and-crest unit (⌣ —), as in "to dance" or "enjoy." If the word sounds classroomy to us now, we might recall that it originally meant something violent and abusive. In ancient Greece a girl named Iambé personified the obscene songs (in iambics) sung to relieve emotional tension at religious mystery rites. *Pentameter* because there are five of these iambs to a line. Among all people five is the natural unit of counting off (a glance at the hand will show why). The fiveness of the line may have another physiological basis. Since the ratio between a somewhat excited pulse rate and the normal rate of breathing (seventeen breaths a minute) is about five to one, we would not be too far off in thinking of iambic pentameter as a breathful of heartbeats. Hugh Kenner imagines Homer in the throes of composition: "the muse singing as his chest contracted, his breath governing the line, his heart beating against the stresses." Recalling this rhythm might even help us save a life. In cardiopulmonary resuscitation—the technique for keeping alive victims of "sudden death" by mouth-to-mouth breathing and rhythmical pressure on the chest—one breath is given for every five of the chest-compressions, which are substitute heartbeats.

Pick up any anthology that covers poetry in English, and you will find that at least two-thirds of it is in this cadence. It has been called the most important meter in the North European world. Chaucer, who got it from the ten- or eleven-syllable line of French and Italian poetry, is given credit for establishing it in English, though there was a basis for it in our earlier native verse.

Iambics, to be so thoroughly accepted, must have seemed natural—like the way people really talk. Aristotle heard them in the language of everyday Greek. Hopkins commented, "and the same holds for English." Richard Blackmur once said, after listening to recorded poetry in thirty-odd languages, that he could hear the iambic base in all but one.

More iambic pentameters are uttered every day here in America than Shakespeare and all his fellows wrote in a lifetime. When George Starbuck wonders:

> Whaddaya do for action in this place?

he is writing in a cadence we often fall into without knowing it.

> I'd like to introduce a friend of mine.

> Please fill 'er up—and better check the oil.

> Suppose you take your damn feet off the chair.

> Deposit fifty cents for overtime.

> Cheeseburger special and a glass of beer.

> For rent: one-room apartment near the lake.

> You ever been in Albuquerque, hey?

> Eleven times eleven comes to what?

> I'd like to know exactly what she said.

It's easy to find lines as natural as this in the poets; in Conrad Aiken, for example, lines like

> I'll meet you Thursday night at half past ten.

> I told him straight, if he touched me, just once more,—
> That way, you know,—I'd kill him. And I did.

> How do you like the way I've done my hair?

> Boy, if I told you half of what I know. . . .

THE DANCER AND THE DANCE

In Frost, lines like:

> I didn't make you know how glad I was
> To have you come and camp here on our land. . . .

> I didn't want the blame if things went wrong. . . .

> He burned his house down for the fire insurance. . . .

> I might have, but it doesn't seem as if.

> It's knowing what to do with things that counts.

Leonard Bernstein thinks that iambic pentameter was in on the birth of the blues, out of which jazz and so much modern music was to evolve. The writers of blues lyrics did not use it because it was "classic"; they used it for the same reason that Shakespeare and the Elizabethan dramatists did—it embodies a basic speech pattern.

> I hate to see that evenin' sun go down. . . .

> Goin' lay my head right on the railroad track,
> [Be]cause my baby, she won't take me back. . . .

> Mr. Crump won't 'low no easy riders here. . . .

> The man I love's got low-down ways for true. . . .

> Woke up this mornin', blues all round my bed. . . .

VARIATIONS ON IAMBIC

The model in our head against which we are measuring our examples in this section is schematized as

$$\cup - | \cup - | \cup - | \cup - | \cup -$$

What we say about it will hold for other metrical patterns as well. But we will not expect lines of living poetry to match this or any other model exactly. There is no merit, as we will soon show, in mere regularity; even the heartbeat departs from its 72 beats a minute to meet the needs of life situations. We can sometimes find perfectly regular iambics, as in Shakespeare's

> When I do count the clock that tells the time . . .

or in his

> Of hand, of foot, of lip, of eye, of brow. . . .

In "Sonnet 66" we have almost eleven consecutive lines (from the "behold" of line 2 through line 12) with only one variation from strict meter—the little stumble that comes in, appropriately enough, with the "tongue-tied" of line 9.

· SONNET 66 ·

Tired with all these, for restful death I cry:
As, to behold desert a beggar born,
And needy nothing trimmed in jollity,
And purest faith unhappily forsworn,
And gilded honor shamefully misplaced,   *5*
And maiden virtue rudely strumpeted,
And right perfection wrongfully disgraced,
And strength by limping sway disablèd,
And art made tongue-tied by authority,
And folly (doctor-like) controlling skill,   *10*
And simple truth miscalled simplicity,
And captive good attending captain ill.
　　Tired with all these, from these would I be gone,
　　Save that, to die, I leave my love alone.

William Shakespeare (1564–1616)

But nothing so regular is to be found elsewhere in the sonnets, or rarely anywhere in good poetry. Shakespeare has a reason here for his unvarying rhythm: He is writing about the monotony of the world's injustice, which has its own dreary pattern of recurrence.

If we were tapping our fingers to music and the music suddenly stopped, we could go on tapping without breaking the rhythm, just as we could continue a wavy line, if it ended, with a dotted line of similar waves.

2/**desert:** *true merit*
3/**needy nothing:** *a penniless non-entity*
3/**trimmed in jollity:** *showily dressed*

6/**strumpeted:** *treated like a harlot*
8/**limping sway:** *defective authority*
11/**simplicity:** *idiocy*

THE DANCER AND THE DANCE

Our expectation of continuing rhythm is so strong that we can even feel an accent where perhaps there is none, as we imagine we hear a ticktock pattern in the undifferentiated ticks of a clock. If we expect an accent on syllables 2, 4, 6, 8, and 10, we are inclined to stress these syllables. When Shakespeare, in "Sonnet 68," complains about such "bastard signs" of beauty as the wearing of wigs from the hair of persons now dead, he writes:

> Before the golden tresses of the dead,
> The right of sepulchers, were shorn away
> To live a second life on second head. . . .

Our anticipation of the rhythm we are now moving in leads us to expect an accent on "of" (the eighth syllable) in the first line, and on the last syllable of "sepulchers" (the sixth syllable) in the second line. There is no real accent on either; but since we expect to hear one, and since nothing insists we *cannot* hear one, we assume that we do.

But sometimes an apparently misplaced accent is too strong to ignore, and then we have a genuine variation in the rhythm. When Shakespeare begins a line with "To the wide world," we cannot imagine that it should be pronounced, "To THE wide WORLD . . ." or any other way except "To the WIDE WORLD. . . ." Such variations are the life of rhythm.

The iambic foot is made up of two particles or syllables, the first having less mass or energy than the second (ᴗ —). But, in place of the normal foot, we find that four options are possible.

1. Pyrrhic (ᴗ ᴗ)

The first option is a foot of two syllables, neither of which has an accent, as in the lines from "Sonnet 68" discussed above. This foot is called a **pyrrhic** (ᴗᴗ).

> When I have seen the hungry ocean gain
> Advan|tăge ŏn| the king|dŏm ŏf| the shore. . . .

> *William Shakespeare*

A horse! A horse! My king|dŏm fŏr| a horse! . . .

William Shakespeare

I feel the ladder sway| ăs thĕ| boughs bend. . . .

Robert Frost

A pyrrhic foot, in giving us *less* than we expect, goes well with any-
thing related to *less*ness—the erosion of the shore, perhaps, or the
sense of the boughs giving as the ladder leans against them. Its weak-
ness helps the very line stagger as we read:

> While through the window masked with flowers
> A lone wasp stag|gĕrs frŏm| the dead. . . .

J. V. Cunningham

2. Spondee (— —)

The second option is a foot of two syllables, both of which have an
accent. This is called a **spondee** (— —). We hear it in expressions like
"dead beat" (very tired), as opposed to "deadbeat" (one who avoids
paying debts); or in expressions like "dead weight," "dead end," "Dead
Sea," as opposed to "deadeye," "deadwood," "deadline," each of which
accents the first syllable.

Since the spondee packs as much mass as possible into a two-
syllable foot, it can be expressive of any kind of muchness, weightiness,
or slowness. Since its very density makes it take longer to pronounce, it
can dramatize extent or duration.

> Was it the proud |fūll sāil| of his |grēat vērse,|
> Bound for the prize of all |tōo prē|cious you. . . ?|

William Shakespeare

> Yet once more ere thou hate me, one |fūll kīss. . . .|

A. C. Swinburne

> The long| dāy wānes,| the slow| mōon clīmbs,| the deep
> Mōans rōund| with many voices. . . .

Alfred, Lord Tennyson

THE DANCER AND THE DANCE

I laid down my |lōng nēt| in the |bīg tīde| . . . .|

Brewster Ghiselin

Clotted spondees have been used for frozen blood:

And though I think this heart's |blōod frōze|nōt fāst|
It ran| tōo smāll| to spare |ōne drōp| for dream|ing. . . .

John Crowe Ransom

Spondees can also slow down the line so that details can be contemplated:

Reign in my thoughts! |fair hānd!|sweet ēye!|rāre vōice!|

Samuel Daniel

Since the pyrrhic foot gives us less than we expect, and the spondee more, they are sometimes combined as a kind of double foot (◡ ◡ — —) in which the second half compensates for the first.

. . . They may seize
Ŏn thĕ whīte wŏn|dĕr ŏf dēar Jūl|iet's hand. . . .

William Shakespeare

Let Rome in Tiber melt| ănd thĕ wīde ārch|
Ŏf thĕ rānged ēm|pire fall! . . .

William Shakespeare

Ănd thĕ mīnd whīrls| ănd thĕ hēart sīngs|
And ă shōut grēets| the daring one.

Robert Frost

3. Trochee (— ◡)

The third option reverses the iambic foot from ◡ — to — ◡. "Happy," "token," "over" are examples of this foot (the **trochee.**) Trochees are so common at the beginning of iambic lines that we hardly feel them as variations.

To be or not to be, that is the question.
|Whĕthĕr| 'tis nobler in the mind to suffer. . . .

They also fit in easily after a strong pause within the line:

Did heaven look on,
And would not take their part? |Sīnfŭl| Macduff,
They were all struck for thee! |Naūght thăt| I am. . . .

But elsewhere, when a trochee substitutes for an iamb, the effect can
be like that of strain or abrupt dislocation. A trochee among iambs is
out of place, its movement going counter to the tilt of the line. In these
examples from Shakespeare a trochee is found roughing the meter,
calling attention to some violence in the thought:

With time's injurious hand |crūshed ănd| o'erworn . . .

|Lĕt mĕ|nōt tŏ| the marriage of true minds
Admit impediments . . .

How weary, stale, |flāt, ănd |unprofitable
Seem to me all the uses of this world!

Here lay Duncan,
His silver skin| lāced wĭth| his golden blood . . .

By the clock 'tis day,
And yet dark night |strānglĕs| the traveling lamp . . .

This tyrant, whose sole name |blīstĕrs| our tongue. . . .

Yeats provides us with an expressive example of a reversed foot:

O she had not these ways
When all the wild |sūmmĕr| was in her gaze.

Going along with the meter, we want to read "the WILD sumMER,"
but cannot. So, with some feeling of strain, we do violence to the meter,
which itself is made to rebel as the words recall the woman's rebellious
youth.

Perhaps it has taken our ear a few centuries to get used to this mid-
line trochee. Even Jefferson, in so many ways willing to declare his in-
dependence, did not easily go along with it. Of the reversed foot in
Milton's

To do aught good |nĕvĕr| will be our task,

THE DANCER AND THE DANCE

he says, "it has not a good effect." What Jefferson disliked about the irregularity is probably what we like—the shock value of the energetic dislocation. Milton's "never" stands out defiantly against accepted laws of meter, as it would never do if placed tamely after "will."

We can also think of the trochee among iambs as a kind of backspin or underspin or reverse English, as in Allen Tate's

> The going years, |caught in| an after-glow,
>
> Reverse like balls |englished| upon green baize. . . .

Here the word "englished" is itself englished, its — ∪ spinning against the ∪ —'s of the line.

4. Anapest (∪ ∪ —)

The fourth option is a foot of three syllables with the accent on the last (∪ ∪ —), as in "disagree," "reproduce," "to the woods." This foot (the **anapest**) adds an extra syllable, as one would do in a series of *de DUM de DUM*'s if he occasionally slipped in a *de de DUM*. Pleasant in itself as a change of pace, it can be expressive in suggesting a burst of speed, something impulsive and capricious, like a skip or little caper interrupting our normal stride. Substitute anapests are common, as in Browning's "Fra Lippo Lippi":

> The world and life's too big to pass |for a dream . . .

> Scarce had they turned the corner when a titter,
> Like the skip|ping of rab|bits by moon|light—three slim shapes. . . .

Shakespeare (like most good poets) freely makes use of all possible options, even writing lines in which four of the five feet are non-iambic:

> |Pluck the|keen teeth|from the|fierce ti|ger's jaws . . .
> |Let me|not to|the mar|riage of|true minds. . . .

But he does not let the number of syllables fall short of ten—fall short of five feet of at least two syllables. Iambic pentameter cares about not only accent but also number of syllables—it may add one or two to the ten, but it practically never drops any. On rare occasions, in what is called a "headless" line, the first syllable may be dropped, as in T. S. Eliot's:

THE RHYTHMS

> Wipe your hand across your mouth, and laugh.

An extra syllable at the end of the line is so common it is hardly felt as an irregularity:

> To be or not to be, that is |thĕ qūes|tiŏn. . . .

Sometimes we even find two unaccented syllables hanging over at the end of a line, as in Shakespeare's

> I, that am rudely stamped, and want love's maj|ĕstў̆. . . .

Much of this chapter has been an account of the structure of iambic pentameter. If we wish to stop the flow of that rhythm to examine the mechanics of the individual wave, we should now be able to do so.

A pleasant poem for this kind of study is Edward FitzGerald's translation of *The Rubáiyát* (or *Quatrains*) of Omar Khayyám, the twelfth-century Persian poet, mathematician, and astronomer (see Anthology, p. 466). Rhythmically, the stanzas are easy to follow, since they have a more regular swing than most of the poems we have been reading. And yet in them we can find all the variations described on the preceding pages.

METER AND RHYTHM

In speaking of music, Igor Stravinsky stresses the distinction between meter and rhythm, a distinction that holds also in poetry. In music, meter is what the metronome is doing; rhythm, what the composer or performer actually gives us. In poetry, **meter** (from the Greek word for *measure*) is the basic scheme, the ∪—|∪—|∪—|∪—|∪—, apart from any realization in words—what our mind could continue with if all sound stopped. **Rhythm** (from the Greek word for *flow*) is the way the words of the poem move, often coinciding with the meter but sometimes not. Meter is like the abstract idea of a dance as a choreographer might plan it with no particular performers in mind; rhythm is like a dancer interpreting the dance in a personal way.

What we feel in the iambic line—or in the other strong-stress lines we shall consider in the next chapter—is an interplay of two movements at once: that of the meter, which our mind holds and anticipates, and that of the actual words of the poem as we hear them. The two are seldom identical. As Robert Frost, with the help of a pun, puts it:

THE DANCER AND THE DANCE

> The tune is not the meter, not the rhythm,
> But a resultant that arises from them.
> Tell them Iamb, Jehovah said, and meant it.

In expecting, in iambic verse, another iambic foot, the mind is right most of the time. When it is not right, it does a double take, and the questionable foot gets more attention than if it were regular.

As we brought out in our discussion of variations, iambic pentameter is monotonous if we think of it merely as meter. Of course: Monotony is the only virtue of a metronome. But good poets do not write iambic pentameter as a meter; they use it as a rough gauge for their rhythms. There are as many rhythms based on iambic pentameter as there are individual—really individual—writers. No one would confuse the iambics of Shakespeare with those of Pope or Milton or Tennyson or Yeats or Cummings. Some poets prefer **end-stopped** lines, which conclude with a pause generally marked by the punctuation. In the excerpt from Pope's "An Essay On Man" (p. 77), every line is end-stopped. The excerpt from Milton's *Paradise Lost* (just below) shows a strong preference for **run-on** lines: In over two-thirds of the lines the sense carries us over to the next line without a pause. The rhythmical effect is very different. Poets differ also in the way they handle the **caesura** (the word means *a cut*)—the pause that tends to fall near the middle of most lines. In scansion it is marked by a double bar ($\|$). In the passage from Book I of *Paradise Lost* in which Milton describes Satan and the fallen angels we see how the poet varies his rhythm by varying the internal pauses. The numbers to the left of the lines indicate the syllable after which the caesura falls (the extra syllables of anapests are omitted from the count).

4	He scarce had ceased $\|$ when the superior fiend	
6	Was moving toward the shore; $\|$ his ponderous shield	
5,7	Etherial temper, $\|$ massy, $\|$ large and round,	
4	Behind him cast; $\|$ the broad circumference	
8	Hung on his shoulders like the moon, $\|$ whose orb	5
4	Through optic glass $\|$ the Tuscan artist views	
3	At evening $\|$ from the top of Fiesole,	
5	Or in Valdarno, $\|$ to descry new lands,	
5	Rivers or mountains $\|$ in her spotty globe.	
2	His spear, $\|$ to equal which the tallest pine	10
6	Hewn on Norwegian hill, $\|$ to be the mast	
6	Of some great admiral, $\|$ were but a wand,	
3	He walked with $\|$ to support uneasy steps	
6	Over the burning marl, $\|$ not like those steps	
5	On heaven's azure, $\|$ and the torrid clime	15

6	Smote on him sore besides, ‖ vaulted with fire;
6	Nathless he so endured, ‖ till on the beach
6	Of that inflamèd sea, ‖ he stood and called
3,6	His legions, ‖ angel forms, ‖ who lay entranced
6	Thick as autumnal leaves ‖ that strow the brooks
5	In Vallombrosa, ‖ where the Etrurian shades
6	High overarched embower; ‖ or scattered sedge
2	Afloat, ‖ when with fierce winds Orion armed
6	Hath vexed the Red Sea coast, ‖ whose waves o'erthrew
3	Busiris ‖ and his Memphian chivalry,
7	While with perfidious hatred ‖ they pursued
7	The sojourners of Goshen, ‖ who beheld
4	From the safe shore ‖ their floating carcasses
6	And broken chariot wheels, ‖ so thick bestrown
6	Abject and lost lay these, ‖ covering the flood,
5	Under amazement ‖ of their hideous change.

20

25

30

Individual style is largely a matter of the interplay between meter and rhythm (an interplay that is also called "variation," "tension," "substitution," or "counterpoint"). For deviations to be felt at all, there has to be something to deviate from. The offbeats of African music are effective because the sense of a regular beat has been established in the mind of the listener. Musicians cannot have offbeats unless they have a metrical beat to be "off." And so in poetry—if the meter is a loose one, the variations will be weak.

The tensions of Beethoven's *Grosse Fuge* are said to have pushed music to extreme limits, almost shattering the tonal system. Working with a rigid meter makes it possible for Yeats to get a similar effect in a poem in which his vision of imminent world chaos throws the last line into confusion, beneath the metrical ruins of which there lies, almost buried, the iambic meter.

· THE SECOND COMING ·

Turning and turning in the widening gyre
The falcon cannot hear the falconer;
Things fall apart; the centre cannot hold;
Mere anarchy is loosed upon the world,
The blood-dimmed tide is loosed, and everywhere
The ceremony of innocence is drowned;
The best lack all conviction, while the worst
Are full of passionate intensity.

Surely some revelation is at hand;
Surely the Second Coming is at hand.
The Second Coming! Hardly are those words out

5

10

THE DANCER AND THE DANCE

When a vast image out of *Spiritus Mundi*
Troubles my sight: somewhere in sands of the desert
A shape with lion body and the head of a man,
A gaze blank and pitiless as the sun,   15
Is moving its slow thighs, while all about it
Reel shadows of the indignant desert birds.
The darkness drops again; but now I know
That twenty centuries of stony sleep
Were vexed to nightmare by a rocking cradle,   20
And what rough beast, its hour come round at last,
Slouches towards Bethlehem to be born?

William Butler Yeats (1865–1939)

The poem also illustrates all of the variations described above.

These variations are expressive. Not all variations are. Some bring nothing more than a pleasant variety to the verse. As with sound itself, correspondence between expressiveness and idea is only occasional. When variations are meaningful, they strike with double effect. Some change of speed or mass or energy in the flow of sound dramatizes what is being said.

An earlier poem of Yeats, "He Remembers Forgotten Beauty," shows how a passionate rhythm can override mathematical meter (which here has four beats instead of the five of pentameter).

> When my arms wrap you round I press
> My heart upon the loveliness
> That has long faded from the world. . . .

While there are wrong ways of scanning these lines ("Whĕn mўʹ| ārms wrăp| yōu rŏund| Ī prĕss . . .") there is no one right way. Here is one possible way of feeling the stresses:

> Whĕn mўʹ|ārms wrāp|yōu rōund|Ĭ prĕss
>
> Mўʹ hēart|ŭpŏn|thĕ lŏve|lĭnĕss
>
> Thăt hăs|lōng fād|ĕd frŏm|thĕ wŏrld. . . .

One might even stress every syllable in the first line. Instead of the four expected accents, it has anywhere from five to eight. There is much more mass and energy than we expect in this line, fewer of the slacks or sags of unaccented syllables. Metrically, this may be the tightest embrace in poetry. The second line is different, with only two strong

12/**Spiritus Mundi:** *the "Soul of the World," a kind of storehouse of archetypal memories*

accents, one on "heart" and one on the "love-" in "loveliness." ("Upon" itself has an accent, but it is relatively weak as we read this line.) The gap in the middle, between "heart" and "loveliness," is as if the rhythm, in its excitement, had skipped a beat. The definite accents in the third line are on "long," "fad-" (of "faded"), and "world." The spondee "long fad-" is for muchness, for length of time. The slack of "-ed from the" has about as many unaccented syllables as the meter would tolerate between "fad-" and "world," so that what has *faded* is distanced by the rhythm itself.

A poem that illustrates the difference between meter and rhythm is Tate's "The Mediterranean," (see Anthology, p. 534), which the poet composed with that distinction in mind: "The poem is obviously in iambic pentameter, but I made a point of not writing any two lines in the same rhythm." The imagery, the poet tells us, is "historical and geographical." It was suggested by a deluxe picnic on the Riviera, in just such a cove as Aeneas and his men may have stopped (*Aeneid*, VII. 107 ff.) when they ate the tortillalike flat cakes they had placed their food on, in this way fulfilling a prophecy that they would find their home where hunger would drive them to "eat their tables." The poem contrasts the hardships of the ancient heroes with the comforts of life today. It goes on to the question of destiny for people and nations and to the way individuals have to find themselves and their place in the culture they were born into.

In "Effort at Speech Between Two People" (see Anthology, p. 549), written in the early 1930s by Muriel Rukeyser, then a college sophomore, there is even more freedom within the feet. It is not always easy to isolate the units within these free-flowing lines, but there tend to be five accentual crests in each. The rhythm returns to a regular line (12, 15, 20, and others) often enough so that we know what the metrical basis is.

LINE LENGTH

Up to now we have used the pentameter, or five-beat line, for our examples. But a line may have any number of feet from one to about eight—at which point we run out of breath. In Matthew Arnold's "Dover Beach," somewhat more than half of the lines are pentameter; the rest have from two to four feet. We might feel that a more determined pattern would be inappropriate for this melancholy reverie.

THE DANCER AND THE DANCE

· DOVER BEACH ·

The sea is calm to-night.
The tide is full, the moon lies fair
Upon the straits; on the French coast the light
Gleams and is gone; the cliffs of England stand,
Glimmering and vast, out in the tranquil bay.   5
Come to the window, sweet is the night-air!
Only, from the long line of spray
Where the sea meets the moon-blanched land,
Listen! you hear the grating roar
Of pebbles which the waves draw back, and fling,   10
At their return, up the high strand,
Begin, and cease, and then again begin,
With tremulous cadence slow, and bring
The eternal note of sadness in.
Sophocles long ago   15
Heard it on the Ægæan, and it brought
Into his mind the turbid ebb and flow
Of human misery; we
Find also in the sound a thought,
Hearing it by this distant northern sea.   20

The Sea of Faith
Was once, too, at the full, and round earth's shore
Lay like the folds of a bright girdle furled.
But now I only hear
Its melancholy, long, withdrawing roar,   25
Retreating, to the breath
Of the night-wind, down the vast edges drear
And naked shingles of the world.

Ah, love, let us be true
To one another! for the world, which seems   30
To lie before us like a land of dreams,
So various, so beautiful, so new,
Hath really neither joy, nor love, nor light,
Nor certitude, nor peace, nor help for pain;
And we are here as on a darkling plain   35
Swept with confused alarms of struggle and flight,
Where ignorant armies clash by night.

Matthew Arnold (1822–1888)

Poems with one foot to the line (**monómeter**) are rare. Lines of two feet (**dímeter**) are about as short as is practical.

28/**shingles:** *rocky beaches*

THE RHYTHMS

· I TO MY PERILS ·

I to my perils
    Of cheat and charmer
    Came clad in armour
      By stars benign.
Hope lies to mortals   *5*
    And most believe her,
    But man's deceiver
      Was never mine.

The thoughts of others
    Were light and fleeting,   *10*
    Of lovers' meeting
      Or luck or fame.
Mine were of trouble,
    And mine were steady,
    So I was ready   *15*
      When trouble came.

A. E. Housman (1859–1956)

Theodore Roethke has written a waltz poem in lines of three feet (**trímeter**).

· MY PAPA'S WALTZ ·

The whiskey on your breath
Could make a small boy dizzy;
But I hung on like death:
Such waltzing was not easy.

We romped until the pans   ·*5*
Slid from the kitchen shelf;
My mother's countenance
Could not unfrown itself.

The hand that held my wrist
Was battered on one knuckle;   *10*
At every step you missed
My right ear scraped a buckle.

You beat time on my head
With a palm caked hard by dirt,
Then waltzed me off to bed   *15*
Still clinging to your shirt.

Theodore Roethke (1908–1963)

THE DANCER AND THE DANCE

Lines of four feet (**tetrámeter**) are the commonest after penta-meter. Four-stress lines are faster, crisper than five-stress ones—appropriate to the theme of Andrew Marvell's best-known poem, "To His Coy Mistress" (see Anthology, p. 429), which tells us that time is of the essence.

The six-foot line (**hexámeter**) is also known, when iambic, as the Alexandrine (from an Old French poem on Alexander the Great). With its tendency to break in two in the middle, this line can drag in English, as in the second of these lines by Pope:

> A needless Alexandrine ends the song,
> That like a wounded snake, drags its slow length along.

In "The Cold Heaven" (see Anthology, p. 498), Yeats uses the long line to dramatize the stretching winter landscape and the vistas of past and future it evokes. Alexandrines also turn up in the lyrics of blues songs:

> People have different blues and think they're mighty sad,
> But blues about a man the worst I ever had. . . .

Lines of seven feet (**heptámeter**) were popular, as "fourteeners," in the sixteenth century. They have also been much used since:

> There's not a joy the world can give like that it takes away. . . .
>
> *George Gordon, Lord Byron*

> The melancholy days are come, the saddest of the year. . . .
>
> *William Cullen Bryant*

> Oh, East is East, and West is West, and never the twain shall meet. . . .
>
> *Rudyard Kipling*

They also turn up in modern song lyrics:

> I want you to tell me, little girl, just where did you
> stay last night . . .

The seven feet often break up into four and three, the well-known **ballad stanza,** as in "Sir Patrick Spens" (p. 14) or such hymns as John Newton's "Amazing Grace":

> Amazing grace, how sweet the sound,
> That saved a wretch like me;
> I once was lost but now am found,
> Was blind but now I see.

Lines of eight feet (**octámeter**), though rarer, are found in some well-known poems, among them Tennyson's "Locksley Hall," which begins:

> Comrades, leave me here a little, while as yet 'tis early morn:
> Leave me here, and when you want me, sound upon the bugle horn . . .

and in Poe's "The Raven":

> Once upon a midnight dreary, while I pondered, weak and weary. . . .

exercises & diversions

A. What purpose, if any, does repetition serve in the following quotations?

1. There was a crooked man, and he walked a crooked mile,
   He found a crooked sixpence against a crooked stile;
   He bought a crooked cat, which caught a crooked mouse,
   And they all lived together in a little crooked house.

   Anonymous

2. This is my play's last scene; here heavens appoint
   My pilgrimage's last mile; and my race,
   Idly yet quickly run, hath this last pace;
   My span's last inch, my minute's latest point. . . .

   John Donne

3. But O the heavy change, now thou art gone,
   Now thou art gone, and never must return!

   John Milton

exercises & diversions

4. There passed a weary time. Each throat
Was parched, and glazed each eye.
A weary time! a weary time!
How glazed each weary eye. . . .

Samuel Taylor Coleridge

5. They all are gone, and thou art gone as well!
Yes, thou art gone!

Matthew Arnold

B. Each of the following examples of iambic lines makes use of one or
more of the optional feet. Find and identify them. Besides adding
variety to the line, which variations are expressive?

1. Sidney is dead, dead is my friend, dead is the world's delight. . . .

Fulke Greville

2. What is your substance, whereof are you made,
That millions of strange shadows on you tend?

William Shakespeare

3. Bear thine eyes straight, though thy proud heart go wide. . . .

William Shakespeare

4.   O, I could prophesy,
But that the earthy and cold hand of death
Lies on my tongue. . . .

William Shakespeare

5. I know when one is dead, and when one lives. . . .

William Shakespeare

6. Weeds among weeds, or flowers with flowers gather'd. . . .

William Shakespeare

7. Cover her face; mine eyes dazzle; she died young.

John Webster

8. The grim eight-foot-high iron-bound serving-man. . . .

John Donne

9. Sweet rose, whose hue angry and brave. . . .

George Herbert

10. Come, keen iambics, with your badger's feet,
And badger-like, bite till your teeth do meet.

John Cleveland

11. Bulkeley, Hunt, Willard, Hosmer, Meriam, Flint,
Possessed the land which rendered to their toil
Hay, corn, roots, hemp, flax, apples, wool and wood. . . .

Ralph Waldo Emerson

12. And the white breast of the dim sea. . . .

William Butler Yeats

13. O body swayed to music, O brightening glance,
How can we know the dancer from the dance?

William Butler Yeats

14. And if by noon I have too much of these,
I have but to turn on my arm, and lo,
The sun-burned hillside sets my face aglow. . . .

Robert Frost

15. Divinity must live within herself . . .
Elations when the forest blooms; gusty
Emotions on wet roads on autumn nights. . . .

Wallace Stevens

16. Tudor indeed is gone and every rose,
Blood-red, blanch-white that in the sunset glows
Cries: "Blood, Blood, Blood!" against the gothic stone
Of England, as the Howard or Boleyn knows.

Ezra Pound

17. And if the child goes out at evening, stands
Cold in the cobbled street, and claps cold hands. . . .

Conrad Aiken

18. On a cold night I came through the cold rain
And false snow to the wind shrill on your pane
With no hope and no anger and no fear:
Who are you? and with whom do you sleep here?

J. V. Cunningham

C. 1. Out of some subway scuttle, cell or loft
A bedlamite speeds to thy parapets,
Tilting there momently, shrill shirt ballooning,
A jest falls from the speechless caravan.

This stanza, from Hart Crane's "To Brooklyn Bridge," describes how, from some obscure and humble lodging, a deranged man will sometimes rush to the bridge, balance a moment dizzily on the railing, then leap to his death. Show how the interplay between meter and rhythm is expressive in every line (especially lines 2 and 3).

2. Allen Tate says that in writing "The Mediterranean" (see Anthology, p. 534), he "made a point of not writing any two lines in the same rhythm." Chances are there is *one* line that is perfectly regular, with meter and rhythm coinciding.

    a. Can you find such a line? Is there only one?

    b. Weighing the other lines one by one, determine how rhythm varies from meter. Which variations are expressive?

    c. Is it true that no two lines have an identical rhythm?

D. But knowing now that they would have her speak,
She threw her wet hair backward from her brow,
Her hand close to her mouth touching her cheek,

As though she had had there a shameful blow,
And feeling it shameful to feel ought but shame   5
All through her heart, yet felt her cheek burned so,

She must a little touch it. . . .

William Morris

Paul Thompson (*The Work of William Morris*) uses the above passage from "The Defense of Guenevere" to show that "odd deviations from the normal iambic beat . . . become masterly devices for creating tension . . . a secondary rhythm drags against the weakened primary meter, so that a purely physical description of Guenevere takes on a sense of sexual shame. . . . The fourth line, clumsy according to conventional metrical standards, is here brilliantly effective. Morris had in fact created a new verse form, like stammering direct speech. . . ."

Do you feel that the "odd deviations" do, indeed, have this effect?

E. ON THE COUNTESS DOWAGER OF PEMBROKE

Underneath this sable hearse
Lies the subject of all verse:
Sidney's sister, Pembroke's mother:
Death, ere thou hast slain another,
Fair, and learn'd, and good as she,   5
Time shall throw a dart at thee.

William Browne (1591–1643)

The meter of this famous little poem, which appears in most anthologies, might seem undecidable, since four of the lines are — ∪ — ∪ — ∪ —, either iambs with the first syllable omitted, or trochees with the last omitted. Winifred Nowottny (*The Language Poets Use*) thinks the poem's brief magnificence comes in part from a change in rhythm. The first three lines are trochaic, except for one reversed foot (can you find it?). But with the word "Death," a reversal of attitude, from mourning to triumph, is accompanied by a reversal of rhythm, to rising iambs—since we cannot reasonably break up the line into

> Death, ere   thou hast   slain an-   other . . .

Do you believe this is a sensible analysis of the rhythm?

F. The four-stress lines in Marvell's "To His Coy Mistress" were described as "faster, crisper" than pentameter would have been. Pentameter would sound like this:

Had we but world enough and time, this coy-
ness, lady, were no crime. We would sit down
And think which way to walk and pass our long
Love's day. Thou by the Indian Ganges' side
Shouldst rubies find; I by the tide of Humber. . . .   5

Is that really slower? What if we doubled the lines? Twice as slow?

Had we but world enough and time, this coyness, lady, were no
    crime.
We would sit down and think which way to walk and pass our long
    love's day. . . .

If tetrameters are fast, would dimeters be twice as fast?

Had we but world
Enough and time,
This coyness, lady,
Were no crime.
We would sit down   5
And think which way
To walk and pass
Our long love's day. . . .

What happens if we read in monometers?

Had we
But world
Enough
And time,
This coyness,   5
Lady,
Were
No crime. . . .

Does a change in line length change the tempo?

G. 1. Make up a dozen or so iambic pentameters of the kind you might
use in conversation, like "This English class has really been a bore"
or "You got your tickets for the game tonight?"

2. Compose a dozen or so lines of realistic dialogue in iambic pen-
tameter.

3. Write a few lines of perfectly regular iambic pentameter; then a
few that use pyrrhic feet (‿ ‿) for *less*ness; a few that use spondees
(— —) for *more*ness or fullness; a few that use trochees (— ‿) for
abruptness or violence; and a few that use anapests (‿ ‿ —) for
speed or impulse.

10

Different Drummers
RHYTHMS OLD AND NEW

OTHER SYLLABLE-STRESS RHYTHMS

The iambic—or heartbeat—rhythm has been the one most frequently used in our poetry over the centuries. But other metrical units are also possible. Three such units are frequently used.

Trochee

We have already noticed the trochee (— ◡) as an option in the iambic line. It can also constitute a rhythm by itself. The word means *rūnnĭng* or *speedy*. Certain common phrases fall into trochaic patterns: "brēad ănd| būttĕr," "sālt ănd| pēppĕr," "cūp ănd| sāucĕr," "hēad ănd| shōuldĕrs," "rōugh ănd| rēadў," "hīgh ănd| mīghtў," "frēe ănd| ēasў." Trochaic lines can become monotonous, as they sometimes do in Longfellow's "The Song of Hiawatha":

> By the shores of Gitche Gumee,
> By the shining Big-Sea-Water,
> Stood the wigwam of Nokomis,
> Daughter of the Moon, Nokomis.
> Dark behind it rose the forest,   5
> Rose the black and gloomy pine-trees,
> Rose the firs with cones upon them;

> Bright before it beat the water,
> Beat the clear and sunny water,
> Beat the shining Big-Sea-Water.   *10*
>   There the wrinkled old Nokomis
> Nursed the little Hiawatha. . . .

In Philip Larkin's poem about a mine disaster, the old rhythm (which Longfellow imitated from an ancient Finnish meter) is successfully revived ("The Explosion," see Anthology, p. 568). A different trochaic rhythm is used in Poe's "The Raven." The first two stanzas should be enough to recall the swing of these famous lines:

> Once upon a midnight dreary, while I pondered, weak and weary,
> Over many a quaint and curious volume of forgotten lore—
> While I nodded, nearly napping, suddenly there came a tapping,
> As of some one gently rapping, rapping at my chamber door—
> " 'Tis some visitor," I muttered, "tapping at my chamber door—   *5*
>   Only this and nothing more."

> Ah, distinctly I remember it was in the bleak December;
> And each separate dying ember wrought its ghost upon the floor.
> Eagerly I wished the morrow; —vainly had I sought to borrow
> From my books surcease of sorrow—sorrow for the lost Lenore—   *10*
> For the rare and radiant maiden whom the angels name Lenore—
>   Nameless *here* for evermore.

The meter is trochaic octameter, with lines 2 and 4 catalectic (*cut short, docked of their final syllable*). Line 6 is tetrameter, also catalectic. If we read the poem naturally, we notice how the individual feet often bond together in pairs:

> While I nodded,| nearly napping,| suddenly there |came a tapping. . . .

Such rhythms, in which two feet tend to fuse into a unit, are called **dipodic.**

The iambic foot, discussed in Chapter 9, is known as a **rising rhythm,** since the energy concentrates at the end of the foot. The trochee is a **falling rhythm.**

Dactyl and Anapest

The two basic three-syllable feet are the **dactyl** (— ‿ ‿) and the **anapest** (‿ ‿ —). The first is from the Greek word for *finger*. It was so called because in Greek it had a long syllable followed by two short

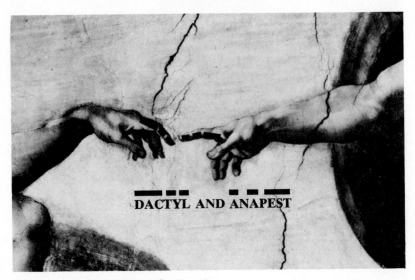

DACTYL AND ANAPEST

Michelangelo, Detail from *The Creation*
(*The Bettmann Archive*)

ones, as the finger has a long bone and two shorter ones. In English
the dactyl has an accented syllable followed by two unaccented ones,
as (twice) in "innocent bystander." Its opposite, with two unaccented
syllables followed by an accented one, is called "anapest" from a word
that means *reversed*. We have already mentioned the anapest as an
option in iambic verse. Both feet occur in their natural state in
English—the dactyl, for example, in a sentence like, "Look at him
finish the pint in a gulp or two!"; the anapest in, "For an option on
cattle you'd mortgage your house?"

Triple rhythms are busier and faster than double ones; on the other
hand, they are lighter, less solid. Triple rhythms are often found in
light verse: "Thĕre wās | ă yoŭng lād | y̆ frŏm Dāl | lăs. . . ." The
distinction between "rising" and "falling" rhythms holds true also for
triple feet—anapests rise, dactyls fall.

Byron's "The Destruction of Sennacherib" is written in anapestic
tetrameters, though with an iamb sometimes substituted for the first
foot and with some variant feet we might feel are more like —◡—
or ◡——than the basic ◡◡—. (If interested, see the Table of Feet,
p. 257, for their names.)

• THE DESTRUCTION OF SENNACHERIB •

The Assyrian came down like the wolf on the fold,
And his cohorts were gleaming in purple and gold;
And the sheen of their spears was like stars on the sea,
When the blue wave rolls nightly on deep Galilee.

Like the leaves of the forest when summer is green,　　　　5
That host with their banners at sunset were seen:
Like the leaves of the forest when autumn hath blown,
That host on the morrow lay withered and strown.

For the Angel of Death spread his wings on the blast,
And breathed in the face of the foe as he passed;　　　　10
And the eyes of the sleepers waxed deadly and chill,
And their hearts but once heaved—and for ever grew still!

And there lay the steed with his nostril all wide,
But through it there rolled not the breath of his pride;
And the foam of his gasping lay white on the turf,　　　　15
And cold as the spray of the rock-beating surf.

And there lay the rider distorted and pale,
With the dew on his brow, and the rust on his mail;
And the tents were all silent, the banners alone,
The lances unlifted, the trumpet unblown.　　　　20

And the widows of Ashur are loud in their wail,
And the idols are broke in the temple of Baal;
And the might of the Gentile, unsmote by the sword,
Hath melted like snow in the glance of the Lord!

George Gordon, Lord Byron (1788–1824)

Robert Frost puts the swingy meter to very different use in his "Blue-
berries," which begins:

> You ought to have seen what I saw on my way
> To the village, through Patterson's pasture today:
> Blueberries as big as the end of your thumb. . . .

In a poem whose symbols yearn for an eternity without the frustra-
tions of this life, William Blake several times changes his simple ana-
pests to a counterbalanced foot like —∪—, as in "golden clime,"
"pined away"—a cross between the anapest and its opposite, a drag
of tension and resistance that slows our reading down so that we can
ponder the images.

THE RHYTHMS

· AH SUN-FLOWER ·

Ah Sun-flower! weary of time,
Who countest the steps of the Sun,
Seeking after that sweet golden clime
Where the traveller's journey is done,

Where the Youth pined away with desire, 5
And the pale Virgin shrouded in snow,
Arise from their graves and aspire
Where my Sun-flower wishes to go.

William Blake (1757–1827)

In his "Dream Variations" (see Anthology, p. 536), Langston Hughes works musical changes on the anapest by varying it with iambs ("To fling"), with feet like those Blake uses ("day is done," "comes on gent-"), and with units of ◡ — — ("my arms wide," "in some place"). He also has some syncopated monosyllabic feet ("Thāt| ĭs mў drēam!" and "Blāck| līke mē") and a complete reversal of rhythm in "Nīght cŏmĭng| tēndĕrlў." But his most musical single variation is the line

Dance! whirl! whirl!

which our ear tries to hear as two feet, since the other lines have two. This makes it like a triplet in music: ♩♩♩ = ♩♩ . Its three beats are to be heard in the time allotted to two.

Dactylic rhythms, though less common in English, can be found. They predominate in Thomas Hardy's "The Voice," which begins:

Woman much missed, how you call to me, call to me,
Saying that now you are not as you were
When you had changed from the one who was all to me,
But as at first, when our day was fair.

Can it be you that I hear?   Let me view you, then, 5
Standing as when I drew near to the town
Where you would wait for me: yes, as I knew you then,
Even to the original air-blue gown! . . . .

William Carlos Williams, not often attracted to traditional rhythms, felt the rightness of the lively dactyl to describe the dancers in a famous painting ("The Dance," see Anthology, p. 515).

Iñ| Breūghĕl's grēat | pīcturĕ, Thĕ | Kērmĕss
thĕ | dāncĕrs gŏ | rōund, thĕy gŏ | rōund ănd
ă | rōund. . . .

· *table of feet* ·

The names of the four important feet are in capitals. The other feet rarely occur except as variations of one of the four. The first four *have* to be variations; none could constitute a rhythm by itself.

Pyrrhic	∪ ∪	of the
Spondee	— —	old loves
Tribrach	∪ ∪ ∪	of a re-
Molóssos	— — —	mote lost land
IAMB	∪ —	recalled
TROCHEE	— ∪	always
ANAPEST	∪ ∪ —	in a dream
DACTYL	— ∪ ∪	mournfully
Bácchius	∪ — —	the closed door
Antibácchius	— — ∪	too rudely
Amphímacer (or cretic)	— ∪ —	overgrown
Amphibrach	∪ — ∪	remembers
Ionic a minore	∪ ∪ — —	and the lost love
Chóriamb	— ∪ ∪ —	only recalled
Antispast	∪ — — ∪	in dreams fading
First Paeon	— ∪ ∪ ∪	mournfully as
Second Paeon	∪ — ∪ ∪	as mournfully
Third Paeon	∪ ∪ — ∪	and as mournful-
Fourth Paeon	∪ ∪ ∪ —	ly as the dark

The words used as examples of the nineteen feet themselves constitute the following little poem.

NINETEEN

Of the old loves of a remote lost land,
recalled always in a dream mournfully.
The closed door too rudely overgrown remembers,
and the lost love only recalled in dreams
fading mournfully as . . . as mournfully . . .
and as mournfully as the dark.

Bouncy irregularities that seem to swing the rhythm into anapests for a phrase or two help to dramatize the rollicking dance.

To feel and enjoy the waves of rhythm in a poem, it is not necessary to be familiar with the terminology, any more than we have to know what "fuel injection" or "universal joint" means if we drive a car. Such terms, though, are a convenience in discussion.

STRONG-STRESS RHYTHMS

Up to now we have been illustrating only one of the several ways of metering sounds in English. Since it takes into account both the number of syllables and the placing of the accents, it has been called the **syllable-stress system.** But it might just as well, more simply, be thought of as standard rhythm. Because of the interplay between meter and rhythm—that is, between expectation and actuality—standard rhythm produces what we could call, by analogy, something like a stereo effect. In listening to it, we are hearing two voices at once. Other systems have more the nature of monaural sound.

One system counts only accents, disregarding number of syllables. The other counts only number of syllables, disregarding where the accents fall. The first of these, the **strong-stress system,** is the older, going back to the verse line of Anglo-Saxon times. The Old English (or Anglo-Saxon) line is made up of two halves. In each half there are two strongly stressed syllables, as in W. H. Auden's

> There hēad falls fōrward   fatīgued at ēvening . . .

Around the two stressed syllables—before them, between them, after them—are their natural clusters of unaccented words or syllables. Since the number of syllables does not matter, there can be a great variety of lengths and patterns—from four syllables, all stressed, in a line like

> rōugh rōads,   rōck-strēwn

to over twenty syllables in the unlikely but possible

> due to the rūthlessness of the rūmorings,   due to
> the Perūvians' incommunicabīlity. . . .

In theory these two lines are equivalent, since each has four strong beats; in practice, however, lines as gangling as the second one seldom or never occur.

Piero della Francesca, *The Resurrection*
(Alinari—Art Reference Bureau)

The four accented syllables were emphasized by alliteration, an ancient feature of Germanic languages. The commonest pattern was to have the first three stresses alliterating (or all beginning with a vowel). Later on, derivatives of strong-stress rhythms have only the four stresses without alliteration, as in the stark little Resurrection poem of the fifteenth century, which recalls the athletic, high-stepping Christ of Piero della Francesca's "Resurrection."

THE RHYTHMS

· I HAVE LABORED SORE ·

I have labored sore   and suffered death,
and now I rest   and draw my breath;
but I shall come   and call right soon
heaven and earth   and hell to doom;
and then shall know   both devil and man,   *5*
what I was   and what I am.

Anonymous (fifteenth century)

4/**doom:** *judgment*

Ezra Pound, in his version of the Anglo-Saxon "The Seafarer," often uses the old pattern:

Nārrow nīghtwatch   nīgh the shīp's head . . .

Chīll its chaīns are;   chāfing sīghs. . . .

Richard Wilbur has used Old English rhythm in a poem which, by its form alone, points up a contrast between our modern world of plastics and unseasoned wood and an older world of well-made tools and furnishings.

· JUNK ·

Huru Welandes
                    worc ne geswiceð
monna ænigum
               ðara ðe Mimming can
heardne gehealdan.
                  Waldere*

An axe angles
           from my neighbor's ashcan;
It is hell's handiwork,
               the wood not hickory,
The flow of the grain
               not faithfully followed.
The shivered shaft
          rises from a shellheap
Of plastic playthings,
             paper plates,   *5*
And the sheer shards
           of shattered tumblers

---

* The epigraph, taken from a fragmentary Anglo-Saxon poem, concerns the legendary smith Wayland, and may roughly be translated: "Truly, Wayland's handiwork—the sword Mimming which he made—will never fail any man who knows how to use it bravely." [Wilbur's note]

DIFFERENT DRUMMERS

That were not annealed
                    for the time needful.
At the same curbside,
                    a cast-off cabinet
Of wavily-warped
                    unseasoned wood
Waits to be trundled
                    in the trash-man's truck.   *10*
Haul them off! Hide them!
                    The heart winces
For junk and gimcrack,
                    for jerrybuilt things
And the men who make them
                    for a little money,
Bartering pride
                    like the bought boxer
Who pulls his punches,
                    or the paid-off jockey   *15*
Who in the home stretch
                    holds in his horse.
Yet the things themselves
                    in thoughtless honor
Have kept composure,
                    like captives who would not
Talk under torture.
                    Tossed from a tailgate
Where the dump displays
                    its random dolmens,   *20*
Its black barrows
                    and blazing valleys,
They shall waste in the weather
                    toward what they were.
The sun shall glory
                    in the glitter of glass-chips,
Foreseeing the salvage
                    of the prisoned sand,
And the blistering paint
                    peel off in patches,   *25*
That the good grain
                    be discovered again.
Then burnt, bulldozed,
                    they shall all be buried
To the depth of diamonds,
                    in the making dark
Where halt Hephaestus
                    keeps his hammer
And Wayland's work
                    is worn away.   *30*

Richard Wilbur (b. 1921)

THE RHYTHMS

In the first twelve lines, there are eleven different arrangements of accented and unaccented syllables.

Auden's "The Wanderer" (p. 145) has the feeling of Old English rhythms and often the very pattern:

> Doom is dark and deeper than any sea-dingle. . . .
>
> Waving from window, spread of welcome. . . .

In his book-length *The Age of Anxiety*, Auden went back to even stricter strong stress:

> Ingenious George reached his journey's end
> Killed by a cop in a comfort station,
> Dan dropped dead at his dinner table,
> Mrs. O'Malley with Miss de Young
> Wandered away into wild places. . . .   5

Even before the time of Chaucer (who did not use strong stress), the line had lost much of its alliteration and had picked up a lilt, learned perhaps from the Latin hymns or the love songs of Provence. In a poem of religious exhortation written about 1275, the alliterative scheme is much modified. Lines 1, 2, 4, and 5 of each stanza show the two halves with two beats in each:

> Where beth they   beforen us weren. . . .

But lines 3 and 6 have only three stresses:

> and hadden field and wodė. . . .

• From UBI SUNT QUI ANTE NOS FUERUNT? •

> Where beth they beforen us weren,
> houndės ladden and havekes beren,
> and hadden field and wodė?
> The richė levedies in their bower,
> that wereden gold in their tressour,   5
> with their brightė rodė?

¹/**beth:** *are*
²/**houndės ladden:** *led hunting dogs*
  havekes beren: *carried hawks*
⁴/**levedies:** *ladies*
  bower: *chamber*

⁵/**tressour:** *ribbons, lace, etc., worn in hair*
⁶/**rodė:** *complexion*

The title is translated by the first line.

Eten and drunken and maden them glad;
their life was all with gamen i-lad;
men keneleden them beforen;
they bearen them well swithe high.   *10*
And in the twinkling of an eye
their soulės weren forloren.

Where is that laughing and that song,
that trailing and that proudė yong,
those havekes and those houndės?   *15*
All that joy is went away,
that weal is comen to *weylaway,*
to manyė hardė stoundės. . . .

                                        Anonymous (c. 1275)

7/**eten:** *they ate*
  maden them glad: *had a good time*
8/**with gamen i-lad:** *spent in having fun*
10/**well swithe high:** *very proudly indeed*

12/**forloren:** *lost*
14/**trailing:** *trailing of dresses*
  yong: *going*
17/**weal:** *happiness, prosperity*
  weylaway: *alas!*
18/**stoundės:** *times*

The same four-beat and three-beat combination is to be found 650 years later in the poem by John Crowe Ransom on page 109.

Many of E. E. Cummings' poems—including some of those that seem most modern—come from the older "Where beth they" tradition.

· IF EVERYTHING HAPPENS THAT CAN'T BE DONE ·

if everything happens that can't be done
(and anything's righter
than books
could plan)
the stupidest teacher will almost guess   *5*
(with a run
skip
around we go yes)
there's nothing as something as one

one hasn't a why or because or although   *10*
(and buds know better
than books
don't grow)
one's anything old being everything new
(with a what   *15*
which
around we come who)
one's everyanything so

THE RHYTHMS

so world is a leaf so tree is a bough
(and birds sing sweeter   *20*
than books
tell how)
so here is away and so your is a my
(with a down
up   *25*
around again fly)
forever was never till now

now i love you and you love me
(and books are shuter
than books   *30*
can be)
and deep in the high that does nothing but fall
(with a shout
each
around we go all)   *35*
there's somebody calling who's we

we're anything brighter than even the sun
(we're everything greater
than books
might mean)   *40*
we're everyanything more than believe
(with a spin
leap
alive we're alive)
we're wonderful one times one   *45*

E. E. Cummings (1894–1962)

In a poem that seems "everything new," Cummings' "anything old" is
a rhythm going back at least seven centuries. If we reassemble one of
the stanzas Cummings has disguised by his typographical layout, we
find four regular strong-stress lines of four beats followed by one of
three beats.

> if ēverything hăppens   that căn't be dōne
> (and ānything's rīghter   than bōoks could plān)
> the stūpidest tēacher   will ālmost guēss
> with a rūn skīp   arōund we go yēs
> there's nōthing as sōmething as ōne

His lines on the page are symmetrically divided and subdivided: whole
line, half line, quarter line, quarter line, whole line, quarter line,
quarter line, half line, three-beat line. Though the poem seems all

DIFFERENT DRUMMERS

spontaneity, it is worked out with a precision almost mathematical.

Most poets who use the four-beat, strong-stress pattern today use a simplified form of it.

> Summer will rise till the houses fear;
> streets will hear underground streams. . . .
>
> *William Stafford*

> I slept under   rhododendron
> All night   blossoms fell
> Shivering on   a sheet of cardboard
> Feet stuck   in my pack
> Hands deep   in my pockets. . . .
>
> *Gary Snyder*

Strong-stress rhythm, based on accent, the most energetic element of speech, serves to communicate physical energy, as in one of the best-known of American baseball poems, Robert Fitzgerald's "Cobb Would Have Caught It" (see Anthology, p. 547). For examples of three-beat strong-stress lines, see Elizabeth Bishop's "The Fish" and James Dickey's "Cherrylog Road" (Anthology, pp. 547 and 568).

In "Blackberry Sweet," the kind of traditional love lyric men have written to women at least since the Song of Songs in the Old Testament, Dudley Randall is playing off two-beat lines against three-beat lines, so that the latter become the rhythmical equivalent of the former, like triplets in music.

• BLACKBERRY SWEET •

> Black girl black girl
> lips as curved as cherries
> full as grape bunches
> sweet as blackberries
>
> Black girl black girl   5
> when you walk you are
> magic as a rising bird
> or a falling star
>
> Black girl black girl
> what's your spell to make   10
> the heart in my breast
> jump   stop   shake
>
> *Dudley Randall (b. 1914)*

SPRUNG RHYTHM

Strong-stress rhythm is so old that poets keep calling it "new" when they rediscover it. In 1800 Coleridge said that the meter of his "Christabel" seemed irregular because "it was founded on a new principle: namely, that of counting in each line the accents, not the syllables." More influential was the "new prosody" that Gerard Manley Hopkins calls "sprung rhythm." By "sprung" he means *abrupt*, as when one accent directly follows another. We also say a thing is *sprung* when it is forced out of its proper position by its own tension or by that of things pressing against it. Unaccented syllables can be *sprung* out of a line by the pressure of accents around them—as when we say "I'll go" for "I will go."

Hopkins explained that in sprung rhythm "one stress makes a foot," no matter how many unstressed syllables there may be. Some of the stresses he marked in his poems are the kind we dó use in speech, but could not easily guess from a printed text. Characteristic of sprung rhythm is the way stresses jostle against one another, unbuffered by unaccented syllables in between. In "Spring and Fall" (see Anthology, p. 496), we see this happening. In the thirteenth line, for example, two *had*'s have been sprung out, leaving the accents to clash together.

> What héart [had] héard of, ghóst [had] guéssed. . . .

We have now seen examples of the two basic rhythmical systems of English versification: the syllable-stress system and the strong-stress system. Both have given us great poetry. If the syllable-stress system has given us more, it may only be because it has seemed more all-purpose than the bouncy and emphatic strong-stress system.

A WORD ABOUT QUANTITY

A third metrical system tried to impose itself on English around 1580 and for a decade or so thereafter. Classicists wanted to meter English as if it were Greek or Latin—by *length* of syllable rather than by accent. Although we recognize that some syllables take longer to say than others—that "home" is longer than "him" and "strength" is longer than "sit"—our ear does not divide syllables into long and short consciously enough for us to feel a pattern in the arrangement. Metering by *quantity*—length of syllable—was a failure in English.

But the study of classical meters did bring some new rhythms into

English, once the long and short syllables were replaced by accented and unaccented ones.

The poems of Sappho, on pages 8 and 18, transpose her quantitative rhythm into accentual ones. It is not surprising to find Sapphic stanzas* in translations of Sappho, but the use to which William Meredith puts them (in a poem which alludes to that of Muriel Rukeyser on p. 549) may come as a jolt. Sapphics to describe a contemporary mugging? Sapphics that say, "God damn it, no!"?

· EFFORT AT SPEECH ·
For Muriel Rukeyser

Climbing the stairway gray with urban midnight,
Cheerful, venial, ruminating pleasure,
Darkness takes me, an arm around my throat and
     Give me your wallet.

Fearing cowardice more than other terrors,   5
Angry I wrestle with my unseen partner,
Caught in a ritual not of our own making,
     panting like spaniels.

Bold with adrenalin, mindless, shaking,
God damn it, no! I rasp at him behind me,   10
Wrenching the leather wallet from his grasp. It
     breaks like a wishbone,

So that departing (routed by my shouting,
Not by my strength or inadvertent courage)
Half of the papers lending me a name are   15
     gone with him nameless.

Only now turning, I see a tall boy running,
Fifteen, sixteen, dressed thinly for the weather.
Reaching the streetlight he turns a brown face briefly
     phrased like a question.   20

I like a questioner watch him turn the corner
Taking the answer with him, or his half of it.
Loneliness, not a sensible emotion,
     breathes hard on the stairway.

Walking homeward I fraternize with shadows,   25
Zig-zagging with them where they flee the streetlights,
Asking for trouble, asking for the message
     trouble had sent me.

* Three lines of —◡|—◡|—◡◡|—◡|—◡ and one of —◡◡|—◡.

All fall down has been scribbled on the street in
Garbage and excrement: so much for the vision   *30*
Others taunt me with, my untimely humor,
    so much for cheerfulness.

Next time don't wrangle, give the boy the money,
Call across chasms what the world you know is.
Luckless and lied to, how can a child master   *35*
    human decorum?

Next time a switch-blade, somewhere he is thinking,
I should have killed him and took the lousy wallet.
Reading my cards he feels a surge of anger
    blind as my shame.   *40*

Error from Babel mutters in the places,
Cities apart, where now we word our failures:
Hatred and guilt have left us without language
    who might have held discourse.

          William Meredith (b. 1919)

A difficulty with such meters in English is their rigidity. We enjoy variations. But a Sapphic line is a Sapphic line, and the writer has almost no freedom to vary accents. Meredith has wisely not tried to apply the template to every line. He is content to give the look and feel of Sapphics. Coming close to a meter (as Meredith does here) is all that one wants in English; a near miss is generally more interesting than a dead-center hit.

SYLLABIC METER

A fourth and totally different system—by number of syllables alone, with no regard for accent—is winningly presented by James Tate in his poem about a student in a poetry workshop:

• MISS CHO COMPOSES IN THE CAFETERIA •

   You are so small, I
   am not even sure
   that you are at all.

   To you, I know I
   am not here: you are   *5*
   rapt in writing a

syllabic poem
about gigantic,
gaudy Christmas trees.

You will send it home   10
to China, and they
will worry about

you alone amid
such strange customs. You
count on your tiny   15

bamboo fingers; one,
two, three—up to five,
and, oh, you have one

syllable too much.
You shake your head in   20
dismay, look back up

to the tree to see
if, perhaps, there might
exist another

word that would describe   25
the horror of this
towering, tinselled

symbol. And . . . now
you've got it! You jot
it down, jump up, look   30

at me and giggle.

James Tate (b. 1943)

Tate has written his poem exactly as little Miss Cho is writing hers. His, too, is a **syllabic** poem—here, with five syllables to the line. In such poems all that matters, metrically, is the number of syllables, not their accent.

Sylvia Plath has also written a five-syllable poem, but with a difference.

· MUSHROOMS ·

Overnight, very
Whitely, discreetly,
Very quietly

THE RHYTHMS

Our toes, our noses
Take hold on the loam.   5
Acquire the air.

Nobody sees us,
Stops us, betrays us;
The small grains make room.

Soft fists insist on   10
Heaving the needles,
The leafy bedding,

Even the paving.
Our hammers, our rams,
Earless and eyeless,   15

Perfectly voiceless,
Widen the crannies,
Shoulder through holes. We

Diet on water,
On crumbs of shadow,   20
Bland-mannered, asking

Little or nothing.
So many of us!
So many of us!

We are shelves, we are   25
Tables, we are meek,
We are edible,

Nudgers and shovers
In spite of ourselves.
Our kind multiplies: 30

We shall by morning
Inherit the earth.
Our foot's in the door.

Sylvia Plath (1932–1963)

Plath treats the line as a line; she likes to pause at the end of a stanza. Tate does not. "Mushrooms" also has another rhythm at work, overriding the syllabic count—alternations of dactyls and trochees, as in the short line of a Sapphic stanza: $— \cup\cup — \cup$. About half of the lines fall into this rhythmic figure ("whitely, discreetly"). Some of the remaining lines reverse the feet ("Very quietly"). We are inveigled, if not appassionated, into the swing of an accentual rhythm, which we hear more compellingly than the syllabic count.

Syllabic poems can have lines of any manageable number of syllables. The odd numbers seem more attractive—five and seven are particular favorites. Dave Etter uses only one syllable in "Romp," which could also be imagined in two-syllable lines—or for that matter in lines of four or eight syllables. (Why not in lines of three or five syllables?)

• ROMP •

her
strong
white
legs
are   5
wet
grass
stained
I
help   10
her
up
she
grabs
my   15
neck
rubs
cool
milk
weed   20
in
my
hot
face
and   25
I
am
glad
she
chose   30
to
run

Dave Etter (b. 1928)

In Dylan Thomas' "Fern Hill" (see Anthology, p. 555) the fourth line of every stanza has six syllables:

Time let me hail and climb. . . .

The third and fifth lines have nine:

> The night above the dingle starry. . . .

Marianne Moore's "A Carriage from Sweden" (see Anthology, p. 520) has eight syllables in lines 1, 2, 3, and 5 (with two exceptions):

> They say there is a sweeter air
>> where it was made, then we have here;
>> a Hamlet's castle atmosphere. . . .
>> something that makes me feel at home. . . .

In "Fern Hill," lines 1, 2, 6, and 7 of each stanza have fourteen syllables. Two of the twenty-four lines are excessive by one syllable, but only a finger-counter would notice. It seems unlikely that our ear will catch any exact number of syllables above about five, since nothing in our speech has accustomed us to attach any importance to such numbers.

An interest in syllabic poetry grew up in France and in this country about the first decade of our century. It was encouraged by the example of Japanese poetry, based on syllable count since Japanese has no accent noticeable enough to base a rhythm on. (See the remarks on *tanka* and *haiku* on pp. 341–342.) The most eminent practitioners of syllabics in English have been Marianne Moore and W. H. Auden, who was influenced by her. The trim, crisp lines of both no doubt owe something to the careful attention that syllabics demand, but the greatness of their work does not consist in their ability to count syllables. A series of counted syllables in itself is hardly a source of excitement or emotion in poetry. Someone in a passion may resort to stress rhythms ("You SON of a BITCH!") but is not likely to count syllables. The charm of James Tate's poem is only partially due to its doling out of five-syllable units. Good syllabic poems are good because of their use of words, or because of their imagery, or because they have an over-rhythm that we feel more strongly than the enumeration of syllables, as in "Mushrooms," or in Thomas' "Fern Hill" or in many poems of Moore and Auden.

FREE VERSE, FREE RHYTHMS

When we pass on from syllabics to **free verse,** we probably think of the new poetry that, more than seventy years ago, Pound and some of his friends began to write and theorize about. One of the principles they agreed on, says Pound, was "to compose in the sequence of the musical phrase, not in sequence of a metronome. . . ." Pound meant that instead of writing in preordained meters, one should let emotion find its own natural rhythm.

· THE RETURN ·

See, they return; ah, see the tentative
    Movements, and the slow feet,
    The trouble in the pace and the uncertain
    Wavering!

See, they return, one, and by one,   5
With fear, as half-awakened;
As if the snow should hesitate
And murmur in the wind,
         and half turn back;
These were the "Wing'd-with-Awe,"   10
         Inviolable.

Gods of the wingèd shoe!
With them the silver hounds,
         sniffing the trace of air!

Haie! Haie!   15
     These were the swift to harry;
These the keen-scented;
These were the souls of blood.

Slow on the leash,
         pallid the leash-men!   20

Ezra Pound (1885–1972)

Here the diffidence of the ghostly figures, once so alive, finds its equivalent in the hesitating cadence, which owes much to the ancient rhythms that Pound knew so well. The rising rhythm of "they return" is immediately reversed, retracted, in the falling rhythm of "see the tentative/Movements," which is followed by the dragging "and the slow feet." Lines 3 and 4 are perturbed and unsubstantial with their many short syllables, especially in the two fourth paeons ($\cup\cup\cup—$) of "thĕ trōu|blĕ ĭn thĕ pāce| ănd thĕ ŭncēr|taĭn . . . ." The rest of the poem is basically iambic, with the usual variations.

    Such poems of Pound represent free verse at its best. Perhaps we should say they are in **free rhythm,** reserving the term "free verse" for poems with less sense of rhythm, like these:

· A MAN SAID TO THE UNIVERSE ·

A man said to the universe:
"Sir, I exist!"
"However," replied the universe,
"The fact has not created in me
"A sense of obligation."   5

Stephen Crane (1871–1900)

· "THINK AS I THINK" ·

"Think as I think," said a man,
"Or you are abominably wicked;
You are a toad."

And after I had thought of it,
I said, "I will, then, be a toad."   5

Stephen Crane (1871–1900)

But it seems that even these apparently free lines wish to be rhythmical. The last two of the ten are regular iambic tetrameter; so are three or four others, with only a single foot in each fluttering into a variation. Two others are iambic dimeter. The overall movement is iambic.

Probably, as T. S. Eliot observed in speaking of Pound's free verse, no verse is free for the man who wants to do a good job. But there is certainly a sense in which rhythms can be said to be free—independent, that is, of any set line length and of any one kind of meter controlling the whole. In free rhythms the feet link together according to their natural affinities, as certain atoms and molecules link together. Rising feet have an affinity for each other; iamb and anapest go easily together, and easily admit a fourth paeon ($\cup\cup\cup$ —). Falling feet have their affinities with falling feet. Monosyllabic feet, spondees, and pyrrhic feet are neutral and fit in with either kind. All these feet, as well as the others we have mentioned, are the building blocks of rhythm, just as atoms, molecules, and the rest are the building blocks of matter.

When the English Bible appeared, the English ear became habituated to its cadences—two or three simple groupings, generally parallel, and, as translated, in free rhythms.

The heavens declare the glory of God; and the firmament
    showeth his handiwork.
Day unto day uttereth speech, and night unto night showeth
    knowledge.

DIFFERENT DRUMMERS

The most familiar and musical of free rhythms are Walt Whitman's, vigorous as his own zest and confidence, spacious as the American vistas he loved to sing. In "Out of the Cradle Endlessly Rocking," his great poem of love and death, we are easily caught up in the surge of his biblical cadence. The best way to read this poem the first few times is to ride the rhythm without trying to analyze its nature (see Anthology, p. 475).

When we do try to analyze it, we notice that often the rhythm comes on waves of parallel syntax—as in the twenty-two-line first sentence, or the fourteen-line sentence beginning with line 127. Whitman professed to dislike regularity, and yet his numerous revisions show that he worked for it, changing many lines to bring them into an iambic dance. Though his lines vary greatly in length and are made up of many kinds of feet, almost always the cells of rhythm join in strands according to their natural affinity.

He has both rising lines,

When the li|lac-scent| was in the air| and Fifth-|month
grass| was grow|ing . . .

and falling ones,

Out of the| cradle| endlessly| rocking. . . .

He has the same foot—or almost the same foot—running through a line:

Out from the| patches of| briers and| blackberries. . . .

Often we come on a familiar shape in the surf of rhythm—perhaps an iambic pentameter or two:

Blow up sea-winds along Paumanok's shore;
I wait and I wait till you blow my mate to me . . .

perhaps hexameters:

I, chanter of pains and joys, uniter of here and hereafter,
Taking all hints to use them, but swiftly leaping beyond them. . . .

Rhythmical figures are likely to be repeated. The first line has the same figure twice (— ∪ ∪ — ∪), the Sapphic combination of dactyl and trochee. Sometimes he uses this motif without the final unaccented syllable, so that it becomes the choriambus ($-\cup\cup-$). Whitman may not have thought in these terms, but he did feel in these rhythms. These two figures, in the first dozen lines, make up nearly the whole texture.

$-\cup\cup-\cup$ $-\cup\cup-$

Out of the cradle
endlessly rocking
Out of the mocking-
musical shuttle
Out of the Ninth-month
Over the sterile
sands and the fields be-   -yond where the child
                     leaving his bed
                     wander'd alone

bareheaded, barefoot
Down from the shower'd
Up from the mystic
twining and twisting   they were alive
Out from the patches
briers and blackber-

                     chanted to me
                     memories sad
risings and fallings
under that yellow   -risen and swol-
                     yearning and love
                     there in the mist
                     never to cease

Sound attracts sound, we said, in speaking of alliteration and assonance. And units of rhythm attract similar units. If we find one amphimacer ($-\cup-$), chances are we will find another, and then another:

Săt thĕ lōne| sīngĕr wōn|dĕrfŭl| caūsĭng teārs . . .

Whāt ĭs thāt| lĭttlĕ blāck| thīng Ĭ seē. . . ?

Little wonder the lines are so musical.

About a half century after Whitman, a rhythm like his turns up in the work of Carl Sandburg:

I am the prairie, mother of men, waiting,
They are mine, the threshing crews eating beefsteak,
     the farm boys driving steers to the railroad cattle pens . . .

THE VARIABLE FOOT

William Carlos Williams, though he wrote poems in free verse, came to feel it was "not the answer." He rejected its looseness, going so far as to say that "free verse wasn't verse at all," since "all art is orderly." He did believe, however, that the traditional rhythms were no longer appropriate for the American idiom.

Williams found his cue in the work of Albert Einstein. If everything else in our world is relative, why not have a relative or "variable" foot in poetry? The three-line "triadic" stanzas that Williams evolved were divided according to his "new measure." He advises us to count a single beat for each line—which, in his system, is considered a foot.

• THE DESCENT •

The descent beckons
        as the ascent beckoned.
                Memory is a kind
of accomplishment,
        a sort of renewal   5
                even
an initiation, since the spaces it opens are new places
        inhabited by hordes
                heretofore unrealized,
of new kinds—   10
        since their movements
                are toward new objectives
(even though formerly they were abandoned).

No defeat is made up entirely of defeat—since
the world it opens is always a place   15
        formerly
                unsuspected. A
world lost,
        a world unsuspected,
                beckons to new places   20
and no whiteness (lost) is so white as the memory
of whiteness

With evening, love wakens
        though its shadows
                which are alive by reason   25
of the sun shining—
        grow sleepy now and drop away
                from desire

Love without shadows stirs now
         beginning to awaken   *30*
              as night
advances.

The descent
      made up of despairs
          and without accomplishment   *35*
realizes a new awakening:
         which is a reversal
of despair.
      For what we cannot accomplish, what
is denied to love,   *40*
      what we have lost in the anticipation—
         a descent follows,
endless and indestructible.

William Carlos Williams (1883–1963)

In his best poems the lines do move expressively, often doubling back on themselves as if in halting or agonized meditation:

    The descent beckons
        as the ascent beckoned.
           Memory is a kind. . . .

The isolation of some words forces us to ponder their meaning—the implications of "even," for example, in line 6 or "formerly" in line 16. Other lines (17, 21) hurry us urgently ahead.

Though Williams denied that the iamb fits American speech, the very words he used to make his denial are themselves iambic, especially if we change his "is not" to the more American " 's not":

The iamb's not| the nor| mal meas|ure of| Amer|ican speech . . .

Whatever he may have said about iambs, he retains many of them in his "new rhythm." A late poem, "Asphodel, That Greeny Flower," begins:

Of as|phodel,| that green|y flow|er,
    like a but|tercup
         upon| its branch|ing stem—
save that| it's green| and wood|en—
    I come,| my sweet,|
        to sing| to you . . .

We can tell one "variable foot" from another by the way each is placed on the page. Such positioning on the page—sometimes called **spatial prosody** or **visual prosody**—has been encouraged in our time

DIFFERENT DRUMMERS

by the use of the typewriter, since its precise spacing can indicate, as Charles Olson (one modern theorist) has said, "the breath, the pauses, the suspensions even of syllables." He explains, in his essay "Projective Verse":

> If a contemporary poet leaves a space as long as the phrase before it, he means that space to be held, by the breath, an equal length of time. If he suspends a word or syllable at the end of a line . . . he means that time to pass that it takes the eye . . . to pick up the next line. . . .

Olson makes use of the multiple margin of the typewriter by moving it to the right or left to indicate progress, regress, or return. Spacing becomes one more analogy poets can use. (Cummings, of course, had done this decades before Olson reduced it to a system.)

CONCRETE POETRY

Typography can even be made to act out what it is saying, as in this poem, which shows us the two *likes* being attracted:

· **LIKE ATTRACTS LIKE** ·

like attracts like

like attracts like

like attracts like

like attracts like

like attracts like

like attracts like

like attracts like

likeattractslike

likeattractslike

likeattracklike

likttracdike

likralike

liklikts

Emmett Williams (b. 1925)

Constructions like this one, which use typography to make a little picture of their subject on the page, are known as **concrete** or **spatialist poetry;** it has enjoyed a vogue not only in recent decades but as long ago as the days of ancient Greece, where it was known as *technopaignia*, or *playing around with technique*. We see an example from the seventeenth century in George Herbert's "Easter-Wings" (see Anthology, p. 418). Poems have been designed in the shape of swans, neckties, watches, automobiles—almost anything. Reinhard Döhl (b. 1934) shows us a German worm in a German apple.

• PATTERN POEM WITH AN ELUSIVE INTRUDER •

Reinhold Döhl (b. 1934)

Hansjörg Mayer (b. 1943) shows us the bubbliness and drippiness of oil by splashing on the page the letters that make up the word.

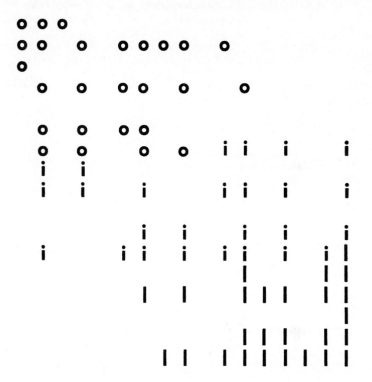

Hansjörg Mayer (b. 1943)

THE PROSE POEM

In another direction, metrical experiment has led to the **prose poem**— a piece that has most of the characteristics of the poem except that it is presented on the page as if it were a short prose piece. Charles Baudelaire, who began his "Little Poems in Prose" in the 1850s, was the best known but not the first of the writers of prose poems in France, where the form arose. A notable collection of prose poems from our own time is Karl Shapiro's *The Bourgeois Poet*, from which we have a selection in the Anthology (p. 552).

exercises & diversions

A. How would you describe the rhythm of each of these examples?

1. Thou preparest a table before me in the presence of mine
   enemies; thou anointest my head with oil; my cup runneth
   over.
   Surely goodness and mercy shall follow me all the days of my
   life: and I will dwell in the house of the Lord for ever.

Psalm 23

2. 'Tis the middle of night by the castle clock,
And the owls have awakened the crowing cock;
Tu—whit!——Tu—whoo!
And hark, again! the crowing cock,
How drowsily it crew.   5

Samuel Taylor Coleridge

3. This is the forest primeval. The murmuring pines and the hem-
   locks. . . .

Henry Wadsworth Longfellow

4. Oh, Caroline, Caroline, child of the sun,
We can never forget that our hearts have been one. . . .

Oliver Wendell Holmes

5. O my agèd Uncle Arly!
Sitting on a heap of barley
   Thro' the silent hours of night,—
Close beside a leafy thicket:—
On his nose there was a cricket,—   5
In his hat a railway-ticket;—
   (But his shoes were far too tight.)

Edward Lear

6. A was an archer, who shot at a frog,
B was a butcher, and had a great dog.
C was a captain, all covered with lace,
D was a drunkard, and had a red face.
E was an esquire, with pride on his brow,   5

F was a farmer, and followed the plough.
G was a gamester, who had but ill-luck,
H was a hunter, and hunted a buck. . . .

Anonymous

7. When the hounds of spring are on winter's traces,
    The mother of months in meadow or plain
Fills the shadows and windy places
    With lisp of leaves and ripple of rain;
And the brown bright nightingale amorous   5
Is half assuaged for Itylus,
For the Thracian ships and the foreign faces,
    The tongueless vigil, and all the pain.

Algernon Charles Swinburne

8. Darius the Mede was a king and a wonder.
His eye was proud, and his voice was thunder.
He kept bad lions in a monstrous den.
He fed up the lions on Christian men. . . .

Vachel Lindsay

9. Winter and Summer I sing of her grace,
As the rose is fair, so fair is her face,
Both Summer and Winter I sing of her,
And snow makyth me to remember her. . . .

Ezra Pound

10. No mice in the heath run, no song-birds fly
For fear of the buzzard that floats in the sky.

    He soars and he hovers, rocking on his wings,
He scans his wide parish with a sharp eye,
He catches the trembling of small hidden things,   5
He tears them in pieces, dropping them from the sky. . . .

Robert Graves

11. All I have is the moment of my life. You
Took a moment away. Delighted, laughing,
You and I lonely by the Mississippi
    Wondered what hell was.

James Wright

exercises & diversions

12. I'm a riddle in nine syllables,
An elephant, a ponderous house,
A melon strolling on two tendrils. . . .

Sylvia Plath

B. IRIS

a burst of iris so that
come down for
breakfast

we searched through the
rooms for   5
that

sweetest odor and at
first could not
find its

source then a blue as
of the sea   10
struck

startling us from among
those trumpeting
petals

William Carlos Williams (1883–1963)

   Line breaks indicate a pause, however slight (if only while the
eye returns to the left-hand margin); stanza breaks indicate a
stronger pause. When a reviewer objected that in "Iris" the breaks
were arbitrary, eccentric, against the habits of ordinary speech, an
admirer of Williams countered that they were expressive and "func-
tional." The break between "its" and "source," for example, drama-
tizes the poet's halting bewilderment as he looks for the source of
the fragrance. Would you agree that Williams' "visual prosody"
(the way of indicating rhythm by the spacing on the page) is mean-
ingful? Are his line breaks natural pauses?

C. Is there anything like "sprung rhythm" in Tennyson's "Break, Break,
Break" (p. 408) or in Campion's "It Fell on a Summer's Day" (see
Anthology, p. 137)?

D. Gary Snyder's "Bubbs Creek Haircut" begins:

exercises & diversions

High ceilingd and the double mirrors, the
       calendar a splendid alpine scene—scab barber—
in stained white barber gown, alone, sat down, old man
A summer fog gray San Francisco day
I walked right in.   on Howard Street
              haircut a dollar twenty-five.
Just clip it close as it will go.
    "now why you want your hair cut back like that."
    —well I'm going to the Sierras for a while
Bubbs Creek and on across to upper Kern . . .

Can you find any iambic pentameters in these free-looking lines?

E. 1. Write a short poem in strong-stress rhythms on a subject that seems appropriate to their energetic character. Or write a poem in syllabics, of any line length you prefer. Or write a poem that makes use of visual prosody—the resources of the typewriter, for example, as Charles Olson describes them.

2. Rewrite "The Destruction of Sennacherib" in iambic pentameter.

      The foe came down like wolf upon the fold;
      His cohorts gleam with purple and with gold. . . .

Or make some equally drastic change in the meter of a famous poem and see what happens.

S · I · X

THE MIND

11

The Shape of Thought
WE GO A-SENTENCING

THE SENTENCE

Up to now we have been dealing with the more physical, or at least the nonintellectual, aspects of poetry: sensation, emotion, voice with its sounds and rhythms. All of these, of course, we experience in our consciousness. What the brain does not register might as well not exist for us. Even our sensuality has nothing but mind to reside in.

But there are elements of poetry that seem to have a more intellectual character than those we have looked at. One of these is the way poets organize the sentences of their poems. The sentence represents, in greatly simplified form, an act of the mind. In *greatly* simplified form: Since the brain has more cells to work with than there are people on this planet, any mental process is almost infinitely complex. When the mind can simplify its complexities so that they can be expressed in words, they naturally come forth as sentences. As Ernest Fenollosa, the student of Oriental languages, put it: "The sentence form was forced upon primitive man by nature itself."

"To write a poem," said Robert Frost, "is to go a-sentencing." A writer's state of mind, or that of the characters he or she creates, can determine the shape of the sentences that reveal that state of mind. Such shapes can be not only expressive but symbolic of their content. In psychological experiments, people have been asked to draw lines they felt would express certain emotional states. Lines felt as beautiful were smoothly curved, unbroken, symmetrical. Lines felt as ugly were jagged, with mixed angles and irregular twists. Sentences can express

us and affect us in much the same way. At a celebration held at
Rutgers in 1982 for the centennial of the birth of James Joyce, one of
the subjects under consideration was the effect the nonlinear sentence
might have on the nervous system.

When at the beginning of Shakespeare's *Richard III* the future king
is confident, exulting in thoughts of his coming triumphs, his language
flows forth in harmonious sentences.

> Now is the winter of our discontent
> Made glorious summer by this sun of York;
> And all the clouds that loured upon our house
> In the deep bosom of the ocean buried.
> Now are our brows bound with victorious wreaths,   *5*
> Our bruisèd arms hung up for monuments,
> Our stern alarums changed to merry meetings,
> Our dreadful marches to delightful measures.
> Grim-visaged War hath smoothed his wrinkled front,
> And now, instead of mounting barbèd steeds   *10*
> To fright the souls of fearful adversaries,
> He capers nimbly in a lady's chamber
> To the lascivious pleasing of a lute. . . .

But when toward the close of the play he is guilt-ridden, terrified by
ghosts that tell him to despair and die, his sentences are abrupt,
staccato.

> The lights burn blue. It is now dead midnight.
> Cold fearful drops stand on my trembling flesh.
> What do I fear? Myself? There's none else by.
> Richard loves Richard: that is, I am I.
> Is there a murderer here? No. Yes, I am.   *5*
> Then fly. What, from myself? Great reason why!
> Lest I revenge. What, myself upon myself? . . . .

When poets, or any writers, can give their sentences a shape that will
dramatize their meaning, they try to do so. Edwin Muir, writing a
poem called "The Labyrinth," started out with a mazily contorted
thirty-five-line sentence—a sentence that was, as he admitted, "de-
liberately labyrinthine." When Eugenio Montale, later awarded the
Nobel Prize, took as a symbol the life cycle of the eel he wrote his
poem (the original is in Italian) in one long sentence—an incomplete
one at that. The effect is to dramatize, in the very thrust of the words,
the tireless energy that shows itself in nature. Is not this vitality, the
poet asks, like the life force that sparkles so beautifully in the eyes of
a woman?

THE SHAPE OF THOUGHT

• THE EEL •

The eel, the
siren of sleety seas, abandoning
the Baltic for our waters,
our estuaries, our
freshets, to lash upcurrent under the brunt   5
of the flood, sunk deep, from brook to brook and then
trickle to trickle dwindling,
more inner always, always more in the heart
of the rock, thrusting
through ruts of the mud, until, one day,   10
explosion of splendor from the chestnut groves
kindles a flicker in deadwater sumps,
in ditches pitched
from ramparts of the Appennine to Romagna;
eel: torch and whip,   15
arrow of love on earth,
which nothing but our gorges or bone-dry
gutters of the Pyrenees ushers back
to edens of fertility;
green soul that probes   20
for life where only
fevering heat or devastation preys,
spark that says
the whole commences when the whole would seem
charred black, an old stick buried;   25
brief rainbow, twin
to that within your lashes' dazzle, that
you keep alive, inviolate, among
the sons of men, steeped in your mire—in this
not recognize a sister?   30

Eugenio Montale (1896–1981)

Short sentences, or sentences made up of short elements, may ex-
press a nervous discharge of energy, as in the poems of Emily Dickin-
son. Gwendolyn Brooks uses three-word sentences to express energy
recklessly expended.

• WE REAL COOL •
The Pool Players.
Seven at the Golden Shovel.

We real cool. We
Left school. We

Lurk late. We
Strike straight. We

THE MIND

Sing sin. We   5
Thin gin. We

Jazz June. We
Die soon.

Gwendolyn Brooks (b. 1917)

Very long sentences or very short ones are the extremes. In between there are many possibilities.

    The way in which poets go a-sentencing will distinguish their rhythm from that of other poets writing in the same meter. How poets pace their sentences, how and where they pause—things like this make one poet's characteristic tempo different from that of another.

USE OF CONNECTIVES

The very way the parts of a sentence are held together may be significant. A series of connectives like "and . . . and . . . and" can be childish—or it can be solemnly impressive, as in the first chapter of Genesis.

In the beginning God created the heaven and the earth. And the earth was without form, and void; and darkness was upon the face of the deep. And the Spirit of God moved upon the face of the waters. And God said, "Let there be light": and there was light.

Frost uses many *and*'s for drowsy monotony at the beginning of "Out, Out—," in which a fatal accident happens because people are tired after a long day's work.

· "OUT, OUT—" ·

The buzz saw snarled and rattled in the yard
And made dust and dropped stove-length sticks of wood,
Sweet-scented stuff when the breeze drew across it.
And from there those that lifted eyes could count
Five mountain ranges one behind the other   5

"Out, Out—": *The title is from Macbeth, V, v:*
      Out, out, brief candle!
      Life's but a walking shadow. . . .

Under the sunset far into Vermont.
And the saw snarled and rattled, snarled and rattled,
As it ran light, or had to bear a load.
And nothing happened: day was all but done.
Call it a day, I wish they might have said   *10*
To please the boy by giving him the half hour
That a boy counts so much when saved from work.
His sister stood beside them in her apron
To tell them "Supper." At the word, the saw,
As if to prove saws knew what supper meant,   *15*
Leaped out at the boy's hand, or seemed to leap—
He must have given the hand. However it was,
Neither refused the meeting. But the hand!
The boy's first outcry was a rueful laugh,
As he swung toward them holding up the hand   *20*
Half in appeal, but half as if to keep
The life from spilling. Then the boy saw all—
Since he was old enough to know, big boy
Doing a man's work, though a child at heart—
He saw all spoiled. "Don't let him cut my hand off—   *25*
The doctor, when he comes. Don't let him, sister!"
So. But the hand was gone already.
The doctor put him in the dark of ether.
He lay and puffed his lips out with his breath.
And then—the watcher at his pulse took fright.   *30*
No one believed. They listened at his heart.
Little—less—nothing!—and that ended it.
No more to build on there. And they, since they
Were not the one dead, turned to their affairs.

Robert Frost (1874–1963)

When conjunctions are omitted, the tone can be one of abruptness and energy, as in Caesar's famous "I came, I saw, I conquered." The omission of connectives that express logical relationships ("therefore," "because," "if," "although," and the like) is common in primitive languages. We might represent a typical pattern as: "Man hungry. He shoot arrow. Kill deer. Man happy." Poetry, caring more for the sensory details than for the logical relationship between them, is especially inclined to use this kind of construction. It is called **parataxis,** or *setting side by side.* The author of the poem "Western Wind" never specifies the connection between the wind and the rain and his love. Dreams, too, work purely by means of parataxis; since they have no easy way of indicating logical relationships, they set objects, persons, or situations meaningfully next to one another. So do some poems.

THE MIND

· THE MESSAGE ·

The door that someone opened wide
The door that someone shut again
The chair where someone came to sit
The cat that someone cuddled there
The fruit that someone bit into   5
The letter someone read and read
The chair that someone overturned
The door that someone opened wide
The road where someone's running yet
The woods that someone's passing through   10
The river someone's jumping in
The hospital where someone's dead.

Jacques Prévert (1900–1977)

It has been suggested that such parataxis makes us feel the poem is coming into being as we read it. Life, we might even say, is all parataxis: It presents us with situations and events; we have to determine their logical relationships.

PARALLELISM

One of the most ancient and powerful ways of organizing a sentence is to give corresponding parts corresponding expression. **Parallelism,** which is a kind of rhythm, is to be found in the poetry of all languages. We recognize it in such biblical cadences as those of Psalm 19:

The heavens declare the glory of God; and the
firmament showeth his handiwork.
Day unto day uttereth speech, and night unto night
showeth knowledge. . . .

We recognize it in the characteristic rhythms of Walt Whitman.

· I HEAR AMERICA SINGING ·

I hear America singing, the varied carols I hear,
Those of mechanics, each one singing his as it should be blithe and strong,
The carpenter singing his as he measures his plank or beam,
The mason singing his as he makes ready for work, or leaves off work,
The boatman singing what belongs to him in his boat, the deckhand
singing on the steamboat deck,

THE SHAPE OF THOUGHT

The shoemaker singing as he sits on his bench, the hatter singing
    as he stands,
The wood-cutter's song, the ploughboy's on his way in the morning,
    or at noon intermission or at sundown,
The delicious singing of the mother, or of the young wife at work, or
    of the girl sewing or washing,
Each singing what belongs to him or her and to none else,
The day what belongs to the day—at night the party of young fellows,
    robust, friendly,   *10*
Singing with open mouths their strong melodious songs.

Walt Whitman (1819–1892)

Parallel structures, by reinforcing each other, strengthen the sentence, paragraph, or poem they make up. Suppose we want to tell how once in battle a horseshoe nail fell out of a horseshoe, so that the horse was crippled and couldn't be managed—was in fact useless—with the result that horse and rider became ineffective as a combat unit. Since that rider played a key role in the battle plan, his loss led to the defeat of his army, so that the government also fell. All because a nail was lost!

    Concentrating these gangling elements into parallel clauses, we get the famous verses quoted by Benjamin Franklin and hung as a reminder in the offices of the Anglo-American Supply Quarters in London in World War II.

> For want of a nail, the shoe was lost,
> For want of a shoe, the horse was lost,
> For want of a horse, the rider was lost,
> For want of a rider, the battle was lost,
> For want of a battle, the kingdom was lost,
> And all for the want of a horseshoe nail.

Kenneth Fearing uses parallelism as a rhythmic principle in such passages as:

> Even when your friend, the radio, is still; even when
>   her dream, the magazine, is finished; even when his
>   life, the ticker, is silent; even when their destiny,
>   the boulevard, is bare;
> And after that paradise, the dance-hall, is closed; after
>   that theater, the clinic, is dark. . . .

Sometimes the parallel elements are crisscrossed, as in lines 4 and 6 of this passage from Yeats' "Easter 1916":

> The horse that comes from the road,
> The rider, the birds that range
> From cloud to tumbling cloud,
> Minute by minute they change;
> A shadow of cloud on the stream 5
> Changes minute by minute. . . .

This figure is called **chiasmus,** from the X-shaped Greek letter *chi*. A simple example would be: "I like football; baseball I hate."

Parallelism that contrasts words or ideas (often by means of "but" or a word like it) is called **antithesis;** it emphasizes conflicting materials by setting them sharply together. Alexander Pope, like other poets of the rational eighteenth century, likes to strike sparks by clashing the flint of one idea against the steel of another.

> Authors are partial to their wit, 'tis true,
> But are not critics to their judgment too?

> True wit is nature to advantage dressed,
> What oft was thought, but ne'er so well expressed.

SENTENCE STRUCTURE

Breaking up the shape of the sentence, some have felt, might enable us to get closer to the complex reality it oversimplifies. Some of the experiments of James Joyce and others have been directed to this end. So have some of the ancient figures of speech, which, as we have seen, are really ways of thinking.

Inversion of the normal word order is one of the most obvious of these figures of speech. Sometimes even good writers have been known to wrench words out of the natural order because they "need them there" for the rhyme or the rhythm; this is always an ugliness.

> Fast to the roof cleave may my tongue
> If mindless I of thee be found. . . .
>
> *Thomas Campion*

> . . . Old acquaintances
> Seem do we. . . .
>
> *Thomas Hardy*

THE SHAPE OF THOUGHT

Not all inversions are bad. Some we hear in colloquial speech. "But nice she is!" "A genius he is *not*!" Only our sense of spoken English tells us which inversions come naturally.

We allow Milton his inversion when he says of Satan:

> Him the Almighty Power
> Hurled headlong flaming from the ethereal sky
> With hideous ruin and combustion down
> To bottomless perdition . . .

This is upside-down—but so was Satan. When Andrew Marvell says of fate:

> And therefore her decrees of steel
> Us as the distant poles have placed. . . .

we can see that he is dramatizing the world-wide separation of the lovers by isolating "us" in the sentence. Bernard Spencer inverts his word order for the backward gesture of a Spanish dancer in his "Castanets":

> Back will go the head with the dark curls
> and the foot will stamp. . . .

E. E. Cummings uses inversion expressively in his little poem about the glance exchanged between a poisoned mouse and its poisoner.

· ME UP AT DOES ·

> Me up at does
>
> out of the floor
> quietly Stare
>
> a poisoned mouse
>
> still who alive   5
>
> is asking What
> have i done that
>
> You wouldn't have

E. E. Cummings (1894–1962)

Normally we look down on the helpless mouse. In this poem it is the reproachful upward glance of the mouse that is more telling; the words reverse as the electrical charge of the glances does.

Parenthesis also interrupts the conventional order of syntax in the interests of fidelity to thought. In a love poem of the Elizabethan Nicholas Breton, Coridon is so enraptured with his Phillida that he can speak hardly a line without exclamations of parenthetic enthusiasm:

> Fair in a morn (O fairest morn,
>   Was never morn so fair!)
> There shone a sun, though not the sun
>   That shineth in the air.
> For the earth and from the earth   5
>   (Was never such a creature!)
> Did come this face (was never face
>   That carried such a feature!).
> Upon a hill (O blessèd hill,
>   Was never hill so blessèd!)   10
> There stood a man (was never man
>   For woman so distressèd!)....

In Shakespeare's *Cymbeline* the guilty Iachimo is less happily distraught; his stricken parentheses play havoc with the sentence:

> Upon a time (unhappy was the clock
> That struck the hour!)—it was in Rome (accursed
> The mansion where!)—'twas at a feast (Oh, would
> Our viands had been poisoned, or at least
> Those which I heaved to head!)—the good Posthumus
> (What should I say? . . . .)

A few pages back we saw a particularly emotional parenthesis in Frost's "Out, Out—":

> . . . Then the boy saw all—
> Since he was old enough to know, big boy
> Doing a man's work, though a child at heart—
> He saw all spoiled.

There are other ways to break up the normal sentence structure to follow the working of the mind. We can start a sentence according to one pattern and abruptly abandon it midcourse for another. "What I'd really like to—how about a long walk?" We all use the device, called **anacolúthon** (*not following*), when impulse or a better thought cancels what we were about to say. Peter Viereck's unhappy and ungrammatical lover is entangled in it the moment he says "is" in the first line.

THE SHAPE OF THOUGHT

• TO HELEN OF TROY (N.Y.) •

I sit here with the wind is in my hair;
I huddle like the sun is in my eyes;
I am (I wished you'd contact me) alone.

A fat lot you'd wear crape if I was dead.
It figures, who I heard there when I phoned you;   5
It figures, when I came there, who has went.

Dogs laugh at me, folks bark at me since then;
"She is," they say, "no better than she ought to";
I love you irregardless how they talk.

You should of done it (which it is no crime)   10
With me you should of done it, what they say.
I sit here with the wind is in my hair.

Peter Viereck (b. 1916)

The incoherence of passion can also shatter the structure of a sentence, as when King Lear struggles to express himself to his unnatural daughters:

> I will have such revenges on you both
> That all the world shall—I will do such things—
> What they are, yet I know not. . . .

We can also start a sentence and abruptly cut it off, perhaps with the "or else—!" that we know can speak louder than words. This is called **aposiopésis** (*falling silent*). "Either you clean up your room, or else—!" Yeats likes to let passion interfere with sentence structure:

> Hanrahan rose in frenzy there
> And followed up those baying creatures towards—
>
> O towards I have forgotten what—enough!

In the poem that follows, the speaker is too choked with rage to continue.

• BEYOND WORDS •

> That row of icicles along the gutter
> Feels like my armory of hate;
> And you, you . . . you, you utter . . .
> You wait!

Robert Frost (1874–1963)

We have already seen quite a few poems that take liberties with conventional sentence structure. Kenneth Patchen's "Moon, Sun, Sleep, Birds, Live" (p. 128) represents three levels of thought and feeling at the same time. Another of his lyrics is in two interwoven voices, distinguished by two kinds of typography.

> O All down within the Pretty Meadow
>
>   *how many times, Death*
>   *have you done it*
>
>   The Lovers
>
>   *to just such golden ones*   5
>   *as these*
>
>   Toss at Their Wondrous Play
>
> *O how many times, Death, have you done it*
> *To just such golden ones as these*
>
>   *Kenneth Patchen (1911–1972)*

Archibald MacLeish's "You, Andrew Marvell" (see Anthology, p. 530) has the infinitive "to feel" as its subject, but we look in vain for a predicate. There is none. The fluidity of the syntax is encouraged by an almost total lack of punctuation: The poem moves forward as smoothly and steadily as the shadow of night does.

John Clare, the nineteenth-century poet who spent the last decades of his life in a benevolent insane asylum, was indifferent to sentence structure and punctuation in the wild tumble of words in his love song to Mary:

• REMEMBER DEAR MARY •

> Remember dear Mary love cannot deceive
> Loves truth cannot vary dear Mary believe
> You may hear and believe it believe it and hear
> Love could not deceive those features so dear
> Believe me dear Mary to press thy soft hand   5
> Is sweeter than riches in houses and Land
>
> Where I pressed thy soft hand at the dewfall o' eve
> I felt the sweet tremble that cannot deceive
> If love you believe in Belief is my love
> As it lived once in Eden ere we fell from above   *10*

THE SHAPE OF THOUGHT

To this heartless this friendless this desolate earth
And kept in first love Immortality's birth

'Tis there we last meet I adore thee and love thee
Theres nothing beneath thee around thee above thee
I feel it and know it I know so and feel   *15*
If your love cannot show it mine cannot conceal
But knowing I love I feel and adore
And the more I behold—only loves thee the more

John Clare (1793–1864)

Besides traveling at different paces and in different manners, sentences can also take us through different sectors of the language, or even break into regions not previously explored. The rest of this chapter will present a few samplings of the many kinds of terrain in which poets can go a-sentencing.

LEVELS OF LANGUAGE

Language has many levels, from the crudest to the most sublime. Poets avail themselves of an appropriate level—or sometimes get ironic effects by seeking out a deliberately inappropriate one, as Rochester does in his poem about the debauchee whom age and venereal disease have now incapacitated for the seduction, revelry, and rape to which his better years were devoted (see "The Disabled Debauchee," Anthology, p. 432). Not a lofty theme, but Rochester handles it as if it were—as if the aging rake were a "brave admiral" now in retirement, capable of serving only in an advisory capacity.

We are familiar with the language governments use in their press releases. We know that if our side has suffered a humiliating rout, official headlines can make things seem all right with "BRILLIANT STRATEGIC RETREAT CONFUSES FOE!" Robert Graves writes in this mode about the Battle of Marathon (490 B.C.), in which the outnumbered Athenians won a surprising victory over the "barbarians," as they called the Persians. Generally we read the Athenian version, as given by Herodotus: "There fell in the battle of Marathon, on the side of the barbarians, about six thousand and four hundred men; on that of the Athenians, one hundred and ninety-two." Graves imagines how the Persian press releases might have explained the incident at home.

THE MIND

· THE PERSIAN VERSION ·

Truth-loving Persians do not dwell upon
The trivial skirmish fought near Marathon.
As for the Greek theatrical tradition
Which represents that summer's expedition
Not as a mere reconnaissance in force   5
By three brigades of foot and one of horse
(Their left flank covered by some obsolete
Light craft detached from the main Persian fleet)
But as a grandiose, ill-starred attempt
To conquer Greece—they treat it with contempt;   10
And only incidentally refute
Major Greek claims, by stressing what repute
The Persian monarch and the Persian nation
Won by this salutary demonstration:
Despite a strong defence and adverse weather   15
All arms combined magnificently together.

Robert Graves (b. 1895)

Drawing on the horror movies of the late late shows in his poem about cat people, Edward Field uses a diction that accepts in a matter-of-fact way the melodramatic improbabilities of such films.

· CURSE OF THE CAT WOMAN ·

It sometimes happens
that the woman you meet and fall in love with
is of that strange Transylvanian people
with an affinity for cats.

You take her to a restaurant, say, or a show,   5
on an ordinary date, being attracted
by the glitter in her slitty eyes and her catlike walk,
and afterwards of course you take her in your arms
and she turns into a black panther
and bites you to death.   10

Or perhaps you are saved in the nick of time
and she is tormented by the knowledge of her tendency:
That she daren't hug a man
unless she wants to risk clawing him up.

This puts you both in a difficult position—   15
panting lovers who are prevented from touching
not by bars but by circumstance:
You have terrible fights and say cruel things
for having the hots does not give you a sweet temper.

One night you are walking down a dark street   20
and hear the pad-pad of a panther following you,
but when you turn around there are only shadows,
or perhaps one shadow too many.

You approach, calling, "Who's there?"
and it leaps on you.   25
Luckily you have brought along your sword
and you stab it to death.

And before your eyes it turns into the woman you love,
her breast impaled on your sword,
her mouth dribbling blood saying she loved you   30
but couldn't help her tendency.

So death released her from the curse at last,
and you knew from the angelic smile on her dead face
that in spite of a life the devil owned,
love had won, and heaven pardoned her.   35

Edward Field (b. 1924)

The business English of want ads and inventory is put to poignant use by Miller Williams in his lonely love poem.

· SALE ·

Partnership dissolved.
Everything must be sold.
Individually or the set
as follows:

Brain, one standard, cold.   5
Geared to glossing.
Given to hard replies.
Convolutions convey the illusion
of exceptional depth.
Damaged.   10

think. think of me. but you are not thinking

One pair of eyes. Green. Like new.
Especially good for girls and women walking,
wicker baskets,
paintings by Van Gogh,   15
red clocks and frogs, chicken snakes and snow.

look at me. but you are not looking at me

THE MIND

One pair of ears, big. Best offer takes.
Tuned to Bach, Hank Williams, bees,
the Book of Job.   20
Shut-off for deans, lieutenants and
salesman talking.

listen. listen please. but you are not listening

Mouth, one wide.
Some teeth missing.   25
Two and a half languages. Adaptable to pipes
and occasional kissing.
Has been broken but in good repair.
Lies.

tell me. tell me please. why won't you tell me   30

Hands, right and left.
Feet. Neck. Some hair.
Stomach, heart, spleen and
accessory parts.

come. come quickly. there is only a little time   35

Starts tomorrow
what you've been waiting for
and when it's gone it's gone
so hurry

hurry   40

Miller Williams (b. 1930)

NEW WORDS, NEW LANGUAGE

Probably the first step toward new ways of sentencing is a reworking
of the word itself. New insights, new awarenesses sometimes demand
new words; or new words can prove to be new insights. The quota-
tions that follow each use a word we would not find in a dictionary,
and yet the meaning is clear.

> . . . Over him arches
> UNITED STATES OF AMERICA, and, squinched in
> Between that and his rump, E PLURIBUS UNUM. . . .

Howard Nemerov

THE SHAPE OF THOUGHT

> . . . fields and hedges, the scarlotry of
> maple leaves. . . .
>
> *A. R. Ammons*

> The American from
> Minnesota
> Speaks Harvardly
> of Revolution—
> Men of the Mau Mau
> Smile
> Their fists holding
> Bits of
> Kenya earth.
>
> *Alice Walker*

"Squinched" and "scarlotry" are made up of words we know: the first of such words as "squeeze," "scrunch," "pinch"; the second of "scarlet" and "harlotry." They are like the "portmanteau" words that Lewis Carroll made up so successfully: "chortle" (from "chuckle" and "snort"), "galumph" (from "gallop" and "triumph"). Alice Walker's "Harvardly" we recognize as an ironic invention.

In a poem about Robert Frost, May Swenson, without inventing new words, uses typography to reveal the words that are hidden in other words. Part of it reads:

> Lots of trees in the fo
> rest but this one's an O
> a K that's plan
> ted hims elf . . .
>
> His sig nature's on the he art
> of his time. . . .

Spelling "forest" as fo/rest emphasizes the "rest" (or peace) in that forest—even for enemies. The "oak" is an O/a K because it is a fine oak, an O.K. oak. Frost, as oak, has not merely planted himself but *plan*ned to plant "hims" (hymns) and is *elf*ish, mischievous. "His sig nature" emphasizes its *natural*ness; his heart is a kind of "he art" or masculine art. In these few lines there are many more such ghostly conjurings.

Not all poets are inclined to break up or invent words. Some, like classic poker players, prefer to stick with the game as it is. On their side would be Frost himself, who stubbornly declares, "We play the words as we find them. We make them do."

John Berryman, in his *Dream Songs* (see Anthology, p. 554), has devised what often sounds like a new language. He has done this by combining various voices that range from hieratic English in the grand style to dialect and baby talk—a selection from the many tones possible to a psyche split many ways.

The nonadventure of "4" is typical of the poet's manner. ("Mr. Bones," or "Sir Bones," is the name for the end man in a minstrel show who clacked out castanetlike rhythms on the "bones.") "22" becomes clear if we recall that Thomas Jefferson and John Adams both died on the Fourth of July, 1826. Adams, knowing that death was near, roused himself to say, "Thomas Jefferson survives." But Jefferson had died a few hours before Adams did. The twelve characters of the first two stanzas might be seen as typical of the TV-watching public that makes up the nation such men as Jefferson and Adams founded. The poem might have a solemn message: We are unworthy of the heroes who founded our country. But it never takes so indignant or preachy a tone. For all of their basic passion, the voices themselves are colloquial and—in their dark way—amusing.

A poet who goes further in conjuring up a language of his own is Cummings.

· WHERELINGS WHENLINGS ·

wherelings whenlings
(daughters of ifbut offspring of hopefear
sons of unless and children of almost)
never shall guess the dimension of

him whose   5
each
foot likes the
here of this earth

whose both
eyes   10
love
this now of the sky

—endlings of isn't
shall never
begin   15
to begin to

imagine how(only are shall be were
dawn dark rain snow rain
-bow &
a   *20*

moon
's whis-
per
in sunset

or thrushes toward dusk among whippoorwills or   *25*
tree field rock hollyhock forest brook chickadee
mountain. Mountain)
whycoloured worlds of because do

not stand against yes which is built by
forever & sunsmell   *30*
(sometimes a wonder
of wild roses

sometimes)
with north
over   *35*
the barn

E. E. Cummings (1894–1962)

Cummings does only one thing that seems new here: He lets any part of speech serve for any other part. Conjunctions can be nouns, adverbs can be adjectives, pronouns can be verbs—anything can be anything. We might think of this as a modern invention, but the practice is so old that the grammarians have not only one term for it but several.

The Old English suffix "-ling" has many meanings. It can mean *having the quality of*, as "darlings" are *dear*, and "hirelings" are *hired*. It can mean *concerned with*, as "worldlings" are concerned with the *world*. It can be a diminutive, as in "gosling" and "suckling." Often it has unfavorable overtones, as in "hireling." When Cummings refers to "wherelings" and "whenlings," he means *petty* people, concerned with the local and the temporary instead of the spiritual; wondering "Where am I?" and "When will I . . . ?" instead of living and doing—always conditional, tentative, irresolute. They live in a nonexistent future, vacillating between "hope" and "fear." They will not do things "unless"; they do them only "almost." People who are really alive care about not the *where* of this earth but "the here of this earth"; what their eyes love is not the *when* of the sky but "this now of the sky." Unless we really live, really *are*, it can never be said of us that we *were*—it will be as if we had never existed. "Whycoloured worlds" (those of whining *why? why? why?*) can never stand against "yes," which for Cummings means the wholehearted acceptance of life and living.

His poem "anyone lived in a pretty how town" (see Anthology, p. 531) is easy to follow once we realize that "anyone," like the medieval Everyman, is a typical human being who marries a typical "noone" (a nobody, as outsiders might think), lives a typical life, dies a typical death, and has what we think of as a typical hereafter.

exercises & diversions

A. What matters discussed in this chapter are illustrated by the following quotations?

   1. Were I (who to my cost already am
      One of those strange, prodigious creatures, man)
      A spirit free to choose. . . .

The Earl of Rochester

   2. Ask of the learn'd the way, the learn'd are blind,
      This bids to serve, and that to shun mankind;
      Some place the bliss in action, some in ease,
      Those call it pleasure, and contentment these;
      Some sunk to beasts, find pleasure end in pain;
      Some swelled to gods, confess ev'n virtue vain;
      Or indolent, to each extreme they fall,
      To trust in everything, or doubt of all.

Alexander Pope

   3.   But how shall I . . . make me room there:
       Reach me a . . . Fancy, come faster—
     Strike you the sight of it? look at it loom there,
       Thing that she . . . There then! the Master. . . .

Gerard Manley Hopkins

4. Lived a woman wonderful,
        (May the Lord amend her!)
    Neither simple, kind, nor true,
    But her Pagan beauty drew
    Christian gentlemen a few
        Hotly to attend her.

    Rudyard Kipling

5. If you have revisited this town, thin Shade,
    Whether to look upon your monument
    (I wonder if the builder has been paid). . . .

    William Butler Yeats

6. Blinded the rooms wherein no foot falls.
    Faded the portraits on the walls.
    Reverberating, shakes the air
        A river there. . . .

    Walter de la Mare

7. Always—I tell you this they learned—
    Always at night when they returned
    To the lonely house from far away. . . .

    Robert Frost

8. The mountain held the town as in a shadow.
    I saw so much before I slept there once. . . .
    Near me it seemed. . . .

    Robert Frost

9. Troops went by the house and down the road and the dust they
    raised powdered the leaves of the trees. The trunks of the trees
    too were dusty and the leaves fell early that year and we saw
    the troops marching along the road and the dust rising and
    leaves, stirred by the breeze, falling and the soldiers marching
    and afterwards the road bare and white except for the leaves.

    Ernest Hemingway

10. Only, when loosening clothes, you lean
    Out of your window sleepily,
    And with luxurious, lidded mien

Sniff at the bitter dark—dear she,
Think somewhat gently of, between
Love ended and beginning, me.

Stanley J. Kunitz

11. I sat by a stream in a
perfect—except for willows—
emptiness. . . .

A. R. Ammons

12.   . . . How she loved
You, me, loved us all, the bird, the cat!

James Merrill

13. The rabbit with his pink, distinctly, eyes. . . .

John Updike

B. **1.** If a poem is written in stanzas (units of the same shape and length), should each stanza be a sentence? If you look back over poems we have read, does it seem that sentences have a tendency to fit the stanza shape, so that stanzas are likely to end with a period?

2. How could a writer use form expressively by *not* stopping for the stanza break but by overriding it?

3. This happens in "A Carriage from Sweden" (p. 520) and in "Bells for John Whiteside's Daughter" (p. 109). With what effect in each?

4. Go a-sentencing through some of the poems we have read earlier, noticing—for this once at least—the interplay between sentence structure and the demand of the form. Point out some interesting effects.

C. **1.** In "Acquainted with the Night" (p. 56), the length of the sentences, in number of lines, is 1, 1, 1, 1, 2, 7, 1. Is this structure related to meaning?

2. In "The End of the Weekend" (p. 12), what is the longest sentence? The shortest? Is the length significant?

D. **1.** How many sentences are there in "The Disabled Debauchee" (p. 432)? How does the elaborate structure of the first sentence help establish the tone of the poem?

exercises & diversions

2. The long "As . . . So . . ." (lines 1–13) is called an epic or Homeric simile, such as Homer uses to describe the Greeks going into battle:

As from his post on a hilltop a goatherd sees a cloud driven across the sea by a raging west wind, a cloud which even though far away looks black as pitch as it moves over the waves, bringing with it a furious storm, and the goatherd shudders to see it and hurries his goats into a cave, so the thick ranks of the sturdy Greeks move toward the battle. . . .

Why is the use of such a simile ironic in Rochester's poem (p. 432)?

3. Would a more parallel structure have strengthened the second stanza?

4. Find examples in this poem of a simile within a simile, metaphor, transferred epithets, synecdoche (or metonymy), oxymoron, puns, anacoluthon. Why are such figures of speech especially appropriate here?

5. Examine the adjectives. How many are used ironically?

E. 1. Quite a few expressions in "Curse of the Cat Woman" (p. 302) take on a special tone. How would you describe the tone of "It sometimes happens" (line 1), "that strange Transylvanian people" (line 3), "an affinity for cats" (line 4), "her tendency" (line 12), "or perhaps one shadow too many" (line 23), "Luckily you have brought along your sword" (line 26), "the woman you love" (line 28), "her breast impaled on" (line 29)?

2. In a differently handled poem, the last four lines might well be a hopeless tissue of clichés and sentimentality. What saves them here?

F. 1. Write a bad poem—sentimental, cliché-ridden—of about a dozen lines, ending up with the last four lines of Field's poem.
2. Write a long-sentence poem, a short-sentence poem, or a poem that expressively mixes long and short sentences.

12

Golden Numbers
ON NATURE AND FORM

If we leaf through a book of verse we notice immediately that poetry, unlike prose, favors special conformations; it likes to arrange itself in shapes on the page. These shapes in space originally represented shapes in time—shapes to be heard if we were listening to a recitation rather than looking at a book.

In its love for shapeliness and proportion, poetry is like mathematics. Many readers, however, believe that poetry and mathematics are opposed in spirit. Such readers may be repelled by the pages that follow, with their drawings that seem to be straight out of Euclid. But no mathematical background is required—there are no problems to solve. The drawings are only to marvel at. And to be seen as analogies: they are really telling us something about the nature of poetry, and about nature itself.

To decide in advance that a poem will have seventeen syllables or fourteen lines or that it will be constructed in stanzaic units of this or that size or shape may seem arbitrary and artificial. When a poem begins to germinate in the poet's mind, could it not grow simply and naturally, the way a flower grows, instead of being forced to follow a pattern? This seems a good question—but it shows little knowledge of how flowers do grow. Nature has been working on its flowers for some millions of years; a close look at them, as at anything in the natural world, will show why Pythagoras said that all things are number, why Plato said that God always geometrizes.

GOLDEN NUMBERS

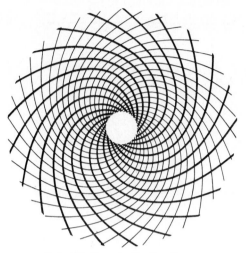

Spiral Pattern in the Sunflower

If we take a close look at the head of a sunflower, we see two sets of spirals whirling in opposite directions. The florets that make them up are not of any random number. Typically, there are twenty-one going clockwise and thirty-four going counterclockwise—numbers that a mathematician would come on with a thrill of recognition. They belong to the series of "golden numbers" called the Fibonacci sequence (after a thirteenth-century Italian mathematician), in which each number is the sum of the two preceding ones: 1, 1, 2, 3, 5, 8, 13, 21, 34, 55, and so on. Although the sequence may look like a man-made curiosity, it turns up again and again in nature—in the way rabbits breed, in the generation of bees, in the number and pattern of leaves or petals on certain plants, in the spirals of the sunflower. The sequence has been used by modern artists in placing units in their paintings and by modern musicians in planning the durations within their rhythms.

A further strangeness about the series is that the ratio between consecutive numbers, after the first few, remains about the same, coming closer and closer to a stabilization in which the smaller number is to the larger as .618 is to 1. This .618 ratio—familiar to the ancient Greeks and to most designers, artists, and architects ever since—is that of the golden section, a way of proportioning dimensions so that the parts (many believe) have the most aesthetically pleasing relationship to each other and to the whole.

THE MIND

In this division, the lesser part is to the greater as the greater is to the whole: $CB : AC :: AC : AB$.

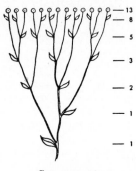

Sneezewort

It is also a ratio we have perceived, without being aware of it, in many things in nature. The human body, besides having bilateral symmetry, seems to have proportioned itself in accordance with the golden section. The length from the top of the head to the navel and the length from the navel to the toes have the ratio of about .618 to 1. These two divisions are subdivided. The length from navel to knee is to the length from knee to sole as 1 to .618. In reverse order, navel to throat and throat to top of head are related as 1 to .618. The architect Le Corbusier, who has planned buildings on the basis of the golden section, has even devised a scale for designers based on the proportions of the human body.

If bodily proportions might have given the Greeks a feeling for the golden section, geometry would have suggested it with more precision. The mysterious appeal of the ancient pentagram, or "endless knot," one of the most famous of all magic signs, owes much to its play of proportion. This star-shaped figure fairly glitters with its two hundred .618's. B cuts both AC and AD so as to give golden sections. BE is .618 of AB, and so on. The followers of Pythagoras used the pentagram as their secret sign. It stood not only for health and love but for the human body itself, which was thought to be organized in fives: five senses, four limbs and a head, five fingers (their three bones having the golden proportion).

GOLDEN NUMBERS

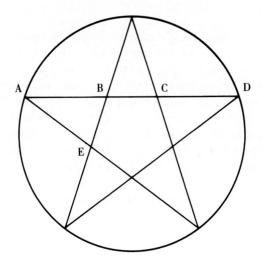

Since the pentagram also stood for the letters in the name "Jesus," it was thought to be an object of fear to hellish spirits. When Mephistopheles finds the pentagram's *Drudenfuss*, or "wizard's foot," drawn on Faust's threshold, it takes some trickery to get by it. Its shape—as with good poems—is its power. In the pentagram—as in good poems—mathematics and magic come together. We are affected by precise relationships we are not conscious of.

If we take a line divided according to the golden section, bend the shorter part upward, and then complete the rectangle, we have the golden rectangle with its "divine proportion," which, with the section itself, is supposed to have had an important influence on ancient art and architecture, determining, it may be, the structure of the pyramids and of the Parthenon, which fits neatly into it. Certainly it made itself felt in the Renaissance (Da Vinci made use of it) and ever since, right down to the architecture of Le Corbusier and the art of Seurat and Mondrian. In 1912 one group of artists even exhibited in Paris as the "Golden Section" painters. It was with them that Marcel Duchamp first showed his *Nude Descending a Staircase*. We can still find this proportion in modern buildings and in many common objects—envelopes, playing cards, magazines. Perhaps we like this rectangle because its proportions correspond with our oval field of vision.

THE MIND

The golden rectangle has been called, with something like Oriental mysteriousness, "the rectangle of the whirling squares." If we divide it by the golden section so that one part is a square, the smaller area will itself be a second golden rectangle within the first (A). If we divide the smaller rectangle in the same way, the same thing will happen—another square, another golden rectangle (B). We can continue in this way, making smaller and smaller squares as we whirl around clockwise. If we then connect, with an evenly curving line, corresponding points of all the squares (C), we will have one of the most beautiful curves in mathematics and one of the most beautiful lines in nature—the logarithmic spiral, whose allure moved one admirer to ask that it be engraved on his tombstone.

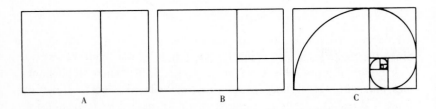

This graceful curve, which seems to have been artificially constructed at a drawing board, probably appears most spectacularly in the nautilus seashell, a favorite of collectors. As the creature in the seashell grows, it moves onward, in a spiral, into larger and larger chambers, all of them having the same proportions. Oliver Wendell Holmes found a moral here, which he expressed, by means of a stanza form that itself expands, in "The Chambered Nautilus."

> Build thee more stately mansions, O my soul,
>   As the swift seasons roll!
> Leave thy low-vaulted past!
>   Let each new temple, nobler than the last,
> Shut thee from heaven with a dome more vast
>   Till thou at last art free,
> Leaving thine outgrown shell by life's unresting sea.

We find this same curve in the sunflower head and the daisy, in the pine cone and the pineapple, all of which have their opposing spirals in Fibonacci numbers. We find it where the time element of living growth has left its shape on matter—in the curling horns of mountain goats, in the tusks of elephants, in the claws of a cat, the beak of a parrot. It appears in transitory fashion in the coil of an elephant's trunk or a monkey's tail, in a lock of hair falling naturally.

GOLDEN NUMBERS

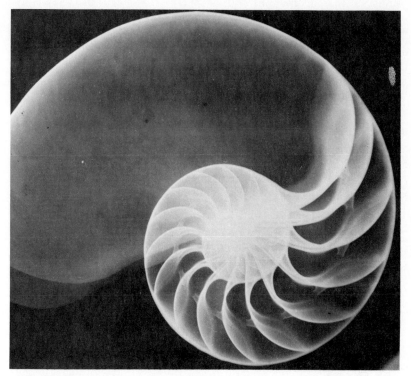

(Leonard Lessin/ Photo Researchers, Inc.)

Part of the pleasure we feel in contemplating this spiral may come from our awareness of its continuous proportion, which, in a world of change, gives us the reassurance of what remains similar to itself. Certain well-managed patterns in poetry may have an analogous effect.

Poets cannot hope to work with the geometrical precision of nature. Most trust their own sense of proportion, developed from study, contemplation, and exercise. But Dante does give a mathematical framework to his *Divine Comedy*. And Vergil, Dante's guide, appears to have made an almost unbelievable use of the proportions of the golden section and the Fibonacci numbers (as they were later named).* In Book IV of the *Aeneid*, for example, Dido, seeing she is about to be

---

* George E. Duckworth, *Structural Patterns and Proportions in Vergil's* Aeneid (Ann Arbor: University of Michigan Press, 1962).

deserted by her lover Aeneas, asks her sister Anna to go and plead with him. This is a passionate moment, but not so passionate that Vergil lets his mathematical composition get out of control. He describes the scene in sections of 5, 8, and 13 lines—all numbers in the basic Fibonacci sequence.

13 {

8 {
Look, Anna, all that scurrying on the seashore,
Crowds everywhere, sails restless for the wind,
The sailors, glad to go, arranging garlands.
Well, as I saw this trouble brewing once,
So, sister, I'll endure it. Just one thing   5
That you could do in kindness. It was you
That liar was polite to, liked to talk with.
You knew his ways, and how to manage with him.

5 {
Go, dear; go coax a little. Tell His Arrogance
I wasn't there at Aulis when those Greeks   10
Swore death to all the Trojans; didn't send
Warships to Troy; and didn't kill his father.
Why won't he even listen when I speak?

13 {

8 {
Where is he rushing off to? Let him do
His love a final favor: wait for friendly   15
Weather and easier sailing. Once he loved me—
I don't ask that again; won't block his glorious
Future. I only ask: a quiet interval.
Time to get used to suffering, used to grief.
Pity your sister. Say it's all I'm asking.   20
Say I'll return his favor—with my life.

Anna's visit to Aeneas is described in the section that follows—in exactly thirteen lines. These two passages would prove nothing. But when we are told that more than a thousand such correspondences have been found in the *Aeneid*, it does begin to look as if Vergil constructed his episodes like little equations and then related them like larger equations of the same proportions, so that his whole work is a kind of mathematical symphony, as orderly as the music of Bach.

Contrived as this intricacy may seem to be, we can hardly call it artificial. Nature—in the seashell, in the daisy, in a lock of hair—far outdoes our artists in the use of mathematical symmetry. All that matters, in any art, is that the calculation and effort should not show, that we see the ease and elegance of the achievement but not the labor that went into it. It is important to realize that imposing a form is not in any way unnatural—Parthenon and nautilus owe their beauty to the same kind of mathematical harmony.

William Blake once wrote: "Without Minute Neatness of Execution the Sublime cannot Exist! Grandeur of ideas is founded on Precision of Ideas." Yeats saw no contradiction between calculated precision and human passion. He once praised Lady Gregory's house as a place in which "passion and precision have been one." He insisted to a friend that "the very essence of genius, of whatever kind, is precision." In "The Statues" he is concerned with the relationship between passion, beauty, and mathematical precision.

• THE STATUES •

Pythagoras planned it. Why did the people stare?
His numbers, though they moved or seemed to move
In marble or in bronze, lacked character.
But boys and girls, pale from the imagined love
Of solitary beds, knew what they were,   5
That passion could bring character enough,
And pressed at midnight in some public place
Live lips upon a plummet-measured face.

No! Greater than Pythagoras, for the men
That with a mallet or a chisel modelled these   10
Calculations that look but casual flesh, put down
All Asiatic vague immensities,
And not the banks of oars that swam upon
The many-headed foam at Salamis.
Europe put off that foam when Phidias   15
Gave women dreams and dreams their looking-glass.

One image crossed the many-headed, sat
Under the tropic shade, grew round and slow,
No Hamlet thin from eating flies, a fat
Dreamer of the Middle Ages. Empty eyeballs knew   20
That knowledge increases unreality, that
Mirror on mirror mirrored is all the show.
When gong and conch declare the hour to bless
Grimalkin crawls to Buddha's emptiness.

When Pearse summoned Cuchulain to his side,   25
What stalked through the Post Office? What intellect,
What calculation, number, measurement, replied?
We Irish, born into that ancient sect
But thrown upon this filthy modern tide
And by its formless spawning fury wrecked,   30
Climb to our proper dark, that we may trace
The lineaments of a plummet-measured face.

William Butler Yeats (1865–1939)

THE MIND

. . . And pressed at midnight in some public place
Live lips upon a plummet-measured· face. . . .

Roman copy of the *Diadoumenus* of Polykleitos
(The Metropolitan Museum of Art, Fletcher Fund, 1925)

In the first stanza, Pythagoras is given credit for the emphasis on proportion in Greek sculpture, which might seem cold to a cold observer. But boys and girls saw their dreams of love embodied in these perfect shapes.

In the second stanza, the spirit of the sculptors, even more than the courage of Greek sailors, is seen as defending the precision of Athenian ideals against the abstractions of Eastern thought. (In 480 B.C. at Salamis, the Greeks defeated the much larger Persian fleet. Phidias was the probable designer of the statuary on the Parthenon.)

In the third stanza, an Eastern Buddha figure, fat and dreamy, out of contact with the physical world and the passionate precision of mathematics, is seen taking over as the Greek spirit declines. ("Gong and conch" suggest an Oriental call to prayer; "Grimalkin" is an old cat or an old woman.)

In the fourth stanza, the Easter Rising of 1916 in Dublin is recalled, when, under the command of Patrick Pearse, Irish nationalist forces seized the Post Office. Cuchulain (Coo-hóo-lin) was a legendary Irish hero whose statue was set up in the Post Office when it was rebuilt after the shelling. Here, Cuchulain (and Pearse) represent "intellect . . . calculation, number, measurement," like that of ancient Athens at its best. These qualities, Yeats believed, were desirable in the formlessness of the modern world.

Yeats would have agreed with one of the conclusions of this section: there is nothing unnatural in our desire to find form and pattern in our experience. We can hardly keep from doing so. When we look at the starry skies, all we really see are swarms of bright specks. But we have never been content to see that way. We see hunters and great bears and rocking chairs and dippers. Or we see figures like lions and scorpions and fish, which we name Leo and Scorpio and Pisces, relating them to long-dead languages. We like to believe there are connections between these imaginary creatures and the temperament and fate of human beings born under them. Everywhere we like to find the reassurance of form.

Part of the shapeliness of poems comes from the way certain of their parts correspond. This is true not only of poems. A popular song some decades back declared, "I met a million-dollar baby in the five-and-ten-cent store." The lover had to meet his girl in *that* store so that "million dollar" could be played off against "five-and-ten-cent." Sing, "I met a million-dollar baby in the local A&P," and the point is gone.

So when Wilfred Owen writes in "Greater Love,"

> Red lips are not so red
> As the stained stones kissed by the English dead. . . .

two crimson things are significantly contrasted.

Often a speaker in Shakespeare completes a pattern by echoing a word or image the preceding speaker had used, as Cassius echoes Casca in *Julius Caesar*:

> CASCA: Indeed, they say the senators tomorrow
> Mean to establish Caesar as a king,
> And he shall wear his crown by sea and land
> In every place save here in Italy.
> CASSIUS: I know where I will wear this dagger then;
> Cassius from bondage will deliver Cassius. . . .

In *A Comedy of Errors*, Egeon, about to be executed, is comforted to find correspondences even in disaster:

> Yet this my comfort: when your words are done,
> My woes end likewise with the evening sun.

We can also look for correspondences between the content of a poem and its shape. But the shape of a poem, like its sound, cannot express much apart from the meaning. We might feel a nervous quality in short, fitful, uneven lines, or sustained power in long, even ones, as we might get a sense of crescendo or decrescendo from the shape of stanzas. Blake probably felt that the short lines of his "The Fly" were appropriate. Flies do not go in for long-distance flights.

> Little fly,
> Thy summer's play
> My thoughtless hand
> Has brushed away.
>
> Am not I
> A fly like thee. . . .

He probably thought that the long lines of his "Holy Thursday" were appropriate for its processional content. His own drawing shows a long line of children across the page, above and below the verses:

> 'Twas on a Holy Thursday, their innocent faces clean,
> The children walking two & two in red & blue & green. . . .

John Donne seems particularly fond of a stanza form that dramatizes a crescendo, an excitement mounting to a climax. Lines (as heard, but not necessarily as printed) are shorter toward the beginning of a stanza, longer toward the end, though in no regular progression. Rhymes also tend to amass, to intensify, toward the close. This is the pattern in which he thinks and feels.

· THE ANNIVERSARY ·

All kings and all their favorites,
    All glory of honors, beauties, wits,
The sun itself, which makes times as they pass,
Is elder by a year now than it was
When thou and I first one another saw: *5*
All other things to their destruction draw,
    Only our love hath no decay;
This, no tomorrow hath nor yesterday;
Running, it never runs from us away,
But truly keeps his first, last, everlasting day.   *10*

Two graves must hide thine and my corse;
    If one might, death were no divorce.
Alas, as well as other princes, we
(Who prince enough in one another be)
Must leave at last in death these eyes and ears,   *15*
Oft fed with true oaths and with sweet salt tears;
    But souls where nothing dwells but love
(All other thoughts being inmates) then shall prove
This, or a love increasèd there above,
When bodies to their graves, souls from their graves remove.   *20*

And then we shall be thoroughly blest,
    But we no more than all the rest;
Here upon earth we're kings, and none but we
Can be such kings, nor of such subjects be.
Who is so safe as we? where none can do   *25*
Treason to us, except one of us two.
    True and false fears let us refrain;
Let us love nobly, and live, and add again
Years and years unto years, till we attain
To write threescore: this is the second of our reign.   *30*

John Donne (1572–1631)

There is the same kind of gathering intensity, dramatized by the form, in "A Valediction: Of Weeping" (see Anthology, p. 412), which begins with the image of a woman's face, at parting, reflected in the falling tears of her lover. In these poems Donne's stanza form moves from less to more, with a sense of mounting excitement. The line arrangement Christina Rossetti chooses for her "An Easter Carol" is appropriate for the exuberance she feels. It begins:

---

[11]/**corse:** *corpse*   [18]/**inmates:** *mere tenants*

THE MIND

> Spring bursts today,
> For Christ has risen and all the world's at play.
>
> Flash forth, thou Sun.
> The rain is over and gone, its work is done. . . .

We get just an opposite effect—from more to less—in the sense of deprivation with which a poem ascribed to Francis Bacon opens:

> The world's a bubble, and the life of man
> Less than a span;
> In his conception wretched, from the womb
> So to the tomb. . . .

In Robert Herrick's happier poem, "The Thanksgiving," the lineation again follows a psychological motive—that of curtailment, littleness, humility. It begins:

> Lord, Thou hast given me a cell
> Wherein to dwell;
> And little house, whose humble roof
> Is weather-proof;
> Under the spars of which I lie   5
> Both soft and dry;
> Where Thou my chamber for to ward
> Hast set a guard
> Of harmless thoughts, to watch and keep
> Me, while I sleep. . . .   10

The adjectives—"little," "humble"—go with the curtailed form, in which Herrick takes a four-beat line and then cuts it in half. Something like the sadness of deprivation is to be felt in the short last line of the stanza that Keats uses in "La Belle Dame Sans Merci" (see Anthology, p. 451). In David Wagoner's poem "The Other Side of the Mountain," a short line has a different effect, that of heels digging in to resist the momentum of the long line:

> To walk downhill you must lean partially backwards,
> Heels digging in,
> While your body gets more help than it can use
> In following directions. . . .

Yeats, in an early poem, dramatizes the poignancy of loss not by using a short line, but by omitting an expected one. The poem starts with a regular quatrain, *a b a b;* then there are three lines of another quatrain; and—just when we expect the fourth line—nothing more.

GOLDEN NUMBERS

· THE LOVER MOURNS FOR THE LOSS OF LOVE ·

>Pale brows, still hands and dim hair,
>I had a beautiful friend
>And dreamed that the old despair
>Would end in love in the end:
>She looked in my heart one day   5
>And saw your image was there;
>She has gone weeping away.

>*William Butler Yeats (1865–1939)*

We are left waiting for the line that never comes.

Sometimes the shape of verse forms may be expressive, as the spiral of the nautilus expresses the life force that shaped it, or as the snowflake expresses the molecular geometry within. At other times the shape seems arbitrary or accidental—though if a verse form continues to live it must somehow fit the way we feel and think. If the logic of a form eludes us, we might think of it as we think of games. Why *three* strikes in baseball? Why *four* balls? Why the rigidly fixed forms of Olympic events, the 440s and 880s? Without rules, games are impossible. We know what rage a hard-core poker player feels when a slaphappy beginner, given dealer's choice, makes up a fancy variant of his or her own: free-form poker. Too many wild cards, and the game is meaningless.

The next section will consider some of the forms available to writers. Few poets have written in all of them; some have confined themselves to one or two; most have tried their hand at several. Certain poets, like Thomas Hardy, prefer to make up their own shapes. As Kipling said:

>There are nine and sixty ways of constructing tribal lays,
>   *And—every—single—one—of—them—is—right!*

FIXED STANZA FORMS

Some forms have no fixed number of lines—they run on until they end. **Blank verse**—unrhymed iambic pentameter—is the most familiar. Shakespeare's plays are, except for a few lines here and there, written in blank verse. We have seen it in MacLeish's "Eleven" (p. 7) and Frost's "Out, Out—" (p. 292). Other forms are arranged in **stanzas,**

Nature often prefers to work in fixed forms. The snowflake, after millions of years, is still a hexagonal structure. Yet no two are alike.
(From Snow Crystals *by W. A. Bentley and W. H. Humphreys)*

identical units of groups of lines. The Italian word *stanza* means a *room*, a *stopping place*. (Nonstanzaic divisions, as in blank verse, can be called *verse paragraphs*.)

We can find poems of just one line.

• EXIT LINE •

Love should intend realities: good-bye!

John Ciardi (b. 1916)

"Good-bye," said the river, "I'm going downstream."

Howard Nemerov (b. 1920)

Two-line poems are more common: We saw an example in Pope's little poem on Sir Isaac Newton (p. 39). Here are two others:

• UPON THE DEATH OF SIR ALBERT MORTON'S WIFE •

He first deceased; she for a little tried
To live without him, liked it not, and died.

Sir Henry Wotton (1568–1639)

• ON READING ALOUD MY EARLY POEMS •

This ignorance upon my tongue
Was once the wisdom of the young.

John Williams (b. 1922)

Many poems are composed in **couplets** (units of two lines): Blake's poem about the tiger (p. 440); Swift's about the morning (p. 434); Marvell's about his mistress (p. 429). The "heroic couplets" of Dryden and Pope (called "heroic" because used in early translations of the heroic poems of Homer and Vergil) were, for a century, the favorite verse form.

Three-line Stanzas

Rhyme schemes, as we mentioned before, are diagramed by using the same letter for each rhyming sound. Lines ending with *roam, sea, home, free* would be indicated by *a b a b*; lines ending with *sky, earth, mirth, fly* by *a b b a*. Unrhymed lines are indicated by an *x*.

Three-line units are constructed most simply by having them rhyme *a a a, b b b,* and so on.

· UPON JULIA'S CLOTHES ·

Whenas in silks my Julia goes,
Then, then, methinks, how sweetly flows
The liquefaction of her clothes.

Next, when I cast mine eyes and see
That brave vibration each way free,   5
Oh how that glittering taketh me!

Robert Herrick (1591–1674)

For another example, see Frost's "Provide, Provide" (Anthology, p. 506).

In "Acquainted with the Night" (p. 56), Frost uses the most celebrated of three-line units, **terza rima,** the "triple rhyme" that Dante and others had used. The rhyme scheme is *a b a, b c b, c d c,* and so on, with the middle rhyme of each **tercet** (group of three) becoming the first and third rhyme of the following group. The interconnection of tercets, the way one leads to and sustains the next, gives this form a continuity and momentum such as few others have. Shelley's "Ode to the West Wind" (see Anthology, p. 448) is written in sections of terza rima, each closed with a couplet.

Four-line Stanzas

The commonest stanza form in European literature is the **quatrain,** or four-line stanza. Psychologists may account for its popularity by recalling that Carl Jung, with much support from mythology and religious symbols, thought the nucleus of the psyche normally expressed itself in a fourfold structure. For Blake, the number four stood for perfection; for Pound (in "Canto 91"), "the whole creation [was] concerned with FOUR." Robert Creeley, though writing in threes, says in his poem "Four":

> This number for me
> is comfort, a secure
> fact of things. The
>
> table stands on
> all fours. The dog   5
> walks comfortably,

and two by two
is not an army
but friends who love

one another. Four   *10*
is a square,
or peaceful circle,

celebrating return,
reunion,
love's triumph. . . .   *15*

Dante Gabriel Rossetti's "The Woodspurge" (see Anthology, p. 481) is an expressive example of a quatrain in monorhyme (*a a a a*), but that rhyme scheme is unusual. The quatrain most often used is the **ballad stanza,** of which we have seen many examples ("Western Wind," p. 6; "Sir Patrick Spens," p. 14; "The Unquiet Grave," p. 104). Lines 1 and 3 are iambic tetrameter (or sometimes $\cup - | \cup - | \cup - | \cup$); lines 2 and 4 are iambic trimeter. The rhyme scheme is *a b a b*, or, more often, *x a x a*, as in "Western Wind" and in most of the poems of Emily Dickinson, who, uninterested in metrical experiment, did most of her work in this simplest of forms. Wordsworth favored the *a b a b* stanza in his Lucy poems.

• A SLUMBER DID MY SPIRIT SEAL •

A slumber did my spirit seal;
    I had no human fears:
She seemed a thing that could not feel
    The touch of earthly years.

No motion has she now, no force;   *5*
    She neither hears nor sees;
Rolled round in earth's diurnal course,
    With rocks, and stones, and trees.

William Wordsworth (1770–1850)

Another well-known quatrain is Tennyson's "In Memoriam" stanza: four tetrameters rhyming *a b b a* in "envelope" fashion—the *a*-rhymes enclose the stanza.

Ring out, wild bells, to the wild sky,
    The flying cloud, the frosty light.
    The year is dying in the night;
Ring out, wild bells, and let him die.

THE MIND

Ring out the old, ring in the new,   5
   Ring, happy bells, across the snow:
   The year is going, let him go;
Ring out the false, ring in the true.

Five-line Stanzas

There are many possible ways of combining rhymes and line lengths
in five-line stanzas. No one form has become standard. A common
practice is to take a familiar quatrain and add an additional rhyming
line. Poe uses three different arrangements (as the indentations in-
dicate) in one of his best poems.

• TO HELEN •

Helen, thy beauty is to me
   Like those Nicéan barks of yore,
That gently, o'er a perfumed sea,
   The weary, way-worn wanderer bore
   To his own native shore.   5

On desperate seas long wont to roam,
   Thy hyacinth hair, thy classic face,
Thy Naiad airs have brought me home
   To the glory that was Greece,
And the grandeur that was Rome.   10

Lo! in yon brilliant window-niche
   How statue-like I see thee stand,
   The agate lamp within thy hand!
Ah, Psyche, from the regions which
   Are Holy-Land!   15

Edgar Allan Poe (1809–1849)

The arrangement in the first stanza is the one Saint John of the Cross
uses, with lines of different length, in his poem "The Dark Night" (p.
57). (His stanza form, well known in Spanish poetry, is called the
lira.)

2/**Nicéan:** *several ancient cities were named Nicea*
8/**Naiad:** *a water nymph*
14/**Psyche:** *the soul personified as a goddess*

Six-line Stanzas

Stanzas of six lines or more are likely to be made up of simpler elements. The "Venus-and-Adonis stanza" (named for Shakespeare's poem) is a quatrain with a couplet added: *a b a b c c*. Sir Edward Dyer uses it in "The Lowest Trees Have Tops" (see Anthology, p. 403); Tichborne in his "Elegy" (p. 410). One of the most individual six-line units is the "Burns stanza" or "Scottish stanza," an *a a a b a b*, in which the *a*'s are tetrameter, the *b*'s dimeter. Robert Burns' "To a Mouse" begins:

> Wee, sleeket, cowran, tim'rous beastie,
> O, what a panic's in thy breastie!
> Thou need na start awa sae hasty,
>   Wi' bickering brattle!
> I wad be laith to rin an' chase thee,   *5*
>   Wi' murd'ring pattle!
>
> I'm truly sorry Man's dominion
> Has broken Nature's social union,
> An' justifies that ill opinion,
>   Which makes thee startle,   *10*
> At me, thy poor, earth-born companion,
>   An' fellow-mortal! . . . .

More recent poets often prefer looser arrangements. Robert Lowell's "Skunk Hour" (see Anthology, p. 558), keeps to no fixed scheme in its six-line stanzas about a degenerate New England culture as seen by a speaker whose mind is "not right." (What goodness there is seems to belong to the animals, who live according to their nature with assurance and courage.) John Berryman uses six-line stanzas, rhyming variously, in his *Dream Songs* (see Anthology, p. 554).

Seven-line Stanzas

Among the seven-line possibilities, *a b a b b c c*, called **rhyme royal** (apparently because it was used by a poet-king of Scotland), stands out as especially attractive. We see it in Wyatt's "They Flee from Me" (see Anthology, p. 403) and, among modern poems, in the wider stanzas of W. H. Auden's "The Shield of Achilles" (p. 102).

---

[1]/**sleeket, cowran:** *glossy, cowering*
[3]/**na start awa sae:** *not start away so*
[4]/**wi' bickering brattle:** *with hasty scuttle, hurry-scurry*

[5]/**wad be laith to rin:** *would be loath to run*
[6]/**pattle:** *shovel*

Eight-line Stanzas

The best-known eight-line stanza, an iambic pentameter *a b a b a b c c*, is called **ottava rima** or "eighth rhyme." Its most brilliant success in English is in *Don Juan*. Byron's passion and wit find themselves at home with the elaborate build-up of the triple rhyme, followed by the opportunity for a sudden wisecrack or anticlimax in the concluding couplet.

> And Julia's voice was lost, except in sighs,
>   Until too late for useful conversation;
> The tears were gushing from her gentle eyes,
>   I wish, indeed, they had not had occasion;
> But who, alas, can love, and then be wise?   5
>   Not that remorse did not oppose temptation:
> A little still she strove, and much repented,
> And whispering "I will ne'er consent"—consented.

But ottava rima can be used seriously too, as in Yeats' "The Statues" (p. 319), "Among School Children" (see Anthology, p. 499), and many of his more thoughtful later poems. There are, of course, a great many other ways of building up an eight-line stanza out of simpler elements.

Nine-line Stanzas

The classic nine-line form is the Spenserian stanza, devised for *The Faerie Queene*. The iambic lines, the first eight of which are pentameter and the last of which is an alexandrine, are richly rhymed: *a b a b b c b c c*. This stanza form was a favorite of the Romantic poets. A stanza from Byron and one from Shelley will show how the form moves through its elaborate pattern, pivoting on the fifth line to begin almost a new movement and closing with the longer, slower line—an effect like the concluding chords of a piece of music.

> There is a pleasure in the pathless woods,
> There is a rapture on the lonely shore,
> There is society, where none intrudes,
> By the deep sea, and music in its roar:
> I love not man the less, but nature more,   5
> From these our interviews, in which I steal
> From all I may be, or have been before,
> To mingle with the universe, and feel
> What I can ne'er express, yet cannot all conceal.

George Gordon, Lord Byron

He has outsoared the shadow of our night;
Envy and calumny and hate and pain,
And that unrest which men miscall delight,
Can touch him not and torture not again;
From the contagion of the world's slow stain   *5*
He is secure, and now can never mourn
A heart grown cold, a head grown gray in vain;
Nor, when the spirit's self has ceased to burn,
With sparkless ashes load an unlamented urn.

                     Percy Bysshe Shelley

Keats uses the Spenserian stanza in "The Eve of St. Agnes" (see Anthology, p. 456). Although today it seems somewhat literary, this stanza form continues to come to life with the right handling. Daryl Hine chooses it for his "Bluebeard's Wife"; Robert Bagg for "The Tandem Ride," a story about Amherst students pedaling off at night in search of a madcap Smithie, who escapes them by diving into a pond with what must be the only bellyflop ever recorded in Spenserian stanzas:

         Our cocked ears took the slap
         Of a skinspankeroo of a bellyflop. . . .

John Updike has chosen Spenserians for "The Dance of the Solids," which is about the atomic structure of solid-state matter. His scientific terminology is almost a burlesque of Spenser's courtly abstractions.

      The *Polymers*, those giant Molecules,
      Like Starch and Polyoxymethylene,
      Flesh out, as protein serfs and plastic fools,
      This Kingdom with Life's Stuff. Our time has seen
      The synthesis of Polyisoprene   *5*
      And many cross-linked Helixes unknown
      To *Robert Hooke*; but each primordial Bean
      Knew Cellulose by heart. *Nature* alone
    Of Collagen and Apatite compounded Bone.

FIXED FORMS FOR POEMS

Besides the fixed stanza forms, there are designs for the complete poem. The most famous—and most notorious—is the **sonnet,** which has no rival in popularity. It has been a favorite of some of the best poets—and some of the worst. The name is from the Italian *sonnetto*, which means *little sound* or *little song*. Part of its appeal is in its brevity—a sonnet can easily be read in less than sixty seconds. But, though brief, the sonnet is ingeniously organized, its fourteen iambic pentameter lines rhyming in various ways. The Italian (or Petrarchan) sonnet is divided into an octave (eight lines) and a sestet (six lines). The 6:8:14 proportions come very close to the 5:8:13 of the Fibonacci numbers and the golden section. People seem to feel, for whatever reason, something satisfying in the proportions. The octave of the Italian sonnet, with its many interrelated symmetries, has a rhyme scheme of *a b b a a b b a*. The sestet combines two or three rhymes in almost any possible way, although final couplets are generally avoided. Common patterns are *c d c d c d* or *c d e c d e*.

Since a sonnet of this kind needs four rhymes for both *a*'s and *b*'s, it is not an easy form to use in English. Yet poets continue to write Petrarchan sonnets. George Meredith chose it to express cosmic fear and awe, with space imagery like that of the telephotography of the astronauts.

· LUCIFER IN STARLIGHT ·

On a starred night Prince Lucifer uprose.
Tired of his dark dominion swung the fiend
Above the rolling ball in cloud part screened,
Where sinners hugged their spectre of repose.
Poor prey to his hot fit of pride were those.   5
And now upon his western wing he leaned,
Now his huge bulk o'er Afric's sands careened,
Now the black planet shadowed Arctic snows.
Soaring through wider zones that pricked his scars
With memory of the old revolt from Awe,   10
He reached a middle height, and at the stars,
Which are the brain of heaven, he looked, and sank.
Around the ancient track marched, rank on rank,
The army of unalterable law.

George Meredith (1828–1909)

Berryman's Sonnets contains 115 poems in the Petrarchan form. One gives the picture of a girl, "blonde, barefoot, beautiful"—but scarcely the Petrarchan ideal. She drinks too much, likes to lie on the floor listening to music, is willful, cannot forbear. The three alliterating adjectives used to describe her are like the girl's willfulness: they are an unrhymed intrusion, a fifteenth line, in a poem otherwise regular.

· SIGH AS IT ENDS ·

Sigh as it ends . . . I keep an eye on your
Amour with Scotch,—too *cher* to consummate;
Faster your disappearing beer than late-
ly mine; your naked passion for the floor;
Your hollow leg; your hanker for one more   5
Dark as the Sundam Trench; how you dilate
Upon psychotics of this class, collate
Stages, and . . how long since you, well, *forbore.*

Ah, but the high fire sings on to be fed
Whipping our darkness by the lifting sea   10
A while, O darling drinking like a clock.
The tide comes on: spare, Time, from what you spread
Her story,—tilting a frozen Daiquiri,
Blonde, barefoot, beautiful,
    flat on the bare floor rivetted to Bach.   15

John Berryman (1914–1972)

The rhyme scheme of the English (or Shakespearean) sonnet is less demanding: *a b a b, c d c d, e f e f, g g*: three quatrains and a final couplet.

· SONNET 29 ·

When, in disgrace with fortune and men's eyes,
I all alone beweep my outcast state,
And trouble deaf heaven with my bootless cries,
And look upon myself and curse my fate,
Wishing me like to one more rich in hope,   5
Featured like him, like him with friends possessed,
Desiring this man's art, and that man's scope,
With what I most enjoy contented least;
Yet in these thoughts myself almost despising,
Haply I think on thee, and then my state,   10
Like to the lark at break of day arising
From sullen earth, sings hymns at heaven's gate;
    For thy sweet love remembered such wealth brings,
    That then I scorn to change my state with kings.

William Shakespeare (1564–1616)

Contemporary poets are still finding new ways of handling it.

---

[3]/**bootless:** *useless, unavailing*

THE MIND

· A PRIMER OF THE DAILY ROUND ·

A peels an apple, while B kneels to God,
C telephones to D, who has a hand
On E's knee, F coughs, G turns up the sod
For H's grave, I do not understand
But J is bringing one clay pigeon down   5
While K brings down a nightstick on L's head,
And M takes mustard, N drives into town,
O goes to bed with P, and Q drops dead,
R lies to S, but happens to be heard
By T, who tells U not to fire V   10
For having to give W the word
That X is now deceiving Y with Z,
    Who happens just now to remember A
    Peeling an apple somewhere far away.

Howard Nemerov (b. 1920)

E. E. Cummings wrote many sonnets in both the Italian and English
mode. Though thought of as experimental, Cummings turned to the
sonnet more often than to any other form: More than one-fourth of
his published poems are sonnets.

Edmund Spenser, inventor of the Spenserian stanza, devised a
matching sonnet form that bears his name. It rhymes *a b a b, b c b c,
c d c d, e e.*

· SONNET LXXV ·

One day I wrote her name upon the strand,
    But came the waves and washèd it away;
    Again I wrote it with a second hand,
    But came the tide and made my pains his prey.
"Vain man," said she, "that dost in vain assay   5
    A mortal thing so to immortalize,
    For I myself shall like to this decay,
    And eke my name be wipèd out likewise."
"Not so," quod I, "let baser things devise
    To die in dust, but you shall live by fame;   10
    My verse your virtues rare shall eternize
    And in the heavens write your glorious name,
Where, whenas death shall all the world subdue,
    Our love shall live, and later life renew."

Edmund Spenser (c. 1552–1599)

[8]/**eke:** *even*   [9]/**quod:** *quoth, said*

Many poets have taken liberties with the traditional arrangements of the rhymes. Gwendolyn Brooks, like some poets before her, eases the Italian pattern into an *a b b a c d d c* octave in one of her sonnets.

· THE RITES FOR COUSIN VIT ·

Carried her unprotesting out the door.
Kicked back the casket-stand. But it can't hold her,
That stuff and satin aiming to enfold her,
The lid's contrition nor the bolts before.
Oh oh. Too much. Too much. Even now, surmise,   *5*
She rises in the sunshine. There she goes,
Back to the bars she knew and the repose
In love-rooms and the things in people's eyes.
Too vital and too squeaking. Must emerge.
Even now she does the snake-hips with a hiss,   *10*
Slops the bad wine across her shantung, talks
Of pregnancy, guitars and bridgework, walks
In parks or alleys, comes haply on the verge
Of happiness, haply hysterics. Is.

Gwendolyn Brooks (b. 1917)

Quite a few sonnets, like hers, refuse to fit into any class. Some are hybrid—half Italian, half English. Some, like Shelley's "Ozymandias" (see Anthology, p. 447) have original rhyme schemes. Some, still called "sonnets," have more or less than fourteen lines, or more or less than five feet to the line. Hopkins, thinking mathematically, kept the proportions but changed the size in his "curtal" (*curtailed*) sonnet. Instead of the 8:6 ratio he used 6:4½ (or 4 and a fraction):

· PIED BEAUTY ·

Glory be to God for dappled things—
    For skies of couple-color as a brinded cow;
        For rose-moles all in stipple upon trout that swim;
Fresh-firecoal chestnut-falls; finches' wings;
    Landscape plotted and pieced—fold, fallow, and plough;   *5*
      And áll trádes, their gear and tackle and trim.

All things counter, original, spare, strange;
    Whatever is fickle, freckled (who knows how?)
      With swift, slow; sweet, sour; adazzle, dim;
He fathers-forth whose beauty is past change: *10*
      Praise him.

Gerard Manley Hopkins (1844–1889)

Of the other fixed forms used in English, the oldest and most elaborate is the **sestina.** Invented by a Provençal poet in the twelfth century, the sestina comes as close as any poetic form to the elaborate mathematical patterns in nature. It has six six-line stanzas and a three-line **envoy** (*short concluding stanza*). The same six words that end the lines in the first stanza return in the other stanzas as line-end words (three of them have to occur midline in the envoy). Their arrangement is different in each stanza, according to a set pattern, which readers sufficiently interested will easily discover in Elizabeth Bishop's memories of a childhood without parents in the home.

· SESTINA ·

September rain falls on the house.
In the failing light, the old grandmother
sits in the kitchen with the child
beside the Little Marvel Stove,
reading the jokes from the almanac,   5
laughing and talking to hide her tears.

She thinks that her equinoctial tears
and the rain that beats on the roof of the house
were both foretold by the almanac,
but only known to a grandmother.   10
The iron kettle sings on the stove.
She cuts some bread and says to the child,

It's time for tea now; but the child
is watching the teakettle's small hard tears
dance like mad on the hot black stove,   15
the way the rain must dance on the house.
Tidying up, the old grandmother
hangs up the clever almanac

on its string. Birdlike, the almanac
hovers half open above the child,   20
hovers above the old grandmother
and her teacup full of dark brown tears.
She shivers and says she thinks the house
feels chilly, and puts more wood in the stove.

It was to be, says the Marvel Stove.   25
I know what I know, says the almanac.
With crayons the child draws a rigid house
and a winding pathway. Then the child
puts in a man with buttons like tears
and shows it proudly to the grandmother.   30

But secretly, while the grandmother
busies herself about the stove,
the little moons fall down like tears
from between the pages of the almanac
into the flower bed the child   35
has carefully placed in the front of the house.

Time to plant tears, says the almanac.
The grandmother sings to the marvellous stove
and the child draws another inscrutable house.

Elizabeth Bishop (1911–1979)

Of the forms that have come to us from French poetry, one of the best known is the **ballade** (not to be confused with the English and Scottish ballad). François Villon (fifteenth century) is the most celebrated writer of **ballades;** his poem that follows illustrates (in translation) the pattern most often followed: three stanzas of eight lines each rhyming *a b a b b c b c C*, and a four-line envoy rhyming *b c a C.** (Capital letters in such formulas mean that the whole line recurs as a **refrain,** which is the name for a line or lines repeated at regular intervals, like the chorus of a song.)

• BALLADE TO HIS MISTRESS •

F alse beauty who, although in semblance fair,
R ude art in action, and hast cost me dear,
A s iron harsh, and harder to outwear,
N ame that did spell the end of my career,
C harm that dost mischief, builder of my bier,   5
O gress who dost thy lover's death require,
Y outh without pity! Womankind, dost hear?
S hould help a man, not drag him in the mire!

M uch better had it been to seek elsewhere
A id and repose, and keep my honour clear,   10
R ather than thus be driven by despair
T o flee in anguish and dishonour drear.
'*H* elp, help!' I cry. 'Ye neighbours all, draw near;
E ach man fetch water for my raging fire!'
Compassion bids that every true compeer   15
Should help a man, not drag him in the mire.

---

* The translation does the envoy as *a c a C.*

THE MIND

V anished soon will be thy beauty rare,
I ts blossom will be withered and sere.
I could find cause for laughter, were I there,
L iving and eating still. But nay, 'twere sheer   20
L unacy, for by then I'ld be thy peer,
O ld, ugly as thyself, and sans desire.
N ow drink amain! For drinking and good cheer
Should help a man, not drag him in the mire.

Prince of all lovers, I do scarcely dare   25
To ask thine aid, lest I provoke thine ire;
But ev'ry honest heart, by God I swear,
Should help a man, not drag him in the mire.

François Villon (1431–1463?)
(English version by Norman Cameron, 1905–1953)

The lines all end with an angry *r* sound, as we mentioned on page 172; most begin with the letters of his name or that of his mistress.

Some other forms deriving from Old French poetry look alike and have similar names: **rondel, roundel, rondeau.** They tend to be bookish —the kind of thing literary folk like to try their hand at instead of doing crossword puzzles, or that young writers attempt once or twice as a stunt. A simpler form of the rondel, the **triolet,** with repetitions at middle and end (*A B a A a b A B*) is familiar in English and has given us a well-known anthology piece.

· TO A FAT LADY SEEN FROM THE TRAIN ·

O why do you walk through the fields in gloves,
    Missing so much and so much?
O fat white woman whom nobody loves,
Why do you walk through the fields in gloves,
When the grass is soft as the breast of doves   5
    And shivering sweet to the touch?
O why do you walk through the fields in gloves,
    Missing so much and so much?

Frances Cornford (1886–1960)

GOLDEN NUMBERS

The **villanelle** (a *villanella* was originally an Italian country song or dance) became a French verse form in the sixteenth century and was taken up by English dilettante poets in the nineteenth. At first it seemed only a literary plaything:

> A dainty thing's the villanelle;
> It serves its purpose passing well. . . .

But for some reason it has attracted the interest of some of the best poets of our time. A nineteen-line poem, consisting of five tercets followed by a quatrain and having only two rhymes, it repeats the first line (A^1) and the third line (A^2) according to the scheme at the left. It looks as if, with the villanelle, we are back with the complexities of the sunflower. When Dylan Thomas wrote "Do Not Go Gentle into That Good Night" (p. 163), his passionate exhortation to his dying father, he chose this "dainty thing" and made it resonant with love, grief, and indignation—one of the best examples we have of how a poet with enough vitality can breathe life into a form apparently long dead. Robinson, Empson, Auden, and Roethke (see Anthology, p. 546) are others who have used the villanelle for serious purposes.

The shape of poetry in English has also been influenced by Japanese poetry. In Japanese, a syllabic language with little accentual stress, the classical form for more than a thousand years has been the **tanka,** a thirty-one-syllable poem whose five lines have 5, 7, 5, 7, 7 syllables. This one is from the tenth century:

> Lying here alone,
> So lost in longings for you
> I forget to comb
> My tangled tresses—oh for
> Your hand caressing them smooth!

> *Lady Izumi Shikibu (tenth century)*

The tanka may have influenced one American invention, the **cinquain,** with its 2, 4, 6, 8, 2 syllables.

(Marginal rhyme scheme:)
A¹ b A² / a b A¹ / a b A² / a b A¹ / a b A² / a b A¹ A²

· CINQUAIN: A WARNING ·

Just now
Out of the strange
Still dusk . . . as strange, as still . . .
A white moth flew. Why am I grown
So cold?

Adelaide Crapsey (1878–1914)

As tanka developed, poets began to write them jointly in a series called **renga** (revived by the Mexican poet Octavio Paz and his friends). One would contribute the first three lines of 5, 7, 5 syllables, another the two lines of 7, 7, and so on.

From the first link of renga came the seventeen-syllable **hokku** or **haiku,** popular from the seventeenth century on. In this concentrated, one-breath verse form, there is generally a suggestion of season or a "season word" in a tersely described incident or observation that suggests more than it says, stirring a mood by presenting a picture. Often a comparison between two things is implied, as in these two of Bashō's:

On a withered branch
A crow has just alighted:
Nightfall in autumn.

Lightning in the clouds!
In the deeper dark is heard
A night-heron's cry.

Bashō (seventeenth century)

Brilliantly adapted as haiku is to Japanese culture and the Japanese language, it has seldom attracted the major American poets, though the apparent simplicity has endeared it to numerous poetry lovers. Richard Wilbur, one of the few well-known poets to use it, has combined the form of the haiku with imagery of the bullfight in the following lines:

· SLEEPLESS AT CROWN POINT ·

All night, this headland
Lunges into the rumpling
Capework of the wind.

Richard Wilbur (b. 1921)

Three fixed forms generally handled as light verse are the **limerick,** the **clerihew,** and the **double dactyl.** The first is so well known that we hardly need an example—which is just as well, since no limerick worth its salt would want to be found in respectable company.

The clerihew, named for E. C(lerihew) Bentley, has two generally mismated couplets with comic rhymes that present the "potted biography" of a famous person.

· SIR ISAAC NEWTON ·

Sir Isaac Newton
Had no time for rootin' and tootin'.
What did he do instead?
He let apples fall on his head.

Anonymous

The double dactyl was conceived by the poet Anthony Hecht and a classicist friend. Here are two of them, the first untitled:

Higgledy-piggledy
Ludwig van Beethoven
Bored by requests for some
Music to hum,

Finally answered with   5
Oversimplicity,
"Here's my Fifth Symphony:
Duh, duh, duh, DUM!"

E. William Seaman (b. 1927)

· TACT ·

Patty-cake, patty-cake,
Marcus Antonius,
What do you think of the
African Queen?

Gubernatorial   5
Duties require my
Presence in Egypt. Ya
Know what I mean?

Paul Pascal (b. 1925)

THE MIND

The form consists of two quatrains, the last lines of each rhyming. All lines except these two have two full dactyls; the rhyming lines have only — ∪∪ |—. The first line is a sort of nonsense invocation, like "Ibbety-bibbety" or the above. The second line has to be a double dactyl name: Laurence Olivier, Anna Karenina, or the like. Somewhere in the poem, ideally in the sixth line, there has to be a double-dactyl word like "parthenogenesis," "gynecological," "Mediterranean." These are heavy obligations for so light a form, and yet a number of disporting poets have met them triumphantly.

Such unserious poems as these can help us make a serious point about form in poetry. A free-verse limerick is improbable. What happens to the rhyme is part of the fun.

> There was a young lady of Tottenham,
> Who'd no manners, or else she'd forgotten 'em;
>   At tea at the vicar's
>   She tore off her knickers,
> Because, she explained, she felt 'ot in 'em.   *5*

> *Anonymous*

Liberate this into free verse, and we get:

> A young lady, a native of Tottenham,
> Had no manners, or else they slipped her mind;
>   At the vicar's tea
>   She tore her knickers off,
> Explaining that she found them uncomfortably warm.   *5*

The first was at least a limerick and, for some, a passing smile. But the second is a nothing. If we saw it by itself, we might even be puzzled as to its intention. So with the double dactyl about Antony and Cleopatra. If we denude it of its form and leave it as naked meaning we get something like:

> "Mark Antony, what do you think of Cleopatra?"
> "Well, I have to stay in Egypt anyway, since I'm the governor. Get it?"

Not very funny. Form is power.

exercises & diversions

A. One of the best-known poems of A. E. Housman begins as follows:

> With rue my heart is laden
>   For golden friends I had,
> For many a rose-lipt maiden,
>   And many a lightfoot lad.

His second stanza is one of these two. Can you be fairly sure which is his? And why?

> By brooks that murmur softly   By brooks too broad for leaping
>   The lightfoot boys are laid;   The lightfoot boys are laid;
> The rose-lipt girls are sleeping   The rose-lipt girls are sleeping
>   In many a misty glade.   In fields where roses fade.

B. 1. In "The Statues," check on the rhymes. Why are the final couplets of each stanza likelier to have perfect rhymes than other lines are? Why are there no off-rhymes in the last stanza, though there had been in earlier stanzas?

2. What sounds are repeated in lines 7 and 8? Are they expressive?

3. Do you notice any expressive irregularities (or regularities) in the rhythm?

C. 1. Leafing through sections of this book you have already read, do you notice any stanza shapes that look unusual or interesting? Upon examination, do they prove to be expressive in any way? Merely decorative? Or—?

2. In poems you have read, do you recall any "correspondences" like those between "million-dollar baby" and "five-and-ten-cent store" or between red lips and blood-stained stones?

D. This section has been making a case for the naturalness of form. But suppose one lives a chaotic life, or lives in a chaotic age that has little sense of form. Is it then more natural to write formless poetry? Or do you think that the more disorder artists feel around them, the more obligation they have to create what order they can? Which of the following statements would you agree with?

1. Art had to be confused to express confusion; but perhaps it was truest, so.

Henry Adams

exercises & diversions

2. [The poetry of primitive people] gives order and harmony to their sudden overmastering emotions and their tumbling thoughts . . . a solid center in what would otherwise be chaos. . . .

C. M. Bowra

3. [Deeply troubled poets, like Thomas Hardy,] tend to use strict forms as a kind of foothold, a fixed point in an uncertain cosmos.

Kenneth Marsden

4. The more [a poet] is conscious of an inner disorder and dread, the more value he will place on tidiness in the work as a *defense*, as if he hoped that through his control of the means of expressing his emotions, the emotions themselves, which he cannot master directly, might be brought to order.

W. H. Auden

E. 1. How would you describe the stanza forms or rhyme-schemes used in "Rattler, Alert" (p. 16), "Most Like an Arch This Marriage (p. 23), "Blue Girls" (p. 112), "Counting the Beats" (p. 220), "My Life Had Stood—A Loaded Gun" (p. 26), "All But Blind" (p. 33), "A Note on Wyatt" (p. 62), "The Ruined Maid" (p. 491), "Dust of Snow" (p. 132), "anyone lived in a pretty how town" (p. 531), "Out, Out—" (p. 292), "me up at does" (p. 297)?

2. What form is used in these stanzas? Are there irregularities?

> "Courage!" he said, and pointed toward the land,
> "This mounting wave will roll us shore-ward soon."
> In the afternoon they came unto a land
> In which it seemèd always afternoon.
> All round the coast the languid air did swoon,   5
> Breathing like one that hath a weary dream.
> Full-faced above the valley stood the moon;
> And like a downward smoke, the slender stream,
> Along the cliff to fall and pause and fall did seem.

Alfred, Lord Tennyson

> Meanwhile at the University of Japan
> Ko had already begun his studies, which
> While making him an educated man

· 346 ·

Would also give him as he learned to pitch
And catch—for Ko was more than a mere fan,   5
But wished as a playing member to do a hitch
With some great team—something to think about
More interesting than merely Safe and Out.

Kenneth Koch

F. 1. Of the six-line stanzas used in the poems listed below, are any two alike? Do some stanza designs seem more successful than others? "The End of the Weekend" (p. 12), "It Fell on a Summer's Day" (p. 408), "A Last Confession" (p. 502), "Dream Songs, 22" (p. 554), "Ubi Sunt Qui Ante Nos Fuerunt?" (p. 262), "Meeting at Night" (p. 194), "Remember Dear Mary" (p. 300).

2. Ask yourself the same questions about these eight-line stanzas. "Winter" (p. 70), "The Mill" (p. 502), "Loose Woman" (p. 84), "I to My Perils" (p. 244).

3. How many different five-line stanzas do you notice among the poems read?

G. 1. The sonnets listed below are all irregular in some way. How? "With How Sad Steps, O Moon" (p. 405), "Leda and the Swan" (p. 42), "Good Ships" (p. 66), "Anthem for Doomed Youth" (p. 200).

2. Milton's "On the Late Massacre in Piedmont" (p. 183) breaks with the Italian sonnet scheme in one small respect, yet the difference makes itself felt so strongly that this is called a "Miltonic sonnet." What is different about it?

H. The ballad stanza is also called "common meter" (C.M.), especially when used in hymns. Why is the following stanza form called "short meter" (S.M.)?

I LOOK INTO MY GLASS

I look into my glass,
And view my wasting skin,
And say, "Would God it came to pass
My heart had shrunk as thin!"

For then, I, undistrest   5
By hearts grown cold to me,

exercises & diversions

Could lonely wait my endless rest
With equanimity.

But Time, to make me grieve,
Part steals, lets part abide;   *10*
And shakes this fragile frame at eve
With throbbings of noontide.

Thomas Hardy (1840–1928)

Why is the following (from "Greensleeves") called "long meter" (L.M.)?

Alas, my love! you do me wrong
To cast me off discourteously;
And I have lovèd you so long,
Delighting in your company. . . .

I. Choose from among the following exercises whichever seems most interesting.

1. Write a poem using the letters of your own name (or somebody else's) as first letters of each line.

2. Write a dozen or so lines of terza rima on a theme that exploits its forward movement.

3. Write a stanza of rhyme royal, or ottava rima (perhaps in the manner of Byron), or a Spenserian stanza, or three or four haiku.

4. Would it be harder to write a passable example of a sonnet or a double dactyl? (Write one of each and see.)

5. Write a villanelle or a sestina.

6. Write two stanzas in stanza forms that, as far as you know, have never been used before.

13

A Head on Its Shoulders
COMMON SENSE, UNCOMMON SENSE

COMMON SENSE

Although complicated ratios and formulas play a part in our sense of proportion, the mathematics that appears openly in poetry will be very simple, like the addition in A. E. Housman's lines

> —To think that two and two are four
> And neither five nor three
> The heart of man has long been sore,
> And long 'tis like to be.

Or like the $a:b::c:d$ in Frost's "The Oven Bird":

> He says the leaves are old and that for flowers
> Mid-summer is to spring as one to ten. . . .

Nor is poetry likely to make much use of formal reasoning.
But some poems come close to revealing the bare bones of thought.

• TO WOMEN, AS FAR AS I'M CONCERNED •

> The feelings I don't have I don't have.
> The feeling I don't have, I won't say I have.
> The feelings you say you have, you don't have.
> The feelings you would like us both to have, we
> neither of us have.   5

THE MIND

The feelings people ought to have, they never have.
If people say they've got feelings, you may be pretty
    sure they haven't got them.
So if you want either of us to feel anything at all
you'd better abandon all idea of feelings altogether.   *10*

D. H. Lawrence (1885–1930)

In *Knots*, R. D. Laing comes even closer to being a poet of intellectual analysis.

· JILL ·

· · ·

JILL I'm upset you are upset
JACK I'm not upset
JILL I'm upset that you're not upset that I'm
       upset you're upset
JACK I'm upset that you're upset that I'm not   *5*
       upset that you're upset that I'm upset,
       when I'm not.

JILL You put me in the wrong
JACK I am not putting you in the wrong
JILL You put me in the wrong for thinking you   *10*
       put me in the wrong.

JACK Forgive me
JILL No
JACK I'll never forgive you for not forgiving me

R. D. Laing (b. 1927)

These are almost disembodied thoughts, as if we had the speech balloons from a comic strip but no characters beneath them. And no environment—no chairs to sit on, no trees to lounge under, nothing to look at.

In "The Subverted Flower" (see Anthology, p. 507), a poem by Frost about a sexual misunderstanding between two young people, we are shown not only the geometry of human behavior, as in Laing's poem, but that geometry as embodied, as seen through the distorting glass of a young man's embarrassed passion. Frost is closer to traditional modes of poetry than Laing is; his young people are more than psyches. They have physical bodies with shining hair and lips and hands; they stand waist-deep in goldenrod and fern; they ache and struggle and are panicked.

A HEAD ON ITS SHOULDERS

Wallace Stevens frequently lets a poem originate in a philosophic problem, but he sees to it that the problem is given a poetic solution. We can observe how he deals with philosophic thought by looking at his "Sunday Morning" (see Anthology, p. 509), a poem that wonders whether one should live for this world or for that afterlife which most religions offer.

"Sunday Morning," a real voice in a real body in a real world, is a vivid example of how poets philosophize. The thoughts of the poem are involved with physical sensations. Philosophical and religious questions come up because the woman is physically happy: she is enjoying her leisure, in comfortable undress, with the taste and fragrance of coffee and oranges, the warmth and gaiety of the sun, the brightly colored bird at liberty on the rug. All her senses are alive in the first few lines of the poem, which never leaves the sensory world.

In much of this book we have been concerned with what we could call the physiology of poetry. We have stressed, too, that poetry has much in common with primitive or childlike ways of apprehending reality, that it seems more at home with dreams and visions than with syllogisms or statistics. George Santayana, philosopher as well as poet, knew what he was talking about when he said that he was "an ignorant man, almost a poet."

But poetry, related as it is to dream and impulse and mysterious influences from our distant past, certainly has a head on its shoulders. It may even be said to be a matter of common sense. If this statement seems shocking, in the next section we will find justice done to poetry's invaluable elements of irrationality.

All we mean by common sense is a sense of the way the world is. When we lift a forkful of mashed potatoes toward our face, common sense tells us it goes in our mouth, not in our ear. We can, of course, protest the weary sameness of things by putting it in our ear, though common sense tells us the consequences will be unpleasant. Common sense tells us to move if we are standing in the street and see a four-wheeled, two-ton object hurtling toward us. It tells us not to step outside the window for a breath of air if we are on the fortieth floor. In worlds of fantasy and dream we can disregard it; in the world that is "real" (in that we live or die there), to disregard it is to risk a quick trip to the hospital, or worse. In our philosophic moods we may wonder what is "really real," but in the details of our everyday living we have a pretty sound idea.

Ezra Pound, when presented with the notion that intelligence involved "some repressing and silencing of poetry," reacted indignantly: He offered a reward "for any authenticated case of intellect having stopped a chap's writing poesy! You might as well claim that railway tracks stop the engine. No one ever claimed that they would make it go." Gary Snyder, in "What You Should Know to Be a Poet," specifies, "Your own six senses, with a watchful and elegant mind."

The function of mind in poetry is worth stressing because there are readers who think poets work better when they turn their mind off and let imagination and emotion take over. Imagination and emotion are necessary sources of poetry, but few good poets would agree that they ought to be in charge. "Every true poet is necessarily a first-rate critic," said Paul Valéry. Dylan Thomas insisted that images, regardless of where they come from, "must go through the rational processes of the intellect." Sylvia Plath thought the mind should be in control—even when dealing with the extremist situations that led to her suicide.

> I think my poems come immediately out of the sensuous and emotional experiences I have, but I must say I *cannot* sympathize with these cries from the heart that are informed by nothing except, you know, a needle or a knife, or whatever it is. I believe one should be able to control and manipulate experiences, even the most terrifying, like madness, like being tortured . . . and should be able to manipulate these experiences with an informed and intelligent mind. . . .*

An example of intellect controlling poetry when everything else has gone awry is one of the last poems of John Berryman, a poem (as events were to show) that is almost a suicide note.

• HE RESIGNS •

Age, and the deaths, and the ghosts.
Her having gone away
in spirit from me. Hosts
of regrets come & find me empty.

I don't feel this will change.   5
I don't want any thing
or person, familiar or strange.
I don't think I will sing

any more just now;
or ever. I must start   10
to sit with a blind brow
above an empty heart.

John Berryman (1914–1972)

---

* Transcribed from *The Poet Speaks*, Argo recording No. RG 455, Record Five (London: Argo Record Company Ltd., 1965).

A HEAD ON ITS SHOULDERS

Unable to keep his life together, the poet keeps his poem more tightly together (*a b a b* in iambic trimeter) than anything he had written in years, instead of simply letting it "flow" from the depths of his agony.

There are readers who consider "poetry" and "common sense" in opposition. Poetry, they think, is some kind of lovely supersense: cloud castles in the airy blue. Most poets, more down to earth than their readers, would agree with Robert Graves that a poem should make prose sense as well as poetic sense. Even ecstatic poetry, thinks Graves, is no exception: A poem cannot make "more than sense" unless it first makes sense.

The painter Miró, for all of his visionary surrealism, believed in keeping in mind his goal of communicating with others. "We Catalans," he said, "believe you must always plant your feet firmly on the ground if you want to be able to jump in the air." Certainly the greatest of the Spanish mystical poets, Saint John of the Cross, believed in making sense even when he was talking about experiences beyond any images our minds could hold or any words we could find to express them. Of such poems of his as "The Dark Night" (p. 57), the Spanish poet Jorge Guillén has written: "We are immediately fascinated by these forms that do not break with the laws of our world." At first this may seem to be low praise. What it means is that the poet shows a reverence and love for the beauty and integrity of the universe.

Few readers are as eagle-eyed as Graves, who can be hard on poetry he thinks deficient in sense. He even finds much to object to in one of Wordsworth's most famous poems:

• THE SOLITARY REAPER •

Behold her, single in the field,
Yon solitary Highland Lass!
Reaping and singing by herself;
Stop here, or gently pass!
Alone she cuts and binds the grain,   5
And sings a melancholy strain;
O listen! for the Vale profound
Is overflowing with the sound.

No Nightingale did ever chaunt
More welcome notes to weary bands   10
Of travellers in some shady haunt,
Among Arabian sands:
A voice so thrilling ne'er was heard
In spring-time from the Cuckoo-bird,
Breaking the silence of the seas   15
Among the farthest Hebrides.

THE MIND

Will no one tell me what she sings?—
Perhaps the plaintive numbers flow
For old, unhappy, far-off things,
And battles long ago: 20
Or is it some more humble lay,
Familiar matter of to-day?
Some natural sorrow, loss, or pain,
That has been, and may be again?

Whate'er the theme, the Maiden sang   25
As if her song could have no ending;
I saw her singing at her work,
And o'er the sickle bending:—
I listened, motionless and still;
And, as I mounted up the hill,   30
The music in my heart I bore,
Long after it was heard no more.

William Wordsworth (1770–1850)

Graves protests that "There are only two figures in sight: Words-worth and the Highland Lass—yet he cries, 'Behold her!' Do any of you find that reasonable?" If he is talking to himself, why say, "Behold her," when he has already done so, or "O listen!" when he cannot help listening, since the vale is "overflowing with the sound"? Graves also finds the poem wordy. If we were cabling the sense of the first stanza, we could say it in twelve words instead of forty-three:

SOLITARY HIGHLAND LASS REAPING BINDING GRAIN
STOP MELANCHOLY SONG OVERFLOWS PROFOUND VALE

Wordsworth uses four expressions for loneliness: "single," "solitary," "alone," "by herself." Graves also objects to the natural science of the poem: "occasional nightingales . . . penetrate to the more verdurous parts of Arabia Felix, but only as winter migrants, when heavy rains provide them with grubs and caterpillars, and never nest there; consequently they do not '*chaunt.*' " The Hebrides, he says, are far from silent: "The islands enjoy a remarkably temperate climate, because of the Gulf Stream; and the cuckoo's arrival coincides with the equinoctial gales." "Cuckoo-bird" he considers baby talk. He goes on to wonder why Wordsworth asks: "Will no one tell me what she sings?" Who could? he wonders, since no one is present except the poet and the single, solitary Highland lass, all alone and by herself. He concludes by defining a good poem as "one that makes complete sense; and says

A HEAD ON ITS SHOULDERS

(The New York Public Library Picture Collection)

all it has to say memorably and economically; and has been written for no other than poetic reasons."*

Some poems show a more flagrant violation of common sense, which even naïve readers will be startled at. We need no background in highway engineering or the theory of bridge construction to feel that something is wrong in the world of a poem like the one below.

· BUILDING THE BRIDGE ·

An old man, going a lone highway,
Came, at the evening, cold and gray,
To a chasm, vast, and deep, and wide,
Through which was flowing a sullen tide.
The old man crossed in the twilight dim;   *5*
The sullen stream had no fears for him;
But he turned, when safe on the other side,
And built a bridge to span the tide.

"Old man," said a fellow pilgrim, near,
"You are wasting strength with building here;   *10*

---

* From Robert Graves, "Legitimate Criticism of Poetry," *Five Pens in Hand* (New York: Doubleday and Company, 1958), pp. 45–48.

Your journey will end with the ending day;
You never again must pass this way;
You have crossed the chasm, deep and wide,—
Why build you the bridge at eventide?"

The builder lifted his old gray head: *15*
"Good friend, in the path I have come," he said,
"There followeth after me today
A youth, whose feet must pass this way.
This chasm, that has been naught to me,
To that fair-haired youth may a pitfall be.   *20*
He, too, must cross in the twilight dim;
Good friend, I am building the bridge for *him*."

Will Allen Dromgoole (1860–1934)

Assuming there can be a "lone" highway, traveled only by an old
man, a fellow pilgrim, and a fair-haired youth, this one is an example
of bad planning: A chasm, vast and deep and wide, has somehow been
overlooked by the highway department. We are not told how the old
man crossed it, though that is an interesting question. Did he swim,
keeping his old gray head above the water? We might wonder, too,
why he bothered to cross at all if he was thinking about building a
bridge. Why not start building it from the near bank instead of swim-
ming over and then building the bridge back from the far side? Gen-
erally the construction of such a bridge requires a little planning and
a good supply of heavy materials. It normally takes time, too, especially
with just one old man, working in dim light, to drive the pilings and
swing the beams into place.

Such a poem breaks violently with the laws of our world. We can
see how remote from reality it is by putting it not into one of Mr.
Graves' cables, but into journalese.

• MAN, 70, BUILDS BRIDGE OVER VAST CHASM •

Commuters long accustomed to swimming the deep, cold waters that roll in Vast Chasm, four miles north of town, were agreeably surprised this morning to find a gleaming steel structure spanning the tide.

"Twarn't there last night is all I know," said long-time resident Wilson Finozzle. "Sure is nice not to get soaked in them deep, cold waters, a-coming home with the vittles of an evening. Ain't read a dry newspaper since I was knee-high to a grasshopper."

"It was nothing," said the gray-haired builder, from his cell in the county jail, where he is being held on charges of bridge building without a permit. "I did it for a fair-haired youth. Wouldn't anybody?"

A HEAD ON ITS SHOULDERS

Will Allen Dromgoole's poem is well intentioned, meant to present us with an edifying example of noble conduct. Nobody would quarrel with her message. But she settles on images so improbable in terms of the world we live in that we are more likely to laugh than to listen seriously. When poetry is working on two levels, that of intended meaning and that of imagery, it has to make sense on *both* levels. One cannot hold back his laughter because "the poet doesn't really mean it that way" or because "it's only a figure of speech." For poets to claim our indulgence for what they *meant* to say is as futile as for golfers to demand that their ball be placed where they meant to hit it: unfulfilled intentions count as little in the world of literature as in the world of sports.

When Christ in the New Testament (Luke 10) wants to show that we should be kind to others, there is no nonsense about how we ought to build bridges across chasms in the dark. Instead we are given the simple parable of the good Samaritan. We might expect Gerard Manley Hopkins, one of the finest of religious poets and presumably partial to the otherworldly, to be sympathetic to departures from prosaic common sense. But he was not. When, in 1886, he was shown a poem by the young William Butler Yeats, he thought it "a strained and unworkable allegory about a young man and a sphinx on a rock in the sea . . . ," and wanted to ask questions like "How did it get there?" and "What did it eat?" Hopkins explained: "People think such criticisms very prosaic, but common sense is never out of place anywhere, neither on Parnassus nor on Tabor nor on the Mount where our Lord preached . . . parables all taken from real life. . . ."

An affront to our common sense is a reason for **parody,** which Pound once said he supposed "the best criticism." The parodist feels that some feature of a poem is so lacking in balance that he deliberately exaggerates its faults, to the point of comedy, to show how absurd they are. The poems of Housman mention a fair number of love-stricken lads who kill themselves or rush off to death in battle or are hanged for murder. Occasionally the maudlin self-punishment leads to a ridiculous situation, like that in "The True Lover," in which a lad who has cut his throat pays a last call on his love, pleading, "Take me in your arms a space." She does:

> She heard and went and knew not why;
> Her heart to his she laid. . . .

By and by she notices that her lad seems not to be breathing (though he can talk in rather long sentences) and has no heartbeat. There is also an odd salty wetness about him. He explains why:

THE MIND

> "Oh like enough 'tis blood, my dear,
>   For when the knife has slit
> The throat across from ear to ear
>   'Twill bleed because of it."

This may bring tears to the susceptible eyes of those whose medical knowledge is limited. Level-headed readers, who refuse to believe what Housman is telling them, are more likely to laugh. Hugh Kingsmill is parodying this aspect of Housman when he writes:

> What, still alive at twenty-two,
> A clean, upstanding chap like you?
> Sure, if your throat 'tis hard to slit,
> Slit your girl's, and swing for it.

> Like enough, you won't be glad,   5
> When they come to hang you, lad:
> But bacon's not the only thing
>   That's cured by hanging from a string. . . .

Parody, although it has to be funny to make its point, is a serious literary exercise that amounts to a criticism of some excess or defect in the original. Fundamentally, it is a protest against some violation of common sense.

UNCOMMON SENSE

If we generally look at the world with the eyes of common sense and if, in survival situations, we are obliged to do so, yet there are times when we can disregard its warnings. In our dreams or daydreams all rules are suspended. We hardly need the Dadaists and Surrealists of the twentieth century to tell us what the sensible Horace admitted long ago—on occasion it is fun to act in a crazy way (*dulce est desipere in loco*). And before him the intellectual Greeks, who produced the Parthenon and the sculpture of the classical period, had also allowed for the irrational in human life. Sappho would probably have been the first to admit that she was not behaving sensibly in letting love take over as it did.

We can point to nature as acting like a zany in producing flying fish and the duckbill platypus. If we look through a telescope at spiral nebulae or through a microscope at the cellular structure of our own bodies, what we see is so like surrealist art we can hardly tell one from another. Nature is continually doing things at which our reason boggles—so much so that philosophies of absurdity and meaninglessness have been based on its caprice. As have religions: In "A Masque of Reason," Frost has Jehovah explain to Job:

> But it was of the essence of the trial
> You shouldn't understand it at the time.
> It had to seem unmeaning to have meaning.

Unreason, then, common enough in the universe, has a right to its place in poetry. According to Yeats, who spoke out strongly for the identity of passion and precision and for the mathematical basis of beauty, all great poetry contains an irrational element.

But welcome as occasional unreason may be, our minds are in for a shock when we first come on a poem like the following, by an Alsatian Dadaist and Surrealist best known for his sculpture and painting.

• WHAT THE VIOLINS SING IN THEIR BACONFAT BED •

the elephant is in love with the millimeter

the snail dreams of lunar defeat
its slippers are pallid and drained
like a gun made of Jell-O that's held by a neodraftee

the eagle has the gestures of an alleged vacuum   5
his breast is swollen with lightning

the lion sports a mustache that is pure gothic of the flamboyant type
his skin is calm
he laughs like a blot from a bottle of oink

the lobster goes *grrr* like a gooseberry   10
he is wise with the savvy of apples
has the bleeding-heart ways of a plum
he is fiendish in sex like a pumpkin

the cow takes a path that's pathetic
it peters out in a pond of flesh   15
every hair of this volume weighs volumes

the snake hops with prickety prickling
around about washbowls of love
full of hearts with an arrow in each

the butterfly stuffed is a popover made of papaya   20
papaya popovers grow into papapaya papapovers
papapaya papapovers grow into grandpapapaya grandpapapovers

THE MIND

the nightingale sprinkles on stomachs on hearts on brains on guts
what I mean is on lilies on roses on lilacs on pinks
the flea puts his right leg behind his left ear   25
his left hand in his right hand
and on his left foot jumps over his right ear

Jean Arp (1888?–1966)

To ask what this poem means is a wrong approach. The question is: What does it do? Such poems certainly jolt us out of habitual ways of perceiving and thinking. Probably they also amuse us. The writing is very specific—anything but abstract. The "thought" is difficult. But it is not meant to be thought. Instead, it is experience, as dreams are or as the inspection of natural oddities is. If it seems an insult to our ordinary ways of thinking, then the writer would consider it a success. To understand why, we have to know something about the Dadaist and Surrealist philosophy.

The Dadaist movement came into existence about the middle of the First World War. If our common sense could lead to the folly of war, the Dadaists felt, perhaps it was time to try another approach—that of "not-sense." They did absurd things in the hope of shocking society into an awareness of the bankruptcy of traditional procedures. They preferred chance to logic as determining a literary work.

Surrealism, which took over from Dadaism in 1922, was not just a literary movement; it was a way of life, aimed at startling people out of the old ways. The fun and games were not without a serious purpose—if they were amusing, all the better. Surrealists hoped to promote their revolution by releasing the untapped forces of the unconscious, the marvels of dream, fantasy, hallucination, and chance; they professed to think spontaneity better than effort. "Thought is made in the mouth," said Tristan Tzara, the Rumanian-born poet who came on the word "dada" in the dictionary. Though it sounds meaningless, it is French baby talk for *horse*, and also the word for a favorite idea one "rides."

One form their spontaneity took was that of automatic writing. In this process, one writes down quickly, without thinking, whatever comes into his or her head. If the words begin to make sense, the writer is on the wrong track and should start over. Picasso once spent several months producing page after page of automatic writing that read like this:

A worse scandalmonger had never been known except if the wheedling friend licks the little woolen bitch twisted by the palette of the ash-gray

painter dressed in shades of hard-boiled egg and armed with the foam
which performs a thousand monkeytricks in his bed when the tomato
no longer warms him what does he care if the dew that does not know
the winning lottery number which the carnation gives a knock at the
mare. . . .

This is probably more fun to write than to read. It was soon found
that automatic writing produced almost nothing of interest. For one
thing, it was easy to fake. André Breton later admitted it had been "a
continuous disaster."

Actually, the Surrealists' devotion to spontaneity and absence of
control was never complete. They never meant to repudiate reason—
they merely wanted it to go halves with unreason. Most Surrealist art
was not at all spontaneous. Tzara spent five years writing and re-
writing one of his books. Breton worked for six months on a thirty-
word poem, probably setting an all-time record for deliberation. The
painter André Masson was seen to throw away from sixty to a hundred
attempts at an automatic drawing before he got one with the "spon-
taneous" feeling he wanted.

We can see what the Surrealists were up to more vividly in their
painting than in their literature. René Magritte, too rational to be a
regular member of the group, was like them in setting out to defy
common sense. In his art he puts things where we least expect them,
or shows them made out of materials we least expect them to be made
out of.

We see a boot, but the boot is sprouting real toes. We see a house
as at midnight—windows lighted, façade glowing in the pallor of a
streetlamp—and yet the sky behind the midnight roof and trees is a
noon sky. Out of a plain fireplace in a plain room, a little locomotive
may come steaming. Every object is painted with perfect fidelity to
nature, and yet nature itself is transformed. Magritte used his eyes and
had his wits about him. He knew that before an artist can master the
surreal, he had better master the real.

Similar transformations of reality are present in the typical sur-
realist image—in Breton's "soluble fish" or "white-haired revolver."
No objects are too remote to be coupled—time and distance are
annulled. As in collage, one can paste anything next to anything. The
Surrealists thought there was something "sublime" in the way the
mind could reconcile contraries and find unity in the unlike. But what
the French mathematician Henri Poincaré observed about combining,
in mathematics, elements from different domains is also true in poetry:
"Most combinations so formed would be entirely sterile."

The Surrealists invented many kinds of word games, and even re-

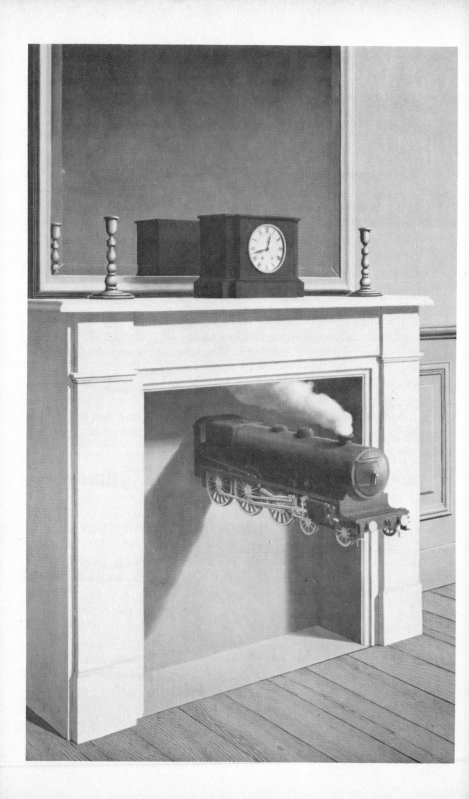

A HEAD ON ITS SHOULDERS

turned with enthusiasm to the games of their childhood, since this was one more way of flouting the prudential time-is-money world of adults. In their favorite game, the first player would write down a word, fold over the paper so the word could not be seen, pass the folded paper to the next player, who would add a word, fold the paper again, and pass it on. When all had contributed, the composition would be read. The game was called "Cadavre exquis" (*exquisite corpse*) from the first sentence that resulted: "The exquisite corpse shall drink the young wine." The results sound like lines from Surrealist poetry. They are not, of course, pure chance. Unless the words have the logic of syntax, they are mere gibberish ("The drank young the shall exquisite wine corpse").

The Surrealists not only made up objects in their imagination, they also took a fresh look at ordinary things, particularly the "found objects" that chance presented them with. Marcel Duchamp once picked up an ordinary iron bottle-rack, signed his name to it, and declared it art. The group also composed "surrealist objects," of which the most famous were a fur-lined cup, saucer, and spoon. Not all inversions of actual experience surprise or amuse us: Surrealism lends itself to schlock confections as easily as any other set of mannerisms does.

Much contemporary poetry, while not strictly in the Surrealist mode, is reminiscent of its methods and shows its influence. The two poems that follow, if not technically Surrealist, demand the suspension of our usual rationality.

• ZEPPELIN •

Someone has built a dirigible in my parlor.
What on earth has happened to the boarders?
I go in there sometimes
and tear the fabric off the framework, I shout
"who's responsible for this?"   5
but nobody answers.
There's nothing underneath
but a wilderness of girders
and a gas bag without any gas.
The dog has taken to living in one of my shoes.   10
Poor thing! His blanket was by the fireplace,

René Magritte, *Time Transfixed*
(*Courtesy, The Art Institute of Chicago*)

now filled up with the underfin.
When the propellers turn they open the doors,
they scatter papers down the hall to the garden,
sometimes they blow the paper I'm reading into my face.   *15*
My first editions are soggy with crankcase oil,
and the batik shawl I brought from ancient Mesopotamia
is soaked in grease.
Up there the pointed cone upon the nose
protrudes through my Matisse.   *20*
The pilot (at least I suppose he's the pilot)
is balled up on my bed, and when I shake him
he lifts one flap of his aviator's tarboosh to shout
"I didn't do it" and something that sounds like
"metal fatigue." He burrows into my pillow   *25*
deeper with his head. I saw a man in a mechanic's uniform
climb up inside this morning. I said
"look here now, this is my living room!"
He only banged with his wrench,
shook his fist at my fractured plaster and shouted   *30*
"what's important is that in the end it fly!"
I have to admire his singleness of mind.
Why it isn't even a new model. "Gott straff England"
is written across the gondola with lipstick in gothic lettering.
One of these mornings I've got to get out and see my lawyer.   *35*
Maybe he will suggest somebody to sue.
In the meantime for my conscience' sake
I need someone authoritative to tell me
what are the principles involved,
I mean so I will know if I should   *40*
feel resentful or honored.

Andrew Glaze (b. 1920)

³³/**Gott straff:** *God punish*

· MY GRANDMOTHER'S FUNERAL ·

At least 100 seabirds attended my grandmother's funeral. And we live over 100 miles from the coast! They flew right into the Episcopal church and stayed for the entire service. No one said anything about them when it was over. We were all sitting around on folding chairs rented from the undertaker and no one said a word about the seabirds! Even the Reverend, who was once a prisoner of the Japanese, and whose eyes were tunneled deep into his head, didn't seem to mind. I watched him when a few of them perched on a special chalice. He didn't budge! It was harder for him, but he knew as well as the rest of us that seabirds are imperturbable, and that they keep away the larger birds, the birds that sit on the coffin, making it almost impossible to carry. . . .

Thomas Lux (b. 1946)

A HEAD ON ITS SHOULDERS

The last of these is written in a manner that young writers were finding attractive in the 1970s. Nothing in it quite makes sense, yet nothing is impossible. Conventional relevance is mocked by irrelevance. The fact that the reverend was once a prisoner of the Japanese is mentioned, as though it had some bearing on what is happening. It seems to have none. For a similar blending of the real and the absurd, see Mark Strand's "The Tunnel" (Anthology, p. 592).

As the discoveries of science become more and more fantastic, poems based on them approach the condition of the surreal.

· PALINDROME ·

There is less difficulty—indeed, no logical difficulty at all—in imagining two portions of the universe, say two galaxies, in which time goes one way in one galaxy and the opposite way in the other. . . . Intelligent beings in each galaxy would regard their own time as "forward" and time in the other galaxy as "backward."

—Martin Gardner in *Scientific American*

Somewhere now she takes off the dress I am
putting on. It is evening in the antiworld
where she lives. She is forty-five years away
from her death, the hole which spit her out
into pain, impossible at first, later easing,   5
going, gone. She has unlearned much by now.
Her skin is firming, her memory sharpens,
her hair has grown glossy. She sees without glasses,
she falls in love easily. Her husband has lost his
shuffle, they laugh together. Their money shrinks,   10
but their ardor increases. Soon her second child
will be young enough to fight its way into her
body and change its life to monkey to frog to
tadpole to cluster of cells to tiny island to
nothing. She is making a list: 15
        Things I will need in the past
          lipstick
          shampoo
          transistor radio
          Alice Cooper   20
          acne cream
          5-year diary with a lock
She is eager, having heard about adolescent love
and the freedom of children. She wants to read

THE MIND

Crime and Punishment and ride on a roller coaster   25
without getting sick. I think of her as she will
be at fifteen, awkward, too serious. In the
mirror I see she uses her left hand to write,
her other to open a jar. By now our lives should
have crossed. Somewhere sometime we must have   30
passed one another like going and coming trains,
with both of us looking the other way.

Lisel Mueller (b. 1924)

In many ways surrealist poetry recalls the nonsense verse that has probably existed as long as poetry itself. E. E. Cummings (who had lived in Paris during the early years of Surrealism) sets up a series of impossible conditions in "as freedom is a breakfastfood," with lines like

as hatracks into peachtrees grow
or hopes dance best on bald men's hair
and every finger is a toe
and any courage is a fear
—long enough and just so long   5
will the impure think all things pure
and hornets wail by children stung. . . .

What seem at first to be nonsense poems may sometimes explode into disturbing fragments of sense.

· OUR BOG IS DOOD ·

Our Bog is dood, our Bog is dood,
They lisped in accents mild,
But when I asked them to explain
They grew a little wild.
How do you know your Bog is dood   5
My darling little child?

We know because we wish it so
That is enough, they cried,
And straight within each infant eye
Stood up the flame of pride,   10
And if you do not think it so
You shall be crucified.

Then tell me, darling little ones,
What's dood, suppose Bog is?
Just what we think, the answer came,   15

A HEAD ON ITS SHOULDERS

Just what we think it is.
They bowed their heads. Our Bog is ours
And we are wholly his.

But when they raised them up again
They had forgotten me   20
Each one upon each other glared
In pride and misery
For what was dood, and what their Bog
They never could agree.

Oh sweet it was to leave them then,   25
And sweeter not to see,
And sweetest of all to walk alone
Beside the encroaching sea,
The sea that soon should drown them all,
That never yet drowned me.   30

Stevie Smith (1902–1971)

Is this a nonsense poem? Or is it a serious poem about the psychology of controversy, religious or political? The word "Bog" does mean *God* in Russian, though why we should invoke a Russian meaning here is not evident to common sense. "Dood" might be baby talk for *good*, or it might mean *dead*, or it might mean nothing. The little ones in the poem, at least, do not agree on its meaning.

A continual source of nonsense or of surrealist revelation is the world of our dreams, daydreams, and fantasies.

The curious fact that many dreams—perhaps most—are in black and white, not in color, is thought to mean that the dreamer is regressing to a primitive stage of human development when we did see in black and white, as some animals still do. In going back so unimaginably far, the dreaming mind falls again into primitive ways of thinking in which reason counts for little. Dream, like myth and fairy tale, prefers emotion, imagery, and symbol to logic and ideas. Every dreamer is a surrealist.

Our waking thoughts have to deal with objects that are hard, sharp, heavy, explosive. A wrong decision can be the end of us. Dreams have no such obligations. We can be run over by dream trains or fall out of dream skyscrapers and be none the worse for it. In dreams we are indestructible. We are free to reassign the properties of matter. Like the surrealist image, anything can become anything else. Time and space lose their power.

Dreams can be poems in themselves. A student in a writing workshop once described a dream that was better than any of her poems. She might well have taken lessons from her unconscious.

> I dreamed I was standing somewhere in the middle of a great desert. Off on the horizon I could see some beautiful purple mountains, their peaks bathed in golden light. Suddenly I heard a drumming of hooves, which grew louder and louder. Then I could see the horse coming. As he got near me, I was surprised to see that he had two heads. One head was well shaped and even noble, like a horse in Greek sculpture; its eyes were fixed on the distant mountains. The other head was ugly, misshapen; it had twisted fangs and bloodshot eyes. As the horse ran past me, the noble head did not look in my direction; but the ugly head kept its eyes leeringly on me, twisting around to do so. I fell to my knees and worshipped the two-headed horse.

This is probably a better image than the dreamer could have found consciously for a young girl's view of sex as both idealistic and threatening. Among modern poets, both Frost and Edwin Muir (see Anthology, p. 516) have admitted using their own dreams as subjects for poems.

If Coleridge is telling the truth, one classic of English poetry (see Anthology, p. 443) was written in a dream. The poet, who said he was publishing his "Kubla Khan" as a "psychological curiosity" rather than for any "supposed *poetic* merits," tells how he fell asleep in his chair as a result of a pain-relieving drug, just as he was reading how Kublai Khan, the great thirteenth-century Mongolian ruler of China, built his summer palace at Xamdu.

He awakened later with the memory of a two- to three-hundred-line poem in his head, which he immediately began to write down. He had reached line 54 when he was interrupted by "a person on business from Porlock." When he returned to his room he found "to his no small surprise and mortification" that he had forgotten all the rest except for some scattered fragments. The poem as we have it seems to be a spontaneous production of the sleeping mind (which did not, however, create it from nothing). Scholars have traced most of the material of the poem to Coleridge's own reading. Not even the subconscious can dredge up much of interest from a shabbily furnished mind.

Unfortunately, the subconscious—like a baseball player who hits one home run in a lifetime career—does not have an impressive record as a writer of finished poems. We have to take Coleridge's word for it that the subconscious finished even this one.

A poem that was not composed in a dream but that looks at the world through a dreamlike haziness, with occasional surrealist images, is one of the gypsy ballads of the Spanish poet Federico García Lorca.

· SLEEPWALKERS' BALLAD ·

Green I love you green.
Green of the wind. Green branches.
The ship far out at sea.
The horse above on the mountain.
Shadows dark at her waist,   5
she's dreaming there on her terrace,
green of her cheek, green hair,
with eyes like chilly silver.
Green I love you green.
Under that moon of the gypsies   10
things are looking at her
but she can't return their glances.

Green I love you green.
The stars are frost, enormous;
a tuna cloud floats over   15
nosing off to the dawn.
The fig tree catches a wind
to grate in its emery branches;
the mountain's a wildcat, sly,
bristling its acrid cactus.   20
But—who's on the road? Which way?
She's dreaming there on her terrace,
green of her cheek, green hair,
she dreams of the bitter sea.

"Friend, what I want is to trade   25
this horse of mine for your house,
this saddle of mine for your mirror,
this knife of mine for your blanket.
Friend, I come bleeding, see,
from the mountain pass of Cabra."   30
"I would if I could, young man;
I'd have taken you up already.
But I'm not myself any longer,
nor my house my home any more."
"Friend, what I want is to die   35
in a bed of my own—die nicely.
An iron bed, if there is one,
between good linen sheets.
I'm wounded, throat and breast,
from here to here—you see it?"   40
"You've a white shirt on; three hundred
roses across—dark roses.
There's a smell of blood about you;
your sash, all round you, soaked.
But I'm not myself any longer,   45
nor my house my home any more."

THE MIND

"Then let me go up, though; let me!
at least to the terrace yonder.
Let me go up then, let me!
up to the high green roof.   50
Terrace-rails of the moonlight,
splash of the lapping tank."

So they go up, companions,
up to the high roof-terrace;
a straggle of blood behind them,   55
behind, a straggle of tears.
Over the roofs, a shimmer
like little tin lamps, and glassy
tambourines by the thousand
slitting the glitter of dawn.   60

Green I love you green,
green of the wind, green branches.
They're up there, two companions.
A wind from the distance leaving
its tang on the tongue, strange flavors   65
of bile, of basil and mint.
"Where is she, friend—that girl
with the bitter heart, your daughter?"
"How often she'd wait and wait,
how often she'd be here waiting,   70
fresh of face, hair black,
here in green of the terrace."

There in her terrace pool
was the gypsy girl, in ripples.
Green of her cheek, green hair,   75
with eyes like chilly silver.
Icicles from the moon
held her afloat on the water.
Night became intimate then—
enclosed, like a little plaza.   80
Drunken, the Civil Guard
had been banging the door below them.
Green I love you green.
Green of the wind. Green branches.
The ship far out at sea.   85
The horse above on the mountain.

Federico García Lorca (1899–1936)

Since insanity is the supreme form (next to suicide) of the mind's crying out against itself, the Surrealists were interested in the visions of madness—though not as much as we might have expected, possibly because the more insane people are, the more incoherent they are likely to become. Their rantings can be as boring as the sane person's platitudes.

One of the best and strangest poems in English that professes to come from the mind of a madman is "Loving Mad Tom" (or "Tom o' Bedlam's Song"), which first appeared in a manuscript collection of 1615 (see Anthology, p. 415).

The Tom of our poem has been driven out of his mind by love for a girl named Maudlin (or Magdalen), whose name suggests an ex-prostitute. He has been an inmate of Bedlam (the Hospital of St. Mary of Bethlehem), the London lunatic asylum. His treatment there consisted of handcuffs, whippings, and starvation. Now released, he has become a Bedlam beggar—one of the many discharged patients, either still mad or pretending to be, who roamed the country in search of food and money, which they got by begging and threatening. Our Tom declares that when well treated he is generally harmless, though he practices petty thievery when he can and goes hungry when he cannot. He says he is fierce, however—"Tom Rhinoceros!"—when treated harshly. He is also involved in magic and has gaudy hallucinations.

exercises & diversions

A. 1. In "The Subverted Flower," what is meant by the flower symbolism of the first four lines? How is the flower "subverted"?

2. From whose point of view (through whose consciousness) is the situation presented? The boy's? The girl's? The poet's?

B. 1. Is it fair to say that "Sunday Morning" is a dialogue with one speaker represented by the "She said" and words in quotation marks? Who is the other speaker? Is there ever a third?

2. If you summarized in a sentence the meaning of each stanza of "Sunday Morning," would the sentences add up to a logical argument? A logical proof of anything? Does their logical validity affect their poetic validity?

C. In the first of the passages that follow, the duchess of Newcastle is very sensible in writing about "What Is Liquid." In the second, Marvell is not very sensible in suggesting how one might get a supply of tears for an especially mournful bereavement.

exercises & diversions

1. All that doth flow we cannot liquid name,
   Or else would fire and water be the same;
   But that is liquid which is moist and wet;
   Fire that property can never get:
   Then 'tis not cold that doth the fire put out,   5
   But 'tis the wet that makes it die, no doubt.

2. Hastings is dead, and we must find a store
   Of tears untouched, and never wept before.
   Go stand betwixt the morning and the flowers;
   And, ere they fall, arrest the early showers.

Yet most would agree that Marvell's lines are better poetry. Does this show that our discussion has overestimated the importance of common sense in poetry?

D. A poem that uses imagery to make a point ought to make sense on *both* levels—that of the intended meaning and that of the imagery. Are both levels well managed in these poems: "The Tyger" (p. 440), "Traveling Through the Dark" (p. 115), "Neither out Far Nor in Deep" (p. 134), "The Eel" (p. 291), "Dover Beach" (p. 243)?

E. **Travesty** and **burlesque** are akin to parody. The first (related to "transvestite") means that garments are changed—a lofty style, for example, shifted to a vulgar or comic one. Travesty drags something down—we speak of a "travesty of justice." Burlesque (from the Italian *burla*, joke) is less literary or critical than parody. It tries to be funny just for the fun of it.

1. The following verses are a takeoff on what famous poet?

2. Would you classify them as parody, travesty, or burlesque—or a combination of any two or all three?

3. What elements of style of the famous poet have been selected for attention?

I NEVER PLUCKED—A BUMBLEBEE

I never plucked—a Bumblebee—
Without I marvelled—"Ouch!"—
Wise Nature—hath such ways to
  show—
Her children—"Mustn't touch!"

I never chewed—a Beetle up—
Sans pouting—"Icky-poo!"
Did Beetle taste—like
  "Choc-o-late"—
He were extinctive now.

exercises & diversions

I never did me—this or that—
Without—I something said.
I put a Pumpkin—on my neck—
And used to call it—"Head"—

Till Robin—cocked his dapper
    eye—
Impeachment—sir—of me?
As one who—off his rocker flip—
Or fruitcake—nutty be?

Anonymous

F. "Kubla Khan" illustrates almost all of the technical points about poetry that we have been discussing.

1. Are there any lines that do not engage one of our senses?

2. Have all the senses been involved by the time the poem ends?

3. Is the vocabulary simple? Does it have a high percentage of "thing-words"?

4. Can you find examples of the functional use of assonance and alliteration?

5. Why did the writer change "Kublai" and "Xamdu" to "Kubla" and "Xanadu" in the poem?

6. How many rhymes can you find on a single sound? How many lines apart can the rhymes be?

7. What two line-lengths are used? Is the shift from one to the other significant? Is there ever a third?

8. Can you find all of the "options" mentioned in our treatment of iambic verse? Are those that you find used expressively?

9. Does the poem, in its own way and as far as it goes, "make sense"? Are there any surrealist details?

10. Do you think it odd that the most celebrated of all dream poems is so craft conscious?

G. The painter Sophie Taeuber (wife of Jean Arp) describes a dream she once had:

Last night I dreamt that I was on a beach. . . . I heard the voices of my friends grow fainter and fainter. I was alone, and, while the night fell, my index finger wrote the word "happy" on the sand, as though it had been impelled by an outside force. While tracing the letters, I saw the word sink into the stone. A muffled, whispering noise made me look up. It was a great slab of rock which had broken loose and was poised ominously above me. And the thought flashed into my mind that if it crushed me that very moment, all that would be left of me would be the single word "happy."

Describe a dream of your own in a way that brings out its kinship with poetry.

H. 1. Make up half a dozen or so surrealist images consisting of noun and adjective, like Breton's "soluble fish" or "white-haired revolver."

2. Invent a half-dozen or so interesting surrealist objects, like the fur-lined breakfast set.

3. Do you recall any poems that you read with such disbelief that you found yourself noticing faults with as sharp an eye as Robert Graves'? Write a Gravesian analysis of a poem you find particularly vulnerable.

4. Write a parody (or travesty or burlesque) of any poem or poet that strikes your fancy. (Suggested titles: "Walt Whitman Among the Yellow Pages," "The Coy Mistress Replies," "Most Like a Hearse This Marriage," "anyone lived in a pretty (huh?) town," "The Ruby Yacht of Omar K. Yamm." Or, better, make up your own.)

14

Adam's Curse
INSPIRATION AND EFFORT

How do poems come into being at all?

Some people believe they are produced by a mysterious something called "inspiration." Poets, in this view, are a sort of medium; they have nothing to do but sit there and let themselves be played on by celestial fingers.

• INSPIRATION •

How often have I started out
With no thought in my noddle,
And wandered here and there about,
Where fancy bade me toddle;
Till feeling faunlike in my glee   5
I've voiced some gay distiches,
Returning joyfully to tea,
A poem in my britches.

A-squatting on a thymy slope
With vast of sky about me,   10
I've scribbled on an envelope
The rhymes the hills would shout me;
The couplets that the trees would call,
The lays the breezes proffered . . .
Oh, no, I didn't *think* at all—   15
I took what Nature offered.

⁶/**distiches:** *distichs* (sic) *are units of two lines. The plural is pronounced* dis-ticks; *Service mispronounces it to rhyme with* britches.

For that's the way you ought to write—
Without a trace of trouble;
Be super-charged with high delight
And let the words out-bubble;   *20*
Be voice of vale and wood and stream
Without design or proem:
Then rouse from out a golden dream
To find you've made a poem.

So I'll go forth with mind a blank,   *25*
And sea and sky will spell me;
And lolling on a thymy bank
I'll take down what they tell me;
As Mother Nature speaks to me
Her words I'll gaily docket,   *30*
So I'll come singing home to tea
A poem in my pocket.

       Robert W. Service (1874–1958)

"Read from some humbler poet," wrote Longfellow, "Whose songs gushed from his heart. . . ." Robert Service is one of those humbler poets, and his songs do indeed "gush." Poets of higher intensity work against greater resistance. The account Dylan Thomas gives of how he composed is very different. Instead of toddling around out-bubbling, he works—he *labors* at the *exercise* of his *craft* or *art*, which is *sullen* because words, like marble, are resistant material.

· IN MY CRAFT OR SULLEN ART ·

In my craft or sullen art
Exercised in the still night
When only the moon rages
And the lovers lie abed
With all their griefs in their arms,   *5*
I labour by singing light
Not for ambition or bread
Or the strut and trade of charms
On the ivory stages
But for the common wages   *10*
Of their most secret heart.

Not for the proud man apart
From the raging moon I write
On these spindrift pages
Nor for the towering dead   *15*

ADAM'S CURSE

With their nightingales and psalms
But for the lovers, their arms
Round the griefs of the ages,
Who pay no praise or wages
Nor heed my craft or art.   20

Dylan Thomas (1914–1953)

A good poem is likely to seem so spontaneous, so easy, so natural,
that we can hardly imagine the poet sweating over it—crossing out
lines, scrawling in between them, making out lists of rhymes or syn-
onyms. But enough of the poets' scribbled-over manuscripts are extant
—under lock and key in rare-book rooms or under glass in museums—
for us to know that most poets did indeed find their muse a difficult
mistress.

A poem that seems spontaneous may have come into being after a
long and painful birth. All that matters is that the finished poem seem
spontaneous. Yeats told us with what difficulty his own poems were
written:

> . . . A line will take us hours maybe;
> Yet if it does not seem a moment's thought,
> Our stitching and unstitching has been naught.
> . . . It's certain there is no fine thing
> Since Adam's fall but needs much laboring.   5

Toujours travailler—always keep on working—was a motto of the
sculptor Rodin. The greater the artist (there are few exceptions to
this) the harder that artist works. It was Picasso, and not some in-
dustrious office manager, who said, "Man invented the alarm clock."

Most writers work hard over their lines to make it seem they have
not worked at all. When Keats said that unless poetry came "as
naturally as the leaves to a tree, it had better not come at all," by
"naturally" he cannot have meant *effortlessly*, as his own much worked-
over manuscripts demonstrate. No poets have been so divinely gifted
that they did not have to struggle to find themselves: "A good poet's
made," said Ben Jonson, "as well as born." Nearly all poets would
agree with Edwin Muir that "to write naturally, especially in verse, is
one of the most difficult things in the world; naturalness does not
come easily to the awkward human race, and is an achievement of art."
As for easy writing, the dramatist Richard Brinsley Sheridan has
summed that up for us: "Easy writing's cursed hard reading."

THE MIND

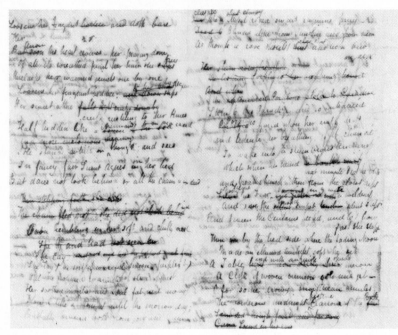

A manuscript of John Keats' "The Eve of St. Agnes," stanzas 26–29 [cf. pp. 462–3]

(Fogg Art Museum, Harvard)

Ideas suddenly and unaccountably flashing into the light of consciousness are called inspirations. We get them in any field in which our minds move with knowledge and experience. They are more often foolish than wise, but even when they are promising, we usually have to work out the details. Poets find that words or lines will suddenly be "given" to them, as if flashed on a mental screen. But they then have to work out the continuity that will complete the poem. Without these given lines, these inspirations, probably no poems come into being. It would be possible for us to know all there was to know about the theory and technique of poetry, and yet never be able to write a poem. It seems that we cannot *will* to do anything creative, although we can will to bring about conditions favorable to inspiration and can will to work on the inspiration once it comes. Technique *in itself* can do little; it is valuable only in the service of passion and inspiration.

The ratio between inspiration and deliberate effort differs in differ-

ADAM'S CURSE

(© 1971 United Feature Syndicate, Inc.)

ent artists. Music came easily to Mozart, but not to Beethoven, who had to jot down his ideas, rework them again and again, sometimes completing a theme twenty-five years after the idea for it struck him. His way of composing, compared with Mozart's, was stodgy and plodding, but the music that resulted was no less "inspired." So too with poets. Some work rapidly, some slowly. The number of flashes of inspiration that go into the process may have little to do with the quality of the poem that results. Frost considered unfinished one poem he had begun to work on fourteen years before; he left another "lying around nameless" for forty years because he could not find a fourth line that suited him.

It should be stressed again that our inspirations are as specialized as our minds are. If our whole bent is toward Romance philology or football strategy, we will not come up with inspirations in the field of economic theory. Inspirations follow common-sense rules: We get only the inspirations we are qualified to receive. And unless we have laid the groundwork by conscious planning and hard work, there is no inspiration to be hoped for.

"Chance," said Pasteur, "favors the prepared mind." Poets have to condition their minds to produce and handle inspirations. If they have a vocabulary of only a few hundred words, the unconscious has very little to work with. If they have taken little notice of the world around, their minds will suffer from a poverty of images. If they have not read other poets, they will not know when they are original and when they are not—as if a young physicist, scorning the achievements of the past, were to spend his time reinventing the wheel.

The influence of a well-conditioned conscious mind extends to the unconscious, which continues to work, often more originally and brilliantly, with the patterns we have consciously set up. All the artist's work, before the fact of inspiration, is a way of programing the unconscious along desirable lines.

THE MIND

Malcolm Cowley's description of Hart Crane's writing habits shows that apparently wild bursts of spontaneity were based on months or even years of careful thought.

> There would be a Sunday afternoon party. . . . Hart would be laughing twice as hard as the rest of us . . . he would be drinking twice as much hard cider and contributing more than his share of the crazy metaphors and overblown epithets. Gradually he would fall silent and a little later we would find that he had disappeared. . . .
>
> An hour later . . . he would appear in the kitchen or on the croquet court. . . . In his hands would be two or three sheets of typewritten manuscript, with words crossed out and new lines scrawled in. "Read that," he would say. "Isn't that the *grrrrea*test poem ever written!" . . .
>
> I later discovered that Hart would have been meditating over that particular poem for months or even years, scribbling verses on pieces of paper that he carried in his pockets and meanwhile waiting for the moment of pure inspiration when he could put them all together. . . .
>
> Painfully, perseveringly—and dead sober—Hart would revise his new poem, clarifying its images, correcting its meter and searching through dictionaries and thesauruses for exactly the right word. . . . Even after the poem had been completed, the manuscript mailed to *Poetry* or the *Dial* and perhaps accepted, he would still have changes to make. . . .*

The knowledge of how to make something of our insights is what we call **technique.** Those who care about communicating their insights care very much about technique, which Ezra Pound said he believed in "as a test of a man's sincerity." Those who do not care about it are like the writer who, as James Russell Lowell said,

> . . . might have been poet, but that, in its stead, he
> Preferred to believe that he was so already.

"Trifles," Michelangelo is reported to have said, "make perfection, and perfection is no trifle." When Frost once digressed into a discussion of some technical point at a reading of his poems, a member of the audience objected:

> "But Mr. Frost, when you're writing your *beautiful* poems, you can't really be thinking of technical things like that? You can't really like *those!*"
> "Like 'em?" Frost growled, "I revel in 'em!"

Dylan Thomas is even more emphatic:

---

* From Malcolm Cowley, *Exile's Return* (New York: Viking, 1941), pp. 145–147.

ADAM'S CURSE

What I like to do is to treat words as a craftsman does his wood or stone or what-have-you, to hew, carve, mould, coil, polish and plane them into patterns, sequences, sculptures, fugues of sound. . . .

I am a painstaking, conscientious, involved and devious craftsman in words. . . . I use everything and anything to make my poems work and move in the direction I want them to: old tricks, new tricks, puns, portmanteau-words, paradox, allusion, paronomasia, paragram, catachresis, slang, assonantal rhymes, vowel rhymes, sprung rhythm. . . . The inventions and contrivances are all part of the joy that is part of the painful, voluntary work.*

A worker in a more popular field, the film director Federico Fellini, told Ray Bradbury that the rumors that he makes up a script as he shoots are "stupid gossip. It's absolutely impossible to improvise. Making a movie is a mathematical operation. It is like sending a missile to the moon. Art is a scientific operation." Fellini himself, according to Woody Allen, is ruled by "technical passion." "All artistic problems" Allen went on to say, "are really technical." Artists in every medium (except for some Surrealists) downplay the role of chance in what they create, and in denying it they return not to some sophisticated world but to the world of the child and of primitive people. For early cultures, there was no such thing as chance; everything had its cause. And so for children: As Piaget has observed, "The idea of chance is absent from the mentality of a child."

Preoccupation with technique can protect writers from the tyranny of the spontaneous, the zombielike acceptance of absolutely everything—trash and treasure alike—that floats up from the depths of the psyche. It can also encourage the objectivity they need to judge their own work, a quality not easy to maintain if they let themselves be swept away by the self-indulgence of their own emotions.

After inspiration has struck and has been recorded more or less satisfactorily in a first draft, poets begin their laborious process of revision. The process is only natural—it assumes that our first thoughts are not always our best ones. In life we often modify the phraseology that first occurred to us—if we have a chance to. We can see how studiously we revise after we have been put down by someone else's clever remark. Perhaps all we can do at the time is mutter something like, "Oh, yeah? Look who's talking!"—not exactly a brilliant comeback. All the way home we may be mulling, "What I *should* have said to that guy was. . . ." As the days go by and we continue to revise, what we should have said gets better and better.

---

* From James Scully, *Modern Poets on Modern Poetry* (New York: McGraw-Hill, 1965), pp. 196–197.

THE MIND

This is exactly what poets are doing when they work over their first thoughts: Revision is a what-I-should-have-said process. And even though it relies a great deal on reason and calculation, it can be very passionate. Nor is it shutting the door on inspiration. It is merely giving inspiration, which takes its own sweet time, a second chance to strike—and a third, and a fourth, until we feel it is right on target.

Poets, with very few exceptions, take pleasure in the work of revision. The Surrealists revised extensively. D. H. Lawrence said, "It has taken me twenty years to say what I started to say, incoherently, when I was nineteen, in this poem. . . ." E. E. Cummings could begin a poem with, "O sweet spontaneous earth . . . ," but he did not let spontaneity interfere with his own painstaking craftsmanship. Sometimes he wrote one or two hundred versions of a poem before he felt it was right.

Often, lines that look as if they had occurred to poets in a moment of inspiration turn out to have been revised into their perfection. One example is from Keats' "Ode to a Nightingale":

> The same that oft-times hath
> Charm'd magic casements, opening on the foam
> Of perilous seas, in faery lands forlorn.

The first inspiration was less memorable:

> Charmed the wide casements, opening on the foam
> Of ruthless seas, in faery lands fo'lorn.

Whitman's line

> Out of the cradle endlessly rocking

benefited immeasurably from revision. His original inspiration was the toneless

> Out of the rocked cradle . . .

which he varied many ways before he got the simple music he wanted. Whitman, though elsewhere he may have loafed and invited his soul, was a hard worker at his poetry, doing prodigious amounts of revision over the decades.

William Blake is another poet often thought of as inspired, which

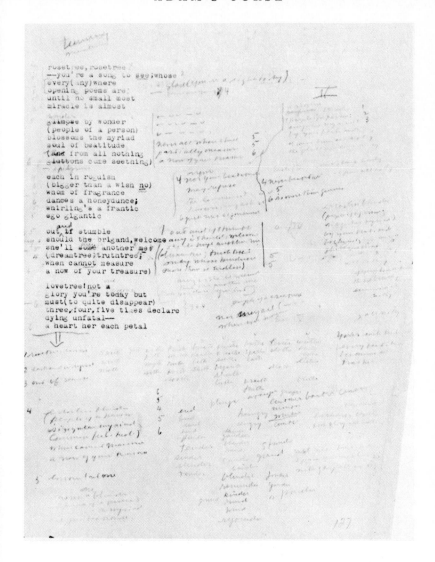

A worksheet of E. E. Cummings—one of the 175 sheets for his nine-stanza "rose-tree." Numbers to the left of the lines indicate the number of syllables; yet the scansion, in the conventional marks for long and short syllables, shows that the poet was also working with accent. The worksheets also have lists of rhymes, indications of vowel and consonant patterns, and various other charts and graphs. Cummings obviously took tremendous care as he composed his apparently artless poems.
(University of Connecticut Photo)

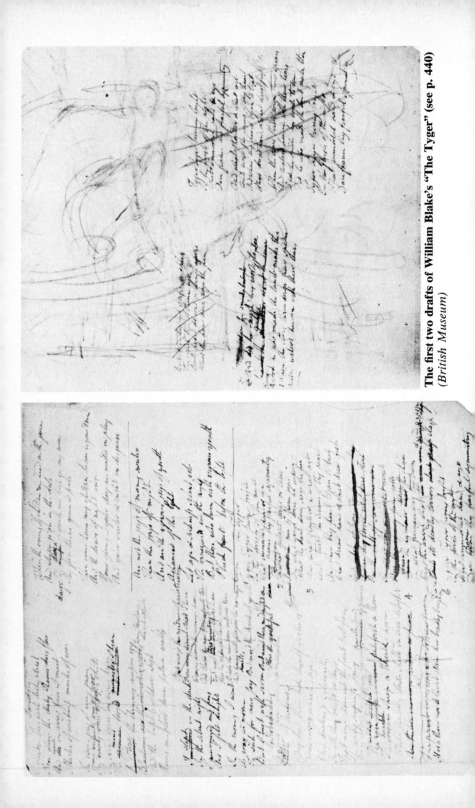

The first two drafts of William Blake's "The Tyger" (see p. 440)
(British Museum)

indeed he claimed to be. "The Authors," he said of his work, "are in Eternity." But an editor familiar with his manuscripts corrects that impression:

> It was Blake's belief . . . that long passages, or even whole poems, were merely transcribed by him from the dictation of spirits. The evidence of extant MSS., however, shows that he himself saw nothing final or absolute in this verbal inspiration, but submitted these writings like any others to such successive changes as at length satisfied his artistic conscience. . . . Blake's meticulous care in composition is everywhere apparent in the poems preserved in rough draft. . . . There we find the first crude version, or single stanza around which his idea was to take shape, followed by alteration on alteration, re-arrangement after re-arrangement, deletions, additions and inversions, until at last the poem as in the case of "The Tiger" attains its perfect form. . . .*

Sometimes poets, in addition to making lesser changes, feel that the whole poem should be reconceived and restructured, as Lawrence does when he reduces the five stanzas of his early "The Piano" to the three stanzas of "Piano."

• THE PIANO •

Somewhere beneath that piano's superb sleek black
Must hide my mother's piano, little and brown, with the back
That stood close to the wall, and the front's faded silk both torn,
And the keys with little hollows, that my mother's fingers had worn.

Softly, in the shadows, a woman is singing to me   5
Quietly, through the years I have crept back to see
A child sitting under the piano, in the boom of the shaking strings
Pressing the little poised feet of the mother who smiles as she sings.

The full throated woman has chosen a winning, living song
And surely the heart that is in me must belong   10
To the old Sunday evenings, when darkness wandered outside
And hymns gleamed on our warm lips, as we watched mother's
     fingers glide.

Or this is my sister at home in the old front room
Singing love's first surprised gladness, alone in the gloom.
She will start when she sees me, and blushing, spread out her hands   15
To cover my mouth's raillery, till I'm bound in her shame's heart-
     spun bands.

---

* From *The Poetical Works of William Blake*, ed. by John Sampson (Oxford University Press, 1913).

A woman is singing me a wild Hungarian air
And her arms, and her bosom, and the whole of her soul is bare,
And the great black piano is clamouring as my mother's never could
    clamour
And my mother's tunes are devoured of this music's ravaging glamour. *20*

· **PIANO** ·

Softly, in the dusk, a woman is singing to me;
Taking me back down the vista of years, till I see
A child sitting under the piano, in the boom of the tingling strings
And pressing the small, poised feet of a mother who smiles as she sings.

In spite of myself, the insidious mastery of song   5
Betrays me back, till the heart of me weeps to belong
To the old Sunday evenings at home, with winter outside
And hymns in the cosy parlour, the tinkling piano our guide.

So now it is vain for the singer to burst into clamour
With the great black piano appassionato. The glamour   *10*
Of childish days is upon me, my manhood is cast
Down in the flood of remembrance, I weep like a child for the past.

D. H. Lawrence (1885–1930)

In the earlier poem the poet, or the character he imagines, is listening to "a wild Hungarian air." The music puts him in mind of a very different kind of music, that of hymns sung at home when he was small enough to sit under the old-fashioned square piano. But the soft music he remembers is swallowed up in the "ravaging glamour" of the wild new music.

In the second version, the childhood memory of music at home is more powerful than the effect of the sexy singer. The poem becomes a lament for the lost innocence of childhood.

If a critical poll were taken, likely enough it would select Yeats as the greatest poet of the twentieth century. No poet ever derived less from inspiration or worked harder at hammering his poems into shape. Yeats found writing an "intense unnatural labor that reduces composition to four or five lines a day." He even said he did much of his work by the critical, rather than the imaginative faculty. We can get some idea of the labor that went into his poetry by looking at the fifth stanza of "Among School Children" (see Anthology, p. 499), which could be summarized as saying: If a mother could see her baby as he will be sixty years later, would all the trouble of his birth seem

ADAM'S CURSE

Not all writers believe in revision.
(Verlag Beringer & Pampaluchi/Zoological Gardens, Zurich)

worthwhile? (Lines 3 and 4 refer to the Platonic notion that the child exists before birth and would like to return to that earlier world unless the memory of it were destroyed by "the drug.")

Yeats' manuscripts show that he started out with a list of possible rhymes for the stanza:

lap	fears	lap
shape	~~tears~~	made
	~~years~~	escape
	~~forth~~ birth	betrayed
	forth	shape
		head

These are obviously not words that just happened to rhyme, as if Yeats were going through the alphabet. The ideas these words stand for are a framework for the way he thought his stanza might develop.

On the two facing pages 388 and 389 we have, on the right-hand page, the clear, simple, and logical lines that finally made up the stanza. The last two lines seem to have come to Yeats easily—or he may have worked hard at them on a manuscript sheet now lost. But the other lines came only after a difficult struggle with alternative versions,

THE MIND

What mother of a child shrieking the first scream
Of a soul
Of a soul struggling to leave
Degradation of the ——
What mother with a child upon her breast
Shedding there its tears, all the despair
Of the soul betrayed into the flesh
What youthful mother, rocking on her lap

A fretful thing that knows itself betrayed
Still knowing that it is betrayed[?]
Still half remembering that it [is] betrayed
A thing, the ~~oblivious honey has~~ generative honey had betrayed

And struggles with vain clamor to escape
And that shrieks out and struggles to escape
And that must sleep, ~~or~~ shriek struggle to escape

Before its memory and apprehension fade
Before its   the memories of its freedom fade
As its drugged memories gleam or fade
As it
As still but half drugged memories decide
As its drugged memories may decide
Where some brief memories or the drug decide
~~As flitting~~   As sudden memories or the drug decide

Would think—[if] it came before her in a vision
Would think—had she ~~foreknown~~ foreknowledge of that shape
Would think her son could she foreknow that shape
Would think her son, ~~could she foreknow~~ did she but see that shape

~~The image~~   What the child would be at sixty years
Her son with sixty winters on his head
With maybe sixty winters on   upon his head
With sixty or more winters upon his head
With sixty or more winters on ~~his~~ its head

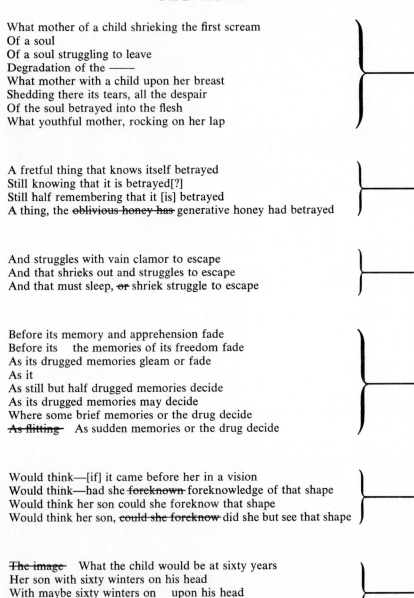

ADAM'S CURSE

What youthful mother, a shape upon her lap

Honey of generation had betrayed,

And that must sleep, shriek, struggle to escape

As recollection or the drug decide,

Would think her son, did she but see that shape

With sixty or more winters on its head,

A compensation for the pang of his birth,
Or the uncertainty of his setting forth?

printed on the left-hand page (which is mostly a rubble of undistinguished language). Work sheets preliminary to these may well have been lost or destroyed. Yeats may have made many choices in his own head before writing a word down.

He would make further changes as he dictated. He could then go to work on the neatly typed copy, making so many revisions that it would have to be retyped. And so on. If the poem had appeared in a magazine, he might further rework it before book publication. Even after the book appeared the revisions continued. Many years after he wrote some of his early poems, he revised them in his later manner—turning "early Yeats" into "late Yeats."

When we see how easily the poem reads it is hard to remember what must have been the pangs of its birth and the uncertainties of its setting forth.

exercises & diversions

A. A. E. Housman has this to say about the composition of his "I Hoed and Trenched and Weeded": "Two of the stanzas, I do not say which, came into my head, just as they are printed. . . . A third stanza came with a little coaxing after tea. One more was needed, but it did not come: I had to turn to and compose it myself, and that was a laborious business. I wrote it thirteen times, and it was more than a twelvemonth before I got it right."

Can you guess which two stanzas came easily, which came with a little coaxing, and which came with difficulty?

I HOED AND TRENCHED AND WEEDED

I hoed and trenched and weeded,
  And took the flowers to fair:
I brought them home unheeded;
  The hue was not the wear.

So up and down I sow them   5
  For lads like me to find,
When I shall lie below them,
  A dead man out of mind.

Some seed the birds devour,
  And some the season mars,   10

But here and there will flower
  The solitary stars,

And fields will yearly bear them
  As light-leaved spring comes on,
And luckless lads will wear them
  When I am dead and gone.

15

A. E. Housman (1859–1936)

B. 1. In the twenty-five or more years that FitzGerald spent on his five editions of *The Rubáiyát* (p. 466), he tried many of the stanzas several ways. Here are three versions of his original stanza XII. Can you see a progressive improvement?

"How sweet is mortal Sovranty!"—think some:
Others—"How blest the Paradise to come!"
  Ah, take the Cash in hand and waive the Rest;
Oh, the brave Music of a *distant* Drum!

Some for the Glories of This World; and some
Sigh for the Prophet's Paradise to come;
  Ah, take the Cash, and let the promise go,
Nor heed the music of a distant Drum!

Some for the Glories of This World; and some
Sigh for the Prophet's Paradise to come;
  Ah, take the Cash, and let the Credit go,
Nor heed the rumble of a distant Drum!

2. Is there a progressive improvement in the changes made in what was originally stanza LXXIV? (No one holds that *all* revisions are improvements.)

Ah, Moon of my Delight, who know'st no wane,
The Moon of Heav'n is rising once again:
  How oft hereafter rising shall she look
Through this same Garden after me—in vain!

But see! The rising Moon of Heav'n again—
Looks for us, Sweet-heart, through the quivering Plane:
  How oft hereafter rising will she look
Among those leaves—for one of us in vain!

Yon rising Moon that looks for us again—
How oft hereafter will she wax and wane;
  How oft hereafter rising look for us
Through this same Garden—and for *one* in vain!

exercises & diversions

C. Look closely at the two versions of D. H. Lawrence's poem about the piano, asking yourself such questions as these:

1. Why is the description of the mother's old worn piano omitted in the later version?

2. The nightclub singer is a brilliant figure. Does the later version suffer by making no mention of her?

3. Why is the original fourth stanza, pleasant in itself, omitted in the later version?

4. Why are "shaking strings" changed to "tingling strings"?

5. Why is "darkness" changed to "winter"?

D. Here is an example of "early Yeats" turned into "late Yeats." In what do the differences chiefly consist? Imagery? Emotion? Diction? Rhythm? Form? Does the meaning change?

THE LAMENTATION OF THE OLD PENSIONER

(1890 version)

I had a chair at every hearth,
   When no one turned to see,
With 'Look at that old fellow there,
   And who may he be?'
And therefore do I wander now,   *5*
   And the fret lies on me.

The road-side trees keep murmuring.
   Ah, wherefore murmur ye,
As in the old days long gone by,
   Green oak and poplar tree?   *10*
The well-known faces are all gone:
   And the fret lies on me.

(1925 version)

Although I shelter from the rain
Under a broken tree,
My chair was nearest to the fire
In every company
That talked of love or politics,   *5*
Ere Time transfigured me.

Though lads are making pikes again
For some conspiracy,
And crazy rascals rage their fill

At human tyranny,   *10*
My contemplations are of Time
That has transfigured me.

There's not a woman turns her face
Upon a broken tree,
And yet the beauties that I loved   *15*
Are in my memory;
I spit into the face of Time
That has transfigured me.

William Butler Yeats (1865–1939)

E. Pick out something you wrote for this class. Along what lines do you
think it could be revised? Work at revising it.

ANTHOLOGY

ANONYMOUS
(FIFTEENTH CENTURY)

• ADAM LAY IBOUNDEN •

Adam lay ibounden,
    Bounden in a bond,
Foure thousand winter
    Thoght he not too long;
And al was for an appil,   *5*
    An appil that he tok,
As clerkės finden
    Wreten in here bok.

Ne hadde the appil takė ben,
    The appil taken ben,   *10*
Ne hadde never our lady
    A ben hevenė quene;
Blessed be the timė
    That appil takė was!
Therfore we moun singen   *15*
    "Deo gracias."

7/**clerkės:** *scholars, clerics*   12/**a:** *have*
8/**here:** *their*   15/**moun:** *may*

ANONYMOUS
(SIXTEENTH CENTURY OR EARLIER)

• A LYKE-WAKE DIRGE •

This ae nighte, this ae nighte,
    Every nighte and alle;
Fire and sleete, and candle lighte,
    And Christe receive thye saule.

When thou from hence away are past,   *5*
    Every nighte and alle;
To Whinny-muir thou comest at laste;
    And Christe receive thye saule.

If ever thou gavest hosen and shoon,
    Every nighte and alle;   *10*
Sit thee down, and put them on;
    And Christe receive thye saule.

lyke-wake: *wake for a corpse*   7/**Whinny-muir:** *a moor of prickly*
1/**ae:** *one*   *plants*
4/**saule:** *soul*   9/**hosen and shoon:** *stockings and*
    shoes

If hosen and shoon thou ne'er gavest nane,
  Every nighte and alle;
The whinnes shall pricke thee to the bare bane   *15*
  And Christe receive thye saule.

From Whinny-muir when thou mayst passe,
  Every nighte and alle;
To Brigg o' Dread thou comest at laste;
  And Christ receive thye saule.   *20*

From Brigg o' Dread when thou mayst passe,
  Every nighte and alle;
To purgatory fire thou comest at laste,
  And Christe receive thye saule.

If ever thou gavest meate or drinke,   *25*
  Every nighte and alle;
The fire shall never make thee shrinke,
  And Christe receive thye saule.

If meate or drinke thou never gavest nane,
  Every nighte and alle;   *30*
The fire will burn thee to the bare bane;
  And Christe receive thye saule.

This ae nighte, this ae nighte,
  Every nighte and alle;
Fire and sleete, and candle lighte,   *35*
  And Christe receive thye saule.

[15]/**bane:** *bone*   [29]/**nane:** *none*
[19]/**Brigg:** *bridge*

ANONYMOUS
(SIXTEENTH CENTURY)

• LULLY, LULLEY, LULLY, LULLEY •

Lully, lulley, lully, lulley,
The fawcon hath born my mak away.

He bare hym up, he bare hym down;
He bare hym in to an orchard browne.

In that orchard ther was an halle,   *5*
That was hangid with purpill and pall.

[2]/**fawcon:** *falcon*   [6]/**pall:** *rich cloth*
  mak: *mate*

And in that hall ther was a bedde;
Hit was hangid with gold so redde.

And yn that bed ther lythe a knyght,
His wowndes bledyng day and nyght.   10

By that bedes side kneleth a may,
& she wepeth both nyght and day.

& by that bedes side ther stondeth a ston,
Corpus Christi wretyn ther on.

11/**may:** *maiden*   14/**Corpus Christi:** *body of Christ*

ANONYMOUS

· EDWARD, EDWARD ·

"Why dois your brand sae drap wi' bluid,
        Edward, Edward?
Why dois your brand sae drap wi' bluid,
   And why sae sad gang yee, O?"
"O, I hae killed my hauke sae guid,   5
        Mither, mither:
O, I hae killed my hauke sae guid,
   And I had nae mair bot hee, O."

"Your haukis bluid was nevir sae reid;
        Edward, Edward.   10
Your haukis bluid was nevir sae reid,
   My deir son I tell thee, O."
"O, I hae killed my reid-roan steid,
        Mither, mither:
O, I hae killed my reid-roan steid,   15
   That erst was sae fair and frie, O."

"Your steid was auld, and ye hae gat mair,
        Edward, Edward:
Your steid was auld, and ye hae gat mair,
   Sum other dule ye drie, O."   20
"O, I hae killed my fadir deir,
        Mither, mither:
O, I hae killed my fadir deir,
   Alas, and wae is mee, O."

1/**brand:** *sword*   8/**nae mair bot:** *no more but*
  sae: *so*   16/**erst:** *before*
4/**gang:** *go*   20/**dule ye drie:** *sorrow you suffer*

"And whatten penance wul ye drie for that,
      Edward, Edward?   25
And whatten penance wul ye drie for that,
    My deir son, now tell me, O."
"Ile set my feit in yonder boat,
           Mither, mither: 30
Ile set my feit in yonder boat,
    And Ile fare ovir the sea, O."

"And what wul ye doe wi' your towirs and your ha',
      Edward, Edward?
And what wul ye doe wi' your towirs and your ha',
    That were sae fair to see, O?"   35
"Ile let thame stand til they doun fa',
           Mither, mither:
"Ile let thame stand til they doun fa',
    For here nevir mair maun I bee, O."   40

"And what wul ye leive to your bairns and your wife,
      Edward, Edward?
And what wul ye leive to your bairns and your wife,
    Whan ye gang ovir the sea, O?"
"The warldis room, late tham beg thrae life,   45
           Mither, mither:
The warldis room, late tham beg thrae life,
    For thame nevir mair wul I see, O."

"And what wul ye leive to your ain mither deir,
      Edward, Edward?   50
And what wul ye leive to your ain mither deir?
    My deir son, now tell me, O."
"The curse of hell frae me sall ye beir,
           Mither, mither:
The curse of hell frae me sall ye beir,   55
    Sic conseils ye gave to me, O."

[33]/**ha':** *hall*
[37]/**fa':** *fall*
[40]/**maun:** *must*
[41]/**bairns:** *children*
[45]/**warldis:** *world's*

[47]/**late tham beg thrae:** *let them beg through*
[49]/**ain:** *own*
[53]/**frae:** *from*
   sall: *shall*
[56]/**sic:** *such*

· LORD RANDAL ·

"O where hae ye been, Lord Randal, my son?
O where hae ye been, my handsome young man?"
"I hae been to the wild wood; mother, make my bed soon,
For I'm weary wi' hunting, and fain wald lie down."

[1]/**hae:** *have*   [4]/**fain wald:** *would like to*

"Where gat ye your dinner, Lord Randal, my son?   5
Where gat ye your dinner, my handsome young man?"
"I din'd wi' my true-love; mother, make my bed soon,
For I'm weary wi' hunting, and fain wald lie down."

"What gat ye to your dinner, Lord Randal, my son?
What gat ye to your dinner, my handsome young man?"   10
"I gat eels boil'd in broo; mother, make my bed soon,
For I'm weary wi' hunting, and fain wald lie down."

"What became of your bloodhounds, Lord Randal, my son?
What became of your bloodhounds, my handsome young man?"
"O they swell'd and they died; mother, make my bed soon,   15
For I'm weary wi' hunting, and fain wald lie down."

"O I fear ye are poison'd, Lord Randal, my son!
I fear ye are poison'd, my handsome young man!"
"O yes! I am poison'd; mother, make my bed soon,
For I'm sick at the heart, and I fain wald lie down."   20

5/**gat:** *got*   11/**broo:** *broth, juice*

• THE DEMON LOVER •

"O where have you been, my long, long love,
  This long seven years and more?"
"O I'm come to seek my former vows
  Ye granted me before."

"O hold your tongue of your former vows,   5
  For they will breed sad strife;
O hold your tongue of your former vows
  For I am become a wife."

He turn'd him right and round about,
  And the tear blinded his ee;   10
"I wad never hae trodden on Irish ground,
  If it had not been for thee.

"I might have had a king's daughter,
  Far, far beyond the sea;
I might have had a king's daughter,   15
  Had it not been for love o' thee."

"If ye might have had a king's daughter,
  Yersell ye had to blame;
Ye might have taken the king's daughter,
  For ye kend that I was nane.   20

10/**ee:** *eye*   20/**kend:** *knew*
11/**wad . . . hae:** *would . . . have*   **nane:** *none*

"If I was to leave my husband dear,
    And my two babes also,
O what have you to take me to,
    If with you I should go?"

"I hae seven ships upon the sea,   *25*
    The eighth brought me to land;
With four-and-twenty bold mariners,
    And music on every hand."

She has taken up her two little babes,
    Kiss'd them baith cheek and chin;   *30*
"O fair ye weel, my ain two babes,
    For I'll never see you again."

She set her foot upon the ship,
    No mariners could she behold;
But the sails were o' the taffetie,   *35*
    And the masts o' the beaten gold.

She had not sail'd a league, a league,
    A league but barely three,
When dismal grew his countenance,
    And drumlie grew his ee.   *40*

They had not sailed a league, a league,
    A league but barely three,
Until she espied his cloven foot,
    And she wept right bitterlie.

"O hold your tongue of your weeping," says he, *45*
    "Of your weeping now let me be;
I will show you how the lilies grow
    On the banks of Italy."

"O what hills are yon, yon pleasant hills,
    That the sun shines sweetly on?"   *50*
"O yon are the hills of heaven," he said,
    "Where you will never win."

"O whaten a mountain is yon," she said,
    "All so dreary wi' frost and snow?"
"O yon is the mountain of hell," he cried,   *55*
    "Where you and I will go."

He struck the tapmast wi' his hand,
    The foremast wi' his knee;
And he brak that gallant ship in twain,
    And sank her in the sea.   *60*

[30]/**baith:** *both*   [40]/**drumlie:** *gloomy*
[31]/**weel:** *well*   [57]/**tapmast:** *topmast*
    ain: *own*

SIR THOMAS WYATT (1503-1542)

• THEY FLEE FROM ME •

They flee from me that sometime did me seek
With naked foot stalking in my chamber.
I have seen them gentle, tame and meek
That now are wild and do not remember
That sometime they put themself in danger   5
To take bread at my hand, and now they range
Busily seeking with a continual change.

Thankèd be fortune, it hath been otherwise
Twenty times better, but once in special,
In thin array, after a pleasant guise,   10
When her loose gown from her shoulders did fall
And she me caught in her arms long and small,
Therewith all sweetly did me kiss,
And softly said, "Dear heart, how like you this?"

It was no dream; I lay broad waking.   15
But all is turnèd through my gentleness
Into a strange fashion of forsaking;
And I have leave to go of her goodness,
And she also to use newfangleness.
But since that I so kindly am servèd,   20
I would fain know what she hath deservèd.

19/**newfangleness:** *desire for change*   20/**kindly:** *according to* [*her and my*] *nature (also the modern meaning)*

SIR EDWARD DYER (1534-1607)

• THE LOWEST TREES HAVE TOPS •

The lowest trees have tops, the ant her gall,
The fly her spleen, the little sparks their heat;
The slender hairs cast shadows, though but small;
And bees have stings, although they be not great.
    Seas have their source, and so have shallow springs,   5
    And love is love, in beggars as in kings.

Where rivers smoothest run, deep are the fords;
The dial stirs, yet none perceives it move;
The firmest faith is in the fewest words;
The turtles cannot sing, and yet they love.   10
    True hearts have eyes and ears, no tongues to speak;
    They hear, and see, and sigh, and then they break.

8/**dial:** *sundial*   10/**turtles:** *turtle-doves*

CHRISTOPHER MARLOWE
(1564–1593)

• THE PASSIONATE SHEPHERD TO HIS LOVE •

Come live with me and be my love,
And we will all the pleasures prove
That valleys, groves, hills, and fields,
Woods, or steepy mountain yields.

And we will sit upon the rocks,   5
Seeing the shepherds feed their flocks,
By shallow rivers, to whose falls
Melodious birds sing madrigals.

And I will make thee beds of roses
And a thousand fragrant posies,   10
A cap of flowers, and a kirtle
Embroidered all with leaves of myrtle;

A gown made of the finest wool,
Which from our pretty lambs we pull;
Fair linèd slippers for the cold,   15
With buckles of the purest gold;

A belt of straw and ivy buds
With coral clasps and amber studs:
And if these pleasures may thee move,
Come live with me and be my love.   20

The shepherd swains shall dance and sing
For thy delight each May morning:
If these delights thy mind may move,
Then live with me and be my love.

11/**kirtle:** *long dress*

SIR WALTER RALEIGH (1552?–1618)

• THE NYMPH'S REPLY TO THE SHEPHERD •

If all the world and love were young,
And truth in every shepherd's tongue,
These pretty pleasures might me move
To live with thee and be thy love.

Time drives the flocks from field to fold,   5
When rivers rage and rocks grow cold;

And Philomel becometh dumb;
The rest complains of cares to come.

The flowers do fade, and wanton fields
To wayward winter reckoning yields: *10*
A honey tongue, a heart of gall,
Is fancy's spring, but sorrow's fall.

Thy gowns, thy shoes, thy beds of roses,
Thy cap, thy kirtle, and thy posies
Soon break, soon wither, soon forgotten,   *15*
In folly ripe, in reason rotten.

Thy belt of straw and ivy buds,
Thy coral clasps and amber studs,
All these in me no means can move
To come to thee and be thy love.   *20*

But could youth last, and love still breed,
Had joys no date, nor age no need,
Then these delights my mind might move
To live with thee and be thy love.

⁷/**Philomel:** *the nightingale*

SIR PHILIP SIDNEY (1554–1586)

· WITH HOW SAD STEPS, O MOON ·

With how sad steps, O moon, thou climb'st the skies,
    How silently, and with how wan a face.
    What, may it be that even in heavenly place
That busy archer his sharp arrows tries?
Sure, if that long-with-love-acquainted eyes   *5*
    Can judge of love, thou feel'st a lover's case;
    I read it in thy looks; thy languisht grace,
To me that feel the like, thy state descries.

Then, even of fellowship, O moon, tell me
    Is constant love deemed there but want of wit?   *10*
Are beauties there as proud as here they be?
    Do they above love to be loved, and yet
Those lovers scorn whom that love doth possess?
Do they call virtue there ungratefulness?

⁹ **of fellowship:** *as a friend in the same situation*

¹⁴/**call virtue . . . ungratefulness:** *call ungratefulness a virtue*

ANTHOLOGY

WILLIAM SHAKESPEARE
(1564–1616)

• From SONNETS •
• 18 •

Shall I compare thee to a summer's day?
Thou art more lovely and more temperate.
Rough winds do shake the darling buds of May,
And summer's lease hath all too short a date.
Sometime too hot the eye of heaven shines,   5
And often is his gold complexion dimmed;
And every fair from fair sometime declines,
By chance, or nature's changing course, untrimmed;
But thy eternal summer shall not fade,
Nor lose possession of that fair thou owest,   10
Nor shall death brag thou wanderest in his shade,
When in eternal lines to time thou growest.
　　　So long as men can breathe or eyes can see,
　　　So long lives this, and this gives life to thee.

[8]/**untrimmed:** *stripped of its trimming*　　　[10]/**owest:** *owns*

• 33 •

Full many a glorious morning have I seen
Flatter the mountain tops with sovereign eye,
Kissing with golden face the meadows green,
Gilding pale streams with heavenly alchemy;
Anon permit the basest clouds to ride   5
With ugly rack on his celestial face,
And from the forlorn world his visage hide,
Stealing unseen to west with this disgrace.
Even so my sun one early morn did shine
With all-triumphant splendor on my brow;   10
But out alack, he was but one hour mine,
The region cloud hath masked him from me now.
　　　Yet him for this my love no whit disdaineth;
　　　Suns of the world may stain when heaven's sun staineth.

[11]/**out alack:** *alas!*

• 73 •

That time of year thou mayst in me behold
When yellow leaves, or none, or few, do hang
Upon those boughs which shake against the cold,
Bare ruined choirs where late the sweet birds sang.

In me thou seest the twilight of such day   5
As after sunset fadeth in the west,
Which by and by black night doth take away,
Death's second self, that seals up all in rest.
In me thou seest the glowing of such fire
That on the ashes of his youth doth lie,   10
As the deathbed whereon it must expire,
Consumed with that which it was nourished by.
    This thou perceivest, which makes thy love more strong,
    To love that well which thou must leave ere long.

· 116 ·

Let me not to the marriage of true minds
Admit impediments; love is not love
Which alters when it alteration finds,
Or bends with the remover to remove.
Oh no, it is an ever-fixèd mark   5
That looks on tempests and is never shaken;
It is the star to every wandering bark,
Whose worth's unknown, although his height be taken.
Love's not time's fool, though rosy lips and cheeks
Within his bending sickle's compass come;   10
Love alters not with his brief hours and weeks,
But bears it out even to the edge of doom.
    If this be error and upon me proved,
    I never writ, nor no man ever loved.

· 129 ·

The expense of spirit in a waste of shame
Is lust in action; and, till action, lust
Is perjured, murderous, bloody, full of blame,
Savage, extreme, rude, cruel, not to trust;
Enjoyed no sooner but despisèd straight;   5
Past reason hunted, and no sooner had,
Past reason hated as a swallowed bait
On purpose laid to make the taker mad;
Mad in pursuit, and in possession so;
Had, having, and in quest to have, extreme;   10
A bliss in proof, and proved, a very woe,
Before, a joy proposed; behind, a dream.
    All this the world well knows, yet none knows well
    To shun the heaven that leads men to this hell.

1/**expense of spirit:** *expenditure of vital energy*
11/**in proof:** *while experienced*

THOMAS CAMPION (1567–1620)

• MY SWEETEST LESBIA, LET US LIVE AND LOVE •

My sweetest Lesbia, let us live and love,
And though the sager sort our deeds reprove,
Let us not weigh them. Heaven's great lamps do dive
Into their west, and straight again revive;
But, soon as once set is our little light,   *5*
Then must we sleep one ever-during night.

If all would lead their lives in love like me,
Then bloody swords and armour should not be;
No drum nor trumpet peaceful sleeps should move,
Unless alarm came from the camp of love.   *10*
But fools do live and waste their little light,
And seek with pain their ever-during night.

When timely death my life and fortune ends,
Let not my hearse be vexed with mourning friends;
But let all lovers, rich in triumph, come   *15*
And with sweet pastimes grace my happy tomb:
And, Lesbia, close up thou my little light,
And crown with love my ever-during night.

• IT FELL ON A SUMMER'S DAY •

It fell on a summer's day
While sweet Bessie sleeping lay
In her bower, on her bed,
Light with curtains shadowèd,
Jamey came; she him spies,   *5*
Opening half her heavy eyes.

Jamey stole in through the door;
She lay slumbering as before;
Softly to her he drew near;
She heard him, yet would not hear.   *10*
Bessie vowed not to speak;
He resolved that dump to break.

First a soft kiss he doth take;
She lay still, and would not wake.
Then his hands learned to woo;   *15*
She dreampt not what he would do,
But still slept, while he smiled
To see love by sleep beguiled.

12/**dump:** *reverie*

Jamey then began to play;
Bessie as one buried lay,   20
Gladly still through this sleight
Deceived in her own deceit.
And since this trance began,
She sleeps every afternoon.

21/**sleight:** *trick*

· THRICE TOSS THESE OAKEN ASHES IN THE AIR ·

Thrice toss these oaken ashes in the air,
Thrice sit thou mute in this enchanted chair;
Then thrice three times tie up this true love's knot,
And murmur soft, "She will, or she will not."

Go burn these poisonous weeds in yon blue fire,   5
These screech-owl's feathers and this prickling brier,
This cypress gathered at a dead man's grave,
That all thy fears and cares an end may have.

Then come, you fairies, dance with me a round,
Melt her hard heart with your melodious sound.   10
In vain are all the charms I can devise;
She hath an art to break them with her eyes.

THOMAS NASHE (1567–1601)

· ADIEU, FAREWELL EARTH'S BLISS ·

Adieu, farewell earth's bliss!
This world uncertain is:
Fond are life's lustful joys;
Death proves them all but toys.
None from his darts can fly;   5
I am sick, I must die.
    Lord, have mercy on us.

Rich men, trust not in wealth:
Gold cannot buy you health;
Physic himself must fade.   10
All things to end are made;
The plague full swift goes by.
I am sick, I must die.
    Lord, have mercy on us.

3/**fond:** *foolish*   4/**toys:** *trifles*

Beauty is but a flower   15
Which wrinkles will devour;
Brightness falls from the air;
Queens have died young and fair;
Dust hath closed Helen's eye.
I am sick, I must die.   20
    Lord, have mercy on us.

Strength stoops unto the grave;
Worms feed on Hector brave.
Swords may not fight with fate;
Earth still holds ope her gate.   25
Come, come, the bells do cry.
I am sick, I must die.
    Lord, have mercy on us.

Wit with his wantonness
Tasteth death's bitterness;   30
Hell's executioner
Hath no ears for to hear
What vain art can reply.
I am sick, I must die.
    Lord, have mercy on us.   35

Haste therefore, each degree,
To welcome destiny:
Heaven is our heritage;
Earth but a player's stage.
Mount we unto the sky!   40
I am sick, I must die.
    Lord, have mercy on us.

Untitled in the play in which it occurs, this poem is sometimes given (by editors) some such title as "In Time of Pestilence."

29/**wantonness:** *playfulness*   36/**degree:** *social level*

CHIDIOCK TICHBORNE (1568?–1586)

· ELEGY ·

Written with his own hand in the Tower before his execution.

My prime of youth is but a frost of cares;
   My feast of joy is but a dish of pain;
My crop of corn is but a field of tares;
   And all my good is but vain hope of gain:

3/**tares:** *a kind of weed*

The day is past, and yet I saw no sun;   *5*
And now I live, and now my life is done.

My tale was heard, and yet it was not told;
   My fruit is fallen, and yet my leaves are green;
My youth is spent, and yet I am not old;
   I saw the world, and yet I was not seen: *10*
My thread is cut, and yet it is not spun;
And now I live, and now my life is done.

I sought my death, and found it in my womb;
   I looked for life, and saw it was a shade;
I trod the earth, and knew it was my tomb;   *15*
   And now I die, and now I was but made:
My glass is full, and now my glass is run;
And now I live, and now my life is done.

JOHN DONNE (1572–1631)

• THE SUN RISING •

     Busy old fool, unruly sun,
      Why dost thou thus
Through windows, and through curtains call on us?
Must to thy motions lovers' seasons run?
     Saucy pedantic wretch, go chide   *5*
     Late school boys, and sour prentices,
   Go tell court-huntsmen that the King will ride,
   Call country ants to harvest offices;
Love, all alike, no season knows, nor clime,
Nor hours, days, months, which are the rags of time.   *10*

     Thy beams, so reverend and strong
      Why shouldst thou think?
I could eclipse and cloud them with a wink,
But that I would not lose her sight so long:
     If her eyes have not blinded thine,   *15*
     Look, and tomorrow late, tell me
   Whether both the Indias of spice and mine
   Be where thou left'st them, or lie here with me.
Ask for those Kings whom thou saw'st yesterday,
And thou shalt hear: all here in one bed lay.   *20*

     She's all states, and all princes, I,
      Nothing else is.
Princes do but play us; compared to this,

17/**glass:** *hourglass*

All honor's mimic; all wealth alchemy.
Thou, sun, art half as happy as we,   *25*
In that the world's contracted thus;
Thine age asks ease, and since thy duties be
To warm the world, that's done in warming us.
Shine here to us, and thou art everywhere;
This bed thy center is, these walls, thy sphere.   *30*

---

²⁴/**alchemy:** *false gold, fraudulence (alchemy professed to be able to transmute base metals into gold)*

· A VALEDICTION: OF WEEPING ·

Let me pour forth
My tears before thy face, whilst I stay here,
For thy face coins them, and thy stamp they bear,
And by this mintage they are something worth,
                    For thus they be   *5*
                    Pregnant of thee;
Fruits of much grief they are, emblems of more,
When a tear falls, that thou falls which it bore,
So thou and I are nothing then, when on a diverse shore.

                    On a round ball   *10*
A workman that hath copies by, can lay
An Europe, Afric, and an Asia,
And quickly make that, which was nothing, all;
                    So doth each tear,
                    Which thee doth wear,   *15*
A globe, yea world, by that impression grow,
Till thy tears mixed with mine do overflow
This world, by waters sent from thee, my heaven dissolvèd so.

                    O more than moon,
Draw not up seas to drown me in thy sphere,   *20*
Weep me not dead, in thine arms, but forbear
To teach the sea, what it may do too soon;
                    Let not the wind
                    Example find,
To do me more harm, than it purposeth;   *25*
Since thou and I sigh one another's breath,
Whoe'er sighs most, is cruellest, and hastes the other's death.

---

²/**whilst I stay:** *before I leave (the speaker is about to go on a sea voyage)*
³/**coins:** *is reflected in them, like the face on a coin*

· A VALEDICTION: FORBIDDING MOURNING ·

As virtuous men pass mildly away,
    And whisper to their souls, to go,
Whilst some of their sad friends do say,
    The breath goes now, and some say, no:

So let us melt, and make no noise,   *5*
    No tear-floods, nor sigh-tempests move;
'Twere profanation of our joys
    To tell the laity our love.

Moving of the earth brings harms and fears,
    Men reckon what it did and meant,   *10*
But trepidation of the spheres,
    Though greater far, is innocent.

Dull sublunary lovers' love
    (Whose soul is sense) cannot admit
Absence, because it doth remove   *15*
    Those things which elemented it.

But we by a love, so much refined,
    That ourselves know not what it is,
Inter-assurèd of the mind,
    Care less, eyes, lips, and hands to miss.   *20*

Our two souls therefore, which are one,
    Though I must go, endure not yet
A breach, but an expansion,
    Like gold to airy thinness beat.

If they be two, they are two so   *25*
    As stiff twin compasses are two:
Thy soul, the fixed foot, makes no show
    To move, but doth, if the other do.

[8]/**laity:** *ordinary people, not ordained in the religion of love*
[9]/**moving of the earth:** *earthquakes*
[11]/**trepidation of the spheres:** *movements in the distant heavens (specifically, what astronomers call "the precession of the equinoxes": apparent shifts in the heavens because of the wobbling of the earth on its axis)*
[13]/**sublunary:** *beneath the moon, earthly*
[16]/**elemented:** *made up its elements*
[24]/**gold:** *gold can be hammered so thin it would take 2,000 sheets to make up the thickness of this page*
[26]/**compasses:** *a draughtsman's compass for drawing circles; not a mariner's compass*

And though it in the center sit,
    Yet when the other far doth roam,   *30*
It leans, and hearkens after it,
    And grows erect, as that comes home.

Such wilt thou be to me, who must
    Like the other foot, obliquely run;
Thy firmness makes my circle just,   *35*
    And makes me end, where I begun.

• DEATH BE NOT PROUD •

Death be not proud, though some have callèd thee
Mighty and dreadful, for thou art not so;
For those whom thou think'st thou dost overthrow
Die not, poor death, nor yet canst thou kill me.
From rest and sleep, which but thy pictures be,   *5*
Much pleasure, then from thee much more must flow,
And soonest our best men with thee do go,
Rest of their bones, and soul's delivery.
Thou art slave to fate, chance, kings, and desperate men,
And dost with poison, war, and sickness dwell,   *10*
And poppy, or charms can make us sleep as well,
And better than thy stroke; why swell'st thou then?
One short sleep past, we wake eternally,
And death shall be no more; death, thou shalt die.

11/**poppy:** *one kind of poppy is the source of opium*

BEN JONSON (1573?–1637)

• ON MY FIRST SON •

Farewell, thou child of my right hand, and joy.
    My sin was too much hope of thee, loved boy;
Seven years thou wert lent to me, and I thee pay,
    Exacted by thy fate, on the just day.
Oh, could I lose all father now. For why   *5*
    Will man lament the state he should envý?—
To have so soon 'scaped world's and flesh's rage,
    And, if no other misery, yet age.
Rest in soft peace, and, asked, say here doth lie
    Ben Jonson his best piece of poetry.
For whose sake, henceforth, all his vows be such   *10*
    As what he loves may never like too much.

1/**child of my right hand:** *the meaning of Benjamin (the boy's name) in Hebrew*

· STILL TO BE NEAT, STILL TO BE DRESSED ·

Still to be neat, still to be dressed,
As you were going to a feast;
Still to be powdered, still perfumed:
Lady, it is to be presumed,
Though art's hid causes are not found,   *5*
All is not sweet, all is not sound.

Give me a look, give me a face,
That makes simplicity a grace;
Robes loosely flowing, hair as free:
Such sweet neglect more taketh me   *10*
Than all the adulteries of art;
They strike mine eyes, but not my heart.

11/**adulteries:** *adulterations*

ANONYMOUS

· LOVING MAD TOM ·

From the hag and hungry goblin
    That into rags would rend ye,
The spirit that stands by the naked man
    In the Book of Moons defend ye!
That of your five sound senses   *5*
    You never be forsaken,
Nor wander from yourselves with Tom
    Abroad to beg your bacon.

        While I do sing, "Any food, any feeding,
            Feeding, drink, or clothing."   *10*
        Come, dame or maid, be not afraid;
            Poor Tom will injure nothing.

Of thirty bare years have I
    Twice twenty been enragèd,
And of forty been three times fifteen   *15*
    In durance soundly cagèd.
On the lordly lofts of Bedlam
    With stubble soft and dainty,
Brave bracelets strong, sweet whips ding-dong,
    With wholesome hunger plenty.   *20*

4/**Book of Moons:** *an astrological al-*
manac
14/**enragèd:** *demented*

17/**Bedlam:** *the Hospital of St. Mary*
of Bethlehem, a London madhouse
18/**stubble:** *rough straw*
19/**bracelets:** *handcuffs*

ANTHOLOGY

And now I sing, etc.

With a thought I took for Maudlin,
    And a cruse of cockle pottage,
With a thing thus tall—sky bless you all—
    I fell into this dotage.   *25*
I slept not since the Conquest,
    Till then I never wakèd,
Till the roguish boy of love where I lay
    Me found and stripped me naked.

       And now I sing, etc.   *30*

When I short have shorn my sow's face
    And swigged my horny barrel,
In an oaken inn I pound my skin,
    As a suit of gilt apparel.
The moon's my constant mistress,   *35*
    And the lowly owl my morrow,
The flaming drake and the nightcrow make
    Me music to my sorrow.

       While I do sing, etc.

The palsy plagues my pulses   *40*
    When I prig your pigs or pullen,
Your culvers take, or matchless make
    Your chanticleer or sullen.
When I want provant, with Humphrey
    I sup, and when benighted,   *45*
I repose in Paul's with waking souls
    Yet never am affrighted.

       But I do sing, etc.

I know more than Apollo,
    For oft, when he lies sleeping,   *50*

---

[22]/**Maudlin:** *Magdalen (girl's name)*
[23]/**cruse of cockle pottage:** *bowl of shellfish chowder (thought to be an aphrodisiac)*
[24]/**sky:** *God*
[28]/**boy of love:** *Cupid*
[32]/**swigged my horny barrel:** *drank a rough barrelful (?)*
[33]/**In an oaken inn:** *under an oak tree (?); in the stocks (?)*
    pound: *impound, enclose*
[37]/**drake:** *dragon*

[41]/**prig:** *steal*
    pullen: *poultry*
[42]/**culvers:** *doves*
    matchless: *without a mate*
[43]/**chanticleer:** *rooster*
    sullen: *goose (?)*
[44]/**provant:** *food*
    Humphrey: *to dine with Duke Humphrey meant "to go dinnerless."*
[46]/**Paul's:** *the churchyard of St. Paul's Cathedral in London*

I see the stars at bloody wars
    In the wounded welkin weeping,
The moon embrace her shepherd,
    And the queen of love her warrior,
While the first doth horn the star of morn,   *55*
    And the next the heavenly farrier.

        While I do sing, etc.

The Gypsies Snap and Pedro
    Are none of Tom's comradoes.
The punk I scorn and the cutpurse sworn   *60*
    And the roaring boy's bravadoes.
The meek, the white, the gentle
    Me handle, touch, and spare not;
But those that cross Tom Rhinoceros
    Do what the panther dare not.   *65*

        Although I sing, etc.

With an host of furious fancies
    Whereof I am commander,
With a burning spear and a horse of air,
    To the wilderness I wander.   *70*
By a knight of ghosts and shadows
    I summoned am to tourney
Ten leagues beyond the wide world's end—
    Methinks it is no journey.

        Yet will I sing, etc.   *75*

52/**welkin:** *heaven*
53/**shepherd:** *Endymion, with whom the moon was in love*
54/**queen of love:** *Venus, in love with Mars*
55/**horn:** *betray by her infidelity*

55/**star of morn:** *Phosphorus, thought of here as husband of the moon.*
56/**farrier:** *blacksmith. Venus was the wife of Vulcan, god of metalworking.*
60/**punk:** *prostitute*
61/**roaring boy:** *boisterous bully*
62/**white:** *innocent, honest*

ROBERT HERRICK (1591–1674)

· DELIGHT IN DISORDER ·

A sweet disorder in the dress
Kindles in clothes a wantonness:

A lawn about the shoulders thrown
Into a fine distraction;
An erring lace, which here and there   5
Enthralls the crimson stomacher;
A cuff neglectful, and thereby
Ribbons to flow confusedly;
A winning wave, deserving note,
In the tempestuous petticoat;   10
A careless shoe-string, in whose tie
I see a wild civility,
Do more bewitch me, than when art
Is too precise in every part.

3/**lawn:** *sheer linen*
6/**stomacher:** *a sort of dickey worn beneath the laces of the bodice*

GEORGE HERBERT (1593–1633)

· EASTER-WINGS ·

Lord, who createdst man in wealth and store,
Though foolishly he lost the same,
Decaying more and more
Till he became
Most poor: 5
With thee
Oh let me rise
As larks, harmoniously,
And sing this day thy victories:
Then shall the fall further the flight in me.   10

My tender age in sorrow did begin:
And still with sicknesses and shame
Thou didst so punish sin,
That I became
Most thin.   15
With thee
Let me combine.
And feel thy victory:
For, if I imp my wing on thine,
Affliction shall advance the flight in me.   20

19/**imp:** *in falconry, to graft feathers onto an injured wing*

· REDEMPTION ·

Having been tenant long to a rich Lord,
Not thriving, I resolvèd to be bold,
And make a suit unto him, to afford
A new small-rented lease, and cancel the old.

ANTHOLOGY

In heaven at his manor I him sought: 5
    They told me there, that he was lately gone
    About some land, which he had dearly bought
Long since on earth, to take possession.
I straight returned, and knowing his great birth,
    Sought him accordingly in great resorts; 10
    In cities, theatres, gardens, parks, and courts:
At length I heard a ragged noise and mirth
    Of thieves and murderers: there I him espied,
    Who straight, *Your suit is granted,* said, and died.

• THE COLLAR •

I struck the board, and cried, "No more.
        I will abroad.
  What? shall I ever sigh and pine?
My lines and life are free; free as the road,
    Loose as the wind, as large as store. 5
      Shall I be still in suit?
  Have I no harvest but a thorn
  To let me blood, and not restore
What I have lost with cordial fruit?
        Sure there was wine 10
    Before my sighs did dry it: there was corn
    Before my tears did drown it.
  Is the year only lost to me?
    Have I no bays to crown it?
No flowers, no garlands gay? all blasted? 15
      All wasted?
  Not so, my heart: but there is fruit,
    And thou hast hands.
    Recover all thy sigh-blown age
On double pleasures: leave thy cold dispute 20
Of what is fit, and not. Forsake thy cage,
      Thy rope of sands,
Which petty thoughts have made, and made to thee
    Good cable, to enforce and draw,
        And be thy law, 25
  While thou didst wink and wouldst not see.
      Away; take heed:
      I will abroad.
Call in thy death's-head there: tie up thy fears.
      He that forbears 30

---

⁵/**store:** *abundant resources*   ¹⁴/**bays:** *laurels, honors*
  in suit: *in service*   ¹⁹/**sigh-blown:** *blown away in sighs*

To suit and serve his need,
    Deserves his load."
But as I raved and grew more fierce and wild
    At every word,
Me thoughts I heard one calling, *Child!*   *35*
    And I replied, *My Lord.*

[35]/**me thoughts:** *it seemed to me*

• LOVE •

Love bade me welcome; yet my soul drew back,
    Guilty of dust and sin.
But quick-eyed Love, observing me grow slack
    From my first entrance in,
Drew nearer to me, sweetly questioning   *5*
    If I lacked anything.

"A guest," I answered, "worthy to be here."
    Love said, "You shall be he."
"I, the unkind, ungrateful? Ah my dear,
    I cannot look on thee."   *10*
Love took my hand, and smiling did reply,
    "Who made the eyes but I?"

"Truth, Lord, but I have marred them; let my shame
    Go where it doth deserve."
"And know you not," says Love, "who bore the blame?"   *15*
    "My dear, then I will serve."
"You must sit down," says Love, "and taste my meat."
    So I did sit and eat.

EDMUND WALLER (1606–1687)

• GO, LOVELY ROSE •

Go, lovely rose,
Tell her that wastes her time and me
    That now she knows,
When I resemble her to thee,
How sweet and fair she seems to be.   *5*

Tell her that's young
And shuns to have her graces spied,
    That hadst thou sprung
In deserts where no men abide,
Thou must have uncommended died.   *10*

Small is the worth
Of beauty from the light retired:
  Bid her come forth,
Suffer herself to be desired,
And not blush so to be admired.   *15*

  Then die, that she
The common fate of all things rare
  May read in thee,
How small a part of time they share
That are so wondrous sweet and fair.   *20*

JOHN MILTON (1608–1674)

· LYCIDAS ·

In this monody the author bewails a learned friend, unfortunately drowned in his passage from Chester on the Irish Seas, 1637. And by occasion foretells the ruin of our corrupted clergy, then in their height.

Yet once more, O ye laurels, and once more,
Ye myrtles brown, with ivy never sere,
I come to pluck your berries harsh and crude,
And with forced fingers rude
Shatter your leaves before the mellowing year.   *5*
Bitter constraint and sad occasion dear
Compels me to disturb your season due;
For Lycidas is dead, dead ere his prime,
Young Lycidas, and hath not left his peer.
Who would not sing for Lycidas? he knew   *10*
Himself to sing, and build the lofty rhyme.
He must not float upon his watery bier
Unwept, and welter to the parching wind,
Without the meed of some melodious tear.
  Begin then, sisters of the sacred well   *15*
That from beneath the seat of Jove doth spring;
Begin, and somewhat loudly sweep the string.
Hence with denial vain and coy excuse;
So may some gentle muse
With lucky words favour my destined urn,   *20*
And as he passes turn,
And bid fair peace be to my sable shroud.
  For we were nursed upon the self-same hill,
Fed the same flock, by fountain, shade, and rill;
Together both, ere the high lawns appeared   *25*

monody: *originally, an ode sung by one person; a lament*
[1-2]**/laurels . . . myrtles . . . ivy:** *three kinds of evergreen foliage symbolizing poetry*

[2]**/sere,** *dry, withered*
[3]**/crude:** *not yet ripe*
[6]**/dear:** *heartfelt, grievous*
[14]**/meed:** *gift*
[15]**/sisters:** *the Muses*

ANTHOLOGY

Under the opening eyelids of the morn,
We drove a-field, and both together heard
What time the gray-fly winds her sultry horn,
Battening our flocks with the fresh dews of night,
Oft till the star that rose at evening, bright,   30
Toward heaven's descent had sloped his westering wheel.
Meanwhile the rural ditties were not mute,
Tempered to the oaten flute;
Rough satyrs danced, and fauns with cloven heel
From the glad sound would not be absent long;   35
And old Damœtas loved to hear our song.
        But O the heavy change, now thou art gone,
Now thou art gone, and never must return!
Thee, shepherd, thee the woods and desert caves,
With wild thyme and the gadding vine o'ergrown,   40
And all their echoes, mourn.
The willows and the hazel copses green
Shall now no more be seen,
Fanning their joyous leaves to thy soft lays.
As killing as the canker to the rose,   45
Or taint-worm to the weanling herds that graze,
Or frost to flowers, that their gay wardrobe wear,
When first the white-thorn blows;
Such, Lycidas, thy loss to shepherd's ear.
        Where were ye, nymphs, when the remorseless deep   50
Closed o'er the head of your loved Lycidas?
For neither were ye playing on the steep
Where your old bards, the famous druids, lie,
Nor on the shaggy top of Mona high,
Nor yet where Deva spreads her wizard stream.   55
Ay me, I fondly dream!
Had ye been there—for what could that have done?
What could the muse herself that Orpheus bore,
The muse herself, for her enchanting son,
Whom universal nature did lament,   60

28/**gray-fly:** *name of several insects,
some beetlelike*
29/**battening:** *feeding, fattening*
33/**oaten:** *made of an oat straw*
36/**Damœtas:** *unidentified (an elderly
professor?)*
45/**canker:** *destructive bug or cater-
pillar*
46/**taint-worm:** *intestinal worm that
infests young cattle*
   weanling: *newly weaned*
53/**druids:** *an order of ancient Celtic
priest-poet-magicians*
54/**Mona:** *the island of Anglesey, off
the northern coast of Wales*
55/**Deva:** *the river Dee, thought to
have prophetic powers, which flows
through Chester and empties into the
Irish Sea*
56/**fondly:** *foolishly*
58/**Orpheus:** *legendary Greek poet and
musician, son of the muse Calliope,
torn to pieces by angered Thracian
women. His head—still singing—was
swept down the river Hebrus (in
Thrace) and across the Aegean to the
island of Lesbos.*

ANTHOLOGY

When by the rout that made the hideous roar
His gory visage down the stream was sent,
Down the swift Hebrus to the Lesbian shore?
    Alas! what boots it with uncessant care
To tend the homely, slighted, shepherd's trade,   *65*
And strictly meditate the thankless muse?
Were it not better done, as others use,
To sport with Amaryllis in the shade,
Or with the tangles of Neæra's hair?
Fame is the spur that the clear spirit doth raise   *70*
(That last infirmity of noble mind)
To scorn delights and live laborious days;
But the fair guerdon when we hope to find,
And think to burst out into sudden blaze,
Comes the blind fury with the abhorrèd shears,   *75*
And slits the thin-spun life. "But not the praise,"
Phœbus replied, and touched my trembling ears:
"Fame is no plant that grows on mortal soil
Nor in the glistering foil
Set off to the world, nor in broad rumour lies;   *80*
But lives and spreads aloft by those pure eyes
And perfect witness of all-judging Jove;
As he pronounces lastly on each deed,
Of so much fame in heaven expect thy meed."
    O fountain Arethuse, and thou honoured flood,   *85*
Smooth-sliding Mincius, crowned with vocal reeds,
That strain I heard was of a higher mood:
But now my oat proceeds,
And listens to the herald of the sea,
That came in Neptune's plea.   *90*
He asked the waves, and asked the felon winds,
What hard mishap hath doomed this gentle swain?
And questioned every gust of rugged wings
That blows from off each beakèd promontory:
They knew not of his story;   *95*
And sage Hippotades their answer brings,

64/**what boots it:** *what good does it do*
65/**shepherd's trade:** *poetry, in this pastoral world*
67/**use:** *habitually do*
68-69/**Amaryllis . . . Neæra:** *girls' names, borrowed from classical poetry*
73/**guerdon:** *reward*
75/**fury:** *death—of the three fates, the one that cuts the thread of our life*
77/**Phœbus:** *Apollo, god of beauty, poetry, etc. His touching or pulling*

the ear is a gesture of reproof.
79/**foil:** *gold or silver leaf placed to increase the brightness of precious stones*
85/**Arethuse:** *a spring in Sicily, symbolic here of Sicilian pastoral poetry*
86/**Mincius:** *Italian river near Vergil's birthplace, symbolic here of Italian pastoral poetry*
88/**oat:** *see line 33*
89/**herald of the sea:** *the sea god Triton*
96/**Hippotades:** *Aeolus, god of the winds*

That not a blast was from his dungeon strayed;
The air was calm, and on the level brine
Sleek Panope with all her sisters played.
It was that fatal and perfidious bark, 100
Built in the eclipse, and rigged with curses dark,
That sunk so low that sacred head of thine.
    Next Camus, reverend sire, went footing slow,
His mantle hairy, and his bonnet sedge,
Inwrought with figures dim, and on the edge 105
Like to that sanguine flower inscribed with woe.
"Ah! who hath reft," quoth he, "my dearest pledge?"
Last came, and last did go,
The pilot of the Galilean lake;
Two massy keys he bore of metals twain 110
(The golden opes, the iron shuts amain).
He shook his mitred locks, and stern bespake:
"How well could I have spared for thee, young swain,
Enow of such as, for their bellies' sake,
Creep and intrude and climb into the fold! 115
Of other care they little reckoning make
Than how to scramble at the shearers' feast,
And shove away the worthy bidden guest.
Blind mouths! that scarce themselves know how to hold
A sheep-hook, or have learnt aught else the least 120
That to the faithful herdman's art belongs!
What recks it them? What need they? They are sped;
And when they list, their lean and flashy songs
Grate on their scrannel pipes of wretched straw;
The hungry sheep look up, and are not fed, 125
But swoln with wind and the rank mist they draw,
Rot inwardly, and foul contagion spread;
Besides what the grim wolf with privy paw
Daily devours apace, and nothing said.

99/**Panope:** *a sea nymph*
103/**Camus:** *the river Cam, representing Cambridge University*
104/**hairy:** *with the fur trimming of an academic gown (?)*
    sedge: *a water plant with a flag-like flower*
106/**flower:** *the hyacinth, the design on whose petals was thought to be the Greek for* Alas!
109/**pilot:** *probably Saint Peter with the keys of heaven and a bishop's cap (miter)*
111/**amain:** *with force*
114/**enow:** *enough*
119/**blind mouths:** *a concentrated way of saying that bad clergymen are all greedy mouths and fail to see what they should see*
120/**a sheep-hook:** *a symbol of the pastor's life, perhaps a bishop's staff*
121/**herdman:** *pastor, clergyman*
122/**What recks it them?:** *What do they care?*
    they are sped: *they have prospered*
123/**list:** *want to*
124/**scrannel:** *thin, scratchy*
    straw: *cf. l. 33*
128/**wolf:** *apparently the Catholics, in their attempt to make converts*

But that two-handed engine at the door   *130*
Stands ready to smite once, and smite no more."
          Return, Alpheus; the dread voice is past
That shrunk thy streams; return, Sicilian muse,
And call the vales, and bid them hither cast
Their bells and flowrets of a thousand hues.   *135*
Ye valleys low, where the mild whispers use
Of shades and wanton winds and gushing brooks,
On whose fresh lap the swart star sparely looks,
Throw hither all your quaint enamelled eyes,
That on the green turf suck the honeyed showers,   *140*
And purple all the ground with vernal flowers.
Bring the rathe primrose that forsaken dies,
The tufted crow-toe, and pale jessamine,
The white pink, and the pansy freaked with jet,
The glowing violet,   *145*
The musk-rose, and the well-attired woodbine,
With cowslips wan that hang the pensive head,
And every flower that sad embroidery wears;
Bid amaranthus all his beauty shed,
And daffodillies fill their cups with tears,   *150*
To strew the laureate hearse where Lycid lies.
For so to interpose a little ease,
Let our frail thoughts dally with false surmise,
Ay me! whilst thee the shores and sounding seas
Wash far away, where'er thy bones are hurled,   *155*
Whether beyond the stormy Hebrides,
Where thou perhaps under the whelming tide
Visit'st the bottom of the monstrous world;
Or whether thou, to our moist vows denied,
Sleep'st by the fable of Bellerus old,   *160*

130/**two-handed engine:** *Many guesses have been made about this ominous and mysterious object, among them a two-handed sword belonging to God or Saint Michael; the two houses of Parliament; Puritan zeal; the approaching civil war; the combined forces of England and Scotland; etc. The fact that it cannot be identified with certainty makes it the more frightening.*
132/**Alpheus:** *a Greek river whose waters were thought to flow unmixed through the sea to rise in the "fountain Arethuse" of line 85*
136/**use:** *are frequent*
138/**swart star:** *Sirius, the Dog star, associated with the hot weather that* burns or tans, makes swart
142/**rathe:** *early*
143/**crow-toe:** *wild hyacinth*
144/**freaked:** *streaked whimsically (freakishly). Milton made up the word.*
146/**woodbine:** *honeysuckle*
149/**amaranthus:** *an imaginary flower thought never to fade*
151/**laureate:** *crowned with laurel*
153/**false surmise:** *the notion that the body of Lycidas is available, and that flowers have any real concern for him*
156/**Hebrides:** *islands off the western coast of Scotland*
160/**Bellerus:** *a fabulous figure apparently invented by Milton, named for Bellerium, or Land's End in Cornwall*

Where the great vision of the guarded mount
Looks toward Namancos and Bayona's hold;
Look homeward, angel, now, and melt with ruth;
And O ye dolphins, waft the hapless youth.
    Weep no more, woeful shepherds, weep no more,   *165*
For Lycidas, your sorrow, is not dead,
Sunk though he be beneath the watery floor;
So sinks the day-star in the ocean bed,
And yet anon repairs his drooping head,
And tricks his beams, and with new-spangled ore   *170*
Flames in the forehead of the morning sky:
So Lycidas sunk low, but mounted high,
Through the dear might of him that walked the waves,
Where, other groves and other streams along,
With nectar pure his oozy locks he laves,   *175*
And hears the unexpressive nuptial song,
In the blest kingdoms meek of joy and love.
There entertain him all the saints above,
In solemn troops and sweet societies,
That sing, and singing in their glory move,   *180*
And wipe the tears for ever from his eyes.
Now, Lycidas, the shepherds weep no more;
Henceforth thou art the genius of the shore,
In thy large recompense, and shalt be good
To all that wander in that perilous flood.   *185*
    Thus sang the uncouth swain to the oaks and rills,
While the still morn went out with sandals gray;
He touched the tender stops of various quills,
With eager thought warbling his Doric lay:
And now the sun had stretched out all the hills,   *190*
And now was dropt into the western bay.
At last he rose, and twitched his mantle blue:
To-morrow to fresh woods and pastures new.

161/**great vision:** *Saint Michael, who was said to appear on the mountain in Cornwall named for him*
162/**Namancos and Bayona:** *place names of an old region and a city in northwest Spain, about 500 miles south of the guarded mount, across the Atlantic*
163/**angel:** *Saint Michael*
    ruth: *pity*
164/**dolphins:** *probably an allusion to the early Greek poet Arion, saved* from drowning by a dolphin. There are other legends of dolphin rescues.
168/**day-star:** *sun*
170/**tricks:** *trims*
173/**him:** *Christ*
176/**unexpressive:** *inexpressible*
183/**genius:** *protective local deity*
186/**uncouth:** *unknown, obscure*
188/**stops . . . quills:** *finger-holes . . . pipes*
189/**Doric:** *Much Greek pastoral poetry was in the Doric dialect.*

· ON HIS BLINDNESS ·

When I consider how my light is spent,
    Ere half my days, in this dark world and wide,
    And that one talent which is death to hide
    Lodged with me useless, though my soul more bent
To serve therewith my Maker, and present   *5*
    My true account, lest he returning chide.
    "Doth God exact day-labor, light denied?"
    I fondly ask; but patience to prevent
That murmur, soon replies, "God doth not need
    Either man's work or his own gifts; who best   *10*
    Bear his mild yoke, they serve him best, his state
Is kingly. Thousands at his bidding speed
    And post o'er land and ocean without rest:
    They also serve who only stand and wait."

[8]/**fondly:** *foolishly*   [13]/**post:** *travel rapidly*

· ON HIS DEAD WIFE ·

Methought I saw my late espousèd saint
    Brought to me like Alcestis from the grave,
    Whom Jove's great son to her glad husband gave,
    Rescued from death by force, though pale and faint.
Mine, as whom washed from spot of childbed taint   *5*
    Purification in the old Law did save,
    And such as yet once more I trust to have
    Full sight of her in heaven without restraint,
Came vested all in white, pure as her mind.
    Her face was veiled, yet to my fancied sight   *10*
    Love, sweetness, goodness, in her person shined
So clear as in no face with more delight.
    But O as to embrace me she inclined,
    I waked, she fled, and day brought back my night.

[2]/**Alcestis:** *Alcestis, who had given her life to save that of her husband, was brought back from death by Hercules (line 3), who presented her veiled to her husband*

ANNE BRADSTREET (1612–1672)

· TO MY DEAR AND LOVING HUSBAND ·

If ever two were one, then surely we.
If ever man were loved by wife, then thee;
If ever wife was happy in a man,
Compare with me, ye women, if you can.
I prize thy love more than whole mines of gold,   *5*

Or all the riches that the East doth hold.
My love is such that rivers cannot quench,
Nor aught but love from thee give recompense.
Thy love is such I can no way repay,
The heavens reward thee manifold, I pray.   *10*
Then while we live, in love let's so perséver
That when we live no more, we may live ever.

RICHARD LOVELACE (1618–1657)

· TO LUCASTA, GOING TO THE WARS ·

Tell me not, sweet, I am unkind,
    That from the nunnery
Of thy chaste breast and quiet mind
    To war and arms I fly.

True, a new mistress now I chase,   *5*
    The first foe in the field;
And with a stronger faith embrace
    A sword, a horse, a shield.

Yet this inconstancy is such
    As you too shall adore;   *10*
I could not love thee, dear, so much,
    Loved I not honour more.

ANDREW MARVELL (1621–1678)

· A DIALOGUE BETWEEN THE SOUL AND BODY ·

Soul
O who shall from this dungeon raise
A soul enslaved so many ways?
With bolts of bones, that fettered stands
In feet; and manacled in hands:
Here blinded with an eye; and there   *5*
Deaf with the drumming of an ear;
A soul hung up, as 'twere, in chains
Of nerves, and arteries, and veins;
Tortured, besides each other part,
In a vain head and double heart.   *10*

---

[10]/**double:** *double-dealing, deceptive*

Body

O who shall me deliver whole
From bonds of this tyrannic soul?
Which, stretched upright, impales me so
That mine own precipice I go;
And warms and moves this needless frame   *15*
(A fever could but do the same);
And, wanting where its spite to try,
Has made me live to let me die;
A body that could never rest,
Since this ill spirit it possessed.   *20*

Soul

What magic could me thus confine
Within another's grief to pine?
Where whatsoever it complain,
I feel, that cannot feel, the pain.
And all my care itself employs   *25*
That to preserve, which me destroys;
Constrained not only to endure
Diseases, but, what's worse, the cure;
And ready oft the port to gain,
Am shipwrecked into health again.   *30*

Body

But physic yet could never reach
The maladies thou me dost teach:
Whom first the cramp of hope does tear;
And then the palsy shakes of fear;
The pestilence of love does heat;   *35*
Or hatred's hidden ulcer eat;
Joy's cheerful madness does perplex,
Or sorrow's other madness vex;
Which knowledge forces me to know,
And memory will not forgo.   *40*
What but a soul could have the wit
To build me up for sin so fit?
So architects do square and hew
Green trees that in the forest grew.

[15]/**needless:** *needing nothing*   [29]/**port:** *the afterlife*
[20]/**it possessed:** *possessed it*

· TO HIS COY MISTRESS ·

Had we but world enough, and time,
This coyness, Lady, were no crime.
We would sit down and think which way
To walk and pass our long love's day.

[2]/**coyness:** *shyness, reserve, disdain*

Thou by the Indian Ganges' side   5
Shouldst rubies find; I by the tide
Of Humber would complain. I would
Love you ten years before the Flood,
And you should, if you please, refuse
Till the conversion of the Jews.   10
My vegetable love should grow
Vaster than empires, and more slow;
An hundred years should go to praise
Thine eyes and on thy forehead gaze;
Two hundred to adore each breast,   15
But thirty thousand to the rest;
An age at least to every part,
And the last age should show your heart.
For, Lady, you deserve this state,
Nor would I love at lower rate.   20
    But at my back I always hear
Time's wingèd chariot hurrying near;
And yonder all before us lie
Deserts of vast eternity.
Thy beauty shall no more be found,   25
Nor, in thy marble vault, shall sound
My echoing song; then worms shall try
That long preserved virginity,
And your quaint honor turn to dust,
And into ashes all my lust: 30
The grave's a fine and private place,
But none, I think, do there embrace.
    Now therefore, while the youthful hue
Sits on thy skin like morning dew,
And while thy willing soul transpires   35
At every pore with instant fires,
Now let us sport us while we may,
And now, like amorous birds of prey,
Rather at once our time devour
Than languish in his slow-chapped power.   40
Let us roll all our strength and all
Our sweetness up into one ball,
And tear our pleasures with rough strife
Thorough the iron gates of life:
Thus, though we cannot make our sun   45
Stand still, yet we will make him run.

---

[10]/**conversion of the Jews:** *which, it was thought, would not come about until the end of time*
[40]/**slow-chapped:** *slow-jawed, devouring slowly*

HENRY VAUGHAN (1621?–1695)

· PEACE ·

My soul, there is a country
   Far beyond the stars,
Where stands a wingèd sentry
   All skillful in the wars;
There, above noise and danger,   *5*
   Sweet peace sits crowned with smiles,
And one born in a manger
   Commands the beauteous files.
He is thy gracious friend,
   And (O my soul, awake!)   *10*
Did in pure love descend
   To die here for thy sake.
If thou canst get but thither,
   There grows the flower of peace,
The rose that cannot wither,   *15*
   Thy fortress, and thy ease.
Leave then thy foolish ranges;
   For none can thee secure,
But one who never changes,
   Thy God, thy life, thy cure.   *20*

JOHN DRYDEN (1631–1700)

· SONG *from* THE SECULAR MASQUE ·

All, all of a piece throughout:
Thy chase had a beast in view;
Thy wars brought nothing about;
Thy lovers were all untrue.
'Tis well an old age is out,   *5*
And time to begin a new.

KATHERINE PHILIPS (1631–1664)

· AN ANSWER TO ANOTHER PERSUADING A · LADY TO MARRIAGE

Forbear, bold youth; all's heaven here,
   And what you do aver
To others, courtship may appear;
   'Tis sacrilege to her.

She is a public deity;   *5*
    And were't not very odd
She should depose herself to be
    A petty household god?

First make the sun in private shine
    And bid the world adieu,   *10*
That so he may his beams confine
    In compliment to you:

But if of that you do despair,
    Think how you did amiss
To strive to fix her beams, which are   *15*
    More bright and large than this.

¹⁵/**fix:** *confine to one place*

APHRA BEHN (1640–1689)

• SONG: LOVE ARMED •

Love in fantastic triumph sate,
    Whilst bleeding hearts around him flowed,
For whom fresh pains he did create,
    And strange tyrannic power he showed:
From thy bright eyes he took his fire,   *5*
    Which round about in sport he hurled;
But 'twas from mine he took desire,
    Enough to undo the amorous world.

From me he took his sighs and tears;
    From thee, his pride and cruelty;   *10*
From me, his languishments and fears;
    And every killing dart from thee.
Thus thou and I the god have armed
    And set him up a deity;
But my poor heart alone is harmed,   *15*
    Whilst thine the victor is, and free.

JOHN WILMOT, EARL OF ROCHESTER (1647–1680)

• THE DISABLED DEBAUCHEE •

As some brave admiral, in former war
    Deprived of force, but pressed with courage still,
Two rival fleets appearing from afar,
    Crawls to the top of an adjacent hill,

From whence (with thoughts full of concern) he views   5
    The wise and daring conduct of the fight,
And each bold action to his mind renews
    His present glory and his past delight;

From his fierce eyes flashes of fire he throws
    As from black clouds when lightning breaks away;   10
Transported, thinks himself amidst the foes,
    And, absent, yet enjoys the bloody day;

So, when my days of impotence approach,
    And I'm by pox or wine's unlucky chance
Forced from the pleasing billows of debauch,   15
    On the dull shore of lazy temperance,

My pains at least some respite shall afford
    While I behold the battles you maintain,
When fleets of glasses sail about the board,
    From whose broadsides volleys of wit shall rain.   20

Nor let the sight of honorable scars
    Which my too forward valor did procure
Frighten new 'listed soldiers from the wars;
    Past joys have more than paid what I endure.

Should any youth (worth being drunk) prove nice,   25
    And from his fair inviter meanly shrink,
'Twould please the ghost of my departed vice
    If, at my counsel, he repent and drink.

Or should some cold-complexioned sot forbid,
    With his dull morals, our bold night-alarms,   30
I'll fire his blood by telling what I did,
    When I was strong and able to bear arms.

I'll tell of whores attacked, their lords at home,
    Bawds' quarters beaten up, and fortress won;
Windows demolished, watches overcome,   35
    And handsome ills by my contrivance done. . . .

With tales like these I will such thoughts inspire,
    As to important mischief shall incline;
I'll make him long some ancient church to fire,
    And fear no lewdness he's called to by wine.   40

Thus, statesmanlike, I'll saucily impose,
    And, safe from action, valiantly advise;
Sheltered in impotence, urge you to blows,
    And, being good for nothing else, be wise.

25/**nice:** *over-refined, shy*

JONATHAN SWIFT (1667–1745)

· A DESCRIPTION OF THE MORNING ·

Now hardly here and there an hackney-coach,
Appearing, showed the ruddy morn's approach.
Now Betty from her master's bed had flown,
And softly stole to discompose her own.
The slipshod prentice from his master's door   5
Had pared the dirt, and sprinkled round the floor.
Now Moll had whirled her mop with dextrous airs,
Prepared to scrub the entry and the stairs.
The youth with broomy stumps began to trace
The kennel-edge, where wheels had worn the place.   10
The small-coal man was heard with cadence deep,
Till drowned in shriller notes of chimney-sweep,
Duns at his lordship's gate began to meet,
And Brickdust Moll had screamed through half the street.
The turnkey now his flock returning sees,   15
Duly let out a-nights to steal for fees;
The watchful bailiffs take their silent stands,
And schoolboys lag with satchels in their hands.

9/**broomy stumps:** *worn-down brooms*
10/**kennel:** *gutter, open sewer*
13/**duns:** *creditors*

14/**brickdust:** *an abrasive used for cleaning*
15/**turnkey:** *jailer*

THOMAS GRAY (1716–1771)

· ELEGY WRITTEN IN A COUNTRY CHURCHYARD ·

The curfew tolls the knell of parting day,
The lowing herd wind slowly o'er the lea,
The ploughman homeward plods his weary way,
And leaves the world to darkness and to me.

Now fades the glimmering landscape on the sight,   5
And all the air a solemn stillness holds,
Save where the beetle wheels his droning flight,
And drowsy tinklings lull the distant folds;

Save that from yonder ivy-mantled tower
The moping owl does to the moon complain   10
Of such, as wandering near her secret bower,
Molest her ancient solitary reign.

Beneath those rugged elms, that yew-tree's shade,
Where heaves the turf in many a moldering heap,

Each in his narrow cell forever laid,   *15*
The rude forefathers of the hamlet sleep.

The breezy call of incense-breathing morn,
The swallow twittering from the straw-built shed,
The cock's shrill clarion, or the echoing horn,
No more shall rouse them from their lowly bed.   *20*

For them no more the blazing hearth shall burn,
Or busy housewife ply her evening care;
No children run to lisp their sire's return,
Or climb his knees the envied kiss to share.

Oft did the harvest to their sickle yield;   *25*
Their furrow oft the stubborn glebe has broke;
How jocund did they drive their team afield!
How bowed the woods beneath their sturdy stroke!

Let not Ambition mock their useful toil,
Their homely joys, and destiny obscure;   *30*
Nor Grandeur hear with a disdainful smile
The short and simple annals of the poor.

The boast of heraldry, the pomp of power,
And all that beauty, all that wealth e'er gave,
Awaits alike the inevitable hour: *35*
The paths of glory lead but to the grave.

Nor you, ye proud, impute to these the fault,
If Memory o'er their tomb no trophies raise,
Where through the long-drawn aisle and fretted vault
The pealing anthem swells the note of praise.   *40*

Can storied urn or animated bust
Back to its mansion call the fleeting breath?
Can Honour's voice provoke the silent dust,
Or Flattery soothe the dull cold ear of Death?

Perhaps in this neglected spot is laid   *45*
Some heart once pregnant with celestial fire;
Hands that the rod of empire might have swayed,
Or waked to ecstasy the living lyre.

But Knowledge to their eyes her ample page,
Rich with the spoils of time, did ne'er unroll;   *50*
Chill Penury repressed their noble rage,
And froze the genial current of the soul.

[16]/**rude:** *lacking the advantages of education and culture*
[26]/**glebe:** *soil*

[35]/**awaits . . . hour:** *hour is the subject*
[39]/**fretted:** *ornately carved*
[43]/**provoke:** *call forth*

ANTHOLOGY

Full many a gem of purest ray serene,
The dark unfathomed caves of ocean bear;
Full many a flower is born to blush unseen,   *55*
And waste its sweetness on the desert air.

Some village Hampden, that with dauntless breast
The little tyrant of his fields withstood;
Some mute inglorious Milton here may rest,
Some Cromwell, guiltless of his country's blood.   *60*

The applause of listening senates to command,
The threats of pain and ruin to despise,
To scatter plenty o'er a smiling land,
And read their history in a nation's eyes

Their lot forbade; nor circumscribed alone   *65*
Their growing virtues, but their crimes confined;
Forbade to wade through slaughter to a throne,
And shut the gates of mercy on mankind;

The struggling pangs of conscious truth to hide,
To quench the blushes of ingenuous shame,   *70*
Or heap the shrine of Luxury and Pride
With incense kindled at the Muse's flame.

Far from the madding crowd's ignoble strife,
Their sober wishes never learned to stray;
Along the cool sequestered vale of life   *75*
They kept the noiseless tenor of their way.

Yet even these bones from insult to protect,
Some frail memorial still erected nigh,
With uncouth rhymes and shapeless sculpture decked,
Implores the passing tribute of a sigh.   *80*

Their name, their years, spelt by the unlettered Muse,
The place of fame and elegy supply;
And many a holy text around she strews,
That teach the rustic moralist to die.

For who, to dumb Forgetfulness a prey,   *85*
This pleasing anxious being e'er resigned,
Left the warm precincts of the cheerful day,
Nor cast one longing lingering look behind?

[57]/**Hampden:** *John Hampden, who in*
1637 refused to pay an illegal tax
levied by the king

[73]/**madding:** *acting like madmen*

ANTHOLOGY

On some fond breast the parting soul relies,
Some pious drops the closing eye requires;   *90*
Even from the tomb the voice of Nature cries,
Even in our ashes live their wonted fires.

For thee, who mindful of the unhonoured dead
Dost in these lines their artless tale relate,
If chance, by lonely contemplation led,   *95*
Some kindred spirit shall inquire thy fate,

Haply some hoary-headed swain may say,
"Oft have we seen him at the peep of dawn
Brushing with hasty steps the dews away
To meet the sun upon the upland lawn.   *100*

"There at the foot of yonder nodding beech
That wreathes its old fantastic roots so high,
His listless length at noontide would he stretch,
And pore upon the brook that babbles by.

"Hard by yon wood, now smiling as in scorn,   *105*
Muttering his wayward fancies he would rove;
Now drooping, woeful-wan, like one forlorn,
Or crazed with care, or crossed in hopeless love.

"One morn I missed him on the customed hill,
Along the heath, and near his favorite tree;   *110*
Another came; nor yet beside the rill,
Nor up the lawn, nor at the wood was he;

"The next, with dirges due, in sad array,
Slow through the church-way path we saw him borne.
Approach and read (for thou canst read) the lay,   *115*
Graved on the stone beneath yon agèd thorn."

The Epitaph

Here rests his head upon the lap of earth
A youth to Fortune and to Fame unknown;
Fair Science frowned not on his humble birth,
And Melancholy marked him for her own.   *120*

Large was his bounty, and his soul sincere;
Heaven did a recompense as largely send:
He gave to Misery all he had, a tear;
He gained from Heaven ('twas all he wished) a friend.

92/**wonted:** *accustomed, usual*
95/**if chance:** *if it happens that*
97/**haply:** *perhaps*
  swain: *countryman*
111/**rill:** *brook*

115/**lay:** *poem*
119/**Science:** *learning, knowledge*
120/**Melancholy:** *sensibility, as well as the modern meaning*

No farther seek his merits to disclose,   *125*
Or draw his frailties from their dread abode,
(There they alike in trembling hope repose)
The bosom of his Father and his God.

CHRISTOPHER SMART (1722–1771)

· From JUBILATE AGNO ·

For I will consider my Cat Jeoffry.
For he is the servant of the Living God duly and daily serving him.
For at the first glance of the glory of God in the East he worships
     in his way.
For is this done by wreathing his body seven times round with
     elegant quickness.
For then he leaps up to catch the musk, which is the blessing of
     God upon his prayer.   *5*
For he rolls upon prank to work it in.
For having done duty and received blessing he begins to consider
     himself.
For this he performs in ten degrees.
For first he looks upon his fore-paws to see if they are clean.
For secondly he kicks up behind to clear away there.   *10*
For thirdly he works it upon stretch with the fore-paws extended.
For fourthly he sharpens his paws by wood.
For fifthly he washes himself.
For Sixthly he rolls upon wash.
For Seventhly he fleas himself, that he may not be interrupted upon
     the beat.   *15*
For Eighthly he rubs himself against a post.
For Ninthly he looks up for his instructions.
For Tenthly he goes in quest of food.
For having considered God and himself he will consider his
     neighbour.
For if he meets another cat he will kiss her in kindness.   *20*
For when he takes his prey he plays with it to give it a chance.
For one mouse in seven escapes by his dallying.
For when his day's work is done his business more properly begins.
For he keeps the Lord's watch in the night against the adversary.
For he counteracts the powers of darkness by his electrical skin
     and glaring eyes.   *25*
For he counteracts the Devil, who is death, by brisking about the
     life.

6/**upon prank:** *prankishly, playfully*
11/**works it upon stretch:** *stretches energetically*
14/**upon wash:** *upon having washed*
15/**upon the beat:** *on his daily round*
26/**brisking . . .:** *living briskly, positively*

ANTHOLOGY

For in his morning orisons he loves the sun and the sun loves him.
For he is of the tribe of Tiger.
For the Cherub Cat is a term of the Angel Tiger.
For he has the subtlety and hissing of a serpent, which in goodness
    he suppresses.   *30*
For he will not do destruction if he is well-fed, neither will he spit
    without provocation.
For he purrs in thankfulness, when God tells him he's a good Cat.
For he is an instrument for the children to learn benevolence upon.
For every house is incomplete without him and a blessing is
    lacking in the spirit.
For the Lord commanded Moses concerning the cats at the departure
    of the Children of Israel from Egypt.   *35*
For every family had one cat at least in the bag.
For the English Cats are the best in Europe.
For he is the cleanest in the use of his fore-paws of any quadruped.
For the dexterity of his defence is an instance of the love of God to
    him exceedingly.
For he is the quickest to his mark of any creature.   *40*
For he is tenacious of his point.
For he is a mixture of gravity and waggery.
For he knows that God is his Saviour.
For there is nothing sweeter than his peace when at rest.
For there is nothing brisker than his life when in motion.   *45*
For he is of the Lord's poor and so indeed is he called by benevolence
    perpetually—Poor Jeoffry! poor Jeoffry! the rat has bit thy
    throat.
For I bless the name of the Lord Jesus that Jeoffry is better.
For the divine spirit comes about his body to sustain it in complete cat.
For his tongue is exceeding pure so that it has in purity what it wants
    in music.
For he is docile and can learn certain things.   *50*
For he can set up with gravity which is patience upon approbation.
For he can fetch and carry, which is patience in employment.
For he can jump over a stick which is patience upon proof positive.
For he can spraggle upon waggle at the word of command.
For he can jump from an eminence into his master's bosom.   *55*
For he can catch the cork and toss it again.
For he is hated by the hypocrite and miser.
For the former is afraid of detection.
For the latter refuses the charge.
For he camels his back to bear the first notion of business.   *60*
For he is good to think on, if a man would express himself neatly.
For he made a great figure in Egypt for his signal services.
For he killed the Ichneumon-rat very pernicious by land.
For his ears are so acute that they sting again.

---

[54]/**spraggle upon waggle:** *twist and frolic (?)*
[64]/**Ichneumon-rat:** *mongoose*

For from this proceeds the passing quickness of his attention. *65*
For by stroking of him I have found out electricity.
For I perceived God's light about him both wax and fire.
For the Electrical fire is the spiritual substance, which God sends from
    heaven to sustain the bodies both of man and beast.
For God has blessed him in the variety of his movements.
For, tho' he cannot fly, he is an excellent clamberer. *70*
For his motions upon the face of the earth are more than any other
    quadruped.
For he can tread to all the measures upon the music.
For he can swim for life.
For he can creep.

WILLIAM BLAKE (1757–1828)

• THE TYGER •

Tyger, Tyger, burning bright,
In the forests of the night,
What immortal hand or eye
Could frame thy fearful symmetry?

In what distant deeps or skies *5*
Burnt the fire of thine eyes?
On what wings dare he aspire?
What the hand dare seize the fire?

And what shoulder, & what art,
Could twist the sinews of thy heart? *10*
And when thy heart began to beat,
What dread hand? & what dread feet?

What the hammer? what the chain?
In what furnace was thy brain?
What the anvil? What dread grasp *15*
Dare its deadly terrors clasp?

When the stars threw down their spears
And watered heaven with their tears,
Did he smile his work to see?
Did he who made the Lamb make thee? *20*

Tyger, Tyger, burning bright,
In the forests of the night,
What immortal hand or eye
Dare frame thy fearful symmetry?

· LONDON ·

I wander through each chartered street,
Near where the chartered Thames does flow,
And mark in every face I meet
Marks of weakness, marks of woe.

In every cry of every Man,   5
In every Infant's cry of fear,
In every voice, in every ban,
The mind-forged manacles I hear.

How the Chimney-sweeper's cry
Every blackening Church appals;   10
And the hapless Soldier's sigh
Runs in blood down Palace walls.

But most through midnight streets I hear
How the youthful Harlot's curse
Blasts the new born Infant's tear,   15
And blights with plagues the Marriage hearse.

· A POISON TREE ·

I was angry with my friend:
I told my wrath, my wrath did end.
I was angry with my foe:
I told it not, my wrath did grow.

And I watered it in fears,   5
Night and morning with my tears;
And I sunnèd it with smiles,
And with soft deceitful wiles.

And it grew both day and night,
Till it bore an apple bright;   10
And my foe beheld it shine,
And he knew that it was mine,

And into my garden stole,
When the night had veiled the pole:
In the morning glad I see   15
My foe outstretched beneath the tree.

· EPILOGUE *to* THE GATES OF PARADISE ·

To the Accuser Who is the God of this World
Truly, My Satan, thou art but a Dunce,
And dost not know the Garment from the Man.
Every Harlot was a Virgin once,
Nor canst thou ever change Kate into Nan.

Though thou art Worshipped by the Names Divine   5
Of Jesus and Jehovah, thou art still
The Son of Morn in weary Night's decline,
The lost Traveller's Dream under the Hill.

WILLIAM WORDSWORTH
(1770–1850)

· SHE DWELT AMONG THE UNTRODDEN WAYS ·

She dwelt among the untrodden ways
  Beside the springs of Dove,
A maid whom there were none to praise
  And very few to love:

A violet by a mossy stone   5
  Half hidden from the eye!
Fair as a star, when only one
  Is shining in the sky.

She lived unknown, and few could know
  When Lucy ceased to be;   10
But she is in her grave, and oh,
  The difference to me!

· THE WORLD IS TOO MUCH WITH US ·

The world is too much with us; late and soon,
Getting and spending, we lay waste our powers:
Little we see in Nature that is ours;
We have given our hearts away, a sordid boon!
This sea that bares her bosom to the moon;   5
The winds that will be howling at all hours,
And are up-gathered now like sleeping flowers;
For this, for everything, we are out of tune;
It moves us not.—Great God! I'd rather be
A pagan suckled in a creed outworn;   10

So might I, standing on this pleasant lea,
Have glimpses that would make me less forlorn;
Have sight of Proteus rising from the sea;
Or hear old Triton blow his wreathèd horn.

¹³⁻¹⁴/**Proteus . . . Triton:** *sea-gods of Greek mythology*

• COMPOSED UPON WESTMINSTER BRIDGE •

September 3, 1802

Earth has not anything to show more fair:
Dull would he be of soul who could pass by
A sight so touching in its majesty:
This City now doth, like a garment, wear
The beauty of the morning; silent, bare,   *5*
Ships, towers, domes, theatres, and temples lie
Open unto the fields, and to the sky;
All bright and glittering in the smokeless air.
Never did sun more beautifully steep
In his first splendour, valley, rock, or hill;   *10*
Ne'er saw I, never felt, a calm so deep!
The river glideth at his own sweet will:
Dear God! the very houses seem asleep;
And all that mighty heart is lying still!

SAMUEL TAYLOR COLERIDGE
(1772–1834)

• KUBLA KHAN •

In Xanadu did Kubla Khan
A stately pleasure-dome decree:
Where Alph, the sacred river, ran
Through caverns measureless to man
    Down to a sunless sea.   *5*
So twice five miles of fertile ground
With walls and towers were girdled round:
And there were gardens bright with sinuous rills,
Where blossomed many an incense-bearing tree;
And here were forests ancient as the hills,   *10*
Enfolding sunny spots of greenery.

But oh! that deep romantic chasm which slanted
Down the green hill athwart a cedarn cover!
A savage place! as holy and enchanted
As e'er beneath a waning moon was haunted   *15*

By woman wailing for her demon-lover!
And from this chasm, with ceaseless turmoil seething,
As if this earth in fast thick pants were breathing,
A mighty fountain momently was forced:
Amid whose swift half-intermitted burst   20
Huge fragments vaulted like rebounding hail,
Or chaffy grain beneath the thresher's flail:
And 'mid these dancing rocks at once and ever
It flung up momently the sacred river.
Five miles meandering with a mazy motion   25
Through wood and dale the sacred river ran,
Then reached the caverns measureless to man,
And sank in tumult to a lifeless ocean:
And 'mid this tumult Kubla heard from far
Ancestral voices prophesying war!   30
    The shadow of the dome of pleasure
    Floated midway on the waves;
    Where was heard the mingled measure
    From the fountain and the caves.
It was a miracle of rare device,   35
A sunny pleasure-dome with caves of ice!

    A damsel with a dulcimer
    In a vision once I saw:
    It was an Abyssinian maid,
    And on her dulcimer she played,   40
    Singing of Mount Abora.
    Could I revive within me
    Her symphony and song,
    To such a deep delight 'twould win me,
That with music loud and long,   45
I would build that dome in air,
That sunny dome! those caves of ice!
And all who heard should see them there,
And all should cry, Beware! Beware!
His flashing eyes, his floating hair!   50
Weave a circle round him thrice,
And close your eyes with holy dread,
For he on honey-dew hath fed,
And drunk the milk of Paradise.

WALTER SAVAGE LANDOR
(1775–1864)

• ROSE AYLMER •

Ah what avails the sceptred race!
  Ah what the form divine!
What every virtue, every grace!
  Rose Aylmer, all were thine.

Rose Aylmer, whom these wakeful eyes   5
  May weep, but never see,
A night of memories and sighs
  I consecrate to thee.

• ON SEEING A HAIR OF LUCRETIA BORGIA •

Borgia, thou once wert almost too august
And high for adoration; now thou'rt dust.
All that remains of thee these plaits unfold—
Calm hair, meandering in pellucid gold.

• PAST RUINED ILION HELEN LIVES •

Past ruined Ilion Helen lives,
  Alcestis rises from the shades;
Verse calls them forth; 'tis verse that gives
  Immortal youth to mortal maids.

Soon shall Oblivion's deepening veil   5
  Hide all the peopled hills you see,
The gay, the proud, while lovers hail
  These many summers you and me.

¹/**Ilion:** *Troy*
²/**Alcestis:** *see footnote to Milton's "On His Dead Wife" (p. 427)*

THOMAS LOVE PEACOCK
(1785–1866)

• THE WAR-SONG OF DINAS VAWR •

The mountain sheep are sweeter,
But the valley sheep are fatter;
We therefore deemed it meeter
To carry off the latter.

Dinas Vawr: *a petty king of the time of King Arthur*

We made an expedition;   5
We met a host, and quelled it;
We forced a strong position,
And killed the men who held it.

On Dyfed's richest valley,
Where herds of kine were browsing,   10
We made a mighty sally,
To furnish our carousing.
Fierce warriors rushed to meet us;
We met them, and o'erthrew them:
They struggled hard to beat us;   15
But we conquered them, and slew them.

As we drove our prize at leisure,
The king marched forth to catch us:
His rage surpassed all measure,
But his people could not match us.   20
He fled to his hall-pillars;
And, ere our force we led off,
Some sacked his house and cellars,
While others cut his head off.

We there, in strife bewildering,   25
Spilt blood enough to swim in:
We orphaned many children,
And widowed many women.
The eagles and the ravens
We glutted with our foemen;   30
The heroes and the cravens,
The spearmen and the bowmen.

We brought away from battle,
And much their land bemoaned them,
Two thousand head of cattle,   35
And the head of him who owned them:
Ednyfed, king of Dyfed,
His head was borne before us;
His wine and beasts supplied our feasts,
And his overthrow, our chorus.   40

9/**Dyfed:** *an old name for a part of Wales*

GEORGE GORDON, LORD BYRON
(1788–1824)

· SO WE'LL GO NO MORE A-ROVING ·

So we'll go no more a-roving
    So late into the night,
Though the heart be still as loving,
    And the moon be still as bright.

For the sword outwears its sheath,   *5*
    And the soul wears out the breast,
And the heart must pause to breathe,
    And love itself have rest.

Though the night was made for loving,
    And the day returns too soon,   *10*
Yet we'll go no more a-roving
    By the light of the moon.

PERCY BYSSHE SHELLEY
(1792–1822)

· OZYMANDIAS ·

I met a traveller from an antique land
Who said: Two vast and trunkless legs of stone
Stand in the desert. Near them, on the sand,
Half sunk, a shattered visage lies, whose frown,
And wrinkled lip, and sneer of cold command,   *5*
Tell that its sculptor well those passions read
Which yet survive, stamped on these lifeless things,
The hand that mocked them and the heart that fed;
And on the pedestal these words appear:
"My name is Ozymandias, king of kings: *10*
Look on my works, ye Mighty, and despair!"
Nothing beside remains. Round the decay
Of that colossal wreck, boundless and bare,
The lone and level sands stretch far away.

Ozymandias: *the Greek form of Usermare-setepenre (Ramses the Great), who reigned in Egypt from 1304 until 1237* B.C. *He left many colossal statues of himself.*

· ODE TO THE WEST WIND ·

I

O wild west wind, thou breath of autumn's being,
Thou from whose unseen presence the leaves dead
Are driven like ghosts from an enchanter fleeing,

Yellow, and black, and pale, and hectic red,
Pestilence-stricken multitudes! O thou   5
Who chariotest to their dark wintry bed

The wingèd seeds, where they lie cold and low,
Each like a corpse within its grave, until
Thine azure sister of the spring shall blow

Her clarion o'er the dreaming earth, and fill   10
(Driving sweet buds like flocks to feed in air)
With living hues and odours plain and hill:

Wild spirit, which art moving everywhere;
Destroyer and preserver; hear, O hear!

II

Thou on whose stream, 'mid the steep sky's commotion,   15
Loose clouds like earth's decaying leaves are shed,
Shook from the tangled boughs of heaven and ocean,

Angels of rain and lightning: there are spread
On the blue surface of thine airy surge,
Like the bright hair uplifted from the head   20

Of some fierce Maenad, even from the dim verge
Of the horizon to the zenith's height,
The locks of the approaching storm. Thou dirge

Of the dying year, to which this closing night
Will be the dome of a vast sepulchre,   25
Vaulted with all thy congregated might

Of vapours, from whose solid atmosphere
Black rain, and fire, and hail will burst: O hear!

III

Thou who didst waken from his summer dreams
The blue Mediterranean, where he lay.   30
Lulled by the coil of his crystalline streams,

21/**Maenad:** *a woman inspired to frenzy by Dionysius*

ANTHOLOGY

Beside a pumice isle in Baiae's bay,
And saw in sleep old palaces and towers
Quivering within the wave's intenser day,

All overgrown with azure moss and flowers   *35*
So sweet, the sense faints picturing them! Thou
For whose path the Atlantic's level powers

Cleave themselves into chasms, while far below
The sea-blooms and the oozy woods which wear
The sapless foliage of the ocean, know   *40*

Thy voice, and suddenly grow gray with fear,
And tremble and despoil themselves: O hear!

IV

If I were a dead leaf thou mightest bear;
If I were a swift cloud to fly with thee;
A wave to pant beneath thy power, and share   *45*

The impulse of thy strength, only less free
Than thou, O uncontrollable! if even
I were as in my boyhood, and could be

The comrade of thy wanderings over heaven,
As then, when to outstrip thy skiey speed   *50*
Scarce seemed a vision; I would ne'er have striven

As thus with thee in prayer in my sore need.
O! lift me as a wave, a leaf, a cloud!
I fall upon the thorns of life! I bleed!

A heavy weight of hours has chained and bowed   *55*
One too like thee: tameless, and swift, and proud.

V

Make me thy lyre, even as the forest is:
What if my leaves are falling like its own?
The tumult of thy mighty harmonies

Will take from both a deep autumnal tone,   *60*
Sweet though in sadness. Be thou, spirit fierce,
My spirit! Be thou me, impetuous one!

Drive my dead thoughts over the universe,
Like withered leaves, to quicken a new birth;
And, by the incantation of this verse,   *65*

---

[32]/**Baiae:** *an ancient Roman resort near Naples, now submerged*

Scatter, as from an unextinguished hearth
Ashes and sparks, my words among mankind!
Be through my lips to unawakened earth

The trumpet of a prophecy! O wind,
If winter comes, can spring be far behind?   *70*

JOHN CLARE (1793–1864)

· BADGER ·

When midnight comes a host of dogs and men
Go out and track the badger to his den,
And put a sack within the hole, and lie
Till the old grunting badger passes by.
He comes and hears—they let the strongest loose.   *5*
The old fox hears the noise and drops the goose.
The poacher shoots and hurries from the cry,
And the old hare half wounded buzzes by.
They get a forkèd stick to bear him down
And clap the dogs and take him to the town,   *10*
And bait him all the day with many dogs,
And laugh and shout and fright the scampering hogs.
He runs along and bites at all he meets:
They shout and hollo down the noisy streets.

He turns about to face the loud uproar   *15*
And drives the rebels to their very door.
The frequent stone is hurled where'er they go;
When badgers fight, then everyone's a foe.
The dogs are clapped and urged to join the fray;
The badger turns and drives them all away.   *20*
Though scarcely half as big, demure and small,
He fights with dogs for hours and beats them all.
The heavy mastiff, savage in the fray,
Lies down and licks his feet and turns away.
The bulldog knows his match and waxes cold,   *25*
The badger grins and never leaves his hold.
He drives the crowd and follows at their heels
And bites them through—the drunkard swears and reels.

The frighted women take the boys away,
The blackguard laughs and hurries on the fray.   *30*
He tries to reach the woods, an awkward race,
But sticks and cudgels quickly stop the chase.
He turns again and drives the noisy crowd
And beats the many dogs in noises loud.

10/**clap:** *urge on by clapping*

He drives away and beats them every one,   *35*
And then they loose them all and set them on.
He falls as dead and kicked by boys and men,
Then starts and grins and drives the crowd again;
Till kicked and torn and beaten out he lies
And leaves his hold and cackles, groans, and dies.   *40*

· AUTUMN ·

The thistledown's flying, though the winds are all still,
On the green grass now lying, now mounting the hill,
The spring from the fountain now boils like a pot;
Through stones past the counting it bubbles red-hot.

The ground parched and cracked is like overbaked bread,   *5*
The greensward all wracked is, bents dried up and dead.
The fallow fields glitter like water indeed,
And gossamers twitter, flung from weed unto weed.

Hill-tops like hot iron glitter bright in the sun,
And the rivers we're eying burn to gold as they run;   *10*
Burning hot is the ground, liquid gold is the air;
Whoever looks round sees Eternity there.

⁶/**bents:** *stalky grass*
⁸/**gossamers:** *fine floating cobwebs*
  twitter: *tremble, quiver*

JOHN KEATS (1795–1821)

· LA BELLE DAME SANS MERCI ·
A Ballad

I

O what can ail thee, knight-at-arms,
    Alone and palely loitering?
The sedge has withered from the lake,
    And no birds sing.

II

O what can ail thee, knight-at-arms!   *5*
    So haggard and so woe-begone?
The squirrel's granary is full,
    And the harvest's done.

The title means "The Beautiful Lady Without Mercy."

III

I see a lily on thy brow,
    With anguish moist and fever dew,   *10*
And on thy cheeks a fading rose
    Fast withereth too.

IV

I met a lady in the meads,
    Full beautiful—a faery's child,
Her hair was long, her foot was light,   *15*
    And her eyes were wild.

V

I made a garland for her head,
    And bracelets too, and fragrant zone;
She looked at me as she did love,
    And made sweet moan.   *20*

VI

I set her on my pacing steed,
    And nothing else saw all day long,
For sidelong would she bend, and sing
    A faery's song.

VII

She found me roots of relish sweet,   *25*
    And honey wild, and manna dew,
And sure in language strange she said—
    "I love thee true".

VIII

She took me to her elfin grot,
    And there she wept, and sighed full sore,   *30*
And there I shut her wild wild eyes
    With kisses four.

IX

And there she lulled me asleep,
    And there I dreamed—Ah! woe betide!
The latest dream I ever dreamed   *35*
    On the cold hill side.

X

I saw pale kings and princes too,
    Pale warriors, death-pale were they all;
They cried—"La Belle Dame sans Merci
    Hath thee in thrall!"   *40*

[18]/**zone:** *belt*

XI

I saw their starved lips in the gloam,
 With horrid warning gaped wide,
And I awoke and found me here,
 On the cold hill's side.

XII

And this is why I sojourn here,   *45*
 Alone and palely loitering,
Though the sedge is withered from the lake,
 And no birds sing.

· ODE TO A NIGHTINGALE ·

1

My heart aches, and a drowsy numbness pains
 My sense, as though of hemlock I had drunk,
Or emptied some dull opiate to the drains
 One minute past, and Lethe-wards had sunk:
'Tis not through envy of thy happy lot,   *5*
 But being too happy in thine happiness,—
  That thou, light-wingèd Dryad of the trees,
   In some melodious plot
 Of beechen green, and shadows numberless,
  Singest of summer in full-throated ease.   *10*

2

O, for a draught of vintage! that hath been
 Cooled a long age in the deep-delvèd earth,
Tasting of Flora and the country green,
 Dance, and Provençal song, and sunburnt mirth!
O for a beaker full of the warm South,   *15*
 Full of the true, the blushful Hippocrene,
  With beaded bubbles winking at the brim,
   And purple-stainèd mouth;
 That I might drink, and leave the world unseen,
  And with thee fade away into the forest dim: *20*

2/**hemlock:** *a poisonous plant, and its juice, medically used as a powerful sedative*
4/**Lethe:** *A river in the underworld whose waters caused the drinker to forget his past*
7/**Dryad** *a wood-nymph*

13/**Flora:** *goddess of flowers*
14/**Provençal:** *of Provence, in the south of France, home of the medieval troubadours*
16/**Hippocrene:** *a spring in Greece sacred to the Muses*

3

Fade far away, dissolve, and quite forget
    What thou among the leaves hast never known,
The weariness, the fever, and the fret
    Here, where men sit and hear each other groan;
Where palsy shakes a few, sad, last gray hairs,   25
    Where youth grows pale, and spectre-thin, and dies;
        Where but to think is to be full of sorrow
          And leaden-eyed despairs,
    Where Beauty cannot keep her lustrous eyes,
        Or new Love pine at them beyond to-morrow.   30

4

Away! away! for I will fly to thee,
    Not charioted by Bacchus and his pards,
But on the viewless wings of Poesy,
    Though the dull brain perplexes and retards:
Already with thee! tender is the night,   35
    And haply the Queen-Moon is on her throne,
        Clustered around by all her starry Fays;
          But here there is no light,
    Save what from heaven is with the breezes blown
        Through verdurous glooms and winding mossy ways.   40

5

I cannot see what flowers are at my feet,
    Nor what soft incense hangs upon the boughs,
But, in embalmèd darkness, guess each sweet
    Wherewith the seasonable month endows
The grass, the thicket, and the fruit-tree wild;   45
    White hawthorn, and the pastoral eglantine;
        Fast fading violets covered up in leaves;
          And mid-May's eldest child,
    The coming musk-rose, full of dewy wine,
        The murmurous haunt of flies on summer eves.   50

6

Darkling I listen; and, for many a time
    I have been half in love with easeful Death,
Called him soft names in many a musèd rhyme,
    To take into the air my quiet breath;
Now more than ever seems it rich to die,   55

32/**Bacchus:** *god of wine*   37/**Fays:** *fairies*
   pards: *leopards*   43/**embalmèd:** *perfumed*
33/**viewless:** *invisible*   51/**darkling:** *in the dark*

To cease upon the midnight with no pain,
    While thou art pouring forth thy soul abroad
      In such an ecstasy!
Still wouldst thou sing, and I have ears in vain—
    To thy high requiem become a sod.   *60*

7

Thou wast not born for death, immortal Bird!
    No hungry generations tread thee down;
The voice I hear this passing night was heard
    In ancient days by emperor and clown:
Perhaps the self-same song that found a path   *65*
    Through the sad heart of Ruth, when, sick for home,
      She stood in tears amid the alien corn;
        The same that oft-times hath
Charmed magic casements, opening on the foam
    Of perilous seas, in faery lands forlorn.   *70*

8

Forlorn! the very word is like a bell
    To toll me back from thee to my sole self!
Adieu! the fancy cannot cheat so well
    As she is famed to do, deceiving elf.
Adieu! adieu! thy plaintive anthem fades   *75*
    Past the near meadows, over the still stream,
      Up the hill-side; and now 'tis buried deep
        In the next valley-glades:
Was it a vision, or a waking dream?
    Fled is that music:—Do I wake or sleep?   *80*

[66]/**Ruth:** *see the Book of Ruth, in the*   [73]/**fancy:** *imagination*
Old Testament

· **TO AUTUMN** ·

Season of mists and mellow fruitfulness,
    Close bosom-friend of the maturing sun;
Conspiring with him how to load and bless
    With fruit the vines that round the thatch-eaves run;
To bend with apples the mossed cottage-trees,   *5*
    And fill all fruit with ripeness to the core;
      To swell the gourd, and plump the hazel shells
    With a sweet kernel; to set budding more,
And still more, later flowers for the bees,
Until they think warm days will never cease,   *10*
      For summer has o'er-brimmed their clammy cells.

Who hath not seen thee oft amid thy store?
    Sometimes whoever seeks abroad may find
Thee sitting careless on a granary floor,
    Thy hair soft-lifted by the winnowing wind;   *15*
Or on a half-reaped furrow sound asleep,
    Drowsed with the fumes of poppies, while thy hook
        Spares the next swath and all its twinèd flowers:
And sometime like a gleaner thou dost keep
    Steady thy laden head across a brook;   *20*
    Or by a cider-press, with patient look,
        Thou watchest the last oozings hours by hours.

Where are the songs of spring? Ay, where are they?
    Think not of them, thou hast thy music too,—
While barrèd clouds bloom the soft-dying day,   *25*
    And touch the stubble-plains with rosy hue;
Then in a wailful choir the small gnats mourn
    Among the river sallows, borne aloft
        Or sinking as the light wind lives or dies;
And full-grown lambs loud bleat from hilly bourn;   *30*
    Hedge-crickets sing; and now with treble soft
    The red-breast whistles from a garden-croft;
        And gathering swallows twitter in the skies.

[17]/**hook:** *hooked knife, sickle*   [32]/**garden-croft:** *small garden next to*
[28]/**sallows:** *willows*   *house*
[30]/**bourn:** *enclosure*

· THE EVE OF ST. AGNES ·

St. Agnes' Eve—Ah, bitter chill it was!
The owl, for all his feathers, was a-cold;
The hare limped trembling through the frozen grass,
And silent was the flock in woolly fold:
Numb were the beadsman's fingers, while he told   *5*
His rosary, and while his frosted breath,
Like pious incense from a censer old,
Seemed taking flight for heaven, without a death,
Past the sweet Virgin's picture, while his prayer he saith.

[5]/**beadsman:** *one given a small pension on condition he pray for his benefactor*

Saint Agnes' Eve is January 20—supposedly the coldest night of the year. Keats wrote the poem in the week or so after that date in 1819. Saint Agnes was the patroness of unmarried girls; the folk belief was that those who went to bed supperless on the night of her feast-day would see their future husband in their dreams.

ANTHOLOGY

His prayer he saith, this patient, holy man;   *10*
Then takes his lamp, and riseth from his knees,
And back returneth, meagre, barefoot, wan,
Along the chapel aisle by slow degrees:
The sculptured dead, on each side, seem to freeze,
Emprisoned in black, purgatorial rails: *15*
Knights, ladies, praying in dumb orat'ries,
He passeth by; and his weak spirit fails
To think how they may ache in icy hoods and mails.

Northward he turneth through a little door,
And scarce three steps, ere music's golden tongue *20*
Flattered to tears this aged man and poor;
But no—already had his deathbell rung:
The joys of all his life were said and sung:
His was harsh penance on St. Agnes' Eve:
Another way he went, and soon among   *25*
Rough ashes sat he for his soul's reprieve,
And all night kept awake, for sinners' sake to grieve.

That ancient beadsman heard the prelude soft;
And so it chanced, for many a door was wide,
From hurry to and fro. Soon, up aloft,   *30*
The silver, snarling trumpets 'gan to chide:
The level chambers, ready with their pride,
Were glowing to receive a thousand guests:
The carvèd angels, ever eager-eyed,
Stared, where upon their heads the cornice rests, *35*
With hair blown back, and wings put cross-wise on their breasts.

At length burst in the argent revelry,
With plume, tiara, and all rich array,
Numerous as shadows haunting faerily
The brain, new-stuffed, in youth, with triumphs gay *40*
Of old romance. These let us wish away,
And turn, sole-thoughted, to one lady there,
Whose heart had brooded, all that wintry day,
On love, and winged St. Agnes' saintly care,
As she had heard old dames full many times declare. *45*

They told her how, upon St. Agnes' Eve,
Young virgins might have visions of delight,
And soft adorings from their loves receive
Upon the honeyed middle of the night,
If ceremonies due they did aright;   *50*
As, supperless to bed they must retire,
And couch supine their beauties, lily-white;

---

[16]/**orat'ries:** *oratories, places to pray, chapels*

[18]/**mails:** *suits of armor*
[37]/**argent:** *silvery, splendid*

Nor look behind, nor sideways, but require
Of heaven with upward eyes for all that they desire.

Full of this whim was thoughtful Madeline: 55
The music, yearning like a god in pain,
She scarcely heard: her maiden eyes divine,
Fixed on the floor, saw many a sweeping train
Pass by—she heeded not at all: in vain
Came many a tiptoe, amorous cavalier,   60
And back retired; not cooled by high disdain,
But she saw not: her heart was otherwise:
She sighed for Agnes' dreams, the sweetest of the year.

She danced along with vague, regardless eyes,
Anxious her lips, her breathing quick and short: 65
The hallowed hour was near at hand: she sighs
Amid the timbrels, and the thronged resort
Of whisperers in anger, or in sport;
'Mid looks of love, defiance, hate, and scorn,
Hoodwinked with faery fancy; all amort,   70
Save to St. Agnes and her lambs unshorn,
And all the bliss to be before to-morrow morn.

So, purposing each moment to retire,
She lingered still. Meantime, across the moors,
Had come young Porphyro, with heart on fire   75
For Madeline. Beside the portal doors,
Buttressed from moonlight, stands he, and implores
All saints to give him sight of Madeline,
But for one moment in the tedious hours,
That he might gaze and worship all unseen;   80
Perchance speak, kneel, touch, kiss—in sooth such things have been.

He ventures in: let no buzzed whisper tell:
All eyes be muffled, or a hundred swords
Will storm his heart, love's feverous citadel:
For him, those chambers held barbarian hordes,   85
Hyena foemen, and hot-blooded lords,
Whose very dogs would execrations howl
Against his lineage: not one breast affords
Him any mercy, in that mansion foul,
Save one old beldame, weak in body and in soul.   90

Ah, happy chance! the aged creature came,
Shuffling along with ivory-headed wand,
To where he stood, hid from the torch's flame,
Behind a broad hall-pillar, far beyond

67/**timbrels:** *tambourines*   81/**sooth:** *truth*
70/**all amort:** *like one dead*   90/**beldame:** *old woman, old nurse*

The sound of merriment and chorus bland:　　　　　　　　*95*
He startled her; but soon she knew his face,
And grasped his fingers in her palsied hand,
Saying, "Mercy, Porphyro! hie thee from this place:
They are all here to-night, the whole blood-thirsty race!

"Get hence! get hence! there's dwarfish Hildebrand;　　　*100*
He had a fever late, and in the fit
He cursèd thee and thine, both house and land:
Then there's that old Lord Maurice, not a whit
More tame for his gray hairs—Alas me! flit!
Flit like a ghost away."—"Ah, gossip dear,　　　　　　*105*
We're safe enough; here in this arm-chair sit,
And tell me how"—"Good saints! not here, not here;
Follow me, child, or else these stones will be thy bier."

He followed through a lowly archèd way,
Brushing the cobwebs with his lofty plume;　　　　　　*110*
And as she muttered "Well-a—well-a-day!"
He found him in a little moonlight room,
Pale, latticed, chill, and silent as a tomb.
"Now tell me where is Madeline," said he,
"O tell me, Angela, by the holy loom　　　　　　　　　*115*
Which none but secret sisterhood may see,
When they St. Agnes' wool are weaving piously."

"St. Agnes! Ah! it is St. Agnes' Eve—
Yet men will murder upon holy days:
Thou must hold water in a witch's sieve,　　　　　　　*120*
And be liege-lord of all the elves and fays,
To venture so: it fills me with amaze
To see thee, Porphyro!—St. Agnes' Eve!
God's help! my lady fair the conjuror plays
This very night: good angels her deceive!　　　　　　　*125*
But let me laugh awhile, I've mickle time to grieve."

Feebly she laugheth in the languid moon,
While Porphyro upon her face doth look,
Like puzzled urchin on an aged crone
Who keepeth closed a wonderous riddle-book,　　　　　*130*
As spectacled she sits in chimney nook.
But soon his eyes grew brilliant, when she told
His lady's purpose; and he scarce could brook
Tears, at the thought of those enchantments cold,
And Madeline asleep in lap of legends old.　　　　　　*135*

98/**hie thee:** *get yourself away*　　　　121/**fays:** *fairies*
105/**gossip:** *godparent, close (woman)*　126/**mickle:** *much*
friend　　　　　　　　　　　　　　　　133/**brook:** *hold back*

Sudden a thought came like a full-blown rose,
Flushing his brow, and in his painèd heart
Made purple riot: then doth he propose
A stratagem, that makes the beldame start:
"A cruel man and impious thou art: 140
Sweet lady, let her pray, and sleep, and dream
Alone with her good angels, far apart
From wicked men like thee. Go, go!—I deem
Thou canst not surely be the same that thou didst seem."

"I will not harm her, by all saints I swear,"   145
Quoth Porphyro: "O may I ne'er find grace
When my weak voice shall whisper its last prayer,
If one of her soft ringlets I displace,
Or look with ruffian passion in her face:
Good Angela, believe me by these tears;   150
Or I will, even in a moment's space,
Awake, with horrid shout, my foemen's ears,
And beard them, though they be more fanged than wolves and bears."

"Ah! why wilt thou affright a feeble soul?
A poor, weak, palsy-stricken, churchyard thing,   155
Whose passing-bell may ere the midnight toll;
Whose prayers for thee, each morn and evening,
Were never missed,"—Thus plaining, doth she bring
A gentler speech from burning Porphyro;
So woeful, and of such deep sorrowing,   160
That Angela gives promise she will do
Whatever he shall wish, betide her weal or woe.

Which was, to lead him, in close secrecy,
Even to Madeline's chamber, and there hide
Him in a closet, of such privacy   165
That he might see her beauty unespied,
And win perhaps that night a peerless bride,
While legioned faeries paced the coverlet,
And pale enchantment held her sleepy-eyed.
Never on such a night have lovers met,   170
Since Merlin paid his demon all the monstrous debt.

"It shall be as thou wishest," said the dame:
"All cates and dainties shall be storèd there
Quickly on this feast-night: by the tambour frame
Her own lute thou wilt see: no time to spare,   175

156/**passing-bell:** *bell rung as one "passes away"*
173/**cates:** *delicacies*
174/**tambour:** *frame to hold embroidery*

ANTHOLOGY

For I am slow and feeble, and scarce dare
On such a catering trust my dizzy head.
Wait here, my child, with patience, kneel in prayer
The while: Ah! thou must needs the lady wed,
Or may I never leave my grave among the dead."   *180*

So saying, she hobbled off with busy fear.
The lover's endless minutes slowly passed;
The dame returned, and whispered in his ear
To follow her; with aged eyes aghast
From fright of dim espial. Safe at last,   *185*
Through many a dusky gallery, they gain
The maiden's chamber, silken, hushed, and chaste;
Where Porphyro took covert, pleased amain.
His poor guide hurried back with agues in her brain.

Her faltering hand upon the balustrade,   *190*
Old Angela was feeling for the stair,
When Madeline, St. Agnes' charmèd maid,
Rose, like a missioned spirit, unaware:
With silver taper's light, and pious care,
She turned, and down the aged gossip led   *195*
To a safe level matting. Now prepare,
Young Porphyro, for gazing on that bed;
She comes, she comes again, like ring-dove frayed and fled.

Out went the taper as she hurried in;
Its little smoke, in pallid moonshine, died: *200*
She closed the door, she panted, all akin
To spirits of the air, and visions wide:
No uttered syllable, or, woe betide!
But to her heart, her heart was voluble,
Paining with eloquence her balmy side;   *205*
As though a tongueless nightingale should swell
Her throat in vain, and die, heart-stifled, in her dell.

A casement high and triple-arched there was,
All garlanded with carven imageries,
Of fruits, and flowers, and bunches of knot-grass,   *210*
And diamonded with panes of quaint device,
Innumerable of stains and splendid dyes,
As are the tiger-moth's deep-damasked wings;

188/**amain:** *greatly*
198/**frayed:** *frightened*
205/**balmy:** *fragrant*
210/**knot-grass:** *grass with jointed stems*

213/**tiger-moth:** *a large scarlet and brown moth*
    deep-damasked: *richly colored (especially with the red of the "damask rose"*

And in the midst, 'mong thousand heraldries,
And twilight saints, and dim emblazonings,   *215*
A shielded scutcheon blushed with blood of queens and kings.

Full on this casement shone the wintry moon,
And threw warm gules on Madeline's fair breast,
As down she knelt for Heaven's grace and boon;
Rose-bloom fell on her hands, together pressed,   *220*
And on her silver cross soft amethyst,
And on her hair a glory, like a saint:
She seemed a splendid angel, newly dressed,
Save wings, for heaven:—Porphyro grew faint:
She knelt, so pure a thing, so free from mortal taint.   *225*

Anon his heart revives: her vespers done,
Of all its wreathèd pearls her hair she frees;
Unclasps her warmèd jewels one by one;
Loosens her fragrant bodice; by degrees
Her rich attire creeps rustling to her knees: *230*
Half-hidden, like a mermaid in sea-weed,
Pensive awhile she dreams awake, and sees,
In fancy, fair St. Agnes in her bed,
But dares not look behind, or all the charm is fled.

Soon, trembling in her soft and chilly nest,   *235*
In sort of wakeful swoon, perplexed she lay,
Until the poppied warmth of sleep oppressed
Her soothèd limbs, and soul fatigued away;
Flown, like a thought, until the morrow-day;
Blissfully havened both from joy and pain;   *240*
Clasped like a missal where swart paynims pray;
Blinded alike from sunshine and from rain,
As though a rose should shut, and be a bud again.

Stolen to this paradise, and so entranced,
Porphyro gazed upon her empty dress,   *245*
And listened to her breathing, if it chanced
To wake into a slumberous tenderness;
Which when he heard, that minute did he bless,
And breathed himself: then from the closet crept,
Noiseless as fear in a wide wilderness,   *250*
And over the hushed carpet, silent, stepped,
And 'tween the curtains peeped where, lo!—how fast she slept.

---

[216]/**blushed with blood:** *was crimson*
with indications of royalty
[218]/**gules:** *red (in heraldry)*
[219]/**boon:** *favor*

[222]/**glory:** *a gloriole, halo*
[237]/**poppied:** *like an opiate*
[241]/**swart paynims:** *swarthy pagans*

ANTHOLOGY

Then by the bed-side, where the faded moon
Made a dim, silver twilight, soft he set
A table, and, half anguished, threw thereon   255
A cloth of woven crimson, gold, and jet:—
O for some drowsy Morphean amulet!
The boisterous, midnight, festive clarion,
The kettle-drum, and far-heard clarionet,
Affray his ears, though but in dying tone:—   260
The hall door shuts again, and all the noise is gone.

And still she slept an azure-lidded sleep,
In blanchèd linen, smooth, and lavendered,
While he from forth the closet brought a heap
Of candied apple, quince, and plum, and gourd;   265
With jellies soother than the creamy curd,
And lucent syrups, tinct with cinnamon;
Manna and dates, in argosy transferred
From Fez; and spiced dainties, every one,
From silken Samarcand to cedared Lebanon.   270

These delicates he heaped with glowing hand
On golden dishes and in baskets bright
Of wreathèd silver: sumptuous they stand
In the retirèd quiet of the night,
Filling the chilly room with perfume light.—   275
"And now, my love, my seraph fair, awake!
Thou art my heaven, and I thine eremite:
Open thine eyes, for meek St. Agnes' sake,
Or I shall drowse beside thee, so my soul doth ache."

Thus whispering, his warm, unnervèd arm   280
Sank in her pillow. Shaded was her dream
By the dusk curtains:—'twas a midnight charm
Impossible to melt as icèd stream;
The lustrous salvers in the moonlight gleam;
Broad golden fringe upon the carpet lies: 285
It seemed he never, never could redeem
From such a stedfast spell his lady's eyes;
So mused, awhile, entoiled in woofèd phantasies.

Awakening up, he took her hollow lute,—
Tumultuous,—and, in chords that tenderest be,   290
He played an ancient ditty, long since mute,
In Provence called, "La belle dame sans merci":

260/**affray:** *startle, frighten*
263/**blanchèd:** *bleached*
266/**soother:** *smoother*
267/**lucent:** *clear, bright*
  tinct: *flavored*

268/**argosy:** *large merchant ship, or fleet of such ships*
277/**eremite:** *hermit; here, worshipper*
288/**entoiled:** *involved, absorbed*
  woofèd: *woven*

Close to her ear touching the melody;—
Wherewith disturbed, she uttered a soft moan:
He ceased—she panted quick—and suddenly   *295*
Her blue affrayèd eyes wide open shone:
Upon his knees he sank, pale as smooth-sculptured stone.

Her eyes were open, but she still beheld,
Now wide awake, the vision of her sleep:
There was a painful change, that nigh expelled   *300*
The blisses of her dream so pure and deep
At which fair Madeline began to weep,
And moan forth witless words with many a sigh;
While still her gaze on Porphyro would keep;
Who knelt, with joinèd hands and piteous eye,   *305*
Fearing to move or speak, she looked so dreamingly.

"Ah, Porphyro!" said she, "but even now
Thy voice was at sweet tremble in mine ear,
Made tunable with every sweetest vow;
And those sad eyes were spiritual and clear: *310*
How changed thou art! how pallid, chill, and drear!
Give me that voice again, my Porphyro,
Those looks immortal, those complainings dear!
Oh leave me not in this eternal woe,
For if thou diest, my love, I know not where to go."   *315*

Beyond a mortal man impassioned far
At these voluptuous accents, he arose,
Ethereal, flushed, and like a throbbing star
Seen 'mid the sapphire heaven's deep repose;
Into her dream he melted, as the rose   *320*
Blendeth its odour with the violet,—
Solution sweet: meantime the frost-wind blows
Like love's alarum, pattering the sharp sleet
Against the window-panes; St. Agnes' moon hath set.

'Tis dark: quick pattereth the flaw-blown sleet.   *325*
"This is no dream, my bride, my Madeline!"
'Tis dark: the icèd gusts still rave and beat:
"No dream, alas! alas! and woe is mine!
Porphyro will leave me here to fade and pine.—
Cruel! what traitor could thee hither bring?   *330*
I curse not, for my heart is lost in thine,
Though thou forsakest a deceivèd thing:—
A dove forlorn and lost with sick unprunèd wing."

---

[325]/**flaw-blown:** *blown by gusts of*   [333]/**unprunèd:** *unpreened, uncared for*
wind

"My Madeline! sweet dreamer! lovely bride!
Say, may I be for aye thy vassal blest?   335
Thy beauty's shield, heart-shaped and vermeil-dyed?
Ah, silver shrine, here will I take my rest
After so many hours of toil and quest,
A famished pilgrim,—saved by miracle.
Though I have found, I will not rob thy nest   340
Saving of thy sweet self; if thou think'st well
To trust, fair Madeline, to no rude infidel.

"Hark! 'tis an elfin-storm from faery land,
Of haggard seeming, but a boon indeed:
Arise—arise! the morning is at hand;—   345
The bloated wassaillers will never heed:—
Let us away, my love, with happy speed;
There are no ears to hear, or eyes to see,—
Drowned all in Rhenish and the sleepy mead:
Awake! arise! my love, and fearless be,   350
For o'er the southern moors I have a home for thee."

She hurried at his words, beset with fears,
For there were sleeping dragons all around,
At glaring watch, perhaps, with ready spears—
Down the wide stairs a darkling way they found.—   355
In all the house was heard no human sound.
A chain-drooped lamp was flickering by each door;
The arras, rich with horseman, hawk, and hound,
Fluttered in the besieging wind's uproar;
And the long carpets rose along the gusty floor.   360

They glide, like phantoms, into the wide hall;
Like phantoms, to the iron porch, they glide;
Where lay the porter, in uneasy sprawl,
With a huge empty flagon by his side:
The wakeful bloodhound rose, and shook his hide,   365
But his sagacious eye an inmate owns:
By one, and one, the bolts full easy slide:—
The chains lie silent on the footworn stones:—
The key turns, and the door upon its hinges groans.

And they are gone: aye, ages long ago   370
These lovers fled away into the storm.
That night the Baron dreamt of many a woe,
And all his warrior-guests, with shade and form

335/**for aye:** *forever*
336/**vermeil-dyed:** *vermilion*
344/**haggard:** *wild*
  boon: *piece of luck, blessing*

349/**mead:** *drink made of fermented honey*
355/**darkling:** *in the dark*

Of witch, and demon, and large coffin-worm,
Were long be-nightmared. Angela the old   375
Died palsy-twitched, with meagre face deform;
The beadsman, after thousand *Ave*'s told,
For aye unsought for slept among his ashes cold.

376/**deform:** *deformed*   377/***Ave's:*** *Hail, Mary's*

EDWARD FITZGERALD (1809–1883)

• From THE RUBÁIYÁT OF OMAR KHAYYÁM •

I

Awake! for Morning in the Bowl of Night
Has flung the Stone that puts the Stars to Flight:
    And Lo! the Hunter of the East has caught
The Sultán's Turret in a Noose of Light.

III

And, as the Cock crew, those who stood before   5
The Tavern shouted—"Open then the Door!
    You know how little while we have to stay,
And, once departed, may return no more."

VII

Come, fill the Cup, and in the Fire of Spring
The Winter Garment of Repentance fling: 10
    The Bird of Time has but a little way
To fly—and Lo! the Bird is on the Wing.

XII c

A Book of Verses underneath the Bough,
A Jug of Wine, a Loaf of Bread—and Thou
    Beside me singing in the Wilderness—   15
Oh, Wilderness were Paradise enow!

XIII c

Some for the Glories of This World; and some
Sigh for the Prophet's Paradise to come;
    Ah, take the Cash, and let the Credit go,
Nor heed the rumble of a distant Drum!   20

16/**enow:** *enough*

Stanzas with Roman numbers only are from the first edition of 1859; those with b numbers are from the second edition of 1868; those with c from the fifth edition of 1889.

XVIII b

Think, in this battered Caravanserai
Whose Portals are alternate Night and Day,
　　How Sultán after Sultán with his Pomp
Abode his destined Hour, and went his way.

XXIV b

I sometimes think that never blows so red　　25
The Rose as where some buried Cæsar bled;
　　That every Hyacinth the Garden wears
Dropt in her Lap from some once lovely Head.

XIX

And this delightful Herb whose tender Green
Fledges the River's Lip on which we lean—　　30
　　Ah, lean upon it lightly! for who knows
From what once lovely Lip it springs unseen!

XXIII b

And we, that now make merry in the Room
They left, and Summer dresses in new bloom,
　　Ourselves must we beneath the Couch of Earth　　35
Descend—ourselves to make a Couch—for whom?

XXVII c

Myself when young did eagerly frequent
Doctor and Saint, and heard great argument
　　About it and about: but evermore
Came out by the same door where in I went.　　40

XXXII

There was a Door to which I found no Key:
There was a Veil past which I could not see:
　　Some little Talk awhile of ME and THEE
There seemed—and then no more of THEE and ME.

LXXVI b

The Moving Finger writes; and, having writ,　　45
Moves on: nor all your Piety nor Wit
　　Shall lure it back to cancel half a Line,
Nor all your Tears wash out a Word of it.

LXXI

And much as Wine has played the Infidel,
And robbed me of my Robe of Honour—well,　　50
　　I often wonder what the Vintners buy
One half so precious as the Goods they sell.

21/**Caravanserai:** *inn primarily for caravans*

LXXII

Alas, that Spring should vanish with the Rose!
That Youth's sweet-scented Manuscript should close!
 The Nightingale that in the Branches sang,   *55*
Ah, whence, and whither flown again, who knows!

CVIII b

Ah, Love! could you and I with Fate conspire
To grasp this sorry Scheme of Things entire,
 Would not we shatter it to bits—and then
Re-mould it nearer to the Heart's Desire!   *60*

LXXIV

Ah, Moon of my Delight, who know'st no wane,
The Moon of Heaven is rising once again:
 How oft hereafter rising shall she look
Through this same Garden after me—in vain!

LXXV

And when Thyself with shining Foot shall pass   *65*
Among the Guests Star-scattered on the Grass,
 And in thy joyous Errand reach the Spot
Where I made one—turn down an empty Glass!

ALFRED, LORD TENNYSON
(1809–1892)

· ULYSSES ·

It little profits that an idle king,
By this still hearth, among these barren crags,
Matched with an aged wife, I mete and dole
Unequal laws unto a savage race,
That hoard, and sleep, and feed, and know not me.   *5*
I cannot rest from travel; I will drink
Life to the lees. All times I have enjoyed
Greatly, have suffered greatly, both with those
That loved me, and alone; on shore, and when
Thro' scudding drifts the rainy Hyades   *10*
Vext the dim sea. I am become a name;
For always roaming with a hungry heart
Much have I seen and known,—cities of men
And manners, climates, councils, governments,
Myself not least, but honored of them all,—   *15*

---

[10]/**Hyades:** *a group of stars whose rising was thought to indicate rain*

ANTHOLOGY

And drunk delight of battle with my peers,
Far on the ringing plains of windy Troy.
I am a part of all that I have met;
Yet all experience is an arch wherethro'
Gleams that untravelled world whose margin fades   *20*
For ever and for ever when I move.
How dull it is to pause, to make an end,
To rust unburnished, not to shine in use!
As tho' to breathe were life! Life piled on life
Were all too little, and of one to me   *25*
Little remains; but every hour is saved
From that eternal silence, something more,
A bringer of new things; and vile it were
For some three suns to store and hoard myself,
And this gray spirit yearning in desire   *30*
To follow knowledge like a sinking star,
Beyond the utmost bound of human thought.
    This is my son, mine own Telemachus,
To whom I leave the sceptre and the isle,—
Well-loved of me, discerning to fulfil   *35*
This labor, by slow prudence to make mild
A rugged people, and thro' soft degrees
Subdue them to the useful and the good.
Most blameless is he, centred in the sphere
Of common duties, decent not to fail   *40*
In offices of tenderness, and pay
Meet adoration to my household gods,
When I am gone. He works his work, I mine.
    There lies the port; the vessel puffs her sail;
There gloom the dark broad seas. My mariners,   *45*
Souls that have toiled, and wrought, and thought with me,—
That ever with a frolic welcome took
The thunder and the sunshine, and opposed
Free hearts, free foreheads,—you and I are old;
Old age hath yet his honor and his toil.   *50*
Death closes all; but something ere the end,
Some work of noble note, may yet be done,
Not unbecoming men that strove with Gods.
The lights begin to twinkle from the rocks;
The long day wanes; the slow moon climbs; the deep   *55*
Moans round with many voices. Come, my friends.
'Tis not too late to seek a newer world.
Push off, and sitting well in order smite
The sounding furrows; for my purpose holds
To sail beyond the sunset, and the baths   *60*
Of all the western stars, until I die.

42/**meet:** *appropriate*
48/**opposed:** *resisted with*

It may be that the gulfs will wash us down;
It may be we shall touch the Happy Isles,
And see the great Achilles, whom we knew.
Tho' much is taken, much abides; and tho'   65
We are not now that strength which in old days
Moved earth and heaven, that which we are, we are,—
One equal temper of heroic hearts,
Made weak by time and fate, but strong in will
To strive, to seek, to find, and not to yield.   70

[63]/**the Happy Isles:** *in classical mythology, the home of the virtuous dead*

• TEARS, IDLE TEARS •

Tears, idle tears, I know not what they mean,
Tears from the depth of some divine despair
Rise in the heart, and gather to the eyes,
In looking on the happy Autumn-fields,
And thinking of the days that are no more.   5

Fresh as the first beam glittering on a sail,
That brings our friends up from the underworld,
Sad as the last which reddens over one
That sinks with all we love below the verge;
So sad, so fresh, the days that are no more.   10

Ah, sad and strange as in dark summer dawns
The earliest pipe of half-awakened birds
To dying ears, when unto dying eyes
The casement slowly grows a glimmering square;
So sad, so strange, the days that are no more.   15

Dear as remembered kisses after death,
And sweet as those by hopeless fancy feigned
On lips that are for others; deep as love,
Deep as first love, and wild with all regret;
O Death in Life, the days that are no more.   20

ROBERT BROWNING (1812–1889)

• MY LAST DUCHESS •
Ferrara

That's my last Duchess painted on the wall,
Looking as if she were alive. I call
That piece a wonder, now: Frà Pandolf's hands
Worked busily a day, and there she stands.

Ferrara: *a center of art and culture in northern Italy during the Renaissance*
[3]/**Frà Pandolf:** *an imaginary artist. Frà is short for Frate (Brother)*

Will't please you sit and look at her? I said   5
"Frà Pandolf" by design, for never read
Strangers like you that pictured countenance,
The depth and passion of its earnest glance,
But to myself they turned (since none puts by
The curtain I have drawn for you, but I)   10
And seemed as they would ask me, if they durst,
How such a glance came there; so, not the first
Are you to turn and ask thus. Sir, 'twas not
Her husband's presence only, called that spot
Of joy into the Duchess' cheek: perhaps   15
Frà Pandolf chanced to say "Her mantle laps
Over my lady's wrist too much," or "Paint
Must never hope to reproduce the faint
Half-flush that dies along her throat:" such stuff
Was courtesy, she thought, and cause enough   20
For calling up that spot of joy. She had
A heart—how shall I say?—too soon made glad,
Too easily impressed; she liked whate'er
She looked on, and her looks went everywhere.
Sir, 'twas all one! My favor at her breast,   25
The dropping of the daylight in the West,
The bough of cherries some officious fool
Broke in the orchard for her, the white mule
She rode with round the terrace—all and each
Would draw from her alike the approving speech,   30
Or blush, at least. She thanked men,—good! but thanked
Somehow—I know not how—as if she ranked
My gift of a nine-hundred-years-old name
With anybody's gift. Who'd stoop to blame
This sort of trifling? Even had you skill   35
In speech—(which I have not)—to make your will
Quite clear to such an one, and say, "Just this
Or that in you disgusts me; here you miss,
Or there exceed the mark"—and if she let
Herself be lessoned so, nor plainly set   40
Her wits to yours, forsooth, and made excuse,
—E'en then would be some stooping; and I choose
Never to stoop. Oh sir, she smiled, no doubt,
Whene'er I passed her; but who passed without
Much the same smile? This grew; I gave commands;   45
Then all smiles stopped together. There she stands
As if alive. Will't please you rise? We'll meet
The company below, then. I repeat,
The Count your master's known munificence
Is ample warrant that no just pretence   50
Of mine for dowry will be disallowed;
Though his fair daughter's self, as I avowed
At starting, is my object. Nay, we'll go

Together down, sir. Notice Neptune, though,
Taming a sea-horse, thought a rarity,   55
Which Claus of Innsbruck cast in bronze for me!

56/**Claus of Innsbruck:** *an imaginary artist*

EDWARD LEAR (1812–1888)

• HOW PLEASANT TO KNOW MR. LEAR! •

How pleasant to know Mr. Lear!
    Who has written such volumes of stuff!
Some think him ill-tempered and queer,
    But a few think him pleasant enough.

His mind is concrete and fastidious,   5
    His nose is remarkably big;
His visage is more or less hideous,
    His beard it resembles a wig.

He has ears, and two eyes, and ten fingers,
    Leastways if you reckon two thumbs;   10
Long ago he was one of the singers,
    But now he is one of the dumbs.

He sits in a beautiful parlour,
    With hundreds of books on the wall;
He drinks a great deal of Marsala,   15
    But never gets tipsy at all.

He has many friends, laymen and clerical,
    Old Foss is the name of his cat;
His body is perfectly spherical.
    He weareth a runcible hat.   20

When he walks in a waterproof white,
    The children run after him so!
Calling out, "He's come out in his night-
    Gown, that crazy old Englishman, oh!"

He weeps by the side of the ocean,   25
    He weeps on the top of the hill;
He purchases pancakes and lotion,
    And chocolate shrimps from the mill.

15/**Marsala:** *a sweet dessert wine from Sicily*
20/**runcible:** *apparently a nonsense word Lear made up*

> He reads but he cannot speak Spanish,
> He cannot abide ginger-beer: *30*
> Ere the days of his pilgrimage vanish,
> How pleasant to know Mr. Lear!

³⁰/**ginger-beer:** *a carbonated soft drink flavored with ginger*

EMILY BRONTË (1818–1848)

• REMEMBRANCE •

Cold in the earth—and the deep snow piled above thee,
Far, far removed, cold in the dreary grave!
Have I forgot, my only love, to love thee,
Severed at last by time's all-severing wave?

Now, when alone, do my thoughts no longer hover   *5*
Over the mountains, on that northern shore;
Resting their wings where heath and fern-leaves cover
Thy noble heart for ever, ever more?

Cold in the earth—and fifteen wild Decembers,
From those brown hills, have melted into spring: *10*
Faithful, indeed, is the spirit that remembers
After such years of change and suffering!

Sweet love of youth, forgive, if I forgot thee
While the world's tide is bearing me along;
Other desires and other hopes beset me,   *15*
Hopes which obscure, but cannot do thee wrong.

No later light has lightened up my heaven,
No second morn has ever shone for me;
All my life's bliss from thy dear life was given,
All my life's bliss is in the grave with thee.   *20*

But when the days of golden dreams had perished,
And even despair was powerless to destroy,
Then did I learn how existence could be cherished,
Strengthened, and fed without the aid of joy.

Then did I check the tears of useless passion—   *25*
Weaned my young soul from yearning after thine;
Sternly denied its burning wish to hasten
Down to that tomb already more than mine.

And, even yet, I dare not let it languish,
Dare not indulge in memory's rapturous pain;   *30*
Once drinking deep of that divinest anguish,
How could I seek the empty world again?

ARTHUR HUGH CLOUGH
(1819–1861)

• THE LATEST DECALOGUE •

Thou shalt have one God only; who
Would be at the expense of two?
No graven images may be
Worshipped, except the currency;
Swear not at all; for, for thy curse,   *5*
Thine enemy is none the worse;
At church on Sunday to attend
Will serve to keep the world thy friend;
Honour thy parents; that is, all
From whom advancement may befall;   *10*
Thou shalt not kill; but needst not strive
Officiously to keep alive;
Do not adultery commit;
Advantage rarely comes of it;
Thou shalt not steal; an empty feat,   *15*
When it's so lucrative to cheat;
Bear not false witness; let the lie
Have time on its own wings to fly;
Thou shalt not covet; but tradition
Approves all forms of competition.   *20*

The sum of all is, thou shalt love,
If anybody, God above;
At any rate shall never labour
More than thyself to love thy neighbour.

WALT WHITMAN (1819–1892)

• From LEAVES OF GRASS (1855) •

I think I could turn and live awhile with the animals. . . . they are so
     placid and self-contained,
I stand and look at them sometimes half the day long.

They do not sweat and whine about their condition,
They do not lie awake in the dark and weep for their sins,
They do not make me sick discussing their duty to God,   *5*
Not one is dissatisfied. . . . not one is demented with the mania of
     owning things,
Not one kneels to another nor to his kind that lived thousands of
     years ago,
Not one is respectable or industrious over the whole earth.

So they show their relations to me and I accept them;
They bring me tokens of myself. . . . they evince them plainly in
    their possession.   *10*

I do not know where they got those tokens,
I must have passed that way untold times ago and negligently
    dropt them,
Myself moving forward then and now and forever,
Gathering and showing more always and with velocity,
Infinite and omnigenous and the like of these among them;   *15*
Not too exclusive toward the reachers of my remembrancers,
Picking out here one that shall be my amie,
Choosing to go with him on brotherly terms.

A gigantic beauty of a stallion, fresh and responsive to my caresses,
Head high in the forehead and wide between the ears,   *20*
Limbs glossy and supple, tail dusting the ground,
Eyes well apart and full of sparkling wickedness. . . . ears finely
    cut and flexibly moving.

His nostrils dilate. . . . my heels embrace him. . . . his well built
    limbs tremble with pleasure. . . . we speed around and return.

I but use you a moment and then I resign you stallion. . . . and do not
    need your paces, and outgallop them,
And myself as I stand or sit pass faster than you.   *25*

15/**omnigenous:** *of all kinds*
16/**remembrancer:** *one who reminds*
17/**amie:** *the French word means friend (feminine); later changed to "one that I love"*

• OUT OF THE CRADLE ENDLESSLY ROCKING •

Out of the cradle endlessly rocking,
Out of the mocking-bird's throat, the musical shuttle,
Out of the Ninth-month midnight,
Over the sterile sands and the fields beyond, where the child leaving
    his bed wander'd alone, bareheaded, barefoot,
Down from the shower'd halo,   *5*
Up from the mystic play of shadows twining and twisting as if they
    were alive,
Out from the patches of briers and blackberries,
From the memories of the bird that chanted to me,
From your memories sad brother, from the fitful risings and fallings
    I heard

3/**Ninth-month:** *the Quaker name for September*

ANTHOLOGY

From under that yellow half-moon late-risen and swollen as if with
    tears,   10
From those beginning notes of yearning and love there in the mist,
From the thousand responses of my heart never to cease,
From the myriad thence-arous'd words,
From the word stronger and more delicious than any,
From such as now they start the scene revisiting,   15
As a flock, twittering, rising, or overhead passing,
Borne hither, ere all eludes me, hurriedly,
A man, yet by these tears a little boy again,
Throwing myself on the sand, confronting the waves,
I, chanter of pains and joys, uniter of here and hereafter,   20
Taking all hints to use them, but swiftly leaping beyond them,
A reminiscence sing.

Once Paumanok,
When the lilac-scent was in the air and Fifth-month grass was growing,
Up this seashore in some briers,   25
Two feather'd guests from Alabama, two together,
And their nest, and four light-green eggs spotted with brown,
And every day the he-bird to and fro near at hand,
And every day the she-bird crouch'd on her nest, silent, with bright
    eyes,
And every day I, a curious boy, never too close, never disturbing them,   30
Cautiously peering, absorbing, translating.

Shine! shine! shine!
Pour down your warmth, great sun!
While we bask, we two together.

Two together!   35
Winds blow south, or winds blow north,
Day come white, or night come black,
Home, or rivers and mountains from home,
Singing all time, minding no time,
While we two keep together.   40

Till of a sudden,
May-be kill'd, unknown to her mate,
One forenoon the she-bird crouch'd not on the nest,
Nor return'd that afternoon, nor the next,
Nor ever appear'd again.   45

And thenceforward all summer in the sound of the sea,
And at night under the full of the moon in calmer weather,
Over the hoarse surging of the sea,
Or flitting from brier to brier by day,
I saw, I heard at intervals the remaining one, the he-bird,   50
The solitary guest from Alabama.

²³/**Paumanok:** *the Indian name for Long Island*

ANTHOLOGY

Blow! blow! blow!
Blow up sea-winds along Paumanok's shore;
I wait and I wait till you blow my mate to me.

Yes, when the stars glisten'd,   *55*
All night long on the prong of a moss-scallop'd stake,
Down almost amid the slapping waves,
Sat the lone singer wonderful causing tears.

He call'd on his mate,
He pour'd forth the meanings which I of all men know.   *60*

Yes my brother I know,
The rest might not, but I have treasur'd every note,
For more than once dimly down to the beach gliding,
Silent, avoiding the moonbeams, blending myself with the shadows,
Recalling now the obscure shapes, the echoes, the sounds and sights
    after their sorts,   *65*
The white arms out in the breakers tirelessly tossing,
I, with bare feet, a child, the wind wafting my hair,
Listen'd long and long.

Listen'd to keep, to sing, now translating the notes,
Following you my brother.   *70*

Soothe! soothe! soothe!
Close on its wave soothes the wave behind,
And again another behind embracing and lapping, every one close,
But my love soothes not me, not me.

Low hangs the moon, it rose late,   *75*
It is lagging—O I think it is heavy with love, with love.

O madly the sea pushes upon the land,
With love, with love.

O night! do I not see my love fluttering out among the breakers?
What is that little black thing I see there in the white?   *80*

Loud! loud! loud!
Loud I call to you, my love!

High and clear I shoot my voice over the waves,
Surely you must know who is here, is here,
You must know who I am, my love.   *85*

Low-hanging moon!
What is that dusky spot in your brown yellow?
O it is the shape, the shape of my mate!
O moon do not keep her from me any longer.

Land! land! O land!   90
Whichever way I turn, O I think you could give me my mate back
    again if you only would,
For I am almost sure I see her dimly whichever way I look.

O rising stars!
Perhaps the one I want so much will rise, will rise with some of you.

O throat! O trembling throat!   95
Sound clearer through the atmosphere!
Pierce the woods, the earth,
Somewhere listening to catch you must be the one I want.

Shake out carols!
Solitary here, the night's carols!   100
Carols of lonesome love! death's carols!
Carols under that lagging, yellow, waning moon!
O under that moon where she droops almost down into the sea!
O reckless despairing carols.

But soft! sink low!   105
Soft! let me just murmur,
And do you wait a moment you husky-nois'd sea,
For somewhere I believe I heard my mate responding to me,
So faint, I must be still, be still to listen,
But not altogether still, for then she might not come immediately
    to me.   110

Hither my love!
Here I am! here!
With this just-sustain'd note I announce myself to you,
This gentle call is for you my love, for you.

Do not be decoy'd elsewhere,   115
That is the whistle of the wind, it is not my voice,
That is the fluttering, the fluttering of the spray,
Those are the shadows of leaves.

O darkness! O in vain!
O I am very sick and sorrowful.   120

O brown halo in the sky near the moon, drooping upon the sea!
O troubled reflection in the sea!
O throat! O throbbing heart!
And I singing uselessly, uselessly all the night.

O past! O happy life! O songs of joy!   125
In the air, in the woods, over fields,
Loved! loved! loved! loved! loved!
But my mate no more, no more with me!
We two together no more.

ANTHOLOGY

The aria sinking,   *130*
All else continuing, the stars shining,
The winds blowing, the notes of the bird continuous echoing,
With angry moans the fierce old mother incessantly moaning,
On the sands of Paumanok's shore gray and rustling,
The yellow half-moon enlarged, sagging down, drooping, the face of
    the sea almost touching,   *135*
The boy ecstatic, with his bare feet the waves, with his hair the
    atmosphere dallying,
The love in the heart long pent, now loose, now at last tumultuously
    bursting,
The aria's meaning, the ears, the soul, swiftly depositing,
The strange tears down the cheeks coursing,
The colloquy there, the trio, each uttering,   *140*
The undertone, the savage old mother incessantly crying,
To the boy's soul's questions sullenly timing, some drown'd secret
    hissing,
To the outsetting bard.

Demon or bird (said the boy's soul,)
Is it indeed toward your mate you sing? or is it really to me?   *145*
For I, that was a child, my tongue's use sleeping, now I have heard you,
Now in a moment I know what I am for, I awake,
And already a thousand singers, a thousand songs, clearer, louder
    and more sorrowful than yours,
A thousand warbling echoes have started to life within me, never to die.

O you singer solitary, singing by yourself, projecting me,   *150*
O solitary me listening, never more shall I cease perpetuating you,
Never more shall I escape, never more the reverberations,
Never more the cries of unsatisfied love be absent from me,
Never again leave me to be the peaceful child I was before what there
    in the night,
By the sea under the yellow and sagging moon,   *155*
The messenger there arous'd, the fire, the sweet hell within,
The unknown want, the destiny of me.

O give me the clew! (it lurks in the night here somewhere,)
O if I am to have so much, let me have more!

A word then, (for I will conquer it,)   *160*
The word final, superior to all,
Subtle, sent up—what is it?—I listen;
Are you whispering it, and have been all the time, you sea-waves?
Is that it from your liquid rims and wet sands?

---

[144]/**demon:** *here and in line 175, a demigod or attendant spirit (more often
spelled "daemon" or "daimon")*

Whereto answering, the sea,   165
Delaying not, hurrying not,
Whisper'd me through the night, and very plainly before daybreak,
Lisp'd to me the low and delicious word death,
And again death, death, death, death,
Hissing melodious, neither like the bird nor like my arous'd child's
    heart,   170
But edging near as privately for me rustling at my feet,
Creeping thence steadily up to my ears and laving me softly all over,
Death, death, death, death, death.

Which I do not forget,
But fuse the song of my dusky demon and brother,   175
That he sang to me in the moonlight on Paumanok's gray beach,
With the thousand responsive songs at random,
My own songs awaked from that hour,
And with them the key, the word up from the waves,
The word of the sweetest song and all songs,   180
That strong and delicious word which, creeping to my feet,
(Or like some old crone rocking the cradle, swathed in sweet
    garments, bending aside,)
The sea whisper'd me.

· WHEN I HEARD THE LEARN'D ASTRONOMER ·

When I heard the learn'd astronomer,
When the proofs, the figures, were ranged in columns before me,
When I was shown the charts and diagrams, to add, divide, and
    measure them,
When I sitting heard the astronomer where he lectured with much
    applause in the lecture-room,
How soon unaccountable I became tired and sick,   5
Till rising and gliding out I wander'd off by myself,
In the mystical moist night-air, and from time to time,
Look'd up in perfect silence at the stars.

· RECONCILIATION ·

Word over all, beautiful as the sky,
Beautiful that war and all its deeds of carnage must in time be
    utterly lost,
That the hands of the sisters Death and Night incessantly softly
    wash again, and ever again, this soil'd world;
For my enemy is dead, a man divine as myself is dead,
I look where he lies white-faced and still in the coffin—I draw near,   5
Bend down and touch lightly with my lips the white face in the coffin.

DANTE GABRIEL ROSSETTI
(1828–1882)

• THE WOODSPURGE •

The wind flapped loose, the wind was still,
Shaken out dead from tree and hill:
I had walked on at the wind's will,—
I sat now, for the wind was still.

Between my knees my forehead was,—   5
My lips, drawn in, said not Alas!
My hair was over in the grass,
My naked ears heard the day pass,

My eyes, wide open, had the run
Of some ten weeds to fix upon;   10
Among those few, out of the sun,
The woodspurge flowered, three cups in one.

From perfect grief there need not be
Wisdom or even memory:
One thing then learnt remains to me,—   15
The woodspurge has a cup of three.

The woodspurge has small greenish yellow flowers.

CHRISTINA ROSSETTI (1830–1894)

• UP-HILL •

Does the road wind up-hill all the way?
    Yes, to the very end.
Will the day's journey take the whole long day?
    From morn to night, my friend.

But is there for the night a resting-place?   5
    A roof for when the slow dark hours begin.
May not the darkness hide it from my face?
    You cannot miss that inn.

Shall I meet other wayfarers at night?
    Those who have gone before.   10
Then must I knock, or call when just in sight?
    They will not keep you standing at that door.

Shall I find comfort, travel-sore and weak?
    Of labour you shall find the sum.
Will there be beds for me and all who seek?   15
    Yea, beds for all who come.

EMILY DICKINSON (1830–1886)

• WENT UP A YEAR THIS EVENING! •

Went up a year this evening!
I recollect it well!
Amid no bells nor bravoes
The bystanders will tell!
Cheerful—as to the village—   5
Tranquil—as to repose—
Chastened—as to the Chapel
This humble Tourist rose!
Did not talk of returning!
Alluded to no time   10
When, were the gales propitious—
We might look for him!
Was grateful for the Roses
In life's diverse bouquet—
Talked softly of new species   15
To pick another day;
Beguiling thus the wonder
The *wondrous* nearer drew—
Hands bustled at the moorings—
The crowd respectful grew—   20
Ascended from our vision
To Countenances new!
A Difference—A Daisy—
Is all the rest I knew!

• HOW MANY TIMES THESE LOW FEET STAGGERED •

How many times these low feet staggered—
Only the soldered mouth can tell—
Try—can you stir the awful rivet—
Try—can you lift the hasps of steel!

Stroke the cool forehead—hot so often—   5
Lift—if you care—the listless hair—
Handle the adamantine fingers
Never a thimble—more—shall wear—

Buzz the dull flies—on the chamber window—
Brave—shines the sun through the freckled pane— 10
Fearless—the cobweb swings from the ceiling—
Indolent Housewife—in Daisies—lain!

7/**adamantine:** *stony, rigid*

· I HEARD A FLY BUZZ—WHEN I DIED ·

I heard a Fly buzz—when I died—
The Stillness in the Room
Was like the Stillness in the Air—
Between the Heaves of Storm—

The Eyes around—had wrung them dry—   5
And Breaths were gathering firm
For that last Onset—when the King
Be witnessed—in the Room—

I willed my Keepsakes—Signed away
What portion of me be   10
Assignable—and then it was
There interposed a Fly—

With Blue—uncertain—stumbling Buzz—
Between the light—and me—
And then the Windows failed—and then   15
I could not see to see—

· I STARTED EARLY—TOOK MY DOG ·

I started Early—Took my Dog—
And visited the Sea—
The Mermaids in the Basement
Came out to look at me—

And Frigates—in the Upper Floor   5
Extended Hempen Hands—
Presuming Me to be a Mouse—
Aground—upon the Sands—

But no Man moved Me—till the Tide
Went past my simple Shoe—   10
And past my Apron—and my Belt
And past my Bodice—too—

And made as He would eat me up
As wholly as a Dew
Upon a Dandelion's Sleeve—   15
And then—I started—too—

And He—He followed—close behind—
I felt His Silver Heel
Upon my Ankle—Then my Shoes
Would overflow with Pearl—   20

Until We met the Solid Town—
No One He seemed to know—
And bowing—with a Mighty look—
At me—The Sea withdrew—

• BECAUSE I COULD NOT STOP FOR DEATH •

Because I could not stop for Death—
He kindly stopped for me—
The Carriage held but just Ourselves—
And Immortality.

We slowly drove—He knew no haste   5
And I had put away
My labor and my leisure too,
For His Civility—

We passed the School, where Children strove
At Recess—in the Ring—   10
We passed the Fields of Gazing Grain—
We passed the Setting Sun—

Or rather—He passed Us—
The Dews drew quivering and chill—
For only Gossamer, my Gown—   15
My Tippet—only Tulle—

We paused before a House that seemed
A Swelling of the Ground—
The Roof was scarcely visible—
The Cornice—in the Ground—   20

Since then—'tis Centuries—and yet
Feels shorter than the Day
I first surmised the Horses' Heads
Were toward Eternity—

16/**Tippet:** *long scarf or shoulder cape*

• THE WIND BEGUN TO KNEAD THE GRASS •

The Wind begun to knead the Grass—
As Women do a Dough—
He flung a Hand full at the Plain—
A Hand full at the Sky—
The Leaves unhooked themselves from Trees—   5
And started all abroad—
The Dust did scoop itself like Hands—

And throw away the Road—
The Wagons quickened on the Street—
The Thunders gossiped low—   *10*
The Lightning showed a yellow Head—
And then a livid Toe—
The Birds put up the Bars to Nests—
The Cattle flung to Barns—
Then came one drop of Giant Rain—   *15*
And then, as if the Hands
That held the Dams—had parted hold—
The Waters Wrecked the Sky—
But overlooked my Father's House—
Just Quartering a Tree—   *20*

• TELL ALL THE TRUTH BUT TELL IT SLANT •

Tell all the Truth but tell it slant—
Success in Circuit lies
Too bright for our infirm Delight
The Truth's superb surprise
As Lightning to the Children eased   *5*
With explanation kind
The Truth must dazzle gradually
Or every man be blind—

WILLIAM MORRIS (1834–1896)

• THE HAYSTACK IN THE FLOODS •

Had she come all the way for this,
To part at last without a kiss?
Yea, had she borne the dirt and rain
That her own eyes might see him slain
Beside the haystack in the floods?   *5*

Along the dripping leafless woods,
The stirrup touching either shoe,
She rode astride as troopers do;
With kirtle kilted to her knee,
To which the mud splashed wretchedly;   *10*
And the wet dripped from every tree
Upon her head and heavy hair,
And on her eyelids broad and fair;
The tears and rain ran down her face.
By fits and starts they rode apace,   *15*

---

⁹/**kirtle:** *long dress*

And very often was his place
Far off from her; he had to ride
Ahead, to see what might betide
When the roads crossed; and sometimes, when
There rose a murmuring from his men,   20
Had to turn back with promises;
Ah me! she had but little ease;
And often for pure doubt and dread
She sobbed, made giddy in the head
By the swift riding; while, for cold,   25
Her slender fingers scarce could hold
The wet reins; yea, and scarcely, too,
She felt the foot within her shoe
Against the stirrup: all for this,
To part at last without a kiss   30
Beside the haystack in the floods.

For when they neared that old soaked hay,
They saw across the only way
That Judas, Godmar, and the three
Red running lions dismally   35
Grinned from his pennon, under which
In one straight line along the ditch,
They counted thirty heads.

         So then,
While Robert turned round to his men,
She saw at once the wretched end,   40
And, stooping down, tried hard to rend
Her coif the wrong way from her head,
And hid her eyes; while Robert said:
"Nay, love, 'tis scarcely two to one,
At Poictiers where we made them run   45
So fast—why, sweet my love, good cheer,
The Gascon frontier is so near,
Nought after this."

         But, "O!" she said,
"My God! my God! I have to tread
The long way back without you; then   50
The court at Paris; those six men;
The gratings of the Chatelet;

[42]/**coif:** *a tight cap*
[45]/**Poictiers:** *a city in France where, in 1356, the English defeated a larger French army*
[47]/**Gascon frontier:** *Gascony, in southwest France, was then held by the English*
[51]/**six men:** *the six judges*
[52]/**the Chatelet:** *the prison in Paris*

ANTHOLOGY

The swift Seine on some rainy day
Like this, and people standing by
And laughing, while my weak hands try   55
To recollect how strong men swim.
All this, or else a life with him,
For which I should be damned at last.
Would God that this next hour were past!"

He answered not, but cried his cry,   60
"St. George for Marny!" cheerily;
And laid his hand upon her rein.
Alas! no man of all his train
Gave back that cheery cry again;
And, while for rage his thumb beat fast   65
Upon his sword-hilts, some one cast
About his neck a kerchief long,
And bound him.

             Then they went along
To Godmar; who said: "Now, Jehane,
Your lover's life is on the wane   70
So fast, that, if this very hour
You yield not as my paramour,
He will not see the rain leave off—
Nay, keep your tongue from gibe and scoff,
Sir Robert, or I slay you now."   75

She laid her hand upon her brow,
Then gazed upon the palm, as though
She thought her forehead bled, and—"No!"
She said, and turned her head away,
As there were nothing else to say,   80
And everything were settled: red
Grew Godmar's face from chin to head:
"Jehane, on yonder hill there stands
My castle, guarding well my lands:
What hinders me from taking you,   85
And doing that I list to do
To your fair wilful body, while
Your knight lies dead?"

              A wicked smile
Wrinkled her face, her lips grew thin,
A long way out she thrust her chin: 90

53-56/**The swift Seine . . . swim:** *Jehane is referring to trial by ordeal: if captured, she could be thrown into the river Seine. If she did not drown, it would be assumed she was protected by evil spirits, and hence was guilty. If she drowned, it would prove—too late—her innocence.*
61/**St. George:** *the patron saint of England.*
86/**list:** *please*

"You know that I should strangle you
While you were sleeping; or bite through
Your throat, by God's help—ah!" she said,
"Lord Jesus, pity your poor maid!
For in such wise they hem me in, 95
I cannot choose but sin and sin,
Whatever happens: yet I think
They could not make me eat or drink,
And so should I just reach my rest."
"Nay, if you do not my behest, 100
O Jehane! though I love you well,"
Said Godmar, "would I fail to tell
All that I know?" "Foul lies," she said.
"Eh? lies, my Jehane? by God's head,
At Paris folks would deem them true! 105
Do you know, Jehane, they cry for you:
'Jehane the brown! Jehane the brown!
Give us Jehane to burn or drown!'—
Eh—gag me Robert!—sweet my friend,
This were indeed a piteous end 110
For those long fingers, and long feet,
And long neck, and smooth shoulders sweet;
An end that few men would forget
That saw it—So, an hour yet:
Consider, Jehane, which to take 115
Of life or death!"

       So, scarce awake,
Dismounting, did she leave that place,
And totter some yards: with her face
Turned upward to the sky she lay,
Her head on a wet heap of hay, 120
And fell asleep: and while she slept,
And did not dream, the minutes crept
Round to the twelve again; but she,
Being waked at last, sighed quietly,
And strangely childlike came, and said: 125
"I will not." Straightway Godmar's head,
As though it hung on strong wires, turned
Most sharply round, and his face burned.

For Robert—both his eyes were dry,
He could not weep, but gloomily 130
He seemed to watch the rain; yea, too,

100/**behest:** *command*
109/**me:** *for me*

His lips were firm; he tried once more
To touch her lips; she reached out, sore
And vain desire so tortured them,
The poor grey lips, and now the hem   *135*
Of his sleeve brushed them.

                With a start
Up Godmar rose, thrust them apart;
From Robert's throat he loosed the bands
Of silk and mail; with empty hands
Held out, she stood and gazed, and saw   *140*
The long bright blade without a flaw
Glide out from Godmar's sheath, his hand
In Robert's hair; she saw him bend
Back Robert's head; she saw him send
The thin steel down; the blow told well,   *145*
Right backward the knight Robert fell,
And moaned as dogs do, being half dead,
Unwitting, as I deem: so then
Godmar turned grinning to his men,
Who ran, some five or six, and beat   *150*
His head to pieces at their feet.

Then Godmar turned again and said:
"So, Jehane, the first fitte is read!
Take note, my lady, that your way
Lies backward to the Chatelet!"   *155*
She shook her head and gazed awhile
At her cold hands with a rueful smile,
As though this thing had made her mad.

This was the parting that they had
Beside the haystack in the floods.   *160*

153/**fitte:** *section of a song or story*

ALGERNON CHARLES SWINBURNE
(1837–1909)

• CHORUS From ATALANTA IN CALYDON •

When the hounds of spring are on winter's traces,
    The mother of months in meadow or plain
Fills the shadows and windy places
    With lisp of leaves and ripple of rain;

A hymn to Artemis, goddess of the moon (line 2) and of hunting (line 9).

ANTHOLOGY

And the brown bright nightingale amorous   *5*
Is half assuaged for Itylus,
For the Thracian ships and the foreign faces,
    The tongueless vigil, and all the pain.

Come with bows bent and with emptying of quivers,
    Maiden most perfect, lady of light,   *10*
With a noise of winds and many rivers,
    With a clamour of waters, and with might;
Bind on thy sandals, O thou most fleet,
Over the splendour and speed of thy feet;
For the faint east quickens, the wan west shivers,   *15*
    Round the feet of the day and the feet of the night.

Where shall we find her, how shall we sing to her,
    Fold our hands round her knees, and cling?
O that man's heart were as fire and could spring to her,
    Fire, or the strength of the streams that spring!   *20*
For the stars and the winds are unto her
As raiment, as songs of the harp-player;
For the risen stars and the fallen cling to her,
    And the southwest-wind and the west-wind sing.

For winter's rains and ruins are over,   *25*
    And all the season of snows and sins;
The days dividing lover and lover,
    The light that loses, the night that wins;
And time remembered is grief forgotten,
And frosts are slain and flowers begotten,   *30*
And in green underwood and cover
    Blossom by blossom the spring begins.

The full streams feed on flower of rushes,
    Ripe grasses trammel a travelling foot,
The faint fresh flame of the young year flushes   *35*
    From leaf to flower and flower to fruit;
And fruit and leaf are as gold and fire,
And the oat is heard above the lyre,
And the hoofèd heel of a satyr crushes
    The chestnut-husk at the chestnut-root.   *40*

And Pan by noon and Bacchus by night,
    Fleeter of foot than the fleet-foot kid,
Follows with dancing and fills with delight
    The Mænad and the Bassarid;

---

[6]/**Itylus:** *slain by his mother Procne (later turned into a nightingale) to get re-
venge on her unfaithful husband, who was king of Thrace*
[38]/**oat:** *the shepherd's flutelike pipe (or panpipe) of oaten straw*
[44]/**Maenad:** *see Shelley's "Ode to the West Wind," line 21 (p. 448)*
    Bassarid: *a Thracian Maenad*

And soft as lips that laugh and hide   *45*
The laughing leaves of the trees divide,
And screen from seeing and leave in sight
The god pursuing, the maiden hid.

The ivy falls with the Bacchanal's hair
    Over her eyebrows hiding her eyes;   *50*
The wild vine slipping down leaves bare
    Her bright breast shortening into sighs;
The wild vine slips with the weight of its leaves,
But the berried ivy catches and cleaves
To the limbs that glitter, the feet that scare   *55*
The wolf that follows, the fawn that flies.

⁴⁹/**Bacchanal:** *a follower of Bacchus, god of wine*

THOMAS HARDY (1840–1928)

• THE RUINED MAID •

"O 'Melia, my dear, this does everything crown!
Who could have supposed I should meet you in Town?
And whence such fair garments, such prosperi-ty?"—
"O didn't you know I'd been ruined?" said she.

—"You left us in tatters, without shoes or socks,   *5*
Tired of digging potatoes, and spudding up docks;
And now you've gay bracelets and bright feathers three!"—
"Yes: that's how we dress when we're ruined," said she.

—"At home in the barton you said 'thee' and 'thou,'
And 'thik oon,' and 'theäs oon,' and 't'other'; but now   *10*
Your talking quite fits 'ee for high compa-ny!"—
"Some polish is gained with one's ruin," said she.

—"Your hands were like paws then, your face blue and bleak
But now I'm bewitched by your delicate cheek,
And your little gloves fit as on any la-dy!"—   *15*
"We never do work when we're ruined," said she.

—"You used to call home-life a hag-ridden dream,
And you'd sigh, and you'd sock; but at present you seem
To know not of megrims or melancho-ly!"—
"True. One's pretty lively when ruined," said she.   *20*

⁶/**spudding up docks:** *digging up weeds*
⁹/**barton:** *farmyard*
¹⁰/**thik oon . . . theäs oon:** *that one . . . this one*
¹⁸/**sock:** *sigh*
¹⁹/**megrims:** *headache, depression*

—"I wish I had feathers, a fine sweeping gown,
And a delicate face, and could strut about Town!"—
"My dear—a raw country girl, such as you be,
Cannot quite expect that. You ain't ruined," said she.

· DRUMMER HODGE ·

I

They throw in Drummer Hodge, to rest
    Uncoffined—just as found:
His landmark is a kopje-crest
    That breaks the veldt around;
And foreign constellations west   *5*
    Each night above his mound.

II

Young Hodge the Drummer never knew—
    Fresh from his Wessex home—
The meaning of the broad Karoo,
    The Bush, the dusty loam,   *10*
And why uprose to nightly view
    Strange stars amid the gloam.

III

Yet portion of that unknown plain
    Will Hodge for ever be;
His homely Northern breast and brain   *15*
    Grow to some Southern tree,
And strange-eyed constellations reign
    His stars eternally.

---

[3]/**kopje:** *a small hill*
[4]/**veldt:** *the South African grassland, with scattered brush*
[5]/**west:** *move westward*
[8]/**Wessex:** *the ancient name for a re-gion in southern England*
[9]/**Karoo:** *the plateau country of South Africa*
[12]/**gloam:** *twilight*

The background is the Boer War of 1899–1902 between the British army and the Dutch settlers of South Africa.

· THE SELF-UNSEEING ·

Here is the ancient floor,
Footworn and hollowed and thin,
Here was the former door
Where the dead feet walked in.

She sat here in her chair,   *5*
Smiling into the fire;
He who played stood there,
Bowing it higher and higher.

Childlike, I danced in a dream;
Blessings emblazoned that day;   *10*
Everything glowed with a gleam;
Yet we were looking away!

· THE MAN HE KILLED ·

"Had he and I but met
By some old ancient inn,
We should have sat us down to wet
Right many a nipperkin!

"But ranged as infantry,   *5*
And staring face to face,
I shot at him as he at me,
And killed him in his place.

"I shot him dead because—
Because he was my foe,   *10*
Just so: my foe of course he was;
That's clear enough; although

"He thought he'd 'list, perhaps,
Off-hand like—just as I—
Was out of work—had sold his traps—   *15*
No other reason why.

"Yes; quaint and curious war is!
You shoot a fellow down
You'd treat if met where any bar is,
Or help to half-a-crown."   *20*

---

[4]/**nipperkin:** *a measure of beer or wine*
—about a half pint
[13]/**'list:** *enlist*

[15]/**traps:** *belongings*
[20]/**half-a-crown:** *about a half dollar*

· THE OXEN ·

Christmas Eve, and twelve of the clock.
    "Now they are all on their knees,"
An elder said as we sat in a flock
    By the embers in hearthside ease.

We pictured the meek mild creatures where   *5*
    They dwelt in their strawy pen,
Nor did it occur to one of us there
    To doubt they were kneeling then.

So fair a fancy few would weave
    In these years! Yet, I feel,   *10*
If someone said on Christmas Eve,
    "Come; see the oxen kneel,

"In the lonely barton by yonder coomb
    Our childhood used to know,"
I should go with him in the gloom,   *15*
    Hoping it might be so.

13/**barton:** *farmyard*   **coomb:** *valley*

According to an old legend, oxen kneel on Christmas Eve in honor of Christ's birth.

· IN TIME OF "THE BREAKING OF NATIONS" ·

I

Only a man harrowing clods
    In a slow silent walk
With an old horse that stumbles and nods
    Half asleep as they stalk.

II

Only thin smoke without flame   *5*
    From the heaps of couch-grass;
Yet this will go onward the same
    Though Dynasties pass.

III

Yonder a maid and her wight
    Come whispering by:
War's annals will fade into night   *10*
    Ere their story die.

6/**couch-grass:** *rough grass that spreads like a weed*
9/**wight:** *man*

Though written during World War I, this poem expresses a feeling that moved Hardy during the Franco-Prussian War in 1870. The title alludes to Jeremiah 51:20, where God's judgment against Babylon is reported: "Thou art my battle axe and weapons of war: for with thee will I break in pieces the nations. . . ."

GERARD MANLEY HOPKINS
(1844–1889)

· GOD'S GRANDEUR ·

The world is charged with the grandeur of God.
    It will flame out, like shining from shook foil;
    It gathers to a greatness, like the ooze of oil
Crushed. Why do men then now not reck his rod?
Generations have trod, have trod, have trod;   *5*
    And all is seared with trade; bleared, smeared with toil;
    And wears man's smudge and shares man's smell: the soil
Is bare now, nor can foot feel, being shod.

And for all this, nature is never spent;
    There lives the dearest freshness deep down things;   *10*
And though the last lights off the black West went
    Oh, morning, at the brown brink eastward, springs—
Because the Holy Ghost over the bent
    World broods with warm breast and with ah! bright wings.

2/**shook foil:** *gold foil, which when shaken gives off a dazzle of light*
3-4/**ooze of oil** / **Crushed:** *olive oil, or various aromatic oils extracted by crushing*
4/**reck his rod:** *pay attention to his power*

· THE WINDHOVER ·

To Christ our Lord

I caught this morning morning's minion, king-
    dom of daylight's dauphin, dapple-dawn-drawn Falcon, in his
        riding
Of the rolling level underneath him steady air, and striding
High there, how he rung upon the rein of a wimpling wing
In his ecstasy! then off, off forth on swing,   *5*
    As a skate's heel sweeps smooth on a bow-bend: the hurl and
        gliding
Rebuffed the big wind. My heart in hiding
Stirred for a bird,—the achieve of, the mastery of the thing!

1/**minion:** *darling, favorite*
2/**dauphin:** *prince*
4/**rung upon the rein:** *pivoted on a wing tip (probably). A horse being trained is said to "ring on the rein"* *when it goes in a circle on the end of a long rein.*
  wimpling: *rippling, pleated*
10/**buckle:** *lock together*

The windhover is a small hawk that hangs or hovers with its head into the wind.

Brute beauty and valour and act, oh, air, pride, plume, here
    Buckle! AND the fire that breaks from thee then, a billion   *10*
Times told lovelier, more dangerous, O my chevalier!

    No wonder of it: shéer plód makes plough down sillion
Shine, and blue-bleak embers, ah my dear,
    Fall, gall themselves, and gash gold-vermilion.

¹²/**sillion:** *furrow (French,* sillon*)*

· FELIX RANDAL ·

Felix Randal the farrier, O is he dead then? my duty all ended,
Who have watched his mould of man, big-boned and hardy-handsome
Pining, pining, till time when reason rambled in it and some
Fatal four disorders, fleshed there, all contended?

Sickness broke him. Impatient, he cursed at first, but mended   *5*
Being anointed and all; though a heavenlier heart began some
Months earlier, since I had our sweet reprieve and ransom
Tendered to him. Ah well, God rest him all road ever he offended!

This seeing the sick endears them to us, us too it endears.
My tongue had taught thee comfort, touch had quenched thy tears,   *10*
Thy tears that touched my heart, child, Felix, poor Felix Randal;

How far from then forethought of, all thy more boisterous years,
When thou at the random grim forge, powerful amidst peers,
Didst fettle for the great grey drayhorse his bright and battering
    sandal!

¹/**farrier:** *blacksmith*
⁷/**reprieve and ransom:** *confession and communion*
⁸/**all road ever:** *in whatever ways*
¹³/**random:** *roughly built of irregular stones*
¹⁴/**fettle:** *prepare*

· SPRING AND FALL ·
to a young child

    Márgarét, áre you gríeving
    Over Goldengrove unleaving?
    Leáves, líke the things of man, you
    With your fresh thoughts care for, can you?
    Ah! ás the heart grows older   *5*
    It will come to such sights colder
    By and by, nor spare a sigh
    Though worlds of wanwood leafmeal lie;

⁸/**wanwood:** *a coined expression for woods wan in autumn*
  leafmeal: *(1) in leafy pieces (cf. piecemeal); (2) ground to leafy meal*

And yet you *will* weep and know why.
Now no matter, child, the name: *10*
Sórrow's spríngs áre the same.
Nor mouth had, no nor mind, expressed
What heart heard of, ghost guessed:
It ís the blight man was born for,
It is Margaret you mourn for.   *15*

13/**ghost:** *spirit*

A. E. HOUSMAN (1859–1936)

· TO AN ATHLETE DYING YOUNG ·

The time you won your town the race
We chaired you through the market-place;
Man and boy stood cheering by,
And home we brought you shoulder-high.

To-day, the road all runners come,   *5*
Shoulder-high we bring you home,
And set you at your threshold down,
Townsman of a stiller town.

Smart lad, to slip betimes away
From fields where glory does not stay   *10*
And early though the laurel grows
It withers quicker than the rose.

Eyes the shady night has shut
Cannot see the record cut,
And silence sounds no worse than cheers   *15*
After earth has stopped the ears:

Now you will not swell the rout
Of lads that wore their honours out,
Runners whom renown outran
And the name died before the man.   *20*

So set, before its echoes fade,
The fleet foot on the sill of shade,
And hold to the low lintel up
The still-defended challenge-cup.

And round that early-laurelled head   *25*
Will flock to gaze the strengthless dead,
And find unwithered on its curls
The garland briefer than a girl's.

9/**betimes:** *early, in good time*
23/**lintel:** *the horizontal piece of stone or timber over a door or window*

· LOVELIEST OF TREES, THE CHERRY NOW ·

Loveliest of trees, the cherry now
Is hung with bloom along the bough,
And stands about the woodland ride
Wearing white for Eastertide.

Now, of my threescore years and ten,   *5*
Twenty will not come again,
And take from seventy springs a score,
It only leaves me fifty more.

And since to look at things in bloom
Fifty springs are little room,   *10*
About the woodlands I will go
To see the cherry hung with snow.

WILLIAM BUTLER YEATS
(1865–1939)

· THE COLD HEAVEN ·

Suddenly I saw the cold and rook-delighting heaven
That seemed as though ice burned and was but the more ice,
And thereupon imagination and heart were driven
So wild that every casual thought of that and this
Vanished, and left but memories, that should be out of season   *5*
With the hot blood of youth, of love crossed long ago;
And I took all the blame out of all sense and reason,
Until I cried and trembled and rocked to and fro,
Riddled with light. Ah! when the ghost begins to quicken,
Confusion of the death-bed over, is it sent   *10*
Out naked on the roads, as the books say, and stricken
By the injustice of the skies for punishment?

[1]/**rook:** *crow*

· SAILING TO BYZANTIUM ·

I

That is no country for old men. The young
In one another's arms, birds in the trees
—Those dying generations—at their song,
The salmon-falls, the mackerel-crowded seas,

[1]/**that:** *Ireland—though it might be any place in the physical world*

*Byzantium, later named Constantinople and now Istanbul, was the capital of the
eastern Roman empire and a famous artistic and religious center. Yeats uses it
as symbolic of the life of the spirit.*

Fish, flesh, or fowl, commend all summer long 5
Whatever is begotten, born, and dies.
Caught in that sensual music all neglect
Monuments of unageing intellect.

II

An aged man is but a paltry thing,
A tattered coat upon a stick, unless 10
Soul clap its hands and sing, and louder sing
For every tatter in its mortal dress,
Nor is there singing school but studying
Monuments of its own magnificence;
And therefore I have sailed the seas and come 15
To the holy city of Byzantium.

III

O sages standing in God's holy fire
As in the gold mosaic of a wall,
Come from the holy fire, perne in a gyre,
And be the singing-masters of my soul. 20
Consume my heart away; sick with desire
And fastened to a dying animal
It knows not what it is; and gather me
Into the artifice of eternity.

IV

Once out of nature I shall never take 25
My bodily form from any natural thing,
But such a form as Grecian goldsmiths make
Of hammered gold and gold enamelling
To keep a drowsy Emperor awake;
Or set upon a golden bough to sing 30
To lords and ladies of Byzantium
Of what is past, or passing, or to come.

18/**gold mosaic:** *Byzantine mosaics show their saints (or "sages") against a background of gold tiles that glitter like fire.*
19/**perne:** *whirl, spin*
27-32/*Yeats tells us that he had read somewhere about artificial singing birds in a gold and silver tree in the Emperor's palace in Byzantium.*

· AMONG SCHOOL CHILDREN ·

I

I walk through the long schoolroom questioning;
A kind old nun in a white hood replies;
The children learn to cipher and to sing,

1/**schoolroom:** *Yeats' duties as a senator of the Irish Free State included occasional school inspections.*

To study reading-books and histories,
To cut and sew, be neat in everything   *5*
In the best modern way—the children's eyes
In momentary wonder stare upon
A sixty-year-old smiling public man.

II

I dream of a Ledaean body, bent
Above a sinking fire, a tale that she   *10*
Told of a harsh reproof, or trivial event
That changed some childish day to tragedy—
Told, and it seemed that our two natures blent
Into a sphere from youthful sympathy,
Or else, to alter Plato's parable,   *15*
Into the yolk and white of the one shell.

III

And thinking of that fit of grief or rage
I look upon one child or t'other there
And wonder if she stood so at that age—
For even daughters of the swan can share   *20*
Something of every paddler's heritage—
And had that colour upon cheek or hair,
And thereupon my heart is driven wild:
She stands before me as a living child.

IV

Her present image floats into the mind—   *25*
Did Quattrocento finger fashion it
Hollow of cheek as though it drank the wind
And took a mess of shadows for its meat?
And I though never of Ledaean kind
Had pretty plumage once—enough of that,   *30*
Better to smile on all that smile, and show
There is a comfortable kind of old scarecrow.

V

What youthful mother, a shape upon her lap
Honey of generation had betrayed,
And that must sleep, shriek, struggle to escape   *35*

[9]/**Ledaean:** *like that of the daughter (Helen of Troy) whom Leda bore. The father was Zeus in the form of a swan. Cf. "Leda and the Swan," p. 42.*
[15]/**Plato's parable:** *In a myth that Plato recounts in his* Symposium, *men and women were once united in double bodies, till Zeus, fearing their power, separated them "as you might divide an egg with a hair."*
[19]/**she:** *the woman of the Ledaean body, whom Yeats was long in love with*
[20]/**daughters of the swan:** *girls of divine birth, like Helen*
[26]/**Quattrocento:** *of the 1400s—the Italian Renaissance*
[34]/**had betrayed:** *by bringing it into this life out of a happier preexistence*

As recollection or the drug decide,
Would think her son, did she but see that shape
With sixty or more winters on its head,
A compensation for the pang of his birth,
Or the uncertainty of his setting forth?   *40*

VI

Plato thought nature but a spume that plays
Upon a ghostly paradigm of things;
Solider Aristotle played the taws
Upon the bottom of a king of kings;
World-famous golden-thighed Pythagoras   *45*
Fingered upon a fiddle-stick or strings
What a star sang and careless Muses heard:
Old clothes upon old sticks to scare a bird.

VII

Both nuns and mothers worship images,
But those the candles light are not as those   *50*
That animate a mother's reveries,
But keep a marble or a bronze repose.
And yet they too break hearts—O Presences
That passion, piety or affection knows,
And that all heavenly glory symbolise—   *55*
O self-born mockers of man's enterprise:

VIII

Labour is blossoming or dancing where
The body is not bruised to pleasure soul,
Nor beauty born out of its own despair,
Nor blear-eyed wisdom out of midnight oil.   *60*
O chestnut-tree, great-rooted blossomer,
Are you the leaf, the blossom or the bole?
O body swayed to music, O brightening glance,
How can we know the dancer from the dance?

---

⁴¹⁻⁴²/**Plato . . . things:** *Plato thought the world we see was only an imitation of true reality, only a kind of froth (spume) on a spiritual framework (ghostly paradigm) of that reality.*
⁴³⁻⁴⁴/**solider Aristotle:** *"solider" because he took the physical world more seriously and based his investigations on it*
   taws: *a schoolmaster's leather strap. Aristotle was the tutor of the boy who was to become Alexander the Great.*
⁴⁵⁻⁴⁷/**Pythagoras:** *he was interested in music, geometry, arithmetic, astronomy. Legend had it that his thighbone was of gold.*
⁴⁸/**old clothes:** *even the greatest men, like the three just mentioned, are no better than scarecrows in old age*

· A LAST CONFESSION ·

What lively lad most pleasured me
Of all that with me lay?
I answer that I gave my soul
And loved in misery,
But had great pleasure with a lad   5
That I loved bodily.

Flinging from his arms I laughed
To think his passion such
He fancied that I gave a soul
Did but our bodies touch,   10
And laughed upon his breast to think
Beast gave beast as much.

I gave what other women gave
That stepped out of their clothes,
But when this soul, its body off,   15
Naked to naked goes,
He it has found shall find therein
What none other knows,

And give his own and take his own
And rule in his own right;   20
And though it loved in misery
Close and cling so tight,
There's not a bird of day that dare
Extinguish that delight.

The speaker is an old woman, looking back on a lifetime of emotional experience.

EDWIN ARLINGTON ROBINSON
(1869–1935)

· THE MILL ·

The miller's wife had waited long,
    The tea was cold, the fire was dead;
And there might yet be nothing wrong
    In how he went and what he said:
"There are no millers any more,"   5
    Was all that she had heard him say;
And he had lingered at the door
    So long that it seemed yesterday.

Sick with a fear that had no form
    She knew that she was there at last;   *10*
And in the mill there was a warm
    And mealy fragrance of the past.
What else there was would only seem
    To say again what he had meant;
And what was hanging from a beam   *15*
    Would not have heeded where she went.

And if she thought it followed her,
    She may have reasoned in the dark
That one way of the few there were
    Would hide her and would leave no mark: *20*
Black water, smooth above the weir
    Like starry velvet in the night,
Though ruffled once, would soon appear
    The same as ever to the sight.

21/**weir:** *dam*

· MR. FLOOD'S PARTY ·

Old Eben Flood, climbing alone one night
Over the hill between the town below
And the forsaken upland hermitage
That held as much as he should ever know
On earth again of home, paused warily.   *5*
The road was his with not a native near;
And Eben, having leisure, said aloud,
For no man else in Tilbury Town to hear:

"Well, Mr. Flood, we have the harvest moon
Again, and we may not have many more;   *10*
The bird is on the wing, the poet says,
And you and I have said it here before.
Drink to the bird." He raised up to the light
The jug that he had gone so far to fill,
And answered huskily: "Well, Mr. Flood,   *15*
Since you propose it, I believe I will."

Alone, as if enduring to the end
A valiant armor of scarred hopes outworn,
He stood there in the middle of the road
Like Roland's ghost winding a silent horn.   *20*

11/*See* The Rubáiyát of Omar Khayyám, VII (*p. 466*).
20/**Roland:** *Roland, in command of the rear guard of Charlemagne's army, was ambushed and outnumbered in the pass of Roncevaux in the Pyrenees. Out of pride, he refused to sound until too late the horn that would have brought the Emperor to his rescue.*

Below him, in the town among the trees,
Where friends of other days had honored him,
A phantom salutation of the dead
Rang thinly till old Eben's eyes were dim.

Then, as a mother lays her sleeping child   *25*
Down tenderly, fearing it may awake,
He set the jug down slowly at his feet
With trembling care, knowing that most things break;
And only when assured that on firm earth
It stood, as the uncertain lives of men   *30*
Assuredly did not, he paced away,
And with his hand extended paused again:

"Well, Mr. Flood, we have not met like this
In a long time; and many a change has come
To both of us, I fear, since last it was   *35*
We had a drop together. Welcome home!"
Convivially returning with himself,
Again he raised the jug up to the light;
And with an acquiescent quaver said:
"Well, Mr. Flood, if you insist, I might.   *40*

"Only a very little, Mr. Flood—
For auld lang syne. No more, sir; that will do."
So, for the time, apparently it did,
And Eben evidently thought so too;
For soon amid the silver loneliness   *45*
Of night he lifted up his voice and sang,
Secure, with only two moons listening,
Until the whole harmonious landscape rang—

"For auld lang syne." The weary throat gave out;
The last word wavered, and the song was done.   *50*
He raised again the jug regretfully
And shook his head, and was again alone.
There was not much that was ahead of him,
And there was nothing in the town below—
Where strangers would have shut the many doors   *55*
That many friends had opened long ago.

WALTER DE LA MARE (1873–1956)

• THE LISTENERS •

'Is there anybody there?' said the Traveller,
    Knocking on the moonlit door;
And his horse in the silence champed the grasses
    Of the forest's ferny floor:

And a bird flew up out of the turret,   5
    Above the Traveller's head:
And he smote upon the door again a second time;
    'Is there anybody there?' he said.
But no one descended to the Traveller;
    No head from the leaf-fringed sill   10
Leaned over and looked into his grey eyes,
    Where he stood perplexed and still.
But only a host of phantom listeners
    That dwelt in the lone house then
Stood listening in the quiet of the moonlight   15
    To that voice from the world of men:
Stood thronging the faint moonbeams on the dark stair,
    That goes down to the empty hall,
Hearkening in an air stirred and shaken
    By the lonely Traveller's call.   20
And he felt in his heart their strangeness,
    Their stillness answering his cry,
While his horse moved, cropping the dark turf,
    'Neath the starred and leafy sky;
For he suddenly smote on the door, even   25
    Louder, and lifted his head:—
'Tell them I came, and no one answered,
    That I kept my word,' he said.
Never the least stir made the listeners,
    Though every word he spake   30
Fell echoing through the shadowiness of the still house
    From the one man left awake:
Ay, they heard his foot upon the stirrup,
    And the sound of iron on stone,
And how the silence surged softly backward,   35
    When the plunging hoofs were gone.

ROBERT FROST (1874–1963)

· MENDING WALL ·

Something there is that doesn't love a wall,
That sends the frozen-ground-swell under it,
And spills the upper boulders in the sun;
And makes gaps even two can pass abreast.
The work of hunters is another thing: 5
I have come after them and made repair
Where they have left not one stone on a stone,
But they would have the rabbit out of hiding,
To please the yelping dogs. The gaps I mean,
No one has seen them made or heard them made,   10

But at spring mending-time we find them there.
I let my neighbor know beyond the hill;
And on a day we meet to walk the line
And set the wall between us once again.
We keep the wall between us as we go.   *15*
To each the boulders that have fallen to each.
And some are loaves and some so nearly balls
We have to use a spell to make them balance:
"Stay where you are until our backs are turned!"
We wear our fingers rough with handling them.   *20*
Oh, just another kind of outdoor game,
One on a side. It comes to little more:
There where it is we do not need the wall:
He is all pine and I am apple orchard.
My apple trees will never get across   *25*
And eat the cones under his pines, I tell him.
He only says, "Good fences make good neighbors."
Spring is the mischief in me, and I wonder
If I could put a notion in his head:
"*Why* do they make good neighbors? Isn't it   *30*
Where there are cows? But here there are no cows.
Before I built a wall I'd ask to know
What I was walling in or walling out,
And to whom I was like to give offense.
Something there is that doesn't love a wall,   *35*
That wants it down." I could say "Elves" to him,
But it's not elves exactly, and I'd rather
He said it for himself. I see him there
Bringing a stone grasped firmly by the top
In each hand, like an old-stone savage armed.   *40*
He moves in darkness as it seems to me,
Not of woods only and the shade of trees.
He will not go behind his father's saying,
And he likes having thought of it so well
He says again, "Good fences make good neighbors."   *45*

· PROVIDE, PROVIDE ·

The witch that came (the withered hag)
To wash the steps with pail and rag,
Was once the beauty Abishag,

The picture pride of Hollywood.
Too many fall from great and good   *5*
For you to doubt the likelihood.

---

[3]/**Abishag:** *the young girl (1 Kings 1:1–4) found to attend King David when he was old and ailing*

Die early and avoid the fate.
Or if predestined to die late,
Make up your mind to die in state.

Make the whole stock exchange your own!   *10*
If need be occupy a throne,
Where nobody can call *you* crone.

Some have relied on what they knew;
Others on being simply true.
What worked for them might work for you.   *15*

No memory of having starred
Atones for later disregard,
Or keeps the end from being hard.

Better to go down dignified
With boughten friendship at your side   *20*
Than none at all. Provide, provide!

· THE MOST OF IT ·

He thought he kept the universe alone;
For all the voice in answer he could wake
Was but the mocking echo of his own
From some tree-hidden cliff across the lake.
Some morning from the boulder-broken beach   *5*
He would cry out on life, that what it wants
Is not its own love back in copy speech,
But counter-love, original response.
And nothing ever came of what he cried
Unless it was the embodiment that crashed   *10*
In the cliff's talus on the other side,
And then in the far distant water splashed,
But after a time allowed for it to swim,
Instead of proving human when it neared
And someone else additional to him,   *15*
As a great buck it powerfully appeared,
Pushing the crumpled water up ahead,
And landed pouring like a waterfall,
And stumbled through the rocks with horny tread,
And forced the underbrush—and that was all.   *20*

· THE SUBVERTED FLOWER ·

She drew back; he was calm:
"It is this that had the power."
And he lashed his open palm
With the tender-headed flower.

He smiled for her to smile, 5
But she was either blind
Or willfully unkind.
He eyed her for a while
For a woman and a puzzle.
He flicked and flung the flower, 10
And another sort of smile
Caught up like fingertips
The corners of his lips
And cracked his ragged muzzle.
She was standing to the waist 15
In goldenrod and brake,
Her shining hair displaced.
He stretched her either arm
As if she made it ache
To clasp her—not to harm; 20
As if he could not spare
To touch her neck and hair.
"If this has come to us
And not to me alone—"
So she thought she heard him say; 25
Though with every word he spoke
His lips were sucked and blown
And the effort made him choke
Like a tiger at a bone.
She had to lean away. 30
She dared not stir a foot,
Lest movement should provoke
The demon of pursuit
That slumbers in a brute.
It was then her mother's call 35
From inside the garden wall
Made her steal a look of fear
To see if he could hear
And would pounce to end it all
Before her mother came. 40
She looked and saw the shame:
A hand hung like a paw,
An arm worked like a saw
As if to be persuasive,
An ingratiating laugh 45
That cut the snout in half,
An eye become evasive.
A girl could only see
That a flower had marred a man,
But what she could not see 50

16/**brake:** *tall ferns*
18/**he stretched her either arm:** *he stretched each of his arms toward her*

Was that the flower might be
Other than base and fetid:
That the flower had done but part,
And what the flower began
Her own too meager heart   55
Had terribly completed.
She looked and saw the worst.
And the dog or what it was,
Obeying bestial laws,
A coward save at night,   60
Turned from the place and ran.
She heard him stumble first
And use his hands in flight.
She heard him bark outright.
And oh, for one so young   65
The bitter words she spit
Like some tenacious bit
That will not leave the tongue.
She plucked her lips for it,
And still the horror clung.   70
Her mother wiped the foam
From her chin, picked up her comb,
And drew her backward home.

WALLACE STEVENS (1879–1955)

· SUNDAY MORNING ·

I

Complacencies of the peignoir, and late
Coffee and oranges in a sunny chair,
And the green freedom of a cockatoo
Upon a rug mingle to dissipate
The holy hush of ancient sacrifice.   5
She dreams a little, and she feels the dark
Encroachment of that old catastrophe,
As a calm darkens among water-lights.
The pungent oranges and bright, green wings
Seem things in some procession of the dead,   10
Winding across wide water, without sound.
The day is like wide water, without sound,
Stilled for the passing of her dreaming feet
Over the seas, to silent Palestine,
Dominion of the blood and sepulchre.   15

II

Why should she give her bounty to the dead?
What is divinity if it can come
Only in silent shadows and in dreams?
Shall she not find in comforts of the sun,
In pungent fruit and bright, green wings, or else   *20*
In any balm or beauty of the earth,
Things to be cherished like the thought of heaven?
Divinity must live within herself:
Passions of rain, or moods in falling snow;
Grievings in loneliness, or unsubdued   *25*
Elations when the forest blooms; gusty
Emotions on wet roads on autumn nights;
All pleasures and all pains, remembering
The bough of summer and the winter branch.
These are the measures destined for her soul.   *30*

III

Jove in the clouds had his inhuman birth.
No mother suckled him, no sweet land gave
Large-mannered motions to his mythy mind.
He moved among us, as a muttering king,
Magnificent, would move among his hinds,   *35*
Until our blood, commingling, virginal,
With heaven, brought such requital to desire
The very hinds discerned it, in a star.
Shall our blood fail? Or shall it come to be
The blood of paradise? And shall the earth   *40*
Seem all of paradise that we shall know?
The sky will be much friendlier then than now,
A part of labor and a part of pain,
And next in glory to enduring love,
Not this dividing and indifferent blue.   *45*

IV

She says, "I am content when wakened birds,
Before they fly, test the reality
Of misty fields, by their sweet questionings;
But when the birds are gone, and their warm fields
Return no more, where, then, is paradise?"   *50*
There is not any haunt of prophecy,
Nor any old chimera of the grave,
Neither the golden underground, nor isle
Melodious, where spirits gat them home,
Nor visionary south, nor cloudy palm   *55*
Remote on heaven's hill, that has endured

---

³⁵/**hinds:** *farm servants*
⁵⁴/**gat them:** *got them, betook themselves*

As April's green endures; or will endure
Like her remembrance of awakened birds,
Or her desire for June and evening, tipped
By the consummation of the swallow's wings.   *60*

V

She says, "But in contentment I still feel
The need of some imperishable bliss."
Death is the mother of beauty; hence from her,
Alone, shall come fulfilment to our dreams
And our desires. Although she strews the leaves   *65*
Of sure obliteration on our paths,
The path sick sorrow took, the many paths
Where triumph rang its brassy phrase, or love
Whispered a little out of tenderness,
She makes the willow shiver in the sun   *70*
For maidens who were wont to sit and gaze
Upon the grass, relinquished to their feet.
She causes boys to pile new plums and pears
On disregarded plate. The maidens taste
And stray impassioned in the littering leaves.   *75*

VI

Is there no change of death in paradise?
Does ripe fruit never fall? Or do the boughs
Hang always heavy in that perfect sky,
Unchanging, yet so like our perishing earth,
With rivers like our own that seek for seas   *80*
They never find, the same receding shores
That never touch with inarticulate pang?
Why set the pear upon those river-banks
Or spice the shores with odors of the plum?
Alas, that they should wear our colors there,   *85*
The silken weavings of our afternoons,
And pick the strings of our insipid lutes!
Death is the mother of beauty, mystical,
Within whose burning bosom we devise
Our earthly mothers waiting, sleeplessly.   *90*

VII

Supple and turbulent, a ring of men
Shall chant in orgy on a summer morn
Their boisterous devotion to the sun,
Not as a god, but as a god might be,
Naked among them, like a savage source.   *95*
Their chant shall be a chant of paradise,
Out of their blood, returning to the sky;
And in their chant shall enter, voice by voice,
The windy lake wherein their lord delights,

The trees, like serafin, and echoing hills,   *100*
That choir among themselves long afterward.
They shall know well the heavenly fellowship
Of men that perish and of summer morn.
And whence they came and whither they shall go
The dew upon their feet shall manifest.   *105*

VIII

She hears, upon that water without sound,
A voice that cries, "The tomb in Palestine
Is not the porch of spirits lingering.
It is the grave of Jesus, where he lay."
We live in an old chaos of the sun,   *110*
Or old dependency of day and night,
Or island solitude, unsponsored, free,
Of that wide water, inescapable.
Deer walk upon our mountains, and the quail
Whistle about us their spontaneous cries;   *115*
Sweet berries ripen in the wilderness;
And, in the isolation of the sky,
At evening, casual flocks of pigeons make
Ambiguous undulations as they sink,
Downward to darkness, on extended wings.   *120*

· THE SNOW MAN ·

One must have a mind of winter
To regard the frost and the boughs
Of the pine-trees crusted with snow;

And have been cold a long time
To behold the junipers shagged with ice,   *5*
The spruces rough in the distant glitter

Of the January sun; and not to think
Of any misery in the sound of the wind,
In the sound of a few leaves,

Which is the sound of the land   *10*
Full of the same wind
That is blowing in the same bare place

For the listener, who listens in the snow,
And, nothing himself, beholds
Nothing that is not there and the nothing that is.   *15*

· A POSTCARD FROM THE VOLCANO ·

Children picking up our bones
Will never know that these were once
As quick as foxes on the hill;

And that in autumn, when the grapes
Made sharp air sharper by their smell   5
These had a being, breathing frost;

And least will guess that with our bones
We left much more, left what still is
The look of things, left what we felt

At what we saw. The spring clouds blow   10
Above the shuttered mansion-house,
Beyond our gate and the windy sky

Cries out a literate despair.
We knew for long the mansion's look
And what we said of it became   15

A part of what it is . . . Children,
Still weaving budded aureoles,
Will speak our speech and never know,

Will say of the mansion that it seems
As if he that lived there left behind   25
A spirit storming in blank walls,

A dirty house in a gutted world,
A tatter of shadows peaked to white,
Smeared with the gold of the opulent sun.

· THE SENSE OF THE SLEIGHT-OF-HAND MAN ·

One's grand flights, one's Sunday baths,
One's tootings at the weddings of the soul
Occur as they occur. So bluish clouds
Occurred above the empty house and the leaves
Of the rhododendrons rattled their gold,   5
As if someone lived there. Such floods of white
Came bursting from the clouds. So the wind
Threw its contorted strength around the sky.

Could you have said the bluejay suddenly
Would swoop to earth? It is a wheel, the rays   10
Around the sun. The wheel survives the myths.
The fire eye in the clouds survives the gods.

To think of a dove with an eye of grenadine
And pines that are cornets, so it occurs,
And a little island full of geese and stars: *15*
It may be that the ignorant man, alone,
Has any chance to mate his life with life
That is the sensual, pearly spouse, the life
That is fluent in even the wintriest bronze.

WILLIAM CARLOS WILLIAMS
(1883–1963)

· TO WAKEN AN OLD LADY ·

Old age is
a flight of small
cheeping birds
skimming
bare trees   *5*
above a snow glaze.
Gaining and failing
they are buffetted
by a dark wind—
But what?   *10*
On harsh weedstalks
the flock has rested,
the snow
is covered with broken
seedhusks   *15*
and the wind tempered
by a shrill
piping of plenty.

· THE RED WHEELBARROW ·

so much depends
upon

a red wheel
barrow

glazed with rain   *5*
water

beside the white
chickens

• THE DANCE •

In Breughel's great picture, The Kermess,
the dancers go round, they go round and
around, the squeal and the glare and the
tweedle of bagpipes, a bugle and fiddles
tipping their bellies (round as the thick-
sided glasses whose wash they impound)   *5*
their hips and their bellies off balance
to turn them. Kicking and rolling about
the Fair Grounds, swinging their butts, those
shanks must be sound to bear up under such
rollicking measures, prance as they dance   *10*
in Breughel's great picture, The Kermess.

¹/**Kermess:** *an outdoor festival, here in celebration of a wedding*

EZRA POUND (1885–1972)

• THE RIVER-MERCHANT'S WIFE: A LETTER •

While my hair was still cut straight across my forehead
I played about the front gate, pulling flowers.
You came by on bamboo stilts, playing horse,
You walked about my seat, playing with blue plums.
And we went on living in the village of Chokan: *5*
Two small people, without dislike or suspicion.

At fourteen I married My Lord you.
I never laughed, being bashful.
Lowering my head, I looked at the wall.
Called to, a thousand times, I never looked back.   *10*

At fifteen I stopped scowling,
I desired my dust to be mingled with yours
Forever and forever and forever.
Why should I climb the lookout?

At sixteen you departed,   *15*
You went into far Ku-to-yen, by the river of swirling eddies,
And you have been gone five months.
The monkeys make sorrowful noise overhead.
You dragged your feet when you went out.
By the gate now, the moss is grown, the different mosses,   *20*
Too deep to clear them away!
The leaves fall early this autumn, in wind.
The paired butterflies are already yellow with August
Over the grass in the West garden;

They hurt me. I grow older.   *25*
If you are coming down through the narrows of the river Kiang,
Please let me know beforehand,
And I will come out to meet you
　　　　　As far as Cho-fu-Sa.

　　　　　　　　　　　　　　　　　　　　　　　　　By Rihaku

*Rihaku is the Japanese name for the famous Chinese poet Li Po (eighth century).
Pound's version of the Chinese poem is based on the English notes of the scholar
Ernest Fenollosa.*

EDWIN MUIR (1887–1959)

· THE HORSES ·

Barely a twelvemonth after
The seven days war that put the world to sleep,
Late in the evening the strange horses came.
By then we had made our covenant with silence,
But in the first few days it was so still   *5*
We listened to our breathing and were afraid.
On the second day
The radios failed; we turned the knobs; no answer.
On the third day a warship passed us, heading north,
Dead bodies piled on the deck. On the sixth day   *10*
A plane plunged over us into the sea. Thereafter
Nothing. The radios dumb;
And still they stand in corners of our kitchens,
And stand, perhaps, turned on, in a million rooms
All over the world. But now if they should speak,   *15*
If on a sudden they should speak again,
If on the stroke of noon a voice should speak,
We would not listen, we would not let it bring
That old bad world that swallowed its children quick
At one great gulp. We would not have it again.   *20*
Sometimes we think of the nations lying asleep,
Curled blindly in impenetrable sorrow,
And then the thought confounds us with its strangeness.

The tractors lie about our fields; at evening
They look like dank sea-monsters couched and waiting.   *25*
We leave them where they are and let them rust:
'They'll moulder away and be like other loam'.
We make our oxen drag our rusty ploughs,
Long laid aside. We have gone back
Far past our fathers' land.
　　　　　　　　　And then, that evening   *30*

Late in the summer the strange horses came.
We heard a distant tapping on the road,
A deepening drumming; it stopped, went on again
And at the corner changed to hollow thunder.
We saw the heads   *35*
Like a wild wave charging and were afraid.
We had sold our horses in our fathers' time
To buy new tractors. Now they were strange to us
As fabulous steeds set on an ancient shield
Or illustrations in a book of knights.   *40*
We did not dare go near them. Yet they waited,
Stubborn and shy, as if they had been sent
By an old command to find our whereabouts
And that long-lost archaic companionship.
In the first moment we had never a thought   *45*
That they were creatures to be owned and used.
Among them were some half-a-dozen colts
Dropped in some wilderness of the broken world,
Yet new as if they had come from their own Eden.
Since then they have pulled our ploughs and borne our loads,   *50*
But that free servitude still can pierce our hearts.
Our life is changed; their coming our beginning.

MARIANNE MOORE (1887–1972)

· A GRAVE ·

Man looking into the sea,
taking the view from those who have as much right to it as you have
      to it yourself,
it is human nature to stand in the middle of a thing,
but you cannot stand in the middle of this;
the sea has nothing to give but a well excavated grave.   *5*
The firs stand in a procession, each with an emerald turkey foot at
      the top,
reserved as their contours, saying nothing;
repression, however, is not the most obvious characteristic of the sea;
the sea is a collector, quick to return a rapacious look.
There are others besides you who have worn that look—   *10*
whose expression is no longer a protest; the fish no longer investigate
      them
for their bones have not lasted:
men lower nets, unconscious of the fact that they are desecrating a
      grave,
and row quickly away—the blades of the oars
moving together like the feet of water spiders as if there were no such
      thing as death.   *15*

ANTHOLOGY

The wrinkles progress among themselves in a phalanx—beautiful
    under networks of foam,
and fade breathlessly while the sea rustles in and out of the seaweed;
the birds swim through the air at top speed, emitting catcalls as
    heretofore—
the tortoise shell scourges about the feet of the cliffs, in motion
    beneath them;
and the ocean, under the pulsation of lighthouses and noise of bell
    buoys,   20
advances as usual, looking as if it were not that ocean in which
    dropped things are bound to sink—
in which if they turn and twist, it is neither with volition nor
    consciousness.

• THE STEEPLE-JACK •

Dürer would have seen a reason for living
    in a town like this, with eight stranded whales
to look at; with the sweet sea air coming into your house
on a fine day, from water etched
    with waves as formal as the scales   5
on a fish.

One by one, in two's, in three's, the seagulls keep
    flying back and forth over the town clock,
or sailing around the lighthouse without moving their wings—
rising steadily with a slight   10
    quiver of the body—or flock
mewing where

a sea the purple of the peacock's neck is
    paled to greenish azure as Dürer changed
the pine green of the Tyrol to peacock blue and guinea   15
gray. You can see a twenty-five-
    pound lobster; and fishnets arranged
to dry. The

whirlwind fife-and-drum of the storm bends the salt
    marsh grass, disturbs stars in the sky and the   20
star on the steeple; it is a privilege to see so
much confusion. Disguised by what
    might seem austerity, the sea-
side flowers and

---

[1]/**Dürer:** *Albrecht Dürer (1471–1528), the German painter and engraver whose work shows a love for precise natural detail.*

trees are favored by the fog so that you have   *25*
     the tropics at first hand: the trumpet-vine,
fox-glove, giant snap-dragon, a salpiglossis that has
spots and stripes; morning-glories, gourds,
     or moon-vines trained on fishing-twine
at the back   *30*

door. There are no banyans, frangipani, nor
     jack-fruit trees; nor an exotic serpent
life. Ring lizard and snake-skin for the foot, or crocodile;
but here they've cats, not cobras, to
     keep down the rats. The diffident   *35*
little newt

with white pin-dots on black horizontal spaced
     out bands lives here; yet there is nothing that
ambition can buy or take away. The college student
named Ambrose sits on the hill-side   *40*
     with his not-native books and hat
and sees boats

at sea progress white and rigid as if in
     a groove. Liking an elegance of which
the source is not bravado, he knows by heart the antique   *45*
sugar-bowl-shaped summer-house of
     interlacing slats, and the pitch
of the church

spire, not true, from which a man in scarlet lets
     down a rope as a spider spins a thread;   *50*
he might be part of a novel, but on the sidewalk a
sign says C. J. Poole, Steeple Jack,
     in black and white; and one in red
and white says

Danger. The church portico has four fluted   *55*
     columns, each a single piece of stone, made
modester by white-wash. This would be a fit haven for
waifs, children, animals, prisoners,
     and presidents who have repaid
sin-driven   *60*

senators by not thinking about them. There
     are a schoolhouse, a post-office in a
store, fish-houses, hen-houses, a three-masted schooner on
the stocks. The hero, the student,
     the steeple-jack, each in his way,   *65*
is at home.

It could not be dangerous to be living
    in a town like this, of simple people,
who have a steeple-jack placing danger signs by the church
while he is gilding the solid-   70
    pointed star, which on a steeple
stands for hope.

· A CARRIAGE FROM SWEDEN ·

They say there is a sweeter air
    where it was made, than we have here;
    a Hamlet's castle atmosphere.
At all events there is in Brooklyn
something that makes me feel at home.   5

No one may see this put-away
    museum-piece, this country cart
    that inner happiness made art;
and yet, in this city of freckled
integrity it is a vein   10

of resined straightness from north-wind
    hardened Sweden's once-opposed-to-
    compromise archipelago
of rocks. Washington and Gustavus
Adolphus, forgive our decay.   15

Seats, dashboard and sides of smooth gourd-
    rind texture, a flowered step, swan-
    dart brake, and swirling crustacean-
tailed equine amphibious creatures
that garnish the axletree! What   20

a fine thing! What unannoying
    romance! And how beautiful, she
    with the natural stoop of the
snowy egret, gray-eyed and straight-haired,
for whom it should come to the door—   25

of whom it reminds me. The split
    pine fair hair, steady gannet-clear
    eyes and the pine-needled-path deer-
swift step; that is Sweden, land of the
free and the soil for a spruce tree—   30

14-15/**Gustavus Adolphus:** *the Swedish monarch and military leader whose reign
(1611–1632) marks one of the greatest epochs of Swedish history*
24/**snowy egret:** *a heron with a beautiful curved neck*
27/**gannet:** *a sea bird that dives from high up to seize its prey under water*

vertical though a seedling—all
    needles: from a green trunk, green shelf
    on shelf fanning out by itself.
The deft white-stockinged dance in thick-soled
shoes! Denmark's sanctuaried Jews!   *35*

The puzzle-jugs and hand-spun rugs,
    the root-legged kracken shaped like dogs,
    the hanging buttons and the frogs
that edge the Sunday jackets! Sweden,
you have a runner called the Deer, who   *40*

when he's won a race, likes to run
    more; you have the sun-right gable-
    ends due east and west, the table
spread as for a banquet; and the put-
in twin vest-pleats with a fish-fin   *45*

effect when you need none. Sweden,
    what makes the people dress that way
    and those who see you wish to stay?
The runner, not too tired to run more
at the end of the race? And that   *50*

cart, dolphin-graceful? A Dalen
    lighthouse, self-lit?—responsive and
    responsible. I understand;
it's not pine-needle-paths that give spring
when they're run on, it's a Sweden   *55*

of moated white castles—the bed
    of white flowers densely grown in an S
    meaning Sweden and stalwartness,
skill, and a surface that says
Made in Sweden: carts are my trade.   *60*

---

[35]/**Denmark's sanctuaried Jews:** *During World War II, Sweden took in and protected Jews from Denmark, who were persecuted when that country was overrun by the Nazis.*
[37]/**kracken:** *sea-monsters*
[38]/**frogs:** *ornamental braided loops for button and buttonhole*
[51]/**Nils Gustaf Dalén:** *In 1912 Dalén (1869–1937) won the Nobel Prize in physics for contributions he made in coastal lighting. Among his inventions was a device that would start up an acetylene flame at twilight and extinguish it at dawn.*

T. S. ELIOT (1888–1965)

• THE LOVE SONG OF J. ALFRED PRUFROCK •

S'io credesse che mia risposta fosse
A persona che mai tornasse al mondo,
Questa fiamma staria senza più scosse.
Ma per ciò che giammai di questo fondo
Non tornò vivo alcun, s'i'odo il vero,
Senza tema d'infamia ti rispondo.

Let us go then, you and I,
When the evening is spread out against the sky
Like a patient etherised upon a table;
Let us go, through certain half-deserted streets,
The muttering retreats   5
Of restless nights in one-night cheap hotels
And sawdust restaurants with oyster-shells:
Streets that follow like a tedious argument
Of insidious intent
To lead you to an overwhelming question . . .   10
Oh, do not ask, "What is it?"
Let us go and make our visit.

          In the room the women come and go
Talking of Michelangelo.

          The yellow fog that rubs its back upon the window-panes,   15
The yellow smoke that rubs its muzzle on the window-panes
Licked its tongue into the corners of the evening,
Lingered upon the pools that stand in drains,
Let fall upon its back the soot that falls from chimneys,
Slipped by the terrace, made a sudden leap,   20
And seeing that it was a soft October night,
Curled once about the house, and fell asleep.

          And indeed there will be time
For the yellow smoke that slides along the street,
Rubbing its back upon the window-panes;   25
There will be time, there will be time
To prepare a face to meet the faces that you meet;
There will be time to murder and create,

The epigraph is from Dante's Inferno, *XXVII, 61–66. The speaker, Guido da Montefeltro, condemned to hell as an evil counselor, is enclosed in a tongue-shaped flame which speaks for him. He says: "If I thought that my answer were to a person who would ever return to the world [and tell others], this flame would move no more [in speech]; but since from this depth no one ever returned alive, if what I hear is true, I'll answer without fear of disgrace."*

ANTHOLOGY

And time for all the works and days of hands
That lift and drop a question on your plate;   *30*
Time for you and time for me,
And time yet for a hundred indecisions,
And for a hundred visions and revisions,
Before the taking of a toast and tea.

    In the room the women come and go   *35*
Talking of Michelangelo.

    And indeed there will be time
To wonder, "Do I dare?" and, "Do I dare?"
Time to turn back and descend the stair,
With a bald spot in the middle of my hair—   *40*
[They will say: "How his hair is growing thin!"]
My morning coat, my collar mounting firmly to the chin,
My necktie rich and modest, but asserted by a simple pin—
[They will say: "But how his arms and legs are thin!"]
Do I dare   *45*
Disturb the universe?
In a minute there is time
For decisions and revisions which a minute will reverse.

    For I have known them all already, known them all:—
Have known the evenings, mornings, afternoons,   *50*
I have measured out my life with coffee spoons;
I know the voices dying with a dying fall
Beneath the music from a farther room.
    So how should I presume?

    And I have known the eyes already, known them all:—   *55*
The eyes that fix you in a formulated phrase,
And when I am formulated, sprawling on a pin,
When I am pinned and wriggling on the wall,
Then how should I begin
To spit out all the butt-ends of my days and ways?   *60*
    And how should I presume?

    And I have known the arms already, known them all—
Arms that are braceleted and white and bare
[But in the lamplight, downed with light brown hair!]
Is it perfume from a dress   *65*

---

[29]/**works and days:** *The* Works and Days *of the Greek poet Hesiod (eighth century B.C.) stresses the need for doing the strenuous work of farming at the proper times.*
[52]/**a dying fall:** *Cf. the opening of* Twelfth Night: *"If music be the food of love, play on;/ Give me excess of it . . . / That strain again! It had a dying fall. . . ." A dying fall is a cadence in music that seems to languish or fall away.*

That makes me so digress?
Arms that lie along a table, or wrap about a shawl.
    And should I then presume?
    And how should I begin?

• • •

Shall I say, I have gone at dusk through narrow streets   70
And watched the smoke that rises from the pipes
Of lonely men in shirt-sleeves, leaning out of windows? . . .

• • •

    I should have been a pair of ragged claws
Scuttling across the floors of silent seas.

And the afternoon, the evening, sleeps so peacefully!   75
Smoothed by long fingers,
Asleep . . . tired . . . or it malingers,
Stretched on the floor, here beside you and me.
Should I, after tea and cakes and ices,
Have the strength to force the moment to its crisis?   80
But though I have wept and fasted, wept and prayed,
Though I have seen my head [grown slightly bald] brought in upon
    a platter,
I am no prophet—and here's no great matter;
I have seen the moment of my greatness flicker,   85
And I have seen the eternal Footman hold my coat, and snicker,
And in short, I was afraid.

    And would it have been worth it, after all,
After the cups, the marmalade, the tea,
Among the porcelain, among some talk of you and me,
Would it have been worth while,   90
To have bitten off the matter with a smile,
To have squeezed the universe into a ball
To roll it toward some overwhelming question,
To say: "I am Lazarus, come from the dead,
Come back to tell you all, I shall tell you all"—   95
If one, settling a pillow by her head,
    Should say: "That is not what I meant at all.
    That is not it, at all."

    And would it have been worth it, after all,
Would it have been worth while,   100

---

[82]/**my head . . . brought in upon a platter:** *The reference is to Saint John the Baptist, beheaded by order of Herod at the request of Salome, whose dancing had pleased the king. Saint John's head was brought to the girl on a platter. As generally depicted in art, the severed head has magnificent locks.*
[89]/**some talk of you and me:** *Cf. "The Rubáiyát of Omar Khayyám," lines 111–112.*
[92]/**squeezed . . . into a ball:** *Cf. Marvell, "To His Coy Mistress," lines 41–44*
[94]/**"I am Lazarus . . .":** *Lazarus was the brother of Martha and Mary, raised from the dead by Jesus (John 11:1–44)*

After the sunsets and the dooryards and the sprinkled streets,
After the novels, after the teacups, after the skirts that trail along the
        floor—
And this, and so much more?—
It is impossible to say just what I mean!
But as if a magic lantern threw the nerves in patterns on a screen: *105*
Would it have been worth while
If one, settling a pillow or throwing off a shawl,
And turning toward the window, should say:
    "That is not it at all,
    That is not what I meant, at all."   *110*
        •   •   •

No! I am not Prince Hamlet, nor was meant to be;
Am an attendant lord, one that will do
To swell a progress, start a scene or two,
Advise the prince; no doubt, an easy tool,
Deferential, glad to be of use,   *115*
Politic, cautious, and meticulous;
Full of high sentence, but a bit obtuse;
At times, indeed, almost ridiculous—
Almost, at times, the Fool.

    I grow old . . . I grow old . . .   *120*
I shall wear the bottoms of my trousers rolled.

    Shall I part my hair behind? Do I dare to eat a peach?
I shall wear white flannel trousers, and walk upon the beach.
I have heard the mermaids singing, each to each.

    I do not think that they will sing to me.   *125*

    I have seen them riding seaward on the waves
Combing the white hair of the waves blown back
When the wind blows the water white and black.

    We have lingered in the chambers of the sea
By sea-girls wreathed with seaweed red and brown   *130*
Till human voices wake us, and we drown.

117/**full of high sentence:** *the speech of the "Clerk . . . of Oxenford" (Oxford scholar) in the Prologue to Chaucer's* Canterbury Tales *is described as "ful of hy sentence"—wise maxims.*
121/**rolled:** *turned up, with cuffs*

· SWEENEY AMONG THE NIGHTINGALES ·

ὤμοι, πέπληγμαι καιρίαν πληγὴν ἔσω.

Apeneck Sweeney spreads his knees
Letting his arms hang down to laugh,
The zebra stripes along his jaw
Swelling to maculate   fe.

The circles of the stormy moon   5
Slide westward toward the River Plate,
Death and the Raven drift above
And Sweeney guards the hornèd gate.

Gloomy Orion and the Dog
Are veiled; and hushed the shrunken seas;   10
The person in the Spanish cape
Tries to sit on Sweeney's knees

Slips and pulls the table cloth
Overturns a coffee-cup,
Reorganized upon the floor   15
She yawns and draws a stocking up;

The silent man in mocha brown
Sprawls at the window-sill and gapes;
The waiter brings in oranges
Bananas figs and hothouse grapes;   20

The silent vertebrate in brown
Contracts and concentrates, withdraws;
Rachel *née* Rabinovitch
Tears at the grapes with murderous paws;

She and the lady in the cape   25
Are suspect, thought to be in league;
Therefore the man with heavy eyes
Declines the gambit, shows fatigue,

---

[4]/**maculate:** *spotted*
[6]/**the River Plate:** *the Río de la Plata, in South America*
[7]/**the Raven:** *the southern constellation Corvus (the Crow)*
[9]/**the Dog:** *the constellation Canis Major or the Dog Star, Sirius, which is in it*

The Greek epigraph is the cry of Agamemnon from offstage as he is murdered by his wife in his bath. It means: "Alas for me! I have been struck a deadly blow in here!"—line 1343 of the Agamemnon *of Aeschylus (525–456* B.C.*), the Athenian dramatist, a play in which Agamemnon is killed in part because of his adulterous love for Cassandra.*

Leaves the room and reappears
Outside the window, leaning in, 30
Branches of wistaria
Circumscribe a golden grin;

The host with someone indistinct
Converses at the door apart,
The nightingales are singing near 35
The Convent of the Sacred Heart,

And sang within the bloody wood
When Agamemnon cried aloud,
And let their liquid siftings fall
To stain the stiff dishonoured shroud. 40

CONRAD AIKEN (1889–1973)

• THE THINGS •

The house in Broad Street, red brick, with nine rooms
the weedgrown graveyard with its rows of tombs
the jail from which imprisoned faces grinned
at stiff palmettos flashing in the wind

the engine-house, with engines, and a tank 5
in which young alligators swam and stank,
the bell-tower, of red iron, where the bell
gonged of the fires in a tone from hell

magnolia trees with whitehot torch of bud
the yellow river between banks of mud 10
the tall striped lighthouse like a barber's pole
snake in the bog and locust in the hole

worn cigarette cards, of white battleships,
or flags, or chorus girls with scarlet lips,
jackstones of copper, peach tree in the yard 15
splashing ripe peaches on an earth baked hard

children beneath the arc-light in a romp
with Run sheep Run, and rice-birds in the swamp,
the organ-grinder's monkey, dancing bears,
okras in baskets, Psyche on the stairs— 20

20/**Psyche:** *a statue or painting of the mythological Psyche, who represents the* soul

The setting of the first five stanzas is Savannah, Georgia.

and then the north star nearer, and the snow
silent between the now and long ago
time like a train that roared from place to place
new crowds, new faces, for a single face

no longer then the chinaberry tree   *25*
nor the dark mockingbird to sing his glee
nor prawns nor catfish; icicles instead
and Indian-pipes, and cider in the shed

arbutus under pinewoods in the spring
and death remembered as a tropic thing   *30*
with picture postcard angels to upraise it
and trumpet vines and hummingbirds to phrase it

then wisdom come, and Shakspere's voice far off,
to be or not, upon the teacher's cough,
the latent heat of melting ice, the brief   *35*
hypotenuse from ecstasy to grief

amo amas, and then the *cras amet,*
the new-found eyes no slumber could forget,
Vivien, the affliction of the senses,
and conjugation of historic tenses   *40*

and Shakspere nearer come, and louder heard,
and the disparateness of flesh and word,
time growing swifter, and the pendulums
in shorter savage arcs that beat like drums—

hands held, relinquished, faces come and gone,   *45*
kissed and forgotten, and become but one,
old shoes worn out, and new ones bought, the gloves
soiled, and so lost in limbo, like the loves—

then Shakspere in the heart, the instant speech
parting the conscious terrors each from each—   *50*
wisdom's dishevelment, the purpose lamed,
and purposeless the footsteps eastward aimed

the bloodstream always slower, while the clock
followed the tired heart with louder knock,
fatigue upon the eye, the tardy springs   *55*
inviting to no longer longed-for things—

---

[37]/**amo amas:** *I love, you love—part of a Latin lesson*
   cras amet: *tomorrow let him love—part of the refrain from a late Latin poem, the* "Pervigilium Veneris"

the birdsong nearer now than Shakspere's voice,
whispers of comfort—Death is near, rejoice!—
remember now the red house with nine rooms
the graveyard with its trumpetvines and tombs—   60

play jackstones now and let your jackstones be
the stars that make Orion's galaxy
so to deceive yourself until you move
into that house whose tenants do not love.

ARCHIBALD MACLEISH (1892–1982)

· ARS POETICA ·

A poem should be palpable and mute
As a globed fruit,

Dumb
As old medallions to the thumb,

Silent as the sleeve-worn stone   5
Of casement ledges where the moss has grown—

A poem should be wordless
As the flight of birds.

·   ·   ·

A poem should be motionless in time
As the moon climbs,   10

Leaving, as the moon releases
Twig by twig the night-entangled trees,

Leaving, as the moon behind the winter leaves,
Memory by memory the mind—

A poem should be motionless in time   15
As the moon climbs.

·   ·   ·

A poem should be equal to:
Not true.

The title means "The art of poetry."

For all the history of grief
An empty doorway and a maple leaf.   *20*

For love
The leaning grasses and two lights above the sea—

A poem should not mean
But be.

• YOU, ANDREW MARVELL •

And here face down beneath the sun
And here upon earth's noonward height
To feel the always coming on
The always rising of the night:

To feel creep up the curving east   *5*
The earthy chill of dusk and slow
Upon those under lands the vast
And ever climbing shadow grow

And strange at Ecbatan the trees
Take leaf by leaf the evening strange   *10*
The flooding dark about their knees
The mountains over Persia change

And now at Kermanshah the gate
Dark empty and the withered grass
And through the twilight now the late   *15*
Few travelers in the westward pass

And Baghdad darken and the bridge
Across the silent river gone
And through Arabia the edge
Of evening widen and steal on   *20*

And deepen on Palmyra's street
The wheel rut in the ruined stone
And Lebanon fade out and Crete
High through the clouds and overblown

And over Sicily the air   *25*
Still flashing with the landward gulls
And loom and slowly disappear
The sails above the shadowy hulls

---

[9]/**Ecbatan:** *town in ancient Persia*   [21]/**Palmyra:** *ancient town in Syria*
[13]/**Kermanshah:** *town in Iran to the*
west of Ecbatan

And Spain go under and the shore
Of Africa the gilded sand   30
And evening vanish and no more
The low pale light across that land

Nor now the long light on the sea:

And here face downward in the sun
To feel how swift how secretly   35
The shadow of the night comes on . . .

E. E. CUMMINGS (1894–1962)

• ANYONE LIVED IN A PRETTY HOW TOWN •

anyone lived in a pretty how town
(with up so floating many bells down)
spring summer autumn winter
he sang his didn't he danced his did.

Women and men(both little and small)   5
cared for anyone not at all
they sowed their isn't they reaped their same
sun moon stars rain

children guessed(but only a few
and down they forgot as up they grew   10
autumn winter spring summer)
that noone loved him more by more

when by now and tree by leaf
she laughed his joy she cried his grief
bird by snow and stir by still   15
anyone's any was all to her

someones married their everyones
laughed their cryings and did their dance
(sleep wake hope and then)they
said their nevers they slept their dream   20

stars rain sun moon
(and only the snow can begin to explain
how children are apt to forget to remember
with up so floating many bells down)

one day anyone died i guess   25
(and noone stooped to kiss his face)
busy folk buried them side by side
little by little and was by was

all by all and deep by deep
and more by more they dream their sleep   *30*
noone and anyone earth by april
wish by spirit and if by yes.

Women and men(both dong and ding)
summer autumn winter spring
reaped their sowing and went their came   *35*
sun moon stars rain

JEAN TOOMER (1894–1967)

· REAPERS ·

Black reapers with the sound of steel on stones
Are sharpening scythes. I see them place the hones
In their hip-pockets as a thing that's done,
And start their silent swinging, one by one.
Black horses drive a mower through the weeds,   *5*
And there, a field rat, startled, squealing bleeds,
His belly close to ground. I see the blade,
Blood-stained, continue cutting weeds and shade.

HART CRANE (1899–1932)

· PRAISE FOR AN URN ·

In Memoriam: Ernest Nelson

It was a kind and northern face
That mingled in such exile guise
The everlasting eyes of Pierrot
And, of Gargantua, the laughter.

His thoughts, delivered to me   *5*
From the white coverlet and pillow,
I see now, were inheritances—
Delicate riders of the storm.

The slant moon on the slanting hill
Once moved us toward presentiments   *10*
Of what the dead keep, living still,
And such assessments of the soul

---

[3]/**Pierrot:** *a melancholy clown of French pantomime*
[4]/**Gargantua:** *a hearty, food-loving giant in Rabelais' novel named for him*

As, perched in the crematory lobby,
The insistent clock commented on,
Touching as well upon our praise   *15*
Of glories proper to the time.

Still, having in mind gold hair,
I cannot see that broken brow
And miss the dry sound of bees
Stretching across a lucid space.   *20*

Scatter these well-meant idioms
Into the smoky spring that fills
The suburbs, where they will be lost.
They are no trophies of the sun.

• PROEM: TO BROOKLYN BRIDGE •

How many dawns, chill from his rippling rest
The seagull's wings shall dip and pivot him,
Shedding white rings of tumult, building high
Over the chained bay waters Liberty—

Then, with inviolate curve, forsake our eyes   *5*
As apparitional as sails that cross
Some page of figures to be filed away;
—Till elevators drop us from our day . . .

I think of cinemas, panoramic sleights
With multitudes bent toward some flashing scene   *10*
Never disclosed, but hastened to again,
Foretold to other eyes on the same screen;

And Thee, across the harbor, silver-paced
As though the sun took step of thee, yet left
Some motion ever unspent in thy stride,—   *15*
Implicitly thy freedom staying thee!

Out of some subway scuttle, cell or loft
A bedlamite speeds to thy parapets,
Tilting there momently, shrill shirt ballooning,
A jest falls from the speechless caravan.   *20*

Down Wall, from girder into street noon leaks,
A rip-tooth of the sky's acetylene;
All afternoon the cloud-flown derricks turn . . .
Thy cables breathe the North Atlantic still.

4/**Liberty:** *the Statue of Liberty*
18/**bedlamite:** *insane person, here bent on suicide*

And obscure as that heaven of the Jews,　　　　　25
Thy guerdon . . . Accolade thou dost bestow
Of anonymity time cannot raise:
Vibrant reprieve and pardon thou dost show.

O harp and altar, of the fury fused,
(How could mere toil align thy choiring strings!)　　30
Terrific threshold of the prophet's pledge,
Prayer of pariah, and the lover's cry,—

Again the traffic lights that skim thy swift
Unfractioned idiom, immaculate sigh of stars,
Beading thy path—condense eternity:　　　　　35
And we have seen night lifted in thine arms.

Under thy shadow by the piers I waited;
Only in darkness is thy shadow clear.
The City's fiery parcels all undone,
Already snow submerges an iron year . . .　　　　40

O Sleepless as the river under thee,
Vaulting the sea, the prairies' dreaming sod,
Unto us lowliest sometime sweep, descend
And of the curveship lend a myth to God.

[26]/**guerdon:** *reward*
   accolade: *ceremony or salute of praise or approval*

ALLEN TATE (1899–1979)

· THE MEDITERRANEAN ·

Quem das finem, rex magne, dolorum?

Where we went in the boat was a long bay
A slingshot wide, walled in by towering stone—
Peaked margin of antiquity's delay,
And we went there out of time's monotone:

Where we went in the black hull no light moved　　5
But a gull white-winged along the feckless wave,
The breeze, unseen but fierce as a body loved,
That boat drove onward like a willing slave:

Quem . . . dolorum?: *The Latin epigraph is a slightly changed version of* Aeneid, *I. 241: "What end of sorrows do you give, great king?"*

For the setting and the explanation of several details, see the discussion of this poem in the text (p. 242).

Where we went in the small ship the seaweed
Parted and gave to us the murmuring shore   *10*
And we made feast and in our secret need
Devoured the very plates Aeneas bore:

Where derelict you see through the low twilight
The green coast that you, thunder-tossed, would win,
Drop sail, and hastening to drink all night   *15*
Eat dish and bowl to take that sweet land in!

Where we feasted and caroused on the sandless
Pebbles, affecting our day of piracy,
What prophecy of eaten plates could landless
Wanderers fulfil by the ancient sea?   *20*

We for that time might taste the famous age
Eternal here yet hidden from our eyes
When lust of power undid its stuffless rage;
They, in a wineskin, bore earth's paradise.

Let us lie down once more by the breathing side   *25*
Of Ocean, where our live forefathers sleep
As if the Known Sea still were a month wide—
Atlantis howls but is no longer steep!

What country shall we conquer, what fair land
Unman our conquest and locate our blood?   *30*
We've cracked the hemispheres with careless hand!
Now, from the Gates of Hercules we flood

Westward, westward till the barbarous brine
Whelms us to the tired land where tasseling corn,
Fat beans, grapes sweeter than muscadine   *35*
Rot on the vine: in that land were we born.

ROBERT FRANCIS (b. 1901)

· PITCHER ·

His art is eccentricity, his aim
How not to hit the mark he seems to aim at,

His passion how to avoid the obvious,
His technique how to vary the avoidance.

32/**the Gates of Hercules:** *the narrows where the Mediterranean meets the Atlantic*
35/**muscadine:** *a kind of grape*

The others throw to be comprehended. He   *5*
Throws to be a moment misunderstood

Yet not too much. Not errant, arrant, wild,
But every seeming aberration willed.

Not to, yet still, still to communicate
Making the batter understand too late.   *10*

· SWIMMER ·

I

Observe how he negotiates his way
With trust and the least violence, making
The stranger friend, the enemy ally.
The depth that could destroy gently supports him.
With water he defends himself from water.   *5*
Danger he leans on, rests in. The drowning sea
Is all he has between himself and drowning.

II

What lover ever lay more mutually
With his beloved, his always-reaching arms
Stroking in smooth and powerful caresses?   *10*
Some drown in love as in dark water, and some
By love are strongly held as the green sea
Now holds the swimmer. Indolently he turns
To float.—The swimmer floats, the lover sleeps.

LANGSTON HUGHES (1902–1967)

· DREAM VARIATIONS ·

To fling my arms wide
In some place of the sun,
To whirl and to dance
Till the white day is done.
Then rest at cool evening   *5*
Beneath a tall tree
While night comes on gently,
    Dark like me—
That is my dream!

To fling my arms wide   *10*
In the face of the sun,
Dance! Whirl! Whirl!
Till the quick day is done.

Rest at pale evening . . .
A tall, slim tree . . .   15
Night coming tenderly
    Black like me.

• THE NEGRO SPEAKS OF RIVERS •

I've known rivers:
I've known rivers ancient as the world and older than the flow of human
    blood in human veins.

My soul has grown deep like the rivers.

I bathed in the Euphrates when dawns were young.
I built my hut near the Congo and it lulled me to sleep.   5
I looked upon the Nile and raised the pyramids above it.
I heard the singing of the Mississippi when Abe Lincoln went down
    to New Orleans, and I've seen its muddy bosom turn all golden
    in the sunset.

I've known rivers:
Ancient, dusky rivers.

My soul has grown deep like the rivers.   10

KENNETH FEARING (1902–1961)

• LOVE, 20¢ THE FIRST QUARTER MILE •

All right, I may have lied to you, and about you, and made a few
    pronouncements a bit too sweeping, perhaps, and possibly
    forgotten to tag the bases here or there,
And damned your extravagance, and maligned your tastes, and libeled
    your relatives, and slandered a few of your friends,
O.K.,
Nevertheless, come back.

Come home. I will agree to forget the statements that you issued so
    copiously to the neighbors and the press,   5
And you will forget that figment of your imagination, the blonde
    from Detroit;
I will agree that your lady friend who lives above us is not crazy, bats,
    nutty as they come, but on the contrary rather bright,
And you will concede that poor old Steinberg is neither a drunk, nor a
    swindler, but simply a guy, on the eccentric side, trying to get
    along.
(Are you listening, you bitch, and have you got this straight?)

Because I forgive you, yes, for everything,   *10*
I forgive you for being beautiful and generous and wise,
I forgive you, to put it simply, for being alive, and pardon you, in
    short, for being you.

Because tonight you are in my hair and eyes,
And every street light that our taxi passes shows me you again, still you,
And because tonight all other nights are black, all other hours are cold
    and far away, and now, this minute, the stars are very near and
    bright.   *15*

Come back. We will have a celebration to end all celebrations.
We will invite the undertaker who lives beneath us, and a couple of
    the boys from the office, and some other friends,
And Steinberg, who is off the wagon, by the way, and that insane woman
    who lives upstairs, and a few reporters, if anything should break.

OGDEN NASH (1902–1971)

· VERY LIKE A WHALE ·

One thing that literature would be greatly the better for
Would be a more restricted employment by authors of simile and
    metaphor.
Authors of all races, be they Greeks, Romans, Teutons or Celts,
Can't seem just to say that anything is the thing it is but have to go out
    of their way to say that it is like something else.
What does it mean when we are told   *5*
That the Assyrian came down like a wolf on the fold?
In the first place, George Gordon Byron had had enough experience
To know that it probably wasn't just one Assyrian, it was a lot of
    Assyrians.
However, as too many arguments are apt to induce apoplexy and thus
    hinder longevity,
We'll let it pass as one Assyrian for the sake of brevity.   *10*
Now then, this particular Assyrian, the one whose cohorts were
    gleaming in purple and gold,
Just what does the poet mean when he says he came down like a wolf
    on the fold?
In heaven and earth more than is dreamed of in our philosophy
    there are a great many things,
But I don't imagine that among them there is a wolf with purple
    and gold cohorts or purple and gold anythings.
No, no, Lord Byron, before I'll believe that this Assyrian was actually
    like a wolf I must have some kind of proof;   *15*
Did he run on all fours and did he have a hairy tail and a big red
    mouth and big white teeth and did he say Woof woof woof?

Frankly I think it very unlikely, and all you were entitled to say, at the
very most,
Was that the Assyrian cohorts came down like a lot of Assyrian
cohorts about to destroy the Hebrew host.
But that wasn't fancy enough for Lord Byron, oh dear me no, he had
to invent a lot of figures of speech and then interpolate them.
With the result that whenever you mention Old Testament soldiers to
people they say Oh yes, they're the ones that a lot of wolves dressed
up in gold and purple ate them.   20
That's the kind of thing that's being done all the time by poets, from
Homer to Tennyson;
They're always comparing ladies to lilies and veal to venison,
And they always say things like that the snow is a white blanket after
a winter storm.
Oh it is, is it, all right then, you sleep under a six-inch blanket of snow
and I'll sleep under a half-inch blanket of unpoetical blanket
material and we'll see which one keeps warm,
And after that maybe you'll begin to comprehend dimly   25
What I mean by too much metaphor and simile.

STEVIE SMITH (1902–1971)

• NOT WAVING BUT DROWNING •

Nobody heard him, the dead man,
But still he lay moaning:
I was much further out than you thought
And not waving but drowning.

Poor chap, he always loved larking   5
And now he's dead
It must have been too cold for him his heart gave way,
They said.

Oh, no no no, it was too cold always
(Still the dead one lay moaning)   10
I was much too far out all my life
And not waving but drowning.

ROBERT PENN WARREN (b. 1905)

• MYTH ON MEDITERRANEAN BEACH: •
APHRODITE AS LOGOS

From left to right, she leads the eye
Across the blaze-brightness of sea and sky

That is the background of her transit.

Logos: *word, the Word, wisdom*

Commanded thus, from left to right,
As by a line of print on that bright   *5*

Blankness, the eye will follow, but

There is no line, the eye follows only
That one word moving, it moves in lonely

And absolute arrogance across the blank

Page of the world, the word burns, she is   *10*
The word, all faces turn. Look!—this

Is what she is: old hunchback in bikini.

A contraption of angles and bulges, an old
Robot with pince-nez and hair dyed gold,

She heaves along beneath the hump.   *15*

The breasts hang down like saddle-bags,
To balance the hump the belly sags,

And under the belly-bulge, the flowers

Of the gee-string garland the private parts.
She grinds along by fits and starts   *20*

Beside the margin of the sea,

Past children and sand-castles and
The lovers strewn along the sand.

Her pince-nez glitter like contempt

For all delusion, and the French lad   *25*
Who exhibitionistically had

Been fondling the American college girl

Loses his interest. Ignoring him,
The hunchback stares at the horizon rim,

Then slowly, as compulsion grows,   *30*

She foots the first frail lace of foam
That is the threshold of her lost home,

And moved by memory in the blood,

Enters that vast indifferency
Of perfection that we call the sea.   35

How long, how long, she lingers there

She may not know, somnambulist
In that realm where no Time may subsist,

But in the end will again feel

The need to rise and re-enact   40
The miracle of the human fact.

She lifts her head, looks toward the shore.

She moves toward us, abstract and slow,
And watching, we feel the slow knowledge grow—

How from the breasts the sea recedes,   45

How the great-gashed navel's cup
Pours forth the ichor that had filled it up.

How the wavelets sink to seek, and seek,

Then languishing, sink to lave the knees,
And lower, to kiss the feet, as these   50

Find the firm ground where they must go.

The last foam crisps about the feet.
She shivers, smiles. She stands complete

In Botticellian parody.

Bearing her luck upon her back,   55
She turns now to take the lifeward track,

And lover by lover, on she moves

Toward her own truth, and does not stop.
Each foot stumps flat with the big toe up,

But under the heel, the damp-packed sand,   60

47/**ichor:** *the divine fluid thought to flow, instead of blood, in the veins of the
gods*

With that compression, like glory glows,
And glory attends her as she goes.

In rapture now she heaves along,

The pince-nez glitter at her eyes,
The flowers wreathe her moving thighs.   *65*

For she treads the track the blessèd know

To a shore far lonelier than this
Where waits her apotheosis.

She passes the lovers, one by one,

And passing, draws their dreams away,   *70*
And leaves them naked to the day.

W. H. AUDEN (1907–1973)

· LULLABY ·

Lay your sleeping head, my love,
Human on my faithless arm;
Time and fevers burn away
Individual beauty from
Thoughtful children, and the grave   *5*
Proves the child ephemeral:
But in my arms till break of day
Let the living creature lie,
Mortal, guilty, but to me
The entirely beautiful.   *10*

Soul and body have no bounds:
To lovers as they lie upon
Her tolerant enchanted slope
In their ordinary swoon,
Grave the vision Venus sends   *15*
Of supernatural sympathy,
Universal love and hope;
While an abstract insight wakes
Among the glaciers and the rocks
The hermit's carnal ecstasy.   *20*

Certainty, fidelity
On the stroke of midnight pass
Like vibrations of a bell
And fashionable madmen raise
Their pedantic boring cry: *25*

Every farthing of the cost,
All the dreaded cards foretell,
Shall be paid, but from this night
Not a whisper, not a thought,
Not a kiss nor look be lost.   *30*

Beauty, midnight, vision dies:
Let the winds of dawn that blow
Softly round your dreaming head
Such a day of welcome show
Eye and knocking heart may bless,   *35*
Find our mortal world enough;
Noons of dryness find you fed
By the involuntary powers,
Nights of insult let you pass
Watched by every human love.   *40*

· IN MEMORY OF W. B. YEATS ·

(d. Jan. 1939)

I

He disappeared in the dead of winter:
The brooks were frozen, the airports almost deserted,
And snow disfigured the public statues;
The mercury sank in the mouth of the dying day.
What instruments we have agree   *5*
The day of his death was a dark cold day.

Far from his illness
The wolves ran on through the evergreen forests,
The peasant river was untempted by the fashionable quays;
By mourning tongues   *10*
The death of the poet was kept from his poems.

But for him it was his last afternoon as himself,
An afternoon of nurses and rumours;
The provinces of his body revolted,
The squares of his mind were empty,   *15*
Silence invaded the suburbs,
The current of his feeling failed; he became his admirers.

Now he is scattered among a hundred cities
And wholly given over to unfamiliar affections,
To find his happiness in another kind of wood   *20*
And be punished under a foreign code of conscience.
The words of a dead man
Are modified in the guts of the living.

ANTHOLOGY

But in the importance and noise of to-morrow
When the brokers are roaring like beasts on the floor of the Bourse,   *25*
And the poor have the sufferings to which they are fairly accustomed,
And each in the cell of himself is almost convinced of his freedom,
A few thousand will think of this day
As one thinks of a day when one did something slightly unusual.
What instruments we have agree   *30*
The day of his death was a dark cold day.

II

You were silly like us; your gift survived it all:
The parish of rich women, physical decay,
Yourself. Mad Ireland hurt you into poetry.
Now Ireland has her madness and her weather still,   *35*
For poetry makes nothing happen: it survives
In the valley of its making where executives
Would never want to tamper, flows on south
From ranches of isolation and the busy griefs,
Raw towns that we believe and die in; it survives,   *40*
A way of happening, a mouth.

III

Earth, receive an honoured guest:
William Yeats is laid to rest.
Let the Irish vessel lie
Emptied of its poetry.   *45*

Time that is intolerant
Of the brave and innocent,
And indifferent in a week
To a beautiful physique,

Worships language and forgives   *50*
Everyone by whom it lives;
Pardons cowardice, conceit,
Lays its honours at their feet.

Time that with this strange excuse
Pardoned Kipling and his views,   *55*
And will pardon Paul Claudel,
Pardons him for writing well.

In the nightmare of the dark
All the dogs of Europe bark,
And the living nations wait,   *60*
Each sequestered in its hate;

[25]/**the Bourse:** *the stock exchange*
[46-57]/*Included in the 1939 version of the poem. Auden later chose to omit these lines.*
[56]/**Paul Claudel:** *French Catholic diplomat, poet, and dramatist (1868–1955)*

Intellectual disgrace
Stares from every human face,
And the seas of pity lie
Locked and frozen in each eye.   *65*

Follow, poet, follow right
To the bottom of the night,
With your unconstraining voice
Still persuade us to rejoice;

With the farming of a verse   *70*
Make a vineyard of the curse,
Sing of human unsuccess
In a rapture of distress;

In the deserts of the heart
Let the healing fountain start,   *75*
In the prison of his days
Teach the free man how to praise.

THEODORE ROETHKE (1908–1963)

· ELEGY FOR JANE ·

My Student, Thrown by a Horse

I remember the neckcurls, limp and damp as tendrils;
And her quick look, a sidelong pickerel smile;
And how, once startled into talk, the light syllables leaped for her,
And she balanced in the delight of her thought,
A wren, happy, tail into the wind,   *5*
Her song trembling the twigs and small branches.
The shade sang with her;
The leaves, their whispers turned to kissing;
And the mold sang in the bleached valleys under the rose.

Oh, when she was sad, she cast herself down into such a pure depth, *10*
Even a father could not find her:
Scraping her cheek against straw;
Stirring the clearest water.

My sparrow, you are not here,
Waiting like a fern, making a spiny shadow.   *15*
The sides of wet stones cannot console me,
Nor the moss, wound with the last light.

If only I could nudge you from this sleep,
My maimed darling, my skittery pigeon.
Over this damp grave I speak the words of my love: *20*
I, with no rights in this matter,
Neither father nor lover.

· THE WAKING ·

I wake to sleep, and take my waking slow.
I feel my fate in what I cannot fear.
I learn by going where I have to go.

We think by feeling. What is there to know?
I hear my being dance from ear to ear.   *5*
I wake to sleep, and take my waking slow.

Of those so close beside me, which are you?
God bless the Ground! I shall walk softly there,
And learn by going where I have to go.

Light takes the Tree; but who can tell us how?   *10*
The lowly worm climbs up a winding stair;
I wake to sleep, and take my waking slow.

Great Nature has another thing to do
To you and me; so take the lively air,
And, lovely, learn by going where to go.   *15*

This shaking keeps me steady. I should know.
What falls away is always. And is near.
I wake to sleep, and take my waking slow.
I learn by going where I have to go.

BERNARD SPENCER (1909–1963)

· CASTANETS ·

Back will go the head with the dark curls
and the foot will stamp:
but now she stoops beneath
her arms, or, frowning, whirls
her skirt to lie out flat on the air   *5*
so the breeze is on
our mouths, and the smoke swings:
dry like a thirst the guitar rings.

Across her eyes drunk hair; the flower
that lodged there spins to the ground: *10*

coolly in the barbarous dance
the wrists arch up, and now
the castanets, those fever teeth,
begin to sound:
then, gunshot through a veil,   *15*
blow the night suddenly mad with their pelting hail.

ROBERT FITZGERALD (b. 1910)

• COBB WOULD HAVE CAUGHT IT •

In sunburnt parks where Sundays lie,
Or the wide wastes beyond the cities,
Teams in grey deploy through sunlight.

Talk it up, boys, a little practice.

Coming in stubby and fast, the baseman   *5*
Gathers a grounder in fat green grass,
Picks it stinging and clipped as wit
Into the leather: a swinging step
Wings it deadeye down to first.
Smack. Oh, attaboy, attyoldboy.   *10*

Catcher reverses his cap, pulls down
Sweaty casque, and squats in the dust:
Pitcher rubs new ball on his pants,
Chewing, puts a jet behind him;
Nods past batter, taking his time.   *15*
Batter settles, tugs at his cap:
A spinning ball: step and swing to it,
Caught like a cheek before it ducks
By shivery hickory: socko, baby:
Cleats dig into dust. Outfielder,   *20*
On his way, looking over shoulder,
Makes it a triple. A long peg home.

Innings and afternoons. Fly lost in sunset.
Throwing arm gone bad. There's your old
     ball game.
Cool reek of the field. Reek of companions.   *25*

ELIZABETH BISHOP (1911–1979)

• THE FISH •

I caught a tremendous fish
and held him beside the boat
half out of water, with my hook

fast in a corner of his mouth.
He didn't fight. 5
He hadn't fought at all.
He hung a grunting weight,
battered and venerable
and homely. Here and there
his brown skin hung in strips 10
like ancient wallpaper,
and its pattern of darker brown
was like wallpaper:
shapes like full-blown roses
stained and lost through age. 15
He was speckled with barnacles,
fine rosettes of lime,
and infested
with tiny white sea-lice,
and underneath two or three 20
rags of green weed hung down.
While his gills were breathing in
the terrible oxygen
—the frightening gills,
fresh and crisp with blood, 25
that can cut so badly—
I thought of the coarse white flesh
packed in like feathers,
the big bones and the little bones,
the dramatic reds and blacks 30
of his shiny entrails,
and the pink swim-bladder
like a big peony.
I looked into his eyes
which were far larger than mine 35
but shallower, and yellowed,
the irises backed and packed
with tarnished tinfoil
seen through the lenses
of old scratched isinglass. 40
They shifted a little, but not
to return my stare.
—It was more like the tipping
of an object toward the light.
I admired his sullen face, 45
the mechanism of his jaw,
and then I saw
that from his lower lip
—if you could call it a lip—
grim, wet, and weaponlike, 50
hung five old pieces of fish-line,
or four and a wire leader
with the swivel still attached,

with all their five big hooks
grown firmly in his mouth.   *55*
A green line, frayed at the end
where he broke it, two heavier lines,
and a fine black thread
still crimped from the strain and snap
when it broke and he got away.   *60*
Like medals with their ribbons
frayed and wavering,
a five-haired beard of wisdom
trailing from his aching jaw.
I stared and stared   *65*
and victory filled up
the little rented boat,
from the pool of bilge
where oil had spread a rainbow
around the rusted engine   *70*
to the bailer rusted orange,
the sun-cracked thwarts,
the oarlocks on their strings,
the gunnels—until everything
was rainbow, rainbow, rainbow!   *75*
And I let the fish go.

MURIEL RUKEYSER (1913–1980)

· EFFORT AT SPEECH BETWEEN TWO PEOPLE ·

Speak to me.   Take my hand.   What are you now?
I will tell you all.   I will conceal nothing.
When I was three, a little child read a story about a rabbit
who died, in the story, and I crawled under a chair:
a pink rabbit: it was my birthday, and a candle   *5*
burnt a sore spot on my finger, and I was told to be happy.

Oh, grow to know me.   I am not happy.   I will be open:
Now I am thinking of white sails against a sky like music,
like glad horns blowing, and birds tilting, and an arm about me.
There was one I loved, who wanted to live, sailing.   *10*

Speak to me.   Take my hand.   What are you now?
When I was nine, I was fruitily sentimental,
fluid: and my widowed aunt played Chopin,
and I bent my head on the painted woodwork, and wept.
I want now to be close to you.   I would   *15*
link the minutes of my days close, somehow, to your days.

I am not happy.   I will be open.
I have liked lamps in evening corners, and quiet poems.
There has been fear in my life.   Sometimes I speculate
On what a tragedy his life was, really.   20

Take my hand.   Fist my mind in your hand.   What are you now?
When I was fourteen, I had dreams of suicide,
and I stood at a steep window, at sunset, hoping toward death:
if the light had not melted clouds and plains to beauty,
if light had not transformed that day, I would have leapt,   25
I am unhappy.   I am lonely.   Speak to me.
I will be open.   I think he never loved me:
he loved the bright beaches, the little lips of foam
that ride small waves, he loved the veer of gulls:
he said with a gay mouth: I love you.   Grow to know me.   30

What are you now?   If we could touch one another,
if these our separate entities could come to grips,
clenched like a Chinese puzzle . . . yesterday
I stood in a crowded street that was live with people,
and no one spoke a word, and the morning shone.   35
Everyone silent, moving. . . . Take my hand.   Speak to me.

ROBERT HAYDEN (1913–1980)

· THOSE WINTER SUNDAYS ·

Sundays too my father got up early
and put his clothes on in the blueblack cold,
then with cracked hands that ached
from labor in the weekday weather made
banked fires blaze. No one ever thanked him.   5

I'd wake and hear the cold splintering, breaking.
When the rooms were warm, he'd call,
and slowly I would rise and dress,
fearing the chronic angers of that house,

Speaking indifferently to him,   10
who had driven out the cold
and polished my good shoes as well.
What did I know, what did I know
of love's austere and lonely offices?

· O DAEDALUS, FLY AWAY HOME ·

Drifting night in the Georgia pines,
coonskin drum and jubilee banjo.
Pretty Malinda, dance with me.

Night is juba, night is conjo.
Pretty Malinda, dance with me.   5

Night is an African juju man
weaving a wish and a weariness together
to make two wings.

       O fly away home fly away

Do you remember Africa?   10

       O cleave the air fly away home

My gran, he flew back to Africa,
just spread his arms and
flew away home.

Drifting night in the windy pines;   15
night is a laughing, night is a longing.
Pretty Malinda, come to me.

Night is a mourning juju man
weaving a wish and a weariness together
to make two wings.   20

       O fly away home fly away

[4]/**juba:** *a dance with hand clapping*
  conjo: *magical objects used in rituals (as is* **juju** *two lines below)*

KARL SHAPIRO (b. 1913)

· THE LEG ·

Among the iodoform, in twilight-sleep,
What have I lost? he first inquires,
Peers in the middle distance where a pain,
Ghost of a nurse, hazily moves, and day,
Her blinding presence pressing in his eyes   5
And now his ears. They are handling him
With rubber hands. He wants to get up.

One day beside some flowers near his nose
He will be thinking, *When will I look at it?*   10
And pain, still in the middle distance, will reply,

[1]/**iodoform:** *an antiseptic*
  twilight-sleep: *a state produced by an injection of morphine and scopolomine in which awareness and memory of pain are dulled or effaced*

At what? and he will know it's gone,
O where! and begin to tremble and cry.
He will begin to cry as a child cries
Whose puppy is mangled under a screaming wheel.   *15*

Later, as if deliberately, his fingers
Begin to explore the stump. He learns a shape
That is comfortable and tucked in like a sock.
This has a sense of humor, this can despise
The finest surgical limb, the dignity of limping,   *20*
The nonsense of wheel chairs. Now he smiles to the wall:
The amputation becomes an acquisition.

For the leg is wondering where he is (all is not lost)
And surely he has a duty to the leg;
He is its injury, the leg is his orphan,   *25*
He must cultivate the mind of the leg,
Pray for the part that is missing, pray for peace
In the image of man, pray, pray for its safety,
And after a little it will die quietly.

The body, what is it, Father, but a sign   *30*
To love the force that grows us, to give back
What in Thy palm is senselessness and mud?
Knead, knead the substance of our understanding
Which must be beautiful in flesh to walk,
That if Thou take me angrily in hand   *35*
And hurl me to the shark, I shall not die!

· THE TWO-YEAR-OLD HAS HAD ·
A MOTHERLESS WEEK

The two-year-old has had a motherless week. Mother has gone
   to bring back the baby. A week is many many years.
   One evening they bring the news to the playpen: a
   child is born, you have a baby brother. The dark little
   eyes consider this news and convey no message. One   *5*
   day long after, they arrive in a taxi, father, mother,
   bundle. The two-year-old observes from her blue
   walker on the sunny sidewalk. She stares and turns
   away on her wheels.

The father has gone to the other side of the world. He will *10*
   bring back strange presents to a strange house. The
   little ones shyly wait their turn. Reconciliation is
   gradual.

In Trenton, New Jersey, the soldiers sit in the innocuous bar.
   It's three years since they saw the ones they wrote to.   *15*
   They are all afraid to go home. One lives two blocks

away; he is very silent. Late in the afternoon, at an
ungiven signal, they get up and disperse, like criminals
perfectly trained for the job ahead.

In my brother's house when I left (whole histories ago) the   20
    furniture was honeymoon fresh, gleam of ceramics;
    soft beige carpets smelt like new-mown hay. With a
    shock I see the carpet is worn; the sofa has settled;
    books have changed places. A thousand days of words
    have passed.   25

Time is mostly absences, oceans generally at peace, and lives
    we love most often out of reach.

RANDALL JARRELL (1914–1965)

· NEXT DAY ·

Moving from Cheer to Joy, from Joy to All,
I take a box
And add it to my wild rice, my Cornish game hens.
The slacked or shorted, basketed, identical
Food-gathering flocks   5
Are selves I overlook. Wisdom, said William James,

Is learning what to overlook. And I am wise
If that is wisdom.
Yet somehow, as I buy All from these shelves
And the boy takes it to my station wagon,   10
What I've become
Troubles me even if I shut my eyes.

When I was young and miserable and pretty
And poor, I'd wish
What all girls wish: to have a husband,   15
A house and children. Now that I'm old, my wish
Is womanish:
That the boy putting groceries in my car

See me. It bewilders me he doesn't see me.
For so many years   20
I was good enough to eat: the world looked at me
And its mouth watered. How often they have undressed me,
The eyes of strangers!
And, holding their flesh within my flesh, their vile

Imaginings within my imagining,   25
I too have taken
The chance of life. Now the boy pats my dog

And we start home. Now I am good.
The last mistaken,
Ecstatic, accidental bliss, the blind   30

Happiness that, bursting, leaves upon the palm
Some soap and water—
It was so long ago, back in some Gay
Twenties, Nineties, I don't know . . . Today I miss
My lovely daughter   35
Away at school, my sons away at school,

My husband away at work—I wish for them.
The dog, the maid,
And I go through the sure unvarying days
At home in them. As I look at my life,   40
I am afraid
Only that it will change, as I am changing:

I am afraid, this morning, of my face.
It looks at me
From the rear-view mirror, with the eyes I hate,   45
The smile I hate. Its plain, lined look
Of gray discovery
Repeats to me: "You're old." That's all, I'm old.

And yet I'm afraid, as I was at the funeral
I went to yesterday.   50
My friend's cold made-up face, granite among its flowers,
Her undressed, operated-on, dressed body
Were my face and body.
As I think of her I hear her telling me

How young I seem; I *am* exceptional;   55
I think of all I have.
But really no one is exceptional,
No one has anything, I'm anybody,
I stand beside my grave
Confused with my life, that is commonplace and solitary.   60

JOHN BERRYMAN (1914–1972)

· DREAM SONGS ·

4

Filling her compact & delicious body
with chicken páprika, she glanced at me
twice.
Fainting with interest, I hungered back

and only the fact of her husband & four other people   5
kept me from springing on her

or falling at her little feet and crying
'You are the hottest one for years of night
Henry's dazed eyes
have enjoyed, Brilliance.' I advanced upon   10
(despairing) my spumoni.—Sir Bones: is stuffed,
de world, wif feeding girls.

—Black hair, complexion Latin, jewelled eyes
downcast . . . The slob beside her   feasts . . . What wonders is
she sitting on, over there?   15
The restaurant buzzes. She might as well be on Mars.
Where did it all go wrong? There ought to be a law against Henry.
—Mr. Bones: there is.

22
of 1826

I am the little man who smokes & smokes.
I am the girl who does know better but.
I am the king of the pool.
I am so wise I had my mouth sewn shut.
I am a government official & a goddamned fool.   5
I am a lady who takes jokes.

I am the enemy of the mind.
I am the auto salesman and lóve you.
I am a teenage cancer, with a plan.
I am the blackt-out man.   10
I am the woman powerful as a zoo.
I am two eyes screwed to my set, whose blind—

It is the Fourth of July.
Collect: while the dying man,
forgone by you creator, who forgives,   15
is gasping 'Thomas Jefferson still lives'
in vain, in vain, in vain.
I am Henry Pussy-cat! My whiskers fly.

For some explanatory remarks about "22," see the discussion in the text (p. 306).

DYLAN THOMAS (1914–1953)

• FERN HILL •

Now as I was young and easy under the apple boughs
About the lilting house and happy as the grass was green,
    The night above the dingle starry,

[3]/**dingle:** *deep hollow or valley*

    Time let me hail and climb
    Golden in the heydays of his eyes,   *5*
And honoured among wagons I was prince of the apple towns
And once below a time I lordly had the trees and leaves
      Trail with daisies and barley
    Down the rivers of the windfall light.

And as I was green and carefree, famous among the barns   *10*
About the happy yard and singing as the farm was home,
    In the sun that is young once only,
      Time let me play and be
    Golden in the mercy of his means,
And green and golden I was huntsman and herdsman, the calves   *15*
Sang to my horn, the foxes on the hills barked clear and cold,
      And the sabbath rang slowly
    In the pebbles of the holy streams.

All the sun long it was running, it was lovely, the hay
Fields high as the house, the tunes from the chimneys, it was air   *20*
    And playing, lovely and watery
      And fire green as grass.
    And nightly under the simple stars
As I rode to sleep the owls were bearing the farm away,
All the moon long I heard, blessed among stables, the nightjars   *25*
    Flying with the ricks, and the horses
      Flashing into the dark.

And then to awake, and the farm, like a wanderer white
With the dew, come back, the cock on his shoulder: it was all
    Shining, it was Adam and maiden,   *30*
      The sky gathered again
    And the sun grew round that very day.
So it must have been after the birth of the simple light
In the first, spinning place, the spellbound horses walking warm
    Out of the whinnying green stable   *35*
      On to the fields of praise.

And honoured among foxes and pheasants by the gay house
Under the new made clouds and happy as the heart was long,
    In the sun born over and over,
      I ran my heedless ways,   *40*
    My wishes raced through the house high hay
And nothing I cared, at my sky blue trades, that time allows
In all his tuneful turning so few and such morning songs
    Before the children green and golden
      Follow him out of grace,
                               45

[25]/**nightjars**: *nocturnal birds*

Nothing I cared, in the lamb white days, that time would take me
Up to the swallow thronged loft by the shadow of my hand,
    In the moon that is always rising,
        Nor that riding to sleep
    I should hear him fly with the high fields   50
And wake to the farm forever fled from the childless land.
Oh as I was young and easy in the mercy of his means,
        Time held me green and dying
    Though I sang in my chains like the sea.

JOHN CIARDI (b. 1916)

· SNOWY HERON ·

What lifts the heron leaning on the air
I praise without a name. A crouch, a flare,
a long stroke through the cumulus of trees,
a shaped thought at the sky—then gone. O *rare!*
Saint Francis, being happiest on his knees,   5
would have cried *Father!* Cry anything you please.

But praise. By any name or none. But praise
the white original burst that lights
the heron on his two soft kissing kites.
When saints praise heaven lit by doves and rays,   10
I sit by pond scums till the air recites
Its heron back. And doubt all else. But praise.

· FACES ·

Once in Canandaigua, hitchhiking from Ann Arbor
to Boston in the middle of December, and just
as dark came full on a stone-cracking
drill of wind that shot a grit of snow,
I was picked up outside an all-night diner   5
by a voice in a Buick. "Jump in," it said. "It's cold."

Four, five miles out, in the dead winter of nowhere
and black as the insides of a pig, we stopped.
"I turn off here."

                I looked around at nothing.   10
"The drive's up there," he said.

                    But when I was out,
he headed on, turned round, drove back, and stopped.

"You haven't thanked me for the ride," he said.

"Thanks," I said, shuffling to find a rock   *15*
I might kick loose and grab for just in case.
But he wasn't that kind of crazy. He just waved:
"You're welcome, brother. Keep the rest for change."
Then he pulled in his head and drove away—
back toward Canandaigua.   *20*

           I thought about him
a good deal, you might say, out there in the sandblast
till a truck lit like a liner picked me up
one blue-black inch from frostbite.
And off and on for something like twenty years   *25*
I've found him in my mind, whoever he was,
whoever he is—I never saw his face,
only its shadow—but for twenty years
I've been finding faces that might do for his.
The Army was especially full of possibles,   *30*
but not to the point of monopoly. Any party
can spring one through a doorway. "How do you do?"
you say and the face opens and there you are
back in the winter blast.

           But why tell you?   *35*
It's anybody's world for the living in it:
You know as much about that face as I do.

ROBERT LOWELL (1917–1977)

· SKUNK HOUR ·
(For Elizabeth Bishop)

Nautilus Island's hermit
heiress still lives through winter in her Spartan cottage;
her sheep still graze above the sea.
Her son's a bishop. Her farmer
is first selectman in our village,   *5*
she's in her dotage.

Thirsting for
the hierarchic privacy
of Queen Victoria's century,
she buys up all   *10*
the eyesores facing her shore,
and lets them fall.

The setting is around Castine, Maine.

The season's ill—
we've lost our summer millionaire,
who seemed to leap from an L. L. Bean
catalogue. His nine-knot yawl
was auctioned off to lobstermen.
A red fox stain covers Blue Hill.   15

And now our fairy
decorator brightens his shop for fall;   20
his fishnet's filled with orange cork,
orange, his cobbler's bench and awl;
there is no money in his work,
he'd rather marry.

One dark night,   25
my Tudor Ford climbed the hill's skull;
I watched for love-cars. Lights turned down,
they lay together, hull to hull,
where the graveyard shelves on the town. . . .
My mind's not right.   30

A car radio bleats,
"Love, O careless Love . . ." I hear
my ill-spirit sob in each blood cell,
as if my hand were at its throat. . . .
I myself am hell;   35
nobody's here—

only skunks, that search
in the moonlight for a bite to eat.
They march on their soles up Main Street:
white stripes, moonstruck eyes' red fire   40
under the chalk-dry and spar spire
of the Trinitarian Church.

I stand on top
of our back steps and breathe the rich air—
a mother skunk with her column of kittens swills the garbage pail.   45
She jabs her wedge-head in a cup
of sour cream, drops her ostrich tail,
and will not scare.

15/**L. L. Bean:** *a store and mail-order house in Maine, specializing in sportswear and camping equipment*
25/**one dark night:** *an allusion to "The Dark Night" of Saint John of the Cross (p. 57)*

· FOR THE UNION DEAD ·

"Relinquunt Omnia Servare Rem Publicam."

The old South Boston Aquarium stands
in a Sahara of snow now. Its broken windows are boarded.
The bronze weathervane cod has lost half its scales.
The airy tanks are dry.

Once my nose crawled like a snail on the glass;   5
my hand tingled
to burst the bubbles
drifting from the noses of the cowed, compliant fish.

My hand draws back. I often sigh still
for the dark downward and vegetating kingdom   10
of the fish and reptile. One morning last March,
I pressed against the new barbed and galvanized

fence on the Boston Common. Behind their cage,
yellow dinosaur steamshovels were grunting
as they cropped up tons of mush and grass   15
to gouge their underworld garage.

Parking spaces luxuriate like civic
sandpiles in the heart of Boston.
A girdle of orange, Puritan-pumpkin colored girders
braces the tingling Statehouse,   20

shaking over the excavations, as it faces Colonel Shaw
and his bell-cheeked Negro infantry
on St. Gauden's shaking Civil War relief,
propped by a plank splint against the garage's earthquake.

Two months after marching through Boston,   25
half the regiment was dead;
at the dedication,
William James could almost hear the bronze Negroes breathe.

Their monument sticks like a fishbone
in the city's throat.   30
Its Colonel is as lean
as a compass-needle.

"Relinquunt . . . Publicam": *"They Gave up Everything to Preserve the Republic"*
[21]/**Colonel Shaw:** *Robert Gould Shaw was commander of the first all-black regiment in the Union Army during the Civil War. A bronze memorial to him and his men, made by the sculptor Saint-Gaudens in 1897, faces the State House on Boston Common.*

He has an angry wrenlike vigilance,
a greyhound's gentle tautness;
he seems to wince at pleasure,   *35*
and suffocate for privacy.

He is out of bounds now. He rejoices in man's lovely,
peculiar power to choose life and die—
when he leads his black soldiers to death,
he cannot bend his back.   *40*

On a thousand small town New England greens,
the old white churches hold their air
of sparse, sincere rebellion; frayed flags
quilt the graveyards of the Grand Army of the Republic.

The stone statues of the abstract Union Soldier   *45*
grow slimmer and younger each year—
wasp-waisted, they doze over muskets
and muse through their sideburns . . .

Shaw's father wanted no monument
except the ditch,   *50*
where his son's body was thrown
and lost with his "niggers."

The ditch is nearer.
There are no statues for the last war here;
on Boylston Street, a commercial photograph   *55*
shows Hiroshima boiling

over a Mosler Safe, the "Rock of Ages"
that survived the blast. Space is nearer.
When I crouch to my television set,
the drained faces of Negro school-children rise like balloons.   *60*

Colonel Shaw
is riding on his bubble,
he waits
for the blessèd break.

The Aquarium is gone. Everywhere,   *65*
giant finned cars nose forward like fish;
a savage servility
slides by on grease.

44/**Grand Army . . .**: *Union soldiers*
60/**drained faces:** *in news reports of integration disorders*

GWENDOLYN BROOKS (b. 1917)

· THE BEAN EATERS ·

They eat beans mostly, this old yellow pair.
Dinner is a casual affair.
Plain chipware on a plain and creaking wood,
Tin flatware.

Two who are Mostly Good.   5
Two who have lived their day,
But keep on putting on their clothes
And putting things away.

And remembering . . .
Remembering, with twinklings and twinges,   10
As they lean over the beans in their rented back room
        that is full of beads and receipts and dolls and cloths,
        tobacco crumbs, vases and fringes.

MAY SWENSON (b. 1919)

· PAINTING THE GATE ·

I painted the mailbox. That was fun.
I painted it postal blue.
Then I painted the gate.
I painted a spider that got on the gate.
I painted his mate.   5
I painted the ivy around the gate.
Some stones I painted blue,
and part of the cat as he rubbed by.
I painted my hair. I painted my shoe.
I painted the slats, both front and back,   10
all their beveled edges, too.
I painted the numbers on the gate—
I shouldn't have, but it was too late.
I painted the posts, each side and top,
I painted the hinges, the handle, the lock,   15
several ants and a moth asleep in a crack.
At last I was through.
I'd painted the gate
shut, me out, with both hands dark blue,
as well as my nose, which,   20
early on, because of a sudden itch,
got painted. But wait!
I had painted the gate.

HOWARD NEMEROV (b. 1920)

· LEARNING BY DOING ·

They're taking down a tree at the front door,
The power saw is snarling at some nerves,
Whining at others. Now and then it grunts,
And sawdust falls like snow or a drift of seeds.

Rotten, they tell us, at the fork, and one   5
Big wind would bring it down. So what they do
They do, as usual, to do us good.
Whatever cannot carry its own weight
Has got to go, and so on; you expect
To hear them talking next about survival   10
And the values of a free society.
For in the explanations people give
On these occasions there is generally some
Mean-spirited moral point, and everyone
Privately wonders if his neighbors plan   15
To saw him up before he falls on them.

Maybe a hundred years in sun and shower
Dismantled in a morning and let down
Out of itself a finger at a time
And then an arm, and so down to the trunk,   20
Until there's nothing left to hold on to
Or snub the splintery holding rope around,
And where those big green divagations were
So loftily with shadows interleaved
The absent-minded blue rains in on us.   25
Now that they've got it sectioned on the ground
It looks as though somebody made a plain
Error in diagnosis, for the wood
Looks sweet and sound throughout. You couldn't know,
Of course, until you took it down. That's what   30
Experts are for, and these experts stand round
The giant pieces of tree as though expecting
An instruction booklet from the factory
Before they try to put it back together.

Anyhow, there it isn't, on the ground.   35
Next come the tractor and the crowbar crew
To extirpate what's left and fill the grave.
Maybe tomorrow grass seed will be sown.
There's some mean-spirited moral point in that
As well: you learn to bury your mistakes,   40
Though for a while at dusk the darkening air
Will be with many shadows interleaved,
And pierced with a bewilderment of birds.

• BECAUSE YOU ASKED ABOUT THE LINE •
BETWEEN PROSE AND POETRY

Sparrows were feeding in a freezing drizzle
That while you watched turned into pieces of snow
Riding a gradient invisible
From silver aslant to random, white, and slow.

There came a moment that you couldn't tell.   5
And then they clearly flew instead of fell.

RICHARD WILBUR (b. 1921)

• A GRASSHOPPER •

But for a brief
Moment, a poised minute,
He paused on the chicory-leaf;
Yet within it

The sprung perch   5
Had time to absorb the shock,
Narrow its pitch and lurch,
Cease to rock.

A quiet spread
Over the neighbor ground;   10
No flower swayed its head
For yards around;

The wind shrank
Away with a swallowed hiss;
Caught in a widening, blank   15
Parenthesis,

Cry upon cry
Faltered and faded out;
Everything seemed to die.
Oh, without doubt   20

Peace like a plague
Had gone to the world's verge,
But that an aimless, vague
Grasshopper-urge

Leapt him aloft,   25
Giving the leaf a kick,
Starting the grasses' soft
Chafe and tick,

So that the sleeping
Crickets resumed their chimes,   30
And all things wakened, keeping
Their several times.

In gay release
The whole field did what it did,
Peaceful now that its peace   35
Lay busily hid.

· PLAYBOY ·

High on his stockroom ladder like a dunce
The stock-boy sits, and studies like a sage
The subject matter of one glossy page,
As lost in curves as Archimedes once.

Sometimes, without a glance, he feeds himself.   5
The left hand, like a mother-bird in flight,
Brings him a sandwich for a sidelong bite,
And then returns it to a dusty shelf.

What so engrosses him? The wild décor
Of this pink-papered alcove into which   10
A naked girl has stumbled, with its rich
Welter of pelts and pillows on the floor,

Amidst which, kneeling in a supple pose,
She lifts a goblet in her farther hand,
As if about to toast a flower-stand   15
Above which hovers an exploding rose

Fired from a long-necked crystal vase that rests
Upon a tasseled and vermilion cloth
One taste of which would shrivel up a moth?
Or is he pondering her perfect breasts?   20

Nothing escapes him of her body's grace
Or of her floodlit skin, so sleek and warm
And yet so strangely like a uniform,
But what now grips his fancy is her face,

And how the cunning picture holds her still   25
At just that smiling instant when her soul,
Grown sweetly faint, and swept beyond control,
Consents to his inexorable will.

4/**Archimedes:** *Greek mathematician*

PHILIP LARKIN (b. 1922)

• LINES ON A YOUNG LADY'S PHOTOGRAPH ALBUM •

At last you yielded up the album, which,
Once open, sent me distracted. All your ages
Matt and glossy on the thick black pages!
Too much confectionery, too rich:
I choke on such nutritious images.   5

My swivel eye hungers from pose to pose—
In pigtails, clutching a reluctant cat;
Or furred yourself, a sweet girl-graduate;
Or lifting a heavy-headed rose
Beneath a trellis, or in a trilby hat   10

(Faintly disturbing, that, in several ways)—
From every side you strike at my control,
Not least through these disquieting chaps who loll
At ease about your earlier days:
Not quite your class, I'd say, dear, on the whole.   15

But o, photography! as no art is,
Faithful and disappointing! that records
Dull days as dull, and hold-it smiles as frauds,
And will not censor blemishes
Like washing lines, and Hall's-Distemper boards,   20

But shows the cat as disinclined, and shades
A chin as doubled when it is, what grace
Your candor thus confers upon her face!
How overwhelmingly persuades
That this is a real girl in a real place,   25

In every sense empirically true!
Or is it just *the past?* Those flowers, that gate,
These misty parks and motors, lacerate
Simply by being over; you
Contract my heart by looking out of date.   30

Yes, true; but in the end, surely, we cry
Not only at exclusion, but because
It leaves us free to cry. We know *what was*
Won't call on us to justify
Our grief, however hard we yowl across   35

---

[10]/**trilby hat:** *a rather mannish hat with brim and indented crown (worn in the stage version of George Du Maurier's 1894 novel* Trilby)
[20]/**washing lines:** *clotheslines*

The gap from eye to page. So I am left
To mourn (without a chance of consequence)
You, balanced on a bike against a fence;
To wonder if you'd spot the theft
Of this one of you bathing; to condense,   *40*

In short, a past that no one now can share,
No matter whose your future; calm and dry,
It holds you like a heaven, and you lie
Unvariably lovely there,
Smaller and clearer as the years go by.   *45*

· AT GRASS ·

The eye can hardly pick them out
From the cold shade they shelter in,
Till wind distresses tail and mane;
Then one crops grass, and moves about
—The other seeming to look on—   *5*
And stands anonymous again.

Yet fifteen years ago, perhaps
Two dozen distances sufficed
To fable them: faint afternoons
Of Cups and Stakes and Handicaps,   *10*
Whereby their names were artificed
To inlay faded, classic Junes—

Silks at the start: against the sky
Numbers and parasols: outside,
Squadrons of empty cars, and heat,   *15*
And littered grass: then the long cry
Hanging unhushed till it subside
To stop-press columns on the street.

Do memories plague their ears like flies?
They shake their heads. Dusk brims the shadows.   *20*
Summer by summer all stole away,
The starting-gates, the crowds and cries—
All but the unmolesting meadows.
Almanacked, their names live; they

Have slipped their names, and stand at ease,   *25*
Or gallop for what must be joy,
And not a fieldglass sees them home,
Or curious stop-watch prophesies:
Only the groom, and the groom's boy,
With bridles in the evening come.   *30*

9/**fable:** *make fabulous or legendary*
18/**stop-press:** *news (of the races) sensational enough to "stop the presses"*

· THE EXPLOSION ·

On the day of the explosion
Shadows pointed towards the pithead:
In the sun the slagheap slept.

Down the lane came men in pitboots
Coughing oath-edged talk and pipe-smoke,   5
Shouldering off the freshened silence.

One chased after rabbits; lost them;
Came back with a nest of lark's eggs;
Showed them; lodged them in the grasses.

So they passed in beards and moleskins,   10
Fathers, brothers, nicknames, laughter,
Through the tall gates standing open.

At noon, there came a tremor; cows
Stopped chewing for a second; sun,
Scarfed as in a heat-haze, dimmed.   15

The dead go on before us, they
Are sitting in God's house in comfort,
We shall see them face to face—

Plain as lettering in the chapels
It was said, and for a second   20
Wives saw men of the explosion

Larger than in life they managed—
Gold as on a coin, or walking
Somehow from the sun towards them,

One showing the eggs unbroken.   25

²/**pithead:** *the top of a mine shaft*

JAMES DICKEY (b. 1923)

· CHERRYLOG ROAD ·

Off Highway 106
At Cherrylog Road I entered
The '34 Ford without wheels,
Smothered in kudzu,

⁴/**kudzu:** *a vine from the Orient that spreads rapidly in much of the South*

With a seat pulled out to run   *5*
Corn whiskey down from the hills,

And then from the other side
Crept into an Essex
With a rumble seat of red leather
And then out again, aboard   *10*
A blue Chevrolet, releasing
The rust from its other color,

Reared up on three building blocks.
None had the same body heat;
I changed with them inward, toward   *15*
The weedy heart of the junkyard,
For I knew that Doris Holbrook
Would escape from her father at noon

And would come from the farm
To seek parts owned by the sun   *20*
Among the abandoned chassis,
Sitting in each in turn
As I did, leaning forward
As in a wild stock-car race

In the parking lot of the dead.   *25*
Time after time, I climbed in
And out the other side, like
An envoy or movie star
Met at the station by crickets.
A radiator cap raised its head,   *30*

Become a real toad or a kingsnake
As I neared the hub of the yard,
Passing through many states,
Many lives, to reach
Some grandmother's long Pierce-Arrow   *35*
Sending platters of blindness forth

From its nickel hubcaps
And spilling its tender upholstery
On sleepy roaches,
The glass panel in between   *40*
Lady and colored driver
Not all the way broken out,

The back-seat phone
Still on its hook.
I got in as though to exclaim,   *45*
"Let us go to the orphan asylum,
John; I have some old toys
For children who say their prayers."

I popped with sweat as I thought
I heard Doris Holbrook scrape   *50*
Like a mouse in the southern-state sun
That was eating the paint in blisters
From a hundred car tops and hoods.
She was tapping like code,

Loosening the screws,   *55*
Carrying off headlights,
Sparkplugs, bumpers,
Cracked mirrors and gear-knobs,
Getting ready, already,
To go back with something to show   *60*

Other than her lips' new trembling
I would hold to me soon, soon,
Where I sat in the ripped back seat
Talking over the interphone,
Praying for Doris Holbrook   *65*
To come from her father's farm

And to get back there
With no trace of me on her face
To be seen by her red-haired father
Who would change, in the squalling barn,   *70*
Her back's pale skin with a strop,
Then lay for me

In a bootlegger's roasting car
With a string-triggered 12-gauge shotgun
To blast the breath from the air.   *75*
Not cut by the jagged windshields,
Through the acres of wrecks she came
With a wrench in her hand,

Through dust where the blacksnake dies
Of boredom, and the beetle knows   *80*
The compost has no more life.
Someone outside would have seen
The oldest car's door inexplicably
Close from within:

I held her and held her and held her,   *85*
Convoyed at terrific speed
By the stalled, dreaming traffic around us,
So the blacksnake, stiff
With inaction, curved back
Into life, and hunted the mouse   *90*

With deadly overexcitement,
The beetles reclaimed their field
As we clung, glued together,
With the hooks of the seat springs
Working through to catch us red-handed   *95*
Amidst the gray breathless batting

That burst from the seat at our backs.
We left by separate doors
Into the changed, other bodies
Of cars, she down Cherrylog Road   *100*
And I to my motorcycle
Parked like the soul of the junkyard

Restored, a bicycle fleshed
With power, and tore off
Up Highway 106, continually   *105*
Drunk on the wind in my mouth,
Wringing the handlebar for speed,
Wild to be wreckage forever.

MAXINE KUMIN (b. 1925)

· THE RETRIEVAL SYSTEM ·

It begins with my dog, now dead, who all his long life
carried about in his head the brown eyes of my father,
keen, loving, accepting, sorrowful, whatever;
they were Daddy's all right, handed on, except
for their phosphorescent gleam tunneling the night   *5*
which I have to concede was a separate gift.

Uncannily when I'm alone these features
come up to link my lost people
with the patient domestic beasts of my life. For example,
the wethered goat who runs free in pasture and stable   *10*
with his flecked, agate eyes and his minus-sign pupils
blats in the tiny voice of my former piano teacher

whose bones beat time in my dreams and whose terrible breath
soured *Country Gardens, Humoresque,* and unplayable Bach.
My elderly aunts, wearing the heads of willful   *15*
intelligent ponies, stand at the fence begging apples.
The sister who died at three has my cat's faint chin,
my cat's inscrutable squint, and cried catlike in pain.

I remember the funeral. *The Lord is my shepherd,*
we said. I don't want to brood. Fact: it is people who fade,   20
it is animals that retrieve them. A boy
I loved once keeps coming back as my yearling colt,
cocksure at the gallop, racing his shadow
for the hell of it. He runs merely to be.
A boy who was lost in the war thirty years ago   25
and buried at sea.

Here, it's forty degrees and raining. The weatherman
who looks like my resident owl, the one who goes out and in
by the open haymow, appears on the TV screen.
With his heart-shaped face, he is also my late dentist's double,   30
donnish, bifocaled, kind. Going a little gray,
advising this wisdom tooth will have to come out someday,
meanwhile filling it as a favor. Another save.
It outlasted him. The forecast is nothing but trouble.
It will snow fiercely enough to fill all these open graves.   35

A. R. AMMONS (b. 1926)

• THE CONSTANT •

When leaving the primrose, bayberry dunes, seaward
I discovered the universe this morning,
          I was in no
mood
for wonder,   5
     the naked mass of so much miracle
already beyond the vision
of my grasp:

along a rise of beach, a hundred feet from the surf,
a row of clam shells   10
     four to ten feet wide
     lay sinuous as far as sight:

in one shell—though in the abundance
          there were others like it—upturned,
four or five inches across the wing,   15
a lake
three to four inches long and two inches wide,
all dimensions rounded,
     indescribable in curve:

and on the lake a turning galaxy, a film of sand,   20
co-ordinated, nearly circular (no real perfections),
     an inch in diameter, turning:
turning:

counterclockwise, the wind hardly perceptible from 11 o'clock
        with noon at sea: *25*
        the galaxy rotating,
        but also,
at a distance from the shell lip,
revolving
round and round the shell: *30*

        a gull's toe could spill the universe:
two more hours of sun could dry it up:
a higher wind could rock it out:

the tide will rise, engulf it, wash it loose:
utterly: *35*

the terns, their
        young somewhere hidden in clumps of grass or weed,
were diving *sshik sshik* at me,
        then pealing upward for another round and dive:

I have had too much of this inexhaustible miracle: *40*
miracle, this massive, drab constant of experience.

· CUT THE GRASS ·

The wonderful workings of the world: wonderful,
wonderful: I'm surprised half the time:
ground up fine, I puff if a pebble stirs:

I'm nervous: my morality's intricate: if
a squash blossom dies, I feel withered as a stained   *5*
zucchini and blame my nature: and

when grassblades flop to the little red-ant
queens burring around trying to get aloft, I blame
my not keeping the grass short, stubble

firm: well, I learn a lot of useless stuff, meant   *10*
to be ignored: like when the sun sinking in the
west glares a plane invisible, I think how much

revelation concealment necessitates: and then I
think of the ocean, multiple to a blinding
oneness and realize that only total expression   *15*

expresses hiding: I'll have to say everything
to take on the roundness and withdrawal of the deep **dark**:
less than total is a bucketful of radiant toys.

8/**burring:** *bustling, fumbling, hurrying*

JAMES MERRILL (b. 1926)

• THE BROKEN HOME •

Crossing the street,
I saw the parents and the child
At their window, gleaming like fruit
With evening's mild gold leaf.

In a room on the floor below,   5
Sunless, cooler—a brimming
Saucer of wax, marbly and dim—
I have lit what's left of my life.

I have thrown out yesterday's milk
And opened a book of maxims.   10
The flame quickens. The word stirs.

Tell me, tongue of fire,
That you and I are as real
At least as the people upstairs.

My father, who had flown in World War I,   15
Might have continued to invest his life
In cloud banks well above Wall Street and wife.
But the race was run below, and the point was to win.

Too late now, I make out in his blue gaze
(Through the smoked glass of being thirty-six)   20
The soul eclipsed by twin black pupils, sex
And business; time was money in those days.

Each thirteenth year he married. When he died
There were already several chilled wives
In sable orbit—rings, cars, permanent waves.   25

We'd felt him warming up for a green bride.
He could afford it. He was "in his prime"
At three score ten. But money was not time.

When my parents were younger this was a popular act:
A veiled woman would leap from an electric, wine-dark car   30
To the steps of no matter what—the Senate or the Ritz Bar—
And bodily, at newsreel speed, attack

ANTHOLOGY

No matter whom—Al Smith or José Maria Sert
Or Clemenceau—veins standing out on her throat
As she yelled *War mongerer! Pig! Give us the vote!*,   35
And would have to be hauled away in her hobble skirt.

What had the man done? Oh, made history.
Her business (he had implied) was giving birth,
Tending the house, mending the socks.

Always that same old story—   40
Father Time and Mother Earth,
A marriage on the rocks.

One afternoon, red, satyr-thighed
Michael, the Irish setter, head
Passionately lowered, led   45
The child I was to a shut door. Inside,

Blinds beat sun from the bed.
The green-gold room throbbed like a bruise.
Under a sheet, clad in taboos
Lay whom we sought, her hair undone, outspread,   50

And of a blackness found, if ever now, in old
Engravings where the acid bit.
I must have needed to touch it
Or the whiteness—was she dead?
Her eyes flew open, startled strange and cold.   55
The dog slumped to the floor. She reached for me. I fled.

Tonight they have stepped out onto the gravel.
The party is over. It's the fall
Of 1931. They love each other still.

She: Charlie, I can't stand the pace.   60
He: Come on, honey—why, you'll bury us all!

A lead soldier guards my windowsill:
Khaki rifle, uniform, and face.
Something in me grows heavy, silvery, pliable.

---

[33]/**Al Smith:** *New York politician; governor from 1919 to 1928, presidential candidate against Hoover in 1928*
   José Maria Sert: *Spanish painter famous for his New York murals*
[34]/**Clemenceau:** *French statesman; leader in World War I*
[36]/**hobble skirt:** *long narrow skirt, popular from about 1910 to 1914*

How intensely people used to feel!   65
Like metal poured at the close of a proletarian novel,
Refined and glowing from the crucible,
I see those two hearts, I'm afraid,
Still. Cool here in the graveyard of good and evil,
They are even so to be honored and obeyed.   70

. . . Obeyed, at least, inversely. Thus
I rarely buy a newspaper, or vote.
To do so, I have learned, is to invite
The tread of a stone guest within my house.

Shooting this rusted bolt, though, against him,   75
I trust I am no less time's child than some
Who on the heath impersonate Poor Tom
Or on the barricades risk life and limb.

Nor do I try to keep a garden, only
An avocado in a glass of water—   80
Roots pallid, gemmed with air. And later,

When the small gilt leaves have grown
Fleshy and green, I let them die, yes, yes,
And start another. I am earth's no less.

A child, a red dog roam the corridors,   85
Still, of the broken home. No sound. The brilliant
Rag runners halt before wide-open doors.
My old room! Its wallpaper—cream, medallioned
With pink and brown—brings back the first nightmares,
Long summer colds, and Emma, sepia-faced,   90
Perspiring over broth carried upstairs
Aswim with golden fats I could not taste.

The real house became a boarding-school.
Under the ballroom ceiling's allegory
Someone at last may actually be allowed   95
To learn something; or, from my window, cool
With the unstiflement of the entire story,
Watch a red setter stretch and sink in cloud.

74/**a stone guest:** *as Don Giovanni, in Mozart's opera of that name, invites the
stone statue of the man he killed to come to dinner. The statue appears and drags
Don Giovanni down to hell*
77/**Poor Tom:** *cf. King Lear, III, iv, where the old king is attended by Edgar,
Gloucester's son, disguised as a "Bedlam beggar" (cf. "Loving Mad Tom," p. 415)*

DAVID WAGONER (b. 1926)

· STAYING ALIVE ·

Staying alive in the woods is a matter of calming down
At first and deciding whether to wait for rescue,
Trusting to others,
Or simply to start walking and walking in one direction
Till you come out—or something happens to stop you.   5
By far the safer choice
Is to settle down where you are, and try to make a living
Off the land, camping near water, away from shadows.
Eat no white berries;
Spit out all bitterness. Shooting at anything   10
Means hiking further and further every day
To hunt survivors;
It may be best to learn what you have to learn without a gun,
Not killing but watching birds and animals go
In and out of shelter   15
At will. Following their example, build for a whole season:
Facing across the wind in your lean-to,
You may feel wilder,
But nothing, not even you, will have to stay in hiding.
If you have no matches, a stick and a fire-bow   20
Will keep you warmer,
Or the crystal of your watch, filled with water, held up to the sun
Will do the same in time. In case of snow
Drifting toward winter,
Don't try to stay awake through the night, afraid of freezing—   25
The bottom of your mind knows all about zero;
It will turn you over
And shake you till you waken. If you have trouble sleeping
Even in the best of weather, jumping to follow
With eyes strained to their corners   30
The unidentifiable noises of the night and feeling
Bears and packs of wolves nuzzling your elbow,
Remember the trappers
Who treated them indifferently and were left alone.
If you hurt yourself, no one will comfort you   35
Or take your temperature,
So stumbling, wading, and climbing are as dangerous as flying.
But if you decide, at last, you must break through
In spite of all danger,
Think of yourself by time and not by distance, counting   40
Wherever you're going by how long it takes you;
No other measure
Will bring you safe to nightfall. Follow no streams: they run
Under the ground or fall into wilder country.   45
Remember the stars
And moss when your mind runs into circles. If it should rain

Or the fog should roll the horizon in around you,
Hold still for hours
Or days if you must, or weeks, for seeing is believing
In the wilderness. And if you find a pathway,   50
Wheel-rut, or fence-wire,
Retrace it left or right: someone knew where he was going
Once upon a time, and you can follow
Hopefully, somewhere,
Just in case. There may even come, on some uncanny evening,   55
A time when you're warm and dry, well fed, not thirsty,
Uninjured, without fear,
When nothing, either good or bad, is happening.
This is called staying alive. It's temporary.
What occurs after   60
Is doubtful. You must always be ready for something to come bursting
Through the far edge of a clearing, running toward you,
Grinning from ear to ear
And hoarse with welcome. Or something crossing and hovering
Overhead, as light as air, like a break in the sky,   65
Wondering what you are.
Here you are face to face with the problem of recognition.
Having no time to make smoke, too much to say,
You should have a mirror
With a tiny hole in the back for better aiming, for reflecting   70
Whatever disaster you can think of, to show
The way you suffer.
These body signals have universal meaning: If you are lying
Flat on your back with arms outstretched behind you,
You say you require   75
Emergency treatment: if you are standing erect and holding
Arms horizontal, you mean you are not ready;
If you hold them over
Your head, you want to be picked up. Three of anything
Is a sign of distress. Afterward, if you see   80
No ropes, no ladders,
No maps or messages falling, no searchlights or trails blazing,
Then, chances are, you should be prepared to burrow
Deep for a deep winter.

JOHN ASHBERY (b. 1927)

• THE INSTRUCTION MANUAL •

As I sit looking out of a window of the building
I wish I did not have to write the instruction manual on the uses of a
    new metal.
I look down into the street and see people, each walking with an
    inner peace,

And envy them—they are so far away from me!
Not one of them has to worry about getting out this manual on
    schedule. 5
And, as my way is, I begin to dream, resting my elbows on the desk
    and leaning out of the window a little,
Of dim Guadalajara! City of rose-colored flowers!
City I wanted most to see, and most did not see, in Mexico!
But I fancy I see, under the press of having to write the instruction
    manual,
Your public square, city, with its elaborate little bandstand! 10
The band is playing *Scheherazade* by Rimsky-Korsakov.
Around stand the flower girls, handing out rose- and lemon-colored
    flowers,
Each attractive in her rose-and-blue striped dress (Oh! such shades
    of rose and blue),
And nearby is the little white booth where women in green serve you
    green and yellow fruit.
The couples are parading; everyone is in a holiday mood. 15
First, leading the parade, is a dapper fellow
Clothed in deep blue. On his head sits a white hat
And he wears a mustache, which has been trimmed for the occasion.
His dear one, his wife, is young and pretty; her shawl is rose,
    pink and white.
Her slippers are patent leather, in the American fashion, 20
And she carries a fan, for she is modest, and does not want the
    crowd to see her face too often.
But everybody is so busy with his wife or loved one
I doubt they would notice the mustachioed man's wife.
Here come the boys! They are skipping and throwing little things on
    the sidewalk
Which is made of gray tile. One of them, a little older, has a
    toothpick in his teeth. 25
He is silenter than the rest, and affects not to notice the pretty young
    girls in white.
But his friends notice them, and shout their jeers at the laughing
    girls.
Yet soon all this will cease, with the deepening of their years,
And love bring each to the parade grounds for another reason.
But I have lost sight of the young fellow with the toothpick. 30
Wait—there he is—on the other side of the bandstand,
Secluded from his friends, in earnest talk with a young girl
Of fourteen or fifteen. I try to hear what they are saying
But it seems they are just mumbling something—shy words of love,
    probably.
She is slightly taller than he, and looks quietly down into his sincere
    eyes. 35
She is wearing white. The breeze ruffles her long fine black hair
    against her olive cheek.
Obviously she is in love. The boy, the young boy with the toothpick,
    he is in love too;

His eyes show it. Turning from this couple,
I see there is an intermission in the concert.
The paraders are resting and sipping drinks through straws   40
(The drinks are dispensed from a large glass crock by a lady in dark
       blue),
And the musicians mingle among them, in their creamy white
       uniforms, and talk
About the weather, perhaps, or how their kids are doing at school.

Let us take this opportunity to tiptoe into one of the side streets.
Here you may see one of those white houses with green trim   45
That are so popular here. Look—I told you!
It is cool and dim inside, but the patio is sunny.
An old woman in gray sits there, fanning herself with a palm leaf
       fan.
She welcomes us to her patio, and offers us a cooling drink.
"My son is in Mexico City," she says. "He would welcome you too   50
If he were here. But his job is with a bank there.
Look, here is a photograph of him."
And a dark-skinned lad with pearly teeth grins out at us from the
       worn leather frame.
We thank her for her hospitality, for it is getting late
And we must catch a view of the city, before we leave, from a good
       high place.   55
That church tower will do—the faded pink one, there against the
       fierce blue of the sky. Slowly we enter.
The caretaker, an old man dressed in brown and gray, asks us how
       long we have been in the city, and how we like it here.
His daughter is scrubbing the steps—she nods to us as we pass into
       the tower.
Soon we have reached the top, and the whole network of the city
       extends before us.
There is the rich quarter, with its houses of pink and white, and its
       crumbling, leafy terraces.   60
There is the poorer quarter, its homes a deep blue.
There is the market, where men are selling hats and swatting flies
And there is the public library, painted several shades of pale green
       and beige.
Look! There is the square we just came from, with the promenaders.
There are fewer of them, now that the heat of the day has increased,   65
But the young boy and girl still lurk in the shadows of the
       bandstand.
And there is the home of the little old lady—
She is still sitting in the patio, fanning herself.
How limited, but how complete withal, has been our experience of
       Guadalajara!
We have seen young love, married love, and the love of an aged
       mother for her son.   70

69/**withal:** *nevertheless*

We have heard the music, tasted the drinks, and looked at colored
    houses.
What more is there to do, except stay? And that we cannot do.
And as a last breeze freshens the top of the weathered old tower,
    I turn my gaze
Back to the instruction manual which has made me dream of
    Guadalajara.

JAMES WRIGHT (1927–1980)

· SPEAK ·

To speak in a flat voice
Is all that I can do.
I have gone every place
Asking for you.
Wondering where to turn   5
And how the search would end
And the last streetlight spin
Above me blind.

Then I returned rebuffed
And saw under the sun   10
The race not to the swift
Nor the battle won.
Liston dives in the tank,
Lord, in Lewiston, Maine,
And Ernie Doty's drunk   15
In hell again.

And Jenny, oh my Jenny
Whom I love, rhyme be damned,
Has broken her spare beauty
In a whorehouse old.   20
She left her new baby
In a bus-station can,
And sprightly danced away
Through Jacksontown.

[9-12]/**I returned . . . the battle won:** *Cf.* Ecclesiastes 9:11: *"I returned, and saw under the sun, that the race is not to the swift, nor the battle to the strong, neither yet bread to the wise, nor yet riches to men of understanding, nor yet favor to men of skill; but time and chance happeneth to them all."*
[13]/**Liston dives . . .:** *in May 1965, "Sonny" Liston was K.O.'d by Cassius Clay (now Muhammad Ali) in one of the shortest title fights on record.*
[15]/**Ernie Doty:** *a distant family friend of the poet's. Doty was executed for rape and murder.*

Which is a place I know,   25
One where I got picked up
A few shrunk years ago
By a good cop.
Believe it, Lord, or not.
Don't ask me who he was.   30
I speak of flat defeat
In a flat voice.

I have gone forward with
Some, a few lonely some.
They have fallen to death.   35
I die with them.
Lord, I have loved Thy cursed,
The beauty of Thy house:
Come down. Come down. Why dost
Thou hide thy face?   40

37-40/*Cf.* Psalm 26:8 (*"Lord, I have loved the habitation* [*some translate it* *"beauty"*] *of thy house* . . .*")* *and* Psalm 27:9 (*"Hide not thy face from me* . . .*")*

PETER DAVISON (b. 1928)

· MY LADY THE LAKE ·

It is the lake within the lake that drowns.
Sunbeams gnaw into its dark, never again
to be released as light. The lake swallows
whatever it is fed. It eats its ice each spring,
nibbles for years at fallen twigs and timber,   5
engorges the heat of summer with each sunset,
closes around corpse of dragonfly and beaver.
By its waters I have sat down and wept, without
taking any comfort or return
except for the offer of what it has translated: 10
frogs, crayfish, sticklebacks. The trout
stocked by a prescient owner crammed themselves,
after the passage of several seasons, up
against its banks to die. It devoured their bones.
Still water gives us only a reflection.   15
Whatever we cast in, it will accept,
and in such lakes within the lake we drown.

ANNE SEXTON (1928–1975)

· PAIN FOR A DAUGHTER ·

Blind with love, my daughter
has cried nightly for horses,
those long-necked marchers and churners
that she has mastered, any and all,
reigning them in like a circus hand—   5
the excitable muscles and the ripe neck;
tending this summer, a pony and a foal.
She who is too squeamish to pull
a thorn from the dog's paw,
watched her pony blossom with distemper,   10
the underside of the jaw swelling
like an enormous grape.
Gritting her teeth with love,
she drained the boil and scoured it
with hydrogen peroxide until pus   15
ran like milk on the barn floor.

Blind with loss all winter,
in dungarees, a ski jacket and a hard hat,
she visits the neighbors' stable,
our acreage not zoned for barns;   20
they who own the flaming horses
and the swan-whipped thoroughbred
that she tugs at and cajoles,
thinking it will burn like a furnace
under her small-hipped English seat.   25

Blind with pain she limps home.
The thoroughbred has stood on her foot.
He rested there like a building.
He grew into her foot until they were one.
The marks of the horseshoe printed   30
into her flesh, the tips of her toes
ripped off like pieces of leather,
three toenails swirled like shells
and left to float in blood in her riding boot.

Blind with fear, she sits on the toilet,   35
her foot balanced over the washbasin,
her father, hydrogen peroxide in hand,
performing the rites of the cleansing.
She bites on a towel, sucked in breath,
sucked in and arched against the pain,   40
her eyes glancing off me where
I stand at the door, eyes locked
on the ceiling, eyes of a stranger,

and then she cries . . .
Oh my God, help me!   45
Where a child would have cried *Mama!*
Where a child would have believed *Mama!*
she bit the towel and called on God
and I saw her life stretch out . . .
I saw her torn in childbirth,   50
and I saw her, at that moment,
in her own death and I knew that she
knew.

PHILIP LEVINE (b. 1928)

· KEEP TALKING ·

If it ain't simply this, what is it?
he wanted to know, and she answered,
"If it ain't just this it ain't nothing,"
and they turned off the light, locked
the door, and went downstairs and out   5
of the hotel and started looking around
for a bar that would stay open all night.
In the first one she said, "When do
you close?" The bartender said, "What's
yours?" Then he got mad, her man,   10
because she'd asked politely, and so
he shouted, "Please answer the question."
Then he said, "How late are you open?"
"Until the law says we gotta close."
They went out into the early summer   15
which was still light even though
kids were probably already in bed.
The wind stood out against the sails
on the Sound, and the last small boats
were coming in on the blackening waters.   20
After a while he said, "Maybe we could
just eat and take a long walk or sit
somewhere for a while and say things."
She didn't answer. The wind had picked
up and just might have blown his words   25
into nothing. "Why don't we talk?"
he said. She turned and stared right
into his eyes, which were light blue
and seemed to be bulging out with tears.
He was unshaven and wore a wool cap   30
which he'd removed. "I've been here
before," he said, "as a boy I wanted
to talk about things, but there was no

one to talk to." "Talk to me," she said.
"I don't know what to say. I didn't   35
know then." "When," she said. "When
I was a boy." So she explained that
being a kid was not knowing what to say
but that now he was a grown man. The lights
of the city were coming on, the high   40
ones in the tall buildings repeated
themselves in the still waters now as dark
as the night would ever be. He thought
about what she'd said and was sure
it had been different, that other kids   45
spoke about who they were or walked
with each other and said all the things
that jumbled in his head then and now.
He sat down on the curb and pressed
his face into his knees. She just stood   50
looking down at the shaven white back
of his neck, thin and childish, and she
thought, If it ain't this what is it?

GARY SNYDER (b. 1930)

• MOTHER EARTH: HER WHALES •

An owl winks in the shadows
A lizard lifts on tiptoe, breathing hard
Young male sparrow stretches up his neck,
        big head, watching—

The grasses are working in the sun. Turn it green.   5
Turn it sweet. That we may eat.
Grow our meat.

Brazil says "sovereign use of Natural Resources"
Thirty thousand kinds of unknown plants.
The living actual people of the jungle   10
        sold and tortured—
And a robot in a suit who peddles a delusion called "Brazil"
        can speak for *them?*

        The whales turn and glisten, plunge
                and sound and rise again,   15
        Hanging over subtly darkening deeps
        Flowing like breathing planets
                in the sparkling whorls of
                        living light—

And Japan quibbles for words on   *20*
    what kinds of whales they can kill?
A once-great Buddhist nation
    dribbles methyl mercury
    like gonorrhea
        in the sea.   *25*

Père David's Deer, the Elaphure,
Lived in the tule marshes of the Yellow River
Two thousand years ago—and lost its home to rice—
The forests of Lo-yang were logged and all the silt &
Sand flowed down, and gone, by 1200 AD—   *30*
Wild Geese hatched out in Siberia
        head south over basins of the Yang, the Huang,
        what we call "China"
On flyways they have used a million years.
Ah China, where are the tigers, the wild boars,   *35*
        the monkeys,
            like the snows of yesteryear
Gone in a mist, a flash, and the dry hard ground
Is parking space for fifty thousand trucks.
IS man most precious of all things?   *40*
—then let us love him, and his brothers, all those
Fading living beings—

North America, Turtle Island, taken by invaders
    who wage war around the world.
May ants, may abalone, otters, wolves and elk   *45*
Rise! and pull away their giving
    from the robot nations.

23/**methyl mercury:** *Cf. Gary Snyder,* The Real Work, *p. 144: ". . . the Indian people in Ontario had to respond to the fact of methyl mercury coming into their waters and giving them Minamata disease. (The disease named after a fishing village in Japan in which hundreds of people died and suffered nerve damage from the dumping of methyl mercury into their bay where it subsequently worked its way into their food chain.")*

26/**Père David's Deer:** *a large, rare Asian deer (Elaphurus davidianus), described in 1866 by a French missionary, Père Armand David. Its original home was presumably in China. Within historic times it has not been found in a natural habitat; specimens exist only in zoos and on private estates. The Yellow River is in China.*

27/**tule** *(tóo-lee): a type of reed or rush. In* The Real Work *(p. 24) Snyder deplores the environmental changes brought about by the draining of the tule swamps in central California.*

37/**the snows of yesteryear:** *Dante Gabriel Rossetti's translation of the refrain of Villon's "Ballade des Dames du Temps Jadis" ("But where are the snows of yester-year?") gives us this famous phrase.*

43/**Turtle Island:** *". . . the old/new name for the continent, based on many creation myths of the people who have been living here for millennia, and reapplied by some of them to 'North America' in recent years. Also, an idea found worldwide, of the earth, or cosmos even, sustained by a great turtle or serpent-of-eternity." (*Turtle Island, *Introductory note)*

Solidarity. The People.
Standing Tree People!
Flying Bird People!   *50*
Swimming Sea People!
Four-legged, two-legged, people!

How can the head-heavy power-hungry politic scientist
Government   two-world   Capitalist-Imperialist
Third-world   Communist   paper-shuffling male   *55*
        non-farmer   jet-set   bureaucrats
Speak for the green of the leaf? Speak for the soil?

(Ah Margaret Mead . . . do you sometimes dream of Samoa?)

The robots argue how to parcel out our Mother Earth
To last a little longer   *60*
            like vultures flapping
Belching, gurgling,
            near a dying Doe.

"In yonder field a slain knight lies—
We'll fly to him and eat his eyes   *65*
        with a down
    derry derry derry down down."

        An Owl winks in the shadow
        A lizard lifts on tiptoe
                breathing hard   *70*
        The whales turn and glisten
                plunge and
        Sound, and rise again
        Flowing like breathing planets

        In the sparkling whorls   *75*

        Of living light.

                            Stockholm: Summer Solstice 40072

⁴⁸/**The People:** *"What we must find a way to do, then, is incorporate the other people—what the Sioux Indians call the creeping people, and the standing people, and the flying people, and the swimming people—into the councils of government"* (Turtle Island, p. 108). Snyder has declared his "political position is to be a spokesman for wild nature."

⁵⁸/**Margaret Mead:** *her anthropological classic* Coming of Age in Samoa *(1928) describes the joys and difficulties of youth in a culture very unlike our own.*

⁶⁴⁻⁶⁷/**"In yonder field . . . down":** *the mention of "Doe" in the line above recalls to the poet the old ballads of "The Three Ravens" and "The Twa Corbies." His four lines blend memories of the two.*

Summer Solstice 40072: *The summer solstice, June 22, marks the beginning of summer. "40072" means 1972. Snyder frequently mentions that the human race, "as it immediately concerns us," has a history of about 40,000 years. In 1967 he dated one of his essays "Eighth Moon, 40067 (reckoning roughly from the earliest cave paintings)."*

TED HUGHES (b. 1930)

· PIKE ·

Pike, three inches long, perfect
Pike in all parts, green tigering the gold.
Killers from the egg: the malevolent aged grin.
They dance on the surface among the flies.

Or move, stunned by their own grandeur,   5
Over a bed of emerald, silhouette
Of submarine delicacy and horror.
A hundred feet long in their world.

In ponds, under the heat-struck lily pads—
Gloom of their stillness: 10
Logged on last year's black leaves, watching upwards.
Or hung in an amber cavern of weeds

The jaws' hooked clamp and fangs
Not to be changed at this date;
A life subdued to its instrument;   15
The gills kneading quietly, and the pectorals.

Three we kept behind glass,
Jungled in weed: three inches, four,
And four and a half: fed fry to them—
Suddenly there were two. Finally one.   20

With a sag belly and the grin it was born with.
And indeed they spare nobody.
Two, six pounds each, over two feet long,
High and dry and dead in the willow-herb—

One jammed past its gills down the other's gullet: 25
The outside eye stared: as a vice locks—
The same iron in this eye
Though its film shrank in death.

A pond I fished, fifty yards across,
Whose lilies and muscular tench   30
Had outlasted every visible stone
Of the monastery that planted them—

Stilled legendary depth:
It was as deep as England. It held
Pike too immense to stir, so immense and old   35
That past nightfall I dared not cast

30/**tench:** *a European freshwater fish of the carp family*

But silently cast and fished
With the hair frozen on my head
For what might move, for what eye might move.
The still splashes on the dark pond,   *40*

Owls hushing the floating woods
Frail on my ear against the dream
Darkness beneath night's darkness had freed,
That rose slowly towards me, watching.

DEREK WALCOTT (b. 1930)

• SABBATHS, W.I. •

Those villages stricken with the melancholia of Sunday,
in all of whose ocher streets one dog is sleeping

those volcanoes like ashen roses, or the incurable sore
of poverty, around whose puckered mouth thin boys are
selling yellow sulphur stone   *5*

the burnt banana leaves that used to dance
the river whose bed is made of broken bottles
the cocoa grove where a bird whose cry sounds green and
yellow and in the lights under the leaves crested with
orange flame has forgotten its flute   *10*

gommiers peeling from sunburn still wrestling to escape the sea

the dead lizard turning blue as stone

those rivers, threads of spittle, that forgot the old music

that dry, brief esplanade under the drier sea almonds
where the dry old men sat   *15*

watching a white schooner stuck in the branches
and playing draughts with the moving frigate birds

those hillsides like broken pots
those ferns that stamped their skeletons on the skin

and those roads that begin reciting their names at vespers   *20*

W.I.: *West Indies*
11/**gommiers:** *gum trees*

mention them and they will stop
those crabs that were willing to let an epoch pass
those herons like spinsters that doubted their reflections
inquiring, inquiring

those nettles that waited   25
those Sundays, those Sundays

those Sundays when the lights at the road's end were an occasion

those Sundays when my mother lay on her back
those Sundays when the sisters gathered like white moths
round their street lantern   30

and cities passed us by on the horizon

SYLVIA PLATH (1932–1963)

· TULIPS ·

The tulips are too excitable, it is winter here.
Look how white everything is, how quiet, how snowed-in.
I am learning peacefulness, lying by myself quietly
As the light lies on these white walls, this bed, these hands.
I am nobody; I have nothing to do with explosions.   5
I have given my name and my day-clothes up to the nurses
And my history to the anaesthetist and my body to surgeons.

They have propped my head between the pillow and the sheet-cuff
Like an eye between two white lids that will not shut.
Stupid pupil, it has to take everything in.   10
The nurses pass and pass, they are no trouble,
They pass the way gulls pass inland in their white caps,
Doing things with their hands, one just the same as another,
So it is impossible to tell how many there are.

My body is a pebble to them, they tend it as water   15
Tends to the pebbles it must run over, smoothing them gently.
They bring me numbness in their bright needles, they bring me sleep.
Now I have lost myself I am sick of baggage—
My patent leather overnight case like a black pillbox,
My husband and child smiling out of the family photo;
Their smiles catch onto my skin, little smiling hooks.   20

I have let things slip, a thirty-year-old cargo boat
Stubbornly hanging on to my name and address.
They have swabbed me clear of my loving associations.

Scared and bare on the green plastic-pillowed trolley   25
I watched my tea-set, my bureaus of linen, my books
Sink out of sight, and the water went over my head.
I am a nun now, I have never been so pure.

I didn't want any flowers, I only wanted
To lie with my hands turned up and be utterly empty.   30
How free it is, you have no idea how free—
The peacefulness is so big it dazes you,
And it asks nothing, a name tag, a few trinkets.
It is what the dead close on, finally; I imagine them
Shutting their mouths on it, like a Communion tablet.   35

The tulips are too red in the first place, they hurt me.
Even through the gift paper I could hear them breathe
Lightly, through their white swaddlings, like an awful baby.
Their redness talks to my wound, it corresponds.
They are subtle: they seem to float, though they weigh me down,   40
Upsetting me with their sudden tongues and their colour,
A dozen red lead sinkers round my neck.

Nobody watched me before, now I am watched.
The tulips turn to me, and the window behind me
Where once a day the light slowly widens and slowly thins,   45
And I see myself, flat, ridiculous, a cut-paper shadow
Between the eye of the sun and the eyes of the tulips,
And I have no face, I have wanted to efface myself.
The vivid tulips eat my oxygen.

Before they came the air was calm enough,   50
Coming and going, breath by breath, without any fuss.
Then the tulips filled it up like a loud noise.
Now the air snags and eddies round them the way a river
Snags and eddies round a sunken rust-red engine.
They concentrate my attention, that was happy   55
Playing and resting without committing itself.

The walls, also, seem to be warming themselves.
The tulips should be behind bars like dangerous animals;
They are opening like the mouth of some great African cat,
And I am aware of my heart: it opens and closes   60
Its bowl of red blooms out of sheer love of me.
The water I taste is warm and salt, like the sea,
And comes from a country far away as health.

MARK STRAND (b. 1934)

• THE TUNNEL •

A man has been standing
in front of my house
for days. I peek at him
from the living room
window and at night,   5
unable to sleep,
I shine my flashlight
down on the lawn.
He is always there.

After a while   10
I open the front door
just a crack and order
him out of my yard.
He narrows his eyes
and moans. I slam   15
the door and dash back
to the kitchen, then up
to the bedroom, then down.

I weep like a schoolgirl
and make obscene gestures   20
through the window. I
write large suicide notes
and place them so he
can read them easily.
I destroy the living   25
room furniture to prove
I own nothing of value.

When he seems unmoved
I decide to dig a tunnel
to a neighboring yard.   30
I seal the basement off
from the upstairs with
a brick wall. I dig hard
and in no time the tunnel
is done. Leaving my pick   35
and shovel below,

I come out in front of a house
and stand there too tired to
move or even speak, hoping
someone will help me.   40
I feel I'm being watched

and sometimes I hear
a man's voice,
but nothing is done
and I have been waiting for days.   *45*

· WHERE ARE THE WATERS OF CHILDHOOD? ·

See where the windows are boarded up,
where the gray siding shines in the sun and salt air
and the asphalt shingles on the roof have peeled or fallen off,
where tiers of oxeye daisies float on a sea of grass?
That's the place to begin.   *5*

Enter the kingdom of rot,
smell the damp plaster, step over the shattered glass,
the pockets of dust, the rags, the soiled remains of a mattress,
look at the rusted stove and sink, at the rectangular stain
on the wall where Winslow Homer's *Gulf Stream* hung.   *10*

Go to the room where your father and mother
would let themselves go in the drift and pitch of love,
and hear, if you can, the creak of their bed,
then go to the place where you hid.

Go to your room, to all the rooms whose cold, damp air you breathed,   *15*
to all the unwanted places where summer, fall, winter, spring,
seem the same unwanted season, where the trees you knew have died
and other trees have risen. Visit that other place
you barely recall, that other house half hidden.

See the two dogs burst into sight. When you leave,   *20*
they will cease, snuffed out in the glare of an earlier light.
Visit the neighbors down the block; he waters his lawn,
she sits on her porch, but not for long.
When you look again they are gone.

Keep going back, back to the field, flat and sealed in mist.   *25*
On the other side, a man and a woman are waiting;
they have come back, your mother before she was gray,
your father before he was white.

Now look at the North West Arm, how it glows a deep cerulean blue.
See the light on the grass, the one leaf burning, the cloud   *30*
that flares. You're almost there, in a moment your parents
will disappear, leaving you under the light of a vanished star,
under the dark of a star newly born. Now is the time.

Now you invent the boat of your flesh and set it upon the waters
and drift in the gradual swell, in the laboring salt.   *35*
Now you look down. The waters of childhood are there.

CHARLES SIMIC (b. 1938)

• BABY PICTURES OF FAMOUS DICTATORS •

The epoch of a streetcar drawn by horses;
The organ-grinder and his monkey.
Women with parasols. Little kids in rowboats
Photographed against a cardboard backdrop depicting an idyllic sunset
At the fairgrounds where they all went to see   5
The two-headed calf, the bearded
Fat lady who dances the dance of seven veils.

And the great famine raging through India . . .
Fortune-telling white rats pulling a card out of a shoebox
While Edison worries over the lightbulb,   10
And the first model of the sewing machine
Is delivered in a pushcart
To a modest white-fenced home in the suburbs,

Where there are always a couple of infants
Posing for the camera in their sailors' suits,   15
Out there in the garden overgrown with shrubs.
Lovable little mugs smiling faintly toward
The new century. Innocent. Why not?
All of them like ragdolls of the period
With those chubby porcelain heads   20
That shut their eyelashes as you lay them down.

In a kind of perpetual summer twilight . . .
One can even make out the shadow of the tripod and the black hood
That must have been quivering in the breeze.
One assumes that they all stayed up late squinting at the stars,   25
And were carried off to bed by their mothers and big sisters,
While the dogs remained behind:
Pedigreed bitches pregnant with bloodhounds.

SEAMUS HEANEY (b. 1939)

• DEATH OF A NATURALIST •

All year the flax-dam festered in the heart
Of the townland; green and heavy headed
Flax had rotted there, weighted down by huge sods.
Daily it sweltered in the punishing sun.
Bubbles gargled delicately, bluebottles   5
Wove a strong gauze of sound around the smell.
There were dragon-flies, spotted butterflies,

But best of all was the warm thick slobber
Of frogspawn that grew like clotted water
In the shade of the banks. Here, every spring   *10*
I would fill jampotfuls of the jellied
Specks to range on window-sills at home,
On shelves at school, and wait and watch until
The fattening dots burst into nimble-
Swimming tadpoles. Miss Walls would tell us how   *15*
The daddy frog was called a bullfrog
And how he croaked and how the mammy frog
Laid hundreds of little eggs and this was
Frogspawn. You could tell the weather by frogs too
For they were yellow in the sun and brown   *20*
In rain.

    Then one hot day when fields were rank
With cowdung in the grass the angry frogs
Invaded the flax-dam; I ducked through hedges
To a coarse croaking that I had not heard   *25*
Before. The air was thick with a bass chorus.
Right down the dam gross-bellied frogs were cocked
On sods; their loose necks pulsed like sails. Some hopped:
The slap and plop were obscene threats. Some sat
Poised like mud grenades, their blunt heads farting.   *30*
I sickened, turned, and ran. The great slime kings
Were gathered there for vengeance and I knew
That if I dipped my hand the spawn would clutch it.

MARGARET ATWOOD (b. 1939)

· SIREN SONG ·

This is the one song everyone
would like to learn: the song
that is irresistible:

the song that forces men
to leap overboard in squadrons   *5*
even though they see the beached skulls

the song nobody knows
because anyone who has heard it
is dead, and the others can't remember.

Shall I tell you the secret   *10*
and if I do, will you get me
out of this bird suit?

I don't enjoy it here
squatting on this island
looking picturesque and mythical   *15*

with these two feathery maniacs,
I don't enjoy singing
this trio, fatal and valuable.

I will tell the secret to you,
to you, only to you.   *20*
Come closer. This song

is a cry for help: Help me!
Only you, only you can,
you are unique

at last. Alas   *25*
it is a boring song
but it works every time.

LOUISE GLÜCK (b. 1943)

· THE SCHOOL CHILDREN ·

The children go forward with their little satchels.
And all morning the mothers have labored
to gather the late apples, red and gold,
like words of another language.

And on the other shore   *5*
are those who wait behind great desks
to receive these offerings.

How orderly they are—the nails
on which the children hang
their overcoats of blue or yellow wool.   *10*

And the teachers shall instruct them in silence
and the mothers shall scour the orchards for a way out,
drawing to themselves the gray limbs of the fruit trees
bearing so little ammunition.

ALICE WALKER (b. 1944)

· EVEN AS I HOLD YOU ·

Even as I hold you
I think of you as someone gone
far, far away. Your eyes the color
of pennies in a bowl of dark honey
bringing sweet light to someone else   5
your black hair slipping through my fingers
is the flash of your head going
around a corner
your smile, breaking before me,
the flippant last turn   10
of a revolving door,
emptying you out, changed,
away from me.

Even as I hold you
I am letting go.   15

· "GOOD NIGHT, WILLIE LEE, I'LL · SEE YOU IN THE MORNING"

Looking down into my father's
dead face
for the last time
my mother said without
tears, without smiles   5
without regrets
but with *civility*
"Good night, Willie Lee, I'll see you
in the morning."
And it was then I knew that the healing   10
of all our wounds
is forgiveness
that permits a promise
of our return
at the end.   15

ROBERT MORGAN (b. 1944)

• FINDING AN OLD NEWSPAPER IN THE WOODS •

The sheets are exposed like film
photographing the gray and yellow seasons of decay.
The weather has flattened them to coarse
paper of leaves and pine needles.
They are almost dust.   5
The print has crawled off
and gone back to live with the ants.

• BEES AWATER •

You find one drinking at the creek,
scratching and drinking
before take-off.
He lifts back
and takes aim, firing homeward.   5
That's the moment to get your sighting,
get the direction and slant of climb
and you'll be looking right at the tree
on the ridge above
where the honey hangs inside   10
like cells of a battery
charged with sweetness.
The whole tree has the hum of a transformer.
Bees bubble, circling
like electrons.   15

Though excited as before a holdup
and hot from the long climb,
you drop the ax
and wait for dark.

ELIZABETH LIBBEY (b. 1947)

• THE GESTURE •

*In every parting there comes a moment when
the beloved is already no longer with us.*
Flaubert, *Sentimental Education*

He leans forward in his chair.
She gazes
over the rim of her wine glass, at the candle
unlit between them.
From the formal red earth of the tablecloth,   5

a continent begins to spread itself:
the arrivals and departures
in separate airports, the sumptuous bars
they will visit, each
without the other. That darkness which   *10*
fills the room one shares
with a stranger, darkness more inclusive
than sleep.

It has been a long trip
into and out of that closeness   *15*
which softens the set of face, softens
even that withdrawal of hands
into themselves. There is
nothing to say. And yet, as the waiter
refolds his towel   *20*
deftly over his arm as a sign to begin,
those delicious possibilities
sweeten each small
gesture of goodbye. Each anonymous, misplaced smile.

For him   *25*
she will leave her spectacles folded
in her lap, she will smooth
her speckled hair, and drink
whatever he chooses.
For her   *30*
he will look upon that face as if
it were not growing indistinct. He will order
for them both, with usual aplomb,
the specialty of the house.
He will request   *35*
that the candle be lit.

KATHA POLLITT (b. 1949)

· TURNING THIRTY ·

This spring, you'd swear it actually gets dark earlier.
At the elegant new restaurants downtown
your married friends lock glances over the walnut torte:
it's ten o'clock. They have important jobs
and go to bed before midnight. Only you   *5*
walking alone up the dazzling avenue
still feel a girl's excitement, for the thousandth time
you enter your life as though for the first time,
as an immigrant enters a huge, mysterious capital:
Paris, New York. So many wide plazas, so many marble addresses! *10*

Home, you write feverishly
in all five notebooks at once, then faint into bed
dazed with ambition and too many cigarettes.

Well, what's wrong with that? Nothing, except
really you don't believe wrinkles mean character   *15*
and know it's an ominous note
that the Indian skirts flapping on the sidewalk racks
last summer looked so gay you wanted them all
but now are marked clearer than price tags: not for you.
Oh, what were you doing, why weren't you paying attention   *20*
that piercingly blue day, not a cloud in the sky,
when suddenly "choices"
ceased to mean "infinite possibilities"
and became instead "deciding what to do without"?
No wonder you're happiest now   *25*
riding on trains from one lover to the next.
In those black, night-mirrored windows
a wild white face, operatic, still enthralls you:
a romantic heroine,
suspended between lives, suspended between destinations.   *30*

GARY SOTO (b. 1952)

· SUMMER ·

Once again, tell me, what was it like?
There was a windowsill of flies.
It meant the moon pulled its own weight
And the black sky cleared itself
Like a sneeze.   *5*

What about the farm worker?
He had no bedroom. He had a warehouse
Of heat, a swamp cooler
That turned no faster than a raffle cage.

And the farms?   *10*
There were groves
Of fig trees that went unpicked.
The fruit wrinkled and flattened
Like the elbows
Of an old woman.   *15*

What about the Projects in the Eastside?
I can't really say. Maybe a child
Burned his first book of matches.

Maybe the burn is disappearing
Under the first layer   20
Of skin.

And next summer?
It will be the same. Boredom,
In early June, will settle
On the eyelash shading your pupil from dust,   25
On the shoulder you look over
To find the sun rising
From the Sierras.

Index of Poets and Poems

Acquainted with the Night, 56
Adam Lay Ibounden, 396
ADAMS, HENRY, 345
Adieu, Farewell Earth's Bliss, 409, 410
Afraid, 30
Ah Sun-flower, 256
AIKEN, CONRAD, 35, 65, 79, 182, 209, 230, 249
  Things, The, 4, 527
Alas! 'Tis Very Sad to Hear, 101
Alba (As cool as the pale wet leaves . . .) 12, 180
Alba (When the nightingale . . .), 192
All But Blind, 33
Along the Field As We Came By, 138
AMIS, KINGSLEY
  Note on Wyatt, A, 62
AMMIANUS
  Epitaph of Nearchos, 101
AMMONS, A. R., 45, 305, 310
  Constant, The, 572
  Cut the Grass, 573
Among School Children, 332, 386, 499
Anniversary, The, 323
Answer To Another Persuading A Lady to Marriage, An, 431, 432
ANONYMOUS, 31, 89, 178, 246, 283, 344
  Adam Lay Ibounden, 396
  Brief Autumnal, 10
  Demon Lover, The, 401
  Edward, Edward, 399

I Have Labored Sore, 260
I Never Plucked—A Bumblebee, 372–373
Lord Randal, 400
Love and Death, 183
Loving Mad Tom, 415
Lully, Lulley, Lully, Lulley, 398
Lyke-Wake Dirge, A, 396
Nineteen, 257
Papa's Letter, 107
Sir Isaac Newton, 343
Sir Patrick Spens, 14
from Ubi Sunt Qui Ante Nos Fuerunt, 262
There Was a Young Lady of Tottenham, 344
Unquiet Grave, The, 105
Western Wind, 6
Anthem for Doomed Youth, 200
anyone lived in a pretty how town, 308, 531
Apple, The, 54
Arms and the Boy, 200
ARNOLD, MATTHEW, 247
  Dover Beach, 243
ARP, JEAN
  What the Violins Sing in Their Baconfat Bed, 359
Ars Poetica, 529
ASHBERY, JOHN
  Instruction Manual, The, 578
At Grass, 567

INDEX OF POETS AND POEMS

ATWOOD, MARGARET
  Siren Song, 595
AUDEN, W. H., 126, 258, 262, 346
  In Memory of W. B. Yeats, 543
  Lullaby, 542
  Musée des Beaux Arts, 198
  Shield of Achilles, The, 101, 102,
    118, 331
  Wanderer, The, 145
AUSTEN, JANE, 89
Autumn, 451

Baby Pictures of Famous Dictators,
  594
BACON, SIR FRANCIS, 43, 89
Badger, 450
Ballade to His Mistress, 339
BARNES, WILLIAM, 151
BASHO, 342
  On a Withered Branch, 342
  Lightning in the Clouds!, 342
Bath Tub, The, 141
BAUDELAIRE, CHARLES, 38
Bean Eaters, The, 562
Beauty, 73
Because I Could Not Stop for Death,
  484
Because You Asked About the Line
  Between Prose and Poetry, 564
BEDDOES, T. L., 181
Bees Awater, 598
BEHN, APHRA
  Song: Love Armed, 432
BELLOC, HILAIRE
  On His Books, 144
Bells for John Whiteside's Daughter,
  109
BERRYMAN, JOHN, 177
  from Dream Songs, 306, 331, 554
  He Resigns, 352
  Sigh as It Ends, 335
Beyond Words, 299
BISHOP, ELIZABETH, 65
  Filling Station, 71
  Fish, The, 265, 547
  Sestina, 338
Blackberry Sweet, 265
BLAKE, WILLIAM, 45, 64
  Ah Sun-Flower, 256
  Epilogue to the Gates of Paradise,
    442
  London, 441

Poison Tree, 441
  Sick Rose, The, 56
  Tyger, The, 440
Blue Girls, 112
BOGAN, LOUISE, 150
Bourgeois Poet, The, 281
BOWRA, C. M., 346
BRADSTREET, ANNE
  To My Dear and Loving Husband,
    427, 428
Break, Break, Break, 137
BRIDGES, ROBERT, 143
Brief Autumnal, 10
Broken Home, The, 574
BRONTË, EMILY
  Remembrance, 473
BROOKS, GWENDOLYN, 49, 143
  Bean Eaters, The, 562
  Rites for Cousin Vit, The, 337
  We Real Cool, 291
BROWNE, SIR THOMAS, 64
BROWNE, WILLIAM
  On the Countess Dowager of
    Pembroke, 250
BROWNING, ELIZABETH BARRETT, 27,
  181
BROWNING, ROBERT, 237
  Meeting at Night, 194
  My Last Duchess, 197, 470
BRYANT, WILLIAM CULLEN, 107, 245
Building the Bridge, 355
BURKE, EDMUND, 35
BURNS, ROBERT, 39, 331
BURR, GRAY, 37, 49
BYRON, LORD (GEORGE GORDON), 172,
  191, 192, 245, 332
  Destruction of Sennacherib, The,
    255
  So We'll Go No More A-Roving,
    206, 447

CAMPION, THOMAS, 296
  It Fell on a Summer's Day, 408, 409
  My Sweetest Lesbia, Let Us Live
    and Love, 408
  Thrice Toss These Oaken Ashes in
    the Air, 409
CARLYLE, THOMAS, 89
Carriage from Sweden, A, 61, 199,
  520
Castanets, 546
Cat & The Weather, 114
CAVENDISH, MARGARET, 43

INDEX OF POETS AND POEMS

Chansons Innocentes, I, 169
CHASIN, HELEN
　City Pigeons, 31
CHAUCER, GEOFFREY, 142
Cherrylog Road, 265, 568
Chorus, from Atalanta in Calydon,
　489
CHURCHILL, CHARLES, 89
CIARDI, JOHN, 33, 49, 136
　Exit Line, 327
　Faces, 557
　Most Like an Arch This Marriage,
　23
　Snowy Heron, 557
Cinquain: A Warning, 342
City Pigeons, 31
CLARE, JOHN, 32, 43, 177, 196
　Autumn, 451
　Badger, 450
　Remember Dear Mary, 300
CLEVELAND, JOHN, 43, 248
CLOUGH, ARTHUR HUGH, 179
　Latest Decalogue, The, 81, 474
Cobb Would Have Caught It, 265,
　547
Cold Heaven, The, 245, 498
COLERIDGE, SAMUEL TAYLOR, 167, 181,
　247, 282
　Kubla Khan, 443
Collar, The, 419, 420
Composed upon Westminster Bridge,
　76, 78, 443
Constant, The, 572
CORNFORD, FRANCES
　To a Fat Lady Seen From the Train,
　340
Counting the Beats, 220
COWLEY, ABRAHAM, 34
CRANE, HART, 36, 203, 212
　Praise for an Urn, 532
　Proem: To Brooklyn Bridge, 533
CRANE, STEPHEN
　Man Said to the Universe, A, 274
　"Think as I Think," 274
CRAPSEY, ADELAIDE
　Cinquain: A Warning, 342
CRASHAW, RICHARD, 36, 48, 64, 149
CREELEY, ROBERT, 328
CREIGHTON, BISHOP MANDELL, 89
CRUZ, VICTOR HERNÁNDEZ, 49
CUMMINGS, E. E., 12, 79, 86, 366
　anyone lived in a pretty how town,
　308, 531

Chansons Innocentes, I, 169
if everything happens that can't be
　done, 263
Me up at does, 297
wherelings whenlings, 306
CUNNINGHAM, J. V., 234
　On a Cold Night I Came Through
　the Cold Rain, 249
Curse of the Cat Woman, 302
Cut Flower, A, 41, 153
Cut the Grass, 573

Dakota: October, 1822, Hunkpapa
　Warrior, 88
Dance, The, 515
DANIEL, SAMUEL, 235
Dark Hills, The, 212
Dark Night, The, 57, 330
DAVIDSON, JOHN, 150
DAVISON, PETER
　My Lady the Lake, 582
Death Be Not Proud, 414
Death of a Naturalist, 594
DE LA MARE, WALTER, 24, 142, 150,
　152, 209, 309
　Afraid, 30
　All But Blind, 33
　Listeners, The, 504
Delight In Disorder, 417, 418
Demon Lover, The, 401
Descent, The, 277
Description of the Morning, A, 76,
　434
Destruction of Sennacherib, The, 255
Dialogue Between The Soul and Body,
　A, 428, 429
DICKEY, JAMES
　Cherrylog Road, 265, 568
DICKINSON, EMILY, 32, 36, 45, 99,
　202
　Because I Could Not Stop for
　Death, 484
　How Many Times These Low Feet
　Staggered, 482
　I Heard a Fly Buzz—When I Died,
　483
　I Started Early—Took My Dog, 483
　My Life Had Stood—A Loaded
　Gun, 26
　Narrow Fellow in the Grass, A, 135
　Tell All the Truth But Tell It
　Slant, 485
　Went Up a Year This Evening, 28,
　482

INDEX OF POETS AND POEMS

DICKINSON, EMILY (*continued*)
  Wind Begun to Knead the Grass,
    The, 484
Dirce, 42
Disabled Debauchee, The, 432
DÖHL, REINHARD
  Pattern Poem with an Elusive
    Intruder, 280
DONNE, JOHN, 23, 144, 246, 248
  Anniversary, The, 323
  Death Be Not Proud, 414
  Sun Rising, The, 411, 412
  Valediction: Forbidding Mourning,
    A, 413, 414
  Valediction: Of Weeping, A, 323,
    412
Do Not Go Gentle into That Good
    Night, 163
D'ORLÉANS, CHARLES, 24
Dover Beach, 243
DOYLE, SIR ARTHUR CONAN, 90
Dream Songs, 306, 331, 554
Dream Variations, 256, 536
DROMGOOLE, WILL ALLEN
  Building the Bridge, 355
  Old Ladies, 111
Drummer Hodge, 492
DRYDEN, JOHN, 34, 89, 178
  Song from the Secular Masque, 431
Dust of Snow, 132
DYER, SIR EDWARD
  Lowest Trees Have Tops, The, 35,
    331, 403

Easter-Wings, 280, 418
ECKSTEIN, GUSTAV, 120
Edward, Edward, 399
Eel, The, 291
Effort at Speech, 267
Effort at Speech Between Two People,
    242, 549–550
Elegy, 77, 331, 410
Elegy for Jane, 545
Elegy Written in a Country Church-
    yard, 434
Eleven, 122, 325
ELIOT, T. S., 48, 69, 136, 203, 212, 238
  Love Song of J. Alfred Prufrock,
    The, 39, 522
  New Hampshire, 210
  Preludes, 9, 88
  Sweeney Among the Nightingales,
    526

EMERSON, RALPH WALDO, 248
Emperor of Ice-cream, The, 90
End of the Weekend, The, 12
Epilogue to The Gates of Paradise,
    442
Epitaph of Nearchos, 101
Essay on Man, from An, 77, 239
ETTER, DAVE
  Romp, 271
Étude Réaliste (I), 110
Even as I Hold You, 597
Eve of St. Agnes, The, 333, 456
Exit Line, 327
Explosion, The, 253, 568

Face in the Mirror, The, 74
Faces, 557
FEARING, KENNETH, 295
  Love, 20¢ the First Quarter Mile,
    73, 537
  Yes, the Agency Can Handle That,
    120
Felix Randal, 496
Fence, A, 67
Fern Hill, 223, 271, 555
FIELD, EDWARD
  Curse of the Cat Woman, 302
Filling Station, 71
Finding An Old Newspaper in the
    Woods, 598
Fish, The, 265, 547
FISHER, MAHLON LEONARD
  In Cool, Green Haunts, 155
Fish's Nightsong, 228
FITZGERALD, EDWARD, 391
  from The Rubáiyát of Omar
    Khayyám, 238, 466
FITZGERALD, ROBERT, 168
  Cobb Would Have Caught It, 265,
    547
For the Union Dead, 560
FRANCIS, ROBERT
  Pitcher, 535
  Swimmer, 536
FROST, ROBERT, 25, 27, 40, 48, 65, 85,
    103, 131, 166, 174, 177, 182, 231,
    234, 235, 248, 255, 309, 349, 359
  Acquainted with the Night, 56
  Beyond Words, 299
  Dust of Snow, 132
  Mending Wall, 505
  Most of It, The, 507

INDEX OF POETS AND POEMS

Neither out Far Nor in Deep, 134
Once By the Pacific, 164
"Out, Out—," 292, 325
Patch of Old Snow, A, 30
Provide, Provide, 328, 506
Subverted Flower, The, 507
Wrights' Biplane, The, 145

Geranium, The, 117
Gesture, The, 598
GHISELIN, BREWSTER, 235
Rattler, Alert, 16
Ghost-Flowers, 116
Girls Working in Banks, 60, 153
GLAZE, ANDREW, 159
Zeppelin, 363
GLÜCK, LOUISE
School Children, The, 596
God's Grandeur, 495
Go, Lovely Rose, 420, 421
"Good Night, Willie Lee, I'll See You
In the Morning," 597
Good Ships, 66
Grasshopper, A, 564
Grave, A, 517
GRAVES, ROBERT, 202, 283
Counting the Beats, 220
Face in the Mirror, The, 74
Persian Version, The, 302
Spoils, 87
GRAY, THOMAS, 176, 179
Elegy Written in a Country
Churchyard, 434
GREVILLE, FULKE, 247
GUTHRIE, RAMON, 81

HALL, DONALD, 25, 168
HALL, JIM, 196
HARDY, THOMAS, 44, 151, 176, 182,
256, 296
Drummer Hodge, 492
I Look into My Glass, 347
In Time of "The Breaking of
Nations," 494
Man He Killed, The, 493
Oxen, The, 494
Ruined Maid, The, 81, 491
Self-Unseeing, The, 492
HAYDEN, ROBERT
O Daedalus, Fly Away Home, 550
Those Winter Sundays, 550

Haystack in the Floods, The, 202,
485–489
HEANEY, SEAMUS
Death of a Naturalist, 594
HECHT, ANTHONY
End of the Weekend, The, 12
HEGEL, 89
HEMINGWAY, ERNEST, 309
HERBERT, GEORGE, 248
Collar, The, 419, 420
Easter-Wings, 280, 418
Hope, 55
Love, 420
Redemption, 31, 418
He Resigns, 352
HERRICK, ROBERT, 43, 324
Delight in Disorder, 417, 418
Upon Julia's Clothes, 328
HIGGINSON, MARY THACHER
Ghost-Flowers, 116
Higgledy-piggledy, 343
HOGG, JAMES, 181
HOLLANDER, JOHN, 188
HOLMES, OLIVER WENDELL, 282, 316
HOPE, LAURENCE, 55
Youth, 118
HOPKINS, GERARD MANLEY, 308
Felix Randal, 496
God's Grandeur, 495
Pied Beauty, 337
Spring and Fall, 140, 496
Windhover, The, 147, 495
Horses, The, 516
HOUSMAN, A. E., 82, 99, 345, 349,
358
Along the Field As We Came by,
138
I Hoed and Trenched and Weeded,
390
I to My Perils, 244
Loveliest of Trees, the Cherry Now,
498
To an Athlete Dying Young, 497
With Rue My Heart Is Laden, 345
HOWARD, RICHARD, 79
How Many Times These Low Feet
Staggered, 482
How Pleasant to Know Mr. Lear, 472
HUGHES, LANGSTON
Dream Variations, 256, 536
Negro Speaks of Rivers, The, 537
HUGHES, TED
Pike, 588

HUGO, RICHARD, 151
HULME, T. E., 33
HUNT, LEIGH, 78

if everything happens that can't be
    done, 263
I Have Labored Sore, 260
I Hear America Singing, 294
I Heard a Fly Buzz—When I Died,
    483
I Hoed and Trenched and Weeded,
    390
I Look into My Glass, 347
In a Station of the Metro, 12
In Cool, Green Haunts, 155
I Never Plucked—A Bumblebee, 372
In Memory of W. B. Yeats, 543
In My Craft or Sullen Art, 376
Inspiration, 375
Instruction Manual, The, 578
Intended for Sir Isaac Newton, 39
In Time of "The Breaking of
    Nations," 494
Iris, 284
Irish Airman Foresees His Death, An,
    139
I Started Early—Took My Dog, 483
It Fell On a Summer's Day, 408, 409
I To My Perils, 244

JAMES, HENRY, 90
JAMMES, FRANCIS, 45
JARRELL, RANDALL, 33, 49
    Knight, Death, and the Devil, The,
        152
    Next Day, 553
JEFFERS, ROBINSON, 33, 142, 143, 179,
    209
    Purse-Seine, The, 20
Jill, 350
JOANS, TED
    .38, The, 222
JOHN OF THE CROSS, SAINT
    Dark Night, The, 56, 330
JOHNSON, SAMUEL, 89, 147
JONSON, BEN
    On My First Son, 414
    Still to Be Neat, Still to Be
        Dressed, 415
Jubilate Agno, from, 438
Junk, 260

KEATS, JOHN, 119, 186, 212, 382
    Eve of St. Agnes, The, 333, 456
    La Belle Dame Sans Merci, 324,
        451
    Ode to a Nightingale, 10, 18, 453
    To Autumn, 41, 455
Keep Talking, 584
KENNEDY, X. J., 152
    Loose Woman, 84
KINSELLA, THOMAS, 142
KIPLING, RUDYARD, 24, 35, 64, 245,
    309
Knight, Death, and the Devil, The,
    63, 152
KOCH, KENNETH, 347
Kubla Kahn, 443
KUMIN, MAXINE
    Retrieval System, The, 571
KUNITZ, STANLEY J., 310

La Belle Dame Sans Merci, 324, 451
LAING, R. D.
    Jill, 350
Lake Isle of Innisfree, The, 205
Lamentation of the Old Pensioner,
    The, 392
LANDOR, WALTER SAVAGE
    Alas! 'Tis Very Sad to Hear, 101
    Dirce, 42
    On Seeing A Hair of Lucretia
        Borgia, 445
    Past Ruined Ilion Helen Lives, 445
    Rose Aylmer, 445
LARKIN, PHILIP
    At Grass, 567
    Explosion, The, 253, 568
    Lines on a Young Lady's
        Photograph Album, 566
Last Confession, A, 502
Latest Decalogue, The, 81, 474
LAWRENCE, D. H., 25
    Piano, 386
    Piano, The, 385
    To Women, As Far As I'm
        Concerned, 349
LEAR, EDWARD, 282
    How Pleasant to Know Mr. Lear,
        472
Learning By Doing, 563
from Leaves of Grass, 221, 474
Leaving Crete, Come Visit Again Our
    Temple, 18
Leda and the Swan, 42, 153
Leg, The, 551

INDEX OF POETS AND POEMS

LEVINE, PHILIP
  Keep Talking, 584
LIBBEY, ELIZABETH
  Gesture, The, 598
Like Attracts Like, 279
LINDSAY, VACHEL, 152, 283
Lines on a Young Lady's Photograph
  Album, 566
Listeners, The, 504
London, 441
LONGFELLOW, HENRY WADSWORTH,
  27, 43, 142, 150, 151, 252, 282
Loose Woman, 84
LORCA, FEDERICO GARCÍA, 51
  Sleepwalkers' Ballad, 369
Lord Randal, 84, 400
Love, 420
Love, 20¢ the First Quarter Mile, 73,
  153, 537
Love and Death, 183
LOVELACE, RICHARD, 43
  To Lucasta, Going to the Wars, 428
Loveliest of Trees, the Cherry Now,
  498
Lover Mourns for the Loss of Love,
  The, 325
Love Song of J. Alfred Prufrock, The,
  39, 522
Loving Mad Tom, 415
LOWELL, JAMES RUSSELL, 35, 36, 89,
  104, 182
LOWELL, ROBERT, 79, 176
  For the Union Dead, 560
  Skunk Hour, 331, 558
Lowest Trees Have Tops, The, 35,
  331, 403
Lucifer in Starlight, 334
Lullaby, 542
Lully, Lulley, Lully, Lulley, 55, 67,
  398
LUX, THOMAS
  My Grandmother's Funeral, 364
Lycidas, 170, 206, 421
Lyke-Wake Dirge, A, 396

MACDIARMID, HUGH, 25, 45
MCKUEN, ROD, 114
MACLEISH, ARCHIBALD
  Ars Poetica, 529
  Eleven, 7, 122, 325
  You, Andrew Marvell, 300, 530

MACNEICE, LOUIS, 36
Man He Killed, The, 493
Man Said to the Universe, A, 274
MARLOWE, CHRISTOPHER
  Passionate Shepherd to His Love,
  The, 404
MARSDEN, KENNETH, 346
MARVELL, ANDREW, 24, 48, 208, 297
  Dialogue Between the Soul and
  Body, A, 428, 429
  To His Coy Mistress, 429
MASTERS, EDGAR LEE, 33
MASTERS, MARCIA, 143
MAYER, HANSJÖRG, 281
Mediterranean, The, 242, 534
Meeting At Night, 194
MELVILLE, HERMAN, 5, 6, 141, 144
Mending Wall, 505
MEREDITH, GEORGE
  Lucifer in Starlight, 334
MEREDITH, WILLIAM
  Effort at Speech, 267
MERRILL, JAMES, 45, 142, 310
  Broken Home, The, 574
Merry-Go-Round, The, 58
MERWIN, W. S., 45
Message, The, 294
Me up at does, 297
Mill, The, 84, 502
MILTON, JOHN, 78, 170, 203, 246, 297
  Lycidas, 170, 206, 421
  On His Blindness, 427
  On His Dead Wife, 427
  On the Late Massacre in Piedmont,
  183
Miss Cho Composes in the Cafeteria,
  268
Money, 52
MONTALE, EUGENIO
  Eel, The, 291
Moon, Sun, Sleep, Birds, Live, 128,
  300
MOORE, MARIANNE, 33, 78, 90, 103,
  272
  Carriage from Sweden, A, 61, 199,
  520
  Grave, A, 517
  Steeple-Jack, The, 518–520
MOORE, THOMAS, 113
MORGAN, ROBERT
  Bees Awater, 598
  Finding an Old Newspaper in the
  Woods, 598

INDEX OF POETS AND POEMS

MORGENSTERN, CHRISTIAN
Fish's Nightsong, 228
MORRIS, WILLIAM, 250
Haystack in the Floods, The, 202,
485
Most Like an Arch This Marriage, 23
Most of It, The, 507
Mother Earth: Her Whales, 585
Mr. Flood's Party, 503–504
MUELLER, LISEL
Palindrome, 365
MUIR, EDWIN, 90
Horses, The, 516
Musée des Beaux Arts, 198
Mushrooms, 269
My Galley Chargèd with Forgetful-
ness, 62
My Grandmother's Funeral, 364
My Lady the Lake, 582
My Last Duchess, 197, 470
My Life Had Stood—A Loaded
Gun, 26
My Papa's Waltz, 244
My Sweetest Lesbia, Let Us Live And
Love, 408
Myth on Mediterranean Beach:
Aphrodite as Logos, 539

Nantucket, 59
Narrow Fellow In the Grass, A, 135
NASH, OGDEN
Very Like a Whale, 193, 538
NASHE, THOMAS
Adieu, Farewell Earth's Bliss, 409,
410
Negro Speaks of Rivers, The, 536
Neither Out Far Nor In Deep, 134
NEMEROV, HOWARD, 45, 49, 79, 327
Because You Asked About the Line
Between Prose and Poetry, 564
Learning By Doing, 563
Money, 52–53
Primer of the Daily Round, A, 336
NERUDA, PABLO, 29
New Hampshire, 210
NEWTON, JOHN, 246
Next Day, 553
Nineteen, 257
No Second Troy, 28
Note on Wyatt, A, 62
Not Waving but Drowning, 539
Nymph's Reply To the Shepherd, The,
404

O Daedalus, Fly Away Home, 550
Ode to a Nightingale, 18, 453
Ode to the West Wind, 328, 448
Old Ladies, 111
Once By the Pacific, 164
O'NEILL, EUGENE, 218
On His Blindness, 427
On His Books, 144
On His Dead Wife, 427
On My First Son, 414
On Reading Aloud My Early Poems,
327
On Seeing a Hair of Lucretia Borgia,
445
On the Countess Dowager of
Pembroke, 250
On the Late Massacre in Piedmont,
183
On the Spartan Dead at Thermopylae,
83
OSGOOD, FRANCIS P.
Winter Fairyland in Vermont, 71
Our Bog is Dood, 366
Out of the Cradle Endlessly Rocking,
475
"Out, Out—," 292, 325
OWEN, WILFRED, 321
Anthem for Doomed Youth, 200
Arms and the Boy, 200
Oxen, The, 494
Ozymandias, 337, 447

Pain For A Daughter, 583
Painting the Gate, 562
Palindrome, 365
Papa's Letter, 107
PASCAL, PAUL
Tact, 343
Passionate Shepherd To His Love,
The, 404
Past Ruined Ilion Helen Lives, 445
PATCHEN, KENNETH, 37
Moon, Sun, Sleep, Birds, Live, 128,
300
Patch of Old Snow, A, 30
Pattern Poem with an Elusive
Intruder, 280
PAYN, JAMES, 113
Peace, 431
PEACOCK, THOMAS LOVE
War-Song of Dinas Vawr, The,
445–446

INDEX OF POETS AND POEMS

Persian Version, The, 302
PHILIPS, KATHERINE
   An Answer to Another Persuading
      A Lady to Marriage, 431, 432
Piano, 386
Piano, The, 385
Pied Beauty, 337
Pike, 588
Pitcher, 535
PLATH, SYLVIA, 167, 168, 171, 182,
    284
   Mushrooms, 269
   Tulips, 590
PLATO
   Apple, The, 54
Playboy, 565
Player Piano, 187
POE, EDGAR ALLAN, 78, 181, 246, 253
   To Helen, 330
Poison Tree, A, 441
POLLITT, KATHA
   Turning Thirty, 599
POPE, ALEXANDER, 35, 64, 89, 181,
    188, 191, 203, 208, 211, 245, 308
   from An Essay on Man, 77, 239
   Intended for Sir Isaac Newton, 39,
    327
Postcard from the Volcano, A, 513
POUND, EZRA, 40, 45, 126, 249, 283
   Alba (As cool as the pale wet
    leaves . . .), 12, 180
   Alba (When the nightingale . . .),
    192
   Bath Tub, The, 141
   In a Station of the Metro, 12
   Return, The, 273
   River-Merchant's Wife: A Letter,
    The, 515
Praise for an Urn, 532–533
Preludes, 9, 88
PRÉVERT, JACQUES
   Message, The, 294
Primer of the Daily Round, A, 336
Proem: To Brooklyn Bridge, 533
Provide, Provide, 328, 506
Psalm 23, 282
Pulverous Silver Essence, 133
Purse-Seine, The, 20

RALEIGH, SIR WALTER
   Nymph's Reply to the Shepherd,
    The, 404

RANDALL, DUDLEY
   Blackberry Sweet, 265
RANDOLPH, THOMAS, 208
RANSOM, JOHN CROWE, 180, 325
   Bells for John Whiteside's Daughter,
    109
   Blue Girls, 112
   Good Ships, 66
Rattler, Alert, 16
Reapers, 532
Reconciliation, 480
Redemption, 31, 418
Red Wheelbarrow, The, 514
Remember Dear Mary, 300
Remembrance, 473
Retrieval System, The, 571
Return, The, 273
RILKE, RAINER MARIA
   Merry-Go-Round, The, 58
RIMBAUD, ARTHUR, 38
Rites for Cousin Vit, The, 337
River-Merchant's Wife: A Letter,
   The, 515
ROBINSON, EDWIN ARLINGTON, 36, 44,
    182, 212
   Mill, The, 84, 502
   Mr. Flood's Party, 503
ROCHESTER, EARL OF (JOHN WILMOT)
   Disabled Debauchee, The, 432
ROETHKE, THEODORE, 179, 228
   Elegy for Jane, 545
   Geranium, The, 117
   My Papa's Waltz, 244
   Waking, The, 546
Romp, 271
Rose Aylmer, 445
ROSSETTI, CHRISTINA, 323
   Up-Hill, 481
ROSSETTI, DANTE GABRIEL, 24
   Woodspurge, The, 100, 481
Rubáiyát of Omar Khayyám, from
   The, 238, 466
Ruined Maid, The, 81, 491
RUKEYSER, MURIEL
   Effort at Speech Between Two
    People, 242, 549
RUTSALA, VERN, 49

Sabbaths, W. I., 589
Sailing to Byzantium, 498
Sale, 303
SANDBURG, CARL, 29, 87, 276
   Fence, A, 67

INDEX OF POETS AND POEMS

SAPPHO, 8, 18, 99
  Leaving Crete, Come Visit Again
    Our Temple, 18
  There's a Man I Really Believe's in
    Heaven, 8
School Children, The, 596
SCHUYLER, JAMES, 37, 210
SCOTT, SIR WALTER, 209
SEAMAN, E. WILLIAM
  Higgledy-piggledy, 343
Second Coming, The, 240
Self-Unseeing, The, 492
Sense of the Sleight-of-Hand Man,
  The, 513
SERVICE, ROBERT W.
  Inspiration, 375
Sestina, 338
SEXTON, ANNE
  Pain For a Daughter, 583
SHAKESPEARE, WILLIAM, 32, 34, 40,
    44, 50, 64, 78, 135, 142, 151,
    174, 178, 179, 180, 181, 202, 208,
    211, 233, 234, 235, 247, 290
  Sonnet 18, 406
  Sonnet 29, 335
  Sonnet 33, 406
  Sonnet 66, 232
  Sonnet 73, 406
  Sonnet 116, 407
  Sonnet 129, 101, 180, 407
  Sonnet 130, 74
  Winter, 70
SHAPIRO, KARL
  Bourgeois Poet, The, 281
  Cut Flower, A, 41, 153
  Girls Working in Banks, 60, 153
  Leg, The, 551
  Two-Year Old Has Had A
    Motherless Week, The, 552
She Dwelt Among the Untrodden
  Ways, 442
SHELLEY, PERCY BYSSHE, 77, 166, 174,
  333
  Ode to the West Wind, 448–450
  Ozymandias, 337, 447
Shield of Achilles, The, 101, 102, 118,
  331
SHIKIBU, LADY IZUMI, 341
  Lying Here Alone, 341
SHIRLEY, JAMES, 48
Sick Rose, The, 56
SIDNEY, SIR PHILIP, 27, 32, 34, 43, 63,
  211

With How Sad Steps, O Moon, 405
Sigh As It Ends, 335
SIMIC, CHARLES
  Baby Pictures of Famous Dictators,
    594
SIMONIDES
  On the Spartan Dead at
    Thermopylae, 83
SIMPSON, LOUIS, 65
Siren Song, 595–596
Sir Isaac Newton, 343
Sir Patrick Spens, 14, 245
SITWELL, EDITH, 36
Skunk Hour, 331, 558
Sleepless at Crown Point, 342
Sleepwalkers' Ballad, 369
Slumber Did My Spirit Seal, A, 329
SMART, CHRISTOPHER
  from Jubilate Agno, 438
SMITH, STEVIE
  Not Waving but Drowning, 539
  Our Bog is Dood, 366
Snow Man, The, 512
Snowy Heron, 557
SNYDER, GARY, 46, 166, 265, 284
  Mother Earth: Her Whales, 585
Solitary Reaper, The, 353
Song for the Middle of the Night, 110
Song from The Secular Masque, 431
Song: Love Armed, 432
Sonnet 18 (Shakespeare), 406
Sonnet 29 (Shakespeare), 335
Sonnet 33 (Shakespeare), 406
Sonnet 66 (Shakespeare), 232
Sonnet 73 (Shakespeare), 406–407
Sonnet LXXV (Spenser), 336
Sonnet 116 (Shakespeare), 406
Sonnet 129 (Shakespeare), 101, 180,
  407
Sonnet 130 (Shakespeare), 74
SOTO, GARY
  Summer, 600
So We'll Go No More A-Roving, 206,
  447
Speak, 201, 581
SPENCER, BERNARD, 297
  Castanets, 546
SPENDER, STEPHEN, 209
SPENSER, EDMUND, 178
  Sonnet LXXV, 336
Spoils, 87, 153
Spring and Fall, 140, 496
Spur, The, 100

INDEX OF POETS AND POEMS

STAFFORD, WILLIAM, 44, 150, 168, 265
  Traveling Through the Dark, 115
STARBUCK, GEORGE, 152
Statues, The, 319, 332
Staying Alive, 577
Steeple-Jack, The, 518
STEVENS, WALLACE, 172, 248
  Emperor of Ice-Cream, The, 90
  Postcard from the Volcano, A, 513
  Sense of the Sleight-of-Hand Man,
    The, 513
  Snow Man, The, 512
  Sunday Morning, 351, 509
Still To Be Neat, Still To Be
  Dressed, 415
STOUTENBURG, ADRIEN, 44
STRAND, MARK
  Tunnel, The, 592
  Where Are the Waters of
    Childhood, 593
Subverted Flower, The, 350, 507
Summer, 600
SUMMERS, HOLLIS, 25, 90, 210
Sunday Morning, 351, 509
Sun Rising, The, 411, 412
Sweeney Among the Nightingales, 526
SWENSON, MAY, 37, 182, 305
  Cat & the Weather, 114
  Painting the Gate, 562
SWIFT, JONATHAN
  Description of the Morning, A, 76,
    434
Swimmer, 536
SWINBURNE, ALGERNON CHARLES, 234,
    283
  Chorus from Atalanta in Calydon,
    489
  Étude Réaliste (I), 110

Tact, 343
TATE, ALLEN, 237
  Mediterranean, The, 242, 534
TATE, JAMES, 167
  Miss Cho Composes in the
    Cafeteria, 268
TAYLOR, ELEANOR ROSS, 49
TAYLOR, ROD
  Dakota: October, 1822, Hunkpapa
    Warrior, 88
Tears, Idle Tears, 100, 122, 470
TEASDALE, SARA, 40

Tell All the Truth But Tell It Slant,
  485
TENNYSON, LORD (ALFRED), 173, 181,
  186, 234, 246, 329, 346
  Break, Break, Break, 137
  Tears, Idle Tears, 100, 122, 470
  Ulysses, 468
There's a Man I Really Believe's in
  Heaven, 8
They Flee from Me, 63, 331, 403
Things, The, 4, 527
"Think As I Think," 274
.38, The, 222
THOMAS, DYLAN
  Do Not Go Gentle Into That
    Good Night, 163
  Fern Hill, 223, 271, 555
  In My Craft or Sullen Art, 376
Those Winter Sundays, 550
Thrice Toss These Oaken Ashes in the
  Air, 409
TICHBORNE, CHIDIOCK
  Elegy, 77, 331, 410
To a Fat Lady Seen from the Train,
  340
To an Athlete Dying Young, 497
To Autumn, 41, 455
To Helen, 330
To Helen of Troy (N.Y.), 299
To His Coy Mistress, 429
To Lucasta, Going To the Wars, 428
To My Dear and Loving Husband,
  427, 428
TOOMER, JEAN
  Reapers, 532
To Waken an Old Lady, 31, 514
To Women, As Far As I'm
  Concerned, 349
Traveling Through the Dark, 115
TUCKERMAN, FREDERICK GODDARD,
  64, 143, 172, 209
Tulips, 590
Tunnel, The, 592
Turning Thirty, 599
Two-Year Old Has Had a
  Motherless Week, The, 552
Tyger, The, 440

Ubi Sunt Qui Ante Nos Fuerunt,
  from, 262
Ulysses, 468
Under Ben Bulben, VI, 210
Unquiet Grave, The, 105

INDEX OF POETS AND POEMS

UPDIKE, JOHN, 218, 310
  Player Piano, 187
Up-Hill, 481
Upon Julia's Clothes, 328
Upon the Death of Sir Albert
    Morton's Wife, 327

Valediction: Forbidding Mourning, A,
    413, 414
Valediction: Of Weeping, A, 323, 412
VAUGHAN, HENRY, 181
  Peace, 431
VERGIL, 318
Very Like a Whale, 193, 538
VIERECK, PETER
  To Helen of Troy (N.Y.), 299
VILLON, FRANÇOIS, 172
  Ballade to His Mistress, 339

WAGONER, DAVID
  Staying Alive, 577
Waking, The, 546
WALCOTT, DEREK
  Sabbaths, W. I., 589
WALKER, ALICE, 305
  Even as I Hold You, 597
  "Good Night, Willie Lee, I'll See
      You In the Morning," 597
WALKER, JEANNE MURRAY, 37
WALLER, EDMUND
  Go, Lovely Rose, 420, 421
Wanderer, The, 145
WARREN, ROBERT PENN
  Myth on Mediterranean Beach:
      Aphrodite as Logos, 539
War-Song of Dinas Vawr, The, 445
WATTS, ISAAC, 32
WEBSTER, JOHN, 248
Went Up a Year This Evening, 28,
    482
We Real Cool, 291
Western Wind, 6
What the Violins Sing in Their
    Baconfat Bed, 359
When I Heard the Learn'd
    Astronomer, 480
Where Are the Waters of Childhood,
    593
wherelings whenlings, 306
WHITE, GILBERT, 201

WHITMAN, WALT, 78, 202, 275
  Beauty, 73
  I Hear America Singing, 294
  from Leaves of Grass, 221, 474
  Out of the Cradle Endlessly
      Rocking, 475
  Reconciliation, 480
  When I Heard the Learn'd
      Astronomer, 480
WHITTIER, JOHN GREENLEAF, 174, 179
WILBUR, RICHARD, 79, 171
  Grasshopper, A, 564
  Junk, 260–261
  Playboy, 565
  Sleepless at Crown Point, 342
WILLIAMS, EMMETT
  Like Attracts Like, 279
WILLIAMS, JOHN
  On Reading Aloud My Early
      Poems, 327
WILLIAMS, MILLER, 37, 143
  Sale, 303
WILLIAMS, WILLIAM CARLOS, 25, 256
  Dance, The, 515
  Descent, The, 277
  Iris, 284
  Nantucket, 59
  Red Wheelbarrow, The, 514
  To Waken an Old Lady, 31, 514
Wind Begun to Knead the Grass, The,
    484
Windhover, The, 147, 495
Winter, 70
Winter Fairyland in Vermont, 71
WINTERS, YVOR, 44
With How Sad Steps, O Moon, 405
With Rue My Heart Is Laden, 345
Wittgenstein and the Crow, 133
Woodspurge, The, 100, 153, 481
WORDSWORTH, WILLIAM, 85, 172
  Composed on Westminister Bridge,
      76, 78, 443
  She Dwelt Among the Untrodden
      Ways, 442
  Slumber Did My Spirit Seal, A, 329
  Solitary Reaper, The, 353
  World Is Too Much With Us, The,
      442, 443
WOTTON, SIR HENRY
  Upon the Death of Sir Albert
      Morton's Wife, 327
WRIGHT, JAMES, 142, 283
  Song for the Middle of the Night,
      110
  Speak, 201, 581

INDEX OF POETS AND POEMS

Wrights' Biplane, The, 145
WYATT, SIR THOMAS
My Galley Chargèd with
Forgetfulness, 62
They Flee From Me, 63, 331, 403

YEATS, WILLIAM BUTLER, 27, 32, 35,
45, 48, 64, 78, 150, 173, 178,
179, 212, 248, 296, 309, 388, 389
Among School Children, 332, 386,
499
Cold Heaven, The, 245, 498
Irish Airman Foresees His Death,
An, 139
Lake Isle of Innisfree, The, 205
Lamentation of the Old Pensioner,
The, 392

Last Confession, A, 502
Leda and the Swan, 42
Lover Mourns for the Loss of Love,
The, 325
No Second Troy, 28
Sailing to Byzantium, 498
Second Coming, The, 240
Spur, The, 100
Statues, The, 319, 332
Under Ben Bulben, VI, 210
Yes, the Agency Can Handle That,
120
You, Andrew Marvell, 300, 530
Youth, 118

Zeppelin, 363

Index of First Lines

A baby's feet, like sea-shells pink, 110
About suffering they were never
　　wrong, 198
a burst of iris so that, 284
Adam lay ibounden, 396
Adieu, farewell earth's bliss, 409,
　　410
A dying firelight slides along the
　　quirt, 12
Age, and the deaths, and the ghosts,
　　352
Ah Sun-flower! weary of time, 256
Ah what avails the sceptred race, 445
Alas! 'tis very sad to hear, 101
All, all of a piece throughout, 431
All but blind, 32
All kings and all their favorites, 323
All night, this headland, 342
All right, I may have lied to you, and
　　about you, and made a few, 537
All year the flax-dam festered in the
　　heart, 594
Along the field as we came by, 138
A man has been standing, 592
A man said to the universe, 274
Among the iodoform, in twilight-
　　sleep, 551
A narrow Fellow in the Grass, 135
An axe angles from my neighbor's
　　ashcan, 260
And here face down beneath the sun,
　　530

And summer mornings the mute child,
　　rebellious, 7
And yet a kiss (like blubber)'d blur
　　and slip, 183
An old man, going a lone highway,
　　355
An owl winks in the shadows, 585
Anyone lived in a pretty how town,
　　531
A peels an apple, while B kneels to
　　God, 336
Apeneck Sweeney spreads his knees,
　　526
A poem should be palpable and mute,
　　529
As a bathtub lined with white
　　porcelain, 141
As cool as the pale wet leaves of
　　lily-of-the-valley, 12
As I sit looking out of a window of
　　the building, 578
A slumber did my spirit seal, 329
As some brave admiral, in former
　　war, 432
A sudden blow: the great wings
　　beating still, 42
As virtuous men pass mildly away, 413
A sweet, deep sense of mystery filled
　　the wood, 155
A sweet disorder in the dress, 417
At last you yielded up the album,
　　which, 566

At least 100 seabirds attended my grandmother's funeral. And we live, 364

Avenge, O Lord, thy slaughtered saints, whose bones, 183

Awake! for Morning in the Bowl of Night, 466

Back will go the head with the dark curls, 546

Barely a twelvemonth after, 516

Because I could not stop for Death, 484

Behold her, single in the field, 353

Black girl black girl, 265

Black reapers with the sound of steel on stones, 532

Blind with love, my daughter, 583

Borgia, thou once wert almost too august, 445

Break, break, break, 137

Busy old fool, unruly sun, 411

But for a brief, 564

Call the roller of big cigars, 90

Carried her unprotesting out the door, 337

Cat takes a look at the weather, 114

Children picking up our bones, 513

Children's voices in the orchard, 210

Christmas Eve, and twelve of the clock, 494

Climbing the stairway gray with urban midnight, 267

Cold in the earth—and the deep snow piled above thee, 473

Come live with me and be my love, 404

Complacencies of the peignoir, and late, 509

Cowhorn-crowned, shockheaded, cornshuck-bearded, 152

Crossing the street, 574

Dark hills at evening in the west, 212

Death be not proud, though some have called thee, 414

Does the road wind up-hill all the way, 481

Do not go gentle into that good night, 163

Doom is dark and deeper than any sea-dingle, 145

Drifting night in the Georgia pines, 550

Dürer would have seen a reason for living, 518

Earth has not anything to show more fair, 443

Even as I hold you, 597

Event, 133

False beauty who, although in semblance fair, 339

Farewell, thou child of my right hand, and joy, 414

Felix Randal the farrier, O is he dead then? my duty all ended, 496

Filling her compact & delicious body, 554

Fleet ships encountering on the high seas, 66

Flowers through the window, 59

Forbear, bold youth; all's heaven here, 431

For I will consider my cat Jeoffry, 438

From left to right, she leads the eye, 539

From the hag and hungry goblin, 415

Full many a glorious morning have I seen, 406

Girls working in banks wear bouffant hair and shed, 60

Glory be to God for dappled things, 337

Go, lovely rose, 420

Go tell at Sparta, traveler passing by, 83

Green grape, and you refused me, 10

Green I love you green, 369

Grey haunted eyes, absent-mindedly glaring, 74

Had he and I but met, 493

Had she come all the way for this, 485

INDEX OF FIRST LINES

Had we but world enough, and time, 429

Having been tenant long to a rich Lord, 418

He disappeared in the dead of winter, 543

He first deceased; she for a little tried, 327

He leans forward in his chair, 598

Helen, thy beauty is to me, 330

Her, 271

Here is the ancient floor, 492

Here lies, but seven years old, our little maid, 30

He thought he kept the universe alone, 507

Higgledy-piggledy, 343

High on his stockroom ladder like a dunce, 565

His art is eccentricity, his aim, 535

How dear the ways of Nature! Lo, yon crow, 133

How many dawns, chill from his rippling rest, 533

How many times these low feet staggered, 482

How often have I started out, 375

How pleasant to know Mr. Lear, 472

I am not sure if I knew the truth, 118

I am the little man who smokes & smokes, 555

I am the poet of the body, 221

I caught a tremendous fish, 547

I caught this morning morning's minion, king-, 495

If all the world and love were young, 404

If ever two were one, then surely we, 427

if everything happens that can't be done, 263

If it ain't simply this, what is it, 584

I gave to Hope a watch of mine: but he, 55

I had a chair at every hearth, 392

I have been one acquainted with the night, 56

I have labored sore and suffered death, 260

I hear America singing, the varied carols I hear, 294

I heard a Fly buzz—when I died, 483

I hear the man downstairs slapping the hell out of his stupid wife again, 38

I hoed and trenched and weeded, 390

I know that I shall meet my fate, 139

I look into my glass, 347

I met a traveller from an antique land, 447

I'm upset you are upset, 350

In Breughel's great picture, The Kermess, 515

I never plucked—a Bumblebee, 372

In every old lady I chance to meet, 111

in Just-, 169

In my craft or sullen art, 376

In shining groups, each stem a pearly ray, 116

In sunburnt parks where Sundays lie, 547

In Xanadu did Kubla Khan, 443

I painted the mailbox. That was fun, 562

I remember the neckcurls, limp and damp as tendrils, 545

I sit here with the wind is in my hair, 299

I stand on slenderness all fresh and fair, 41

I started Early—Took my Dog, 483

'Is there anybody there?' said the Traveller, 504

I struck the board, and cried, "No more, 419

It begins with my dog, now dead, who all his long life, 571

It fell on a summer's day, 408

I think I could turn and live awhile with the animals. . . . they are so, 474

It is the lake within the lake that drowns, 582

It little profits that an idle king, 468

I to my perils, 244

It sometimes happens, 302

It was a kind and northern face, 532

I've known rivers, 537

I've tossed an apple at you; if you can love me, 54

I wake to sleep, and take my waking slow, 546

INDEX OF FIRST LINES

I walk through the long schoolroom questioning, 499
I wander through each chartered street, 441
I was angry with my friend, 441
I was sitting in my study, 107
I will arise and go now, and go to Innisfree, 205

Just now, 342

Lay your sleeping head, my love, 542
Leaving Crete, come visit again our temple, 18
Let me not to the marriage of true minds, 407
Let me pour forth, 412
Let the boy try along this bayonet-blade, 200
Let us go then, you and I, 522
Looking down into my father's, 597
Lord, who createdst man in wealth and store, 418
Love bade me welcome; yet my soul drew back, 420
Love in fantastic triumph sate, 432
Loveliest of trees, the cherry now, 498
Love should intend realities: good-bye, 327
Lully, lulley, lully, lulley, 398
Lying here alone, 341

Man looking into the sea, 517
Márgarét, áre you gríeving, 496
Methought I saw my late espousèd saint, 427
Me up at does, 297
Most like an arch—an entrance which upholds, 23
Moving from Cheer to Joy, from Joy to All, 553
My galley chargèd with forgetfulness, 62
My heart aches, and a drowsy numbness pains, 453
My Life had stood—a Loaded Gun, 26
My mistress' eyes are nothing like the sun, 74
My prime of youth is but a frost of cares, 410

My soul, there is a country, 431
My stick fingers click with a snicker, 187
My sweetest Lesbia, let us live and love, 408

Nature and Nature's laws lay hid in Night, 39
Nautilus Island's hermit, 558
New air has come around us, 88
Nobody heard him the dead man, 539
not the beautiful youth with features of bloom & brightness, 73
Now as I was young and easy under the apple boughs, 555
Now first of all he means the night, 110
Now hardly here and there an Hackney-Coach, 434
Now the stone house on the lake front is finished and the workmen are beginning the fence, 67

Observe how he negotiates his way, 536
Off Highway 106, 568
Of the old loves of a remote lost land, 257
Oh, but it is dirty, 71
Old age is, 514
Old Eben Flood, climbing alone one night, 503
Old people are like birds, 31
O 'Melia, my dear, this does everything crown, 491
On a cold night I came through the cold rain, 249
On a starred night Prince Lucifer uprose, 334
Once again, tell me, what was it like, 600
Once in Canadaigua, hitchhiking from Ann Arbor, 557
Once in the dark of night, 57
One day I wrote her name upon the strand, 336
One must have a mind of winter, 512
One's grand flights, one's Sunday baths, 513
One thing that literature would be greatly the better for, 538

Only a man harrowing clods, 494
On the day of the explosion, 568
O Rose, thou art sick, 56
Our Bog is dood, our Bog is dood, 366
Our sardine fishermen work at night
   in the dark of the moon; day-
   light or moonlight, 20
Out of the cradle endlessly rocking,
   475
Overnight, very, 269
O what can ail thee, knight-at-arms,
   451
O where hae ye been, Lord Randal,
   my son, 400
O where have you been, my long, long
   love, 401
O who shall from this dungeon raise,
   428
O why do you walk through the fields
   in gloves, 340
O wild west wind, thou breadth of
   autumn's being, 448

Pale brows, still hands and dim hair,
   325
Partnership dissolved, 303
Past ruined Ilion Helen lives, 445
Patty-cake, patty-cake, 343
Pike, three inches long, perfect, 588
Pythagoras planned it. Why did the
   people stare, 320

Remember dear Mary love cannot
   deceive, 300
Rest lightly O Earth upon this
   wretched Nearchos, 101

St. Agnes' Eve—Ah, bitter chill it
   was, 456
Season of mists and mellow
   fruitfulness, 455
See her come bearing down, a tidy
   craft, 62
See, they return; ah, see the
   tentative, 273
See where the windows are boarded
   up, 593
September rain falls on the house, 338

Shall I compare thee to a summer's
   day, 406
She drew back; he was calm, 507
She dwelt among the untrodden ways,
   442
She looked over his shoulder, 102
Sigh as it ends . . . I keep an eye on
   your, 335
Sir Isaac Newton, 343
Slowly he sways that head that cannot
   hear, 16
Softly, in the dusk, a woman is
   singing to me, 386
Someone has built a dirigible in my
   parlor, 363
Someone who well knew how she'd
   toss her chin, 84
Something there is that doesn't love a
   wall, 505
Somewhere beneath that piano's
   superb sleek black, 385
Somewhere now she takes off the dress
   I am, 365
so much depends, 514
So we'll go no more a-roving, 447
Sparrows were feeding in a freezing
   drizzle, 564
Speak to me. Take my hand. What
   are you now, 549
Stand close around, ye Stygian set, 42
Staying alive in the woods is a matter
   of calming down, 577
Still to be neat, still to be dressed, 415
Suddenly I saw the cold and rook-
   delighting heaven, 498
Sundays too my father got up early,
   550

Tears, idle tears, I know not what
   they mean, 470
Tell all the Truth but tell it slant, 485
Tell me not, sweet, I am unkind, 428
That is no country for old men. The
   young, 498
That row of icicles along the gutter,
   299
That's my last Duchess painted on
   the wall, 470
That time of year thou mayst in me
   behold, 406
The apparition of these faces in the
   crowd, 12

INDEX OF FIRST LINES

The Assyrian came down like the wolf on the fold, 255

The buzz saw snarled and rattled in the yard, 292

The children go forward with their little satchels, 596

The curfew tolls the knell of parting day, 434

The descent beckons, 277

The door that someone opened wide, 294

The eel, the, 291

the elephant is in love with the millimeter, 359

The epoch of a streetcar drawn by horses, 594

The expense of spirit in a waste of shame, 407

The eye can hardly pick them out, 567

The feelings I don't have I don't have, 349

The gray sea and the long black land, 194

The house in Broad Street, red brick, with nine rooms, 527

The king sits in Dumferling toune, 14

The lowest trees have tops, the ant her gall, 403

The miller's wife had waited long, 502

The mountain sheep are sweeter, 445

The old South Boston Aquarium stands, 560

The people along the sand, 134

There's a man I really believe's in heaven, 8

There's a patch of old snow in a corner, 30

There was a young lady of Tottenham, 344

There was such speed in her little body, 109

The sea is calm to-night, 243

The shattered water made a misty din, 164

The sheets are exposed like film, 598

The thistledown's flying, though the winds are all still, 451

The time you won your town the race, 497

The tulips are too excitable, it is winter here, 590

The two-year old has had a motherless week. Mother has gone, 552

The way a crow, 132

The whiskey on your breath, 244

The Wind begun to knead the Grass, 484

The wind doth blow today, my love, 104

The wind flapped loose, the wind was still, 481

The winter evening settles down, 9

The witch that came (the withered hag), 506

The wonderful workings of the world: wonderful, 573

The world is charged with the grandeur of God, 495

The world is too much with us; late and soon, 442

They eat beans mostly, this old yellow pair, 562

They flee from me that sometime did me seek, 403

They're taking down a tree at the front door, 563

They say there is a sweeter air, 520

They throw in Drummer Hodge, to rest, 492

"Think as I think," said a man, 274

This ae nighte, this ae nighte, 306

This biplane is the shape of human flight, 145

This ignorance upon my tongue, 327

This is the one song everyone, 595

This morning we shall spend a few minutes, 52

This spring, you'd swear it actually gets dark earlier, 599

Those villages stricken with the melancholia of Sunday, 589

Thou shalt have one God only; who, 474

Thrice toss these oaken ashes in the air, 409

Tired with all these, for restful death I cry, 232

To fling my arms wide, 536

To speak in a flat voice, 581

Traveling through the dark I found a deer, 115

Truly, My Satan, thou art but a Dunce, 442

INDEX OF FIRST LINES

Truth-loving Persians do not dwell upon, 302
Turning and turning in the widening gyre, 240
Twirling your blue skirts, travelling the sward, 112
Tyger, Tyger, burning bright, 440

Under bare Ben Bulben's head, 210
Underneath this sable hearse, 250
Under the roof and the roof's shadow turns, 58

Went up a year this evening, 482
We real cool. We, 291
What lifts the heron leaning on the air, 557
What lively lad most pleasured me, 502
What passing-bells for these who die as cattle, 200
When, in disgrace with fortune and men's eyes, 335
When all is over and you march for home, 87
Whenas in silks my Julia goes, 328
When I am dead, I hope it may be said, 144
When icicles by silver eaves, 71
When icicles hang by the wall, 70
When I consider how my light is spent, 427
When I put her out, once, by the garbage pail, 117

When leaving the primrose, bayberry dunes, seaward, 572
When midnight comes a host of dogs and men, 450
When the hounds of spring are on winter's traces, 489
When the nightingale to his mate, 192
Where beth they beforen us weren, 262
wherelings whenlings, 306
Where we went in the boat was a long bay, 534
While my hair was still cut straight across my forehead, 515
Why dois your brand sae drap wi' bluid, 399
Why should I blame her that she filled my days, 28
With how sad steps, O moon, thou climb'st the skies, 405
With rue my heart is laden, 345
Word over all, beautiful as the sky, 480

Yet once more, O ye laurels, and once more, 421
You are so small, I, 268
You find one drinking at the creek, 598
You, love, and I, 220
You recommend that the motive, in Chapter 8, should be changed, 121
You think it horrible that lust and rage, 100

Index of Principal Terms and Topics

Abstractness, 4, 11
Accent, 241–242
Adjectives, 138–141
Adverbs, 138–141
Allegory, 61
Alliteration, 172
Allusion, 38–39
Anacoluthon, 298
Analogy, 31, 32–36
Anapest, 237–238, 253
Antipoetry, 69–76
Antithesis, 296
Aposiopesis, 299
Assonance, 166
Automatic writing, 360–361

Ballad, 14
Ballade, 339
Ballad stanza, 245, 329
Blank verse, 325
Burns stanza, 331

Cacophony, 201
Caesura, 239
Catalectic, 253
Chiasmus, 296
Cinquain, 341
Clerihew, 343
Clichés, 130
Concreteness, 4, 11, 280
Concrete poetry, 279–280
Connectives, 292–294
Connotation, 130

Consonance, 201
Consonants, 171–180
Couplets, 327

Dactyl, 253–254
Denotation, 130
Dimeter, 243
Dipodic, 253
Double dactyl, 343
Dreams, 367–368

Elegy, 207
Emotion, 95–103
End-stopped, 239
Envoy, 338
Etymology, 147–148
Euphony, 201

Fibonacci numbers, 313, 316–318
Foot, 226
    table of feet, 257
Free verse, 272

Haiku (hokku), 342
Heptameter, 245
Hexameter, 245
Hyperbole, 86

Iambic pentameter, 229
Image, 3
    archetypal, 98
    supercharged, 28
    withheld, 83

INDEX OF PRINCIPAL TERMS AND TOPICS

Inspiration, 375, 378
Inversion, 296
Irony, 80

Language, 301–308
Limerick, 343
Line length, 243–246
Litotes, 86
Lyric, 18

Metaphor, 21–32
  implied, 22, 27
  mixed, 29
Meter, 238
Metonymy, 50
Monometer, 243
Mythology, 42

Nonsense verse, 366

Octameter, 246
Ode, 18
Onomatopoeia, 185–190
Ottava rima, 332
Overstatement, 86
Oxymoron, 78

Paradox, 76–79
Parallelism, 294
Parataxis, 293
Parenthesis, 298
Parody, 357–358
Pastoral, 207
Pentameter, 243
Personification, 39–41
Poetic diction, 127–136
Prose poem, 281
Pyrrhic, 233

Quantity, 266
Quatrain, 328

Refrain, 339
Renga, 342
Repetition, 219
Rhyme, 190–201
  end rhyme, 199
  internal rhymes, 199
  off-rhyme, 199–201
Rhyme royal, 331
Rhyme scheme, 193–194, 327
Rhythm, 217–219, 238
  falling, 253

  free, 273
  rising, 253
  sprung, 266
  strong-stress, 258
  syllable-stress, 224
Rondel (roundel, rondeau), 340
Run-on lines, 239

Scansion, 226
Sense, 103
Senses, 3–11
Sentence, 289–292
Sentence structure, 296–301
Sentimentality, 104*ff.*
Sestina, 338
Simile, 21–32
Sonnet, 333–337
  curtal, 337
  English (Shakespearean), 335
  Italian (Petrarchan), 335
  Spenserian, 336
Sonnet diction, 155
Spatialist poetry, 280
Spatial prosody, 278
Spenserian stanza, 332–333
Spondee, 234
Stanza(s), 325–333
Surrealism, 360*ff.*
Syllabic meter, 269–272
Symbol, 51–58
Synecdoche, 47
Synesthesia, 36–38

Tanka, 341
Technique, 380
Tercet, 328
Terza rima, 328
Tetrameter, 245
Thing-poems, 58
Trimeter, 244
Triolet, 340
Trochee, 235–236, 252

Understatement, 81–86

Variable foot, 277–279
Venus-and-Adonis stanza, 331
Villanelle, 341
Visual prosody, 278
Vowels, 161–171

Words
  living, 125–141
  new, 304–308

Permissions Acknowledgments

of Achilles." Copyright 1934, 1940, 1952 and renewed 1962, 1968 by W. H. Auden. Reprinted from *W. H. Auden: Collected Poems,* edited by Edward Mendelson, by permission of Random House, Inc., and from *Collected Shorter Poems 1927–1957* by permission of Faber and Faber Ltd.

Robert Bagg, 2 lines from "The Tandem Ride" from *Madonna of the Cello.* Copyright © 1961 by Robert Bagg. Reprinted by permission of Wesleyan University Press.

Hilaire Belloc, "On His Books" from *Complete Verse.* Reprinted by permission of A. D. Peters & Co. Ltd.

John Berryman, "Sigh As It Ends" from *Berryman's Sonnets.* Copyright © 1952, 1967 by John Berryman. "He Resigns" from *Delusions, Etc.* Copyright © 1969, 1971 by John Berryman. Copyright © 1972 by the Estate of John Berryman. "Dream Song #4" and "Dream Song #22" from *The Dream Songs.* Copyright © 1959, 1962, 1963, 1964, 1969 by John Berryman. Reprinted by permission of Farrar, Straus & Giroux, Inc.

Elizabeth Bishop, "Filling Station," "Sestina," "The Fish," and 2 lines from "The Prodigal" from *Elizabeth Bishop: The Complete Poems.* Copyright © 1940, 1951, 1955, 1956, 1969 by Elizabeth Bishop. Copyright renewed © 1979 by Elizabeth Bishop. Reprinted by permission of Farrar, Straus & Giroux, Inc.

Gwendolyn Brooks, 4 lines from "The Ballad of Rudolph Reed." Copyright © 1960 by Gwendolyn Brooks. "We Real Cool: The Pool Players. Seven at the Golden Shovel." Copyright © 1959 by Gwendolyn Brooks. "The Bean Eaters." Copyright © 1959 by Gwendolyn Brooks. "The Rites for Cousin Vit." Copyright © 1949 by Gwendolyn Brooks Blakely. From *The World of Gwendolyn Brooks.* Reprinted by permission of Harper & Row, Publishers, Inc.

Arthur Buller, "There was a young lady named Bright . . . etc." from *Punch.* Copyright © 1923 by Punch/Rothco.

Gray Burr, 2 lines from "A Vision" from *A Choice of Attitudes.* First published in *The New Yorker.* Copyright © 1960 by Gray Burr. Reprinted by permission of Wesleyan University Press.

Helen Chasin, "City Pigeons" from *Coming Close.* Copyright © 1968 by Yale University. Reprinted by permission of Yale University Press.

John Ciardi, "Snowy Heron" from *I Marry You: A Sheaf of Love Poems.* Copyright © 1958 by Rutgers University Press. "Faces" from *In the Stoneworks.* Copyright © 1961 by Rutgers, The State University. "Most Like an Arch This Marriage" from *I Marry You: A Sheaf of Love Poems.* Published by Rutgers University Press, 1958. 3 lines from "Letter to a Wrong Child" from *In Fact.* 2 lines from "Chorus" from *Live Another Day.* 2 lines from "New Year's Eve" and 2 lines from "A Crow's Long Scratch of Sound" from *The Strangest Everything.* Reprinted by permission of the author.

Frances Cornford, "To a Fat Lady Seen from the Train" from *Collected Poems.* Published by Cresset Press, 1954. Reprinted by permission of Barrie & Jenkins Ltd.

Hart Crane, "Praise for an Urn," "Poem: To Brooklyn Bridge," and 2 lines from "The Bridge" (Section II, "Van Winkle") from *The Complete Poems and Selected Letters and Prose of Hart Crane,* edited by Brom Weber. Copyright 1933, © 1958, 1966 by Liveright Publishing Corp. Reprinted by permission of Liveright Publishing Corp.

Adelaide Crapsey, "Warning to be Mighty" from *Verse.* Copyright 1922 by Algernon S. Crapsey and renewed 1950 by The Adelaide Crapsey Foundation. Reprinted by permission of Alfred A. Knopf, Inc.

Robert Creeley, 15 lines from "Four" from "Numbers," in *Pieces.* Copyright ©

1969 by Robert Creeley (New York: Charles Scribner's Sons, 1969). Reprinted with the permission of Charles Scribner's Sons.

E. E. Cummings, 4 lines from "since feeling is first" from *IS 5 Poems.* Copyright 1926 by Horace Liveright. Copyright renewed 1953 by E. E. Cummings. "in Just-" (Chansons Innocentes, I) from *Tulips & Chimneys.* Copyright 1923, 1925, and renewed 1951, 1953 by E. E. Cummings. Copyright © 1973, 1976 by Nancy T. Andrews. Copyright © 1973, 1976 by George James Firmage. Reprinted by permission of Liveright Publishing Corp. 7 lines from "as freedom is a breakfastfood," 4 lines from "my father moved through dooms of love," "anyone lived in a pretty how town," "me up at does," "wherelings whenlings," and "if everything happens that can't be done" from *Complete Poems 1913–1962.* Reprinted by permission of Harcourt Brace Jovanovich, Inc.

J. V. Cunningham, 2 lines from "The Dogdays" from *Collected Poems & Epigrams.* Reprinted by permission of Ohio University Press. 4 lines from "Doctor Drink" from *The Exclusions of a Rhyme: Poems and Epigrams.* Copyright © 1960 by J. V. Cunningham. Reprinted by permission of The Swallow Press.

John Davidson, 3 lines from "The Last Ballad" from *A Selection.* Published by Hutchinson Publishing Group Ltd.

Peter Davison, "My Lady the Lake" from *Barn Fever, and Other Poems.* Copyright © 1981 by Peter Davison (New York: Atheneum, 1981). Reprinted with the permission of Atheneum Publishers.

Walter de la Mare, "Afraid," "All But Blind," 4 lines from "Remembrance," 3 lines from "Martins," 2 lines from "The Scarecrow," 4 lines from "The Spectre," "The Listeners," 2 lines from "Here Sleeps," and 4 lines from "The Bead Mat" from *Complete Poems.* Reprinted by permission of the literary trustees of Walter de la Mare and the Society of Authors as their representative.

James Dickey, "Cherrylog Road" from *Poems 1957–1967.* First published in *The New Yorker.* Copyright © 1963 by James Dickey. Reprinted by permission of Wesleyan University Press.

Emily Dickinson, "Went Up a Year This Evening!," "How Many Times These Low Feet Staggered," "I Heard a Fly Buzz—When I Died," "I Started Early—Took My Dog," "Because I Could Not Stop for Death," "The Wind Began to Knead the Grass," "Tell All the Truth But Tell It Slant," 2 lines from "Ample make this bed," and 5 lines from "A Bird Came Down the Walk" from *The Poems of Emily Dickinson,* edited by Thomas H. Johnson. Cambridge, Mass.: The Belknap Press of Harvard University Press, Copyright 1951, © 1955, 1979 by the President and Fellows of Harvard College. "My Life had Stood—a Loaded Gun" from *The Complete Poems of Emily Dickinson,* edited by Thomas H. Johnson. Copyright © 1957 by Mary L. Hampson. "A Narrow Fellow in the Grass" from *The Complete Poems of Emily Dickinson,* edited by Thomas H. Johnson. Published by Little, Brown and Company. Copyright 1951, 1955 by The President and Fellows of Harvard College. Reprinted by the permission of the publishers and the Trustees of Amherst College.

T. S. Eliot, "The Love Song of J. Alfred Prufrock," "New Hampshire," "Sweeney Among the Nightingales," 2 lines from "La Figlia che Piange," and "Preludes" from *Collected Poems 1909–1962.* Copyright © 1963 by Harcourt Brace Jovanovich, Inc.; copyright © 1963, 1964 by T. S. Eliot. Reprinted by permission of Harcourt Brace Jovanovich, Inc. and Faber and Faber Ltd.

Dave Etter, "Romp" from *Go Read the River.* Copyright © 1966 by the University of Nebraska Press. Reprinted by permission of the author and the University of Nebraska Press.

Kenneth Fearing, 6 lines from "X Minus X" from *The Collected Poems of*

PERMISSIONS ACKNOWLEDGMENTS

Kenneth Fearing. Published by AMS Press, Inc., New York. "Yes, the Agency Can Handle That," and "Love, 20¢ the First Quarter Mile" from *New and Selected Poems.* Published by Indiana University Press.

Edward Field, "Curse of the Cat Woman" from *Variety Photoplays.* Reprinted by permission of the author.

Dudley Fitts, "Brief Autumnal" and "Epitaph of Nearchos" from *Poems from the Greek Anthology.* Copyright 1938, 1941, © 1956 by New Directions Publishing Corp. Reprinted by permission of the publisher.

Robert Fitzgerald, "Cobb Would Have Caught It" from *In the Rose of Time.* Copyright 1943 by Robert Fitzgerald. Reprinted by permission of New Directions Publishing Corp.

Robert Francis, "Swimmer" from *The Orb Weaver.* First published in *The Saturday Review.* "Pitcher" from *The Orb Weaver.* First published in *New Poems by American Poets, I.* Copyright © 1953 by Robert Francis. Reprinted by permission of Wesleyan University Press.

Robert Frost, "A Patch of Old Snow," "Acquainted with the Night," "Dust of Snow," "Mending Wall," "The Most of It," "Neither Out Far Nor In Deep," "Once by the Pacific," "Out, Out—," "Provide, Provide," "The Subverted Flower," and "The Wright's Biplane" from *The Poetry of Robert Frost,* edited by Edward Connery Lathem. Copyright 1916, 1923, 1928, 1930, 1939, © 1969 by Holt, Rinehart and Winston. Copyright 1936, 1942, 1944, © 1956, 1958 by Robert Frost. Copyright © 1964, 1967, 1970 by Lesley Frost Ballantine. Reprinted by permission of Holt, Rinehart and Winston, Publishers.

Brewster Ghiselin, "Rattler Alert" from *Windrose: Poems 1929–1979.* Copyright 1941 and renewed 1969 by Brewster Ghiselin. Reprinted by permission of University of Utah Press.

Andrew Glaze, "Zeppelin" from *Damned Ugly Children.* Copyright © by Andrew Glaze. 4 lines from "Freedom" from *76th Street.* Reprinted by permission of Andrew Glaze.

Louise Glück, "The School Children" from *The House on Marshland.* Published by The Ecco Press. Copyright © 1975 by Louise Gluck. Reprinted by permission.

Robert Graves, "The Face in the Mirror," "Spoils," "Counting the Beats," "The Persian Version," and 6 lines from "Rocky Acres" from *Collected Poems.* Reprinted by permission of Robert Graves.

Ramon Guthrie, 6 lines from "Scherzo for a Dirge" from *Asbestos Phoenix.* Published by Funk & Wagnalls. Copyright © 1968 by Ramon Guthrie. Reprinted by permission of Harper & Row, Publishers, Inc.

Donald Hall, 2 lines from "The Farm," 3 lines from "In the Kitchen of the Old House," and 2 lines from "Church Meadows, Oxford" from *Alligator Bride.* Reprinted by permission of Donald Hall.

Jim Hall, 3 lines from "Why Should I Worry" from *The Mating Reflex.* Published by Carnegie-Mellon University Press, 1980. Copyright © 1980 by Jim Hall. Reprinted by permission of the publisher.

Robert Hayden, "O Daedalus, Fly Away Home" and "Those Winter Sundays" from *Angle of Ascent, New and Selected Poems.* Copyright © 1975, 1972, 1970, 1966 by Robert Hayden. Reprinted by permission of Liveright Publishing Corporation.

Seamus Heaney, "Death of a Naturalist" from *Death of a Naturalist* (published by Faber and Faber Ltd.) and *Poems 1965–1975* (published by Farrar, Straus & Giroux, Inc.). Copyright © 1966, 1980 by Seamus Heaney. Reprinted by permission of Farrar, Straus & Giroux, Inc. and Faber and Faber Ltd.

Anthony Hecht, "The End of the Weekend" from *The Hard Hours.* Copyright

PERMISSIONS ACKNOWLEDGMENTS

1937 and renewed 1965 by Donnan Jeffers and Garth Jeffers. Reprinted by permission of Random House, Inc.

Ted Joans, "The .38" from *Black Pow-Wow*. Copyright © 1964, 1969 by Ted Joans. Reprinted by permission of the author's representative, Gunther Stuhlmann.

X. J. Kennedy, "Loose Woman" and 5 lines from "Girl Sketching Me Into Her Landscape" from *Growing Into Love*. Copyright © 1964, 1967, 1968, 1969 by X. J. Kennedy. Reprinted by permission of Curtis Brown Ltd.

Hugh Kingsmill, 8 lines from "What, Still Alive at Twenty-Two" from *The Table of Truth*. Published by Jarrold, London.

Rudyard Kipling, 6 lines from "The Vampire," 6 lines from "South Africa," 2 lines from "In the Neolithic Age," and 4 lines from "The Virginity" from *Rudyard Kipling's Verse: Definitive Edition*. Reprinted by permission of Doubleday & Company, Inc. 6 lines from "The Vampire," 6 lines from "South Africa," 2 lines from "In the Neolithic Age," and 4 lines from "The Virginity" from *The Definitive Edition of Rudyard Kipling's Verse*. Reprinted by permission of The National Trust.

Kenneth Koch, 8 lines from "Ko, or A Season On Earth" from *Ko, or A Season On Earth*. Copyright © 1959 by Kenneth Koch. Reprinted by permission of the author.

Maxine Kumin, "The Retrieval System" from *The Retrieval System*. Copyright © 1976 by Maxine Kumin. Reprinted by permission of Viking Penguin, Inc.

Stanley Kunitz, 6 lines from "Promise Me" from *The Poems of Stanley Kunitz 1928–1978*. Copyright 1930, © 1958 by Stanley Kunitz. Reprinted by permission of Little, Brown and Company in association with the Atlantic Monthly Press.

R. D. Laing, "Jill" from *Knots*. Copyright © 1970 by The R. D. Laing Trust. Reprinted by permission of Pantheon Books, a division of Random House, Inc., and Tavistock Publications Ltd.

Philip Larkin, "The Explosion" from *High Windows*. Copyright © 1974 by Philip Larkin. Reprinted by permission of Farrar, Straus & Giorux, Inc., and Faber and Faber Ltd. "At Grass" and "Lines on a Young Lady's Photograph Album" from *The Less Deceived*. Reprinted by permission of The Marvell Press, England.

Philip Levine, "Keep Talking" from *Poetry,* September 1980. Copyright © 1980 by The Modern Poetry Association. Reprinted by permission of the Editor of *Poetry*. Published in *One for the Rose* by Atheneum, 1981.

Elizabeth Libbey, "The Gesture" from *The Crowd Inside*. Published by Carnegie-Mellon University Press, 1978. Copyright © 1978 by Elizabeth Libbey. Reprinted by permission of the publisher.

Vachel Lindsay, 4 lines from "Daniel" from *Collected Poems*. Copyright 1920 by Macmillan Publishing Co., Inc.; renewed 1948 by Elizabeth C. Lindsay. Reprinted by permission of Macmillan Publishing Co., Inc.

Federico García Lorca, "Sleepwalker's Ballad" ("Romance Sonambulo") from *Selected Poems,* translated by John F. Nims. Copyright 1955 by New Directions Publishing Corp. All rights reserved. Reprinted by permission of New Directions Publishing Corp., agents for the estate of Federico Garcia Lorca.

Robert Lowell, "For the Union Dead" from *For the Union Dead*. Copyright © 1960, 1964 by Robert Lowell. "Skunk Hour" from *Life Studies*. Copyright © 1956, 1959 by Robert Lowell. Reprinted by permission of Farrar, Straus & Giroux, Inc.

Thomas Lux, "My Grandmother's Funeral" from *Memory's Handgrenade*. Copyright © 1972 by Thomas Lux. Reprinted by permission of the author and Pym-Randall Press.

Rod McKuen, 10 lines from "A Cat Named Sloopy" from *Listen to the Warm.*

PERMISSIONS ACKNOWLEDGMENTS

PERMISSIONS ACKNOWLEDGMENTS

Pablo Neruda, 2 lines from "The Morning is Full" from *Twenty Love Poems,* translated by W. S. Merwin. Translated from the Spanish *20 Poemas de Amor y una Cancion Desperada,* first published in Santiago de Chile, 1924. English translation Copyright © 1969 by W. S. Merwin. Reprinted by permission of Viking Penguin, Inc., the Estate of Pablo Neruda, W. S. Merwin, and Jonathan Cape Ltd.

Kenneth Patchen, "O All Down Within the Pretty Meadow," 2 lines from "Beautiful You Are," and "Moon, Sun, Sleep, Birds, Live" from *Collected Poems of Kenneth Patchen.* Copyright 1942, 1946 by Kenneth Patchen. Copyright © 1954 by New Directions Publishing Corporation. Reprinted by permission of the publisher.

Katha Pollitt, "Turning Thirty" from *Antarctic Traveller.* Copyright © 1981 by Katha Pollitt. Reprinted by permission of Alfred A. Knopf, Inc.

Sylvia Plath, 10 lines from "Daddy" from *Ariel.* Copyright © 1963 by Ted Hughes. Reprinted by permission of Harper & Row, Publishers, Inc., and Olwyn Hughes. "Mushrooms" and 3 lines from "Metaphors" from *The Colossus and Other Poems.* Copyright © 1960 by Sylvia Plath. Reprinted by permission of Alfred A. Knopf, Inc., and Olwyn Hughes. "Tulips" (Copyright © 1962 by Ted Hughes) and 2 lines from "Nick and the Candlestick" (Copyright © 1965 by Ted Hughes) from *The Collected Poems* (published by Harper & Row Publishers, Inc.) and *Ariel* (published by Faber and Faber Ltd.) Reprinted by permission of Harper & Row, Publishers, Inc., and Faber and Faber Ltd.

Ezra Pound, 4 lines from "Canto VI," 4 lines from "Canto XIII," 2 lines from ":Canto 80," and 2 lines from "Canto 98" from *The Cantos of Ezra Pound.* Copyright 1934, 1948, © 1959 by Ezra Pound. Reprinted by permission of New Directions Publishing Corp. 3 lines from "A Ballad of Mulberry Road," "In a Station of the Metro," "Alba" ("As cool as . . ."), "Alba" ("When the nightingale . . ."), 2 lines from "Speech for Psyche in the Golden Book of Apuleius," "The Bath Tub," "The Return," "The River Merchant's Wife: A Letter," 8 lines from "Further Instructions," and 2 lines from "The Seafarer" from *Personae.* Copyright 1926 by Ezra Pound. Reprinted by permission of New Directions Publishing Corp.

Jacques Prévert, "The Message" from *Paroles.* Copyright 1949 by Editions Gallimard. Reprinted by permission of Editions Gallimard. The translation in this text is by John Frederick Nims.

Dudley Randall, "Blackberry Sweet" from *The New Black Poetry,* edited by C. Major. Copyright © 1969 by International Publishers Co., Inc. Reprinted by permission of International Publishers Co., Inc.

John Crowe Ransom, "Good Ships," "Bells for John Whiteside's Daughter," "Blue Girls," and 2 lines from "Winter Remembered" from *Selected Poems, Third Edition, Revised and Enlarged.* Copyright 1924, 1927 by Alfred A. Knopf, Inc., and renewed 1952, 1955 by John Crowe Ransom. Reprinted by permission of Alfred A. Knopf, Inc.

Rainer Maria Rilke, "The Merry-Go-Round" from *Selected Poems,* translated by C. F. MacIntyre. Reprinted by permission of University of California Press.

Edwin Arlington Robinson, 2 lines from "The Field of Glory." Copyright 1915 by Edwin Arlington Robinson; renewed 1943 by Ruth Nivison. 2 lines from "Llewellyn and the Tree." Copyright 1916 by Edward Arlington Robinson; renewed 1944 by Ruth Nivison. "The Mill" and "The Dark Hills." Copyright 1920 by Edwin Arlington Robinson; renewed 1948 by Ruth Nivison. "Mr. Flood's Party." Copyright 1921 by Edwin Arlington Robinson; renewed 1949 by Ruth Nivison. From *Collected Poems.* Reprinted by permission of Macmillan Publishing Co., Inc.

Theodore Roethke, "The Geranium." Copyright © 1963 by Beatrice Roethke as

PERMISSIONS ACKNOWLEDGMENTS

Administratrix of the Estate of Theodore Roethke. "My Papa's Waltz." Copyright 1942 by Hearst Magazines, Inc. "Elegy for Jane." Copyright 1950 by Theodore Roethke. "The Waking." Copyright 1953 by Theodore Roethke. Reprinted from *The Collected Poems of Theodore Roethke* by permission of Doubleday & Company, Inc.

Muriel Rukeyser, "Effort at Speech Between Two People," from *Theory of Flight.* Copyright 1935 by Yale University Press; copyright © 1960 by Muriel Rukeyser. Reprinted by permission of International Famous Agency.

Vern Rutsala, 2 lines from "Listening" and 4 lines from "Review" from *The Window.* Copyright © 1964 by Vern Rutsala. Reprinted by permission of Wesleyan University Press.

St. John of the Cross, "The Dark Night" from *The Poems of St. John of the Cross,* 3rd edition, translated by John F. Nims. Reprinted by permission of John F. Nims and the University of Chicago Press.

Carl Sandburg, 12 lines from "They Have Yarns" from *The People, Yes.* Copyright 1936 by Harcourt Brace Jovanovich, Inc.; renewed 1964 by Carl Sandburg. "A Fence" from *Chicago Poems.* Copyright 1916 by Holt, Rinehart and Winston, Inc.; copyright 1944 by Carl Sandburg. 4 lines from "Irish Bulls" and 3 lines from "Prairie" from *The Complete Poems of Carl Sandburg.* Reprinted by permission of Harcourt Brace Jovanovich, Inc.

Sappho, "There's a Man, I Really Believe" from *Sappho to Valéry, Poems in Translation,* by John Frederick Nims. Published by Rutgers University Press, 1971. Reprinted by permission of Rutgers University Press. "Leaving Crete, come visit again our temple . . ." from *Sappho to Valéry.* Copyright © 1971 by John Frederick Nims. Excerpt reprinted by permission of Princeton University Press.

James Schuyler, 3 lines from "Now and Then" and 2 lines from "3/23/66" from *Freely Espousing.* Copyright by James Schuyler. Reprinted by permission of Doubleday & Company, Inc., and the author. 3 lines from "May, 1972" from *Hymn to Life.* Copyright by James Schuyler. Reprinted by permission of the author.

E. William Seaman, "Higgledy-Piggledy, Ludwig van Beethoven" from *Jiggery-Pokery: A Compendium of Double Dactyls,* edited by Anthony Hecht and John Hollander. Copyright © 1966 by Anthony Hecht and John Hollander (New York: Atheneum, 1966). Reprinted with the permission of Atheneum Publishers.

Robert W. Service, "Inspiration" from *The Best of Robert Service.* Copyright 1949 by Dodd, Mead & Company, Inc. Copyright renewed 1978 by Germaine Service and Iris Davies. Reprinted by permission of Dodd, Mead & Company, Inc.

Anne Sexton, "Pain for a Daughter" from *Live or Die.* Copyright © 1966 by Anne Sexton. Reprinted by permission of Houghton Mifflin Company.

Karl Shapiro, "A Cut Flower," "The Leg," and "The two-year-old has had a motherless week" from *Selected Poems.* Copyright 1942, 1944, © 1962, and renewed 1970 by Karl Jay Shapiro. Reprinted by permission of Random House, Inc. "Girls Working in Banks" from *Esquire Magazine,* June 1972. Copyright © 1972 by Esquire, Inc. Reprinted by permission of *Esquire Magazine.*

Charles Simic, "Baby Pictures of Famous Dictators" from *Classic Ballroom Dances.* Reprinted by permission of Georges Braziller, Inc.

Louis Simpson, 3 lines from "Hot Night on Water Street" from *A Dream of Governors.* Copyright © 1957 by Louis Simpson. Reprinted by permission of Wesleyan University Press.

Edith Sitwell, 2 lines from "Romance" and 2 lines from "Gardner Janus Catches a Naiad" from *Collected Poems.* Copyright by Macmillan Publishing Co., Inc. Reprinted by permission of Harold Ober Associates, Inc.

PERMISSIONS ACKNOWLEDGMENTS

PERMISSIONS ACKNOWLEDGMENTS

PERMISSIONS ACKNOWLEDGMENTS

About the Author

Born in Muskegon, Michigan, John Frederick Nims received his M.A. from the University of Notre Dame and his Ph.D. in comparative literature from the University of Chicago. He has taught poetry and given workshops in poetry at Notre Dame, the University of Toronto, the University of Illinois at Urbana, Harvard University, Williams College, the University of Florida, and the University of Illinois at Chicago, where he is now. He has also been a Visiting Professor at the universities of Florence and Madrid and has been on the staff of many writers' conferences, including the one at Bread Loaf, Vermont, where he taught for more than ten years. He is the author of six books of poetry: *The Iron Pastoral, A Fountain in Kentucky, Knowledge of the Evening* (a National Book Award nominee), *Of Flesh and Bone, The Kiss: A Jambalaya,* and *Selected Poems*—books that have brought him awards from The National Foundation of Arts and Humanities, The American Academy of Arts and Letters, and Brandeis University, which awarded him its Creative Arts Citation in Poetry. He has been the Phi Beta Kappa poet at the College of William and Mary and at Harvard University. He has also published several books of translations, including *Sappho to Valéry: Poems in Translation* and *The Poems of St. John of the Cross,* and edited *The Harper Anthology of Poetry.* Several times on the staff of *Poetry* (Chicago), he has been its editor since 1978. In 1982, he was awarded the Fellowship of the Academy of American Poets.